Library of
Davidson College

VOID

In the Collected Studies Series:

STEPHAN KUTTNER
The History of Ideas and Doctrines of Canon Law in the Middle Ages

WALTER ULLMANN
Jurisprudence in the Middle Ages

WALTER ULLMANN
The Church and the Law in the Earlier Middle Ages

WALTER ULLMANN
The Papacy and Political Ideas in the Middle Ages

WALTER ULLMANN
Scholarship and Politics in the Middle Ages

BRIAN TIERNEY
Church Law and Constitutional Thought in the Middle Ages

JEAN GAUDEMET
La formation du droit canonique médiéval

JEAN GAUDEMET
La société ecclésiastique dans l'Occident médiéval

RAYMONDE FOREVILLE
Gouvernement et vie de l'Eglise au Moyen-Age

GILES CONSTABLE
Religious Life and Thought (11th-12th Centuries)

GILES CONSTABLE
Cluniac Studies

PAUL MEYVAERT
Benedict, Gregory, Bede and Others

EDMOND-RENÉ LABANDE
Spiritualité et vie littéraire de l'Occident, Xe-XIVe s.

EDMOND-RENÉ LABANDE
Histoire de l'Europe occidentale, XIe-XIVe s.

BERNHARD BLUMENKRANZ
Juifs et Chrétiens – Patristique et Moyen-Age

A. H. ARMSTRONG
Plotinian and Christian Studies

MILTON V. ANASTOS
Studies in Byzantine Intellectual History

Medieval Councils, Decretals, and Collections of Canon Law

Stephan Kuttner

Medieval Councils, Decretals, and Collections of Canon Law

Selected Essays

VARIORUM REPRINTS
London 1980

British Library CIP data   Kuttner, Stephan
　　　　　　　　　　　　　　Medieval councils, decretals and collections
　　　　　　　　　　　　　　of Canon law. — (Collected studies series;
　　　　　　　　　　　　　　CS126).
　　　　　　　　　　　　　　1. Canon law — History
　　　　　　　　　　　　　　2. Church history — Middle Ages, 600-1500
　　　　　　　　　　　　　　I. Title   II. Series
　　　　　　　　　　　　　　262.9'094   BV760.2

　　　　　　　　　　　　　　ISBN 0-86078-071-6

Copyright © 1980 by   Variorum Reprints

Published in Great Britain by   Variorum Reprints
　　　　　　　　　　　　　　　　20 Pembridge Mews London W11 3EQ

Printed in Great Britain by   Galliard (Printers) Ltd
　　　　　　　　　　　　　　　Great Yarmouth Norfolk

　　　　　　　　　　　　　　　VARIORUM REPRINT CS126

TABLE OF CONTENTS

Preface		i—ii
I	Quelques observations sur l'autorité des collections canoniques dans le droit classique de l'Église	305—312
	in: Actes du Congrès de droit canonique, Paris 22-26 Avril 1947 (Paris 1950)	
II	Some Roman Manuscripts of Canonical Collections	7—29
	in: Bulletin of Medieval Canon Law, New Series 1 (Berkeley 1971)	
III	The So-called Canons of Nîmes (1096)	175—189
	In collaboration with Robert Somerville, in: Tijdschrift voor Rechtsgeschiedenis 38 (Groningen-Brussels-The Hague 1970)	
IV	Gerland of Besançon and the Manuscripts of his 'Candela': A Bibliographical Note	71—84
	in: Parádosis: Studies in Memory of Edwin A. Quain (New York 1976)	
V	The 'Extravagantes' of the Decretum in Biberach	61—71
	in: Bulletin of Medieval Canon Law, New Series 3 (Berkeley 1973)	
VI	The Decretal 'Presbiterum' (JL 13912) — a Letter of Leo IX	133—135
	in: Bulletin of Medieval Canon Law, New Series 5 (Berkeley 1975)	
VII	Collectio Francofortana	370—380
	in: Zeitschrift der Savigny-Stiftung für Rechtsgeschichte, Kan. Abt. 22 (Weimar 1933)	

| VIII | A Collection of Decretal Letters of Innocent III in Bamberg | 41—56 |

*in: Medievalia et Humanistica,
New Series 1 (In Honor of S. Harrison
Thomson; Cleveland-London 1970)*

| IX | A New Eyewitness Account of the Fourth Lateran Council | 115—178 |

*In collaboration with A. García y García,
in: Traditio 20 (New York 1964)*

| X | Johannes Teutonicus, das vierte Laterankonzil und die Compilatio quarta | 608—634 |

*in: Miscellanea Giovanni Mercati,
V (Studi e Testi 125; Città del
Vaticano 1946)*

| XI | Die Konstitutionen des ersten allgemeinen Konzils von Lyon | 70—131 |

*in: Studia et documenta historiae
et iuris 6 (Rome 1940)*

| XII | Conciliar Law in the Making: The Lyonese Constitutions of Gregory X in a Manuscript at Washington | 39—81 |

*in: Miscellanea Pio Paschini, II
(Lateranum N.S. 15; Rome 1949)*

| XIII | The Date of the Constitution 'Saepe', the Vatican Manuscripts, and the Roman Edition of the Clementines | 427—452 |

*in: Mélanges Eugène Tisserant,
IV (Studi e Testi 234; Città del
Vaticano 1964)*

| | Retractationes | 1—18 |
| | Index | 1—23 |

PREFACE

In this volume a number of studies have been brought together that reflect the writer's concern, over the years, with understanding the processes by which canon law was made, recorded, and circulated in the medieval Latin Church. The papers here selected for republication first appeared between 1933 and 1975. They deal with decretal letters and conciliar enactments from the eleventh century to the Council of Vienne; with textual transmission by planning and by the accidents of accretion; with the purposes of compilers in making collections and, as the case may be, with the stages of official publication. In short, these papers try to describe aspects of the medieval counterpart to what today we would call the legislative process. They do not include the work of Gratian: in this respect the volume is something like a playbill for Hamlet with the Prince of Denmark left out. But republishing my efforts at dealing with the central figure in the history of canonical collections must wait for another occasion.

Somewhat reluctantly, I excluded certain essays from this volume that would have considerably swelled its size. They are mostly studies dealing the work of scholars in the sixteenth century and beyond who broke the ground in exploring the sources of medieval canon law. The great Antonio Agustín (d. 1586) at least receives some attention in the second paper here republished. But it was not feasible to print again the monograph which was a companion study to the one on the constitutions of the first Council of Lyons (No. XI of this volume): *L'édition romaine des Conciles généraux et les actes du premier concile de Lyon* (Miscellanea historiae pontificiae 3.5, Rome 1940).

I wish to express my sincere thanks for permission to reprint these essays to the editors and publishers of the *Tijdschrift voor Rechtsgeschiedenis*, of the *Zeitschrift der Savigny-Stiftung für Rechtsgeschichte*, of *Medievalia et Humanistica*, of the Vatican Library's *Studi e Testi* and the Lateran University's *Studia et Documenta historiae et iuris*, as well as to the managers of Fordham University Press (New York) and the publishing house of Letouzey et Ané (Paris). I wish to thank in particular my colleagues and friends, Antonio García y García (Universidad Pontificia, Salamanca) and Robert Somerville (Columbia University, New York) who generously allowed me to include in this volume papers of which they share the authorship with me.

In a spirit of abiding friendship Professor Stanley Chodorow (University of California, San Diego) once more took upon himself the exacting task of programming the computer, with the assistance of Dr. Constance Bouchard, for typesetting the table of contents, the preface, the appended material, and the index. The appended material, as on an earlier occasion, bears the title of *Retractationes*: it is meant to bring my earlier efforts somewhat up to date by new information, new insights, and the correction of errors of fact or judgment.

University of California　　　　　　　　　　　　　　　　Stephan Kuttner
Berkeley,
May 1980

In the earlier volume of collected studies, *The History of Ideas and Doctrines of Canon Law in the Middle Ages*, Article I, page 6, section III, lines 10-12 should read as follows:

[...] The Visigothic *Breviarium* (*Lex Romana Visigothorum,* 506 A.D.), which combined a small selection of epitomized writings of imperial consitutions [...]

I

Quelques observations sur l'autorité des collections canoniques dans le droit classique de l'Église

Malgré les immenses progrès que des générations de savants ont réalisés dans l'histoire des sources et de la littérature du droit canon, nous sommes encore bien loin d'une connaissance intégrale de ce qu'on pourrait appeler l'histoire de la pensée canonique. Pour atteindre ce but, il ne suffira pas de reconstruire le développement des règles et des doctrines particulières sur tel ou tel sujet — reconstruction qui elle-même est encore à faire ou à refaire pour la plupart des institutions canoniques, vu la multiplication formidable des textes anciens et médiévaux que nous devons aux recherches de la science moderne : une telle histoire doctrinale resterait vaine si on l'édifiait en commettant l'erreur de croire à une identité constante de la pensée juridique, c'est-à-dire si l'on supposait que la manière de raisonner et de concevoir les opérations du droit dans son ensemble, dans ses règlements individuels, dans son application aux données particulières, n'a pas subi au cours des siècles des transformations profondes.

On ne saurait nier, par exemple, qu'une mentalité très différente de la nôtre se manifeste au ve siècle (et encore plus tard), dans les variations de la réception et de la tradition des plus anciens *syntagmata canonum* ou bien des anciennes décrétales des papes; qu'au haut Moyen Age la réalité des institutions ecclésiastiques, gouvernée par des forces féodales, se sépare nettement des règles transmises dans les textes canoniques, de sorte que les collections successives de ces textes, surtout depuis l'époque des grands faussaires, prennent plutôt la nature d'ouvrages programmatiques, où les compilateurs se servent des *sacri canones* pour exprimer leurs propres idées, soit réformatrices, soit conservatrices.

En ce qui concerne, en particulier, l'interprétation historique des doctrines et des institutions, on fera bien de se rappeler, entre autres, que du temps des Pères le souci des terminologies techniques et des distinctions précises, quoique développé à merveille au cours des grandes controverses christologiques, ne s'attache que rarement aux problèmes de droit canon; le besoin même de soumettre les dispositions canoniques aux règles de l'exégèse ne se fait pas fortement sentir avant la fin du xie siècle. Aussi ne faut-il pas chercher la précision et la logique de ce qui est calculable — qui caractérise, par exemple, le décret d'Alexandre III sur les élections papales — dans le régime des élections en droit ancien, qui ne connaît (même après la réforme de Nicolas II) ni la compétence absolue d'un collège électoral, ni le principe de la majorité.

Seul l'historien qui s'efforce de comprendre que les variations historiques de la manière de raisonner ne sont pas moins réelles que les données palpables des faits extérieurs et des règles formulées dans les textes se gardera des malentendus anachroniques. Or, nous nous proposons, dans la présente communication, de démontrer qu'un tel malentendu existe, dans la théorie des sources du droit canonique, à l'égard des collections qui forment le *Corpus juris canonici*. Nous faisons allusion ici à la doctrine commune selon laquelle le *Décret* de Gratien, étant un ouvrage d'autorité purement privée, n'aurait jamais eu, en tant que collection, force obligatoire dans l'Église, de sorte que chaque canon qui y est contenu n'aurait pu jouir d'aucune autre autorité que celle qui lui était propre d'après son origine individuelle; tandis que les collections officielles des décrétales — les *Grégoriennes*, le *Sexte* et les *Clémentines* — étant promulguées par le pouvoir législatif suprême de l'Église, se trouvaient revêtues dans toutes leurs parties dispositives d'une autorité obligatoire et absolue.

Cette distinction correspond parfaitement aux notions précises sur la nature des lois ecclésiastiques et leur relation nécessaire avec le pouvoir législatif, telles qu'elles ont pris leur forme définitive dans la philosophie thomiste, et qui du moins depuis l'époque tridentine étaient devenues le fondement traditionnel de la théorie générale du droit canonique. Personne ne songerait à nier l'exactitude de ces notions fondamentales et la nécessité de leur application aux livres médiévaux du *Corpus juris canonici*, dans un système intégral de droit positif comme celui qui s'est formé, au cours des siècles, autour de ces recueils, par les interprétations et innovations innombrables qui y ont été apportées constamment par la législation et la jurisprudence pontificales. Mais ne nous dissimulons pas, d'une part, que c'était un processus assez lent et difficile pour la pensée juridique que de parvenir à une harmonie entre la théorie abstraite des lois et la réalité des collections hétérogènes qui faisaient toujours partie du droit positif (1). Ne nous dissimulons pas non plus qu'à l'époque de l'origine de ces collections, leur fonction véritable comme sources de droit était bien différente de celle qu'elles allaient remplir dans les âges à venir. C'est peut-être seulement depuis que le Code pio-bénédictin a mis fin à leur rôle d'éléments du droit en vigueur que nous avons gagné la distance nécessaire pour les voir dans la juste perspective historique.

Pour ce qui est de l'œuvre de Gratien, nous dirons d'abord que le problème de son autorité ne pouvait se poser aux canonistes du XIIe siècle dans ces termes : collection privée ou collection officielle. C'étaient là des catégories qui n'existaient pas dans la pensée d'une époque qui n'avait

---

(1) Voir les opinions divergentes citées par Gonzalez Tellez, dans l'*Apparatus* introductoire (n. 49 sq.) de ses *Commentaria perpetua*, ou par Schmalzgrueber, dans la *Dissertatio prooemialis* (§ 262 sq.) de son *Jus ecclesiasticum universum*.

pas encore vu la papauté faire usage de son droit incontestable de publier des compilations autorisées. Certes, le pouvoir législatif universel du Souverain pontife était, grâce aux clarifications acquises pendant la querelle des Investitures, désormais un fait acquis pour la doctrine (bien que la discussion continuât sur les limites possibles de ce pouvoir); mais, pour les glossateurs, il ne s'ensuivait pas qu'un recueil de la tradition canonique millénaire eût besoin — à la différence, par exemple, d'un florilège patristique — d'une autorisation formelle (1).

D'autre part, les glossateurs n'ignoraient point que les observations personnelles du maître lui-même (les *dicta* ou *paragraphi*) ne faisaient pas partie de la tradition canonique; ils savaient également qu'on pouvait toujours citer des canons traditionnels mais omis par Gratien — ils seront plus tard incorporés dans les manuscrits à titre de *palea*. Mais si l'on prétend en déduire le caractère « privé » de la *Concordia discordantium canonum* dans l'opinion des contemporains, on oublie que la notion complémentaire d'une collection « officielle » n'existait pas. (En fait, la légende de l'approbation du *Décret* par Eugène III n'a pris et ne pouvait prendre naissance qu'à une époque postérieure.) Ce n'est pas par ces notions qu'on arrive à comprendre dans quelle mesure l'œuvre du moine bolonais faisait autorité dans les écoles, les tribunaux et la Curie romaine au Moyen Age.

Il faut se rappeler que le droit classique de l'Église naquit dans les écoles comme partie du mouvement scolastique. Conçu dès son origine comme un sententiaire raisonné pour l'élaboration dialectique d'un système de droit, le livre de Gratien restait à Bologne, et partout où la science nouvelle se répandit, le texte fondamental, le dossier établi des *auctoritates* et *rationes* par l'interprétation desquelles il devenait possible aux maîtres d'ériger l'édifice harmonieux du droit commun de l'Église. Gratien lui-même avait indiqué dans ses *paragraphi* le cours qu'il fallait suivre; on pouvait affiner la méthode par tous les moyens disponibles de l'exégèse, de l'analyse et de la synthèse, mais les *auctoritates* du passé (avec l'addition de quelque *palea* çà et là) se présentaient désormais telles que Gratien les avait réunies et disposées. Changer ce système (on connaît l'échec du cardinal Laborans qui le tenta vers 1180) aurait entraîné la chute de tout l'édifice. La question de savoir si le *Décret* avait force obligatoire ne se posait pas.

C'est pourquoi les papes, dans leur nouvelle pratique d'interpréter et de développer le droit positif par un nombre toujours croissant de lettres décrétales, ont pris le *Décret* de Gratien comme point de départ. On a observé très justement que l'usage fait du Décret par les papes ne constitue pas une approbation, formelle ou implicite. Pourtant, cette

---

(1) Le *Dictatus papæ* de Grégoire VII, en déclarant qu'il ne peut y avoir de *liber canonicus* sans l'autorisation du Saint-Siège (c. 17), ne vise pas, dans notre opinion, les collections canoniques, mais le canon des Écritures. — Voir notre étude, *Liber canonicus : a Note on Dictatus papæ c. 17*, dans Studi Gregoriani, II, Rome, 1947, p. 387 sq.

observation n'a rien à voir avec l'autorité réelle de l'œuvre. C'est son autorité comme *Corpus* de la tradition canonique qui comptait, pour la Curie non moins que pour les écoles — et il ne faut pas oublier que les grands juristes sous la tiare étaient des élèves des écoles. On ne saurait s'imaginer un Alexandre III ou un Innocent III concevant le droit ancien séparé de la forme que Gratien lui avait donnée.

Mais, dira-t-on peut-être, cela devait changer au moment où les recueils officiellement promulgués des décrétales firent leur apparition. Ne devait-on pas s'apercevoir alors qu'il y avait une différence fondamentale entre un ouvrage composé par un maître privé et un texte envoyé par le Souverain pontife aux écoles avec l'ordre de l'appliquer? On ne s'en apercevait pas. Les Compilations authentiques d'Innocent III et d'Honorius III (la *tertia* et la *quinta* parmi les *antiquæ*) ne retiraient de leur promulgation officielle aucune autorité prééminente qui les distinguât, dans l'usage des écoles et des tribunaux, des trois Compilations privées d'Extravagantes également adoptées comme textes du droit nouveau. Quant au *Liber decretalium* de Grégoire IX, sa promulgation en 1234 constituait sans doute un des événements les plus marquants dans l'histoire du droit classique. Pour la première fois un pape abolissait des textes — les *Compilationes antiquæ* — du droit positif, en les remplaçant par une rédaction définitive et authentique de tous les textes qu'il entendait retenir du droit nouveau. Il interdisait pour l'avenir la confection de collections privées. Mais — et c'est là le point essentiel — il ne touchait pas à l'autorité, établie depuis près d'un siècle, du *Corpus* de la tradition ancienne. De plus, la parenté (tant pour le but que pour les matériaux employés) entre la compilation grégorienne et le *Code* de Justinien était trop frappante pour ne pas suggérer l'analogie (moins précise, il est vrai) entre le *Décret* et le *Digeste*.

Le droit commun de l'Église devait désormais s'étudier dans les deux grands livres, celui du moine et celui du pape, qui pendant tout le Moyen Age resteront les *libri ordinarii* dans les programmes des universités. Et, s'il est vrai que le premier était souvent modifié par le second — car *lex posterior derogat legi priori* — celui-ci supposait toujours l'existence de l'autre : il restait toujours un livre d'*Extravagantes*, de textes nouveaux « en dehors » du *Liber decretorum* (1). Le régime en vigueur pour une institution quelconque ne pouvait se déterminer que par un examen des *auctoritates* contenues dans les deux livres (avec l'addition, plus tard, de celles du *Sexte* et des *Clémentines*); examen raisonné à faire selon toutes les règles dialectiques. Mais on chercherait en vain chez les glossateurs du XIIIe siècle, soit dans les prologues des Sommes et commentaires (endroits traditionnels pour expliquer la théorie des sources), soit dans les interprétations particulières, une argumentation qui distinguât entre

---

(1) Au XVe siècle, l'Abbas Panormitanus nous dira (*Lectura in Decretales*, ad proœm. *Rex pacificus*, n. 7) qu'il y avait des auteurs qui s'opposaient à l'usage de citer les Grégoriennes par l'abréviation *X;* elle ne correspondrait plus à l'autorité de l'ouvrage.

l'autorité privée du *Liber decretorum* et l'autorité officielle des Décrétales, ou qui prît comme points de départ les notions de force obligatoire et de pouvoir législatif. Ce problème, semble-t-il, ne fut pas mentionné avant Jean d'André, et encore ce dernier ne l'effleura-t-il qu'en passant et pour la seule question de savoir si la citation d'une loi civile dans un *dictum* de Gratien peut déroger comme *lex canonizata* à un canon opposé. Dans sa réponse négative, l'argument d'autorité appuie seulement d'autres arguments; on ne peut en conclure que Jean d'André l'aurait appliqué à un texte proprement canonique faisant partie de la tradition ancienne reproduite par Gratien (1).

Avec les remarques du grand docteur du xɪvᵉ siècle, nous passons au deuxième élément de la doctrine commune moderne, à savoir la proposition sur la force de loi des canons individuels : force relative, dans le cas de Gratien, selon le degré d'autorité propre à chaque texte de par son origine; force absolue et universelle dans le cas des collections de décrétales. Comme corollaire d'une distinction entre les autorités respectives des collecteurs, la conclusion serait logiquement inévitable. C'est pourquoi le fait que la conclusion ne correspond pas à la réalité historique prouve mieux qu'aucun argument d'ordre général que la distinction précitée ne jouait aucun rôle dans le droit classique de l'Église.

En fait, les canonistes médiévaux ne songèrent pas à appliquer aux sources une herméneutique faite sur mesure, selon les échelons de la hiérarchie de juridiction ecclésiastique. A cet égard il importe de ne pas se méprendre sur la nature des fameuses règles concernant les sources du droit et leur harmonisation, qui, depuis la fin du xɪᵉ siècle, préparèrent le climat pour une science dialectique du droit canon. Dans ces théories, l'idée de ce qu'on a récemment appelé « la hiérarchie des textes » servait surtout à expliquer la genèse du droit et à définir les textes qui pouvaient être considérés comme faisant partie de la discipline ecclésiastique; mais, du moment qu'un canon d'origine particulière était une fois admis, il sortait de la sphère du droit particulier et s'intégrait dans le droit commun (2). Sa place désormais se déterminait, non par le rang de son auteur,

---

(1) Jean d'André, *Novella*, ad X, 1, 3, c. 2, in gl. ult., vᵒ *secundum leges;* voir aussi Panormitanus, ad loc.

(2) Cela se trouve exprimé très clairement, par ex. chez Bernold de Constance, *Apologeticus,* c. 4 : *De excommunicatis vitandis,* § 50 (éd. Thaner, dans *Mon. Germ. hist., Libelli de lite,* II, 63 et 135). MM. Fournier et Le Bras ne nous semblent pas avoir donné toute sa valeur à cette idée importante. Cf. aussi les articles récents de Mgr A. Van Hove, *Een inleiding tot de bronnen van het Kerkelijk Recht* (dans les *Miscellanea historica Alberti De Meyer,* I, Louvain, 1946, p. 367); *De oorsprong van het Kerkelijke Rechtswetenschap en de Scholastiek* (dans *Mededeelingen van de Koninklijke Vlaamsche Academie, Klasse der Letteren,* vɪ, 1946, n. 3, p. 20). — Ce que nous venons de dire sur le sens véritable de la « hiérarchie des sources » dans la pensée médiévale s'applique surtout à la règle dite de S. Isidore, si fréquemment citée à l'époque préscolastique (cf. J. de Ghellinck, *Le mouvement théologique du XIIᵉ s.,* 2ᵉ éd., 1948, p. 64 et 482 sq.) : *...ut quotiescumque in gestis conciliorum discors sententia invenitur, illius concilii magis teneatur sententia, cujus aut antiquior aut potior extat auctoritas* (lettre à l'évêque Massona, *P. L.,* LXXXIII, 901 —

mais par des catégories objectives; précepte ou conseil, droit strict ou dispense, interprétation du contexte, etc. Et l'on sait que les canons particuliers furent admis de nouveau par centaines après que la sévérité intransigeante des canonistes de la réforme grégorienne envers la tradition non romaine eut fait place aux conceptions plus conciliatrices des Yves, des Bernold, etc.

C'est ainsi que chez Gratien lui-même il n'y a plus de rapport entre la rigueur de la théorie des sources exprimée dans certains *dicta* — où il dénie par exemple la qualité de droit aux sentences des Pères et aux actes des conciles provinciaux non contrôlés par le Saint-Siège — et l'inclusion inconditionnée dans son texte de tout ce que la tradition commune lui offrait de sentences patristiques, de canons provinciaux, de canons pénitentiels, etc. (1). Et de même que Gratien n'applique pas l'argument hiérarchique dans ses solutions des problèmes posés par les *discordantes canones*, les glossateurs eux non plus, ni avant ni après la publication des Décrétales grégoriennes, ne pensent à donner aux canons de Gratien « seulement le poids que leur confère l'autorité inhérente à leurs auteurs respectifs ». Qu'on ouvre les Sommes, les commentaires, les distinctions, les questions disputées et autres écrits quelconques des auteurs médiévaux, chaque page fournira des exemples d'une méthode juridique et scolastique basée sur la discussion de nombreux *argumenta* puisés dans Gratien pour et contre telle ou telle solution, mais qui ne se demande jamais d'où l'*argumentum* est dérivé en dernière analyse. Si les auteurs classiques, conformément aux conceptions de la théorie plus récente, s'étaient posé la question de la force obligatoire de tel ou tel texte (le problème épineux des faux textes mis à part !), ils auraient dû écarter plus de la moitié de leur dossier — ou bien on devrait recourir, pour justifier la validité de leurs citations, à la construction, évidemment artificielle, d'un droit coutumier.

La théorie plus rigoureuse des sources, inopérante donc en ce qui concerne le droit ancien, devait pourtant fournir la base de la création du droit nouveau, irrévocablement concentrée désormais entre les mains des papes. On sait qu'ils exerçaient cette prérogative moins souvent par la législation universelle que par les *mandata, commissoria* et *responsa* qu'à la façon des empereurs romains ils envoyaient à des particuliers. On n'ignore pas non plus les discussions des canonistes du XIIe siècle sur la question de savoir dans quelle mesure ces lettres décrétales pouvaient

---

reléguée parmi les faux par Dom P. Séjourné, *S. Isidore de Séville*, Paris, 1929, p. 75 sq.; mais voir G. Le Bras, dans *Revue des sciences religieuses*, x, 1930, p. 224 sq.). Elle ne limite pas la portée des canons comme tels; elle n'est que très rarement mise au service des solutions pratiques; voir par ex. Petrus Blesensis, *Speculum*, c. 1, § 1 (éd. Reimarus, p. 7), ou Rufinus, *Summa*, dist. L, c. 28 (éd. Singer, p. 122). Les glossateurs mettront en doute le principe « isidorien » lui-même; voir *Glos. ord.*, dist. L, c. 28, v° *discors*.

(1) Voir les observations faites par M. Le Bras à l'égard de *La doctrine, source des collections canoniques*, dans le *Recueil d'études... en l'honneur de F. Gény*, I, Paris, 1935, p. 69 sq., et particulièrement p. 74.

changer le droit commun (1). Ce n'est qu'après l'introduction des recueils d'Extravagantes dans les écoles (à partir du *Bréviaire* de Bernard de Pavie, 1190 environ) que l'autorité des nouveaux textes devint incontestée. Mais il faut se rendre compte qu'à la différence des statuts des nouveaux conciles œcuméniques la fonction générale des décrétales individuelles, citées soit dans les compilations, soit en dehors d'elles, était toujours celle d'un argument et non pas celle d'un commandement de loi abstrait.

Innocent III fut le premier pape à désigner lui-même les décrétales de son pontificat qu'il estimait propres à remplir cette fonction générale (2). C'était là le premier pas dans la voie de la détermination officielle de toutes les *auctoritates* du droit nouveau qui devait s'accomplir par la compilation grégorienne. La bulle *Rex pacificus* nous dit tout ce que Grégoire IX s'était proposé de faire : abolir la confusion des textes, éliminer le superflu et le contradictoire, compléter le *corpus* de la tradition et résoudre, le cas échéant, ce qui y restait de douteux par l'insertion de ses propres missives, prescrire l'usage exclusif du livre pour le droit des Extravagantes et en interdire des compilations privées. Il n'y a rien dans les paroles du pape qui revendiquerait pour son *Liber decretalium* les qualités ultérieures qu'une interprétation extensive lui donnera plus tard. En premier lieu, Grégoire ne voulait pas créer une codification abstraite qui aurait transformé tous les textes recueillis en des normes, des commandements absolus, revêtus d'une nouvelle force obligatoire, comme s'ils étaient tous des lois uniformément et simultanément promulguées pour la première fois le 5 septembre 1234. Le fameux *omnia nostra facimus*, proclamé par Justinien dans la constitution introductoire du *Digeste* (3), Grégoire IX ne le prononça pas.

Et, pour l'historien, ce serait une spéculation entièrement gratuite que de chercher à découvrir si un sens pareil ne se cachait pas derrière le langage si clair et si simple de la bulle : pour le pape, il s'agit d'une réforme officielle des manuels à l'usage des écoles et des tribunaux, et non pas d'un bouleversement des méthodes législatives, qui, du reste, n'aurait guère échappé aux décrétalistes de l'époque. Or, pour eux, les *extravagantes* individuelles ne changeaient pas de nature par leur nouvelle promulgation. Elles restaient des *auctoritates* dans le sens traditionnel, et qui

---

(1) C.-à-d. si toutes les décrétales *possint trahi ad consequentiam*.

(2) La part de la Curie dans la circulation des décrétales d'Alexandre III reste assez douteuse (voir W. Holtzmann, dans *Quellen und Forschungen aus ital. Arch. and Bibl.*, xxx, 1940, p. 16 sq.). Quant à Innocent III, rappelons que, d'une part, il a publié la *Compilatio III*ᵃ et que, d'autre part, il a refusé d'approuver les collections de Bernard de Compostelle (voir Tancrède) et de Jean le Teutonique (voir notre art., dans les *Miscellanea Mercati*, vi, 608-634). Voir aussi, pour un cas où le pape tenait à exclure toute fonction générale, la décrétale dans la collection d'Alain (app., 79; deuxième rédaction, II, 6, 5) : ...*nos per consultationem quam nuper edidimus in casu consimili derogare nolentes oppinionibus aliorum*... (éd. R. von Heckel, *Zeitschr. der Sav.-Stift., Kan. Abt.*, xxix, 1940, p. 326).

(3) Const. *Deo auctore* (= *Cod.*, l. I, tit. xvii, lex 1), § 6; voir aussi const. *Hæc quæ necessario* (pour le Code de 529), § 2.

n'étaient plus importantes que les *auctoritates* du droit ancien que dans la mesure où elles changeaient effectivement le droit matériel.

Par conséquent, pour les canonistes de l'âge classique, il n'existe pas encore de doute qu'on puisse résoudre le conflit éventuel entre deux décrétales du livre grégorien par l'argument chronologique (1); ainsi donc, point de simultanéité fictive. Et rappelons-nous que parmi les *extravagantes* il y avait bon nombre de canons du droit ancien que Gratien avait omis de citer, que Bernard de Pavie avait puisés dans les sources prégratiennes, et qui de là avaient passé dans la compilation officielle. L'idée que de la sorte, parmi plusieurs textes anciens d'origine identique, l'un aurait acquis par un pur hasard un nouveau titre d'autorité universelle, tandis que les autres, chez Gratien, seraient restés des lois de portée relative, allait être prise au sérieux au XVe siècle. Pour le droit classique, c'était une proposition absurde.

En conclusion, nous ne croyons pas que la doctrine traditionnelle sur l'autorité des collections du *Corpus juris canonici* rende justice à leur rôle dans la théorie et la pratique canoniques du Moyen Age. Nous ne prétendons pas avoir résolu le problème par nos remarques sommaires et, peut-être, quelque peu frondeuses. Mais si nous avons pu démontrer à quel urgent besoin répondrait une analyse historique détaillée de la théorie générale du droit à l'âge classique — dans la pensée pure comme dans son application — nos observations n'auront pas été entièrement inutiles.

---

(1) Voir, par ex., la *Glose ordinaire*, ad *Decr.*, l. III, tit. v, c. 7, vo *quam voluerit;* c. 14, vo *maluerit;* c. 28, vo *contenderit.*

II

Some Roman Manuscripts of Canonical Collections*

I. THE COLLECTIONS OF MS. VAT. LAT. 4977

In his pioneer article, 'Le premier manuel canonique de la réforme du xie siècle', Paul Fournier discussed Vat. lat. 4977 and distinguished two collections, 'rapprochées par le hazard de la reliure', fol. 1-23 and fol. 24-end (89).[1] The second of these is derived in part from the pre-Gregorian Collection in Five Books;[2] we are here concerned with the first part, which Fournier has identified as a fragment of the Collection in 74 Titles. But to be precise, this fragment covers fol. 6v-23v only and contains cc. 1-129 of the 74T, as John Gilchrist has pointed out in the *Prolegomena* of his forthcoming edition.[3] Fournier was also wrong in assuming a composite MS ('hazard de la reliure'): fol. 24, the first of the second collection, is actually the last leaf of the third quire (fol. 17-24) in the MS. Thus the end of the fragment from 74T and the beginning of Coll. II, although written by different scribes s. xii, are part of the same quire.

The first to identify the initial portion of the MS was not Fournier but Antonio Agustín (†1586), whose autograph notes are found scattered in the margins, and who wrote on the paper fly-leaf the shelf-mark '2.8' and two descriptive lines, 'Fragmentum corporis canonum', 'et varia collectio N.' Vat. lat. 4977 must thus be added to the Roman MSS that came from Agustín's library;[4] it fits Nr. 285 in his *Bibliotheca latina*: 'Corporis canonum aliud

---

* These *notulae* owe much to the generous help of friends in Rome and the Vatican, especially Professors Claudio Leonardi, Augusto Campana, Vittorio Peri, and Msgr. José Ruysschaert.

[1] *Mélanges d'archéologie et d'histoire* 14 (1894) 150; see also his 'De l'influence de la collection irlandaise...', Nouv. RHD 23 (1899) 67; 'Un groupe de recueils canoniques italiens...', *Mém. Acad. Inscr.* 40 (1916) 206-8.

[2] Fournier, *Mém. Acad. Inscr.* 40.207; Fournier-Le Bras, *Histoire des collections canoniques* II 126f. For an unidentified text inscribed 'Gregorii pape et urbani pape' fol. 50r (*ibid.* II 127) see F. J. Gossman, *Pope Urban II and Canon Law* (Catholic University of America Canon Law Studies 403; Washington D. C. 1960) 18.

[3] *Diuersorum patrum sententie siue Collectio in LXXIV titulos digesta* ed. J. T. Gilchrist (Mon. iur. can. series B: Corpus collectionum 1; to appear in Spring 1972) *Proleg.* § 160 at n. 8.

[4] A large number of such MSS was identified by C. Leonardi, 'Per una storia dell'edizione romana dei concili ecumenici (1608-1612): da Antonio Agustín a Francesco Aduarte', *Mélanges Eugène Tisserant* (Studi e Testi 231-7; Vatican City 1964) VI 583-637, esp. 606ff. In an earlier note (see Bulletin for 1968, *Traditio* 24.505) this writer called attention to the autograph Agustín MS Vat. lat. 4895. The present article adds nine of his codices (and one which he had borrowed and returned; *infra* after n. 55): Vat. lat. 4886, 4977, 4979, 4983,

fragmentum. Liber in membranis annorum CD. forma quadrati'.⁵ The terse note, 'et varia collectio N.' shows once more—if such proof were needed—the penetrating historical acumen of the Archbishop of Tarragona: 'N.' was the symbol he gave to the collection of Anselm of Lucca⁶ in the unpublished draft of an Epitome of Canon Law which this writer found in the autograph MS Vat. lat. 4895. In other words, Antonio Agustín was aware of a close relationship between Anselm and 74T, the collection which Thaner, three hundred years later, still would call 'Collectio minor'.

The fragmentary collection found on fol. 1-6v was copied into the MS at the same time as the fragment of 74T which it precedes,⁷ but must be kept distinct from it. (Fournier's failure to do so explains Bishop Gossman's astonishment at finding texts from Urban II in this copy of 74T.⁸) One may characterize it as an *abbreviatio* or (better) *reconcinnatio* from Gratian's *Concordia*,⁹ written in an archaic script, partly in full lines, partly in two columns, and mixed with extraneous pieces. The Gratian pieces have in most cases been identified in Antonio Agustín's marginal notations. Here is a brief analysis; the MS gives almost all chapters with Gratian's inscriptions and rubrics.

    1r-v   Grat. C.2 q.6 dict.p.c.31, c.32 (no rubric), p.c.32
                 C.3 q.4 c.8, c.10
                 C.6 q.1 c.15
                 C.7 q.1 c.7
                 C.31 q.2 c.3 (with addition in the margin, *al. man.*: C.31 q.2 dict.fin.; C.31 q.3 pr.)

5003, 6093, 6381, Barb. lat. 897, and Vallicell. C.24.—Other Roman MSS to be added to Leonardi's list include Vat. lat. 4897, Council of Ephesus, s. XVI (No. 246 of the *Bibliotheca latina ms.* cited in the next note); 4985, *Vitae Rom. pont.* copied s. XVI from Vat. lat. 3762 (*Bibl.* No. 209); 4988, *Regulae Cancelleriae etc.* s. XV (*Bibl.* No. 275). For Vallicell. MS C.26, identified by G. Martínez Díez, see n. 72 *infra*. But I have great doubts on the authenticity of the note in Ottob. lat. 2461, fol. 1r, which prompted Msgr. Ch. Lefebvre to assign to Agustín the little treatise *ibid.* fol. 500r-513v: Antonii Augustini *Praxis Rotae* [et] Jacobi Emerix *Tractatus seu notitia s. Rotae Romanae* (Monumenta christiana selecta 8; Tournai etc. [1961]) 7-27.

⁵ *Aeternae memoriae viri Antonii Augustini Bibliothecae graeca manuscripta, latina manuscripta, mixta ex libris editis variarum linguarum* (Tarragona 1586), published posthumously in 1587 by M. Bailó; cf. Kuttner, *L'édition romaine des conciles généraux* ... (Miscell. historiae pontif. 5; Rome 1940) 27 n. 49.

⁶ Proof of this must be left for another occasion.

⁷ Folios 1-3 are the counter leaves of 8, 7, 6 in the first quire; 74T begins on 6v: there can be no doubt that this was a quire from the beginning.

⁸ Gossman, *op. cit.* 16.

⁹ Hence the MS cannot be s. xi, or s. xi/xii, as Fournier, *Mél. d'archéol.* 14.150, *Mém. Acad. Inscr.* 40.206, and Gilchrist *loc. cit.* assume. Gossman, in suggesting that Gratian may have used this or a similar collection as source (*op. cit.* 17), reversed the actual relationship.

C.32 q.1 c.1 (no rubric), cc.4 (shortened), 13, 14 (all with rubrics)
C.32 q.2 c.8

This is followed, fol. 2r-v, by a *quaestio* with the title *De his qui occulte nubunt* . . . , beg. 'Quidam uxorem duxit sine presentia testium . . .', with a rather rigoristic solution for the problem of clandestine marriages; perhaps written to illustrate C.30 q.5 (edited below, pp. 25-6).

2v-4v § De affinitate. Cum nouerca—consummatus est = Ivo Decr. 9.28, Pan. 7.62 (not identified by Antonio Agustín)
§ De spirituali germanitate. Dictum etiam nobis' = Grat. C.30 q.1 c.4
§ De eodem. Simili ratione qui spiritualem habet compatrem gener eius fieri non prohibetur—uxorem accipere non probibeatur. (Not C.30 q.4 c.4 *Qui spiritualem*, contrary to Antonio Agustín's marginal notation.)
C.30 q.4 c.3—dict.fin.[10] (At the top of fol. 3r a note of identification, 'hec sunt Gratiani . . . ', in a hand which I believe to be that of Pedro Chacón,[11] one of the *Correctores Romani.*)
C.30 q.5 c.6, dict.p.c.6, c.8-dict.fin. (p.c.11)
Julius pp. Habet sacrosancta—uoluerit (*al. m.*) = Ivo Pan. 4.12 (cf. Grat. C.9 q.3 cc.17-18).—fol. 4v blank.

5r-v D.32 c.6 II § 5 Proibentur (marg. 'Gregorius': see the preceding line in Gratian), cc.6-13, 15, 16; D.33 c.6

5v-6v C.11 q.1 pr. and cc.1, 3, 31, dict.p.c.31
C.11 q.3 cc.11, 14, 27, 28, 40, 106, 107

The Collection in 74 Titles begins here, in a different hand. Vat. lat. 4977 thus offers significant evidence for the continuing interest in copying 'antiquated' collections of the eleventh century—74T and the 'Corporis canonum aliud fragmentum' (Coll. II: fol. 23ff.)[11a]—at a time when Gratian's *Concordia* was already in use.

II. The Collection in XIII Books of MS Vat. lat. 1361 (s. xii)

Fournier described this collection in his study on Ivo of Chartres and again in the *Histoire des collections canoniques*; he characterized it as derived es-

---

[10] This piece, being covered by a tissue screen on fol. 3r of the MS, is hardly legible on microfilm; c.6 (Urban II) was therefore missed by Gossman.

[11] By comparison with his autograph marginalia in Vat. lat. 8922, fol. 1-76, on which see G. Card. Mercati, *Opere minori* (Studi e Testi 76-80; Vatican City 1937-41) III 367. The best bio-bibliographical information on Chacón (Ciaconius; 1527-1581) is still André Schott, S. J., *Hispaniae Bibliotheca* (Francof. 1608) 556-64, on whom all later notices are ultimately based. Chacón is frequently mentioned in Agustín's Dialogues; but according to Schott, *Bibl. Hisp.* 559, Chacón destroyed his own *castigationum notae* on Gratian.

[11a] References to 'Corp. can.' in Antonio Agustín's hand are frequent in the margins of Coll. II (e.g. fol. 24r, 31r-v, . . . 79v, 80r, 83r-v, 84v, 85r) wherever he could not identify a given text in Gratian. *Corpus canonum* for him was the *Dionysio-Hadriana*—see III *infra*, App. (III), No. 284 of his Latin MSS, and his copy of the Wendelstein edition (Mainz 1525) in Leonardi's list, p. 622 No. 80.

sentially from Anselm of Lucca but with a marked influence of Ivo's Panormia; and as containing later material, down to texts from the councils of Innocent II.[12] It was not his intention to give an exhaustive analysis, but like many other Italian collections of the early twelfth century—such as the 3L of Vat. lat. 3831 and Pistoia 135 (109)[13]—the 13L of Vat. lat. 1361 deserves a much closer study. There are for instance many indications that the Anselm text which is at its base was one of the late recensions, probably of the C-type.

13L shares with Ans. C many of the chapters added to the original form (A) of Anselm's collection at the end of the individual 'books'. We may note one instance in passing: both Ans. C and 13L present at the end of Book IV—as does the Naples MS of Ans. A—the canons of the First Lateran Council (1123), in the long form (Leonardi's β),[14] providing thus the much-desired twelfth-century evidence for the β-recension.[15] It was the first text of Pope Calixtus's council to come to light in the sixteenth century, and again Antonio Agustín was the first to discover it, in the MS he owned of Ans. C.[16] But before we have a satisfactory study of the various 'appendices', and indeed of the composition, of each book in the extant Anselm MSS, no precise statement will be possible as to the version of his collection which is at the basis of 13L.

One major feature of Vat. lat. 1361 which escaped Fournier's attention is its strong monastic bias, with an overtone of little esteem for the canons regular. It is a bias much stronger than the interest in matters monastic expressed by the several secondary Anselm recensions in their additions to Book 5, where we find after Ans. A 5.64 that Ans. B has 83 additional chapters (and more in the appendix of Vat. lat. 1364); that Ans. Bb has 82 and Ans. C 95 (plus 5 unnumbered) additional chapters. The additions in 13L, numbered 52-119 (c.51 = Ans. 5.64) are less in bulk but more significant. They begin with Pseudo-Boniface IV 'Sunt nonnulli' JE †1996 (5.52, fol. 112rb-vb), followed by what thus far appears to be the only copy, outside of Pisa, Semin. MS 59, of Peter Damiani's *opusculum* 28, here inscribed *Tractatus domini petri religiosissimi cardinalis romane ecclesie aduersus clericos et canonicos* (beg. 'Cunc-

---

[12] 'Les collections canoniques attribuées à Yves de Chartres', BEC 58 (1897) 430-33; Fournier-Le Bras, *Hist. des coll.* II 225-6. See also Gossman, *op. cit.* 89-93 for material from Urban II.

[13] Cf. the brief note in this Bulletin, *Traditio* 24 (1968) 504-5.

[14] Ans. (C) *post* 4.55; 13L (*post* 4.33=Ans.[A] 4.55) 4.34-42, followed by ten more chapters, 43-52. Cf. P. Fournier, BEC 58.433 nn. 1-2; 'Observations sur diverses recensions de la collection canonique d'Anselme de Lucques', *Annales de l'Université de Grenoble* 13 (1901) 434 (the Naples MS), 446 (rec. C); Fournier-Le Bras II 197, 225. F. does not discuss which form of the Lateran canons was used in these texts.

[15] C. Leonardi, in COD 165 found no medieval MS for this recension.

[16] See III 2 *infra*.

tis amantissimis': 5.53, fol. 112vb-114ra).¹⁷ Among the texts that follow next,¹⁸ two astonishing forgeries should be singled out:

lviii. *De factis clericis monachis et de omnibus ministris sancte ecclesie.* Placuit omnibus residentibus in sanctis synodis—quia sanctus dominus sanctos uult ministros. (fol. 114vb-115ra)

lxviii. *Quod monachi et canonici regulariter debent uiuere.* Placuit omnibus sanctis constitutionibus—et omnem odit iniquitatem. (fol. 115vb-116ra)

Astonishing, for both fabrications use the vocabulary and phraseology of two well-known anti-monastic forgeries, the Pseudo-Nicene 'Placuit omnibus' and the canon ascribed to Eugenius II 'Placuit communi' (cf. Grat. C. 16 q.1 cc.1, 8), but turn their meaning into exactly the opposite. The 'original' forgeries seem to have made their first appearance in the *Polycarpus*—that is, between 1109 and 1113¹⁹—whence they were copied into several of the secondary recensions of Anselm, to be eventually incorporated into Gratian's book. In 13L 5.58 and 68, however, the prohibition for monks to exercise any pastoral or clerical ministry, from baptism to burial, has been turned into an unrestricted permission, to be respected by all; and the monastic life is held up as a model to all canons regular, even to the point that 'nullus quippe dici potest canonicus qui monachus rennuit fore' (5.68). This reverses the well-known prohibitions for canons to become monks at will which go under Urban II's name in many twelfth-century collections (cf. Grat. C.19 q.3 cc.2, 3)¹⁹ᵃ and appear also in 13L: 4.51, 48. One has the impression of forgers on both sides of the controversy trying to outwit one another, especially so if the texts in the *Polycarpus*, in turn, should prove to be a response to a still earlier set of forgeries, Pseudo-Gregory 'Oportet' and Pseudo-Boniface 'Sunt nonnulli' (JE †1951, †1996), which were in circulation since the mid-eleventh century.

Monastic rights are emphasized again in Bk. 13 towards the end with a cluster of forgeries (fol. 244vb-246ra),

xli. *De decimis dandis monachis.* Beatissimo pape damaso Ieronimus presbiter in domino salutem. Inter alia—pauperum est.

---

[17] Cf. S. Kuttner and R. Somerville, 'The So-called Canons of Nîmes (1096)', TRG 38 (1970) 177-8.

[18] 13L 5.54-57, for instance, correspond to: (54-55) Ivo Pan. 2.67-68, (56) JL 5778, (57) Ans. B 5.74 = C 5.97 (not numbered: c. 2 *post* 5.95). For 5.56 see Gossman, *Urban II* 90.

[19] For the date see H. W. Klewitz, 'Die Entstehung des Kardinalskollegiums', ZRG Kan. Abt. 25 (1936) 165, 212. The wrong date in Fournier-Le Bras II 171 (1104-6) is still repeated by all manuals.

[19a] The source of c.2 *Mandamus* is unknown. It made its first appearance in the *Polycarpus* 4.31.83. 'Anselm of Havelberg' (actually Arno of Reichersberg), whom Friedberg n. 3 *ad loc.* cites (following Berardi), is a derivative, not a source of Gratian. C.3 is an excerpt from Urban II JL 5763, ed. U. Chevalier, *Codex diplomaticus ordinis s. Rufi* (Valence 1891) No. 5, pp. 8-9.

II

12

 xlii. *Item de decimis et oblationibus.* Syricius papa ad theodorum cordubiensem episcopum. Litteris a tua fraternitate—fidei caritas.
 xliii. *Item quod monachi non dent decimas* ex decretis g̅g̅. (gregorii). Statuimus secundum priorem diffinitionem ut monasteria—carissime fili, patiantur,

preceding Urban II's canon of Clermont, 'Quesitum est de episcopis' C.1 q.3 c.4 (here: 'xliiii. § Vrbanus pp.ii.de decimis') and an unknown letter of Paschal II, 'Litterarum uestrarum', numbered xlv. and addressed 'clericis sci. alexandri': the earliest extant papal document in the long-drawn quarrel between the two cathedrals, St. Vincent's and St. Alexander's, at Bergamo. The decision is based in part on a report the pope received from Guido, *preclarus iudex Cremonensis.*

To complete the dossier of this case as given in Kehr's *Italia pontificia*,[20] Paschal's letter will be edited below (pp. 28-9). Also, as an addition to the corpus of *epistolae spuriae* established by Erasmus, Vallarsi, and Maffei for St. Jerome,[21] 'Inter alia' will be edited below from 13L 13.41 and Vatican MS Barb. lat. 1450 (prov. Monte Amiata), where it is found at the end of Burchard's *Libri decretorum*,[22] while only a fragment appears in Gratian C.16 q.1 c.68 (repeated in part in C.1 q.2 c.6). This letter is not to be confused with another Pseudo-Jerome, *ep. spur.* 43 = C.10 q.1 c.13, to Pope Damasus, which made its first appearance in the *Polycarpus*, 3.9.11.[23]

Among the pieces following at the end of Bk. 13 in Vat. lat. 1361, mention should be made of a cluster of texts on *consuetudo* (13.49-57, also c.64; fol. 247va-248rb). The collection ends with 13.101-105 on *mendacium* (fol. 255rb-257rb) and six chapters on oaths and perjury (257rb-258vb): 13.106-111 =

---

[20] Kehr, *Ital. pont.* 6.1.366ff. 377ff. where the earliest papal document is by Innocent II.
[21] Clavis 633 (pp. 144-6).
[22] The MS is described by F. Pelster, 'Das Dekret Bischof Burkhards von Worms (1000-1025) in vatikanischen HSS.', *Miscellanea Giovanni Mercati* (Studi e Testi 121-6; Città del Vaticano 1946) II 145-6, but Pelster did not trace the provenance ('... eines Zisterzienserklosters, dessen Name nicht mehr zu entziffern ist'); actually, fol. 1r marg. sup. [s.xiv] gives us: 'Hic liber est sacristie mon^{rii} s^{ti} saluatoris monte Amiato or^{is} Cist^{is} usuj m(ih)i sigismu(n)do'); nor did he identify all the appendices on fol. 165r-166v. The Burchard text breaks off in 19.48 (not 20.48); it is followed by Greg. M. JE †1366, Zachar. JE 2306, Urb. II JL 5760, an explanation of the Mass, beg. 'Introitus misse conuenit patriarcharum prophetarumque preconiis...' (the same in Paris, B.N. lat. 11579, fol. 21 according to Hauréau), and the Pseudo-Jerome. A hand s. xiii then records a feudal oath to the abbot *s. Saluatoris* (cf. Pelster 145).
[23] Not mentioned in Fournier's list of *spuria* which entered twelfth-century canon law through this collection, 'Les deux recensions de la collection canonique romaine dite le Polycarpus', *Mélanges d'archéol. et d'histoire* 37 (1918-19) 73-5. The Pseudo-Jerome is followed in *Polyc.* 3.9.12 by Pseudo-Damasus 'Quoniam perniciosa' (source of Gratian C. 10 q. 1 c. 15 'Hanc consuetudinem' [JK †249 lists only this incipit]). Friedberg's notes on c. 13 are unsatisfactory.

Ivo Pan. 8.84, 89. 105-108 (in one), 115-116 (in one), 111, 122. The last two leaves (259ra-260ra) contain an incomplete *Chronicon mundi*, beg. 'PRIMA etas in exordio sui continet creationem mundi'; ends 'Julius v. v̄. liiii. (*leg.* v̄.c. liiii. = 5154) hic primo manarchiam (*sic*) tenuit. SEXTA ETAS.'

The provenance of the book needs further investigation, but it seems likely that the collection originated in a monastic house in or near Bergamo.

III. ANSELM OF LUCCA: THE MANUSCRIPTS OF THE CORRECTORES ROMANI AND OF ANTONIO AGUSTÍN

It is no secret that in the unfinished edition of Anselm, Friedrich Thaner gave us less than one might have expected from his great scholarship. Little would be gained by completing the edition (from Ans.11.16 to the end of Bk.13) on the lines of what Thaner published. New MSS have come to light: G. Fransen some years ago discovered a new copy of recension A in Florence, Bibl. Laur. MS San Marco 499 (s.xii), and a sixteenth-century copy of recension C in Huesca, Bibl. Provincial MS 20. Also, the classification of some of the known MSS, never reexamined after Fournier (1901), needs revision. (Naples, B.N. MS XII·A.37-39 is a case in point, combining the basic features of A, as it seems, with some of the interpolations and appendices characteristic of C.)[24] A future editor would also have courageously to break with the illusion that something like the 'original' Anselm could be produced: he would have to find typographical devices for presenting the basic collection (A) together with all its accretions in the MSS of A and in the variant or expanded forms B, Bb, and C. Even a mere tabulation showing the composition of individual books and their appendices in the MSS would be most helpful—if only for understanding the references to Anselm in the margins and the *Notae* of the Roman edition of Gratian; references which must appear inconsistent and contradictory unless one realizes that the *Correctores* used several MSS side by side. (Friedberg, having at his disposal only Haenel's copy of an artificial, seventeenth-century combination of Bb and C, was never able to grasp this.)

1. The booklist of the *Correctores Romani* mentions codices 'ex Vaticana et Hieronymi Parisetti'. Parisetti (Parisetus) was one of the *doctores* in the commission. His MS was cited as *Authentica canonum* by the *Correctores* in the early stages of their work.[25] As Fournier saw, it belonged to class C; how-

---

[24] See Fournier, *Annales Grenoble* 13 (n. 14 *supra*) 431-7.
[25] See, e.g. the minutes of the *congregatio* of 30 September 1567, Vat. lat. 4889, fol. 64r ad D. 38 c. 5: '... et Auth. cano. quae est apud D. Parisetum referatur in Cong. gen.'; also num. xiv of the *Leges constitutae et obseruatae in correctione* (*ibid.* fol. V-VIr, whence published in Appendix I of Theiner's *Disquisitiones criticae* [Rome 1836], reprinted by Friedberg, *Corp. iur. can.* I lxxvii-viii). The material of the *Correctores* in Vat. lat. 4889-4894 was briefly mentioned in this Bulletin, *Traditio* 24 (1968) 505.

ever, since the *Correctores* repeatedly call it a *vetustus codex*,[26] this cannot have been the sixteenth-century paper MS, now Vat. lat. 4983,[27] which corresponds in almost every detail to the peculiarities mentioned in their notes[28] but must rather be considered a direct copy taken from Parisetti's thus far untraced codex.

How many Anselm MSS 'ex Vaticana' the *Correctores* had at their disposal can be deduced from a tabulation of their references, as recorded in the minutes of their meetings, Vat. lat. 4889, 4891-92; in the printed edition of 1582; occasionally also in the draft of the *Notae*, by their secretary, Michael Thomasius (of whom more later), Vat. lat. 4890. A few samples must suffice here:[29]

	Vat.lat. 1363 (A)	Vat.lat. 1364 (B)	Vat.lat. cod. Pari- 6381 (B) seti (C)	Vat.lat. 3531 (Bb)	Correctores Congregat. ed. Rom.	
D.38 c.1	7.100	7.107	7.*105*	7.*114*	7.*118*	7.105 *al*.118	7.114
2	99	108	*104*	*113*	*117*	104 *al*.117	113
3	101	109	*107*	116	*119**	107 *al*.119	119
4	102	110	*108*	117	[120]	108	108
5	103	111	*109*	*118*	[121]	109 *al*.118	109
		*Vat.lat. 3531 ends here					
D.74 c.4	7.86	7.93	7.*91*	7.98	7.*103*	7.91	6.103**
7	6.58-9	6.60-1	6.*60-1*	6.64-5	6.*66-7*	6.60,71*al.66	6.66-7
8	7.65	7.72	7.*70*	7.74	7.*75*	7.70 *al*.75	7.75
9	7.85	7.92	7.*90*	7.97	7.*102*	7.90 *al*.102	7.102
		*mistake for 61 **misprint					

Several conclusions can be drawn: (1) the *Correctores* ignored the Vatican MS of recension A, although it had been identified as early as Marcello Cer-

---

[26] See e.g. the draft for the *Notae* by Michael Thomasius (Miguel Tomás Taxaquet, of whom more later), Vat. lat. 4890, fol. 137v (No. 1942) ad C. 24 q. 3 c. 24, v. *conversos*: '. . . quae absunt a plerisque exemplaribus Gratiani et uetusto codice Pariseti in cuius calce hic et alij tres Canones tamquam fragmentum alicuius concilij descripti sunt'; fol. 92v ad C. 12 q. 2 c. 37 (No. 1156): 'Ad finem codicis antiqui, collectionis Anselmi, qui est penes Hieron. Parisetum habetur fragmentum alicuius concilij Vrbani 2^i ubi in principio ita legitur. Alienationes quae. . .' In the printed *Notae* the first reference appears as '. . . et vetusto quodam codice', the second as 'Post collectionem Anselmi in codice perantiquo habetur. . .'.

[27] As Fournier, *Ann. Gren.* 13.443 assumes.

[28] To give only one example: the four canons mentioned as 'fragmentum alicuis concilij', '. . . concilij Vrbani 2^i,' in Thomasius's notes (see n. 26) appear in Vat. lat. 4983, fol. 621v, at the end of the appendices to Ans. C Book 13, but without any inscription. The source of Thomasius's error in calling this fragment of Conc. I Later. a council of Urban II (as does Gratian) can be traced to an error in MS Vallicell. C.24 (mentioned p. 18 *infra*).

[29] In the draft of Thomasius, the quire containing his notes for D.17-D.56 is missing after fol. 14v of Vat. lat. 5890, and for D. 74 his notes give nothing new as compared with the minutes of the *congregationes*. The source or sources of the citations by the *Correctores* are printed in italics (in the case of Parisetti's codex, I am inferring the numbers from the 16th-cent. copy).

vini's catalogue;³⁰ it must have come so late to their attention that only very few citations can be found.³¹ (2) They disposed of a copy of Bb, which must have been the copy made for Cardinal Antonio Carafa from MS Barb. lat. 535 (XI.175)—the Barberini codex itself does not appear in the booklist of the *Correctores*—and which Carafa as member and, from 1569 on, as chairman, evidently put at the disposal of the commission. Their copy, now Vat. lat. 3531, came to the Vatican Library only after his death in 1591,³² but the references to Gratian entered in the margins of Carafa's book must go back to the days of the *Correctores*. They are in Pedro Chacón's elegant, minute hand. The MS breaks off with Ans. Bb 7.119: hence the references to its chapter numbers stop here in the example given above from Grat. D.38, while in the Barberini codex Book 7 has 209 numbered chapters (plus appendix). (3) The copy of recension B was certainly not Vat. lat. 1364, although this MS, too, had been identified as 'Anselmi Decretum' in the Cervini catalogue.³³ But much as one might want to consider Vat. lat. 6381 the source of the *Correctores* for B, it can't be done: this MS, as we shall presently see, was not at the Vatican in their time but in Spain; it came to Rome only after the death of its owner, Antonio Agustín (1586). Yet in all cases of discrepancy between the two B codices, the references of the *Correctores* would correspond to this MS. We must therefore assume that they had 'ex Vaticana' a now lost Anselm MS, closely akin to Agustín's codex. Since they had the privilege of borrowing books from the Vatican Library,³⁴ the existence and disappearance of such a MS would not be too daring a conjecture. (4) As for recension C, it has been observed above that Parisetti's *codex vetustus* rather than its copy in Vat.lat. 4983 was the book which served the *Correctores*.

---

³⁰ Vat. lat. 3968, fol. 56v No. 1870: 'Liber de potestate et primatu apostolice sedis' with Cervini's addition 'Decretum Anselmi'. For Vat. lat. 3968 and other early inventories F. Ehrle, 'Zur Geschichte der Katalogisierung der Vatikana', *Historisches Jahrbuch der Görres-Gesellschaft* 11 (1890) 718-27 remains fundamental.

³¹ E. g. *Nota Corr.* C. 1 q. 3 c. 9 (Alex. II, JL 4722, Kehr, *Ital. pont.* 3.339 No. 7): 'Exstat integra haec epistola in bibliotheca Vaticana post librum Anselmi Lucensis', — thus only in Vat. lat. 1363 fol. 241r-v. (JL 4722 is also found in the Coll. 7L of Turin MS D.IV.33 [cf. Fournier-Le Bras II 166] and, shortened and interpolated, in Deusdedit, *Libellus contra invasores* 2.19 [ed. Sackur, MGH *Libelli* 2.338.24-29] = Deusd. *Coll. can.* 4.95. The source for the text in Mansi 20.963 No. 35 was Gratian, not Ivo.—This by way of emendation of Kehr's entry *loc. cit.*)—Another rare reference of the *Correctores* is at C. 16 q. 1 c. 65, cited as Ans. 6.167 (from the second B codex) in ed. Rom. but as 6.167, *al.* 160 (=A), *al.* 177 (mistake for Bb 6. 176) in the minutes.

³² Verso of second fly-leaf: 'Antonij Card. Carafae Bibliothecarij. Munus ex testamento.' See also Fournier, *Annales Grenoble* 13.428, 450.

³³ Vat. lat. 3968, fol. 56v No. 1857.

³⁴ *Breve* of 18 February 1567; see Pastor, *Geschichte der Päpste* VIII (Freiburg 1925) 146 n. 3.

2. For a first effort at critical evaluation of the various recensions, we must again turn to Antonio Agustín. In his essay 'De quibusdam veteribus canonum ecclesiasticorum collectoribus', which his nephew and namesake, Antonio Agustín S. J., first published posthumously in 1611 from the archbishop's autograph notes (Vat. lat. 6252), mention is made of three codices of Anselm of Lucca.[35] Two of these Agustín owned himself: they appear as Nos. 282 and 283 in the catalogue of his library.[36] He used to call one his *liber vetus* and the other, his *exemplum Romanum*.[37] Already the Ballerini identified them correctly, but without giving their reasons, as Vat. lat. 4983 and 6381 (misquoted as '6361'); they could not trace the third.[38] Neither could Fournier, who moreover remained vague about the two Vatican codices and would not commit himself further than saying that Antonio Agustín 'knew' both MSS, even though he had seen the copy made from Vat. lat. 4983 in Ottob. lat. 224, dated 'Romae Anno iubilaei M.DC.' and inscribed 'Decretum Anselmi excerptum ab alio Antonij Augustini Archiēpi Tarraconen.'[39]

We have, however, a perfect key to the identity of these MSS in his *De emendatione Gratiani*, dialogues 4 and 5 of the second book, in which the discourse is 'de Callisti secundi Romana synodo', i. e. the Lateran Council of 1123.[40] Here A. (Antonius Augustinus) tells his interlocutors B. and C. (Francisco Aduarte and Martín Agustín, the archbishop's nephew)[41] that he obtained the first Anselm codex from the library of Luis Gomez, his predecessor as auditor of the Rota, bishop of Sarno (1534-1543), and that he collated it with a second codex, of Niccolò Ormaneto, bishop of Padua (1570-77).[42] The saintly Ormaneto,

---

[35] Vat. lat. 6252 (cf. Leonardi, *Mél. Tisserant* [n. 4 *supra*] VI 599-601, 608 No. 20) fol. 279; *Epitome iuris pontificii* II (Rome 1611) fol. †††† 2v = *Opp.* III (Lucca 1767) 239-40.

[36] *Bibl. lat.* (n. 5 *supra*) 282: 'ANSELMI Episcopi Lucensis decretorum libri XIII. quib. praeponitur ordo Pontificum Romanorum. Liber in membranis annor. ccc et vltra forma quadrati.' *Ibid.* 283: 'ANSELMI iterum decretorum libri siue collectio regularum, et sententiar. sanctorum Patrum, ac concilior. quibus item praeponitur idem ordo, et de celebrando concilio. Ambrosii libellus de vita, et ordinatione Episcoporum. Gregorii Papae epistula ad Joannem CP. et alios. Liber recens in charta forma folii.' ('praeponitur' in No. 283 is an error: it should be 'postponitur idem ordo, et praeponitur de celebr. conc.')

[37] *Loc. cit.* n. 35 *supra*.

[38] *De antiquis. . . collectionibus et collectoribus canonum* (Opera S. Leonis Magni III; Venice 1757) ccxcvi = PL 56.327B; cf. Fournier, *Annales Grenoble* 13.429 n. 1, 430 n. 3.

[39] Fournier *loc. cit.* and pp. 443, 458.

[40] Ant. Augustini archiep. Tarraconensis *De emendatione Gratiani dialogorum libri duo* (Tarragona 1587) 237-48 = pp. 271-84 in Baluze's edition (Paris 1670, 1672) = *Opp.* III 117-22.

[41] They are identified in n. 1 (p. 221) of Bk. 2 dial. 1 in the original edition, and in the margin of dial. 1 in Baluze's ed. (p. 245) and *Opp.* III 108. On Aduarte see C. Leonardi, *art. cit.* (n. 4 *supra*) 626-37.

[42] *De emend. Grat.* 2.4: 'Tria volumina eius collectionis, quam Anselmi Lucensis appellamus, ad manus meas peruenerunt sine nomine collectoris. Primum ex Ludouici Gometii

friend of Giberti and Pole and at one time Vicar General of St. Charles Borromeo, became nunzio to the court of Philip II in 1572; he died in Spain in 1577, having been denied his wish to return to his diocese.[43] It appears that he repeatedly lent manuscripts to Antonio Agustín.[44] These two Anselm MSS Agustín calls *satis antiqua*, while the third, which he acquired 'recently' from the library of Michael Thomasius, bishop of Lérida, was a copy 'ex bibliotheca Vaticana nuper, ut suspicor, exscriptum'[45] (here he was wrong, for the source was Dr. Parisetti's, not a Vatican codex).

To begin with this last-named MS. Miguel Tomás Taxaquet, a protégé of Agustín and secretary of the *Correctores Romani*, was appointed bishop of Lérida in 1577 to succeed Antonio Agustín upon the latter's transfer to the metropolitan see of Tarragona. Miguel Tomás left Rome for his bishopric in the spring of 1578 but died already in July of that year.[46] The 'exemplum Romanum' had evidently been copied for him during his years as secretary in Rome, and it was eventually to return to Rome with other books from Antonio Agustín's estate, after the archbishop's death in 1586, its margins filled with innumerable notes in his own hand—among them the identification of Pope Calixtus's Lateran Council at the end of Bk. 4, mentioned above.[46a]

But how was it possible, we may ask with Francisco Aduarte in the dialogue, that with this book in hand Michael Thomasius, Pedro Chacón, and their fellow *Correctores* did not recognize the text of this council as the source of the canons ascribed to Calixtus in Gratian? Perhaps, Agustín replies, because the council appears here without any inscription and without separation of its canons, 'as you can see here with your own eyes'.[47] And indeed, Vat.lat.

Episcopi Sarnensis, cui ego Romae suffectus fui sacri Palatii auditor, bibliotheca accepi: idque contuli cum alio exemplo Nicolai Ormaneti Episcopi Patauini' (p. 237).

[43] F. M. Carini S. I., *Monsignor Niccolò Ormaneto Veronese vescovo di Padova, nunzio Apostolico alla corte di Filippo II re di Spagna 1572-1577* (Rome 1894); excerpts from this in C. Robinson, *Nicolo Ormaneto: A Papal Envoy in the Sixteenth Century* (London 1920).

[44] See *infra*, Appendix (II) on Vat. lat. 4886.

[45] *De emend. Grat.* 237.

[46] Nicolaus Antonius, *Bibliotheca hispanica nova* II 147; Hurter, *Nomenclator* III 90; K. Schellhass, 'Deutsche und kuriale Gelehrte im Dienste der Gegenreformation', QF 14 (1911) 289 *et passim*; P. M. Baumgarten, *Hispanica* I: *Spanische Beiträge zur Emendatio Decreti Gratiani* (Krumbach 1927) 3-6. Miguel Tomás signs a letter to Antonio Agustín on 25 May 1573 (F. Miguel Rosell, 'Epistolario Antonio Agustín: Ms. 53 de la Biblioteca universitaria', *Analecta Sacra Tarraconensia* 13 [1937-40] 152-4: 'su menor servidor y capellán El doct. Mi. Thomas.') For his departure from the Curia see the minutes of the *congregatio* of 6 May 1578 in Vat. lat. 4913, fol. 76r-v, printed poorly (and without indication of the source) in Theiner's *Disquisitiones crit.* App. I pp. 35-7.

[46a] II *supra*, at n. 16.

[47] *Loc. cit.*: 'A: . . . Aperi, C. hunc librum, et quaere librum quartum extremum.—B: Cur Romani selecti viri ex hoc libro emendationem Callisti capitum non fecerunt? praesertim cum ipse Thomasius, et Pet. Ciacconius eius sodalis eodem libro fuerint vsi?—A:

II

18

4983 fol. 199v shows the words 'Calist.2. in concilio' (Later. *add.al.m.*) and the chapter divisions inserted in Antonio Agustín's own hand.

The dialogue goes on identifying the Lateran canons one by one in Gratian and discussing the variant readings. (The identifications include c.18(ii) of the vulgate recension = Gratian C.16 q.7 c.39,[48] which Friedberg, three hundred years later, still considered a *caput incertum*!) The discussion turns to the canons of the council which appear under the name of Urban II in Gratian. They appear, as Aduarte remarks, 'sine nomine... in extremo hoc Anselmo Romano', that is, toward the end of Vat.lat. 4983, fol. 621v, but he had seen them also ascribed to Urban 'in quibusdam schedis' (p. 245), 'in Romanorum schedis veteribus, quae a Pariseto docto viro inventae sunt' (p. 246). Without going here into the complex issue of the false Urban attribution, we may only note that the Roman *schedae*, initialed by 'M.T.' (Michael Thomasius) and marked in his (or Aduarte's) hand, 'Haec sunt accepta ex cod. Doct. Pariseti', were later bound together with other material on councils and decretals; and that they can be traced today in MS C.24 of the Biblioteca Vallicelliana in Rome, fol. 92. This miscellaneous book, too, had first passed into Antonio Agustín's library and was annotated by him, before returning to Rome after his death.[49]

The Anselm MS which had come to Antonio Agustín from the library of Gomez is Vat. lat. 6381. Fournier, who concentrated for recension B on the time-honored Vat. lat. 1364,[50] gave this MS only a perfunctory glance. Yet it is a very fascinating book which represents the critical endeavors of Agustín, based on his collations with Ormaneto's codex. Vat. lat. 6381 actually consists of two MSS: a vellum codex s.xii, fol. 1-256 (old 257), and a paper codex s. xvi, fol. 258-326 (old 258-324), with a paper leaf of larger format, folded over and originally not numbered (new 257) in between. This contains some material pertaining to the work of the *Correctores* and was apparently a loose sheet found in the book at the time of rebinding.

The first MS contains Anselm's recension B, ending incomplete fol. 256v at (B) 12.17, which corresponds to A 13.16 (Book 11 of A being omitted in recension B), while the *capitulatio* gives 29 chapters for Book 12 (fol. 253r). A paper slip pasted onto the verso of the fly-leaf has an autograph note by Agustín, with the title 'Anselmi $\overline{\text{epi}}$ Lucen̄' followed by a brief biographical notice from 'SIGIBERTVS IN Chronicis'. On fol. 1, where the *Ordo Romanorum*

Cur id factum sit, plane ignoro. In caussa tamen fuisse existimo, quod sine vlla inscriptione canonum verba posita sint, ipsaq. canonum distinctio nulla sit, vt vestris oculis inspicere potestis' (p. 237).

[48] *De emend. Grat.* 2.5 (p. 245 = 280 Baluze).

[49] A full analysis of Vallicell. C. 24 will be published by Dr. Laura Menichetti-Gasparri, Rome.

[50] *Annales Grenoble* 13.348ff.

pontificum from St. Peter to Paschal II (1-4r) begins, with three lines of verse preceding, there are a shelf-mark 466 and the ownership note 'Ludouici gomez epi Sarnen. auditoris Rote' at the top. At the bottom the wrong title 'Brocardus Vormacien. eps.' (s. xvi) has been canceled, and directly above it an erased line becomes legible under ultraviolet light: 'Antonius eps Ilerden.' Underneath, the shelf mark 'Cod. V. 6381' was later entered. This may indicate that Agustín acquired the book from the estate of Gomez († 1543) only after his transfer from Alife to Lérida in 1561. The folios are numbered throughout in his hand,[51] and likewise autograph are the marginal identifications of chapters with the corresponding texts in Gratian, as well as occasional variants or corrections entered from another MS. In books 11 and 12 Agustín emended the rubrics to 'duodecimus' and 'tertius decimis', and the right-hand running heads from XI and XII to XII and XIII. Certain *capitula* of the collection have a zero (Ø) put against them in the margin, evidently indicating their absence in the MS he collated, i. e. in Ormaneto's MS. A spot check of Fournier's sampling of texts which Ans. B has added to Ans. A[52] leads to the conclusion that Ormaneto's MS belonged to the latter type.

The second MS, which Agustín numbered consecutively from 258 to 324, apparently has never been examined;[53] Fournier doesn't even mention it. It is a supplement on paper to Gomez's codex, in the hand of a copyist, beginning with the missing chapters of Bk. 13 and an appendix to that book (fol. 258-268), the chapters through xxvii (= Ans. A 13.27) numbered by the scribe, and from 28 to 45 (in arabic) by Agustín. From fol. 270 (old 268) on we find, always in the scribal hand, first some texts marked 'Ante initium libri' by Antonio Agustín; then chapters seemingly out of sequence, beginning with two texts of Leo I, numbered xc. and xli. (error for xci.), identified and marked in the margin 'pag. 34' by Agustín: they were to go to fol. 34 of the first MS, that is to the end of Bk. 1 which ends there (B 1.90). The chapters which follow Agustín destined for insertion in Bk. 3,

(scribe) xxxiii.-xxxiiii.	(Antonio Agustín)	pa. 63
lv.		p. 68. In Ro. lvii
lvij.		p. 74 in Ro. xcii

that is, always by referring to the folios of the first MS and indicating, as the case may be, the presence of the texts 'in Ro.' i. e. in Agustín's *exemplum Romanum*, Vat. lat. 4983 (here = C 3.57 and *post* c. 91). This supplement, book by book, is followed, fol. 324v-326v (322-324v), by some additional chapters to be inserted in Books 6-8. An autograph index of sources by Agustín

---

[51] With a mistake: the count jumps from 187 to 189, which explains the difference from the present pagination.
[52] *Ann. Gren.* 13.440-42.
[53] The only brief mention of its nature as a supplement is in A. Stickler, 'Il potere coattivo materiale della Chiesa... secondo Anselmo di Lucca', *Studi Gregoriani* 2 (1947) 243 n. 15.

II

20

follows fol. 328r-336r—to this day the only index to Anselm's collection—arranged by popes from *Adrianus* to *Zosimus*; incipits from *Abbatem* to *Vt subdiaconus*; councils from *Affricanum* to *Zachariae Sy*(*nodus*).

A comparison between Agustín's supplement and the few peculiarities mentioned by Fournier[54] for the Venice MS of recension A made a further inquiry into this codex appear worthwhile. Examination of a partial microfilm of Venice, S. Marco MS lat. IV.55,[55] proved that the hunch was correct: it is indeed the codex from which Agustín had his supplemental texts copied—it is Ormaneto's book. We find chapters marked with a cross: they are the ones copied in the Vatican supplement; we find errors in rubrication and numbering: they are reproduced in the Vatican supplement and corrected there by Agustín; we find, to clinch the argument, his autograph identifications of chapters in the margins of the Venice MS. Only a chapter-by-chapter tabulation could fully demonstrate the truth of these assertions; here it may suffice to single out an error in numbering of the chapters of Bk 11 in the Venice MS (fol. 227r-v), where chapters xlvi-lii should actually be li-lvii; they appear, however, with the same wrong numbering in the supplement of the Vatican MS (fol. 306v-307v) where the error has been corrected in another hand—probably Agustín's.

A label on the inside of the cover of the Venice MS reads as follows: 'MSS. latini Cl. 4. No. 55. Provenienza Biblioteca di Padova. Collocazione 2243.' Niccolò Ormaneto, therefore, must have been given back his codex by Antonio Agustín and left it to the library of his church.

It would be interesting to investigate whether the elaborate arrangement and expansion of *liber vetus meus* meant that Antonio Agustín planned an edition of the collection. There is no hint of it in his published work and letters; but one must bear in mind that much of his correspondence remains to be printed. It should also be investigated whether the sixteenth-century copy of Anselm in Huesca has any connection with the learned Archbishop of Tarragona. Whether such an edition, if planned, would have become a *recensio mixta* from the codices he knew, or whether it would have distinguished the traditions, remains a purely speculative question.

Appendix: (I) *Antonio Agustín's Paenitentiale Romanum.* In his marginal notes to Anselm's Book 11, Agustín often refers to titles and chapters of a *Pen-*(*itentiale*),[56] which is the *Paenitentiale Romanum* he included, from a MS once in the library of Michael Thomasius, in his edition of six penitential treatises (Tarragona 1582) and which he showed to be a compilation of the twelfth cen-

---

[54] *Op. cit.* 437-8.
[55] Valentinelli VIII.15; num. progr. 2243. I wish to thank Dr. Mario Fornasari for the loan of his microfilm of Books 11-13.
[56] E.g. Vat. lat. 6381, fol. 305r-313r (old 303-311), seven references: *Pen.* 1.16, 1.31, 1.13, 9.4, 4.10, 6.3, 7.3.

tury, made after Gratian.[57] In discussing the council of Calixtus II (*De emendatione Gratiani* dial. 2.5), he refers to a chapter inscribed 'Calixtus papa' in *Paenitentiale Romanum meum*, tit. 8 c.8, as identical with Grat. D.27 c.8. In turn, in the edition of the Penitential we find at this point a note 'Callist. II in concil. Romano cap. xx. Refert Anselm. lib. 4. cap. ult. in Rom(ano exemplari) et Grat. dist. 27. cap. 8 . . .'.

In the catalogue of Agustín's *Bibliotheca latina* the MS appears under No. 349:

> INCERTI Paenitentiale, ab Antonio Augustino felicis memoriae Romanum appellatum, quia ex Vrbe ad eius manus peruenit, et ab eo editum est cum ipsius notis. Liber in membranis annorum cc. forma minori quadrati.

It can now be identified as Vat. lat. 5003.

(II) Antonio Agustín's copy made 'ex libro Veronensi Nic. Ormanetti' of the *Collection of Vat. lat. 3829*, is now MS Vat. lat. 4886,[58] part II, bound together with other materials from Agustín's library, including in part III an index to the *Collectio Avellana* (of which he owned a recent copy).[59] This collection of materials will be discussed in detail on another occasion; it was sent from Spain to Rome through the Nunzio Filippo Sega, in 1577 or early 1578, for the use of the *Correctores Romani*.[60] They cite its part II as 'Liber decretorum Antⁱⁱ Augustini' in connection with letters of Alexander II in their rough notes for the *Index librorum*;[61] Michael Thomasius has the same book in mind when in the draft for the *Notae* in C. 16 q.7 c.18 he speaks[62] of an *epistola* of Alexander

---

[57] *Canones Paenitentiales*, praef. (Tarragona 1582, fol. prelim. [vi]r-v = *Opp*. III 253). Cf. H. Wasserschleben, *Die Bussordnungen der abendländischen Kirchen* (Halle 1851) 95.

[58] Cf. Fournier-Le Bras II 210-11, where the provenance from Agustín's library is, however, not recognized.

[59] Part II: fol. 91-126; part III: fol. 127-140. The index of *Coll. Avell.* by Agustín is made 'Ex libro Marcelli pp. ii.' (autogr. entry fol. 123r) and has thus far not been known. On the codex of Pope Marcellus II (Vat. lat. 4961, Günther's *a*), see O. Günther, *Coll. Avell.* (CSEL 35) p. xxiiii ff. Antonio Agustín owned a copy of it, No. 264 of his *Bibliotheca latina*, now Escorial MSç.II.264, on which see P. Ewald, in *Neues Archiv* 6 (1881) 235 (misnumbered p. 335).

[60] Vat. lat. 4886, fol. 140: 'hoc volumen misit P. episcopus placentinus ex Hispa(nia) ad Congregationem.' Sega was Nunzio in Spain from 1577 to 1582 (cf. Pastor, *Geschichte der Päpste* IX [1925] 114, 257-267), and returned on a special mission in 1583 (*ibid*. 272ff.). He was a personality very unlike his predecessor Ormaneto, as shown by the pressure he brought on Philip II for the invasion of England and the support of the Irish revolution (Pastor IX 301, 309, 321ff.); he ended his long diplomatic career as cardinal (1591; † 1596). If the note above calls him bishop of Piacenza, this would mean that it was written after his transfer to that see from Ripatransone, 3 October 1578; but the book itself must have reached the *Correctores* before Michael Thomasius left Rome in Spring 1578 (see n. 46 *supra*), since it has marginalia in his hand, and was used in his notes.

[61] Vat. lat. 4891, fol. IIr.

[62] Vat. lat. 4890, fol. 109v No. 1436.

II

II... 'quam Ant. Aug^{nus} Archi$\overline{eps}$ Tarraconensis ex vetusto codice descriptam misit'—which in the printed *Nota ad loc.* has become '... quae epistola ex vetusto codice descripta Romam ex Hispania missa est'. In all these cases the reference is to the text of JL 4501 in Vat. lat. 4886 (fol. 115r).[63]

(III) Only the briefest mention will here be made of Antonio Agustín's copy of a fragment of the Dionysio-Hadriana, No. 284 in his *Bibliotheca latina*,

> CORPORIS canonum, quod sub titulo CANONES Apostolor. et aliorum concilior. circumfertur, fragmenta a Sardicensis concilii canonib. vsq. ad Symmachi Papae decreta. Liber in membranis annor. CD. et vltra forma quadrati,

which can be identified as the ninth-century Vat. lat. 4979. It includes some contemporary glosses which Professor Claudio Leonardi hopes to discuss in a separate paper and which he considers to be possibly autograph entries by Ratherius of Verona.

(IV) We need not dwell very long on Agustín's MSS of two canonical collections which have long been known to be in the Vatican Library. They are

(1) *Liber B. Mariae Populeti*, No. 288 in the catalogue of his *Bibliotheca latina*, which is an eleventh-century copy of his so-called *Liber Tarraconensis* (No. 287 *ibid.*). The latter belonged to Petrus Galesius at the time of the Dialogues *de emendatione Gratiani*;[64] it is now MS 26 of the Biblioteca Provincial of Tarragona.[65] Fournier seems to have considered *Liber Tarrac.* and *Liber Populeti* merely two names for the same MS.[66] He was unaware of the MS at Tarragona and would not commit himself to more than the probable identity of the book from the Abbey of Poblet with Vat. lat. 6093. Antonio Agustín had

---

[63] Another copy of Ormaneto's codex remained in Antonio Agustín's library until his death, *Bibliotheca latina* No. 269: 'Epistolae diuersor. Rom. Pontificum ab Honorio Papa ad Innocentium II. ex libro Tridentino veteri. Liber in charta recenter scriptus in forma folii.' If the original is called here *liber Tridentinus* instead of *Veronensis*, this must be a mistake: both No. 269 and Vat. lat. 4886 pt. II were copies of the same book, as shown by this entry in Agustín's *manuductio* (edited from MS Vat. lat. 3958 by C. Leonardi [n. 4 *supra*] p. 620 No. 59): 'Epistolae diuersorum... Innocentium secundum, *quarum exemplum Romam missum est* (corr. ex *misi*) ad Congregationem eorum qui praeerant emendationi Gratiani' (italics mine).

[64] *De emend. Grat.* 1.4 (p. 29 = ed. Bal. 33 = *Opp.* III 31a): '... et tuus, B. Tarraconensis'.

[65] First identified by G. Fransen, cf. *Congrès de Droit canonique médiéval, Louvain et Bruxelles*... (Louvain 1959) 102 (discussion).

[66] 'Le Liber Tarraconensis', *Mélanges L. Havet* (Paris 1895) 259f, 278-80; Fournier-Le Bras II 240. (There is an erroneous reference to Taragona MS 26, *ibid.* II 14 n. 2, as containing the *Coll. 74 tit.*) The source of this confusion of two MSS was the archbishop's nephew, Antonio Agustín S.J., in his edition of the posthumous 'De quibusdam veteribus...' (n. 35 *supra*) c. 33: 'Tarraconensis quem alias Populeti nominat archiepiscopus....' (*Epitome iuris pont.* II fol. ††††4ra = *Opp.* III 242b); whence Baluze in his *Notae ad Ant. Augustinum* 427, the Ballerini, *De antiquis collect.* (n. 38 *supra*) cccxix = PL 56.351, and Fournier *loc. cit.*

sent copies of individual texts from it to the *Correctores*, who mention the *Liber Populeti* in their booklist and in the *Notae* on C.16 q.1 c.25 (the Pseudo-Boniface IV, JE † 1996), but the MS itself came to the Vatican only after his death.

(2) MS Barb. lat. 897 (2864; xvi. 104), a sixteenth-century copy of the *Collectio Caesaraugustana* with marginal notes by Agustín, and others in a modern hand (A. Theiner?). Antonio Agustín had this copy made (and sent to Rome) [ex] 'libro Caesaraugustano Cartusianor. qui Hieronymi Zuritae fuit';[67] the Barberini MS bears his autograph note 'Liber caesar. Aulae Dei/ Hier. Zuritae' at the top of fol. 1. No evidence has been found that the *Correctores* used the copy.[68] The original, still given as lost in Fournier-Le Bras, was actually identified by the Abbé Tarré in a thèse at the École des Chartes (1927) as 'Bibl. du Roi à Madrid VII-E-3'; it is today in the University Library at Salamanca, MS 2644.[69] The line of provenance can be thus reconstructed: Aula Dei (O. Carth.) - Zurita - Ant. Aug. - Colegio de Cuenca (Salamanca) - Bibl. Real VII.E.3 - Madrid, Palacio II.554. The Vatican copy (listed with the wrong shelf-mark Barb. 535 in Fournier-Le Bras)[70] was correctly identified by the Ballerini as a copy of the original codex from the Charterhouse of Zaragoza.[71]

This concludes our list of canonical collections in the Vatican Library that once belonged to Antonio Agustín.[72]

IV. The Collections of Vallicelliana MS F. 54

This MS has been studied for several of its components by a number of scholars;[73] a complete critical analysis remains to be given. It is actually a composite

---

[67] *De emend. Grat.* 1. 5 (p. 42 = ed. Bal. 49 = *Opp.* III 36).

[68] Contrary to the assertion in Fournier, 'La collection canonique dite Caesaraugustana', *Nouv.* RHD 45 (1921) 53; Fournier-Le Bras II 269.

[69] J. Tarré, 'Les sources de la législation ecclésiastique dans la province tarraconnaise...', *École des Chartes, Position des thèses* 1927, p. 133; C. M. Batlle, in *Pelagii I papae epp.* (Montserrat 1956) proleg. xxxvii; F. Marcos Rodríguez, 'Tres manuscritos del siglo xii con colecciones canónicas', *Anal. sacra Tarrac.* 32 (1959) 35-44.

[70] Fournier, *Nouv.* RHD 45.53; Fournier-Le Bras II 269. Another wrong shelfmark in Friedberg, *Corp. iur. can.* I col. lxxi, 'No. 286', is probably derived from the old Barberini number (2864; XVI.104). For Barb. lat. 535 see *supra* after n. 31.

[71] *De antiquis collectionibus* cccxix = PL 56.352.

[72] It is not quite clear whether G. Martínez Díez, *La colección canónica Hispana* I (Madrid 1966) 54 means to say that Vat. lat. 4887—a collation made of the lost *codex Lucensis* of the *Hispana* by Juan Bautista Pérez († 1597)—once belonged to Antonio Agustín. Elsewhere (p. 44) Martínez Díez states correctly that the book was sent to Gregory XIII in 1575 by Gaspar de Quiroga, then bishop of Cuenca (later cardinal archbishop of Toledo). Quiroga also gave a copy to Agustín, cf. C. García Goldáraz, *El códice Lucense de la colección canónica Hispana* (Madrid 1954) I 105-6. Perhaps this is MS Vallicell. C.26, identified with No. 259 in Agustín's *Bibl. latina* by Martínez Díez, *op. cit.* 46, 55, 191 (Vallicell. C.18 and C.21, cited *ibid.* 46, 54-5, 189-90 for *Bibl.* 258, 257, appear already in Leonardi's list, p. 608, Nos. 63, 66).

[73] (see p. 24).

book made up from three MSS. Only a few essentials will be pointed out here for MSS I and II; MS III seems not to have been seriously examined before. MS I (fol. 1-130), s. xi, contains the *Collection in 74 Titles* (fol. 1-62v) and will be designated *Rv* in Gilchrist's forthcoming edition. 74T is followed here by another substantial collection (62v-130) of conciliar and patristic canons, which includes the apocryphal council of 'Pope Sylvester' edited in 1886 by Charles Poisnel from this MS (fol. 103v-111r).

MS II (fol. 131-169), in Beneventan script s. xi/xii, is a collection mostly but not entirely of penitential texts, largely based on the *Collection in Five Books*.[74] From fol. 158v to 169r, conciliar canons have in their rubrics the designation *hera* instead of *capitulum*, e. g. fol. 159r, 'Canone ancirano hera xxi. et xxv.' This rare term (= *aera*) is characteristic, as Hubert Mordek has shown, of the *Collectio Vetus Gallica* and of its influence, direct or indirect.[75] In a letter to this writer, Dr. Mordek considers the folios in question 'eine meines Wissens bisher unbekannte Überlieferung des *Poenitentiale Vallicellianum primum*, das vermutlich von der *Herovalliana* formal beeinflusst worden ist'.

On fol. 169v, another hand (s. xii, no longer Beneventan) entered Paschal II's Lateran Council of 7 March 1110, cc. 1-4 (the MS was not used in Weiland's[76] or any other edition), and still another hand, again in Beneventan script, Calixtus II's Lateran Council of 1123, c.9 (vulg. 5).

MS III (fol. 170-226), s. xii, is a canonical collection which does not have any formal division by *tituli* but mostly groups the material roughly by topics. Thus, at the beginning of the MS as preserved, all chapters deal with tithes;then follows a cluster of texts on negligence, etc. The collection includes letters and councils of eleventh-century popes down to Urban II. Its most striking feature, however, is its manner of composition. Texts from Ivo's Decretum and from the Collection of Deusdedit are serially juxtaposed, with texts from other sources in between. Thus we have at the beginning (fol. 170r-177r).

Ivo D. 3.195-7; ... Deusd. 3.59, 61-65; ... Ivo D.3.179; Deusd. 3.182-3, 176-7 ...

The compiler reproduced also rubrics and inscriptions of his models, in one case even the numbering of a chapter: 'cxlv. Imperator Iustinianus a(ugustus) Mene archiepiscopo constantinopoli. Sancimus ut nulli liceat ...' (fol. 177r),

---

[73] Duchesne, *Liber Pontificalis* (Paris 1886) I cxxxvii; Ch. Poisnel, 'Un concile apocryphe du pape Silvestre', *Mélanges d'arch. et d'hist.* 6 (1886) 3-13; Fournier, 'Le premier manuel...' 150; also Nouv. RHD 23.64-5, *Mém. Acad. Inscr.* 40.101-2 (with a brief mention of pt. III, p. 101 n. 3) — all cited n. 1 *supra*; Fournier-Le Bras I 444-5; Gilchrist, *Diuersorum patr. sent.* (n. 3 *supra*) proleg. §37.

[74] Fournier-Le Bras *loc. cit.*

[75] H. Mordek, 'Aera', DA 25 (1969) 216-22.

[76] MGH *Const.* I 567-9.

which is from Deusd. 3.177 in the numbering of Wolf von Glanvell's edition but counted as cxlv. in the original, Vat. lat. 3833. At least in one instance, the source seems to have been Ivo's *Tripartita* rather than the *Decretum*: on fol. 180v, without inscription, the complete letter of Urban II to the priest Vitalis of Brescia appears thus:

> Super quibus consuluit—compatres effecti sunt. (JL 5741)
> Quod autem uxor—iniungi debet. (JL 5742)
> Porro eos qui—sanctorum canonum preiudicio. (JL 5740)

This is the same sequence as in *Tripart.* A, Urban Nos. 5, 6A-B; *Coll. 13L* (Vat. lat. 1361) 9.120, 121A-B; *Catalaun. I* fol. 2v-3r; *Caesaraug.* 4.127A-C,[77] and 'in veteri codice MS monasterij Rivipullensis', where Étienne Baluze found the letter *integra* and with the correct inscription.[78] The codex from S. Maria de Ripoll is probably lost and, owing to Friedberg's rather vague notation of Baluze's report,[79] the letter to Vitalis still appears as three separate items in Jaffé-Lowenfeld, and as two in Kehr's *Italia pontificia*.[80]

The influence of Deusdedit on later canonical collections is generally assessed as slight. The combination of texts from his work and that of Ivo in part III of Vallicell. F. 54 would therefore deserve a full analysis.

University of California,
Berkeley.

---

[77] Cf. Gossman, *Pope Urban II* (n. 2 *supra*) 50, 60, 77, 91.
[78] *Notae ad Gratianum*, C.1 q.5 c.2 (JL 5740), p. 482 of Baluze's edition of Ant. Aug. *De emend. Grat.*
[79] Friedberg *ad loc.* (*Corp. iur. can.* I 423 n. 12).
[80] *It. pont.* 6.1.334 Nos. 3, 4.

TEXTUS TRES SELECTI

1.

De his qui occulte nubunt uel postquam nupserint aliqua uerenda contra coniugium faciunt.

Quidam uxorem duxit sine presentia testium solo ad inuicem maritali consensu firmato. Postea breui tempore interiecto, priusquam consensum
5 occultum facto manifesto probasset, de facto penituit, eam quam in hunc modum uxorem duxerat dimisit, aliam duxit celebri apparatu manifeste coram ecclesia. Fortassis cum parentum traditione, cum sacerdotis benedictione nuptias fecit, filios genuit. Venit illa prior ad ecclesiam, iudicium interpellat, iusticiam postulat, iniuriam sibi illatam palam exponens. Ne-

---

Vat. lat. 4977, fol. 2r-v = V

II

gat ille. Nec sunt testes qui possunt probare quod occultum est. Hic queris quid facere debeat ecclesia, quia utrumque inconueniens aliquod concurrere uidetur. Si enim illi mulieri <credatur> que quidem uerum dicit, set tamen occultum est et probare non potest pro eo quod incertum est et occultum, hic quod certum et manifestum est dissoluitur. Poterit deinceps quelibet uel quilibet in alium uel aliam quodcumque uoluerit fingere ut sibi simili ratione credatur. Quod si admissum fuerit, magna confusio proueniet, neque deinceps in ecclesia aliquid firmum stabit.

Considerandum est quomodo supra memorate questionj responderi oporteat. Dubium non est quia id quod ecclesia probare non potest, ecclesia ipsa iudicare non potest. Et rursum: dubium non est quia id quod manifesto et legitimo ecclesie iudicio factum est, sine legitima, rationabili et manifesta causa rescindi non potest. Ergo non potest quod occultum est id quod manifestum est infirmare. Quapropter oportet ut secundum copulam, que iudicio ecclesie legitime facta est, ipsa ecclesia iudicet ratam esse debere. Ideo ad continentiam cogenda est prima mulier: ita sane, quia negligentiam cauere noluit, iustum est ut penam sustineat. Quare in manifesto non nupsit? Si prius in nubendo testimonium ecclesie habere contempsit, qua ratione nunc iudicium ecclesie interpellat? Ipsa igitur se obligauit: sustineat itaque nunc penam negligentie, ut alijs mulieribus, ne idem presumant, correptionis et cautele exemplum fiat. Continere peccatum non est nec impossibile est, etiam si difficile est. Si ergo mulieres nolunt continere, caueant in occulto nubere. Ibi nubant ubi testes habere possunt, si maritos consentientes habere non possunt. Quod si culpam uitare nolunt, sustineant penam. Qui ergo coniugium suscipere uult, cogitet primum, quia cum illud susceperit, legem eius portare debet. Non ergo ecclesia aliud dicere potest quam ut in matrimonio quod eius attestatione firmatum est fidem seruet.

2.

Beatissimo pape Damaso Hieronimus presbiter in Domino salutem. Inter alia que scripsisti etiam illud annectere placuit ut rationem oblationum quas a fidelibus offerri cotidie cernimus beatitudini uestre notam facere curaremus, uidelicet quare dentur et quibus et ad quorum usus

---

10 probari V   11 *mallem* utrimque *vel* utcumque   12 credatur *scripsi* : *om.* V
15 quelibet] quemlibet V   23 infirmarj V   37 seruat V

Barb. lat. 1450 fol. 166va-b (ult.) = B; Vat. lat. 1361 fol. 244vb-245rb = V; Grat. C.16 q.1 c.68 (ad lin. 34-52 supra) = G; C.1 q.2 c.6 (ad lin. 48-52) = G2. Quoniam B integrum textum praebet quamvis saepe corruptum, lectiones eius secutus sum etiam in dubiis (v.g. 2 scripsisti, oblationum, 22 stipendia, 44 auctoritatibus), non autem in erroribus nec in mere orthographicis, secundum principia quae apud *Monum. iuris can.* vigent. Quae in V adduntur in fine uncis inclusi. Lect. varias G quandoque rettuli nonnullis codd. et edd. inspectis, seposito app. Friedbergiano.

1-33 *om.* G, 1-48 subnixa *om.* G2   1 Ieronimus V   2 alias B   scripsistis V   2-3 oblationum] decimarum <et?> *praem.* V   3 afferri B (*sed vide lin.* 32)   cernimus] decreuimus V   4 curamus B   ad] a B

5 debeant prouenire. ⌜Metiris nos uiribus tuis et turbidum riuulum fontem putas, cumque sit nobis parua supplex sensuum et uerborum, magnis nos questionibus honeras, ut deficere potius quam satisfacere uideamur. Tritum uulgi prouerbium est quod si asinus cum lapsus fuerit in uia, diuerticulum querit seque cum honere quod habuerit humi prosternit. Cum essem
10 adulescentulus et adhuc calerem recentibus studiis litterarum, post Quintiliani facundiam, post fluuium Ciceronis tam eram in dictando uelox et agilis, ut omnium meorum contemporalium uiderer ingenia superare et quicquid dicere uolebam et promtum et in ore erat. Set efeto iam corpore cum ipsis uiribus corporis uis et acumen ingenii, sensus et ratio quodam
15 modo defecerunt.⌝ Verum quia filialis obedientia me coegit, ⌜immo Christi caritas compulit,⌝ trium dierum laborem arripui cunctorumque Grecorum auctorum opuscula in unum contuli, uidelicet Cirilli et Petri, Origenis et Didimi, Johannis Osaurei et Gregorii Nazanzeni preceptoris mei, et quid de his sentirent studio quesiui. Quid multa? Omnes quos supra
20 memorauimus quasi quedam Spiritus sancti organa consonis uocibus predicant, protestantur et clamant, omnes decimas et oblationes deberi solis episcopis propter exsecutionem episcopalis officii, sicut terrena stipendia et tributa debentur solis potestatibus seculi propter amministrationem publice functionis. Sicut illi, habentes uasa interfectionis, in eo subseruiunt
25 subditis quod malos a malo reprimunt et bonos in bonis nutriunt et omnibus equitatis iura ponunt ac per hoc omnium subiectorum stipendium consequuntur, sic ecclesiastici principes, christiane reipublice curam gerentes et ecclesie sacramenta singulari priuilegio ministrantes, oblationes et decimas singulariter sortiuntur in usus suos suarumque familiarum
30 deputandas. Solis enim illis congruit chrisma conficere, pueros consignare, sacros ordines distribuere, consecrationes ecclesiarum celebriter agere. Quocirca quicquid in decimis, quicquid in oblationibus offertur et mittitur, in ius et dominium cedit illorum.
Et quoniam quicquid habent pauperum est et domus illorum omnibus
35 esse debent communes, susceptionibus peregrinorum et hospitum inuigilare

---

5-15 Metiris-defecerunt B : *om.* V   12 ut] u B   15 quia *om.* B   15-16 immo—compulit V : ira movit caritas compulit B *(forsan male legit compend.* īmoxī*)*   16 cunctorumque] cum ceterorumque B   20-21 predicatur B   21 et² *om.* B   22 exsequutionem V, excusationem B   22 stipendia] vectigalia *add.* V   23 seculi] scilic& B   24 functionis] fluctuationis B   Sicut] enim *add.* V   29 singulariter] et specialiter *add.* V   suorumque B   30 deputanda B   crismam B   31 consecrationes] et *praem.* V   31-32 Quocirca] Idcirco V   32 quicquid in²] et V   34-52 Quoniam (*om.* Et) — bibunt G, *praem. paragr.* Quod autem decime episcoporum consensu monachis licite tribuantur b. Ieronimus Damaso pape scribit dicens, *et rubr.* Liberum est clericis monachis decimas concedere   34 habent] clerici *add.* G   35 debent esse *tr.* VG   susceptioni G   hospicium V

8-9 *asinus — diuerticulum querit*: cf. Hieron. ep. 107.10 (ed. Vallarsi, PL 22.875; ed. Hilberg, CSEL 55.301.8-9)   9-11 *Cum essem—fluuium Ciceronis*: cf. Hieron. ep. 125.12 (Vallarsi 1079; Hilberg 56.131.9-13)   18 *preceptoris mei*: cf. Hieron. 52.8 (Vallarsi 534; Hilberg 54.429.4)   20 *Spiritus—uocibus*: similia, forsan ex eodem (nescio quo) fonte, leguntur in Quaestionibus cod. Oxon. coll. Oriel 53, fol. 338vb: 'Audi quanta sit armonia quantusque concentus in organis que Dei spiritu insufflantur'.

debent. Maxime curandum est illis ut decimis et oblationibus ⌜cenobiis et xenodochiis⌝ qualem uoluerint et potuerint sustentationem impendant. Liberum est enim illis monachis et spiritualibus uiris Deum timentibus et colentibus decimas et oblationes ceteraque remedia concedere et de iure
40 suo in dominium illorum et usum transferre, nec tam in pauperibus paupertatem quam religionem attendere.

Quod autem beatitudo tua quesiuit, utrum decimarum usus et oblationum secularibus prouenire posset, nouerit uestra sanctitas penitus non licere, protestantibus hoc omnibus diuinis ⌜auctoritatibus⌝. Quam ob rem
45 si aliquando fuerint ab huiusmodi male detenta que diuini iuris esse noscuntur et in usum et dominium transierint monachorum et seruorum Dei, episcopo tamen loci prebente consensum, constabunt eis omnia perpetua stabilitate et firmitate subnixa. Clericos autem illos conuenit ecclesie stipendiis sustentari quibus parentum et propinquorum nulla subsidia
50 suffragantur. Qui autem bonis parentum et opibus sustentari possunt, si quod pauperum est accipiunt, sacrilegium profecto committunt et per abusionem talium iudiciis sibi manducant et bibunt. [Et infra. Par sacrilegium est rem pauperum non pauperibus dare. At uero quicquid habet episcopus, quicquid ecclesia, pauperum est.]

3.

Paschalis II clericis ecclesiae s. Alexandri (Bergomensis) decimam adiudicat si quadragenalem possessionem probare potuerint.
JL—. It. pont.—.   Romae, 7 oct. (1103-4 vel 1110-13)

Pascalis episcopus seruus seruorum Dei dilectis in Christo filiis clericis sancti Alexandri salutem et apostolicam benedictionem. Litterarum uestrarum lectione et Guidonis preclari iudicis Cremonensis relatione comperimus

---

36 maximeque V   decimis] de (*var.* in) *praem. plurimi codd.* G   36-37 cenobiis et xenodochiis BG : ipsis *post* 35 sustentationem V   38 illis *om.* G   spiritualibus] spiritualiter B   39 ceteraque] cunctaque G   39-40 suo iure *tr.* V   40 et usum *om.* V   42 tua] uestra G *var.*   usus decimarum *tr.* VG   43 possit G   nouit G   sanctitas uestra *tr.* V   penitus] omnino G   44 hoc *om.* G *var.*   omnibus *om.* G *var.*   auctoritatibus B : auctoribus et auctoritatibus canonum paternorum V, auctoritatibus paternorum canonum G   45 huiusmodi] his G   46 et dominium *om.* G   monachorum transierint *tr.* G   47 tamen] tantum B   loci] illius *add.* G   48 firmitate et (*var.* ac) stabilitate *tr.* G   48-52 Clericos—bibunt G2, *praem. rubr.* Qui sumptibus propriis sustentari possunt ab ecclesia stipendia non accipiant (*var.* potest . . . accipiat) *et inscr.* Item Ieronimus ad Damasum papam   48 ecclesiis (*leg.* ecclesiasticis ?) B   49-50 nulla subsidia suffragantur] nulli suffragantur G, nulla suffragantur G *ed. Rom.* G2 (nulla suffragantur stipendia [*vel* bona] *vel* nulla stipendia suffragantur GG2 *varr.*)   50 opibus] suis *add.* G2 *ed. Rom.*   51 quod] quid V   committunt] incurrunt et *praem.* G (*praeter ed. Rom.*)   52-54 Et infra—pauperum est V : *om.* BGG2   53 mallem sacrilegii *vel* sacrilegio

Vat. lat. 1361 fol. 246ra-b = V
1 *num.* xlv. *et rubr.* De possessione .xl. annorum *praem.* V   3 relationis V

ad hoc uos de controuersia que inter uos et clericos sancti Vincentii de
5 decima agitur conuenisse, ut ipsa causa duorum uestrorum ciuium iudicio
committeretur, et quod ipsi pariter sensu iudicassent ab utraque parte firmiter seruaretur. Set quoniam ipsi in iudicio dissentiunt, uos a nobis
queritis quid uobis de hoc faciendum sit. Nos autem beati Gregorii sententiam in hoc imitandam credimus, qui ad Petrum diaconum ita scribit:
10 'Ideo, inquid, uolumus questionem ipsam tali ratione discutere, dominio
rei apud possessorem sicut hactenus possessum est uidelicet permanente,
ut si monasterium fines ipsos de quibus causatio mota est inconcussis
.xl. annis possedisse repperitis, nullam deinceps patiaris sustinere calump-
niam.' Et uos itaque, si iuxta predictam beati Gregorii sententiam eandem
15 decimam uos inconcusse per annos .xl. tenuisse probare potueritis, sine
omni deinceps calumpnia eam retinere et habere debetis. Data Rome
nonis octobris.

---

4 clerici V   8 (et 14) Gregorii] gg¹ V   9 immitandam V   10 Ideo—uo-
lumus] Et ideo uolumus accendentem te ad Panormitanam ciuitatem *orig.*   11 ac-
tenus V   12 monasterium] praefatum sancti Theodori *add. orig.*   inconcussis
scripsi cum orig. (*et* V *lin.* 15 inconcusse): in conclusis V   13 deinceps] etiam
si quid sanctae Romanae ecclesiae competere potuit *add. orig.*   14 iusta V
16 omni] omnium V

10-14 abbrev. ex Greg. M. ep. 1.9 (JE 1076; MGH *Epp.* 1.11.6-11), forsan ex ipso registro. Collectionum canonicarum quas novimus nulla v. 'ideo' servat in excerptis ex
orig.; duæ tantum a v. 'Volumus' incipiunt, sc. *3 Lib. 2.31.5 (cod. Vat. lat. 3831 fol. 71ra)
et Grat. C.16 q.4 c.2, omnes aliae a vv. 'Si monasterium' (= V lin. 12), sc. Ans. 5.57, Deusd.
3.92, Ivo *Tripart. (in serie epp. Greg. partis I, cod. Par. lat. 3858 fol. 84v), Decr. 3.146,
Pan. 2.66, *Polyc. 3.12.1. (Quas asterisco signavi non laudant Corr. Rom. nec Friedb.)

III

THE SO-CALLED CANONS OF NÎMES (1096)

In collaboration with Robert Somerville

In separate notes appearing in the 1968 Bulletin of the Institute of Medieval Canon Law, the authors called attention to the manner in which post-Reformation scholarship has created certain 'pseudo-problems' for the student of the medieval Reform-papacy. A short collection of decrees from the end of Avranches MS 146, wrongly ascribed since d'Achery to the 1114 legatine Council of Beauvais, and a series of problematic texts assigned to the pontificate of Urban II, pointed out the pitfalls which plague users of the editions in Mansi, in Friedberg, and elsewhere [1]. One of the instances cited was 'the pretended "confirmation", in Urban II's Council of Nîmes (1096), of two monastic forgeries circulating under the names of Gregory the Great and Boniface IV' [2]: a case of confusion which we want to take up today.

From the mid-eleventh century these twin fabrications in favor of monastic *cura animarum* were copied widely and in various forms [3]. Eventually they entered Gratian's *Decretum*, with a

---

[1] R. Somerville, *The Council of Beauvais, 1114,* Traditio 24 (1968) 493—503; S. Kuttner, *Brief Notes, ibid.* 504—5: *Urban II and Gratian.*

[2] Kuttner, *loc. cit.* 504.

[3] For modern bibliography reference should be made to H. Frank, *Zwei Fälschungen auf den Namen Gregors des Grossen und Bonifatius' IV.*, Studien und Mitteilungen zur Geschichte des Benediktinerordens 55 (1937) 19—47; J. J. Ryan, *St. Peter Damiani and His Canonical Sources* (Pontifical Institute of Mediaeval Studies, Studies and Texts 2; Toronto 1956) 55—8; G. Constable, *The Treatise „Hortatur nos" and Accompanying Canonical Texts . . .,* Speculum historiale [Festschrift for J. Spörl] (Munich 1966) 569—70.

full text for the Pseudo-Boniface (JE †1996: *C.*16 *q.*1 *c.*25: *Ex decreto Bonifacii pape. Sunt nonnulli...*), preceded by the concluding sentence of the Pseudo-Gregory (JE †1951: *ibid. c.*24: *Idem* [*i.e.* Greg. M.]. *Ex auctoritate*...). Philippe Labbe and Gabriel Cossart, S.J., were the first to call attention, in 1671, to the identity of these chapters with *cc.*2 and 3 of the Council of Nîmes. A set of *Decreta Vrbani papae in Nemausensi Concilio, Anno Christi MXCVI. celebrato* had been published ten years earlier (1661) from a manuscript at St. Aubin in Angers by Dom Luc d'Achery [4]; Labbe and Cossart published this series again, but with a different numbering of the canons, and using a copy their late confrère Jacques Sirmond (†1651) had taken many years before from the same St. Aubin manuscript [5]). In the marginal notes of their edition the learned Jesuits identified Nîmes *c.*2 with *C.*16 *q.*1 *c.*25 (also with Ivo, *Decr.* 7.22), and the end of *c.*3 with *C.*16 *q.*1 *c.*24 [6]).

The parallel was pointed out again in 1672 by Baluze; actually he had observed it much earlier, even before the appearance of d'Achery's edition, as is shown by his unpublished papers [7]). A hundred years later, Carlo Sebastiano Berardi, who knew that the attributions to St. Gregory and Boniface IV were spurious, went even further and concluded that the two texts probably originated in Pope Urban's Council of Nîmes [8]). If this were

---

[4]) L. d'Achery, *Spicilegium sive collectio veterum aliquot scriptorum* ... IV (Paris 1661) 234; the codex had been pointed out to him by Émeric Bigot (*ibid.* preface p. 12). The second edition (Paris 1723), 1. 628—9, includes Baluze's variant readings from a second St. Aubin MS, on which more below.

[5]) Labbe-Cossart, *Sacrosancta concilia* ... 10 (Paris 1671) 605—9, with the introductory note referring to the copy by „Sirmondus noster ex cod. S. Albini Andegavensis". Reproduced in J. D. Mansi, *Sacrorum conciliorum nova et amplissima collectio* 20 (Venice 1775) 931—7.

[6]) Labbe-Cossart *c.*1 corresponds to d'Achery *cc.*1 and 2, LC. 2 = d'A. 3 + 4; LC. 3 = d'A. 5, etc.

[7]) E. Baluze, *Notae ad Gratianum*, in Antonius Augustinus, *De emendatione Gratiani dialogorum libri duo* (ed. Paris 1672) 516—7; for the unpublished notes see *infra*.

[8]) C. S. Berardi, *Gratiani canones genuini ab apocryphis discreti* ... (Venice 1777) III 140—1, 151—2. He is followed by Ae. Friedberg, *Corpus iuris canonici* I

THE SO-CALLED CANONS OF NÎMES

true, the false inscriptions would have been invented between 1096 and the time of Gratian. This was indeed assumed by F. Patetta when in his eulogy of Paul Fournier (1937) he argued that Ivo's *Decretum* — where JE †1996 appears with the Boniface inscription — must be dated *post* 1096 [9]). He proposed as Ivo's source the little collection of five monastic canons in Turin MS Accad. MM.V.21 (fol. 97v—98) which, twenty years earlier, he had assigned to France and the last years of the eleventh century, simply by identifying its opening canons, 'Boniface' and 'Gregory', with Nîmes cc. 2 and 3 [10]).

This speculation is ruled out by the fact that the two texts were known and used as 'Gregory' and 'Boniface' long before Nîmes, i.e. since the mid-eleventh century [11]). St. Peter Damiani is a key witness: his *opusculum* 28 refers to the decree *quod Bonifacius in nostrorum tuitione composuit* [12]). A date not long after 1058 is accepted for this tract even by G. Lucchesi, who has questioned Damiani's authorship [13]). (His doubts, based on the observation that *opusc.* 28 is known from a single manuscript [14]),

---

(Leipzig 1879; reprinted 1955) 767 nn. 163 and 166.

[9]) F. Patetta, *Paolo Fournier*, Rendiconti Accad. Lincei, Classe di Scienze morali [6] 13 (1937) 429 n. 1; reprinted in the collection of Patetta's papers, *Studi sulle fonti giuridiche medievali*, ed. G. Astuti (Turin 1967) 1002 n. 1.

[10]) *Di alcuni manoscritti posseduti dalla Reale Accademia delle Scienze di Torino (Nota III)*, Atti Accad. Torino 53 (1917—18) 925—6.

[11]) Examples in P. Fournier, *Le Liber Tarraconensis*, Mélanges Julien Havet (Paris 1895) 279; Frank, *loc. cit.;* Ryan, *loc. cit.;* Ch. Dereine, *Le problème de la cura animarum chez Gratien*, Studia Gratiana 2 (1954) 307—18. — It is difficult to understand how L. Hödl, *Die Geschichte der scholastischen Literatur und der Theologie der Schlüsselgewalt* (Beiträge zur Geschichte der Philosophie und Theologie des Mittelalters 38.4; Münster 1960) 169—70, could suggest for the pseudo-Boniface a dependence on the twelfth-century theologians Rupert of Deutz and Honorius of Autun, since he is aware of the presence of the text in Ivo's *Decretum*.

[12]) Migne, *Patrologia latina* 145.511 sqq.

[13]) G. Lucchesi, *Clavis s. Petri Damiani*, Studi su San Pier Damiani in onore del Cardinale Amleto Giovanni Cicognani (Biblioteca Cardinale Gaetano Cicognani 5; Faenza 1961) 313—4. His doubts have been declared „non necessari" by G. Miccoli, *Chiesa Gregoriana: Richerche sulla Riforma del sec. XI* (Firenze 1966) 99 n. 2.

[14]) Pisa, Seminary, Bibl. Cateriniana MS 59 (s. xii), fol. 13r—14v; also (within the canonical collection of Anselm of Lucca) fol. 87v—89r: see K. Reindel, *Studien*

will perhaps be dispelled by the existence of another, thus far unrecorded copy, entitled *Tractatus domini Petri religiosissimi cardinalis romane ecclesie aduersus clericos et canonicos*, in the canonical collection of MS Vat. lat. 1361) [15]).

Even after the Council of Nîmes, no medieval writer quoted the texts of 'Boniface' and 'Gregory' with any other attribution [16]). Is it still possible, then, to accept that Urban II re-enacted the spurious canons at the Council? Charles Dereine has pointed out how slight the textual basis is for our knowledge of the printed canons of Nîmes [17]) — that is, as we should say more precisely, of all its canons except *c*.1, which is the restatement of Clermont *cc*.3 and 4 (Cencius-Polycarpus series). This text occurs, always as *decretum* of Pope Urban from Nîmes, in several twelfth-century manuscripts [18]). The series of fifteen remaining canons is, however, peculiar to the codex of St. Aubin's that served d'Achery and Sirmond-Labbe. No series of Nîmes appears in such twelfth-century collections of canons from reform councils of Urban and other popes as those one finds appended to certain manuscripts of the Polycarpus (e.g. Paris lat. 3881, Vatican Reg.

---

zur Überlieferung der Werke des Petrus Damiani, I, Deutsches Archiv 15 (1959) 45.

[15]) Collection in XIII Books (s. xii) 5.53, fol. 112vb—114ra, within a very interesting section on monastic privileges and discipline (5.52—119) which Fournier (cf. P. Fournier and G. Le Bras, *Histoire des collections canoniques en Occident* II 225—6, with bibliography) seems to have overlooked, but which presents the key to the monastic origin of the collection. This material will be discussed elsewhere.

[16]) Dereine, *op. cit.* 318. A single, inconsequential exception could be the inscription *Hormisdas* for JE † 1996, in the Naples MS XII. A. 37—39 of Anselm of Lucca (Book 5, app.), if Fournier's notes are correct; *Observations sur les diverses recensions . . . d'Anselme de Lucques*, Annales de l'Université de Grenoble 13 (1901) 435.

[17]) Dereine, *op. cit.* 315, 317—8. See also F. Kempf, S.J., in *Die mittelalterliche Kirche* I (Handbuch der Kirchengeschichte 3.1; Freiburg 1966) 447 n. 9.

[18]) Thus Rouen MS E. 49 (704) fol. 257v—258r (for this MS see Fournier, *De quelques collections canoniques issues du Décret de Burchard*, Mélanges Paul Fabre [Paris 1902] 191—5, especially 195); Paris, Mazarine MS 4310 (711), fol. 34r (see at n. 44 *infra*); and Vatican Reg. lat. 982, fol. 35r. In two identical appendices to Ivo's *Panormia* the second part of Nîmes *c*.1 alone appears (from *Quia monachorum* . . .): Paris B.N. lat. 4284, fol. 163r, and Vatican Reg. lat. 972, fol. 110r. Baluze recorded another occurrence, see *infra*.

THE SO-CALLED CANONS OF NÎMES 179

lat. 987 and 1026) [19]) or to the Collection in VII Books of Turin (B.N. MS D.IV. 33=Pasini lat. 239) [20]).

Nearly three hundred years ago Etienne Baluze demolished the authority of the St. Aubin tradition for the Nîmes series in one of the *Notae* of his *Capitularia regum Francorum*, published in 1677. Discussing the *decretum Bonifacii IV de libertate monachorum* he rejected the argument which would cite Nîmes *c*.2 in defense of its authenticity [21]):

> ... sed ego decretum illud [*i.e.* of Boniface IV] omnino supposititium esse arbitror. Neque me movet auctoritas Bedae [*i.e.* Bede, *Hist. eccl.* 2.4 on the Roman synod of Boniface IV in 610 [22]), usually quoted in conjunction with JE † 1996 by seventeenth-century scholars [23])] ... Opponi quoque potest auctoritas canonum Nemausensium, inter quos reperitur Bonifaciana isthaec constitutio. Primùm reponi potest eam non esse auctoritatem Concilij Nemausensis ut novis inventis tribuere possit auctoritatem vetustatis ...

He went on to state that most of the canons of Nîmes as edited do not belong to this council but are later additions by various hands found in one MS alone; that in two *vetustissima exemplaria* the inscription of the first canon (*cc*.1 and 2 in d'Achery's numbering) runs in the singular, *Decretum Urbani papae in Nemausensi concilio*; and that d'Achery changed this to read *Decreta* ... [24]):

> Deinde certum est plerosque canones qui sub nomine canonum Nemausensium editi sunt, synodi illius non esse, et additos diversis temporibus fuisse constitutionibus eiusdem Concilii. Vidimus nos duo vetustissima illius exemplaria in quibus descripti tantùm sunt duo priores canones cum hoc titulo: *Decretum Vrbani PP. in Nemausensi Concilio*. Pro quo vir clarissimus Lucas Dacherius emendavit: *Decreta Vrbani papae in Nemausensi Concilio*.

---

[19]) On these appendices see P. Fournier, *Les deux recensions de la collection canonique romaine dite le Polycarpus*, Mélanges d'archéologie et d'histoire 37 (1918—19) 58—9; J. Rambaud-Buhot, in *L'Age classique* (Histoire du droit et des institutions de l'Eglise en occident 7; Paris 1965) 57—8.
[20]) Fournier-Le Bras, *Histoire* II 166.
[21]) *Capitularia regum Francorum* II (Paris 1677) 1243—4 (*Notae ad libros capitularium);* reprinted in Mansi, *Conc.* 18.827.
[22]) Ed. Plummer (Oxford 1896) I 88.
[23]) E.g. Labbe-Cossart 5.1617.
[24]) Baluze *loc. cit.*

> Sanè fatendum est in uno exemplari extare omnia capitula Concilij Nemausensis quae edita à Dacherio sunt. Sed illa multò post tempora habiti Concilij addita sunt à diversis hominibus, quia paginae vacabant. Sciunt autem eruditi hunc veterum monachorum morem fuisse ut vacantes pagellas implerent interdum malis rebus, plerunque bonis . . .

Baluze here did not say where he had seen the *duo vetustissima exemplaria*, but it stands to reason that they are the same which he had mentioned in 1663 as *codex ms. duplex sancti Albini Andegavensis, uterque vetus*, when he discussed the equivalence of Clermont *c*.3 with the first part of Nîmes *c*.1 in the Notes on Clermont, published with his edition of Pierre de Marca's *De concordia sacerdotii et imperii* [25]). It is true that the somewhat ambiguous language of the *Notae in libros Capitularium* could at first sight be construed to mean that the *unum exemplar* with the full series edited by d'Achery was a third MS rather than one of the *duo vetustissima* (and in that case one of these would not be from St. Aubin); especially since Baluze elsewhere noted that he had come across a third copy of Nîmes *c*.1 in a cartulary of Vendôme [26]). But this construction is impossible: he refers d'Achery's emendation *Decretum*] *Decreta* expressly to one of the *duo vetustissima*; thus they can confidently be identified as the two MSS from St. Aubin which Baluze knew by 1663.

This is borne out by certain of his unpublished papers concerning the history of councils, bound together as MS Baluze 7 at the Bibliothèque Nationale. They contain various sets of copies from MSS and drafts of notes, written, corrected, and added to at different times. When they are properly arranged and integrated with the printed material, they show the development of Baluze's knowledge and critical thought on the Council of Nîmes, which was to culminate in the published verdict of 1677.

1.— MS Baluze 7, fols. 316r—321v are bound in reverse order and must be read beginning with fol. 321v:

---

[25]) P. de Marca, *Dissertationum de concordia sacerdotii et imperii . . . libri octo* 6.31 (Paris 1663) II 191—3; ed. Frankfurt (1708) I 959—60.
[26]) Paris, B.N. MS Baluze 7, fol 199r *marg.;* see *infra*, No. 4 and n. 41.

THE SO-CALLED CANONS OF NÎMES

Concilium Nemausense cui præfuit Vrbanus II. Papa, habitum anno M.XCVI. mense Julio.

Ex Codice MS. S. Albini [27]) Andegavensis.

In Arvernensi — serventur.

marg. Canon est Concilii Claromontani qui repetitus est in Nemausensi. Sunt nonnulli — (fol. 321r) — potentior.

marg. xvi. q.1 c.25. Ex concilio Bonifacii Papae.

fol. 321r] Oportet eos — (fol. 320v) — peccata solvere.

fol. 320v—320r] the other canons follow, numbered IV—XVI.

fol. 320r] Ex archiuo Monasterij Riuipullensis.

Anno dominicae incarnationis — (fol. 319v) — Regis Francorum. [28])

fol. 319v] Notae Stephani Baluzii Tutelensis ad Concilium Nemausense.

Canones huius concilij debemus Codici Ms. S. Albini Andegauensis [29]), unde descripsit Jacobus Sirmondus, nosque ex authentico. [30]) Confirmationem vero priuilegiorum Monasterij Riuipullensis à Berengario Archiepiscopo Tarraconensi factam descripsimus ex schedis Illustrissimi viri Petri de Marca Archiepiscopi Tolosani, qui eam exscribi curauerat ex ipsis veteribus schedis monasterij Riuipullensis, dum visitationis munere pro Rege Christianissimo fungeretur in Principatu Cataloniae ... Nos, tam (fol. 319r) ex hoc monasterij Riuipullensis instrumento ...

fol. 319r] a list of prelates and nobles present at the council, with additions and references to 'Spicil. to. VI pag. 20' and 'Labbe pag. 575', entered at various times. [31]) — fol. 318 blank.

fol. 317v—317r] an incomplete copy of the Ripoll material on Nîmes.

fol. 316v—316r] a clean copy of the list of participants:

Synodo Nemausensi interfuerunt Archiepiscopi, Episcopi, Cardinales, Abbates et Proceres, qui sequuntur:

---

[27]) A canceled word follows, not legible.

[28]) Settlement made during the Council of Nîmes, 11 July 1096, between the Archbishop of Tarragona and the monks of S. Maria de Ripoll, ed. Baluze, *Miscellanea* 7 (Paris 1715) 72; republished first by N. Coleti, *Sacrosancta concilia* ... 12 (Venice 1730) 941—2, then by Mansi, *Steph. Baluzii Miscellanea novo ordine digesta* 1 (Lucca 1761) 127 and in his *Concil. coll. amplissima* 20.439—40.

[29]) *Post corr.*

[30]) *Post corr.:* apographo *del.*, autographo *del.*

[31]) Many of the names come from the list of witnesses to the charter of Count Raymond of Toulouse, Nîmes, 12 July 1096, ed. d'Achery, *Spicilegium* 6 (1664) 19—20 (= 2nd ed. 1.629—30), carelessly reproduced with omissions by Cossart in Labbe-Cossart, *Conc.* 10.609—10 = Mansi 20.937—8. — 'Labbe pag. 575' refers to the edition of Guido of Auxerre's *Gesta abbatum s. Germani Autissiodoren.* in Labbe's *Nova bibliotheca manuscript. librorum* I (Paris 1657), where on p. 575 the resignation of Abbot Guibert at the council *in praesentia domini Vrbani papae* is recorded (a detail of Nîmes overlooked by Cossart, Mansi, Hefele-Leclercq, etc.).

182

> Vrbanus ii. Pontifex Romanus/ Daibertus [32]) Archiepiscopus Pisanus/ .../Lambertus Abbas s. Bertini/ Raymundus Comes Tholosanus/ ... Rainerius de Posquerias.

The *Notae* were drafted at a time when Baluze's patron, Pierre de Marca, was still archbishop of Toulouse (1652, confirmed 1654; transferred to Paris in 1662), even though he resided most of the time at Paris, where Baluze had become his secretary in 1656 [33]). Since the Notes mention Sirmond's copy taken from the St. Aubin codex but not d'Achery's edition, they would not be written later than 1661. In that year, Baluze tells us elsewhere, he was in Angers with his patron and copied manuscript material at St. Aubin's [34]). (The document from S. Maria de Ripoll had been copied for de Marca at a much earlier time, during the years of his office as *visiteur général* of Catalonia, 1644—51). Some of the additions were made in or after 1664[35]); however, they do not affect Baluze's position as regards the St. Aubin series of canons, which he uncritically accepted as authentic at this stage. The identity of *c*.1 with Clermont *cc*.3—4, and of *c*.2 with the 'Boniface' text in Gratian, he already noted.

2.— MS Baluze, fols. 264r—265r: Notes on the repetition of Clermont *cc*. 3—4 in Nîmes. These may belong to the same period as the material above, or to the time when Baluze prepared his notes for the edition of Pierre de Marca's *Concordia*, which represent the next stage of his investigation.

---

[32]) *Corr. ex* Daimbertus.

[33]) For de Marca's dates see C. Eubel, *Hierarchia cath. mediae et rec. aetatis* 4.247, 340, and the *Vita* by Baluze in front of the 1669 and 1708 editions of the *De concordia* (Frankfurt 1708: I 26—8, 41, 49—50); this is a revised and enlarged version of the *Epistola ad ... Samuelem Sorberium De vita, rebus gestis, moribus et scriptis ... Petri de Marca* (Paris 1663), also published in front of the 1663 edition of the *De concordia* (see *ibid*. I 13—4, 22—3, 25—6). Baluze speaks of his entering de Marca's service *ibid*. (1663) 15—6; (1708) 45.

[34]) Baluze, *Concilia Galliae Narbonensis* (Paris 1668), praefatio fol. *ā vi verso*: „... Nam canones Concilij Monspeliensis ... descripsimus ex veteri codice MS. monasterij sancti Albini Andegavensis, cum illic ageremus anno MDCLXI. in comitatu illustrissimi Archiepiscopi ..." For de Marca's visit at Angers see F. Gaquère, *Pierre de Marca* (Paris 1932) 223.

[35]) References to 'Spicil. to. VI pag. 20'; see n. 31 *supra*.

THE SO-CALLED CANONS OF NÎMES

3.— *Notae in aliquot Canones Concilii Claromontani* printed in Pierre de Marca, *Dissertationum de concordia sacerdotii et imperii* ... 6.31, ed. Paris 1663, II pp. 191—3 (= ed. Frankfurt 1708, I 959—60): first mention of two MSS from St. Aubin [36]); criticism of d'Achery for careless copying of the Nîmes text (*c*.1); no discussion of the long and the short text.

4.— MS Baluze 7, fols. 201r—203r, 199r—200r, 197r—198r (should have been bound in this order).

> fol. 201r—203r] text of the 16 canons of Nîmes. The last sentence of *c*.1 *Et sic cuique sua iura seruentur*, is marked *abhinc alia manu;* similarly before *c*.4 (fol. 202v): *Dein alia manu sed antiqua*. Marginal notes to the sections of *c*.1 establish the identity with Clermont *cc*. 3—4 and explain why Gratian does not cite from the Council of Nîmes:
> ... Grat. 16. q.2. *Sane quia monachor*. ubi ita legitur: *Item Urbanus II*. ubi Sirmondus censet addendum, *in concilio Nemausensi*. At non adeo fortassis cognitum erat concilium Nemausense, ut huic potius hic canon tribuendus sit quam Claromontano, unde petitus est.
> fol. 199r] Notae ad Concilium Nemausense sub Vrbano II.
> Concilium istud Nemausense publici juris jampridem fecit vir optimus Dacherius in Tomo IV Spicilegii ex apographo quod multorum manibus terebatur et in meas quoque peruenerat. Verum tot mendis scatet apographum illud, ut dici vix possit. Itaque visum est synodum illam reuidere ad fidem vetustissimi codicis manuscripti monasterii sancti Albini Andegauensis, unde primitus descripta est, quemque nos illic repertum Lutetiam deferri curauimus ad Illustrissimum virum Petrum de Marca Parisiensem Archiepiscopum, vt [37]) merito nobis synodus isthaec debitura sit suam laudem, cuius statutis longam damus senectutem.
> Can. I) Praeter codicem illum, in quo extant omnes canones huius concilii, hic primus canon extat etiam in alio veteri codice ms. eiusdem monasterii cum hoc titulo: *Decretum Vrbani Papae in Nemausensi Concilio*. Eodemque modo scriptum est in alio codice, ubi primitus descriptus tantum fuerat primus hic canon: ceteri deinde adiecti sunt a manu diuersa sed antiqua. Quod cum aliqui non intellegerent, existimarunt heic peccatum fuisse a librario proque *Decretum* reponendum esse *Decreta*. Vide porro Notas nostras ad canonem III. Concilii Claromontani.
> *marg*. Extat etiam cum eodem titulo in Chartulario monasterii Vindocinensis. [later addition]

---

[36]) See *supra*, at n. 25.
[37]) Archiepiscopum. Vt *cod*.

> Can. II) Refertur hic Canon apud Gratianum 16. q.1. c.25 ex decreto [38]) Bonifacii Papae. Correctores vero Romani docent, caput hoc cum nonnullis alijs missum ex Hispania, Tarraconensi videlicet, descriptum ex veteri codice MS. monasterii Populeti . . . [39]). Integrum verò caput edidit Holstenius in Collectione sua Romana bipartita. Itaque canon iste Nemausensis est tantùm epitome canonis in Concilio Bonifacii Papae conditi.
>
> fol. 199r—200r, 197r—198r] Notes on can. V and can. XVI, partly cancelled later by long diagonal strokes.

Baluze apparently drafted this set of *Notae* at about the time when his Notes on Clermont were published (1663) or at least were ready for publication. For he refers explicitly to these Notes at the end of his remarks on Nîmes *c.*1; and the two opening sentences, *Concilium istud — ut dici vix possit*, are repeated verbatim from the printed criticism of d'Achery's text. In the meantime, Lucas Holste's *editio princeps* of the Pseudo-Boniface decree had appeared in 1662 [40]), and Baluze had arranged for the St. Aubin codex with the long version of the Nîmes canons to be brought to Pierre de Marca, who had become archbishop of Paris in the last weeks of his life (nominated 26 February, transferred 5 June, died 29 June 1662).

It is remarkable that in these *Notae* Baluze recorded all that is of critical importance — the difference between the two MSS, the change of hand *in alio codice*, the substitution of the title *Decreta* by the *aliqui* (*i.e.* Sirmond and d'Achery) who did not understand the singular — and that still he failed to draw the conclusion at which he would eventually arrive by 1677. Rather, *c.*2 remained to him a re-enactment (*epitome*) of the Boniface decree, itself taken for genuine. A similar passage occurs in the long note on *c.*16:

> . . . Arbitror autem id primo statutum fuisse in Claromontano Concilio, deinde vero repetitum in Nemausensi . . . (fol. 198r).

It confirms the fact that at this time Baluze had no suspicions. At some later date (to judge from ink and writing), he entered the

---

[38]) Concilio *ante corr.*
[39]) Here the *Nota Correctorum* to Gratian *loc. cit.* is reproduced *verbatim*.
[40]) L. Holstenius, *Coll. Romana bipartita* (Rome 1662) I 242—5.

additional note on the presence of Nîmes *c*.1 in the Vendôme cartulary [41]), but changed nothing concerning the Pseude-Boniface text.

5.— MS Baluze 7, fols. 259r—258v (again, the order is reversed) are two tear-sheets from the 1663 edition of *De concordia sacerd. et imp.* II pp. 191—194, with copious marginal corrections for the second (or a later) edition [42]). Nothing of relevance to the Nîmes problem.

6.— The *Notae ad Gratianum*, in Baluze's edition of Antonio Agustín, *De emendatione Gratiani dialogorum libri duo* (Paris 1672) pp. 516—7, contain his first published statement on the identity of Nîmes *c*.2 and the canon of Boniface, again without questioning the authenticity of either text. Five more years went by before this point was reached.

7.— The *Notae ad libros Capitularium* (*Capitularia regum Francorum* II, Paris 1677) 1243—4 = Mansi 18.827, as discussed above, and culminating in the statement: „Certum est plerosque canones qui sub nomine canonum Nemausensium editi sunt, synodi illius non esse, et additos diversis temporibus fuisse constitutionibus euisdem concilii".

Baluze's verdict of 1677 was hidden in such an unexpected place

---

[41]) This must be the text printed as No. 368 in the edition by Ch. Métais, *Cartulaire de l'Abbaye cardinale de la Trinité de Vendôme* (Paris 1893—94) II p. 119f.: „*Decretum Urbani pape II*. In Arvernensi — soliti sunt." Baluze may have seen the copy extant at the Jesuit Collège de Clermont (now Paris B.N. lat. 10402), or the one taken by Dom Lemichel (now Paris B.N. lat. 13820). Note however that the Vendôme *decretum* presents merely the section corresponding to Nîmes *c*. 1 ed. d'Achery (= *c*. 1 part I in Baluze's apograph and Labbe-Cossart), and that it is not attributed to the council.

[42]) Ed. 2 (1669); ed. 3 (1704). It would be the latter if these marginalia belong to the same period as those of fol. 118r—119v (concerning the texts of the First Lateran Council = ed. 1663, II pp. 363—366 with corrections), where we read: „Je l'ay corrigé sur le MS. d'Aniane (i.e. Paris lat. 3881) dans mon exemplaire de la seconde edition to. 2 pag. 436" (fol. 118r).

— an *obiter dictum* in his commentary on *c*.19 of the second Appendix of Book VII of Benedict the Levite — that it remained unnoticed. It escaped Louis-François-Joseph de la Barre in the 1723 edition of d'Achery's *Spicilegium*; it escaped Hardouin, Coleti, and Mansi, all of whom reproduced Labbe's text; it even escaped Dom Labat and his confrères of St. Maur in their preparations for the never-completed new collection of *Concilia Galliae* [43]). All later historians simply relied on the standard editions.

It is now possible to confirm Baluze's judgment, since his two codices from St. Aubin can be identified. The 'short' text, containing only Nîmes *c*.1, is found in a one-leaf fragment which today forms part (fol. 34) of the miscellaneous MS 4310 (711) at the Bibliothèque Mazarine [44]). Identification is warranted by the presence in the same fragment of two items that Baluze edited in his Notes on Clermont [45]) as occurring in the second St. Aubin MS with the single Nîmes decree: a letter of Paschal II (JL 5820) and a letter of Bishop Geoffrey of Chartres in favor of the monks of St. Aubin.

The 'long' text, giving all of the so-called Nîmes decrees, is found appended to a codex of Burchard's *Liber decretorum* at the Bibliothèque Nationale, MS lat. 3860. This is the *vetustissimus codex* which Baluze had sent to the archbishop of Paris. He later acquired it himself: the shelfmark 'Bal. 28' appears on the first page [46]). Here we find:

---

[43]) Only the first volume of the Maurists' *Concilia Galliae* was published (Paris 1789), and proof sheets exist for vol. II cols. 1—695; see S. Kuttner, *L'Edition romaine des Conciles généraux* ... (Miscell. Historiae Pontificiae 5; Rome 1940) 34, with bibliography cited. In their unpublished notes and drafts, MSS Vat. lat. 9862—9875, the material for Nîmes 1096 is assembled in Vat. lat. 9867 fols. 318r—327v. — For the second edition of d'Achery's *Spicilegium*, see n. 4 *supra*.

[44]) Cited n. 18 *supra*. MS 4310 is analyzed in A. Molinier, *Catalogue des mss. de la Bibliothèque Mazarine* II (Paris 1890) 293—4.

[45]) *loc. cit.* n. 25 *supra*.

[46]) Par. lat. 3860 should be added to the MSS from St. Aubin d'Angers at the B.N. in Delisle's list, *Le Cabinet des manuscrits de la Bibliothèque nationale* II (Paris 1874) 401, and likewise to the MSS discussed in J. Rambaud-Buhot, *Baluze, bibliothécaire et canoniste*, Etudes d'histoire du Droit canonique dédiées à Gabriel

fol. 138rb—va, immediately after the explicit of Burchard's Bk. XX, the *Decretum urbani pape in nemausensi concilio*, written in two paragraphs (*In Arvernensi* and *Sane quia monachorum* = cc.1—2 ed. d'Achery = c.1 Labbe-Cossart etc.); [47]

fol. 138va—vb, in another hand, the two monastic forgeries *Sunt nonnulli* and *Oportet* — the pretended second and third canons of Nîmes — without inscriptions, but with marginal instructions for the rubricator, *Bonefatius* and *Gregorius;*

fol. 138vb—139ra, in yet another hand and without inscriptions or marginal aids, the remaining 'canons of Nîmes'.

In 1744 the printed catalogue of the Bibliothèque du Roi described MS lat. 3860, *olim Baluzianus*, and correctly assessed the additions to Burchard [48]:

... accedunt ad calcem 1) decretum *Urbani* papae, in Nemausensi concilio; 2) *Bonifacii*, papae IV. decretum de libertate Monachorum; 3) decreta nonnulla quae in collectionibus Conciliorum ponuntur tanquam decreta concilii Nemausensis, quamvis ad illud concilium nullatenus pertineant.

This caveat, however, like Baluze's criticism, went unheeded.

There remains one last problem of identification. This Burchard MS with the appended 'canons of Nîmes' was certainly at St. Aubin's Abbey in Angers in Sirmond's, d'Achery's, and Baluze's days. Whether it was also written at that house [49] is another question, although the presence of the two forgeries (JE †1996 and †1951) points to a monastic *scriptorium*. The difficulty lies in the fact that a mid-twelfth-century catalogue of St. Aubin's library, published by Delisle, lists a single Burchard codex [50], and that there are three candidates for its identification: MS Angers

---

Le Bras (Paris 1965) I 325—42.

[47] The last sentence of *Sane quia* shows a change of ink but not, *pace* Baluze [MS 7 fol. 201r], of hands.

[48] *Catalogus codicum mss. bibl. regiae* III (Paris 1744) p. 522—3. Here pseudo-Gregory *Oportet* is overlooked, probably because the rubricator had not filled in the initial *O*. The Maurists, in copying from the cod. Regius, also did not recognize that here a new text begins (Vat. lat. 9867 fol. 318v).

[49] The provisional card index in the office of the MSS Division of the B.N. gives: „copié à St. Aubin, fin XIe siècle".

[50] L. Delisle, *Le Cabinet des mss.* II 485—7, at No. 62 (p. 486a).

368 (s. XI), as affirmed by Molinier's catalogue of the Bibliothèque municipale and by L. W. Jones [51]); MS 678 (s.XI) of the Bibliothèque de l'Arsenal in Paris, which has an old St. Aubin *ex libris* on fol.1 and was identified 'sans doute' with the MS in Delisle's list by H. Martin [52]); and finally, our Par. lat. 3860 with the 'Nîmes canons'.

Bernard de Montfaucon in 1739 still recorded a Burchard MS as extant in the monastery [53]). By then, Baluze's codex had long been removed from Angers; likewise, the present-day Arsenal MS 678 could well have left St. Aubin before Montfaucon's time [54]). But only a palaeographic investigation could determine which of the three Burchard codices, if not all three, originated in the abbey's *scriptorium* [55]) and was on its shelves in the twelfth century — the medieval catalogue could easily be incomplete.

In conclusion, three points can be made. First, it is nearly always rewarding to examine the writing, published or unpublished, of Etienne Baluze. As with Antonio Agustín in the century before him, his notes still can yield much new information for the historian of canon law [56]). Secondly, canons 2—16 of the

---

[51]) A. Molinier, in *Catalogue général des mss. des bibliothèques publiques* . . . 31 (Paris 1898) p. 320; Leslie W. Jones, *The Library of St. Aubin's at Angers in the Twelfth Century*, Classical and Mediaeval Studies in honor of E.K. Rand (New York 1938) 151—2. Cf. Dereine, *op. cit.* (n. 11 *supra*) 318 n. 52, who cites the Angers Burchard by its number in Montfaucon (n. 53 *infra*) as No. 265.

[52]) H. Martin, *Catalogue des mss. de la Bibliothèque de l'Arsenal* II (Paris 1886) p. 32—3, overlooked by both Molinier and Jones. The writers wish to thank Professor G. Fransen, who called this MS to their attention.

[53]) *Bibliotheca bibliothecarum* (Paris 1739) II 1228, No. 265.

[54]) Without further research all that can be said is that the Marquis de Paulmy, founder of the Arsenal library, acquired the Burchard MS in 1785, a few months before his death, at the sale of the library of Jean-Baptiste-Paulin d'Aguesseau, who had inherited it from his father, the Chancelier d'Aguesseau (1668—1751): H. Martin, *Catalogue* . . . VIII (*Histoire de la Bibl.;* Paris 1899) 274, 275 n. 2, 277.

[55]) None of the codices in question appears among those mentioned in the abstract of the thesis of J. Vezin, *Les „scriptoria" d'Angers au XIe siècle* (Ecole des Chartes, *Positions des thèses*, 1958 pp. 131—8).

[56]) See e.g. W. Holtzmann, in Nachrichten Akad. Göttingen phil.-hist. Klasse 1945 p. 24 No. 53, and Festschrift Akad. Göttingen 1951 p. 89 (on MS Baluze 77: notes from a collection, now lost, of 12th-cent. decretals in Marmoutier Abbey,

supplement to Burchard in Paris lat. 3860 are not from Nîmes, and for most of them (*c*.4 sqq.) further study is needed to determine their identity. Finally, since one can no longer maintain that the forgeries ascribed to Boniface and Gregory were officially adopted by Pope Urban II, the whole of his attitude towards the pastoral activity of monks requires a fundamental re-interpretation [57]. It is tempting to speculate how delighted the scribes of St. Aubin might have been, had they known that inadvertently they would manage to endow two monastic fabrications for centuries with the authority of one of the great reform popes of the Middle Ages.

Tours); or H. Mordek, in Traditio 25 (1969) 485—8 (on MSS Baluze 2, 4, and 9: notes from codices of the *Coll. Herovalliana*). For the history of councils, one should also examine the copy of Labbe's *Conciliorum generalium, nation. provinc. ... historica synopsis* (Paris 1661) with manuscript notes by Baluze in Grenoble MS 512 (not seen); cf. the *Catalogue* and A. De Backer-C. Sommervogel, *Bibliothèque de la Compagnie de Jésus* IV (1893) 1318 No. 63. — For Ant. Agustín see C. Leonardi, in Mélanges Eugène Tisserant VI (Studi e Testi 236; Città del Vaticano 1964) 583—637; cf. also Kuttner, in Traditio 24 (1968) 505.

[57] Dereine, *op. cit.* 317—8, already suggested as much.

Additional Note.

ad n. 31 (a detail of Nîmes overlooked ...): but not overlooked in the *Vita* of Urban II by Ruinart (1724), PL 151.167 B.

ad n. 33: For Baluze's entering the service of de Marca see also his fragmentary autobiography, published by Pierre de Chiniac in the *ed. nova* of the *Capitularia regum Francorum* (Paris 1780) 63a.

IV

GERLAND OF BESANÇON AND THE MANUSCRIPTS OF HIS 'CANDELA': A BIBLIOGRAPHICAL NOTE

I

Two anonymous French canonists shortly before or around 1170, the author of the Parisian *Summa Magister Gratianus in hoc opere* and, in his footsteps, the author of the fragmentary *Summa Antiquitate et tempore*, cited a book they called 'Candela Gerlandi' (or 'Gelandi').[1] Neither Schulte nor the writer of these pages, in his *Repertorium* (1937), was able to make much of the citation, save for connecting it with one 'Jarlandus Chrysopolitanus' whose name appears in some bibliographies of the seventeenth and the eighteenth century, and with a few manuscript references.[2] To the codex Victorinus (now Paris, B. N. lat. 14618), first mentioned in 1666 by Erich Mauritius, professor at the then recently opened University of Kiel, in his dissertation *De libris iuris communis*, Schulte added two more manuscripts of the *Candela* he had noted at random in the catalogues of Troyes and Montpellier.[3]

Historians of theology and canon law, however, should have been aware that the prologue of Gerland of Besançon (Chrysopolis, Vesuntio) for his *Candela* has existed in print ever since Martène and Durand published it from a Clairvaux manuscript (now Troyes MS 668) in the *Thesaurus novus anecdo-*

---

[1] *Summa Magister Gratianus in hoc opere* D.11 c.5 v. *scriptura*, first noted by J. F. von Schulte, 'Zur Geschichte der Literatur über das Dekret Gratians: Zweiter Beitrag,' *Sb. Akad. Vienna* 64 (1870) 35; see now *The Summa Parisiensis on the Decretum Gratiani* ed. T. P. McLaughlin (Toronto 1952) p. 11, cf. xxii. *Summa Antiquitate et tempore* D.11 c.5 v. *que orientem*, first noted—with wrong attribution to Rufinus—by Schulte, *Geschichte der Quellen und Literatur des canonischen Rechts* I (Stuttgart 1875; repr. Graz 1956) 46; cf. the introduction of his edition, *Die Summa magistri Rufini* (Giessen 1892) lxii.

[2] Schulte, 'Zweiter Beitrag' 35; *Geschichte der Quellen* II (1877; repr. 1956) 557; S. Kuttner, *Repertorium der Kanonistik (1140–1234)* (Vatican City 1937; repr. 1973) 179 n. 1, 455.

[3] *De Libris juris communis horumque Usu . . . praeside* Erico Mauritio *. . . publico eruditorum examini submittit* Christian Ehrenfriedt Charisius . . . (Kiel, n.d.) § 28; republished posthumously in his *Dissertationes et opuscula* (Frankfurt 1692; Strasbourg 1724). The date 1666 there given is confirmed by Mauritius' reference in § 16 to Pithou's edition of the *Epitome Juliani* (Basel 1576) as 'ante annos nonaginta.' On the career and writings of Mauritius (1631[?]–91) see R. Stintzing, *Geschichte der deutschen Rechtswissenschaft* II (Munich–Leipzig 1884) 238–44. Cf. Schulte *loc. cit.* (n. 2); his reference to Mauritius came from B. G. Struve's *Bibliotheca juris selecta* (Jena 1756).

torum (1717). The prologue, beginning 'Studiorum omnium theologia gubernatrix,' is preceded by a greeting to the reader:[4]

> Omnibus in Christo degentibus Jarlandus crisopolitanus sancti Pauli scolarum preceptor et canonicus fidei doctrinam et studii salutaris candelam.

The author continues by exalting theology over the 'ficta compositio philosophorum,' over Plato, Ovid, and 'Tullius'; but also over the study of *physica* which teaches only things about the body. He concludes by announcing that he has assembled many texts from many doctors, mostly from Sts. Jerome, Ambrose, Augustine, and Gregory; that he has arranged them in twenty-six parts, and given the whole corpus the name of *Candela*:[5] 'quia sicut ardens candela tenebras pellit, ita pene in omnibus capitulis unde scriptum sit quod dicitur quasi quadam tituli candela reperitur.'

The most substantial account of the *Candela* and its author was published in 1873 by Ulysse Robert, then a young graduate of the École des Chartes; but the paper, *De Gerlandi vita et operibus*, likewise escaped the attention of nearly all medievalists for a long time.[6] In most respects it has not been outdated by modern research. In a hundred years, only a few more manuscripts of the collection have been added to those Robert knew or mentioned; and only in one major point was his account corrected, when Charles Homer Haskins in 1924 showed by chronological calculations that Gerlandus, the author of a widely read treatise on *computus*, wrote in 1093 and must have been an earlier namesake, preceding by at least one generation the canon of St. Paul's at Besançon, to whom Robert, with all earlier bibliographers, had ascribed the work.[7] But Robert's study was not even mentioned in the otherwise well-informed observations on the *Candela* and on the two Gerlands which Ludwig Ott tucked away in a lengthy footnote in his book on twelfth-century *theologische Briefliteratur* (1937).[8]

When A. Cordoliani in 1945 published the first of his two articles on Gerland of Besançon in the newly founded *Revue du moyen âge latin*, he could inscribe

---

[4] E. Martène et U. Durand, *Thesaurus novus anecdotorum* I (Paris 1717; repr. New York 1968) 372 'ex ms. Clarevallis'; collated with the Ste.-Geneviève MS as quoted by U. Robert (see n. 6) col. 601 n. 3, and my own notes from Par. lat. 14618.

[5] *Thesaurus* I 373: '... corporique voluminis totius partium omnium Candelae nomen imposui.' Some writers give the name as 'Fidei doctrina et candela studii salutaris'; but this is derived from the closing words of the *salutatio*, and is not a formal title.

[6] U. Robert, 'De Gerlandi vita et operibus,' *Analecta juris pontificii* 12 (1873) 596–614. I find no reference earlier than C. H. Haskins, *Studies in the History of Mediaeval Science* (Cambridge, Mass. 1924; 2nd ed. 1927) 85 n. 13.

[7] Haskins, *op. cit.* 85; as against Robert 609–12, the *Histoire littéraire de la France* 12 (Paris 1763; reissued 1869) 278 *s.v.* Gerland and others.

[8] L. Ott, *Untersuchungen zur theologischen Briefliteratur der Frühscholastik* (Beiträge zur Geschichte der Philosophie und Theologie des Mittelalters 34; Münster 1947) 454 n. 5.

it with some justification, 'Notes sur un auteur peu connu.'[9] But Cordoliani's articles are disappointing, to say the least: in his first footnote he labels Robert's basic paper as 'étude peu précise,' and then goes on in his text and notes to incorporate, as if it were his own, most of Robert's information.[10] The second article, on Gerland's *computus*, is based on careful original research but is apparently ignorant of Haskins' fundamental *Studies*, which had come to the same results long before. There followed (to complete this rapid bibliographical *tour de l'horizon*) an article in 1948 by Bernard Jacqueline, who resumed the biographical data, announced that he was working on an edition of the *Candela*, and published the *tabula* of its twenty-six books, beginning 'Prima pars continet de Deo, de Trinitate et unitate,' from Troyes MS 668.[11]

II

Gerland's styling himself, in the *salutatio* of his book, 'master of the schools and canon of St. Paul's,' evidently antedated his election as prior by the reforming party of that collegiate church at Besançon, during the struggle to transform the collegiate chapter into a chapter of canons regular.[12] The charter Bishop Anseric addressed on May 4, 1131 'dilecto filio Gerlando priori S. Pauli et fratribus regularibus' marks the end of this turmoil and the *terminus ad quem* for the *Candela*.[13] It was reinforced in a papal charter Innocent II

---

[9] A. Cordoliani, 'Notes sur un auteur peu connu: Gerland de Besançon (avant 1100–après 1148),' *Revue du moyen âge latin* 1 (1945) 411–19; and 'Le comput de Gerland de Besançon,' *ibid.* 2 (1946) 309–13.

[10] One would have to quote page after page to show the unacknowledged borrowings.

[11] B. Jacqueline, 'Un recueil théologique et canonique inédit du xiie siècle: La "candela" de Gerland de Besançon,' *Ephemerides iuris canonici* 4 (1948) 462–9 (the first word of the *tabula* is misprinted 'Priora,' p. 466). In 1956 Msgr. Jacqueline deposited a list of the *capitula* of Book 5, with inscriptions, incipits and explicits, transcribed from the Montpellier MS, at the Institute of Medieval Canon Law.

[12] For all the biographical data here summarized see Robert's article (n. 6) 597–9, to be corrected only in minor points of detail.

[13] This agrees with the date 'Anno circiter 1130' given by Martène and Durand *loc. cit.* (n. 4 *supra*). Robert, *art. cit.* 599, maintained that Gerland witnessed — after the *terminus ad quem* just mentioned — a charter of July 25, 1131 as *scholasticus* of St. Paul, together with Zachary, master of the schools of St. Jean (the cathedral of Besançon), and again with the same title in 1134. But here Robert's memory was at fault: in his paper, 'Zacharie le Chrysopolitain,' *Bibliothèque de l'École des Chartes* 34 (1873) 580–82, the witness list of the 1131 charter is quoted: 'testes . . . Gerlandus *prior canonicorum* sancti Pauli . . . et Zacharias magister scholarum sancti Johannis Evangelistae . . .' (p. 581 n. 3, emphasis added); and for the charter of 1134, note 4 *ibid.* refers to *Gallia christiana* 15 (1860), Instr. eccl. Vesunt. no. 25, but there only 'Zacharias doctor scholarum' appears among the witnesses and no Gerlandus at all. By a further misunderstanding Jacqueline, *art. cit.* (n. 11) 463, has Gerland succeed Zachary in 1131 as *écolâtre* of the cathedral school.

sent from Cluny on February 3, 1132.¹⁴ In the last year of his life Master Gerland of Besançon was invited with Master Thierry of Chartres to accompany Archbishop Albero of Trier on his river voyage to the court King Conrad held at Frankfurt in 1147 — it must have been a spectacular fleet, forty covered ships, not counting the light brigs and the rafts for luggage and cooking supplies. The archbishop, his biographer tells us, greatly enjoyed the debates and conversations of the 'two outstanding doctors of our times' in his cabin, and upon returning dismissed them with handsome presents.¹⁵

In between these dates a few more records exist of Prior Gerland's activities in affairs of the canons regular; and it is possible that before coming to Besançon he was a master of the schools in Metz.¹⁶ Some authors have asserted that he was the 'Gerlandus scientia trivii quadruviique oneratus et honoratus' to whom Hugo Metellus, that effusive writer of theological letters from St. Leo's in Toul, sent a stinging rebuke upbraiding him for his teaching on the Eucharist.¹⁷ But even Mabillon expressed doubts about the addressee of this letter, arguing that this Gerlandus was the same person as one 'Gerardus monachus' to whom Hugo had written another letter on the Eucharistic Presence, and that the basic manuscript has a scribal mistake for the name in one of the two epistles.¹⁸ This may or may not be true. What is more important, no proof has ever been offered that the master of Besançon actually taught the heretical doctrine for which Hugo Metellus took his correspondent to task: i.e., that (with Berengar) he gave to Christ's words, 'this is my body . . . this is my blood' only a figurative meaning. The praise of theology in the preface of the *Can-*

---

¹⁴ JL 7532 (formerly dated February 5).
¹⁵ *Gesta Alberonis archiepiscopi auctore Balderico* ed. G. Waitz, MGH Scriptt. 8 (1848) 257 lin. 20ff. = PL 154.1333A–B. 'Ego Baldricus qui hanc scriptiunculam feci' was part of the archbischop's retinue; he calls Master Jarlandus Bisuntinus and Master Teodericus Carnotensis 'duos fama et gloria doctores nostri temporis excellentissimos' (lin. 25f.). Cf. Robert, 'De vita' 598; Haskins, *op. cit.* (n. 6) 85.
¹⁶ I am indebted to Mr. Charles McCurry for having pointed out to me the reference to a Master Garland among the *écolâtres* at Metz, 1128, in M. Parisse, 'Formation intellectuelle et universitaire en Lorraine . . . ,' *L'Université de Pont-à-Mousson et les problèmes de son temps: Actes du Colloque . . . 1972* (Annales de l'Est, Mémoire 47; Nancy 1974) 20 n. 2. For records of other activities see Robert 598–9.
¹⁷ Hugo Metellus, *ep.* 33, ed. J. Mabillon, *Vetera analecta* (Paris 1723) 475–7; ed. C. L. Hugo, *Sacrae antiquitatis monumenta historica, dogmatica, diplomatica* II (Saint-Dié 1731) 372–4. Gerland of Besançon is claimed as addressee by Hugo p. 372 note *a* (cf. 361 note *a* on *ep.* 26); *Hist. litt. de la France* 276; Robert 505–7; Ott, *Untersuchungen* (n. 8) 53; Jacqueline 463. I have not seen the book of the Marquis de Fortia d'Urban, *Histoire et ouvrages de Hugues Métel* (Paris 1839), cited by Cordoliani, 'Notes sur un auteur . . . ' (n. 9) 411 n. 2, and Jacqueline 462 n. 1.
¹⁸ Mabillon, *Vetera anal.* 476b–77a, with a partial edition of *ep.* 26 (ed. Hugo 361–3); cf. also J. de Ghellinck, 'Eucharistie au xii⁰ siècle en Occident,' DThC 5.2 (1913) 1245. *Contra*: the writers cited in note 17.

dela, with its warning against the study of the philosophers and the ruin it brings upon the soul,[19] would not sit well with one who is ironically greeted as weighed down with the knowledge of the seven liberal arts. But it would be pointless to argue any further before someone studies the sixteenth book of the *Candela*, 'De mysterio corporis et sanguinis Domini.'

III

All we have been told thus far of Gerland's collection is that its twenty-six books encompass theology, canon law, and liturgy, covering practically the whole range of topics in these three, as yet undifferentiated, fields; and that the work is composed of texts taken not only from the Fathers — 'a doctoribus multis,' as the preface says — but also from councils and decretals.[20] We have also been told that

> le Recueil de Jarlandus . . . pourroit être de quelque utilité pour la restitution de plusieurs Textes des Auteurs qui y sont cités, & en général pour éclairer plusieurs points des Antiquités Ecclésiastiques. Je pourrois, Messieurs, donner bien des preuves de ce que j'avance ici . . . .

Thus the writer of an unsigned letter dated March 22, 1763 to the editors of the *Mémoires de Trévoux* and printed in the May issue of that year.[21] The letter was meant to correct, from the writer's knowledge of the manuscripts, some misapprehensions he had found in the article which the German jurist and legal antiquary, Baron Heinrich Christian von Senckenberg, had published

---

[19] 'Quo tibi nugacitas auctorum? Quo eloquentia rhetorum? Quo ficta compositio philosophorum? . . . in quorum studiis non solum nullus est animae vel corporis fructus, verum potius quidam carnis marcor et fluxus; et quod miserrimum est, animae pernicies et mortis secundae laqueus' (edd. Martène and Durand 371E–F).

[20] Robert, 'De vita . . .' 602–8, with a description of the contents; J. de Ghellinck, *Le mouvement théologique du XIIe siècle*[2] (Museum Lessianum, Section historique 10; Bruges–Brussels–Paris 1948) 464: 'grande encyclopédie de théologie et de droit canon.'

[21] 'Lettre aux auteurs de ces Mémoires sur un Ouvrage de Jarlandus, Chanoine de St. Paul de Besançon, intitulé CANDELA,' *Mémoires pour l'Histoire des Sciences et des Beaux-Arts. Commencés d'être imprimé l'an 1701 à Trévoux* . . . [Année 1763] (Mai 1763) 1315–27, at p. 1319. This very rare item would hardly have attracted the present writer's attention, were it not for the typewritten copy we found in sorting out the papers left by the late Friedrich Heyer of Bonn (1878–1973) and acquired in 1974 by the Robbins Collection of the School of Law, University of California at Berkeley. A penciled note in Heyer's hand on the first page of the transcription, 'Berlin K[önigliche] B[ibliothek] Ac 2870' indicates that his interest in Gerland went back to the time before the end of the monarchy in Germany (November 1918). Only one reference to the *Lettre* of 1763 seems to exist in print: Ch. Kohler's notice for the Ste.-Geneviève MS 2768, in *Catalogue général des manuscrits des bibliothèques publiques de France: Paris, Bibliothèque Sainte-Geneviève* II (1898) 497–8.

in 1761 on the *Candela* and other canonical collections.²² The writer cited two examples for the point he wished to make in the passage quoted above: Gerland apparently made use (*Cand.* 10.74) of a source for the council of Thionville (821) which was unknown to Baluze, Sirmond, '& tous ceux qui ont ramassé les actes des Conciles ou les Capitulaires de nos Rois'; and he showed himself well informed on the ritual precepts outlined by Amalarius of Metz on the repeated examinations of catechumens before baptism, as well as on the different customs followed for these *scrutinia* in different churches (*Cand.* 13.1).²³ It is strange that Robert, otherwise so punctilious a bibliographer, would take over these observations (and a few other details) from the *Mémoires de Trévoux*, paraphrasing them in Latin without revealing his source.²⁴

IV

A full analytical study of the *Candela* seems to be indicated. Since no one has yet investigated its *auctoritates* and the structure of its *partes* in relation to the canonical collections or to the books of Sentences which circulated in France during the early-twelfth century, it is thus rather premature to contemplate editing Gerland's work. But, above all, no edition should be planned before a thorough inquiry has been made into its manuscript diffusion. (The mistaken notice of an edition printed in Cologne, 1527, has long been discarded: that book contains a similarly entitled tract against Luther.²⁵)

The most recent publications on Gerland unaccountably speak only of three or — by adding de Ghellinck's new information (1948) on a copy at Admont — four manuscripts, while no fewer than seven were known to eighteenth-century

---

²² Henrici Christiani baronis de Senkenberg [sic] 'Commentatio de veteribus Canonum Collectionibus, praecipue de Jarlandi Chrysopolitani Candela,' in Ios. Ant. Riegger, *Bibliotheca iuris canonici* (Vienna 1761) II 65ff. [not seen], and again in Riegger's *Oblectamenta historiae et iuris ecclesiastici* (Ulm 1776; also Freiburg/Br. 1779) I 95–130. On Sen(c)kenberg (1704–68, knighted as *Reichsfreiherr* in 1751) see Stintzing's continuator, E. Landsberg, *Geschichte der deutschen Rechtswissenschaft* III 1 (Munich–Leipzig 1898) 245–9 and *Noten* (separate pagination) 162–7. The Senckenbergische naturforschende Gesellschaft in Frankfurt is named after his brother, the naturalist and physician Johann Christian.

²³ 'Lettre aux auteurs . . .' 1319–22.

²⁴ See Appendix, *infra*.

²⁵ Thus already the letter in the *Mémoires de Trévoux* (1773) 1318; *Hist. litt. de la France* 12 ('Notes' of the 1869 reissue) 727; Robert 509f. But the old biographical legend is still repeated in Hurter, *Nomenclator totius theologiae* II² (Innsbruck 1906) 96 n. 2 and M. Grabmann, *Geschichte der scholastischen Methode* II (Freiburg 1911; repr. Graz 1957) 116 n. 2, though certainly not 'par tous les auteurs,' as Cordoliani maintains ('Notes sur un auteur peu connu' 414).

writers.[26] Even without attempting any systematic search one can muster nine extant codices and two which apparently are lost, or at any rate have not yet been traced. This count does not include the manuscript which Pierre-François Chifflet, s.j. (1592–1682), mentioned in passing in a note in his edition of Fulgentius (1649) but without giving its location;[27] nor the one which is described in the unpublished papers, preserved at Besançon, of Père François Xavier Laire, O.Min. (1738–1801), a scholar who is best remembered for his role in saving ecclesiastical libraries during the Revolution and to whom Pius VI once offered a post in the Vatican Library.[28] Either of these manuscripts may be identical with one which is known from the records compiled here.

Let us hope that the notes which follow will one day lead others to examine the manuscripts themselves.

Admont, Benedictine Abbey MS 90, fols. 1–118; s. xii.
Dijon, Bibl. municipale MS 195 (158), from Cîteaux; s. xii.
Montpellier, École de Médecine MS 403, from St. Bénigne, Dijon; s. xiii in.
Paris, B. N. MS lat. 10623, from the Dominicans of St. Étienne, Troyes; s. xiii.
— lat. 14618, from St. Victor; s. xii.
— lat. 18119, from the Dominicans of St. Jacques, Paris; s. xii.
Paris, Bibl. Ste.-Geneviève MS 2768 (D.I.4), from Hérivaux; s. xiii in.
Troyes, Bibl. municipale MS 668, from Clairvaux; 2 vols. s. xii.
— 1082, from the Dominicans of St. Étienne, Troyes; s. xii/xiii.
†MS formerly at the Cathedral Chapter of Città di Castello; *ante* 1144.
†MS formerly at the Cistercian Abbey of Vauluisant, dioc. Sens; old shelf-mark H.13.

The identity of the three manuscripts at the Bibliothèque Nationale with those which had been seen before the French Revolution in the libraries of St. Victor and of the 'Jacobins' (Dominicans) at Paris and Troyes can be established by consulting Léopold Delisle's *Cabinet des manuscrits* and the in-

---

[26] Cordoliani 416–17 refers only to Montpellier 403, Paris lat. 14618, and Troyes 668 as extant MSS; for Admont 90 see de Ghellinck, *Mouvement théologique* (n. 20) 463–4. These four are given in Jacqueline, *art. cit.* 464 and in his recent *Épiscopal et papauté chez saint Bernard de Clairvaux* (Saint-Lô 1975) 34 n. 62. Ott, *Untersuchungen*, has two MSS at Paris (lat. 14618 and 18119, the latter from an *obiter dictum* in Grabmann *loc. cit.* n. 25 *supra*), two at Troyes (668 and 1082), and the Montpellier MS (the two last probably from Schulte). The better information available in the eighteenth century is discussed below.

[27] *Fulgentii Ferrandi Carthaginiensis ecclesiae diaconi Opera iunctis Fulgentii et Crisconii ... opusculis ...* (Dijon 1649) 323. Cf. Robert 600 n. 2.

[28] Besançon, Bibl. de la ville MS 1260 (see the entry in A. Castan's catalogue, *Catal. gén. des mss. des bibl. publ. de France* 32 [1897] p. 940: 'Pièces relatives à l'histoire de l'imprimerie, par le P. Laire ...'; fol. 252-255: 'Observations sur le manuscrit intitulé *Candela* qui ne porte pas de nom d'autheur, mais est d'un célèbre chanoine régulier de St Paul de Besançon au xie siècle nommé Jarland ou Gerland....' On Laire see the entry in the *Biographie nouvelle des Contemporains* 10 (Paris 1823) 350–51; also in Michaud's *Biographie universelle* 22 (2nd ed.) 581–3.

ventories which he published periodically in the *Bibliothèque de l'École des Chartes* between 1862 and 1871.[29] Ulysse Robert identified and used only one of these (Par. lat. 10623).[30] The earliest notice of any of them had been given by Erich Mauritius (1666), who saw the *Candela* of Jarlandus Chrysopolitanus at St. Victor's, probably in 1657/58 when he stayed in Paris as tutor to the young prince of Holstein.[31] He spoke, however, of only twenty-two books, presumably by misreading his own notes (xxii for xxvi) or by a slip of the pen.[32] Next, Quétif and Échard reported in 1719 that the work could be found 'apud nostros Sanjacobeos Parisienses.' The manuscript (now Par. lat. 18119) is incomplete; according to the writer in the *Mémoires de Trévoux* of 1763, it ends in Book Fourteen c. 20.[33]

The manuscript of the 'Jacobins de Troyes' was first mentioned by Abbé Jean Lebeuf (1687–1760), the tireless historian of Paris, of his native Auxerre, of Verdun, etc., who had seen it in 1731; his observations were quoted by the Baron von Senckenberg (1761). The writer in the *Mémoires de Trévoux* had more details to offer, but only 'à l'aide d'un ami qui a bien voulu l'examiner,' for the Dominicans let him know they could not send out their manuscripts without incurring excommunication.[34] Par. lat. 10623 indeed carries an entry at the end marking the book as a gift of King Charles V to the Dominicans of Troyes (1375), not to be removed from their library under pain of excommunication. The manuscript lacks a title, the preface, and the first four books.[35]

---

[29] L. Delisle, *Le cabinet des manuscrits de la Bibliothèque impériale (nationale) à Paris* (Histoire générale de Paris 6; Paris 1868–81). — B.N. lat. 10623: *Le cabinet des mss.* I (1868) 45 and n. 1; 'Inventaire des mss. . . .,' *Bibl. Éc. Ch.* 24 (1863) 194. — B.N. lat. 14618: *Bibl. Éc. Ch.* 30 (1869) 31. — B.N. lat. 18119: *Le cabinet des mss.* II (1874) 6, 244–5, 328; *Bibl. Éc. Ch.* 31 (1870) 542. Designation of the Dominicans as 'Jacobins,' from their French motherhouse, St. Jacques in Paris, was common in the Ancien Régime.

[30] Robert 601. He also cited the older bibliographical sources for the St. Victor (p. 500 n. 3), the St. Jacques (*ibid.* n. 5), and the Clairvaux (*ibid.* n. 6, 602 n. 1) codices, but without identifying any of them with extant manuscripts.

[31] Mauritius, *De Libris juris communis* (n. 3) § 28: 'saepe vidi in Bibliotheca eximia, quae plus quam mille quingentos Codices Mssto continet, Canonicorum ad S. Victorem Lutetiae Parisiorum, volumine 819.' On his stay in Paris see Stintzing, *Geschichte* II 241.

[32] The error was first noted in the *Mémoires de Trévoux* (1763) 1316. Cf. also Robert 602.

[33] J. Quétif and J. Échard, *Scriptores Ordinis Praedicatorum* I (Paris 1719) 189; *Mémoires de Trévoux* (1763) 1325–6; brief mention of Par. lat. 18119 in Grabmann *loc. cit.* n. 25 and Ott *loc. cit.* n. 26 *supra*.

[34] J. Lebeuf, *Dissertations sur l'histoire ecclésiastique et civile de Paris suivies de plusieurs éclaircissements sur l'histoire de France* (Paris 1739–43) III 481; Senckenberg, 'Commentatio . . .' (n. 22) 113 and note (*b*) at p. 114; *Mémoires de Trévoux* 1327–8. On Lebeuf see *Biographie universelle* 23.481; a list of his writings (236 titles) is found at the end of the 'Notice biographique' in the revised edition of his *Mémoires concernant l'histoire civile et ecclésiastique d'Auxerre . . .* (Auxerre 1848) xlvii–lxii.

[35] See Delisle, *Le cabinet des manuscrits* I 45 and n. 1; Robert 601 n. 1, 602.

The fourth Paris manuscript, Ste.-Geneviève 2768, had been acquired in the seventeenth century from the Abbey of Hérivaux. First, Joseph Barre, a canon regular of Ste.-Geneviève and chancellor of the University of Paris (†1764), sent a note describing it to the Baron von Senckenberg; a few years later the writer in the *Mémoires de Trévoux* also published a brief description. The manuscript breaks off at the beginning of Book Twenty-three and has a lacuna at the end of Book Nine.[36]

Troyes MS 668 originally belonged to the Abbey of Clairvaux and was known to Casimir Oudin (†1717), in whose posthumously published *De scriptoribus ecclesiae* (1722) it is mentioned.[37] The codex was temporarily misplaced at the time the writer in the *Mémoires de Trévoux* asked the monks of Clairvaux about it: since they were engaged in the remodeling of their library, they 'auroient inutilement cherché le Ms. de Jarlandus dans l'endroit où ils ont déposé pêle-mêle leurs livres.'[38] One would hardly have to repeat that this was the 'ms. Clarevallis' from which Martène had copied Gerland's preface for the *Thesaurus*, were it not for a bibliographical legend which attributes a Clairvaux origin also to MS 403 of the Faculté de Médecine of Montpellier.

It has long been known that in the eighteenth century this manuscript belonged to the great library in Dijon which had been partly assembled, partly inherited, by Jean Bouhier (1673–1746), president of the Parlement de Bourgogne, the last and most renowned of a long line of *noblesse de robe*. We further know that the Bouhier library was sold in 1782 to Clairvaux by a later heir, the Comte d'Avaux; and that the Gerland codex was one of the 323 among the abbey's manuscripts which after the Revolution were assigned to the École de Médecine of Montpellier, while the bulk went to Troyes.[39] Now,

---

[36] See Senckenberg 114; the description by Barre (on whom see Michaud, *Biographie universelle* 3.146–7) is quoted in Robert 600–1, without further reference. *Mémoires de Trévoux* 1326; Kohler, *loc. cit.* n. 21 *supra*.

[37] C. Oudin, *Commentarius de scriptoribus Ecclesiae antiquis . . . a Bellarmino, Possevino . . . et aliis omissis* (ed. 2; Leipzig 1722) II 1289: '. . . extat MS. in insigni Bibliotheca Archicoenobii Clarae Vallis, Ordinis Cisterciensis'; cf. Robert 600. Oudin had no entry on Gerland in his first edition, *Supplementum de scriptoribus vel scriptis ecclesiasticis a Bellarmino omissis . . .* (Paris 1686).

[38] *Mémoires de Trévoux* (1763) 1327–8. Cordoliani 416 and Jacqueline 464 mistakenly identify the Clairvaux MS of Troyes with the one given by Charles V to the Troyes Dominicans (Paris lat. 10623).

[39] See A. Harmand, introd. to the Troyes catalogue, *Cat. gen.* (quarto) 2 (Paris 1855) pp. ii–vii (with the list drawn up at the time of the MSS destined for Montpellier, pp. xvi–xxiv); Delisle, *Le cabinet des manuscrits* II 266–79 ('Le cabinet de la famille Bouhier'), esp. 278f.; and recently the definitive monograph by A. Ronsin, *La Bibliothèque Bouhier: Histoire d'une collection formée du XVIe au XVIIIe siècle par une famille de magistrats bourguignons* (Mém. Acad. Dijon 118; 1971).

if we are to believe Guglielmo Libri's catalogue of the Montpellier manuscripts (1849), Bouhier apparently thought that his *Candela* (with the shelfmark E.6) could be the codex from Clairvaux which had been mentioned by Oudin. But Bouhier, who drew up the catalogue of his manuscript collection in 1721 (with some later additions), never said anything of the sort. What Libri here attributed to the president was in fact his own invention: another piece of dishonesty on the part of the great embezzler.[40]

Modern studies in the history of the Bouhiers' library have established that the *Candela* was recorded as early as the 1660s in a catalogue made during the last years of the president's grandfather, Jean III Bouhier (†1671). It was one of the thirty-odd manuscripts the family had acquired at one time or another from the Abbey of St. Bénigne in Dijon.[41] We thus can safely identify Montpellier MS 403 (Bouhier E.6) with the codex from St. Bénigne which Quétif and Échard in the *Scriptores Ordinis Praedicatorum* mentioned from Abbot Nicolas Janin's catalogue as having belonged to that house in 1621. It appears no longer in Dom Benetôt's list of 1653:[42] acquisition by the Bouhiers falls between those two dates.

Among the Gerlandus manuscripts of which eighteenth-century bibliographers knew, there remains one which has not yet been traced and may indeed be lost: this is the codex of Vauluisant (Vallis Lucensis O.Cist.) 'pulpito 13. littera H.' which Oudin cited together with the one of Clairvaux.[43]

In the nineteenth century it was Johann Friedrich von Schulte who first drew attention, in 1870, to MS 1082 of Troyes (from Harmand's catalogue) and, a few years later, from the catalogue of Libri, to the manuscript of Montpellier whose antecedents were discussed above.[44] Troyes 1082, like Paris B.

---

[40] Notice by G. Libri, *Cat. gén.* (quarto) 1 (Paris 1849) p. 443 for Montpellier, Fac. de Méd. MS 403 = Bouhier E.6. For the date of the president's catalogue see Ronsin (n. 39) 108, 219. It is preserved in MS H.19 of the Faculté de Médicine. I am greatly indebted to Professor André Gouron in Montpellier for having examined both Bouhier's Gerlandus and his catalogue entry, also for first having called Ronsin's book to my attention. On the notorious Libri (1803–69) see G. A. Bogeng, *Die grossen Bibliophilen* (Leipzig 1922) I 505–7; III 346–7 (bibliography).

[41] See the concordance of the president's and Jean III's catalogues by A. Vernet and R. Étaix, 'Appendice,' in Ronsin, *La Bibl. Bouhier* 222ff. (E.6 = Jean III D.35, p. 227) and the list of provenances, *ibid.* 238ff. (E.6: St. Bénigne, p. 240). For the date of Jean III's catalogue see Ronsin 107; for other MSS from St. Bénigne, Vernet's index *ibid.* 243.

[42] Quétif-Échard (n. 33) I 189: 'Hoc idem opus erat anno 1621 in monasterio S. Benigni Divionensis et recensetur in catalogo codd. MS bibliothecae Janinianae.' Cf. H. Omont, *Cat. gén.* 5 (1889) 453–7, at p. 456a. Dom Benetôt's catalogue is summarized in B. Montfaucon, *Bibliotheca bibliothecarum manuscriptorum nova* (Paris 1739) II 1284–7: Professor Vernet of the École des Chartes kindly pointed out to me this important clue to the St. Bénigne MSS in the Bouhier collection (letter of April 7, 1976).

[43] Oudin, *Comm. de scriptoribus* II 1289. Cf. Robert 600.

[44] Schulte, as cited nn. 1, 2 *supra*.

N. lat. 10623, comes from the 'Jacobins' of Troyes. Garland's collection here forms part of a miscellaneous codex (with a grammatical treatise preceding and a series of sermons following); and like the manuscript now in Paris it lacks the first four books of the *Candela*.[45] Future study will have to establish whether one manuscript was copied from the other or both came from a common model.

H. Omont recorded Dijon MS 195 (158) from Cîteaux in his catalogue (1889); otherwise it has remained unnoticed, even though Jacqueline's article refers to the presence of the *Candela* in the old Cîteaux inventory which Omont printed in the same volume.[46]

Admont MS 90, to which J. de Ghellinck first drew attention in 1948, thus far is the only manuscript known outside of France. It would be different if only we could trace the copy owned by Pope Celestine II (Master Guido of Castello, †1144), who left it with his other books to the cathedral of St. Floridus in his native Città di Castello. When Dom Wilmart identified this interesting book list in 1923, he did not comment on the entry 'Candelam';[47] it is worth noting, however, that the work of Gerlandus, like the *Sic et non* of Guido's teacher Abailard, found its way into the pope's personal library in the lifetime of the author.

Is it an accident, we may ask at the end of this survey, that so many of these manuscripts come from monastic centers? That the literary references to the 'Candela Gerlandi' of which we know during the twelfth century all occur in the context of liturgical rather than canonical or theological questions?[48]

---

[45] Harmand, *Cat. gén.* (quarto) 2 p. 447; cf. Kuttner, *Repertorium* 178 n. 1.

[46] *Cat. gén.* 5 (1889) p. 57; cf. Appendice p. 369 (Jean de Cirey's inventory No. 276), cited by Jacqueline 465 n. 2.

[47] A. Wilmart, 'Les livres légués par Célestin II à Città di Castello,' *Revue bénédictine* 35 (1923) 98–102. The list is at the end of Pope Celestine's copy of the letters of St. Jerome, now Escorial MS a.II.12, whence first printed, without identification, by G. Antolín, *Catálogo de los códices latinos de la R. Biblioteca del Escorial* 1 (Madrid 1910) pp. 45–51. See 'Candelam' (Wilmart 101 lin. 16), 'Sic et non' (lin. 26). Professor Robert Somerville, who drew my attention to Wilmart's paper, is engaged in a study on the contents of Celestine II's library. Professor Vernet (in his letter cited n. 42 *supra*) has likewise noted this copy of the *Candela*.

[48] The two canonists mentioned at the beginning of this paper cite Gerlandus in commenting on Gratian's D.11 c.5 (Basilius *de spiritu sancto* c.27: PG 32.187), ad v. 'que enim scriptura ... salutifere crucis signaculo fideles docuit insigniri?' (*Sum. Par.*) and 'que orientem uersus nos orare litterarum forma docuit?' (*Antiq. et temp.*). An anonymous letter *de ordine legendi s. Scripturam* (PL 213.713–18, at 716c) cites the *Candela Gerlandi* for the 'rationes singulorum que per anni curriculum fiunt'; noted by Martène–Durand, *Thesaurus novus anecd.* I 489 note (a) *ad loc.*; Ott, *Untersuchungen* (n. 8) 454 n. 5; Jacqueline 465 n. 3.

Probably not: by the time Gerland disappeared from the scene, the future of canon law and theology no longer lay with unreflected collections but with the reasoned assimilation of *auctoritates* in the dialectic discourse of the new schools. And yet, if such an old-fashioned book as Gerland's continued to be copied and recopied, it must have attracted readers even in the expanding intellectual universe of the Scholastic age. In short, his *Candela* remained a part, however modest, of medieval tradition: it thus deserves to be recorded in a volume designed to honor the memory of that distinguished guardian of παράδοσις, Father Edwin Quain.

University of California
Berkeley

APPENDIX

ULYSSE ROBERT AND THE 'MÉMOIRES DE TRÉVOUX' (cf. note 24 *supra*)

Not many libraries own a complete set of the *Mémoires pour l'Histoire des Sciences et des Beaux Arts* (*Mémoires de Trévoux*; 1701–67). It will therefore be best to quote in full some sample passages of the *Lettre* published in the May issue of 1763 which Robert evidently used, without indicating his source. The French text is taken from Heyer's typescript (see n. 21 *supra*), Robert's text from the *Analecta juris pontificii* 12 (1873) 596ff.

La *Candela* . . . est une collection de passages des Peres, de Canons des Conciles, & de Décrétales des Papes, telles que celles que nous ont données *Burchard*, Evêque de Worms, *Yves* de Chartres, *Gratien* & plusieurs autres: . . .	Fere tamen omnia . . . e patrum scriptis, canonibus, pontificum decretis, qualia a Burchardo, Wormacensi episcopo, Yvone Carnotensi, etc. excerpsit. . . .
Il a mis à contribution tous les Ouvrages des Écrivains Ecclésiastiques à mesure qu'ils sont tombés sous sa main; outre S. Jerôme, S. Augustin, S. Jean Chrisostôme & S. Grégoire, dont il tire le plus grand nombre de ses Extraits,	Ut enim confitetur ipse, praesertim ab Hieronymo, Augustino, Chrysostomo et Gregorio multa;
il a puisé encore dans Amalarius, dans Julien Pomerius, dans Paterius, Evipius [*sic*], Jean Diacre, Haymon & plusieurs autres dont la liste serait trop longue.	ab Amalario, Juliano Pomerio, Paterio, Edipio [*sic*], Johanne Diacono, Haymone, etc. depromsit pauciora.
Pour les Décrétales des Papes, il se sert également des authentiques & de celles dont la supposition a été si bien démontrée dans le dernier siècle. (pp. 1316–18)	Quod autem ad Romanorum pontificum decretales attinet, aeque veris utitur et falsis. (col. 602)

GERLAND OF BESANÇON 83

(Note especially: the substitution of Chrysostom for Ambrose [cf. *supra*, before n. 5] among the major Fathers; the list of minor authors, with the 'emendation' of the error 'Evipius' for Eugippius.)

Je pourrois, Messieurs, donner bien des preuves de ce que j'avance ici; mais je me borne à une ou deux qui vous feront juger des autres: Sirmond, Baluze & tous ceux qui ont ramassé les actes des Conciles ou les Capitulaires de nos Rois, rapportent la décision du Concile de Thionville tenu en 821, contre ceux qui maltraitoient les membres du Clergé; mais aucun de ces Compilateurs ne dit que Charles-le-Chauve assista à ce Concile, circonstance que nous apprend Jarlandus qui ajoute sur ce sujet des détails intéressants, & que je copie au bas de la page (*a*).
[Note] (*a*) Ludovico Imperatore adhuc superstite, *dit-il*, (Lib. x. Cap. 74.). . . .
. . . Je crois devoir remarquer que dans les trois Mss. de Jarlandus, l'Archevêque de Mayence qui présida à ce Concile s'appelle *Agistolphus*, tandis que les autres Collecteurs des Conciles le nomment *Aistolphus*, & qu'il porte le nom d'*Haistuphus* [sic] dans son Epitaphe rapportée par Serarius. (Moguntiac. rer. Lib. iv.) (1319-21)

in hoc capite, res est memoratu digna, scilicet Carolum Calvum Ludovici imperatoris filium, Theodonisvillae concilio adfuisse: 'Ludovico imperatore, inquit Gerlandus, adhuc superstite . . . Agistolphus Mangonciensis [sic], etc.' Illud de Carolo omiserunt Sirmundus, Baluzius et caeteri qui concilii hujus mentionem injecerunt.

Notandum etiam est quod in Gerlandi codice episcopus Moguntinus nomine Agistolphus nominatur, dum apud caeteros conciliorum scriptores Aistolphus et in suo epitaphio a Serario memorato (Mogunt. rer. lib. iv) Haistuphus [sic] nominatur. (604)

(Note especially: the observation on 'Sirmond, Baluze and others' having failed to mention the presence of Charles the Bald at Thionville; the observation on the forms of Archbishop Aistulph's name, with the same spelling error found in both texts.)

Pour peu qu'on soit versé dans la connoissance des anciens rits Ecclésiastiques, on sait que les *scrutins* étoient des épreuves ou examens par lesquels on faisoit passer les Cathécumenes avant de les admettre au Baptême.
Les Liturgistes anciens s'accordent presque tous sur le nombre de ces scrutins; mais ils diffèrent entre eux sur l'ordre que l'on gardoit dans la pratique de ces usages, aussi bien que sur le tems où on les observoit: Jarlandus qui traite ce sujet . . .

Quicumque vel paululum in antiquis ecclesiae ritibus versatur, non ignorat scrutinia fuisse disquisitiones quibus ante baptismum catechumeni subjiciebantur.

Scrutiniorum de numero consentiunt fere omnes qui de liturgia scripserunt; dissentiunt autem de ritibus adhibitis, necnon de tempore.

Hanc rem satis fuse tractat Gerlandus . . .

IV

84

[Excerpts in note (*b*), including a piece of Amalarius, and ending 'septimum alicubi fieri solet, alicubi minimè.']

... & ce qu'il dit donne la plus grande vraisemblance à l'opinion de ceux qui pensent que le tems des scrutins varioit dans la très-grande partie des Eglises qui ne suivoient pas le Rit Romain. (1321-23)

[A long excerpt follows, including a piece of Amalarius, and ending 'septimum ... alicubi minime.']

Quibus dictis merito conjiciendum est scrutiniorum tempus non fuisse unum et idem in ecclesiis quae Romanum ritum non tenebant. (605)

V

THE 'EXTRAVAGANTES' OF THE DECRETUM IN BIBERACH

In his description of the Decretum of Gratian that has recently come to light in Biberach an der Riss, Spitalarchiv MS B 3515, Professor R. Weigand briefly listed decretals and other supplemental texts which are found entered by various hands throughout the volume where space was available in partially unused columns, in blank pages, and sometimes also in the margins. Some of these are scattered entries of single texts, others appear in clusters, particularly on fols. 236-237 and 280.¹ One may doubt that material of this kind was haphazardly assembled; it seemed reasonable therefore to look for parallels in decretal collections, or in short appendices mixed of decretals, *paleae*, and other *extravagantes* as we know them from other Gratian MSS.²

A first clue comes from the series of texts on fol. 280rb which begins with three letters addressed to the archbishop of Ravenna: JL 14074, 14073, 14072 = W. Holtzmann, *Kanonistische Ergänzungen* Nos. 58, 57, 61. They appear in sequence only here and in the *Collectio Cusana* (cc. 22, 20, 21), where they form part of that singular set of five decretals concerning Ravenna (cc. 20-24 = *Kan. Erg.* 57, 61, 58, 59, 55) which points to a local tradition behind the *exemplar* of *Cus*.³ All three texts of *Bib.* exist also in *Coll. Lipsiensis* but without serial cohesion (Lips. 51.4; 47.26; 47.8). *Bib.* 3 is otherwise present only in *Coll. Rotomagensis* 31.18 (with c.1 given in *Rot.* 17.6) while *Bib.* 1 and 2 are found, but never as a pair, in several other collections (e.g. *Bamb.*, *Cass.*, *Tann.*,*Sang.*, *Frcf.*).⁴ Thus the unique parallelism of *Bib.* and *Cus.* eliminates any other known collection as model for these three texts, and this kinship is confirmed when we extend the comparison to some of the other clusters of texts. In all these cases we may postulate a common source for *Bib.* and *Cus.* This source may be once or twice removed, but in any event the principle of economy, i.e.that sources are not to be multiplied without necessity, bids us not to look farther afield where *Cus.* satisfies our needs. Only in those instances where no parallel with *Cus.* exists should we try to find possible sources elsewhere.

Professor Weigand has given us separate lists of the *paleae* and of the *extravagantes* (decretals, papal councils, etc.) in Biberach. In the survey that follows I have departed from this division whenever such materials appear in combination, as is typical of early decretal collections and appendices. Some minor additions and corrections have been made.

(i) fol. 77 va/b, 159rb.

> Alexander seruus seruorum dei fratri suo Wigornensi episcopo salutem et apostolicam benedictionem. *De appellatione que fit super incidenti causa.* Super eo quod a nobis tua sollicitudo — nichilominus supersedeatur. (f)

---

[1] BMCL 2 (1972) 76-81, at 78f. In the meantime the Institute has obtained a microfilm of the Biberach MS through the kindness of Professor Weigand.

[2] Cf. *Repertorium der Kanonistik* 273-6; W. Holtzmann, *Kanonistische Ergänzungen* 4 (QF 37 [1957] 58); J. Rambaud-Buhot, in *L'âge classique* (Histoire du droit et des institutions de l'Église 7; Paris 1965) 115-19. Many more of these appendices could be listed; they are mentioned as early as Stephen of Tournai's *Summa* C.13 q.2 p.c.7: '...non in uolumine isto set inter cetera extrauagantia in fine scribitur' (cf. p.219 Schulte).

[3] See Holtzmann's commentary to *Kan. Erg.* No.57 and his 'Zu den Dekretalen bei Simon von Bisignano', Bulletin for 1962, *Traditio* 18.450-59, at 453.

[4] For details see *Kan. Erg.* Nos. 58, 57, 61.

De appellatione que fit de falsi suggestione. Si autem aduersa pars —
   obstaculum inhibeatur. (g)
De appellationibus que fiunt pro minimis causis. De appellationibus vero
   que pro causis — negotiis deferendum. (h)
De non prosequentibus appellationem. Verum si appellantes — districte conpellas. (i)
De his qui cum affinibus suis carnaliter commiscentur. Quod si aliquis
   parochianorum — (77vb) — penitentia iniungenda. (j)
De donationibus que fiunt absque consensu conuentus. Ceterum si abbatem — irritum iudicandum. (k)
De terris datis ecclesie per conditionem. Verum cum alicui — robur
   habere. (l)
De his qui coram episcopo se uouent ad religionem transituros. (Alex'.
   Wirgorn. ep̄o *add.al.m.*) Meminimus[5] nos ex parte tua — matrimonium rescindere. (a)
*De his qui post factam scitationem uel ante iter ad dominum papam arri-
   piunt.* Ceterum cum aliquam — aliquatenus obseruandum. (d)
De lite que infra certum terminum decidi precipitur. Si autem lis infra
   certum — non est dubium expirare. Dat. ben(euenti) secundo Nonas sept(embris). (e)
(fol. 159rb, after the end of C.11 q.3:)
(D)e monachis autem — conuenit respondere. (b)
(*al.m.*) Preterea illi qui episcopo — censuales facere. (c)

This is JL 13162 (WH 649) 'Meminimus', in an inverted order. I have indicated the correct sequence of the sections by the letters (a)-(l).[6] Of the two missing pieces, (b) is supplied on fol. 159r in the same hand as the bulk of the decretal (fol. 77v), (c) by another hand, which also wrote after the date line of the main text fol. 77v in the margin:

§ partem huius decretalis///
inuenies et nou///
unam decretalem ri///
Wigornensi sc///

Still in another hand we have the marginal note next to the rubric of (d): 'pars hic (huius?) est que habetur infra///'. (The rest of the two notes, in the fold of the page, is not visible on the film.)

While the Italian collections, including *Cus.* 106-107, present the correct order of the decretal, the inversion 'Super eo — robur habere' (f-l), 'Meminimus — expirare' (a-e) occurs also in two English 'primitive' collections, 1 *Cantuariensis* 22 and *Roffensis* 112, though not exactly as here and without rubrics.[7] The

---

[5] Erasure between the large initial M and 'eminimus'.

[6] The WH number is that of Holtzmann's index of decretals at the Institute. In No. 649 he used a slightly different lettering, which treats (f) (g) and (h) (i) each as one (f I, II; g I, II) and divides (l) in two.

[7] Both have (a)-(e) in proper sequence but invert (h) (j) (i). See also C. Duggan, *Twelfth-Century Decretal Collections* (London 1963) 164, 181.

pieces are still more scrambled in two others that begin with 'Super eo': *Wigorn. altera* 4-5[8] and *Fontanensis* 1.1-3, 4b; 3.11-13. Much closer to Biberach is the *Fragmentum Parisiense* from St. Victor in B.N. lat. 15001 (fol. 121vb-122r) cc.1 and 3:[9] the sections are presented in the sequence (d) (e) = c.1, with the same date as in *Bib.*, and (f)-(l) = c.3. All sections have the same rubrics as in *Bib.*:[10] a unique parallelism which overrides such differences as the contradictory second date, 'Beneuento kal. septembris', at the end of c.3, or the lack in the Paris fragment not only of sections (b) (c) as in *Bib.* fol. 77v, but also of the opening section (a). Both texts are derived from a source with full address; and *Bib.* should settle the variants of dating in favor of September 4 (ii.non.) 1167-9.[11]

(ii) fol. 94ra/vb: an inserted leaf, dividing C.1 q.5 c.3 (fol. 93vb)... esse te- (95ra) stentur tamen quia culpam...'.

    1. (94ra) Qualiter uero commendaticias — (94va) — idest euangelium (*palea* Dist. 73).
    2. Prohibentur alii accusare — audiuntur (C.2 q.1 c.14).
    3. Alex. Cantuar. archiep. Qua fronte—non est tradendum sepulture (JL 14312, WH 755).

Each piece is by a different hand. As pointed out by Weigand (p. 77), c.2, which is compiled from Dig. 48.2.8-11, 13, appears again in a shortened form in its proper place, fol. 99vb.[12] This provides new evidence for the late insertion of this Roman text and the uncertainty of its early MS tradition.[13] There is no parallel for c.3 in *Cus.*

The *palea* D. 73 includes here a tabulation of the Greek alphabet with its letter values and numerial values in four ornamental columns (in the manner of canon tables), *inc.* 'I.|A^a|alpha|Mia.' This table serves to illustrate the principle of *litterae formatae*.

(iii) fol. 159va/vb (for 159rb see (i) *supra*), after supplying C.6 q.4 c.5 through q.5, which was missing from its proper place fol. 129 (cf. Weigand p.77), the same hand continues:

---

[8] *Repertorium* 284 ('Londinensis IV'); Duggan 153.

[9] *Repertorium* 286-7, where the folio indication must be corrected as above. 122r is written in whole lines.

[10] In the rubric of *Par.* c.3e = section (j) the last word should read 'commiscentur'. The preceding c.3d = section (i) ends correctly 'districte compellas': the aberration mentioned *Repert.* 287 was mine, not the scribe's.

[11] In *Font.* 1.4 the garbled form 'beñ. v̄. R non. sept.' also stands probably for 'beneṽ. 2 non. sept.'

[12] 'Prohibentur — euocari^{219} non possunt etc. usque diuus Seuerus^{238} — audiantur' (I have indicated Friedberg's exponents in C.2 q.1 c.14 for better orientation).

[13] See Kuttner, 'New Studies on the Roman Law in Gratian's Decretum', *Seminar* 11 (1953) 33; J. Rambaud-Buhot 'Le "Corpus iuris civilis" dans le Décret...', BEC 111 (1954) 61.

V

65

1. Ex registro gregorii.vii. Peruenit ad nos — absoluimus (JL 5153/4, WH 709).
2. Idem. Quod latenter — subsistere (cf. JE 1259).
3. Ex concilio triburiensi. Nobilis homo — ferro se expurget (*palea* C.2 q.5 c.15).

None of this is related to *Coll. Cus.* but cc.1 and 2 appear in frequent combination in appendices of Gratian, thus e.g. Innsbruck 90 fol. 276ra; Darmstadt 907 cc.9, 10; Harvard Law School 64 cc.7-8. JL 5153/4, absolving Bishop Henry of Liège from his oath, was first paraphrased from Greg. VII, *Reg.* 7.13-14 by Deusdedit *Coll. can.* 1.246 (197), then further shortened in the collections of the twelfth century, and so handed down to 1 *Comp.* 2.17.9 (X 2.24.2). The sentence 'Quod latenter et per uim et illicite introductum est, nulla debet stabilitate subsistere' (c.2) may originally have been a gloss to this, lifted from Greg. M. *Reg.* 3.54 (JE 1259).[14] In *Coll. Francofortana* 46.8 we find the two texts conflated into one, and shall likewise encounter them in this form in *Bib.* fol. 237v (see (vi) c.12 *infra*); elsewhere they drifted apart, and the short excerpt from Gregory the Great became a *regula iuris* in 1 *Comp.* 5.37.4 (X 5.41.5). — The *palea* 'Nobilis homo' on compurgation (c.3) appears also in some collections (2 *Par.* 31.2; *Lips.* 38.4) and entered the Decretals (1 *Comp.* 5.30.1; X 5.34.1), but nowhere in the same context as in *Bib.*

(iv) fol. 208va, *marg. inf.* near end of C.21 q.4.

Presbiterum cuius duos digitos — scandalum generari. (*al.m.marg.:*) Eugenius papa Jocel' sarum episcopo (JL 8959, WH 736).

The decretal is found, undivided as here, in several collections, among which *Cus.* 59.

(v) fol. 224rb, *marg. sup.* near C.23 q.4 cc.26-27.

§Anathema separationis, maledictionis, abhominationis et occasionis iuxta illud apostoli, 'optabam esse anathema pro fratribus meis' (Rom. 9.3), i.e. occidi secundum carnem. (*al.m.* on top:) Heimo super epistola ad Rom.

This *divisio*, based on Haimo of Auxerre's Commentary on the Pauline letters (PL. 117.440C; cf. Weigand p. 78), is probably not meant as an additional text but a gloss on C.23 q.4 c.27 v. *anathematizatumque*.

(vi) fol. 236rb-237vb, a major insertion between C.23 q.6 c.3 and c.4, beginning with the misplaced chapters C.24 q.1 cc.35-37[14a] (another hand in the top margin notes 'vacat', and a third adds 'ab hoc loco usque Jam uero', i.e. from here to 23 q.6 c.4); then :

1. (fol. 236va) Item ex decreto Hormisde pape ad Eusebium episcopum. Qua (*leg.* Tua) sanctitas — tenenda mandamus (*palea* C.31 q.2 c.2; JK † 869).
2. Idem. Duobus modis — se suscipiunt (*palea* C.27 q.2 c.51).

---

[14] MGH *Epp.* 1.213.6.
[14a] Not cc. 25-27, cited by Weigand 77.

V

3. Item Benedictus seruus seruorum dei. Lex diuine constitutionis — nulla ratio docet (*palea* C.27 q.2 c.8; JL 3773; WH 610, *Kan. Erg.* No. 145).
4. Quociens frater — (236vb) — quod uerum iurauerit. (*marg. al.m.:*) Innocentius Venerabilibus episcopis (fratribus *suprascr.*) aquilegensi patriarche <M.> Mantuano g. Flectrensi (*leg.* Feltrensi) .j. uincentino et p. cumensi episcopis (*palea* C.2 q.5 c.17; JL 8289; WH 842, *Kan. Erg.* No. 141; ends near Friedb. n.194 *ad loc.*).
5. Item ex magu<n>tiensi. A sancto concilio decretum est — subiacebunt (*palea* C.2 q.7 c.7).

The first four *paleae* appear at different locations in several decretal collections; only the Italian *Coll. Ambrosiana* 10, 12, 13, 52 presents at least *Bib.* cc.1-3 closely together; one may also note the sequence of cc.3, 1 in 2 *Par.* 81 (80).2, 1. But *Cus.* gives one chapter (4) only: *Cus.* 13 = *Ambr.* 52. The elaborate address of Inn. II 'Quotiens frater' is not infrequent, and in several collections (among them *Ambr.* 52 and 2 *Par.* 30.4) the text ends at the same point as in *Bib.* c.4. — Mme Rambaud has excluded C.2 q.7 c.7 (*Bib.*c.5) from her revised list of *paleae*, under the assumption that it makes its appearance only in fourteenth-century MSS.[15] The argument — in itself questionable as a *petitio principii* — is voided by our MS. In *Bib.* c.5 (and also *Coll. Fontanensis* 1.6) the chapter begins with the words 'A sancto concilio decretum est' where the later Gratian MSS and editions have only 'Decretum est'. In any case, it should be restored to the list of *paleae*, together with a few others that no longer figure there.

6. (236vb) Item eugenius seruus seruorum dei dilectis suis magistro O. et Ar. subdiacono nostro salutem et apostolicam benedictionem. Litteras dilationis (*sic*) — salutem (JL 9654; WH 625, *Kan. Erg.* No. 67).
7. Item Stephanus apostolice et uniuersalis romane ecclesie episcopus episcopis omnibus in domino salutem. Sanctorum patrum — alienus (*cap. incert.* cf.X 2.26.3).
8. Item Gregorius episcopo siracusano. Ne (*corr. ex* De) religio<so>rum — prescriptione seruata (JE 1482).
9. Item Gregorius papa Petro subdiacono. Ego episcopus Petrus — (237ra) — sancta euangelia (JL—; WH 382).[16]
10. (A)drianus episcopus seruus seruorum dei uniuersis monachis pontis domini (*sic*) salutem et apostolicam benedictionem. Nobis in eminenti — datum est hoc decretum captie (*leg.* Capue) tercio nonas decembris (JL 10444, WH 664; *Kan. Erg.* No. 90).

While the combination of cc.7 and 8 is quite frequent (although usually with the attribution to Gregory also of c.7),[17] the series cc.6-10 finds a parallel only in *Cus.* 145, 148-151. — The singular inscription of c.7 is borrowed from the Ps.-Isidorian letter JK †131 of Stephen (Hinschius p. 183).

---

[15] *L'âge classique* 108.

[16] Now edited by H.E.J. Cowdrey, *The Epistolae Vagantes of Pope Gregory VII* (Oxford 1972) 172 No. 69 from *Coll. Berol.* and *Duac.*, with reference to the Holtzmann papers; cf. also p.v.

[17] *Cus.* 148 (*sine inscr.*), 149; *Flor.* 26 ('Alexander iii'), 27; *App.* 38.7, 6; *Bamb.* 41.3, 4, etc. down to 1 *Comp.* 2.18.4, 5.

11. (237ra) *Decreta Turonensis con(cilii) a diuino ore summi pontificis pape Alexandri promulgata regnantibus christianissimis principibus Lodouico rege Francorum et Henrico inuictissimo rege Anglorum duce Normannie et Aquitanie.*

Under this formal rubric there follow the canons of Tours 1163 in the frequently attested sequence (237ra/b) 5-7, 4, 8, followed (237va) by 3, 2, 1.[18] *Cus.* 95-102 differs slightly (cc.5-7, 8, 4, 1-3) but there is no parallel for the general rubric nor for the elaborate rubrics of the individual canons. They differ from those of the vulgate text (Mansi 21.1175-81) and are somewhat akin to, though not identical with, the equally elaborate rubrics of the eight chapters as they appear in a previously unrecorded appendix of decretals and canons at the end of the *Abbreviatio 'Quoniam egestas'*, Paris B.N. lat. 15001, fol. 236v-238v (at 237r-238r) — the second instance of a relationship between materials in the two MSS (see (i) *supra*):[19]

(5) Ne sub annuo precio sacerdotes ad ecclesiarum regimen statuantur *Bib. Par.*

(6) Ne ab his qui ad religionem transire uolunt aliqua pecunia exigatur neue prioratus aut capellanie quelibet uendantur aut pro sepultura aut sacri olei aut crismatis perceptione ulla exactio intercedat *Bib.*

Ne ab his qui ad religionem conuerti uolunt pecunia exigatur *Par.*

(7) Ne aliqui constituti in clero ad agendas uices episcoporum seu archidiaconorum in causis ecclesiasticis terminandis sub annuo precio constituantur *Bib.*

Ne decani uel archipresbiteri ad agendas uices episcoporum seu archidiaconorum et terminandas causas sub annuo precio statuantur *Par.*

...

(1) Prebende in suo statu permaneant et dignitatum permutationes non fiant *Bib.*

Ne diuisio prebendarum ac dignitatum permutatio fiat *Par.*

In the three texts that follow (237vb) space has been left for rubrics:

12. Ex registro Gregorii. Peruenit ad nos...doluimus asserentes eius eius (*sic*) fraternitatem a iuramenti uinculis non pos<se astringi...quo>d' latenter et per uim ... nulla stabilitate subsistere potest (see (iii) *supra*, cc.1, 2).
13. Ex con. Cartaginiensi. Si quis contra suam professionem uel subscriptionem uenerit, si clericus est deponatur, si laicus anathematizetur (cf. 2 Conc. Carth. c.13, Bruns I 122).[20]
14. Item ex conc. lugdunensi. Non liceat presbitero — ambarum faciat (Burch. 3.24).
15. Item celestini pape decretum florentine ecclesie missum.

---

[18] See C.N.L. Brooke, 'Canons of English Church Councils in the Early Decretal Collections', Bulletin for 1957, *Traditio* 13.480, with my supplementary notes, Bull. for 1961, *ibid.* 17.536-7. Weigand p. 79 gives c.9 instead of c.3.

[19] A description of this appendix, of two more collections of *extravagantes* (fol. 124r-125r, 247r), a collection of 46 pre-Gratian canons (122v-123v, 125r-126v), and other entries in Par. lat. 15001 must be left to another occasion. For '*Quoniam egestas*' see *Repert.* 263.

[20] Not *Cod. eccl. Afr.* c. 11 (Bruns I 162 [= 2 Carth. c.8, p. 120]), cited by Weigand 79.

The series ends with this inscription, which belongs to the *palea* C.35 q.6 c.2, i.e. the decretal 'Videtur nobis' (JK †384), actually by Celestine II (WH 1084, *Kan. Erg.* No.22). Two erased lines follow (so it appears from the microfilm). The four texts seem to exist nowhere else as a series. — The conflation from two texts of Gregory VII and Gregory the Great in c.12 has already been mentioned;[21] what is missing between the meaningless letters $p^g d$' may be presumed to have been similar to *Frcf.* 46.8: '... posse astringi tunc quia nefandissima coactus iurauit, tunc quia id quod latenter ...'. — c.13 is found in appendices of several Gratian MSS,[22] and c.14 in a few collections (e.g. *Frcf.* 30.6); it was to enter eventually 1 *Comp.* 3.11.1 (X 3.13.1).

As a whole, the long sequence of *Bib.* (vi) 1-15 must have come from at least four different sources. Nothing certain can be said of cc.5, 12-15, but cc.1-4 came from an Italian collection of the class of the *Ambrosiana*, cc. 6-10 from the ancestor common to *Bib.* and the *Cusana*, and the canons of Tours (c.11) from a source where they showed the same sequence and similar rubrics. This source must have been a collection which combined Tours with decretals, and was glossed. For we find two strings of glosses consisting of references (*allegationes*) on fol. 237va, at Tours cc.3 and 2. The first (*Quamuis* v. *quod laici*) cites C.16 q. 7 cc.3, 24, 13, 38; the second is of greater interest as it includes three decretal references (*Plures* v. *aliud usure*):

```
di. xlvii. episcopus (c.l)
di. xlvi. c. ult. (c.10)
di. xlvi. quoniam multi (D.47 c.2)
c. xxiiij. q. iii c.j et ij. (C.14 q.3 cc.1, 2)
in deč. ad nostram noueritis.
c. xiiij. q. iii. c.j.
c. xiij. q. iii. plerique. (C.14 q.3 c.3)
in deč. nuntios et litteras.
in deč. super eo quod.
```

The decretals can be identified: 'Nuntios' is JL 14157 + 14155 (WH 691) of Alexander III and refers to the section that deals with usury = 1 *Comp.* 5.15.6 (X—). Among the many letters beginning 'Ad nostram noueritis' the one discussing usury is JL 13804 (WH 79) = X. 2.24.7, and among the many that have 'Super eo quod' the proper reference would be Eugenius III JL 9667 (WH 1011, *Kan. Erg.* No.131), printed from *Lucensis* 52 by Mansi, in *Steph. Baluzii Miscellanea* III 377, and from *Cantab.* 60 by Friedberg, *Canonessamml.* p.16. Among the few collections which contain all three texts undivided we have the *Floriana* (cc.86, 85, 132), probably from Bologna, and its relative *Cus.* 8, 7, 152. What is more, on the canons of Tours, *Flor.* presents with very slight variants

---

[21] See (iii) *supra*.
[22] Rambaud, *L'âge classique* 116 n.6.

the same two glosses (among others) as *Bib.*;[23] only that there the three decretals are appropriately cited as 'jnfra e. (eodem *or* eadem) Ad nostram' etc. Again, as in the case of *Cus.*, the striking coincidence bespeaks a common ancestor: the different order of the conciliar canons in *Flor.* (cc. 3, 4, 8, 5-7, 1, 2) excludes a direct filiation.

(vii) fol. 271vb, at the end of C.27 q.2 (dict. p.c. 50)
1. Cum teneamur ex debito — duxeris exequendum. Data anag. ij. kal. marcij (JL 13994, WH 317).
2. Adrianus cantuar. archiepiscopo. Commissum nobis — absque diminutione persolui (JL 11660, WH 134).

Cus. 28, 26 provides a satisfactory parallel tradition. In 'Cum teneamur' (Alexander III to the Bishop of London) both *Cus.* and *Bib.* omit the inscription and only they give a date, but *Cus.* 28 remains ambiguous (dat'. anag' ii. kl'. aug. maij). The more probable choice is between 'maij' and 'marcij'; according to Alexander's itinerary this gives us 30 April 1173-76 or 28(29) February 1174-76. — For c.2 the attribution to Hadrian IV is in accordance with *Cus.* 26 and at least four other collections; the more frequent reading which gives Alexander III as writer and (beatus) Thomas of Canterbury as addressee was adopted in JL 11660 but need not be the better one.[24]

(viii) fol. 280rb/vb, after the end of C.30 q.5 and on the upper half of a page (280v) containing a diagram of the *arbor affinitatis*.
1. (280rb) Alex.iii. G. archiepiscopo ravenne. Si quando tue fraternitati aliqua — suggestum (JL 14074; WH 911, *Kan. Erg.* No.58).
2. Alex.iii. G. ravennatj archiepiscopo. Inter cetera super negotio uitalis Sicardo et uxore eē. (*leg.* eius) etcet. et jnfra. Super eo quod — non ualemus (JL 14073; WH 588, *Kan. Erg.* No.57).
3. Item abbati s. ar/.(*leg.* Apollinaris) in classe. Significauit nobis — iudicem conuenire (JL 14072; WH 982, *Kan. Erg.* No.61).
4. Idem londonensi episcopo. Secundum instituta — teneantur (Conc. Westmonast. 1175 c.10; JL [†]13999; WH 901a).[25]
5. Juuenis ille — ab eo diuidas. (*marg.al.m.*:) Eugenius papa presbitero esculapio (JL 9655; WH 596).

The unique relation between *Bib.* 1-3 and *Cus.* 22, 20, 21 has been pointed out in the beginning of this inquiry. It continues with *Bib.* c.4 = *Cus.* 19, while *Bib.* c.5 finds only substantial but no serial correspondence in *Cus.* 142. — Another

---

[23] Some of the numerals are given correctly where *Bib.* is mistaken, and *vice versa*; there is no repetition of C.14 q.3 c.1; the order of the last two references is inverted. On the Bologna provenance of *Flor.* see Holtzmann, *art. cit.* (n. 3) 451-2.

[24] Holtzmann noted in his papers that a presumptive 'A(drianus) Th(eobaldo) Cantuar.' would have been more easily misinterpreted by scribes as 'A(lexander) Th(ome)' than the other way round.

[25] See Weigand 79, with reference to Brooke (note 18 *supra*) *Trad.* 13.478; add E. Seckel, 'Canonistische Quellenstudien, I', *Deutsche Zeitschr. für Kirchenrecht*³ 9 (1899-1900) 159-89, at 170, 182-3.

V

hand provided rubrics in the upper margin of the page (the first: 'R(ubrica). assignare tenetur causam summo pontifici quare non possit quis eius obedire mandatis') and marked them *a, b, c, d*, with corresponding letters placed near cc. 1, 2, 4, 5; c.3, which does not begin on a new line, was apparently overlooked.
— There are three marginal glosses evidently referring to other decretals in the *exemplar*,

> (c.1) jnfra in decr. in fin. ex parte
> (c.1) supra prox. vii. penult. decl' (dec't?)
> (c.3) supra in quaterno decretalium Sicut ex tenore contra,

for which at present we can offer no convincing interpretation.

6. (280va) Leo episcopus seruus seruorum dei omnibus fidelibus in Christo per totam italiam. (R)elatum est auribus — gladio subiaceat (JL 4269; WH 864, *Kan. Erg.* No.224).
7. (280vb) Alex.iij. tetrathonensi (*leg.* Tarraconensi) archi. Significasti nobis — non debet admitti (JL 14107; WH 956).
8. Eugenius paduano episcopo. Super eo quod a nobis — usura est (JL 9667; WH 1011, *Kan. Erg.* No.131).
9. Ex conscilio triburiensi. Fures et latrones — non denegamus (*palea* C.13 q.2 c.31).
10. Eugenius in concilio remensi. Temerariam militum — careat sepultura (Reims 1148 c.12; cf. 1 *Comp.* 5.11.2).

All five pieces are found in *Cus.* cc.53, 25, 152-154; the last three exist likewise in sequence in *Flor.* 132-134, which has also *Bib.* c.5 = *Flor.* 57; it does not, however, transmit Leo IX's 'Relatum'. To this chapter, *Bib.* c.6, another hand[26] entered an interesting gloss at the top of the page (280va):

> Idem leo (postea *add. supra lin.*) seipsum quasi et hanc decretalem corrigendo conuersum in monasterium uolentem conuerti, precipue si in uita, idest sanus uelit conuerti, tertiam tantum partem debere relinquere <censuit>[27] ecclesie sue parrochiali de bonis que pro anima sua dare decreuerat. [Pro (?) i *add. et del.*] Et hoc statuit in decretali que incipit 'nulli'. Videtur etiam quibusdam hodie quemlibet posse eligere liberam sepulturam ubi uoluerit.

The reference is to 'Nulli tamen denegamus', i.e. the second sentence of 'Nos instituta' (JE 2536, WH 676), a decretal which all collections, down to X 3.28.1 ascribe to Leo III. But already Rufinus assumed that both rulings — 'Relatum', which required one-half, and 'Nos instituta', requiring only one-third to be left to the parish church—were by the same Leo (IX); he was perplexed by the contradiction: 'Sed quod horum magis tenendum est nobis non est diffiniendum, potius summi patriarche oraculum implorandum'.[28] And when Celestine III in 1193 answered an inquiry from Lérins about funeral rights (JL 16941, WH 129;

---

[26] Different from the hand that wrote the rubrics at the top of fol. 280r (see *supra*) and also began rubrics for c.7 etc. here at the top of 280vb.

[27] I have supplied this in accordance with the text referred to, JL 2536: 'tertiam partem... ecclesie iure dare censemus'.

[28] Rufinus, *Summa* C.13 q.1 pr. (334-5 Singer).

X 3.28.9) he also supposed that *one* Leo had designated 'iustitiam illam quandoque tertiam partem, quandoque uero mediam'.[29] Our gloss evidently was written before, or at least without knowledge of, Celestine's decretal.

(**ix**) fol. 316ra, *marg. inf.* near C.33 q.5 c.4:

Quidam intrauit monasterium — set m(ulier). (*marg.al.m.*:) Alex. archiepiscopo Pisano (JL 14061; WH 814, *Kan. Erg.* No.35).

Among several other collections transmitting this decretal we find also *Cus.* 203.

Looking back over the nine insertions of *extravagantes* in the Biberach MS, we can point to the *Cusana* as the most closely related collection for *Bib.* (vi) 6-10, (vii), and (viii), and as a satisfactory parallel tradition for (iv), (vi) 11, and (ix). Special affinities exist with the St. Victor MS Paris lat. 15001 for *Bib.* (i) and (vi) 11; with some traditional Gratian appendices for (iii) 1-2; with the *Francofortana* for (vi) 12, and with the glosses of the *Floriana* for (vi) 11. The Biberach MS offers thus an interesting example for the way in which *extravagantes* were collected from various sources and appended to individual copies of Gratian.

University of California,
Berkeley.

---

[29] See Holtzmann's commentary on Leo IX 'Relatum' in *Kan. Erg.* No. 224. For the author and date of JL 16941 — 12 March 1193 — see his 'Die Benutzung Gratians in der päpstlichen Kanzlei', SG 1 (1953) 335 No. 6.

Additional note on the canons of Tours (p. 67 *supra*). — As Professor R. Somerville kindly pointed out to me, what has been said above concerning the rubrics of *Bib.*(vi) 11 needs correction. *Coll.* 3 *Dunelm.* (cf. *Repert.* 280; Holtzmann, *Traditio* 18 [n. 3 *supra*] 455-6), which begins with *Turon.* cc.5-8, 4, 1-3, presents the same general inscription with only two variants (*om.* 'christianissimis principibus' and 'duce—Aquitanie'). The individual chapters too, although their sequence differs somewhat, have the same rubrics as *Bib.*, again with slight variants (e.g. *Bib.* 6 Ne] Non *Dun.*   olei aut] olei uel   7 constituantur] statuantur   1 suo statu] sua integritate). Therefore MS Durham C.III.1 fol. 14rbc/va instead of Paris lat. 15001 should be considered the closest known relative of *Bib.* for these canons.

VI

The decretal 'Presbiterum' (JL 13912) — a letter of Leo IX

The decretal letter beginning 'Presbiterum etiam istum in homicidii crimine lapsum' made its first known appearance in the so-called *Appendix Concilii Lateranensis*, in the title 'De depositione clericorum et dispensatione circa eosdem', as a letter of Alexander III to the bishop of Exeter (*App.* 26.13, JL 13912). The Leipzig manuscript of this collection in a marginal gloss identifies the chapter as part of the decretal 'Tanta' addressed to the same bishop: 'pars capituli est Tanta uis matrimonii';[1] this decretal in turn was abstracted at an early time from Alexander's letter to Bartholomew of Exeter, 'Meminimus nos fraternitati tue super causa' (JL 13917), whose juridical conclusions it epitomizes.[2] From the *Appendix* tradition the chapter 'Presbiterum' found its way to the margins of two manuscripts of the *Collectio Francofortana*: it appears as 'Idem exon. episcopo. Presbiterum etiam istum' next to *Francof.* 56.28 in the Egerton MS (from St. Maximin's, Trier) and as 'Alexander exonen. episcopo. Meminimus et infra (uel (T)anta est uis *add. al. m.*). Presbiterum istum' next to *Francof.* 59.1 in the Paris MS (from Rouen).[3]

The Anglo-Norman canonists who criticized Pope Alexander's permissive decision as running counter to the established doctrine that deposition of a priest for murder was irreparable, likewise cited the precedent sometimes as 'Presbiterum', sometimes as part of 'Tanta'.[4] One can understand why twelfth-century collectors and glossators tried to link the two decretals together: for one, the wording 'Presbiterum etiam istum' pointed to a portion of text that must have gone before; and secondly, if one were to pick a text among the many decretal letters Alexander wrote to Bartholomew of Exeter, the famous ruling on the legitimation of natural children by subsequent marriage would offer itself as the most suitable piece on which to graft another startling decision. But this was mere conjecture: none of the known decretal collections presents a text of either 'Meminimus' or 'Tanta' with our chapter attached to it.

There is more. Three collections from another branch of the English decretal tradition (Holtzmann's 'Wigorniensisgruppe') give us a text of JL 13912 which evidently antedates the form the compiler of *Appendix* (or his source) had given the letter. In the *Collectio Cheltenhamensis* 13.13, the *Petrihusensis* 4.32, and

---

[1] Leipzig Univ. MS 1242, fol. 99rb.

[2] In his unpublished papers W. Holtzmann preferred to list 'Tanta' separately as JL 13906 together with another derivative of 'Meminimus'; i.e., *Coll. Cantab.* c. 100, inc. 'Fraternitati tue duximus respondendum quod tanta est uis . . .', rather than as merely a section of JL 13917 (the number he used for 'Tanta', like everybody else, in all his published writing). In abridging and paraphrasing the original text, 'Tanta' indeed belongs into the same class as *Cantab.* 100, save for the first five words.

[3] B. M. (British Library) MS Egerton 2901, fol. 85v; Paris B.N. MS lat. 3922A, fol. 296va, with a reference note (*al.m.*), 'Supra in supl. de matrimonio Meminimus uel tanta'. The 'suplementum' referred to is *Coll. Rotom.* in the same codex; the chapters cited are *Rot.* 1.21 and 1.29 (fol. 148vb, 149rb).

[4] See several texts in S. Kuttner and E. Rathbone, 'Anglo-Norman canonists of the twelfth-century', *Traditio* 7 (1949/51) at p. 310. Critical glosses on the text itself in *App.* (cod. Lips. *loc. cit.*) and *Francof.* (cod. Egert. *loc. cit.*).

VI

134

the *Cottoniana* 5.28, instead of 'Presbiterum etiam istum' we read 'Hunc Andream presbiterum'.[5] This opening indicates that the priest himself was the bearer of the letter by which the pope informed Bishop Bartholomew that he had restored the one-time criminal to the priesthood. Also the conclusion of the letter shows that the *Appendix* tradition had garbled an earlier, better text:

Pet.	*App.* (etc.)
Vnde Calixtus papa, Errant, inquid, qui putant sacerdotem post lapsum si dignam egerit penitentiam ministrare non posse, set a malis abstineat.	Vnde Calixtus papa: Errant quidam qui putant post dignam penitentiam sacerdotem lapsum non posse reparari et ministrare posse si a malis abstineat.
3 egerint *Pet.* non posse ministrare *Ch. Cott.* 4 set] si *Ch. Cott.* malis] suis *add. Ch.*	

Several glossators of the later version recognized this as a (free) quotation from D. 50 c. 14,[6] but no one remarked on the nonsense produced by the redundant second 'posse' (if any repetition, it should have read 'non posse' or 'nec ... posse').

Finally, the two traditions became conflated in two collections of the 'Sangermanensis group': *Tanner* 2.15.21 and *Abrincensis* 2.11.4 present the letter under the same title ('de depositione' etc.) and with the same closing sentence as in the *Appendix,* but with the opening 'Hunc Andream' conforming to the earlier form of the text. By way of further contamination, *Tann.* 2.15.21 prefixed 'pars c. Tanta est uis' to this opening.[7]

Such is the information we can gather from twelfth-century decretal collections and the discussions on *reparatio lapsorum* in the schools. And now the recent discovery by Dr. Robin Aronstam of an unknown letter of Pope Leo IX in the Bodleian MS Barlow 37[8] eliminates the case of Andrew the priest altogether from the dossier of Alexander III — of which Dr. Aronstam remained

---

[5] B. M. Egerton 2819 (formerly Phillipps 11726), fol. 71 ra/b; Cambridge, Peterhouse MS 180, fol. 54vb; B. M. Cotton MS Vitellius E.xiii, fol. 257rb/va (practically illegible).

[6] 'di. l. Ponderet', i.e. the end of the Pseudo-Calixtus chapter D.50 c.14 is cited in glosses of *App.* (cod. Lips.), *Francof.* (cod. Par.), *Tanner* 2.15.21 (on which more presently).

[7] Bodleian MS Tanner 8, p. 621 (formerly 619), cf. W. Holtzmann's analysis, 'Die Sammlung Tanner', *Festschrift zur Feier des 200 jährigen Bestehens der Akad. der Wiss. in Göttingen* (phil. hist. Kl. 1951) 83-145, at p. 113; Avranches MS 149, fol. 85ra, ed. Singer, *Neue Beiträge* p. 365. Cf. also S. Kuttner, 'Notes on the presentation of text and apparatus', Bulletin for 1959, *Traditio* 15.464.

[8] R. A. Aronstam, 'Pope Leo IX and England: an unknown letter', *Speculum* 49 (1974) 535-41; see also her paper, 'Penitential pilgrimages to Rome in the early Middle Ages', AHP 13 (1975) 65-83. For other canonical texts in MS Barlow 37 (Sum. cat. 6464) see W. Holtzmann, *Papsturkunden in England* III (Abh. Akad. Göttingen³ 33; 1952) 19, where the wrong shelfmark 36 must be corrected (cf. Aronstam, *Spec.* 49.537 n. 15); P. Brommer, 'Die bischöfliche Gesetzgebung Theodulphs von Orléans', ZRG Kan. Abt. 60 (1974) 1-120 at p. 16 etc. — A series of *distinctiones*, beg. 'Tria consideranda sunt in electione' (fol. 1v) was copied in the margins of the pre-Gratian material in the later 12th cent. It seems to be related to the circle of the *Summa Inperatorie maiestati* and deserves further study.

unaware since this lay outside the confines of her investigation — and moves it back to the first half of the eleventh century. A small collection of papal and episcopal letters from Archbishop Wulfstan's time on penitential pilgrimages to Rome is extant in several manuscripts; in Barlow MS 37 it includes a letter (c. 1049-50) of Leo IX to Archbishop Eadsige of Canterbury :[9]

> Leo episcopus seruus seruorum Dei E. anglorum archiepiscopo sal. et ap. ben. Hunc Andream presbiterum uestrum in homicidii crimine lapsum ... et a malis abstineat. Peccator post penitentiam iam non est qui fuit ... per Ihesum Christum dominum nostrum.

One further piece of evidence for this letter exists. It comes from the file of summary notices the late Walther Holtzmann kept of all twelfth-century decretals in three boxes of octavo-sized sheets. There he recorded — in the manner of his *Kanonistische Ergänzungen zur Italia pontificia* — the textual transmission of each letter, with brief discussions of authorship, addressees, dates, and historical context as the case may be. On the *verso* of his summary for JL 13912 (= WH 737) he jotted down, without comment, that in the Gratian codex Durham C.iii.1 our text is found on fol. 63v *marg. inf.* after D.50 c.37 as 'Leo ep. s. s. D. e. Anglorum archiepō sal. Hunc Andream—abstineant'. Had he lived longer, Holtzmann would no doubt have followed up on this note.

It may be rewarding to scan other Gratian manuscripts in England for similar entries. The Durham text takes the first step in an 'editing' process by omitting the last sentence, 'Peccator post penitentiam ...' etc. of Leo's letter and by shortening its quotation from 'Calixtus'.[10] Thereafter, the connection with Leo IX is lost: In *Chelt.* 13.13 'Hunc Andream' lacks any inscription, while *Cott.* 5.28 writes 'Idem', meaning Alexander III, whose name is spelled out in *Pet.* 4.32. In the body of the letter these three have the shortened version of the Pseudo-Calixtus text in common with Durham. The new recipient, '... Exoniensi episcopo', has replaced Archbishop E(adsige) in *App.* 26.13 and all the other collections with the altered beginning and/or ending.

The medieval tendency to give recent texts the appearances of a venerable age is well known. The decretal recorded for Alexander III in JL 13912 is one of the rare instances where the textual history goes in the opposite direction.

University of California, Berkeley.

---

[9] Full text published by Aronstam, *Spec.* 49.541 and again in AHP 13.82 No. 9.

[10] By good luck, fol. 63v is among the selected photostats of Durham C.iii.1 which the Institute received many years ago as a gift from Msgr. Daniel Shanahan. Differently from all others, the Durham version uses the plural, 'sacerdotes ... si egerint ... abstineant' in its last sentence.

VII

COLLECTIO FRANCOFORTANA

[Collectio Francofortana.] Unter diesem Namen, der nach kanonistischem Brauch den Fundort (die Stadtbibliothek zu Frankfurt am Main) anzeigt, soll hier kurz eine neuentdeckte Dekretalensammlung des 12. Jahrhunderts bekanntgemacht werden, deren genauere Analyse einer späteren Arbeit vorbehalten werden muß.[4])
Cod. Francof. 60, ehemals der Bibliothek des St. Bartholomäus-Doms zu Frankfurt gehörig, ist ein Lederband in Kleinfolio, in dem mehrere Pergamenthandschriften verschiedener Zeit zusammengebunden sind. Der alte Lederdeckel mit Metallknöpfen trägt auf einem Schildchen von einer Hand des 15. Jahrhunderts in gotischer Zier-

---

[1]) Cod. Bibl. Jag. nr. 356 f. 189.
[2]) Friedberg a. a. O. C. XVI qu. 7 n. 389.
[3]) Die nähere Beschreibung der Handschrift nr. 356 der Jagellonischen Bibliothek in Krakau erscheint nunmehr in der Studie der Frau Dr. Zofja Ameisenowa unter dem Titel: Les principaux manuscrits à peintures de la Bibliothèque Jagellonienne à Cracovie im Bulletin de la Société pour réproduction des manuscrits à peintures, Paris 1933.
[4]) Eine weitere, noch nicht bearbeitete Dekretalensammlung befindet sich im Cod. 229 (fol. 67—123^v) der Bibliothek des Hospitals zu Kues (J. Marx, Verzeichnis der Handschriftensamml. d. Hospitals zu Kues, Trier 1905).

schrift die Angabe: *Tractatus de sponsalibus et quamplurima alia circa rubricas decretalium. Item tytulus de electione magistri gwilhelmi. Item breviarium ad omnes materias in iure canonico inveniendas secundum Bernhardum.* Der erste Satz betrifft die Coll. Francof. Sie steht auf foll. 2—85 (nach einem neuen weißen Papiervorsatzblatt und einem fol. 1, das recto nur den Stempel der Stadtbibliothek, verso ein z. T. fehlerhaftes Verzeichnis der Titelrubriken der Sammlung von einer Hand des späten 13. oder des beginnenden 14. Jahrhunderts enthält). Die Collectio[1]) ist von mehreren einander sehr ähnlichen Händen des ausgehenden 12. Jahrhunderts in kräftiger klarer Schrift, die Seite zu zwei Kolumnen, geschrieben. Die breiten, unbeschnittenen Blattränder, wohl zur Aufnahme von Glossen bestimmt, lassen die Linienvorzeichnung noch deutlich erkennen. Die abwechselnd blau und roten Initialen gehen nur bis fol. 83^v.

Die Fr(ancofortana) gehört unter den Sammlungen zwischen Gratian und der Compilatio prima zu der späteren Gruppe, die das Material bereits systematisch in Titeln geordnet enthält (Parisiensis II, Appendix Conc. Lat., Bambergensisgruppe usw.).[2]) Über Verwandtschafts- und Filiationsverhältnisse sowie über Alter und Heimat der Sammlung — es bestehen m. E. unmittelbare Verbindungslinien zur Comp. I, zur Appendix, zur Brugensis und zur Parisiensis II — wird erst nach einer eingehenden Analyse kritisch Gesichertes gesagt werden können. Im folgenden habe ich lediglich die Absicht, einen kurzen Überblick über Umfang und Material zu geben, auf einige Besonderheiten der Sammlung hinzuweisen sowie eine vorläufige Liste von neuen[3]) Ver-

---

[1]) Die weiteren Teile des Miszellenbandes, die ich nicht untersucht habe, sind:
 a) Guilelmus de Mandagoto, Super electionibus faciendis et eorum processibus ordinandis, mit der Glosse (vor 1294; vgl. v. Schulte, Gesch. d. Quellen u. Lit. des kan. Rechts, Bd. II 1877 S. 183 und namentlich Paul Viollet in der Hist. littér. de France XXXIV 1911 p. 25 ss.), (fol. 86—105).
 b) Das auf dem Deckel angegebene Breviarium, ein verbreitetes Nachschlagewerk aus dem 13. Jahrhundert (vgl. v. Schulte, Gesch.QL. II S. 485 f.) (fol. 105—109).
 c) Ein Traktat über Fragen der fratres mendicantes, 15. Jahrhundert (fol. 109^v—110^v).

[2]) Einen Überblick über die Geschichte der Gattung gibt Fr. Heyer in seiner Besprechung von Singers Neuen Beiträgen über die Dekretalensammlungen usw., in dieser Zeitschrift XXXIV Kan. Abt. III S. 615f. — Die Abhandlung von J. Juncker, Collectio Berolinensis, in dieser Zeitschrift XLIV Kan. Abt. XIII S. 284ff. enthält viele Mitteilungen und Bemerkungen, die gleichfalls die Gattung im ganzen betreffen.

[3]) Die Bestätigungen von bereits anderweit bekanntgewordenen Jaffé-Emendationen durch den Inhalt von Fr. sind dabei fortgelassen. — Herr Dr. Lohmann hatte die Freundlichkeit, meine Liste von Jaffé-Nummern mit dem Manuskript seiner in diesem Bande (oben S. 36ff.) erscheinenden Abhandlung zur Collectio Wigorniensis zu kollationieren und so Doppelregistrierung zu verhindern. Für diese Bemühung und für manche andere Hinweise bin ich ihm zu herzlichem Dank verpflichtet.

besserungen zu Jaffé-Löwenfelds Regestenwerk zusammenzustellen, die sich bei der ersten Durchsicht der Sammlung ergaben. Ich füge schließlich den Text einiger Dekretalen Alexanders III. und Hadrians IV. bei, die m. W. bisher unbekannt sind.

Fr. umfaßt 65 Titel und einen Anhang von 11 extra titulos stehenden Stücken. Die 726 capitula der Sammlung setzen sich aus folgendem Material zusammen:

    300 vorgratianische Canones
      1 Dekr. Innocenz II.
      9 Dekr. Eugens III.
      5 Dekr. Hadrians IV.
    371 Dekr. Alexanders III.
      1 Dekr. Lucius III.
      1 Dekr. Clemens III.
      1 canon des Konzils von Reims (1148).
      9 canones des Konzils von Tours (1163).
     27 canones des III. Laterankonzils (1179).
      1 Glossenfragment (offenbar zu D. 50 des Decr. Grat.).[1])

Wir haben damit die bisher umfänglichste der Sammlungen vor Bernhard von Pavia vor uns. Besonders ist die Anzahl der vorgratianischen Canones gegenüber den anderen Sammlungen auffallend gesteigert und erreicht fast die Zahl dieser Canones in der Comp. I (in Friedbergs Ausgabe: 311). Dabei hat Fr. vielfach Stücke, die weder in die Comp. I eingegangen, noch in einer der gedruckten älteren Canonessammlungen nachweisbar sind. Nach welchen Quellen (außer Burchard und Ivo) der Verfasser von Fr. hier gearbeitet haben mag, habe ich vorläufig noch nicht feststellen können[2]); es wird sich auch ohne Handschriften nicht ermitteln lassen.

Hinsichtlich des übrigen Materials verdient die Tatsache Erwähnung, daß die Canones der unter Alexander III. zelebrierten Konzilien (Turonense und Lateranense III.) bereits zerstückt und in die Titel der Sammlung eingeordnet sind; eine vor der Comp. I bisher nur in der Brugensis festgestellte Erscheinung.[3]) Von Dekretalen nach

---

[1]) tit. 62 de dispensatione c. 7 (Fr. fol. 80): „*Quandoque valet restitui sacerdos ad honorem suam post peractam penitentiam, licet inde diversi diversa sentiant, dicentes non posse restitui ad honorem. Set sicut dictum est, propter dissimulatas penitentias quorumdam et propter affectatas honorum dignitates.*" — Zur Sache vgl. etwa Dict. p. c. 24 D. 50 und, von gedruckten Dekretisten, etwa Rufinus zu pr. D. 50. Woher das Stück stammt, habe ich nicht feststellen können; von den namentlich bekannten Dekretisten kommt keiner in Frage, ebensowenig die bekannten anonymen Summen (Colon. Paris. Bamb. Monac. Lips. Hal. [Ye. 52]) zum Dekret.

[2]) Auch nicht mit Hilfe von Theiners Index der Kapitelanfänge in den älteren Canonessammlungen (Augustini Theineri Disquisitiones criticae usw., Romae 1836, appendix secunda), einem freilich heute unzureichenden Hilfsmittel.

[3]) Friedberg, Canonessammlungen, Leipzig 1897, S. 138.

Alexander III. hat Fr. nur je eine Lucius' III. und Clemens' III. aufzuweisen; die Clemensdekretale¹), Ja(ffé-L.) 16596, ist datiert (s. unten S. 278) und ermöglicht es, als terminus a quo für Fr. das Jahr 1189 anzunehmen.

Fr. gibt in vielen Abschnitten ausführliche Kapitelrubriken, was von den älteren Sammlungen nur Aureaevall.²), von den jüngeren nur Appendix und Lips.³) tun. — Ganz besondere Aufmerksamkeit vom literarhistorischen Gesichtspunkt aus verdient jedoch die bei Dekretalensammlungen einzigartige Einschiebung von Überleitungssätzen, paragraphi, zwischen einzelne Stücke, wodurch teils diese miteinander in Beziehung gebracht, teils ihre Gegensätze beleuchtet und gelöst werden sollten. Der Verfasser⁴) der Fr. wandte also die Konkordanzmethode auf die neue Dekretalengesetzgebung an. Die andern Dekretalensammler hatten ihre Aufgabe sonst in anderem gesehen: sie wollten Rechtsquellen aufzeichnen, aber nicht — wie Gratian — zugleich selber theoretische Erkenntnisse liefern. So bildet unter ihnen der Autor der Fr. eine Ausnahme. In seinen Überleitungssätzen ist bereits eine literarische Behandlung der gesammelten Quellen angebahnt, wenn auch nur in knappster Form und wenn auch diese Paragraphen nur streckenweise vorkommen. Oft beschränken sie sich auf ein „*Hiis contrarium videtur . . .*" oder ein „*Huic consonat . . . .*".

---

¹) Sie befindet sich (als c. 4) unter den am Ende der Sammlung extra titulos stehenden Stücken. Dieser gesamte Anhang von 11 capitula bietet jedoch keinen Anlaß, spätere Entstehung gegenüber den rubrizierten Teilen zu argwöhnen: Die Schreiberhand ist die gleiche wie in den letzten Titeln, das Material besteht neben der Clemensdekretale nur aus Stücken, die der Verf. der Fr. bestimmt bereits gekannt hat: so z.B. 4 cc. Conc. Lat. III.; so das erste Stück der Dekretale *Nobis in eminenti* Hadrians IV. (Ja. 10444), deren zweites Stück, *Dilecti filii nostri*, sich bereits tit. 19 *de decimis* c. 16 befindet. — Wir haben es bei diesem ganzen Anhang m. E. mit einem authentischen Nachtrag zu tun, wie ihn z. B. später auch die Sammlungen Gilberts und Alanus (Codd. D 5 und D 14 der Landesbibl. Fulda) aufweisen. Vgl. zu diesen v. Schulte, Sitz.-Ber. d. phil.-histor. Cl. der k. Akad. d. Wissensch. LXV 1870 S. 595 ff. (600f.) und Fr. Heyer, in dieser Zeitschrift XXXV Kan. Abt. IV 1914 S. 583 ff. (597f.).

²) W. Holtzmann, in dieser Zeitschrift XLVII Kan. Abt. XVI 1927 S. 78 u. 97.

³) J. Juncker, Coll. Berol., in dieser Zeitschrift XLIV Kan. Abt. XIII 1924 S. 288.

⁴) Man darf ihn wohl so nennen, da er ja eben über das reine Sammeln hinausgeht. Stephanus Tornacensis freilich hatte nicht einmal Gratian den Titel eines „auctor" zuerkennen wollen: „*Compositorem huius operis recte dixerim Gratianum, non auctorem. Capitula namque a sanctis patribus edita in hoc volumine composuit, i. e. ordinavit. Non eorum auctor vel conditor fuit, nisi forte quis eum auctorem idcirco dicere velit, quoniam multa ex parte sua sanctorum sententias distinguendo et exponendo in paragraphis suis ponit.*" (ed. v. Schulte, Die Summa des St. T. über das Decretum Gratiani, Gießen 1891, p. 5). Die Vorrede Stephans, der dieses Stück entnommen ist, ist überhaupt für die Auffassung der älteren Kanonisten vom Begriff ihrer Wissenschaft sehr instruktiv.

VII

In manchen Partien aber sind sie auch reicher; z. B. im Tit. 19 *de decimis*:

fol. 30   (cc 1—7). . . . . .

§ *Unde Alexander Trece[te]nsi epō:*
(c 8) Ex parte tue frat. — vendicare. (= c 10 Comp I 3 26; Ja. 14117)

§ *Vel in omnibus auctoritate apostolica. Unde Alexander scribit Eboracensi archiēpo. dicens:*
(c 9) Fraternitatem tuam — a nobis fieri postulares (= c 8 Comp I h. t.; Ja. 13873)

§ *Hij quidem non sunt conpellendi nisi in fraude faciant, sc. ut veteres*
fol. 30ᵛ   *ecclesias iuribus suis defraudent. Unde Alexander scribit Cantuarensi archiēpo.:*
(c 10) Fraternitati tue — cessare. (= c 4 Comp I 3 37; Ja. 13807)
(c 11) *Idem monachis de Neblosia.*

     a) Dilecti filij — manus extendere. (= c 6 Comp I 3 26; Ja. 14023)

     b) Sane laborum — pontificum. (= c 12 Comp I h. t.; Ja. 14173)[1])

§ *Alexandro consonat Paschalis II^{us} qui clericos ecclesie deservientes generaliter a solutione decimarum absolvit, ita dicens*:
(c 12) Novum exactionis — labores accipiunt. (c 7 Comp I h. t., Ja. 6605)

§ *Gregorius vero tantum monasteria absolvit ita dicens:*
(c 13) Statuimus subdunt. (c 14 Comp I h. t.; cap. incert.)

§ *Ceterum hijs contradicit Adrianus, qui monasteria tantum a solutione decimarum de novalibus absolvit, ita dicens.*
(c 14) Pervenit ad nos — persolvi. (c 18 Comp I h. t.; Ja. 11660)[2])

fol. 31   (cc 15 u. 16) . . . . .

fol. 31ᵛ   § *Hijs consonat triburiense concilium, in quo sic legitur:*
(c 17) Ut nullus abbas — firmamus. (c 20 Comp I h. t., cap. incert.)

§ *Hijs tamen decime possunt dari, sicut ait Johannes papa:*
(c 18) Certam habemus — investitur. (c 21 Comp I h. t., cap. incert.)

Sane cum ob paupertatem et caritatem religiosis viris data sunt super decimis privilegia et iam propter eorum multitudinem antique graventur ecclesie, eos ad trans[s]i⟨g⟩endum super decimis ipse hortatur Alexander, ita scribens monasterio[3]) *de Loregio:*

(c 19) Suggestum — deponunt (c 9 Comp I h. t.; Ja. 14004)
(c 20) . . . .

---

[1]) Die Zusammengehörigkeit der Trennstücke ist bereits durch Par. II 56 10 und Berol. 108 bekannt.

[2]) Der Brief Alexanders wird Hadrian gleichfalls zugeschrieben in Par. II 56 4 und Brug. 17 12. Vgl. Juncker zu Coll. Berol. 52; a. a. O. S. 369. — Alle Sammlungen außer Fr. beginnen mit *Commissum nobis* oder *Commissae nobis*; der erste Satz fehlt hier.

[3]) *monasterij* Hs.

§ *Potest enim de decimis transigi. ut Alexander scribit Eboracensi epō.*
ita dicens:
  Titulus (20). *de transactione.*
    usw.

Die Feststellung von Konkordanzen und Kontrarietäten wechselt hier mit Erklärungen des Zusammenhangs der Kapitel. Daß die eigenartige Literaturgattung, die in Fr. durch solche Behandlung des Rechtsstoffes versucht wurde, sich nicht durchsetzte, kann aus inneren Gründen wohl begriffen werden. Der Charakter der kirchlichen Rechtsquellen hatte sich durch die gewaltige rechtsschöpferische Tätigkeit Alexanders III. verändert. Der Rechtsstoff der älteren Zeit hatte im Werke Gratians seine endgültige, die Schule beherrschende Gestalt gewonnen — die großangelegte Kanonessammlung des Kardinals Laborans (1182)[1] blieb gänzlich einflußlos —, und die neue päpstliche Gesetzgebung[2] bot als Rechtsquellenstoff gegenüber den discordantes canones, die Gratians Quellen gewesen waren, ein ganz anderes Bild. Vermöge der praktischen Erweiterung der Gerichtsbarkeit und vermöge der theoretischen Begründung der obersten Gesetzgebungsgewalt des apostolischen Stuhls durch die Kanonisten[3] erwuchs die vom Willen zur exakt juristischen Gestaltung und Fortentwicklung des kirchlichen Rechtsstoffs getragene einheitliche Schöpfung des Dekretalenrechts: Materiell jeweils nur Entscheidung eines Einzelfalls, boten die Dekretalen doch zugleich die Normen für eine Einfassung des kirchlichen Rechtslebens in präzise juristische Begriffsgebilde, wurden sie Quellen einer zentralen Rechtsbildung, welche als ius canonicum dem ius romanum zur Seite trat. Gerade das römische Recht hatte ja in der rechtschaffenden Wirkung der Kaiserreskripte das Vorbild für diese Entwicklung gegeben[4], welche bei den Dekretalen nur auf der Grundlage einer aus dem Bezirk der Theologie zur Rechtswissenschaft verselbständigten Kanonistik sich entfalten konnte. — (Eine Herausarbeitung der „inneren" Urkundenmerkmale der Papstbriefe, insbesondere der litterae de iustitia[5], für die Epoche seit der Mitte des 12. Jahrhunderts, würde m. E. den Umschwung zur Juris-

---

[1] v. Schulte, Gesch. QL I S. 148. — Seit Theiners disquisitiones criticae (oben S. 372 Anm. 2), p. 401 ff., ist das quellengeschichtlich wichtige Werk leider nicht mehr analysiert worden, und Theiners Abhandlung erschöpft den Gegenstand nicht. — Die einzige Handschrift des Werkes befindet sich im Archiv von St. Peter in Rom, Cod. C. 110. Signatur und Beschreibung der Hs. bei G. B. Sirugusa, Il regno di Guilelmo I. in Sicilia¹ 1885 I S. 181, dazu II S. LIII f. (In der 2. Aufl. 1929 gestrichen).

[2] Zu diesem Problem manche Bemerkungen bei E. Seckel, Dtsch. Liter. Ztg. XVIII 1897 Sp. 658 (in der Besprechung von Friedbergs „Canonessammlungen").

[3] Hinschius, System des kath. KR., IV. Bd. Berlin 1883, S. 730 ff.

[4] v. Schulte, Gesch. QL I S. 101 Anm.

[5] Zu diesem Begriff: Breßlau, Hdb. d. Urkundenlehre I² 1912 S. 82, mit Lit.

prudenz auch stilistisch erhärten können[1]) und damit eine historisch lebensvollere Einteilung als die herrschende, welche die Periode von Leo IX. bis zu Coelestin III. diplomatisch als eine einzige ansieht, ermöglichen.)

Diesen neuen Dekretalen gegenüber bestand wohl für die Wissenschaft noch eine Aufgabe methodischer Ordnung nach Materien (wie sie Bernhard von Pavia dann für die nächsten Jahrhunderte richtungweisend leistete); aber die Konkordanzaufgabe, die gegenüber dem historisch geschichteten Rechtsstoff, wenn man ihn zu dogmatischer Einheit bringen wollte, die wichtigste gewesen war, konnte es bei einem zentralen, einheitlichen Material von Rechtsquellen nicht mehr geben. Die Aufgabe, das Verhältnis der neuen Dekretalengesetzgebung zum bereits gesammelten, alten Recht im einzelnen festzustellen, war freilich in hervorragendem Maße Konkordanzaufgabe; sie fiel aber den Glossatoren, nicht mehr den Sammlern des neuen Rechtsstoffes zu. Die Überleitungsparagraphen in Fr. bleiben eine am Ende des 12. Jahrhunderts rückständige Verwischung der Grenzen von Rechtsquellen und Rechtsliteratur. —

Zu Jaffé-Löwenfelds Regesta pontificum Romanorum (Bd. II² Leipzig 1888) ergeben sich aus Fr. folgende Verbesserungen (mit Ausnahme der letzten Nummer alle zum Pontifikat Alexanders III.):

Ja. 12 668. (Fr. 55 de appellationibus c 25.) *Idem Gradensi patriarche et eodem*[a]) *titulo sancti Vitalis presb. cardinali et priori sancte Cecilie.*[b]) Constitutis in presentia — terminetis. Ceterum etc.[c]) *Datum Angaie*[d]) X. kal. augusti. cr. 1176 Juli 23.

Bei Jaffé auf 1173—1176 angesetzt; etwa 1176 nach Kehr, Italia Pontificia, VII 2, Berlin 1925 S. 92. — [a]) verderbt aus *et Teodino*? [b]) sonst überall *Crucis*. [c]) Diese Andeutung einer Fortsetzung auch in Aureaev. 3 (W. Holtzmann a. a. O. S. 84). Das könnte vielleicht auf das Fragment Ja. 13944 bezogen werden, das an einen Patriarcha Gradensis adressiert ist. [d]) lies *Anagnie*.

Ja. 13 798. (Fr. 21 de iure patron. c. 7.) *Idem eidem.*[a]) Veniens ad nos G. pauper clericus sollicita nobis et constanti assertione proposuit, quod cum ipse in cappella de Stratona canonice fuisset institutus, R. Britto qui ius patronatus in ipsa ecclesia ab eodem, ad quem representatio pertinebat, se conparasse proponat, ipsum multis molestijs et gravaminibus fatigat et ei dampna gravia irrogare presumpsit. Quoniam igitur prefati clerici iuri pastorali volumus sollicitudine providere et presumptionem memorati R. pontificali auctoritate reprimere,

---

[1]) Die inneren Merkmale der Papsturkunden sind freilich bisher nur auf dem Gebiet der formalen Einteilung und des formalen Aufbaus untersucht; Zusammenfassendes bei Breßlau, Hdb. d. Urkundenlehre I² S. 72ff.; Schmitz-Kallenberg, Lehre v. d. Papsturk. (in Meisters Grundriß d. Geschichtswiss. I 1906) S. 182ff. Zum kritischen Studium der Stilmerkmale, insbesondere des Eindringens der Rechtssprache in die Diktion der Papstbriefe, fehlen bisher noch die Vorarbeiten.

fraternitati tue per apostolica scripta precipiendo mandamus, quatenus eundem R. studiose commoneas et omni districtione conpellas, ut illata dampna eidem clerico resarciat et de iniuriis satis faciat, aut exinde coram te appellatione remota non differat iustitie plenitudinem exhibere. De iure vero [b]) patronatus — revocare.

> Bisher war nur der letzte Teil überliefert. Holtzmann a. a. O. S. 95 zu Aureaev. 107 vermutet bereits die Existenz eines Anfangskapitels. — [a]) Das vorangehende cap. hat keinen Adressaten. Ja. 13798 ist an den archieps. Cantuarensis gerichtet.   [b]) *vero* sonst nur in Aureaev. 107.

Ja. 13843. (Fr. 44 de accusat. c 18) *Alexander Arelatensi*[a]) $\overline{epo}$. Insinuatum est auribus — peierare. *Datum Feriarum*[b]) *VI. kal. julii.* 1175. Juni 26 (?).

> Bei Jaffé 1159—1181. Die hier vorgeschlagene Datierung ist jedoch nur möglich, wenn man für die entstellte Ortsbezeichnung *Ferentini* konjiziert. Liest man *Ferrarie*, so käme das Jahr 1177 in Betracht; dann ist aber der 26. Juni unmöglich. Vgl. das Itinerar. — [a]) sonst überall *Cestriensi*.   [b]) *feriaȥ* geschrieben. Ein Ort dieses Namens existiert nicht.

Ja. 13854. (Fr. 2 que impediant .... matrimonium c 6.) *Idem magistro Fidantie civitatis.*[a]) Ad nostram noveris audientiam pervenisse — denuncies. *Datum Capue XII kal. ian.* 1176 Dez. 21.

> Bei Jaffé 1179—1181. Urkunden Alexanders III. aus Capua kommen sonst m. W. nicht vor. Der Papst hat sich ausweislich dieser Dekretale auf seiner Reise von Anagni „per terram Laboris" nach Benevent (6.—25. Dez. 1176; Itinerar b. Jaffé) in Capua aufgehalten. Andere Zeugnisse für diesen Aufenthalt fehlen. — [a]) sonst meist *Civitatensi*. Vgl. Juncker zu Berol. 112.

Ja. 13878 (false **14346**)[a]) (Fr. 21 de iure patron. c 3) *Unde idem scribit Eboracensi* $\overline{epo}$. Inter cetera. et infra. Ad hec[b]) cum laici — ordinare. *Datum Agan. IIII° kal. mart.* 1160, 1174, 1176 Februar 27 (26)?

> Bei Jaffé 1159—1181. Der Ortsname ist verderbt; ich wüßte jedoch nur *Anagnie* dafür zu setzen. — [a]) Über die Zugehörigkeit von „*(Ad hec) cum laici*" zur Dekretale *Inter ceteras*, und nicht zu Ja. 14346 vgl. Juncker, Berol. 40, Vorbemerkung (a. a. O. S. 364) und Lohmann in diesem Bande S. 72 zur Coll. Wigorn.   [b]) Wie in Berol. Cantabr. Claustron. (Juncker S. 365).

Ja. 13937. (Fr. 2 que impediant ... matrimonium c 24). *Idem abbati de Fontibus et magistro Vocario.*[a]) Significavit nobis O. andegavensis — in uxorem. *Datum Venetiis in rivo alto. II*[e] *kal. julij.* 1177 Juni 30.

> Bei Jaffé 1159—1181. Savigny, Gesch. des röm. Rechts im MA. IV 1850 S. 421 setzt das Schreiben auf 1164 oder später an. — [a]) Über die Lesarten des Namens s. Friedberg, Note 2 zu c 2 X 4 7. Über den englischen Glossator Vacarius handelt Savigny a. a. O. S. 411ff.

Ja. 13944 mit 12668 zu vereinigen? s. daselbst.

Ja. 13 960 (Fr. 21 de iure patron. c 10). *Unde Alexander sic ait fratribus templi.* Cum seculum relinquitis — non audeatis. *Datum Ferentini IIII° kal. iulii.* 1175 Juni 28.

Bei Jaffé 1159—1181.

Ja. 14188 (Fr. 22 de symonia . . . . c 17). *Idem Remensi archiepo.* Dilectus filius noster — patiatur.

Die bisher nur in Appendix 2 16 überlieferte Dekretale ist dort nicht inskribiert.

Zum Pontifikat Clemens' III:

Ja. 16 596 (Fr. extra titulos c 4) *Clemens eps servus servorum Dei venerabili fratri Seguntino epo salutem et apostolicam benedictionem.* Pervenit ad nos — relinquendum. *Datum Lateranis V. non. iulii, pontificatus nostri anno secundo.* 1189 Juli 3.

Bei Jaffé 1187—1191. Die Wiedergabe der vollen Intitulatio und Inskriptio könnte auf eine Kenntnis des Verf. der Fr. von der Originalurkunde oder ihrer Überlieferung (Archiv von Siguenza?) und damit auf die Heimat der Sammlung deuten.

Von den sonst unbekannten Stücken der Fr. möchte ich vorläufig die folgenden mitteilen:

tit. 6 *sine iudicio ecclesie uxor relinqui non debet.*

fol. 13 (c 5) *de eodem.*[1])[2]) Ex parte cuiusdam mulieris B. nomine nostris auribus est intimatum, quod cum inter patrem et matrem fuisset secundum morem ecclesie nullo prohibente contractum matrimonium, discordia postmodum inter eos emergente pater eius a lege mulieris, cum Berta adhuc haberetur in utero, fuit ecclesie iudicio conpaternitatis vinculo separatus. Qui cum aliam nomine C. postmodum duxisset in uxorem, et ex ea minime prolem suscepisset, ipsam Berta exhered⟨it⟩ata bonorum suorum tam mobilium quam immobilium heredem instituit. Sane cum Berta patre defuncto vellet ei sicut ab intestato succedere et ad bona paterna pervenire, ea que illi secundo nupserit non permisit. Quoniam igitur sepe dicta B⟨erta⟩ paternis bonis non debuit hac occasione fraudari, fraternitati tue per apostolica scripta precipiendo mandamus, quatenus veritatem super hijs diligenter inquiras et si cognoveris quod parentes Berte publice et sine contradictione ecclesie antequam ipsa nasceretur, matrimonium inter se contraxissent et ipsam illis in matrimoniali fide existentibus conceptam fuisse, facias eam sicut legitimam ad paternam hereditatem admitti. Quoniam si quis filius est, et heres iuxta apostolum, qui hoc in suis epistolis protestatur. Si enim sepe dicta C. aut alii duxerint resistendum quominus mandatum apostolicum exsequaris, eos contradictione et appellatione cessante per excommunicationis sententiam conpescere non obmittas.

[1]) c 4 hat die Rubrik: *Matrimonium accusare non potest qui diu mansit cum uxore et eam in facie ecclesie duxit.*

[2]) Inskription fehlt. — Wegen des Inhalts vgl. Alexanders III. c 2 X qui fil. sint leg. 4 17.

fol. 14ᵛ (c 15) *de eodem.*¹) *Idem*²) *Januensi epo.* Cum in civitate tua matrimonia sepius illicita contrahantur, nobis imminet pastorali sollicitudine precavendum, ne contrahentes in sua possint diutius iniquitate permanere. Inde est quod fraternitati tue per apostolica scripta precipiendo mandamus, quatenus cum ad audientiam tuam pervenerit, quod in civitate tua matrimonia contrahantur que non debent contrahari, vel contracta durare, publicos testes tue civitatis, qui ad hoc iure iurando sunt instituti, ad tuam presentiam convoces et eorumdem testium dicta in scriptis redacta appellatione remota recipias, etiamsi contrahentes legitime citatos habere nequiveris et nisi ap⟨er⟩te fuerit in pronu⟨n⟩tiatione processum vel appellatum, in sentencia ferenda procedas. In matrimoniis sane que publice contrahuntur, non nisi ordine iudiciario vel secundum consuetudinem ecclesie Januensis cum iusta deliberatione procedas.

tit. 19 *de decimis.* (vgl. oben S. 374)

fol. 31 (c 15) *Adrianus Senonensi archiepo et Antiodorensi epo.* Dilectus filius abbas H. monasterij sancti Petri directa nobis conquestione monstravit, quod sanctimoniales H. decimam, quam monachis ecclesie sancti Florencij ad eius ius specialiter pertinentis debent exsolvere, violenter detinere presumunt et eam ipsis dare modis omnibus contradicunt. Pontumacenses etiam monachi decimam, quam idem abbas apud sanctas virtutes habere dinoscitur, ei sicut nobis dicitur, ex integro non persolvunt. Pontumacenses etiam fratres quandam terram ipsi abbati contra iustitiam auferre presumunt. Preterea Firminus, frater Senonensis archiepe, parrochianus tuus, cum quandam terram prefato abbati, ut ab eo accepimus, vendidisset et cum non velit secundum legem statuta super ipsa vendicione tueri, coram domino ad cuius dominium terra pertinebat, XXIIII libras abbas se eidem conqueritur persolvisse. Quia vero ex iniuncto nobis a Deo apostolatus officio cunctis Xpi fidelibus et hijs presertim qui divino sunt obsequio mancipati, in suo iure existimus debitores, fraternitatibus vestris per apostolica scripta precipiendo mandamus, quatenus tam predictas sanctimoniales quam monachos et memoratum G. infra XXX dies post harum susceptionem litterarum cum omni districtione compellatis ut predictas decimas vel terram atque pecuniam eidem abbati sub celeritate restituant et de cetero ab ipsarum decimarum detentione desistant vel plenam sub presentia vestra iusticiam ei super hijs omnibus non differant exhibere. Vos igitur utrisque partibus in conspectu vestro congruo loco et tempore constitutis, ipsorum auditis et cognitis rationibus causam appellatione cessante mediante iusticia terminetis; ita quidem, ut aliquod privilegium, in quibus decime laborum eis concedantur, in ipsa causa eis non debeat suffragari. Nos enim

---

¹) c 14: *Crimen occulte commissum cum matre vel sorore illius que postea ducta est, non solvit matrimonium.*

²) c 14: *Alexander III.*

religiosis viris non alias decimas, nisi eas que de novalibus provenire noscuntur, duximus indulgendas. Quodsi predicte moniales ac monachi ct idem G. restituciones predictorum facere vel in presentia vestra ipsi abbati complementum iusticie noluerint exhibere, canonicam in eos sententiam non differa⟨ti⟩s ullatenus promulgare. *Datum Beneventi XIIII. kal ian.* (1155 Dez. 19)

An dieser Stelle möchte ich zu meiner Abhandlung über Johannes Teutonicus im vorjährigen Bande dieser Zeitschrift (Kan. Abt. XXI) folgendes berichtigen: Zu S. 158: ad c. 6 D. 25, Glosse ad v. Primum sine crimine (rechte Spalte) Zeile 13: statt „§ 1. — respondeo" zu lesen: „I. responso (D. 21, 1, 17, 1)". Letzte Zeile: statt „turpis" zu lesen „temporis". — Zu S. 174 Anm. 1: Die Bemerkung „notavi XV q. ult. in summa" bezieht sich nicht auf ein „Summa" heißendes Werk, sondern auf eine eigene Glosse zum Dictum Grat. vor C. 15 q. 8; diese Anfangsdicta hießen bei den Dekretisten allgemein „summae". — Gegen die Bezeichnung des im Cod. Pal. überlieferten Werkes des Joh. Teutonicus als Summa bestehen überhaupt Bedenken, auf die mich Herr Prof. H. Kantorowicz gütigst aufmerksam gemacht hat (Fehlen der Praefatio, Übernahme fremder Glossen mit Siglen u. a.). Damit gewinnt es größere Wahrscheinlichkeit, daß das Werk von Johannes als Glossenapparat (Vorläufer der ordinaria) verfaßt, ohne Legaltext abgeschrieben und darum schon von einem gleichzeitigen Benutzer als Summa bezeichnet worden ist. Die Frage nach der litterarischen Gattung ist, bei der geringen sachlichen Differenz zwischen Summen und Apparaten, hier schwierig zu entscheiden; ich hoffe noch unter Heranziehung weiteren Materials darauf zurückzukommen.

VIII

A Collection of Decretal Letters of Innocent III in Bamberg

THE TWENTY LETTERS of Innocent III in MS. Bamberg Patr. 132 (Q. VI. 42) fol. 110r–118r were briefly identified in 1903 by H. Fischer in his *Katalog*;[1] more recently, the present writer suggested that this collection deserved the attention of canonists as a link in the history of papal decretals.[2]

Bamb. Patr. 132 is a composite manuscript, *saec.* xiii, beginning with Robert of Flamborough's Manual for Confessors (fol. 1–64v), followed by penitential canons based on Burchard's *Corrector* (fol. 65–80v).[3] My knowledge is limited to microfilm reproductions of fol. 81–118r, containing in a formal book hand the text of the seventy constitutions of the IV Lateran Council together with the constitution *Ad liberandam* for the Crusade and the quasi-official notice[4] on the participants of the Council (fol. 81–110r); after which, without any interruption, the same scribe copied the collection of twenty decretal letters from Innocent's years xiii–xviii which we shall call *Collectio Bambergensis secunda*;[5] they alone are our concern here. Notes in a cursive hand on fol. 119 pertain to the conciliar controversies of the fifteenth century. The codex formerly belonged to the cathedral library; beyond this, we have no indications of provenance.

It is obvious that after the promulgation of Pope Innocent III's official collection of decretals — completed during his twelfth year, in the summer of 1209 and commonly known in the schools as *Compilatio tertia* — there existed a practical need for supplementing the official book with decisions and responses from the pope's later years. This need accounts for the private circulation of small collections arranged in a roughly chronological fashion, such as the three interrelated texts which Professor C. R. Cheney analyzed some years ago (*Pragensis, Palatina I*, and *Abrincensis II*).[6] A common core can be isolated in these three, which points to a process of selection of letters from Innocent's years xii and xiii by canonists in the Chancery; this core was subsequently added to in various ways. It is also apparent that these collections are connected, "though in an indeterminate and unproved way," with the *Compilatio quarta*, where most of their material reappears.[7] It has been argued elsewhere[8] that Johannes Teutonicus did not work from the papal registers when he composed this systematic arrangement of Innocent's "new" law — conciliar and extra-conciliar — but from intermediate collections. Texts like those of *Coll. Pragensis* and its relatives must have been available at Bologna.

Bambergensis II presents another intermediate collection of the chronological type, a welcome complement to the *Pragensis* group, with which it has only one decretal in common.[9] It provides the full text of fourteen of the thirty papal letters used in *Comp. IV* that can be definitely dated to the period from December 1210 (*Bamb.* 1: 11 Dec. 1210) to Innocent's eighteenth year.[10] Together with another nine letters from *Coll. Pragen.*[11] this accounts for all but seven decretals of this period in *Comp. IV*.[12] In addition, *Bamb. II* contains three letters (Nos. 9, 12, 14) which are not in *Comp. IV* but later reappeared in the decretals of Gregory IX: presumably Raymond of Peñafort, like our collector, took these from Innocent's registers. Only three of the twenty letters in Bamberg (Nos. 10, 17, 18) did not find their way into any of the standard compilations. No. 10 is otherwise known from the register (*Reg.* xvi. 3: PL 216. 786); Nos. 17 and 18 are printed below: they come from the seventeenth year, for which the register is lost. No other copies seem to exist, although another trace for No. 17 is found in the *Indice* 254 of the Vatican Archives.

The letters of *Bamb. II* present a strictly chronological order. This points to the origin of the collection — not necessarily of its Bamberg copy — in the circles of the Chancery. Also, addresses are in general closer to the register than those of either *Comp. IV* or *Liber Extra*. A few examples must suffice.[13]

> *Bamb.* 1 (*Reg.* xiii. 187) "Innocentius iii. Placentino [Palentino *Reg.*] et Burgensi episcopis et abbati de arnundo [Morimundo *Reg.*] Cistersiensis ordinis" shows some confusion. But Palencia is likewise confused with Piacenza in MSS. of *Comp. IV* and *Extra*, with others (and *Extra ed.*) giving Valencia. "de arnundo" becomes "de ar." in *Comp. IV* and "de N." in *Extra*. *Bamb.* 4 (Reg. xv. 6) "Idem G. [S. *Comp. IV*] de uallibus, magistris [magistro *Reg. Comp. IV Extra*] G. et P. de fumiis [Fimiis *Reg.*] canonicis laudunensibus." "G. de uallibus" omitted in *Extra*; "de fumiis can. laudun." becomes "de Fimiscano," "de Fumiscano," "de Firmisca," etc., in *Comp. IV* and *Extra*.

A Collection of Decretal Letters of Innocent III in Bamberg

Bamb. 5 (*Reg.* xv. 118) "Idem lingonensi [Legionensi *Comp. IV*] episcopo"; no address in *Extra*.
Bamb. 8 (*Reg.* xv. 191) "Idem episcopo Gebenensi et Vienensi sacriste": the sacristan of Vienne is either omitted or distorted in *Comp. IV* ("et Vienen. vel Ateste") and *Extra* ("et N. Valentinensi," etc.).[14]
Bamb. 11 (*Reg.* xvi. 26) "Idem Slewirensi [Sleswicensi *Reg.*] episcopo": the several sections appear inscribed to "Vicensi" or "Seuicensi" in *Comp. IV*, to "S." or "Senonensi," or without address in *Extra*.
Bamb. 13 (*Reg.* xvi. 118) "Idem archiepiscopo lundensi apostolice sedis legato": in all the sections that appear in *Comp. IV* and *Extra*, Lund is confused with either London or Lyons.
Bamb. 15 and 16 (*Reg.* xvi. 165, 166) "Idem episcopo Wastisslauensi [Wratislaviensi *Reg.*]" and "Idem eidem" reproduce two successive letters of the register; the outlandish name of Wrocław-Breslau is even more disfigured in *Comp. IV* (("Vratismen.," "Veteranen," etc.) and *Extra* ("Veratisamensi").

The texts of the register appear unabridged, with one exception (No. 11, discussed below), as far as the substance of the letters is concerned. Only the conventional, final clauses of chancery usage ("Tu denique, frater episcope . . ."; "Quod si non ambo . . .")[15] are often omitted. The textual quality of the copy is average.[16] Dates are usually in order[17] and given in a slightly shortened form, thus: "Dat'. later. iiii. non. octobris anno xiiii." The fuller ending ". . . pontificatus nostri anno . . ." is written out only once (No. 20). A few dates are omitted or incomplete, but even there the chronological sequence is kept.[18] On the other hand, Nos. 19 and 20 provide dates, from the lost register volumes, that were previously unknown.[19]

As for the date of the collection itself, only a guess is possible. Its last letter (No. 20) was written early in the eighteenth year, 28 March 1215. By contrast, Johannes Teutonicus presented four letters of that year, one from after the close of the Council, while another could be even later.[20] This suggests that *Bamb. II* was completed by the middle of 1215 and that its juxtaposition in the manuscript with the conciliar texts of IV Lateran means no more than that it was convenient to have material of this kind copied into one book. We find the same combination of Council and decretals in the Prague manuscript:[21] yet *Coll. Pragen.* certainly was not composed after Innocent's sixteenth year, of which it includes one letter only.[22]

A single fact could be construed as possibly indicating a post-conciliar origin of *Bamb. II*: No. 11 (Potth. 4722), addressed to the bishop of Schleswig, omits after its third section ("Cimeteria uero") the short piece "Procurationes autem — impendis" (PL 216. 815c2–5), the concluding chancery formula "Tu denique, frater episcope . . . ," and the date. The same omission occurs in *Comp. IV* and *Liber Extra*.[23] Already Baluze observed that this rule on *procurationes* is also found in *IV Later.* c. 33 = *Extra* 3. 39. 23 (*IV Comp.* 3. 18. 2).[24] It stands to reason that *Comp. IV* and *Extra* omitted the clause on *procurationes* in Potth. 4722 in order to avoid repetition.

Reg. xvi. 26	*IV Conc. Later.* c. 33
Procurationes autem quae visitationis ratione debentur, sine manifesta et necessaria causa non exigas, nisi cum personaliter officium visitationis impendis.[25]	Procurationes que ratione uisitationis debentur episcopis, archidiaconis uel quibuslibet aliis, etiam apostolice sedis legatis aut nuntiis, absque manifesta et necessaria causa non exigantur, nisi quando personaliter officium uisitationis impendunt . . .[26]

If the same reasoning is applied to *Bamb. II*, it would argue for composition after the Council. But differently from Johannes Teutonicus — and, later, from St. Raymond of Peñafort — our compiler nowhere else shows any interest in "editing" his texts. He does not shun repetitious material, as can be seen in No. 17 (printed below): thus there exists no conclusive argument for a post-conciliar origin. The inclusion of only one letter an. xviii points rather in the opposite direction.

As for the person or persons who compiled or commissioned *Bamb. II*, it may be tempting to look for clues among the addressees of the letters, in particular of those that are *unica*. But once we admit that the source of our collection must be a choice of texts made in the Chancery, any argument is fallacious in which the accidental loss of a given register volume makes some letters appear — today — as though they came from another source, such as a recipient's archives. For this reason it is inadmissible to deduce, for instance, specific Scandinavian connections from the fact that No. 17, to the archbishop of Lund, is not preserved anywhere else and that *Bamb. II* contains another letter to the same archbishop and one to the bishop of Schleswig (Nos. 11, 13). Like these two letters, No. 17 was once contained in the register (xvii. 6); and with the same logic one could postulate French connections because No. 10, to the archbishop of Reims (Potth.

A Collection of Decretal Letters of Innocent III in Bamberg

4678), is not contained in other compilations, and several other letters of *Bamb. II* are addressed to French prelates (Nos. 4, 5, 7, 9, 14, 19).[27] As for the other *unicum*, No. 18, it is true that we have no date and no positive indication that it was ever enregistered; moreover it is the only letter which would seem out of place in a collection of decretals, being a piece of strictly theological teaching. Still, its position between two letters of the seventeenth year makes it unlikely that it should have been copied from a source other than the Chancery records, let alone the difficulty of finding an unequivocal solution for the garbled address "episcopo Ketinensi."

In conclusion, we may classify *Bamb. II* as representing a selection of decretals chosen from the registers by a curial canonist early in the eighteenth year of Innocent III. It adds two pieces to our knowledge of the Innocentian corpus; it adds in no small way to our knowledge of the stuff from which the *Compilatio quarta* was made.

CONCORDANCE OF COLLECTIONS AND PAPAL REGISTER

BAMB.	REG.	DATE	POTTH.	4 COMP.	EXTRA	INCIPIT AND EXPLICIT
1	xiii. 187	1210 Dec. 11	4143	5. 14. 1	5. 38. 10	Noua quedam — celorum commisit.
2	xiv. 107	1211 Oct. 4	4312	5. 6. 4	5. 12. 20	Sicut ex tenore — officio abstinere.
3	xiv. 140	1212 Jan. 10	4360	3. 3. 2	3. 8. 5	Postulasti per sedem — non debet.
4	xv. 6	1212 Mar. 2	4400	1. 2. 2	1. 3. 25	Olim ex litteris — plena fides.
5 (a)	xv. 118	1212 Jun. 7	4523	—	5. 6. 14	Postulasti per sedem — commercia exercere.
(b)	”	”	”	—	—	Consequenter quesiuisti — sustentandum.
(c)	”	”	”	3. 10. 1	3. 31. 21	Tertio quesiuisti — mutare.
6	xv. 162	1212 Sep. 18	4598	5. 12. 3	5. 23. 20	Petisti per sedem — licentia abbatis.
7	xv. 166	1212 Oct. 7	4603	3. 14. 1	3. 40. 6	Ligneis edificiis — denuo consecrari.

VIII

BAMB.	REG.	DATE	POTTH.	4 COMP.	EXTRA	INCIPIT AND **EXPLICIT**
8 (a)	xv. 191	1212 Dec. 20	4628	5. 1. 4	5. 1. 21	Inquisitionis negotium — facere presumatur.
(b)	"	"	"	"	"	Quesiuisti preterea — non existit.
9	xv. 202	1213 Jan. 9	4641	—	5. 39. 45	Contingit interdum — noscitur instituta.
10	xvi. 3	1213 Mar. 14	4678	—	—	Etsi apostolatus — prouocet ultionem.
11 (a)	xvi. 26	1213 Apr. 29	4722	2. 2. 3	2. 2. 14	Postulasti per sedem — facienda.
(b)	"	"	"	"	5. 12. 21	Quesiuisti preterea — duricie imputandum.
(c)	"	"	"	3. 15. 1	3. 40. 7	Cimeteria uero — dedicationibus consueuit.
12	xvi. 93	1213 Aug. 8	4789	—	3. 34. 10	Per tuas nobis — de te factum
13 (a)	xvi. 118	1213 Oct. 3	4820	1. 10. 1	1. 21. 6	Quia circa minima — curauerint continenter.
(b)	"	"	"	—	—	De presbyterorum uero — quod pretendunt.
(c)	"	"	"	5. 15. 1	—	Quesiuisti preterea — exegerit clericorum.
(d)	"	"	"	5. 12. 5	5. 33. 22	Subsequenter etiam — set et futuri.
(e)	"	"	"	—	—	Sane quia contingit — sit subortum.
(f)	"	"	"	—	4. 14. 6	Porro de nobili — scandalum imminere.
14	xvi. 158	1214 Jan. 2	4869	—	5. 34. 16	Accepimus litteras — nostris expressam.
15	xvi. 165	1214 Jan. 8	4873	1. 2. 4	1. 3. 27	Postulasti per sedem — litteris mentionem.

A Collection of Decretal Letters of Innocent III in Bamberg

BAMB.	REG.	DATE	POTTH.	4 COMP.	EXTRA	INCIPIT AND EXPLICIT
16	xvi. 166	1214 Jan. 8	4974	3. 2. 3	3. 5. 26	Vacante in quadam — beneficio competenti.
17	(xvii. 6)	1214 Mar. 1	—	—	—	Tua nos duxit — uiderimus expedire.
18	—	(1214 Mar./Nov.)	—	—	—	Auditis litteris — minime contradicant.
19	—	1214 Nov. 11	—	2. 1. 2	2. 25. 5	Cum inter dilectos — materiam extendatur.
20	(xviii. .)	1215 Mar. 28	5038	5. 7. 1	5. 19. 16	Salubriter conscientie — matrimonii supportanda.

NOTES ON THE CONCORDANCE

The main characteristics of *Bamb. II* as regards addresses, text, and dates have been indicated in the opening pages. A full apparatus of readings should not be expected here; the following notes are only meant to give some information on letters or portions of letters that do not appear in *Comp. IV* and *Extra*. The two letters that were previously unknown will be edited in the end.

Bamb. 5 (b) shows no significant variants from the text as printed in PL 216. 630c5–12. The section deals with a person "qui se falso episcopum asserens altaria consecrauit et alia plura exercuit que ad officium pertinent presulatus." The bishop of Langres is to declare all these acts invalid "et ipsum perpetuo carceri facias mancipari, pane doloris et aqua angustie sustentandum": a penal clause which Innocent used also in Potth. 4683 (*Reg.* xvi. 10, PL 216. 794) and which echoes 3 Regum 22: 27 (cf. Baluze's note col. 630 *ad loc.*).[28]

Bamb. 10: text as in PL 216. 786; a mandate to the archbishop of Reims and his suffragans to suppress the evil practice of blasphemous oaths: many persons in France "non solum per diuinos manus et pedes iurare non metuunt, uerum etiam ipsius Christi et sanctorum eius secretiora membra lingua sacrilega perscrutantes, ea non formidant intimare iurando que nos scribendo sumus ueriti nominare."

Bamb. 13: full text as in the register, printed in PL 216. 914–16 and *Diplomat. Danicum,* I, 5, pp. 58–60 (No. 37). *Comp. IV* and *Extra* omit the final clause, "si uiuere curauerint continenter" of section (a), as well as section (b), in which Innocent cites the rule that priests' sons may not be ordained, except in monastic or regular houses, "ex decreto Urbani ii." (D. 65 cc. 1, 11) and "ex concilio Pictauensi" (*I Comp.* 1. 9. 1 = *Extra* 1. 17. 1), and continues: "de presbyteris autem Suethie certum non possumus dare responsum, nisi uiderimus priuilegium quod pretendunt" (PL 216. 914c10–915A1; *Dipl. Dan.* p. 58. 14–19). The two compilations also omit section (e), which deals with the denunciation of marriages concluded within the forbidden degrees of kindred (PL 216. 915c1–916A1; *Dip. Dan.* p. 59. 15–24); here, the old editions of the register disfigured the rare term *iuramentalis* (compurgator, oath-helper) in the passage "ad denominationem iuramentalium [iumentalium *Reg. ed.*], ut tuis uerbis utamur, procedere . . ."; cf. Skyum-Nielsen, *Dipl. Dan.* p. 57 (introd. to No. 37). The word obviously was unfamiliar to Innocent III; it is therefore interesting to note that the only instances listed by DuCange occur in the *Liber legis Scaniae,* i.e., the Latin version which Archbishop Anders Sunesen of Lund (1201–24; d. 1228) made of the old *Skånske Lov* (*Skånelag*),[29] and that the prelate to whom Pope Innocent wrote about "the appointment of *iuramentales,* to use your expression," should be none but Archbishop Anders.

Bamb. 19, from the lost register an. xvii, provides the address and the date that are lacking in the compilations: "Idem abbati monasterii noui, ph. decano et ph. subdiacono Pictauiensibus. Cum inter . . . Dat. later. iii. Jdus nou. anno xvii." (The inscription "Idem monachis Farfensibus" in the Roman edition of *Extra* 2. 25. 5 is not borne out by manuscripts but due to aberration from c. 6 *ibid.*: see Friedberg's note 2 *ad loc.*) The readings of *Bamb.* generally are closer to *Comp. IV* than to Raymond's text, but at one point *Bamb.* ". . . coram nobis et dil'. n̄." badly distorts the original "coram uobis ex delegatione nostra" which the compilations have preserved.[30]

Bamb. 20, to the bishop-elect of Otranto, likewise presents a previously unknown date; it also gives us the stilted first sentence, which was cut short ("Salubriter, et infra") in the compilations. *Bamb.*: "Idem electo Ydrotinensi.[31] Salubriter conscientie tue consulis sedem apostolicam in dubiis consulendo, que se consulentibus non inconsulte consulere consueuit. Sane generum . . . matrimonii supportanda. Tu denique et cet. Dat. later. kal. aprilis anno pontificatus nostri octauo decimo."

A Collection of Decretal Letters of Innocent III in Bamberg

NEW TEXTS

Bamb. 17

Idem Lundonensi archiepiscopo apostolice sedis legato. [1] Tua nos duxit fraternitas consulendos utrum,[a] cum homines prouincie tue proni sint ad periuria et testes aut instrumenta[b] de more terre examinari non consueuerint[c] et uix absque animarum periculo coniugia inter eos qui se in quinto consanguinitatis uel quarto affinitatis gradu contingunt possint rescindi contracta, utrum tibi dissimulare liceat coniugia quinti gradus, si uideris inter eos unanimem cohabitationis consensum aut ex diuortio periculum imminere. [2] Quesiuisti etiam utrum illi presbyteri qui duas successiue focarias habuerunt irregulares existunt, ut cum eis in executione officii ualeas dispensare si promiserint celibatum. [3] Et utrum monachi Omnium Sanctorum uti ualeant priuilegio bone memorie E. predecessoris tui ad episcopales decimas retinendas de possessionibus acquirendis sicut et illo tempore acquisitis; [4] quasdam tam super matrimoniis quam presbyterorum filiis ac dispensatione super matrimonio inter Necui. et N. uxorem eius contracto, falsa[d] suggestione obtenta, et comitatu Alsatie adiciens questiones. [5] Nos ergo fraternitati tue taliter respondemus quod, cum tuam in proximo expectemus presentiam ad concilium generale, supersedendum duximus id ad presens, quoniam auctore Domino super hiis et aliis plenius instrueris. [6] Preterea quesiuisti utrum,[e] cum homines[f] ipsius regni Suetie censum apostolice sedis, prohibente ipsorum rege, tibi iuxta mandatum nostrum soluere non curant, nitentes per census subtractionem ab obedientie iugo subtrahere semetipsos, utrum ipsorum excessus, ne rex Datie offendatur in offensa predicti regis, cum sit ei affinitate coniunctus, debeas tolerare uel in eos censuram ecclesiasticam exercere. [7] Ad hoc autem fraternitati tue taliter respondemus ut, cum tu regni Suetie primas existas, censum sedis apostolice firmiter exigas et diligentia exquisita procures ut census preteriti temporis integre persoluatur et in futuri solutione non adhibeatur aliqua difficultas; [8] Vbsalensem archiepiscopum et episcopos regni illius sollicite commonens et diligenter exhortans et, si necesse fuerit, per censuram ecclesiasticam appellatione remota[g] compellens ut ad concilium ueniant generale, in quo auctore Domino super premissis et aliis statuemus quod uiderimus expedire. Tu denique et cet. Dat'. Rome apud s. Petrum kal. martii anno xvii.[h]

[a] ū *Cod.* [b] iuramenta *Cod.* [c] consueuerunt *Cod.* [d] *leg.* falsi ? [e] ut *Cod.*
[f] homines *om. Cod.* [g] ap. se. *Cod.* [h] xvi. *Cod.* (*sed vide infra in commento*)

Bamb. 18

Idem episcopo Ketinensi. Auditis litteris tuis et intellectis que dilectus filius abbas Casemarij proposuit coram nobis, fraternitati uestre breuiter respondemus quod credendum est pariter et docendum sanctorum animas etiam ante iudicii diem in celo regnare cum Christo, ad quod probandum inter alia testimonia scripturarum, que pro multitudine subticemus, sufficere potest quod Dauid legitur prophetasse de Deo, "Ascendens in altum captiuam duxit captiuitatem."[a] Ipse quidem descendens ad inferos[b] in sanguine testamenti sui uinctos suos emisit de lacu in quo non erat aqua,[c] captiuitatem illam sanctorum ducens in altum captiuitatem[d] captiuam. Haut dubium quin in celum, ubi est ad dexteram Dei sedens. Vnde cum per mortem eius ianua uite sit aperta, dubitare te nolumus quin, etiam cum nunc patrie porta sit reserata, talium anime a peccatorum nexibus et penarum uinculis absolute in celum cum Christo regnature transmigrent, quemadmodum desiderat Apostolus dicens, "Cupio dissolui et esse cum Christo."[e] Quecumque igitur auctoritates aliud forsitan innuere uideantur, ita sunt exponende ut huic sententie minime contradicent. Dat'. lateran'.

[a] c. d. c. *Cod.*—*Ephes. 4:8 (ex Ps. 67:19)* [b] *cf. Ephes. 4:9* [c] *cf. Zach. 9:11*
[d] captiuitate *Cod.* [e] *cf. Phil. 1:23*

NOTES ON THE NEW TEXTS

Bamb. 17 (fol. 116v–117r), to Archbishop Anders Sunesen of Lund, is recorded in *Indice* 254 of the Vatican Archives as c. 6 of an. xvii:[32] "In primis quod archiepiscopus Lundensis est primas regni Suetie. Vt legitur 'Tua nos' etc." Accordingly, the date of *Bamb.* (". . . anno xvi.") has been corrected above. 1 March 1214 (not 1213) is also required by the reference to the archbishop's presence at the future General Council, the summons to which had gone out only on 19 April 1213 (Potth. 4706).

The letter, which we have divided for convenience into eight sections, consists of two main parts. Sections 1–4 recite a number of queries to which the pope proposes to reply later when the archbishop will be in Rome (section 5). In the second part (sections 6–8) the pope turns to matters on which he prefers to give immediate instructions. Now it is very strange that the first four sections repeat queries which Innocent III had, for the most part, already answered on 3 October

1213 in his decretal letter Potth. 4820, our No. 13, "Quia circa minima" (= Q):[33]

Sec. 1 "Tua nos — imminere": though differently formulated, *Bamb. 13* (e) likewise deals with the problem whether to proceed or not to proceed against marriages among *consanguinei* and *affines* (see notes on No. 13 *supra*); Q 59. 15–24.

Sec. 2 "Quesiuisti — celibatum": cf. *Bamb. 13* (a); Q 58. 4–7, 11–14; *Extra* 1. 21. 6.

Sec. 3 "Et utrum monachi — acquisitis": cf. *Bamb. 13* (d); Q 59. 5–14; *Extra* 5. 33. 22. The "predecessor E." is Archbishop Eskil, 1138–77.

Sec. 4 "quasdam tam super matrimoniis": no parallel in Q.

———— "quam presbyterorum filiis": cf. *Bamb. 13* (b); Q 58. 7, 14–17; see notes on No. 13 *supra*.

———— "ac dispensatione — obtenta": cf. *Bamb. 13* (f); Q 59. 25–60. 3; *Extra* 4. 14. 6.

———— "et comitatu Alsatie": no problem concerning the county of Holstein is mentioned in Q.

Have we to do, then, with two papal responses to one inquiry, because of inefficiency in chancery procedures? Or did Archbishop Anders not receive the first letter (Potth. 4820) and therefore write again to Rome? One can only speculate on this, and on the reasons for the pope's almost brusque refusal (sec. 5) to enter into the substance of the questions from Lund. It is a most unusual reply for Pope Innocent, who always loved to teach in his decretals — especially if we consider that the Lateran Council, at which the archbishop would "soon" (*in proximo*) receive his instructions, was still twenty months away.

In the opening of the second part (sec. 6) emendation of the text was required by grammar and borne out by the parallelism with the sentence structure of section 1.[34] Collection of Peter's Pence (*census apostolice sedis*) in Denmark and Sweden was the responsibility of Lund ever since Paschal II had raised the see to metropolitan rank in 1104;[35] the *mandatum nostrum* in the present text is Innocent's letter of 6 November 1204 to Archbishop Anders (Potth. 2320).[36] The actual controversy with King Eric of Sweden over the payment of the *census* and its political implications here alluded to ("lest the king of Denmark take offense") must be left to the investigation of Swedish church historians;[37] Pope Innocent seems to have returned to the matter in a lost letter to all the faithful in Schleswig, May or June 1216 (Potth. 5291).[38]

Section 8, "Vbsalensem archiepiscopum . . . ," is an admonition tacked on to the papal response that has nothing to do with the archbishop's inquiry. We can sense how strongly Innocent must have felt about the presence of the Scandinavians at the future council if he sent this reminder to Lund only eight days after his letter of 21 February 1214 (Potth. 4900), in which he had rebuked the archbishop for seeking an excuse from attending and ordered him to convey the papal exhortation also to Upsala and its suffragans.[39] The new letter differs only in that it adds the authority for Archbishop Anders to enforce compliance by ecclesiastical censure.

Nonetheless, attendance from the northern countries was very poor at the Lateran Council. The only extant list gives one bishop *de Dacia*.[40] But it has been argued with good reason[41] that Archbishop Anders, after all, did come to the Council and that he stayed in Rome until the spring of 1216. The *rubricellae* of *Reg. Vat.* 8A for the lost registers an. xviii/xix include the record of a privilege granted to him of collating to the vacant bishopric of Roskilde (Potth. 5289, 5290).[42] On 25 January 1217, Honorius III confirmed this right, which ". . . dudum *cum esses apud sedem apostolicam constitutus*, b. m. Innocentius papa predecessor noster fraternitati tue interuenientibus nobis indulsit" (Potth. 5432).[43] The original indult, with a batch of other letters on Danish matters, belongs to the last months of Innocent III (May/June 1216).[44] By the testimony of Honorius III, the archbishop was then in person at the Curia. It would be unreasonable to assume that this was anything but a continuation of his presence at the Lateran Council.

Bamb. 18 (fol. 117r-v) is undated, but its position in the sequence of letters permits us to assign it to the months between March and November 1214. Identification of the addressee is less certain. The name as written, "episcopo Ketineñ.," would most likely be a misspelling for "Katinensi" — which may mean Catania in Sicily (Gr. *Katanē*) or Caithness in Scotland: the adjectival form *Catinensis* is attested for either of these sees. Pope Innocent's letter gives no clue as to which of the two bishops might have sent the inquiry. Since the abbot of Casamari (in the diocese of Veroli) is mentioned as having spoken before the pope — apparently he was the bearer of the letter of inquiry — one would be inclined to decide for a bishop from the South. On the other hand, an abbot of Casamari (the same?) had been Innocent's legate to France and England in 1203-4.[45] Connections between Scotland and the abbey were at least possible. A year after

A Collection of Decretal Letters of Innocent III in Bamberg

the present letter, both bishops attended the Lateran Council, according to the only known list of participants,[46] although the Chronicle of Melrose does not mention Bishop Adam of Caithness among the four prelates who traveled from Scotland to Rome *generalis concilii gratia*: he thus would have been one of the *ceteri* who merely sent their proctors.[47]

But whoever was the bishop to whom Innocent III wrote this piece of doctrinal teaching, it deserves the historian's attention. The controversy over the state of the blessed souls prior to the Last Judgment was to erupt into a serious crisis in the days of John XXII, over a hundred years later.[48] The letter of Innocent indicates an early phase of this theological controversy, and an interesting papal effort to resolve it with an uncommon scriptural exegesis.

NOTES

1. H. Fischer, *Katalog der Handschriften der königlichen Bibliothek zu Bamberg*, I, 1. 3 (Bamberg, 1903), p. 520.
2. S. Kuttner, "Notes on Manuscripts," *Traditio*, XVII (1961), 536; ibid., XXIV (1968), 507.
3. *Katalog*, p. 519.
4. See S. Kuttner and A. García y García, "A New Eyewitness Account of the Fourth Lateran Council," *Traditio*, XX (1964), 118, where MSS., editions, and a possible trace in the register are briefly discussed.
5. The well-known *Bambergensis* (see, e.g., W. Deeters, *Die Bambergensisgruppe der Dekretalensammlungen des 12. Jhdts.*, Bonn, 1956) should henceforth be called *Bamb. I*.
6. C. R. Cheney, "Three Decretal Collections before Compilatio IV," *Traditio*, XV (1959), 464–83. For the date of completion of *Comp. III*, see S. Kuttner, "Johannes Teutonicus, das vierte Laterankonzil und die Compilatio quarta," *Miscellanea Giovanni Mercati*, V (Studi e Testi, 125; Città del Vaticano, 1946), 621.
7. Cheney, *Trad.*, XV, 469.
8. *Miscell. Mercati*, V, 622.
9. *II Bamb.* 8 = *II Abr.* 1 (*IV Comp.* 5. 1. 2). This decretal is also entered as an addition in the appendix to Rainer of Pomposa, Reims MS. 692, fol. 31v; cf. Kuttner, *Repertorium der Kanonistik* (Studi e Testi, 71; Città del Vaticano, 1937), p. 310; Cheney, *Trad.*, XV, 472, n. 32.
10. A. Potthast, *Regesta Pontificum Romanorum* (Berlin, 1874–75), Nos. 4143 (an. xiii); 4312, 4360 (an. xiv); 4400, 4523, 4598, 4603, 4628 (an. xv); 4722, 4820, 4873, 4874 (an. xvi); *IV Comp.* 2. 1. 2 (Potth. —; an. xvii), and Potth. 5038 (an. xviii) = *II Bamb.* 1–8, 11, 13, 15, 16, 19, 20. For details, see the Concordance, *infra*.
11. Potth. 4163, 4164, 4174 (an. xiii); 4195, 4379 (an. xiv); 4401, 4577, 4614

(an. xv); 4844 (an. xvi) = *Prag.* 14, 13, 15, 20, 19, 18, 17, 25, 34; see Cheney's tabulation, *Trad.*, XV, 473–75. It is possible, though unproved, that five more letters, covered by *Coll. Prag.* but undated, equally belong in this time span: Potth. 2360, 5022, 5025, 5028, *IV Comp.* 2. 7. 2 (Potth. —) = *Prag.* 16, 24, 21, 23, 22 (cf. the tabulation and Cheney, pp. 477–78). If so, our figures would be: thirty-five letters, of which fourteen in *II Bamb.* and fourteen in *Prag.*

12. Potth. 4337 (*IV Comp.* 3. 19. 1), 4587 (2. 11. 1), 4847 (3. 2. 3), 4956 (2. 10. 2), 4989 (1. 3. 2), 5009 (5. 5. 1), 5298 (3. 9. 3: an. xviii/xix). This list does not include *IV Comp.* 1. 18. 2, which Potthast 4957 dates 1214–15 (an. xvii): actually the decretal is of uncertain date, perhaps 1208–15 (if the archbishop of Pisa here addressed was Lotharius the Glossator).

13. The readings here given from the registers (*Reg.*) are those of the Migne text in PL; readings of *Comp. IV* and *Liber Extra* are taken from Friedberg's text and apparatus, checked for *Comp. IV* against Antonio Augustín's edition (Lérida, 1576). — *II Bamb.* 3, 5, 9, 12, 14, 16, 20 have no addresses in *Extra*; the address of No. 19, from the lost register an. xvii, was previously unknown (see Notes on the Concordance, *infra*).

14. The address is correct in Reims 692 (n. 9 *supra*), but garbled in *II Abr.* 1: "Innoc. iii. tenm [with suspension marks: cenomanen ?] episcopo et dilecto filio sacriste uianensi."

15. A convenient list of these common forms will be found in C. R. Cheney and Mary G. Cheney, *The Letters of Pope Innocent III (1198–1216) Concerning England and Wales* (Oxford, 1967), pp. 195–96.

16. Some poor readings will be found in the texts edited below; see also Notes on the Concordance for No. 19. The opening word of No. 14 is "Accepimus" as in *Extra* 5. 34. 16, where the register, at least in the edition, has "Recepimus." At No. 4 the rubricator blundered and made "Cum" out of the initial "Olim" of Potth. 4400.

17. The following differ from the registers: No. 1 "iii. idus nouembris [decembris *Reg.*] an. xiii"; No. 7 "non. kal. [non. *Reg.*] octobris an. xv"; No. 9 "v. kal. [v. id. *Reg.*] ianuarii an. xv"; No. 12 "v. [vi. *Reg.*; vii. *Gall. christ.*] id. augusti an. xvi." But it should be remembered that *Reg. Vat.* 8, which covers the years xiii–xvi, is not the original register but a copy made under Urban V (1362–70).

18. Nos. 11, 14, 18 (undated); No. 15, "Dat. Later."; No. 16, "Dat." ("Dat. ut supra" *Reg.*)

19. Notes on the Concordance, *infra*.

20. Potth. 5009 (*IV Comp.* 5. 5. 1) of 14 December 1215; Potth. 5298 (3. 9. 3) an. xviii or xix. The other two are Potth. 5038 (5. 7. 1) = *II Bamb.* 20, and Potth. 4989 (1. 3. 2) of July 1215.

21. Prague, Univ. MS. XXIII. E. 59 (*ol.* Lobkowitz 439), fol. 2r–23v, 24r–45r.

22. *Prag.* 34: Potth. 4844 of 6 November 1213.

23. *IV Comp.* 3. 15. 1, *Extra* 3. 40. 7; both cite the beginning of the letter wrongly as "Consuluisti et infra. Cimeteria . . ." ("Proposuisti" *Reg.*, *Bamb.*).

24. PL 216. 816, notes 37, 38. See also Niels Skyum-Nielsen, *Diplomatarium*

A Collection of Decretal Letters of Innocent III in Bamberg

Danicum, Ser. I, Vol. 5: *1211–1223* (Copenhagen, 1957), p. 52, in his introductory note to the critical edition of this letter (No. 33).
25. PL, *ut supra* (Baluze's text); *Diplomat. Danicum* I, 5, p. 54, lin. 3–5 (from the archival tradition, collated with the register).
26. Text established by A. García y García for the forthcoming edition in the *Monumenta Iuris Canonici.* Variant readings in the vulgate editions (from Crabbe to Mansi): lin. 1 "visitationis ratione"; lin. penult. "praesentialiter" (for "personaliter") — noted as a false reading already by Baluze, see PL 216. 816, n. 38. *Comp. IV* and *Extra* agree with the correct readings. (I am indebted to Fr. García for the permission to use his text.)
27. Laon (4), Langres (5, 14), Besançon (7), Thérouanne (9), Poitiers (19).
28. Had Friedberg, in his edition of the *Liber Extra,* been consistent in his efforts to restore the portions of the text omitted by Raymond of Peñafort and by the respective *Compilationes antiquae,* then the text of PL 216. 630c5–12 should have been printed in italics and included in brackets at the end of *Extra* 5. 6. 14. But Friedberg arbitrarily decided to drop all the passages that appear at the end, rather than in the middle of a decretal (cf. his *Prolegomena,* col. xlv). This makes no sense in a case where the "end" actually occurs in the middle of the original text, as here or as in *II Bamb.* 13 (b) and (e), which are likewise bypassed in Friedberg.
29. DuCange, *Glossarium,* IV, 452 col. *b,* s.v. *iuramentum.* See *Lex Scaniae* 5. 6 ". . . testes totidem quam iuramentales"; 6. 10, 13; 7. 4, 9; 15. 3 ". . . et duodecim iuramentalibus"; also 7. 2, 3, 5, 13; 16. 3: ed. P. G. Thorsen, in *Skånske Lov* (Nordiske Oldskrifter, XVIII; Copenhagen, 1854), pp. 133, 155–56, 159–62, 166, 169, 199. I have not seen the edition by S. Aakjaer and E. Kroman in *Danmarks gamle Landskabslove,* I, 2 (Copenhagen, 1933), 467–667. The original title seems to be "Liber legis Scaniae" as in the colophon (p. 204 *ed.*), not "Lex Scaniae provincialis" as chosen by Thorsen.
30. In Antonio Augustín's edition of *IV Comp.* 2. 1. 2 the word "nostra" (not "delegatione nostra," as Friedberg, n. 6 ad *Extra* 2. 25. 5, asserts) is lacking; it is present in the MSS. Also, Friedberg's n. 14 *ad loc.* should be corrected: all MSS. read "debeat," not "abeat."
31. "Ydotonen." and other variants in *IV Comp.* (garbled in *ed.*); no address in *Extra.*
32. A. Haidacher, "Beiträge zur Kenntnis der verlorenen Registerbände Innozenz' III.," *Römische historische Mitteilungen,* IV (1960/61), 58, No. 1 with note 1; cf. Kuttner, *Trad.,* XXIV (1968), 507.
33. Q (= PL 216. 914–16) will be cited here by page and line numbers in Skyum-Nielsen's edition, *Diplomat. Danicum* I, 5, 58–60.
34. Sec. 6 would lack a subject without inserting "homines"; the reading "ut[rum] cum . . . , utrum . . ." is needed in both sections in order to tie together the long recital of facts with the actual question: an unusual sentence structure, perhaps, but an effective one.
35. Ph. Jaffé, *Regesta Pontificum Romanorum* . . . , ed. 2 (Berlin, 1885–88), No. 6335; for text and date see P. Fabre and L. Duchesne, *Le Liber Censuum de l'Église Romaine* (Paris, 1889–1910), I, 227; L. Weibull and N.

Skyum-Nielsen, *Diplomatarium Danicum*, I, 2 (Copenhagen, 1963), p. 67, No. 30. Also, for Sweden, Anastasius IV on 28 November 1154, Jaffé (ed. 2) 9938.
36. PL 215. 461; N. Skyum-Nielsen, *Diplomat. Dan.* I, 4 (1958), p. 194, No. 94.
37. The issue is not mentioned in Y. Brilioth, *Den påfliga beskattningen af Sverige intill den stora schismen* (Uppsala, 1915), which deals specifically with papal taxation in Sweden.
38. For the date, see *Dipl. Dan.* I, 5, No. 77.
39. PL 216. 965; *Dipl. Dan.* I, 5, No. 41: ". . . unde plurimum admiramur quod te super hoc excusare aliquatenus uoluisti" (p. 64. 23–24).
40. J. Werner, "Die Teilnehmerliste des Laterankonzils vom Jahre 1215," *Neues Archiv der Gesellschaft für ältere deutsche Geschichtskunde*, XXXI (1906), 586, from Zurich MS. Car. C. 148; also in R. Foreville, *Latran I, II, III, et Latran IV* (Histoire des Conciles Oecuméniques, VI; Paris, 1965), p. 392. The authentic list, in the register an. xviii, No. 234, is lost; cf. Kuttner and García (n. 4 *supra*), pp. 118, n. 18, 122.
41. Skyum-Nielsen, *Dipl. Dan.* I, 5, p. 92 (introd. to No. 59).
42. *Ibid.*, Nos. 75, 76 (*Reg. Vat.* 8A, fol. cxviii).
43. *Ibid.*, No. 102 (p. 149f).
44. Cf. *Dipl. Dan.* I, 5, Nos. 74–83, 85–90 (Potth. 5107–8, 5110, 5114, 5116, 5118–19, 5121, 5263–64, 5289–94.
45. See Cheney and Cheney, *Letters of Pope Innocent* (note 15, *supra*), Nos. 484–87, 506–11, 531–32, 555–56, 569 (Potth. 1921–22, 2009–12, 2081, 2181, 2275); cf. H. Tillmann, *Die päpstlichen Legaten in England* . . . (Bonn, 1926), pp. 90–92.
46. Werner (n. 40 *supra*), pp. 587, 592: Foreville, pp. 392, 395.
47. *The Chronicle of Melrose*, from the Cottonian Manuscript, . . . introd. by A. O. and M. O. Anderson, index by W. C. Dickinson (facsimile edition, London, 1936), p. [61] = fol. 32r: "profecti sunt de scotia ad curiam romanam generalis concilii gratia. . . . Ceteri uero prelati personaliter romam non adierunt, set legatos suos miserunt." Cf. A. Bellesheim (tr. Dom. O. H. Blair), *History of the Catholic Church of Scotland*, I (Edinburgh-London, 1887), 339.
48. The documentation in H. Denifle and E. Chatelain, *Chartularium Universitatis Parisiensis*, II (Paris, 1891), 414–42, and in the article by X. Le Bachelet, "Benoît XII," *Dictionnaire de Théologie catholique*, II, 1 (Paris, 1910), 653–704, remains fundamental. For theologians immediately preceding Innocent III, see Le Bachelet, p. 690 f.

IX

A NEW EYEWITNESS ACCOUNT OF THE FOURTH LATERAN COUNCIL

In collaboration with Antonio García y García

Two years ago we briefly announced the discovery of a new document of great interest for the history of the Fourth Lateran Council.[1] Written in Spring 1216 as a letter from Rome, presumably by a German, it was copied by a thirteenth-century scribe into a manuscript now at the Universitätsbibliothek of Giessen, where it follows directly after the *constitutiones* of the council. With its detailed and vivid description of the three plenary sessions and of many events that took place in between, the anonymous report adds considerably to the information we possess from other sources. But although other portions of the Giessen codex have been known and used by many scholars ever since the eighteenth century, this text has been overlooked to the present day. It is a happy coincidence that we are able to present this eyewitness account of the greatest of the ecumenical councils of the Middle Ages while the Second Vatican Council is in session.[2]

I. The Giessen Manuscript

MS 1105 of the University Library[3] is a codex made up from three different vellum manuscripts (fols. 1-46, 47-60, 61-142) assembled in a fourteenth- or fifteenth-century binding, pigskin over wooden boards (34.5 × 25 cm), with traces of five nails on front and back, which are no longer preserved, and two clasps, only one of which is extant. At the time of binding the codex belonged to the Cistercian monastery of Haina (Hayna) in Hesse, which was suppressed in 1527. The white monks had come to Haina in 1221 by the transfer of their original house from Aulesburg, founded as a Benedictine abbey in 1144, where they had been established by 1188.[4] On fol.

---

[1] Bulletin of the Institute of Research and Study in Medieval Canon Law, *Traditio* 18 (1962) 449.

[2] The text was discovered by A. García in 1961. Description of the MS, edition and general evaluation of the letter (chs. I-III) are the result of our joint labors. S. Kuttner is responsible for most of the commentary (IV) and for Appendices A and C; A. García for Appendix B.

[3] J. V. Adrian, *Catalogus codicum mss. bibliothecae academicae Gissensis* (Frankfurt 1840) p. 342.

[4] Cf. L. H. Cottineau, *Répertoire topo-bibliographique des abbayes et prieurés* I (Mâcon 1935) 1370; LThK[2] 4 (1960) 1326; for the Benedictine foundation see C. Will (mit Benut-

61ʳ and fol. 142ʳᵛ, that is on the first and the last pages of the third MS of the volume, the original ownership is entered: 'Liber gloriose (*al.* sancte) uirginis Marie de Aulesburg.' The old shelfmark is 3.6, and on the front cover the contents are given as 'Breuiarium extrauagantium. Haymo super Isaiam. Item concilium Lateranense iv.' in a contemporary hand.

I. fol. 1ʳᵃ-46ᵛᵇ, late 12th-cent. script in two columns, 52 lines per col.; rubrics and red initial letters; sparse glosses by two hands. Seven quires, numbered I-VII at the bottom of the respective last pages. With the exception of the *sexternio* VII (fol. 42-46), all consisted originally of eight folios each, but the first fol. of quire II (now consisting of fols. 9-15), the six middle fols. of III (now 16-17), and the last, presumably blank, fol. of VII are missing; small strips of parchment can still be seen before fol. 9 and after fol. 46, also traces of lost leaves between fol. 16 and 17.[5]

> INCIPIT BREUIARIUM EXTRAUAGANTIUM B. PREPOSITI PAPIENSIS. ANNO DOMINICE INCARNATIONIS M.C.LXXVIII. PRESIDENTE S. ROMANE ECCLESIE SANCTISSIMO PAPA ALEXANDRO III. PONTIFICATUS ANNO XX. MENSE MARTII INDICTIONE XII. ET V. Q. (*leg.* ET) VII. ET VIII. DIE MENSIS, SEDATA IAM DISCORDIA QUE INTER ECCLESIAM ROMANAM ET IMPERIUM . . . IN QUA SINODO XXVIII. CANONES PROMULGAUIT SANCTUS PAPA ALEXANDER. Iuste iudicate filii hominum . . . (ends:) Quod non est licitum—non tenetur reus.[6] Explicit.

This copy of the so-called *Compilatio prima* of decretals, composed by Bernard of Pavia between 1188 and 1192, here with two sets of early glosses, was already known by scholars of the eighteenth century.[7] The curious rubric 'Anno dominice incarnationis . . . ', a formalized notice of the Third Lateran Council, appears also in a few other manuscripts between title and prologue of the work; it has misled some modern authors into believing that Bernard's *Breviarium* was originally composed at the time of that council (1179) and that all later decretals are interpolations.[8]

---

zung des Nachlasses von J. F. Böhmer), *Regesten zur Geschichte der Mainzer Erzbischöfe* I (Innsbruck 1877) p. 327 No. 35.

[5] We wish to thank Dr. Schawe, Director of the University Library, for reexamining the codex and supplying some of the physical detail given above.

[6] 1 *Comp.* 5.37.12.

[7] H. Chr. Senckenberg, *Meditationum de universo iure et historia volumen* (Giessen 1740) 372-83; J. Chr. Koch, *Programma de Breviario extravagantium Bernardi Circae cod. ms. membran. Biblioth. Acad. Giessensis* . . . (Giessen 1772; microfilm kindly supplied by Dr. Schawe). Jos. Anton Riegger used the MS in his unfinished edition, *Bernardi praepositi Papiensis Breviarium extravagantium cum Gregorii IX. P. Decretalium collectione ad harmoniam revocatum* Pars I (Freiburg Br. 1779; no more publ.).

[8] Cf. Kuttner, *Repertorium der Kanonistik* (Studi e Testi 71; Città del Vaticano 1937) 322 n. 1.

Because of the loss of leaves in quires II and III, the Giessen copy lacks 1 *Comp.* 1.23.2 - 1.27.1 (before fol. 9) and 2.20.12 - 3.9.4 (before fol. 17). Otherwise it shows approximately the same variants of transmission—omissions, additions, datings, and other peculiarities — as the Brussels MS 1407-9 in Fransen's pioneering study on the textual stages of *Comp.* I,[9] thus representing an intermediary stage between his groups Σ and Φ.

The first stratum of glosses represents mostly the 'Ad hunc titulum spectant . . . ' type, which goes back to Bernard himself; a slightly later hand added other parallel and adversative references.

II. fol. 47ra-60vb: four pieces, of which Nos. 1-2 are by the same hand, Nos. 3 and 4 by two other hands, all of the first half of the 13th cent. Two columns throughout, 43 lines per col. in Nos. 1-2, with Nos. 3 and 4 each filling only part of a column. No rubrics; alternating red and blue initials; marginal Roman numerals in red for the individual Lateran constitutions in No. 1. Two quires originally of eight folios each, but the first fol. of quire (i) and the last of quire (ii) are missing, with loss of text only before fol. 47. A slash goes through fols. 55-68, without serious impairment of the text.

(1) fol. 47ra-58vb:

< . . . > quibuscumque nominibus censeantur. . . . (ends:) sub pena excommunicationis firmiter prohibemus < . . . >

These are the constitutions of the Fourth Lateran Council, beginning in c. 3,[10] and ending with the unnumbered const. *Ad liberandam*, which lacks the last two paragraphs, breaking off in § *Licet autem*[11] with half a column left blank. Between c. 70 and *Ad liberandam*, the scribe included also the beginning of Innocent III's conciliar sermon 'Desiderio desideravi . . . ' (fol. 57va).[12] The ample margins left for glosses (the two columns fill only 25 × 16.5 cm on a 33 × 24 cm page) was never used.

---

[9] G. Fransen, 'Les diverses formes de la *Compilatio prima*,' *Scrinium Lovaniense: Mélanges historiques Étienne Van Cauwenbergh* (Louvain 1961) 235-53; and his paper 'La tradition manuscrite de la *Compilatio prima*,' read at the Second International Congress of Medieval Canon Law, Boston, August 12-16, 1963, to be published in the forthcoming volume of *Proceedings*. These studies also show that the earliest form of *Comp.* I does not antedate the pontificate of Clement III (1187-91) as proposed by A. Vetulani, 'Deux intéressants manuscrits de la "Compilatio prima",' *Traditio* 12 (1956) 605-11.

[10] Mansi 22.986 lin. E5; *Conciliorum oecumenicorum decreta*, ed. Centro di Documentazione, Istituto per le Scienze Religiose . . . (Herder: Basel-Barcelona-Freiburg etc. 1962) 209 lin.12. In this new edition (hereafter COD) C. Leonardi, who signs as responsible for the medieval councils from I Lateran to Vienne, has collated Mansi's text of IV Lateran with Crabbe's *editio princeps* (1538) and the Roman edition (1612); cf. pp. viii, 204-5.

[11] Mansi 1066 E8; COD 246.23.

[12] Ends at ' . . . multa sunt et uaria desideria hominum' (Mansi 968E).

118

The Giessen codex is one of the earliest and best copies of the Lateran constitutions and will be used in A. García's forthcoming edition for the *Monumenta iuris canonici*.[13]

(2) fol. 59ra-60va:

> Serenitati uestre transcribere non sufficiens . . . uerum est testimonium eius.

This eyewitness report of the Lateran Council is edited and discussed below. Some underlinings and short marginal notations by a 17th.-cent. German reader.[14]

(3) fol. 60va:

> Anno ab incarnatione uerbi M.cc.xv. celebrata est sancta et uniuersalis synodus rome in basilica saluatoris . . . Ciuitatum etiam aliorumque locorum ingens affuit multitudo. Amen.

This official or quasi-official notice of the council appears in many MSS of the Lateran constitutions[15] and in many medieval chronicles;[16] it is printed in the conciliar collections, from Binius (1606) to Mansi.[17] Possibly it corresponds to No. 162 in the lost Register of Innocent's eighteenth year: 'clxii. Item quoddam inuentarium de synode (*sic*) celebrata.'[18]

(4) fol. 60vb, about two-thirds of the column:

> Quoniam ea que in meliuitano (*sic*) et kartaginensi concilio statuta sunt in desuetudinem abierunt, statuit hoc sanctum concilium . . . ipsos subiacere decreuimus.

---

[13] On the MSS and editions of the constitutions see, for the time being, A. García, 'El Concilio IV de Letrán (1215) y sus comentarios,' *Traditio* 14 (1958) 484-500; C. Leonardi, in COD 204-5. A fuller account will be given in García's edition.

[14] Fol. 60rb: 'Sigfr. Arep̄s. Moguntinus' (to line 170 of the text edited below); 'Siciliae' (to line 182); 'lignum S. Crucis' (to line 185).

[15] Cf. García, in *Trad*. 14.487; A. Luchaire, 'Un document retrouvé,' reprinted from *Journal des savants* 1905 pp. 557-68 in Hefele-Leclercq, *Histoire des conciles* 5.ii (Paris 1913) 1722-33, at 1724 n.2. We may cite, e.g., the following MSS : Bern 22, fol. 2rb; Cambrai 556 (514), fol. 196^v; Cambridge, Corpus Christi Coll. MS 450, p. 201; Giessen; Kassel Jur. 11 (no foliation); Lisbon B. N. Alcob. 304 (173) fol. 1^r; London, Lambeth Palace 210, fol. 148^r; Munich lat. 8596, p. 255; Oxford, Bodl. e Mus. 82, fol. 120^v; Merton Coll. B. I. 7, fol. 45ra; Paris, B. N. lat. 12249, fol. 108^v; Rome, Casanat. 1910, fol. 15rb-15va; Rouen 706, fol. 268vb; 759, fol. 77^v; Toledo 15-26, fol. 36rb-36va; Vatican, Vat. lat. 3555, fol. 61^v; Reg. lat. 448, fol. 1^r; Zurich Car. C. 148, fol. 46^{rv}.

[16] E. Winkelmann, *Philipp von Schwaben und Otto IV von Braunschweig* II (Leipzig 1878) 513.   [17] Mansi 22.1079.

[18] Vatican Archives, Indice 254 fol. 13^v. On this *Indice* and its importance for the reconstruction of the lost volumes of the Register see A. Haidacher, 'Beiträge zur Kenntnis der verlorenen Registerbände Innocenz' III,' *Römische historische Mitteilungen* 4 (1961) 37-62; this entry, given p. 61 n.1 (reading recollated by Dr. Peter Herde), must refer to something different from No. 234 (Haidacher p. 49 n. 49), 'Item expressio nominum prelatorum in synodo ipsa presentium.'

THE FOURTH LATERAN COUNCIL 119

Two constitutions of an unnamed council, edited and discussed below, Appendix A.

III. fol. 61r-142rb, first half of 14th cent.; biblical text in center of pages, 23 lines, surrounded by commentary (61 lines), without division into columns. Rubric in red, fol. 61r; two tri-color initials (red, blue, green), fol. 61va and 63ra. For the slash in fol. 55-68 see No. II above; for the ownership notes on the first and last pages, see the remarks on provenance, before No. I.

> INCIPIT EXPOSITIO HAYMONIS SUPER YSAIAM PROPHETAM. Sciendum quod diuiso populo propter salomonis offensam . . . (ends:) . . . de hiis qui habitant in terra, dicit Dominus omnipotens, qui est uia, ueritas et uita. Deo gratias.

Pseudo-Haymo of Halberstadt, *In Isaiam libri tres*, a ninth-century commentary, was most probably written by Haymo of Auxerre, a monk of St. Germain, and exists in two versions: (i) beg. 'Isaias propheta nobili prosapia ortus' (ed. Cologne 1531, iv. id. Febr.=PL 116.715-1086); (ii) our version, beg. 'Sciendum . . . ' (ed. Cologne 1531, 16 kal. Apr.=Paris 1531).[19] The Cologne printer, Eucharius, knew two MSS, from Altenburg and Heisterbach, of this version, but modern authorities cite MSS only for the first. The Giessen copy, however, was discussed in 1741 by Chr. Fr. Ayrmann.[20] The text is followed by copyist's verses and a *Confessio brevis et utilis* (another hand).

Fol. 61r and 142v:

> Qui sursum corda tenditis
> et terrena despicitis . . .
> (ends:) . . . et iniustis supplicia. Amen.

The *Vita rhythmica* of St. Marina, edited by the Bollandists from another MS.[21]

II. GENERAL NOTES ON THE GIESSEN REPORT OF THE COUNCIL

Beginning without an address and taking leave from the reader without a final greeting, our writer nonetheless makes it clear in the first lines that

---

[19] Cf. E. Riggenbach, *Historische Studien zum Hebräerbrief* (Forschungen zur Geschichte des neutestamentlichen Kanons 8; Leipzig 1907) 93-100, 157; F. Stegmüller, *Repertorium biblicum medii aevi* 3 (Madrid 1951) Nos. 3083, 3084; cf. 3066.

[20] 'Nachricht von einer Merkwürdigkeit des ehemaligen Klosters Aulesburg in Hessen,' in J.F.C. Retter, *Hessische Nachrichten, darinnen allerlei zur Historie* . . . 3 (Frankfurt 1741) 1-14, 15ff. (not seen).

[21] *Analecta Bollandiana* 11 (1892) 264-9; cf. U. Chevalier, *Repertorium hymnologicum* 2 (1897) No. 16520; *Bibliotheca hagiographica latina* No. 5530. Also printed from the Giessen MS by Ayrmann, *op. cit.*, 74ff. according to J. V. Adrian's *Catalogus*, where likewise an edition by Ayrmann (p. 7) of the *Confessio* fol. 142r is cited.

he is writing a letter ('Sinceritati uestre transcribere non sufficiens singula que in urbe..., notum uobis facio quod...'); that he is writing from Rome as an eyewitness of the council ('... de sollempnitate concilii... prout uisu comprehendi secundum ordinem edisseram'); and that he hopes to complete his account later in oral communication ('... sperans tamen quod super huiusmodi uobiscum conferendis tandem aliquando ueniet... hora...'). A clue for the approximate date of his letter is given toward the end, where he says that it would be tedious to commit to writing all that was done from the time of the council until mid-lent (lines 198-201). The *media quadragesima*, Thursday of the third Lenten week, in 1216 fell on 17 March, and it is unlikely that he would have chosen this expression if he had written during Holy Week or after Easter (10 April).

There is every reason to believe that our writer was a German and that he was reporting back to a prelate, or prelates, in Germany. Perhaps he sent at the same time a copy of the council's constitutions; for both the *constitutiones* and the letter were copied at Aulesburg or Haina by the same scribe into the codex which is now at Giessen. More important, however, than the medieval location of the MS are certain internal criteria of the letter itself.

Either a German or a Sicilian could speak of Frederick II as *noster rex* (line 49), but if we compare our text with that of Richard of San Germano, the chronicler from the southern kingdom,[22] the difference in the knowledge of names and places is revealing. Where Richard of San Germano speaks of 'B(erardus) uenerabilis Panormitanus archiepiscopus' (ed. Garufi p. 71 lines 12-14 [=R 71.12-14]), our author (=G) mentions him merely as 'episcopus Palermitanus' (line 85); on the other hand, G 168ff. describes an otherwise unrecorded episode which involves 'Sifridus, sancte Moguntine sedis archiepiscopus' and the 'principes Alimanie'; he identifies the nunnery at Quedlinburg ('Quidelincburc' G 101, 142) where R 72.21-2 gives us only 'quoddam monialium monasterium'; and where R vaguely reports one of the accusations made against the ex-Emperor Otto, 'quia episcopum quemdam quem dominus papa... excommunicauerat nisus est fouere' (72.12-4), G 104-5 specifies the charge: 'quod episcopo Bremensi excommunicato et destituto regalia porrexerit.'[23] He discusses relations between Germany and England (G 168ff.), and finally he mentions that after the council many bish-

---

[22] *Ryccardi de Sancto Germano Chronica*, long version, ed. A. Gaudenzi, in Società Napoletana di storia patria, *Monumenti storici* ser. 1: *Cronache* (1888) 89-94; ed. C. A. Garufi, in RIS² 7.ii (1936-38) 61-73, left columns. (Unless otherwise noted, texts will be cited from Garufi.)

[23] We may assume that in the original letter also the bishop of Münster was correctly identified where the MS has the corrupt reading, 'quod Manifestime episcopum captiuauerit' (G 100, *app. crit.*), but R 72.15-6 has merely: 'legatum alium episcopum capere...'

ops, 'maxime de Alemannia' stayed on at the curia (G 196-8). All this can leave no doubt but that our writer came from Germany—perhaps from Mainz[24]—to assist at the council.

He was a cleric of some education. The *captatio benevolentiae* at the beginning, the whole texture of the opening paragraph, and the rhetorical devices he employs where he wishes to abridge his tale,[25] all show that he was familiar with the arts and the precepts of *dictamen*. He quotes Horace, Vergil and Ovid unobtrusively but effectively,[26] and biblical phrases easily flow from his pen. They may—as for instance the closing sentence borrowed from St. John's gospel (G 201-3)—not always agree with our standards of taste but are in perfect accordance with the literary habits of his time. His prose is lively and of remarkable descriptive power, not without a fine sense of humor, as in the scene where Innocent III makes the archbishop of Mainz sit down three times (G 174-8). He has a flair for the blunt directness and sarcasm Innocent displayed at times during the debates[27] and is full of praise for the pope's effective Latin oratory (G 110-11). Again, it is an elegant instance of medieval *parodia* when he adapts a liturgical text to describe how a papal procession was met by the people (G 66-8).

The chief purpose of the Giessen Anonymous, however, is that of presenting a faithful record. He carefully distinguishes between the events he had witnessed himself ('prout uisu comprehendi' G 10-11) and those he reports on hearsay (cf. G 53-5, 57-9) or as his own conjecture (cf. G 178-80). Where he missed out, as in the case of the pope's opening sermon, which he could not hear very well 'propter tumultum populi,' he made an effort to obtain the text later (G 28-30).

At the outset, the writer announces that he plans to describe the *sollempnitas*, the *gesta*, and the *instituta* (enactments) of the council (G 9-10). His own interests were certainly not canonistic: he relates the dogmatic decrees well enough (G 152-8), but passes over the sixty-eight constitutions on ecclesiastical reforms with a few words: 'deinde leguntur constitutiones domini pape' (G 184). On the other hand, he dwells at length on discussions, during and between the sessions, that bear on the great political issues of the day: the fifth Crusade, the case of the count of Toulouse, the appeal to the coun-

---

[24] See below, commentary on lines 170-1.
[25] '... hanc secundum ordinem explanare non sufficiens breuiter perstringo' (G 74-5); '... ne lectori forte fastidium occasione prolixitatis gignerent, stilo mandare recusaui' (G 200-1). Also to be noted are the Ciceronian 'satis superque' (G 2) or the rare word 'barrientibus' (G 65; cf. ThLL s.v. *barrire*).
[26] See the edition, notes 4, 5, 9, 10.
[27] See G 109-10, 174-5. Jests and sarcastic remarks by Innocent were reported by not a few contemporary writers, cf. H. Tillmann, *Papst Innocenz III.* (Bonn 1954) 50, 154 n. 11, 237-8.

cil of the ex-Emperor Otto IV, the excommunication of the English barons. He briefly records some important ecclesiastical issues: the provision of the vacant see of Constantinople and the primatial claims of Toledo.

On all these *gesta in concilio* our writer has interesting new material to contribute, sometimes implementing, sometimes correcting, sometimes corroborating information we possess from other sources. But what arrests in particular our attention is his painstaking description of the *sollemnitas concilii*. From the opening Mass which the pope celebrated at dawn, with only the cardinals, archbishops, and bishops present, to the final blessing he gave with a relic of the True Cross at the dismissal, we read in G many details of the liturgy and the ceremonial that are not known from any other source. Of especial interest is his colorful account of the consecration of the church of S. Maria in Trastevere on the Sunday after the first session, which appears here as one of the great public events of the council. Another liturgical event he commemorates is the feast of the Dedication of St. Peter's (18 November), with the crowds through which the pope can barely make his way to the Basilica.

All things considered, the only account of the Lateran Council that bears comparison with the Giessen text is the Chronicle of Richard of San Germano, in the long recension published by Gaudenzi (1888) and Garufi (1936-38). An official record of the proceedings, such as the *Breves notae* which the papal chancery was to produce later in the century for the two general councils of Lyons,[28] does not exist. Only a formal, dry notice of a few lines was circulated, giving the numbers of prelates and ambassadors present at the Lateran in 1215; the Giessen MS contains one of its many medieval copies.[29] Of greater importance is the detailed list, discovered sixty years ago in Zurich MS Car. C.148, of the archbishops and bishops who attended;[30] but obviously this document, which stems from an entry in the lost volume of the Register for Innocent's eighteenth year,[31] regards the prosopography of the council rather than its history. Some narrative sources, to be sure, throw light on one or another of the conciliar events,[32] but in general they do not

---

[28] Mansi 23.610-13; 24.61-8.

[29] See above, I, at nn. 15-16.

[30] Luchaire, 'Un document retrouvé' (n. 15 above); his text, reprinted in Hefele-Leclercq 5 ii.1726-8, is inferioɪ to the one published by J. Werner, 'Die Teilnehmerliste des Laterankonzils vom Jahre 1215,' *Neues Archiv der Gesellschaft für ältere deutsche Geschichtskunde* 31 (1906) 575-93. It was actually Werner who had first shown the MS to Luchaire.

[31] *Rubricella* in Reg. Vat. 8A, ed. A. Theiner, *Vetera monumenta Slavorum meridionalium historiam illustrantia* (=VMS; Rome 1864) p. 63 No. 14: ' Item sunt ibi nomina cardinalium, patriarcharum, archiepiscoporum et episcoporum qui interfuerunt in dicto concilio'; cf. also Vat. Arch. Indice 254, fol. 13ᵛ No. 234 (see n. 18 above).

[32] For details see the commentary below, *passim*. Other affairs mentioned in connection with the council by chroniclers (Stephen Langton's suspension, the York election

endeavor to record more than what happened to be of interest to the individual chronicler. In this respect, Richard of San Germano was thus far the only known exception, and his report was evidently still read in the fourteenth century.[33] The German writer's no less vivid, and in many respects better informed account was destined to be forgotten after a monk at Aulesburg or Haina copied it from the original letter.

The scribe's work is uneven. In a number of places his mistakes may be attributable to poor Latinity;[34] in one case he grossly disfigured a place name;[35] and twice he missed portions of his text.[36] In our edition we have retained his spelling but not his obvious mistakes. Punctuation and the use of capitals have been normalized and paragraph numbers have been inserted.

III. Text

1. Sinceritati uestre transcribere non sufficiens singula que in urbe satis superque ammiratione digna uidentur, notum uobis facio quod tot linguarum genera, tot uenerabilium personarum agmina que ex omni natione que sub celo est[1] ad presens apud sedem apostolicam confluxe-
5 runt, nec oculus quidem uidit nec auris audiuit nec in cor hominis ascendisse crederentur.[2] Parti namque et Medi et Elamite cum hiis habitant Iherosolimam etc.[3] Sperans tamen quod super huiusmodi uobiscum conferendis tandem aliquando ueniet narratibus hora tempestiua meis,[4] imprimis ea que maxime audire deposcitis, uidelicet de sollempnitate
10 concilii et in ipso gestis et institutis, benignitati uestre prout uisu comprehendi secundum ordinem edisseram:

Segnius etenim irritant animos demissa per aurem
<quam> que sunt oculis subiecta fidelibus.[5]

---

case, the foundation of the bishopric of Chiemsee, the reorganization of Cyprus, etc.) are discussed in A. Luchaire, *Innocent III* (vol. VI): *Le Concile de Latran et la réforme de l'Église* (Paris 1908) 26-7, 43-54; Hefele-Leclercq 5 ii.1321, 1397-8.

[33] See MS Vat. lat. 3555, Appendix B below.
[34] See below, *app. crit.* to G 13, 50, 111, 161, 167, 178; also 130 (haplography), 137 (dittography).
[35] See *app. crit.* G 100 and n. 23 above.
[36] See G 28, 57.

[1] Cf. Act. 2.5   [2] Cf. 1 Cor. 2.9; Is. 64.4
[3] Cf. Act. 2.9   [4] Ov. *Metam.* 5.499-500
[5] Hor. *Ars poet.* 180-1

---

1 (*fol.* 59ra)   2 satis *bis* G^{ac} [= G *ante corr.*]   6 *vel* creduntur (cred'utur) G
8 hora] N *add.* G^{ac}   13 quam *om.* G

2. In die igitur beati Martini inchoatum est concilium. Dominus papa apud Lateranum in ecclesia Saluatoris que Constantiniana dicitur summo diluculo, intromissis solummodo cardinalibus, archiepiscopis et episcopis, eodem die missam inprimis celebrauit. Qua celebrata et episcopis cum abbatibus ad differentiam episcoporum non infulatis per sedes proprias dispositis, milia milium, immo decies centena milia,[6] tam clerici quam populi intra gremium ecclesie iam dicte admittuntur. Quamplurimis itaque intromissis et in eadem ecclesia, cum sit amplissima, nullo fere loco uacante, dominus papa, homo super homines discretus et uere spiritu sapientie et intellectus[7] adimpletus, cum suis cardinalibus et ministris in eminentiori loco constitutus hunc ymnum 'Veni Creator' etc. inchoauit. Quo sollempniter ac Deo digne nec sine lacrimis pre spirituali gaudio emanantibus decantato, dominus papa huiusmodi collectam subiunxit 'Actiones nostras, quesumus, Domine' etc.[8] <...> de quo, proh dolor, perpauca propter tumultum populi quem nemo compescere ualuit intelligere potui. Pro quo tamen potui inuestigare non desii donec ipsum optinui et scripto commendaui. In eodem sermone inter cetera pro redemptione terre sancte | plurimum exhortatus est. Deinde patriarcha Iherosolimitanus sermonem in idipsum arripuit. Asseruit etiam dominus papa in eodem sermone quod si principes consulent ad terram sanctam, personaliter sibi laborem uellet assumere; sin autem, in preparationem nauium insuper peregrinorum ab urbe proficientium promisit expendere. Hec in prima die concilii et his similia in Lateranensi ecclesia sunt pertractata.

3. Sequenti die in maiori palatio de patriarcha apud Constantinopolim statuendo, quod ecclesie Romane numquam hactenus licuit, multumque diuque sermo uertebatur.

4. Tercia uero die litem que inter Compostellanum et Tolletanum episcopos super optinendo primatum hucusque durauit, dominus papa dirimere et rationabiliter inde diffinire conabatur.

5. Postmodum uero pluribus diebus tractatum est de comite de Tolosa qui propter hereticos aliquando in terra sua commorantes et ob hoc de heresi accusatus, per regem Francie castella et magnam partem terre amisit, immo penitus per alios etiam signatos qui contra eum destinati fuerant est destructus. Verum quia idem comes cum uxore sua aliquando, que est soror uxoris domini Friderici nostri regis, extitit presens et cruce

---

[6] Cf. Dan. 7.10   [7] Cf. Is. 11.2
[8] Vide infra in comment.

---

28 *post* etc. *aliqua omissa esse patet*   perpauca] ppᵃ (= papa) G   29 quem] que G   32 (*fol.* 59ʳᵇ)   44 Tolose G

THE FOURTH LATERAN COUNCIL

50 signatus est, dominus papa xl. marcas ultra mare perpetuo mansuro de omnibus reditibus quos Deus contulerat sibi, ei assignauit in sustentationem. Comitisse uero quicquid tenuit de rege Francie ultra Iordanem assignauit. Ut dicitur, regem Francie per excommunicationis sententiam intendebat compellere ut quiete ei dimitteret. Comes uero de Munfort
55 totam terram residuam de manibus domini pape ac beati Petri tenebit. Filius enim . . . adhuc existens in curia, per gratiam domini pape expectans <. . .>. Multa talium, que hic pertranseo, utpote non certa michi plenarie fama referente cognoui, que ueris addere sepe falsa solet[9] suaque mobilitate uigens uires acquirit eundo.[10]

60 6. Prima dominica post Martini quis adesse non cuperet in tanta gloria? Summus pontifex ad consecrandam ecclesiam beate Marie que ad Oleum fundentem | nuncupata est honorificentissime conducitur. Romanorum nobilissimi, sericis et purpureis circumamicti,[11] in timpano et choro, in cordis et organo,[12] necnon et in tubis quodam concrepanti so-
65 nitu[13] barrientibus, subsequente infinita cleri et populi multitudine ipsum precedebant. Pueri Romanorum, tollentes ramos oliuarum, obuiauerunt domino clamantes et dicentes, sicut sui moris est, Kyrieleyson, Christeleyson[14] indesinenter. Statim ex altera parte pontis per quem ad predictam iter est ecclesiam, lampades innumerabiles per uicos et
70 plateas[15] in funibus dependentes proprie claritatis ardore serenitatem illius diei sibi cedere contendebant. Vexillorum et purpurarum que in domibus et in altis turribus Romanorum expanduntur certus non estimabatur numerus. Set quidem de hiis cum pocius ad sollempnitatem dedicationis ecclesie iam dicte sermo uerteretur, hanc secundum ordinem
75 explanare non sufficiens, breuiter perstringo quod fere totus ille dies ad consecrationem illius ecclesie deductus est. Nam circa uesperas primum dominus papa non cum minori sollempnitate rursum a Romanis ad palatium reducitur.

7. In octaua beati Martini uidi turbam quasi harenam que est in
80 litore maris[16] ad ecclesiam beati Petri et Pauli ob anniuersarium sue dedicationis diem ex uniuersis mundi partibus confluentem, et dominum papam per multitudinem hominum, in pressura maxima et uicos et plateas[17] ambulantium, uix accessum ad ecclesiam beati Petri habuisse.

---

[9] Ov. *Metam.* 9.138-9   [10] Virg. *Aen.* 4.175
[11] Cf. Esth. 8.15   [12] Cf. Ps. 150.4
[13] Cf. 1 Paral. 15.28; 2 Paral. 5.12, 29.27   [14] Vide infra in comment.
[15] Cf. Cant. 3.2   [16] Cf. 3 Reg. 4.29 cum concordantiis
[17] Cf. Cant. 3.2

---

50 mansurus G   52 quicquic G   56 *post* enim *lacuna fere decem litt.*
57 *post* expectans *aliqua omissa esse patet*   62 (*fol.* 59ᵛᵃ)   65 clerici G
66-7 obui. d. c. *abbr.* G   68 Christeleyson] X. *abbr.* G   79 est] se G

8. Proxima vi. feria post octauam Martini iterum sollempnizatum est concilium, in quo primum episcopus Palermitanus litteras regis Friderici recitauit et sermonem postea pro ipso fecit. Postmodum quidam Mediolanenses uiri discreti nuntii Ottonis quondam imperatoris cum instantia postularunt ut littere ipsius Ottonis admitterentur. Ad hoc multi archiepiscopi et episcopi, abbates et clerici siue prelati quorum non erat numerus reclamabant, et precipue marchio de Munferrato, qui asserebat ipsos legatos non esse audiendos tribus de causis. Prima, quod essent periuri. Secunda quod fouerent hereticos. Tercia, quod ipsum marchionem tali federe sibi peterent assistere et domino Ottoni quod ab ipsis nullo modo, nec etiam pro excommunicatione domini pape, diuerteret. Ipsum uero dominum Ottonem non debere absolui vii. de causis: Prima, quod cum idem Otto semel periurauerit, iam cautio iuratoria non sufficeret ad ipsius absolutionem. Secunda, quod de dampnis ecclesie Romane illatis non posset satisfacere. Tercia, quod regem Fridericum impecierit et bona ipsius occupauerit que de Romana tenet ecclesia, et adhuc detineat occupata. Quarta, quod Monasteriensem episcopum captiuauerit. Quinta, quod monasterium in Quidelincburc destruxerit et castrum ibidem fecerit. Sexta, quod regem Fridericum, quem principes imperii in imperatorem elegerant, subsannando regem solummodo presbiterorum esse dixerit. Septima, quod episcopo Bremensi excommunicato et destituto regalia porrexerit.

9. Tandem dominus papa ipsum marchionem et alios contra dominum Ottonem clamantes compescuit dicens quod ob hoc sanctum concilium sit institutum, ut culpabilis et inculpabilis, simul in unum diues et pauper,[18] ibidem audiantur, adhiciens etiam quod si diabolus posset penitere, certe recipiendus esset. Et in latino sermone, quo maxime pollet et effluit, predictas marchionis exceptiones interpretari cepit. Quibus expletis factum est silentium et leguntur littere domini Ottonis quondam imperatoris, premissa salutatione in hunc modum: 'Venerabilibus dominis kardinalibus, archiepiscopis, episcopis, prelatis et toti concilio Otto Dei gratia Romanorum imperator et semper Augustus salutem in Domino et bone uoluntatis exhibitionem.' In sequentibus supplicando deuote ut pro ipsius absolutione apud dominum papam interueniant,

---

[18] Cf. Ps. 48.3

---

87 Ottonis] O. *hic et in seqq. abbr.* G   90 Munf'ra. G   92 quod² *om.* G
(*fol.* 59ᵛᵇ)   96 periurauerat Gᵃᶜ   100 Monasteriensem *scripsimus*: Manifestime G (*cf. infra in comm.*)   101, 102, 104 Quinta ... sexta ... septima] vᵃ ... viᵃ ... viiᵃ G   102 destruxit G   103 subsanando G   105 porrexit G   107 compescuit *bis* Gᵃᶜ   111 interprecari G   111-12 expletis *scripsimus*: exceptis G

quoniam ipsum peccasse peniteat et uelit stare mandatis, quod nuntii
sui pro ipso spoponderint.

120 10. Perlectis litteris ac diligenter auditis, lector eorumdem contra
singulos marchionis articulos respondit excipiendo. Contra primum,
uidelicet quod essent nuntii periuri, sic: quod non esset uerum, et hoc
uellent probare incontinenti. Quod fouerent hereticos, respondit similiter quod non esset uerum, quoniam ubicumque apud eos esse scirentur
125 heretici, aut ipsos penis afficiendo extra suum consortium eicerent aut
qui eos in domibus suis lo|carent, tota ciuitate et episcopo cum cruce
illuc usque procedentibus exterminarent, domos eorum destruerent;
et x. libras illos qui eos hospitarentur dare oporteret. Ad tertium sic
respondit, quod ipsum marchionem in communitatem suam quam
130 uellet, uellent asciscere, salua omni reuerentia sedi apostolice debita.
Contra articulos domino Ottoni obiectos sic excepit; et ad primum,
uidelicet quod idem Otto esset periurus, sic: 'Pater sancte, aut tibi
constat eum esse periurum uel non.' Respondit papa quod ei constaret.
Ad quod ille: 'Penitet igitur, Pater sancte, eum peierasse. Querit ueniam
135 et offert satisfactionem. Ergo recipiendus est.' Ad secundum, quod de
dampnis non posset satisfacere, respondit quod Mediolanenses, Placentini et alie ciuitates sibi coniurate parate sint ad iuramentum, fidem et
obsides super omnibus dampnis que imperator ecclesie Romane intulit satisfacere. Ad quod papa respondit quod licet omnes ciuitates ille sint di-
140 tissime, tamen ad restituendum dampnum per ipsum Ottonem ecclesie
Romane illatum nequaquam possent sufficere. Ad hoc quod claustrum
de Quidelincburc destruxerit, respondit quod claustrum non destruxerit
set castrum in monte supra claustrum sito, quem ab hostibus suis occu-
pari timebat, construxerit, nec propter hoc aliquid mali ecclesia aut
145 moniales inde perceperint. Super aliis, licet ipsum Ottonem penitus
excusare nequiuerit, tamen in his sicut et in premissis pro ipso ueniam
et absolutionis beneficium postulauit. Et hec in secunda sollempnitate
concilii gesta sunt hoc modo.

11. Item tercio sollempnizatum est concilium in die beati Andree.
150 Dominus papa, summo mane missa celebrata et omnibus episcopis per
sedes suas dispositis, in eminentiorem locum cum suis kardinalibus et
ministris ascendens, sancte Trinitatis fidem et singulos fidei articulos
recitari fecit. Quibus recitatis quesitum est ab uniuersis alta uoce: 'Cre-

---

118 quoniam] quō (= quomodo) G   122 esset] essent G^{ac} 124 quoniam] Quō G
    126 (fol. 60ra)   128 oportet G   tertium] iii. G   130 uellet uellent
scripsimus: uellet G (haplogr.)   137 parate coniurate parate male G   141 tamen
(140) post nequaquam iterum G   142 destruxit^1 G   143 castrum scripsimus:
claustrum G   145 moniales G

ditis hec per omnia?' Responderunt omnes: 'Credimus.' Postmodum
dampnati sunt omnes heretici et reprobate quorumdam sententie, Ioachim uidelicet et Emelrici Parisiensis. Quibus recitatis iterum quesitum est: 'An reprobatis sententias Ioachim et Emelrici?' At illi magis inualescebant[19] clamando: 'Reprobamus.'

12. Postea tractatum de negocio sancte Crucis et expeditione signatorum, firmissima pace ipsius constituta et inducta. | Qua occasione omnes barones Anglie et uniuersi tam consilio quam auxilio ipsis contra regem suum cruce signatum assistentes, districta excommunicatione percelluntur. Proposuitque dominus papa quam potens esset idem rex tam in persona quam in rebus terre sancte prebere subsidium, et quod ipse tanquam specialis ecclesie Romane filius terram suam singulis eidem ad mille marcas sterlingorum fecerit tributariam, et eam de manu sua iure beneficiario receperit, et quantam honoris prerogatiuam in hoc sedi apostolice contulerit. Quia uero illud regnum Anglie ad imperatoriam, ut dicitur, pertinet potestatem, ne ius suum in hoc principes imperii in posterum amittant, surgens pre ceteris Sifridus, sancte Moguntine sedis archiepiscopus, dictum regnum quod Romanorum imperatori et principibus Alimanie de iure attineret asserere et probare conabatur. Cui dominus papa, hoc considerato eleuata manu silentium indicens ut ab incepto sermone desisteret, et taliter contra ipsum locutus est: 'Audias me modo, posthac audiam te.' Et sic dictus archiepiscopus tamquam promptus obedientie filius, ut decuit et oportuit, contra uoluntatem patris et domini minime processit, licet uero tribus uicibus super eodem ei respondendo surrexerit. Verum quia ex huiusmodi commendatione et defensione regis Anglie dominus papa Ottonem quondam imperatorem, ut puto, restituere credebatur, subiunxit hinc dominus papa dicens hec uerba: 'Nulli debet esse dubium: Quod principes Alimannie et imperii circa Fridericum Cecilie regem fecerunt, ratum habemus, immo ipsum fouere et promouere in omnibus uolumus et complebimus.'

13. Deinde leguntur constitutiones domini pape. Quibus perlectis, cum iam plus quam nona hora diei esset, magnam partem de ligno sancte crucis de Constantinopoli allato omnibus demonstrauit. Qua ab uniuersis geniculatim adorata, ipse papa 'Te Deum laudamus' inchoauit. Quo sollempniter ab omnibus decantato hanc collectam papa subiunxit: 'Omnipotens sempiterne Deus, fac nos et deuotam tibi semper gerere uoluntatem' etc.[20] et benedictionem per lignum sancte Crucis ad omnes

---

[19] Cf. Luc. 23.5   [20] Vide infra in comment.

160 (fol. 60rb)   161 ipsius G   163 percellentur G   165 specialis] spˉali G
167 et scripsimus: in G   178 huius G   189-90 semper g. v. abbr. G

faciendo concilium absoluit et terminauit. Hec in ultima festiuitatis die, cum sollempniter | tantum tribus diebus predictis in ecclesia Lateranensi concilium extiterit, coram infinita catholicorum uirorum multitudine pertractatum esse dinoscitur.

195 14. Altera autem die post concilium terminatum multi episcopi cum aliis prelatis a domino papa licentiati recesserunt. Quamplures tamen et maxime de Alemannia episcopi per totum aduentum et quidam usque ad quadragesimam pro specialibus negotiis in curia remanserunt. Que medio tempore, uidelicet usque ad mediam quadragesimam ab ineunte
200 concilio ibidem gesta et tractata sunt, ne lectori forte fastidium occasione prolixitatis gignerent, stilo mandare recusaui. Et testimonium perhibet de his qui uidit et scripsit hec, et scitur quia uerum est testimonium eius.[21]

IV. COMMENTARY

1. *Arenga*

The arenga is constructed according to rhetorical precepts: note the forms of address, 'sinceritati uestre' (1), 'benignitati uestre' (10), and the scriptural allusions (3-4, 5-7) surrounded by classical turns of phrase ('satis superque' 2; 'edisseram' 11) and capped by classical quotations (8, 12-13).

2. *First Session: Opening Ceremonies; Sermon of the Pope, Sermon of the Patriarch of Jerusalem; Crusading Matters.*
15 November 1215

Cf. Richard of San Germano, *Chronica* ed. Garufi (=R) 62.21-71.5 (left col.). There are certain differences between the two accounts, which will be discussed presently.

14 *In die igitur beati Martini:* Wednesday, 11 November 1215. R 62.12 gives 'x⁰ intrante mense Nouembris' as St. Martin's day. This error does not seem to be the scribe's, since later on (71.5) Richard speaks of the second session, 20 November, as held 'post dies decem.'

16-18 *summo diluculo . . . quesumus Domine etc.:* G is our only source for the full liturgical detail: the pope's Mass at dawn ('summo diluculo'), with only the higher prelates admitted (16); the seating of bishops and abbots —the latter wearing no mitres (18)—before the basilica is opened to the

---

[21] Cf. Jo. 21.24, 19.35

---

192 (*fol.* 60ᵛᵃ)   194 pertractatur Gᵃᵉ   198, 199 quadragesimam] xlᵃᵐ G

masses of clergy and people (19-21); the reservation of an *eminentior locus* for the pope, his cardinals and attendants (24-5). The pope intones the hymn 'Veni creator spiritus' (25) taken up by all, and sings the collect (27).

19-22 *milia milium . . . nullo fere loco uacante:* Several chroniclers mention the immense crowds, taking their cue from the words ' . . . ingens adfuit multitudo' of the official Notice[1] of the council. We read the biblical 'milia milium' (Dan. 7.10) also in the fourteenth-century *Cronicon* of Reinhardsbrunn and in the *Chronica* of St. Peter's, Erfurt (*c.* 1276),[2] both of which incorporate for the years 1209-1215 the text of the lost *Historiae* (*c.* 1217) of Reinhardsbrunn.[3] That same source has here a fantastic tale of mass suffocation of prelates: 'sub pressura multitudinis episcopi, abbates et quamplurimi alii nouissimum in concilio spiritum exalarunt . . . ';[4] and indeed one or several fatal accidents may have occurred, even though most of the sources recording such accidents are relatively late and differ in their versions. Still, the monk Bernard Itier of St. Martial in Limoges, who says that 'tres episcopi vi obpressionis obierunt,'[5] was a contemporary (d. 1225); one would also assume a sound local tradition behind the *Chronicon Amalphitanum* (*c.* 1294), when it reports that the aged Bishop Matthew of Amalfi was crushed to death 'in ostio ecclesiae S. Joannis ubi concilium celebrabatur.'[6] This could be the 'episcopus quidam' who, according to the Chronicle of Melrose Abbey (*c.* 1275) died of suffocation in the crowds, whereupon the pope 'iurauit per s. Petrum quod mausoleum eius lapide marmoreo signaretur.'[7] In the fourteenth century, finally, Jean Le Long of Ypres asserts

---

[1] Mansi 22.1079. Cf. Winkelmann *loc. cit.* (I n. 16 above) on the use of the Notice by the medieval chroniclers.

[2] ed. O. Holder-Egger, MGH SS 30.i (1896) 588.24; 384.28; also in *Monumenta Erphesfurtensia* (MGH in usum schol.; 1899) 214.

[3] Cf. Holder-Egger's introduction to both texts, SS 30.339, 494-8.

[4] *Ibid.* 588.25-8, 384.29-31. Cf. Luchaire, *Le Concile de Latran* (II n. 32 above) 7-8 for a résumé (uncritical) of this and of some of the texts cited in nn. 5-8.

[5] ed. Holder-Egger, MGH SS 26 (1882) 436.1-2; ed. H. Duplès-Agier, *Chroniques de Saint-Martial de Limoges* (Paris 1874) 94.

[6] *Chron. Amalph.* c. 47, ed. L. A. Muratori, *Antiquitates Italicae medii aevi* 1 (Milan 1738) 210; ed. A. A. Pelliccia, *Raccolta di varie croniche, diarj . . . appartenenti alla storia del Regno di Napoli* 5 (Naples 1782) ii.160. Cf. Ughelli, *Italia sacra* 7 (2nd ed. Venice 1721) 218, who adds (without giving proof) that the bishop was buried 'in eadem ecclesia.' Nothing is recorded in V. Forcella's *Iscrizioni delle chiese . . . di Roma* (Rome 1869-84), nor did a search kindly undertaken by Professor Robert Brentano of Berkeley yield any inscription at the Lateran basilica. — A notice on Matthew's death, very similar to that of the *Chron. Amalph.*, as Professor Brentano points out, exists in the *Liber pontificalis ecclesiae Amalfitanae* (ed. P. Pirri, *Il duomo di Amalfi e il Chiostro del Paradiso* [Rome 1941] at p. 181), which is based on old traditions, although its last entry is for 1547.

[7] *Chronica de Mailros* ed. J. Stevenson (Bannatyne Club; Edinburgh 1835) 121; ed R. Pauli, MGH SS 27 (1885) 438.

that the bishop of Amalfi was trampled to death on the first day 'in ingressu ecclesie Lateranensis,' and one archbishop on the second.[8] It remains an open question what credence can be given to any of these gruesome stories, especially since the two detailed eyewitness accounts, G and R, are silent. All that G complains about is that 'propter tumultum populi quem nemo compescere ualuit' he could not hear the pope's sermon (28-9).

22-24 *homo super . . . adimpletus:* Admiration for Innocent III's exceptional intellect and learning was frequently expressed by contemporary canonists.[9]

24 *in eminentiori loco:* Cf. R 62.22 'cum . . . pater ipse patrum altius resideret'; 62.29 'de supernis sedibus'; *Annales Ceccanenses*: ' . . . dominus papa ascendit in thalamum';[10] all this refers probably to a dais.

25 *ymnum 'Veni Creator'*: Cf. R 62.27-8.

27-28 *collectam 'Actiones nostras quesumus Domine'*: Cf. *Annales Ceccanenses*: ' . . . et ibi celebrata oratione et benedictione super conventum' (*loc. cit.*). The collect 'Actiones nostras'—familiar from the *Gratiarum actio post Missam* of the Roman Missal—does not appear in the conciliar *ordines* of the various stages of the medieval Roman *Pontificale*. There is, however, some evidence for the conciliar use of this prayer outside of Rome.[11] The earliest instance—and the only one, it seems, before 1215—is from Limoges, in the 'Ordo qualiter fit concilium apud Lemouicam urbem' for a council of the province of Bourges in 1031 (Martène's *Ordo* III).[12] In the second half of the thirteenth century 'Actiones nostras' appears as a conciliar prayer in the Meaux Pontifical,[13] and by the fourteenth it was commonly used in French synods.[14]

28-29 *de quo . . . perpauca . . . intelligere potui:* The line or lines dropped by the scribe of G before 'de quo' referred to Innocent's famous opening

---

[8] ed. Holder-Egger, MGH SS 25 (1880) 831-2.

[9] Vincentius Hispanus, *Apparatus Comp. III*, prologue: ' . . . pater eminentis scientie et perspicacissimi ingenii' (MS Vat. lat. 1378, fol. 1ra); Anonymous, prologue to the Lateran constitutions: ' . . . patre perspicacissimi ingenii et summe intelligentie, cui a longissimis temporibus non fuit inuentus similis in cathedra piscatoris . . . ' (Lisbon, B. N. MS Alcob. 381, fol. 225r).

[10] ed. G. H. Pertz, MGH SS 19 (1866) 300.33.

[11] We owe the information which follows to the kindness of Dr. Richard Kay of the University of Kentucky, who sent abundant notes with a letter dated 10 June 1963.

[12] Berlin MS Phillipps lat. 93, fol. 117v (from the Jesuit College of Clermont), ed. E. Martène, *De antiquis Ecclesiae ritibus* III (Rouen 1702) 404; ed. L. Delisle, 'Notice sur les manuscrits originaux d'Adémar de Chabannes,' *Notices et extraits des manuscrits de la Bibliothèque Nationale* . . . 35 (1896) 267.

[13] Paris, B. N. MS nouv. acq. lat. 1202; also Martène and Durand, *Thesaurus novus anecdotorum* 4 (Paris 1717) 891.

[14] Various Sens Pontificals; *Liber synodalis* of Lodève.

sermon (cf. 31 'in eodem sermone'), the full text of which (beg. 'Desiderio desideraui') is given in R 62.31-70.36 and, from another, unidentified source, in the great conciliar collections, beginning with the *Editio Romana* 4 (1612),[15] down to Mansi 22.968-79.

30-31 *donec ipsum optinui et scripto commendaui:* The text of the papal sermon must have been circulated immediately after the council, since our chronicler, just as R, did eventually obtain a copy. It was therefore probably not by coincidence that a few lines of the sermon were inserted in the copy of the *constitutiones* which precedes our letter in the Giessen MS, between c.70 and *Ad liberandam* (fol. 57va).[16] Similarly, the sermon is found in connection with the constitutions in Paris, B.N. MS lat. 12249 (from Saint-Germain-des Prés), but after *Ad liberandam*.[17] — A fourteenth-century chronicler made the fine observation that in choosing the text of Luke 22.15 'Desiderio desideravi hoc pasca manducare vobiscum antequam patiar,' the pope 'ignorans horam sue mortis prophetavit.'[18]

31-32 *inter cetera pro redemptione terre sancte . . . exhortatus est:* Elsewhere the sermon is more precisely described as bearing also on Church reform; cf. R 62.15-16, the Reinhardsbrunn Chronicle, etc. Developing his text allegorically, Innocent spoke of the liberation of the Holy Land as his *pascha temporale*, and reform as his *pascha spirituale*.[19]

32 *patriarcha Iherosolimitanus:* Cf. R 70.37-41, who adds that the patriarch also 'quedam in laudem protulit domini pape.' His name was Radulfus.[20]

---

[15] An examination of the manuscript materials of the *editores Romani* (cf. S. Kuttner, *L'édition romaine des Conciles généraux et les actes du premier Concile de Lyon* [Miscellanea historiae pontificiae 3; Rome 1940] 13f.) is not possible at present. But a collation of R with *ed. Rom.* shows that the two texts came from different archetypes; one example must suffice here: R 70.35-6 . . . qui cum patre et spiritu sancto uiuit in secula seculorum. Amen] cui est honor et gloria in secula seculorum. Amen *ed. Rom et seqq.* — It is worth noting that the two sermons of Innocent III (on the second, which is spurious, see below, to lines 152-158) were inserted in *ed. Rom.* at the last moment. They are not mentioned in the table of contents of vol. 4, fol. a ijv, and occupy four unnumbered leaves intercalated in signature D between pp. 42 and 43. Page 42 (= fol. D iiiv), at the end of Innocent's *epistolae ad concilium spectantes* (= Mansi 22.956-68), has in the lower right corner the custos *DECRE-*, which refers to the beginning of p. 43 = fol. D iiii: DECRETA GENERALIS CONCILII LATERANENSIS . . . , but the printer marked the first of the inserted sheets again as D iiii.

[16] See above, I at n. 12.

[17] Luchaire, *ap.* Hefele-Leclercq 5 ii.1725.

[18] Jacques de Guise, *Annales Hannoniae*, ed. E. Sackur, MGH SS 30.272.29.

[19] Mansi 22.969E, 970 D; R 64.42ff., 66.4ff. For a brief analysis of the sermon see Hefele-Leclercq 5 ii.1321-3; Luchaire, *Le Concile de Latran* 18-20 (who finds 'rien de bien original').

[20] Cf. Potthast 4954; C. Eubel, *Hierarchia catholica medii aevi* I (2nd ed. Münster 1913) 275.

33-36 *Asseruit etiam ... expendere*: The awkward position of this sentence, resuming the pope's sermon after the speech of the patriarch of Jerusalem, raises the suspicion that in the original letter the writer may have inserted 'Asseruit etiam' *rell.* by afterthought, perhaps in the margin, to be read after '... exhortatus est' (32), and that the scribe misplaced the sentence. But it appears doubtful that the pope said all this 'in eodem sermone.' The text of *Desiderio desideraui* is much less specific on the Crusade; it bears out only the first of the two papal statements reported in G, although the writer could have refreshed his memory from the copy he had obtained after the session: while G 34-5 'quod si principes ... assumere' echoes a passage of the sermon ('Ecce ergo, dilectissimi fratres, totum me uobis committo ... paratus iuxta consilium vestrum ... personalem subire laborem et transire ad reges et principes'),[21] nothing is found there that corresponds to the promise G 35-6 'sin autem, in preparationem nauium ... expendere.' This promise, however, is contained in one of the provisions of the conciliar constitution 'Ad liberandam,' the so-called *Expeditio pro recuperanda terra sancta:*.[22]

> § Ne vero: ... ecce nos de his quae ... potuimus reservare triginta milia librorum in hoc opus concedimus et donamus; praeter navigium quod crucesignatis de Urbe atque vicinis partibus conferimus, assignaturi nihilominus ad hoc ipsum tria milia marcarum argenti ...

In the manuscripts of the constitutions, 'Ad liberandam' is always found after c.70, without number;[23] being rather a bundle of *ad hoc* ordinances and administrative measures enacted 'sacro approbante concilio,' it did not have the same character of general legislation as the dogmatic and the reform decrees.[24] In its full form the *Expeditio* seems to have been published separately, after the end of the council, on 14 December 1215.[25] In any event, G indicates that part of the provisions for the Crusade were announced in the first, and others in the third session (see § 12), before they were cast into the final form as we know it.

Independent evidence for such a procedure exists in the text of the *Expeditio* which Roger of Wendover inserted in his account of the council; its

---

[21] Mansi 22.970B-C; R 65.25-30.
[22] Mansi 22.1059C-D; COD 244.30-36.
[23] Cf. Mansi 1058; COD 243; García, in *Trad.* 14 (1958) 487.
[24] In the First and the Second Council of Lyons, neither Innocent IV nor Gregory X were to publish their respective crusading decrees together with the conciliar *constitutiones*, cf. Kuttner, 'Conciliar Law in the Making,' *Miscellanea Pio Paschini* (Lateranum N. S. 15; Rome 1949) 48-9.
[25] Potthast 5012. The date (18 kal. jan. an. 18) is based on the printing in L. Cherubini's *Bullarium* (1585; 1617), whence it passed in all later editions of the Roman *Bullarium*. The source of Cherubini's text is, however, unknown; all other traditions are undated.

difference from the published form of 'Ad liberandam' has thus far escaped the attention of scholars. Without distinguishing sessions, Wendover reports that all prelates were assembled and seated according to rank, and that the pope preached a *sermo exhortationis*; then sixty (!) *capitula* were recited, and 'tandem de negotio Crucifixi et subsidio terrae sanctae verbum praedicationis exorsus subiunxit dicens: "Ad haec sane ne quid ... (ends:) ... ad salutem. Amen".'[26] In Wendover's text, whatever must have preceded the words 'Ad haec' is unfortunately not preserved. But what is more important, the lengthy document shows a partly different sequence of sections than the official text of 'Ad liberandam'; there are also textual variants, some substantial; there are different phrases of transition and different clauses of conclusion for the individual sections; one short sentence on the Jews is recast into a long decree in the official text, and two of the latter's important clusters of ordinances are altogether absent from the text of Wendover.[27]

It is obvious, then, that this text represents a preliminary stage of 'Ad liberandam.' It includes the provision mentioned in G for the first session, but not the one G specifically reports in the third (G 160).[28] Thus it seems reasonable to conclude (1) that Roger of Wendover had a copy of that partial draft which was read in sess. I;[29] (2) that this part was read after the pope and the patriarch had spoken, and (3) that the narrator of G, in writing down his afterthought 'Asseruit etiam ... ,' contracted into one his recollection of two different phases (the pope's sermon and the decree) of the first day. It might even be argued that also the clause G 34-5 'quod si principes consulent ... ,' notwithstanding the verbal parallel in the pope's sermon, refers not to this sermon but to the passage 'ubi et nos personaliter, Domino annuente, disposuimus tunc adesse ... ' in the *Expeditio*;[30] if so, the whole 'Asseruit etiam ... ' would hang together and be in its right place; the words 'in eodem sermone' would then be G's only mistake.

---

[26] Roger of Wendover, *Chronica sive Flores historiarum*, ed H. O. Coxe III (London 1841) 342-4; ed. H. G. Hewlett (Rolls Series; London 1886-89) II 156-9. Repeated from Wendover in Matthew Paris, *Chronica majora*, ed H. R. Luard II (R. S.; London 1874) 631-3.

[27] For details, see Appendix C, below.

[28] It is interesting that also Rainier of Liège (d. 1230) in his Annals singles out only a few crusading provisions of Innocent III which correspond to G's report for the first session and are contained in Wendover's text (ed. G. H. Pertz, MGH SS 16 [1859] 674.49-54). See also the 14th-cent. account of MS Vat. lat. 3555, below, Appendix B, lines 19-21.

[29] Similarly, Matthew Paris was to include a draft, not the official text of the constitutions of the Council of Lyons (1245) in his *Chronica*, cf. Kuttner, 'Die Konstitutionen des ersten allgemeinen Konzils von Lyon,' *Studia et documenta historiae et iuris* 6 (1940) 97-100.

[30] Mansi 22.1059A; COD 243.22-5; Wendover ed. Coxe III 344.

37 *et his similia:* With these words G passes over the speech of the bishop of Agde on the Albigensian heresies, which is reported at this point in R 70.41-71.2.

3. Discussions on the Vacant See of Constantinople.
12 November 1215

38-39 *Sequenti die . . . de patriarcha apud Cp. statuendo:* G is the only source to give us this date for the beginning of the deliberations on a new patriarch for the see of Constantinople, vacant by the death (1211) of Thomas Morosini.[31] While R is silent on the whole affair, we have the fuller but garbled information from the *Chronica regia Coloniensis* that 'Constantinopoli duo in patriarchas electi Romam ad concilium venerunt. Quos ambos consilio cardinalium deposuit et tertium substituit et investivit et ad propriam sedem remisit.'[32] In fact, there was no *tertius substitutus* but one of the two rivals, Archbishop Gervase of Heraclea, was confirmed by Innocent. A bundle of letters concerning his confirmation and related matters existed in the lost volume of Innocent's Register for the eighteenth year.[33]

39 *quod ecclesie Romane numquam hactenus licuit:* Cf. *Chron. regia Colon.* (*loc. cit.*).: 'in hoc concilio . . . orientalis ecclesia, quod antea inauditum fuit, se subditam Romanae ecclesiae exhibuit.' Such assertions are hardly correct: it was not the 'oriental' Church but the Latin Church in the East which 'se subditam . . . exhibuit'; and 'de patriarcha . . . statuendo' (G) Innocent had given an example before with Morosini's elevation and various regulations concerning elections at Constantinople.[34] The similarity of phrase in G and the Cologne chronicler is striking, but any direct relationship is ruled out; for the Cologne chronicler knew more than G about the background of the election controversy (see above, to 38-9) but much less on the council in general; or else he could not have written that in the council, except for this affair, 'nichil dignum memoriae . . . actum est' (*loc. cit.*).

---

[31] For the whole election dispute (1211-15) see L. Santifaller, *Beiträge zur Geschichte des Lateinischen Patriarchats von Konstantinopel (1204-1261) und der venezianischen Urkunde* (Weimar 1938) pp. 28-30, and in particular R. L. Wolff, 'Politics in the Latin Patriarchate of Constantinople, 1204-1261,' *Dumbarton Oaks Papers* 8 (1954) 225-303, at 244-55.

[32] ed. G. Waitz, MGH *Script. in usum schol.* (1880) 237 (previously known as Godfrey of St. Pantaleon and so quoted in Mansi 22.1075). Cf. Wolff, *op. cit.* 252.

[33] *Rubricellae* in Theiner, VMS (above, II n. 31) I 66 Nos. 83-94; Potthast *5193-*5204.

[34] Cf. Wolff, *op. cit.* 227-9. The constitution 'Licet apostolice sedis' of May 1205 on patriarchal elections, Po. 2508, edited by Wolff 297 No. ii from Honorius III's 'Cum a nobis petitur' (22 March 1218, Pressutti 1174), where it is inserted, had actually been published before from Reg. Vat. 7 by L. Delisle, 'Lettres inédites d'Innocent III,' *Bibliothèque de l'École des Chartes* 34 (1873) 409 No. ix. Cf. Potthast, *Addenda* to 2508 (II p. 2047).

39-40 *multumque diuque sermo uertebatur:* G indicates the difficulties but not their outcome, and the letters to Gervase all seem to date from after the council. But the confirmation must have taken place before the last session (30 November), for in the official Notice of the council as well as in the Zurich list[35] *patriarcha C.politanus* is mentioned as one of the participants.

4. The Primatial Claims of Toledo. 13 November 1215

41-42 *litem que . . . hucusque durauit:* The 'Spanish question' at the IV Lateran Council was apparently of no interest to R, who passes it over in silence; but it has become one of the perennial points of controversy among Spanish historians ever since García de Loaysa in 1593 published 'ex libro manuscripto qui asseruatur in bibliotheca Ecclesiae Toletanae' an account of the pleadings entered for and against the primatial claims of Toledo 'in pleno consistorio' during the council, 'octavo idus octobris,' in speeches by Archbishop Rodrigo Jiménez and his opponents, the archbishops of Braga, Compostela, Tarragona (represented by the bishop of Vich), and Narbonne (who was absent but entered his plea the next day).[36] It is in particular Don Rodrigo's speech referring to the Spanish apostolate of St. James as an old wives' tale[37] which has engendered so much heat in the learned controversy; it has prompted modern defenders of the glory of Compostela not only to dismiss the speeches of the litigating metropolitans as pure invention, but even to deny the presence of the archbishop of Toledo and the hearing of his suit at the council.[38] Loaysa, it is true, embroidered his source, the 'Pars Concilij lateranij,' fol. 22^r-23^v of the 'Notule de primatu, nobilitate et dominio ecclesie Toletane' in MS 15-22 of the Chapter of Toledo (now Madrid, B. N. Vitr. 15 n.5 Hh. 144).[39] But critics have overshot their mark in discounting these pages as a fourteenth-century insertion into the mid-thirteenth-century codex:[40] the script clearly belongs to the thirteenth century.[41]

Whatever one may think of the authenticity of the speeches as reported in this text, there exists supporting evidence for several significant details

---

[35] Above, II n. 30.

[36] García de Loaysa, *Collectio conciliorum Hispaniae* (Madrid 1593) 287-92, reproduced in the conciliar collections, e.g. Mansi 22.1071-5.

[37] Mansi 1074D.

[38] Thus F. Fita, 'Santiago de Galicia: Nuevas impugaciones y nueva defensa (IV),' *Razón y Fe* 2 (1902) 35-45, where the early history of the controversy is given; *id.* (V), *ibid.* 178-95 and (VI-VII), *ibid.* 3 (1902) 49-61. Cf. also H. Flórez, *España sagrada* 3 (Madrid 1754) 39-58.

[39] Fita, *art. cit.* (V) 178-95, with a parallel printing of the original and Loaysa's text. (The Madrid shelfmark is given in Erdmann, *art. cit. infra* n. 42, p. 223 n. 2.)

[40] So Fita, *ibid.* 178.

[41] See the plates, *ibid.* 181, 193.

THE FOURTH LATERAN COUNCIL 137

of the colorful account;[42] and the fact that Archbishop Rodrigo was present at the council and presented his claim is unassailable. Another, much shorter Toledo document of the thirteenth century (inserted as fol. 1 in the 'De priuilegiis et primatu ecclesie Toletane' of Toledo MS 42-21) contains a brief statement of the complaint (*querimonia*) of Don Rodrigo in the consistory, the formal rejoinders of the above-named prelates, and a long list of 'testes de yspania qui ea audierunt et uiderunt.' All this is drawn up as an official record ('Notum igitur sit omnibus hominibus presentem paginam inspecturis') and dated 'Laterani viii. <ydus N>ouembris' in the year of the Incarnation 1215, the 18th year of the pontificate of Innocent III.[43] A comparison with the list of prelates in the Zurich MS shows that this document deserves full credence.[44]

Further confirmation comes from the important collection of *allegationes* which was prepared for the case of Braga against the claims of Toledo in 1216-17 (Lisbon, Arq. Nac. da Torre do Tombo, Coll. Especial pte. II, caixa 43) and in which reference is made to a papal document (Hadrian IV, JL 10141) 'quo usus fuit [*scil.* archieps. Toletanus] in iure cum in presentia domini In. illud legit contra nos et alios.'[45] By its first-hand testimony, G now provides additional corroboration for the hearing at the council, though it singles out only Compostela among the opponents of Toledo.

41 *Tercia uero die:* G gives the final solution for the problem of the date of these proceedings: 13 November. As indicated above, the basic Toledo document (MS 42-21) has a lacuna here, which the editors restored to read 'viii. <ydus N>ouembris.' From this date (= 6 November) specious objections have been raised against the 'pretended' connection with the Lateran Council,[46] even though 6 November could be called 'in the council,' since

---

[42] C. Erdmann, 'Mauritius Burdinus (Gregor VIII.),' *Quellen und Forschungen aus italienischen Archiven und Bibliotheken* 19 (1927) 207 n.1, 208 n.1, points out that the (in part fantastic) story told of Burdinus by Archbishop Rodrigo in his rebuttal of Braga's defense (Mansi 22.1072 E-73E; Fita 187-90) has a parallel in Rodrigo's book *De rebus Hispaniae* 6.28 (ed. Schott [1603]= 6.27 ed. F. de Lorenzana, *Patrum Toletanorum quotquot extant opera* 3 [Madrid 1793] 140-42) and that details of the Toledo account are borne out by the Braga dossier mentioned below.

[43] ed. Fita, *art. cit.* (IV) 40-43; J. F. Rivera, 'Personajes hispanos asistentes en 1215 al IV Concilio de Letrán,' *Hispania sacra* 4 (1951) 335-55, at 336-7. The letters within pointed brackets are supplied by the editors. See also J. Gorosterratzu, *Don Rodrigo Jiménez de Rada* (Pamplona 1925) 160-76, at 169f.

[44] Gorosterratzu, *op. cit.* 166-8 and Rivera, *art. cit.* in refutation of Fita's arguments against the authenticity, *art. cit.* (IV) 44-5; (VII) 52-7.

[45] C. Erdmann, *Papsturkunden in Portugal* (Abh. Ges. der Wiss. Göttingen N. F. 20.3; Berlin 1927) 383 No. 13 and note; on the Braga dossier in general see *ibid.* 105-9, 142, 381-4. For other 12th-cent. antecedents of the great suit see J. F. Rivera Recio, 'La primacía eclesiástica de Toledo en el siglo xii,' *Anthologica annua* 10 (1962) 11-87.

[46] Fita, *art. cit.* (IV) 44.

Innocent had summoned it for November 1st. At any rate, 'viii. ouembris' must be a corruption (of an original 'ydibus nouembris'?), and it can easily be seen how 'oūbris' became 'octobris' in the derivative texts of Toledo MS 15-21 and Loaysa.

43 *dirimere et . . . diffinire conabatur:* Innocent tried but failed to impose an equitable solution: we know that the litigation continued under Honorius III and beyond.

5. *The Case of Raymond VI of Toulouse. After 13 November 1215*

While R 73.3-8 offers merely a rather vague, and in part even incorrect statement on the decision announced by Innocent III at the closing session of 30 November, G shows himself better informed of the fact that the papal sentence against Raymond of St. Gilles, count of Toulouse, was but the last act in a long drama, and that it was preceded, during the council, by considerable manoeuvering and debate. On the other hand, G misses out on a speech concerning the Albigensians in the first session, which is mentioned by R (see above, to line 37).

44 *pluribus diebus tractatum est*: The anonymous continuator of Guilhem de Tudèle's *Chanson de la croisade contre les Albigeois* gives us a dramatic recital of these protracted debates, the pleas and counterpleas by which the reluctant pope was finally swayed to pronounce judgment against Raymond.[47] The *Chanson* is not only a piece of great literary quality but certainly—with all due allowance for poetic licence and for its Albigensian bias—based on first-hand information.[48] Also those contemporary chroniclers who were hostile to the count of Toulouse report that 'fuerunt ibi aliqui . . . qui pro restitutione dictorum comitum laborabant' (Pierre des Vaux-de-Cernay)[49] and that Innocent 'comitem Sancti Egidii, qui vocabatur Tolosanus, et eius filium damnatos de heresi videbatur velle restituere ad terras suas . . . ' (Guillaume le Breton).[50] Innocent's desire for a policy of conciliation and for a fair procedure are apparent throughout his acts, from 1209 to the council; this desire had led him more than once to oppose the actions of his own leg-

---

[47] *La Chanson de la croisade contre les Albigeois* ed. P. Meyer (Société de l'Histoire de France; Paris 1875-79) verses 3150-3665; ed. E. Martin-Chabot (Les Classiques de l'hist. de France au moyen âge; Paris 1931-61) II 40-89, sections 143-151.

[48] Cf. P. Belperron, *La croisade contre les Albigeois et l'union de Languedoc à la France* (Paris 1942) 306.

[49] *Petri Vallium Sarnaii monachi Hystoria Albigensis* ed. P. Guébin and E. Lyon (Soc. de l'Hist. de France; Paris 1926-39) II 261-2, § 571; ed. M. Bouquet, *Recueil des historiens des Gaules et de la France* 19 (1833; 1880) 104, c.83. This chapter also in Mansi 22.1069.

[50] *Gesta Philippi Augusti* c. 216, ed. H. F. Delaborde, *Oeuvres de Rigord et de Guillaume le Breton* I (Paris 1882) 306. Repeated in Aubrey of Trois-Fontaines' *Chronica* (ed. P. Scheffer-Boichorst, MGH SS 23 [1874] 904), whence Mansi 22.1082.

ate and the other leaders of the Albigensian crusade;[51] it had dictated his interim decision of 2 April 1215, to bestow on Simon of Montfort only a wardship of the conquered lands ('ut eas custodias et defendas') and to leave the final disposition of the case to the coming council.[52]

45-46 *et ob hoc de heresi accusatus:* This reflects correctly the attitude of Innocent III before the conciliar sentence, cf. his letter *Licet Raimundus* of May/June 1212,[53] 'quia tamen nondum est damnatus de heresi,' and the cautious language of the sentence itself (see below); whereas Guillaume le Breton calls the count and his son already before the sentence of the council 'damnatos de heresi' (see above).

46-47 *per regem Francie . . . amisit:* G erroneously believes that Philip Augustus had taken part, or even the lead, in the Albigensian crusade.

47 *signatos:* i. e. *cruce signatos;* so also in line 159, likewise in other sources.[54]

48-49 *comes cum uxore sua . . . extitit presens:* It is known from the *Chanson* and Pierre des Vaux (§ 571 [c.83]) that the count of Toulouse, the young count (Raymond VII), the count of Foix, and other barons had come to the council to plead their case. The presence of the countess—whose possessions, too, were at stake (see line 52) —is nowhere else recorded. G had a special reason to mention her, since she was the sister-in-law of his own king: of the sisters of Pedro II of Aragon, Eleanor was married to Raymond of Toulouse and Constance was the queen of Frederick II.

49-50 *et cruce signatus est:* Raymond himself had taken the cross against the heretics, cf. *Chanson* v. 264.[55]

50-57 *dominus papa . . . expectans:* This summarizes the final sentence (Potthast 5009), without saying when it was actually passed and made public. According to R 73.3-8 this was done in Innocent's speech at the opening of the third session, 30 November, but of this sermon we have only the short *rubricella* for the lost entry in the papal Register,[56] and other narrative sources

---

[51] Cf. H. Tillmann, *Papst Innocenz III.* (Bonn 1954) 189-200; A. P. Evans, 'The Albigensian Crusade,' in K. M. Setton, *A History of the Crusades* II (ed. R. L. Wolff and W. Hazard, Philadelphia 1962) 297-8, 304-5; O. Hageneder, 'Studien zur Dekretale "Vergentis" (X. V, 7, 10),' *Zeitschrift der Savigny-Stiftung für Rechtsgeschichte*, Kan. Abt. 49 (1963) 158-61; id., 'Das päpstliche Recht der Fürstenabsetzung,' *Archivum historiae pontificiae* 1 (1963) 60-69.

[52] Potthast 4967: Pierre des Vaux, *Hyst. Albig.* § 556 (Guébin II 250; = c. 82, Bouquet 19.102; Mansi 22.938); cf. Potthast 4968-69.

[53] PL 216.613C-614A (Potthast 4517). Cf. also *Chanson* v. 3482 ed. Meyer (= 149.4 ed. Martin-Chabot), where Innocent calls the count a true Catholic.

[54] E. g. *Hyst. Albig.* § 571 (c. 83); Rainier of Liège, MGH SS 16.674.16, 40, 50.

[55] Cf. Meyer's note, II 520 (to p. 15 n.2); Martin-Chabot I 39 n. 6.

[56] Theiner, VMS I 63 No. 14. Cf. below, to lines 152-8.

do not specify the day.[57] In its written form, the sentence was published only after the council, on 14 December 1215, as a general *ordinatio*,[58] beg. 'Quantum ecclesia laborauerit,' with the address 'Uniuersis Christifidelibus ad quos littere iste peruenerint.' Probably on the same day, special mandates in execution of the judgment concerning the count and the countess went out to the archbishop of Narbonne and Simon de Montfort;[59] the mandates in the case of the count of Foix were issued on 21 December.[60] The full text of the general sentence itself became known only in the eighteenth century when De Vic and Vaissete published it from an original bull (Baluze Arm. 385) in their *Histoire générale de Languedoc*.[61] Among the thirteenth-century canonists it circulated in a truncated form, without address or date. This tradition is represented above all by the *Compilatio IV* of Johannes Teutonicus, where *Quantum ecclesia* appears as c.1 of the title *De hereticis* (5.5.1, inscribed 'Idem'),[62] but also by some manuscripts where it is found appended to the Lateran constitutions: so in Paris MS lat. 12249 (fol. 129^{rv}, from St.-Germain-des Prés), Kassel MS jur. 11 (no foliation), Rouen MS 706 (fol. 268^v, from Jumièges),[63] and—with the last two sentences missing—in the codex of the Abbey of Lyre (Normandy) from which it was published in 1666 by d'Achéry.[64] This manuscript, no longer traceable,[65] seems to have been closely related to the one from St.-Germain.[66] [See Additional Note, p. 178.]

---

[57] See, however, *infra* at n. 121 for the Chronicle of St. Martin's of Tours.

[58] So the *rubricella* in Theiner, VMS I 63 No. 15: 'Uniuersis Christifidelibus significatur ordinatio facta quod comes Tholosanus . . . '

[59] Theiner Nos. 16-17; Potthast 5010-11.

[60] Theiner Nos. 19-20; Potthast 5014-15.

[61] (Paris 1730-45) III, preuves p. 251; new ed. by A. Molinier, VIII (Toulouse 1879) 681. The text is badly reproduced in Bouquet 19.598. Another original exists in Paris, Archives Nationales J. 430 n.13, cf. Guébin-Lyon, *Petri . . . Hyst. Albig.* II 263 n.1 (cited as 'Trésor des chartes, Bulle contre les hérétiques n°. 13' by Molinier, *Hist. gén. de Languedoc* V 474 n.1).

[62] ed. Antonius Augustinus (Agustín), *Antiquae collectiones decretalium* (Lérida 1576) fol. 24rb-24va; Friedberg, *Quinque Compilationes antiquae* (Leipzig 1881) 147.

[63] Cf. Luchaire, 'Un document retrouvé,' *Journ. des savants* 1905 p. 560 (= Hefele-Leclercq 5 ii. 1725); García (above, I n. 13), *Trad.* 14.487.

[64] L. d'Achéry, *Spicilegium* 7 (Paris 1666) 210; 2nd ed. (1723) 1.707 (reference in Potthast 5009 not correct); whence reproduced e. g. in Mansi 22.1069.

[65] It is not among the bulk of the abbey's MSS in the Bibliothèque Municipale of Évreux, nor apparently among the scattered books from Lyre which ended up in Rouen or Paris, listed by H. Omont in *Catalogue général des manuscrits . . . , Départements* 2 (Paris 1888) 383 nn. 2-3 and G. Nortier, in *Revue Mabillon* 48 (1958) 16-19.

[66] According to d'Achéry, the Lyre MS contains the traditional brief Notice of the council, 'Anno ab incarnatione . . . ,' ending ' . . . non fuit certus numerus comprehensum. In ea Synodo fuerunt haec instituta quae sequuntur, *videlicet* (d'Achéry adds) *Canones ejusdem Concilii et sub finem post orationem Innocentii Papae*: Sententia de terrà Albigensi. Quantum ecclesia . . . videbitur expedire.' This sequence corresponds to Paris lat. 12249

In the original document,⁶⁶ᵃ the pope speaks 'sacro consulto concilio' (*Comp. IV* has 'sacri concilii consilio'), but Pierre des Vaux's *Hystoria Albigensis* records a significant qualification, 'approbante pro maiori ac saniori parte sacrosancto concilio in hunc modum ordinavit ... '; the lack of unanimity is also apparent in Guillaume le Breton, who states that against the pope's original intentions (cf. at n. 50, above) 'universum fere concilium reclamabat.'⁶⁷

50-52 *dominus papa xl. marcas ... in sustentationem*: G mentions only the annual pension, giving the erroneous figure of 40 marks instead of 400 (so the original, Potthast 5009); the chief point, however, of the decision, 'ab eius [*scil.* terre] dominio, quod utique praue gessit, perpetuo sit exclusus,'⁶⁸ is left to be inferred from the adjudication of the lands to Simon of Montfort (lines 54-5). This has a certain parallel in the elliptic accounts of Pierre des Vaux ('statuit ... quod Tolosa civitas et alie terre a crucesignatis obtente concederentur comiti Montis Fortis')⁶⁹ and R 73.5-8 (' ... et mandante ut terram ipsius a comite Montisfortis acceptam [!] custodire idem comes ... deberet'), both of whom do not even mention the annuity for Raymond. R is particularly inadequate in having Innocent speak of the count of St. Gilles 'qui lapsus fuerat in heresim' (73.4), for the tenor of the papal *ordinatio* avoids an explicit condemnation of the count for heresy: in the decisive clause, 'ut Raimundus Tolosanus comes, qui culpabilis repertus est in utroque, ... ab eius dominio ... sit exclusus,'⁷⁰ the sentence refers back to the opening clause, 'Quantum ecclesia laborauerit ... ad exterminandum hereticos et ruptarios de prouincia Narbonensi ... ,'⁷¹ and the phrase 'culpabilis in utroque' leaves it open, with almost studied ambiguity, whether Raymond was found *culpabilis*, 'negligent' in exterminating the heretics and routiers, or *culpabilis*, 'guilty' as a heretic and leader of rou-

---

(as given by Luchaire *loc.cit.*), while in the Kassel and Rouen MSS *Quantum ecclesia* follows immediately after *Ad liberandam* and is in turn followed by the brief Notice. [Possibly Par. lat. and d'Achéry's MS are identical; see Additional Note, p. 178.]

⁶⁶ᵃ All quotations are from De Vic-Vaissete (ed. Molinier). Friedberg in his edition of 4 *Comp.* 5.5.1 used the faulty reprint of Bouquet 19.598 for collating the decretal text with the 'original'; and even these collations are unreliable. In the notes which follow, variant readings of the decretal text (from Agustín and Friedberg) will be recorded (= D). H. J. Warner, *The Albigensian Heresy* II (London 1928) 88-9 merely reproduces d'Achéry's edition, cf. Guébin-Lyon *loc. cit.* (n. 61).

⁶⁷ *Hyst. Albig.* § 572 (Guébin II 262; = c. 83 Bouquet); *Gesta Phil. Aug.* c. 216 (Delaborde I 306).

⁶⁸ utique *om.* D.

⁶⁹ *Hyst. Albig. loc. cit.*

⁷⁰ Raimundus—qui] quoniam R. quondam comes Tolosanus D   utrisque D.

⁷¹ exterminandos D   ruptarias D (?)

tiers himself. If the second were meant, 'reus in utroque' would have been the proper technical term. The continuation, ' . . . (in utroque) nec umquam sub eius regimine terra posset in pacis et fidei statu seruari,'[72] points in the same direction, especially if taken together with the leniency shown in the granting of a pension. Raymond emerged from the council as somehow *culpabilis*, but not a convicted heretic, as the *rubricella* for the lost Register entry, some chroniclers, and some modern historians would have it.[73]

50 *ultra mare perpetuo mansuro:* In the sentence, Raymond was merely ordered to stay 'extra terram ipsam in loco idoneo ubi dignam agat penitentiam de peccatis';[74] G must have conjectured the 'ultra mare' because of the preceding 'cruce signatus' (49-50).

52-53 *Comitisse uero . . . assignauit:* In the *ordinatio* this part of the sentence provides that 'uxor uero ipsius comitis . . . terras ad suum dotalicium pertinentes integre habeat et quiete' because of her good reputation as a 'catholica mulier et honesta'; but she must have these lands watched so that 'per ipsas negotium pacis et fidei non ualeat perturbari,' and, as an alternative, 'uel pro illis secundum apostolice sedis arbitrium recompensationem accipiat competentem.'[75] In a letter of the same day the archbishop of Narbonne was ordered to assign 150 marks to the countess from the castle of Beaucaire (Potthast 5010). G 'quicquid tenuit de rege Francie ultra Iordanem' seems again to be a conjecture, similar to the 'ultra mare' (line 50).

53-54 *Ut dicitur . . . ei dimitteret:* this is frankly a rumor.

54-55 *Comes uero . . . tenebit:* In reporting the assignment of the conquered lands of Raymond to Simon of Montfort, G wrongly assumes that Simon was to hold them as papal fief. This was indeed what Montfort had wished for a long time,[76] but the *ordinatio* provides expressly that the land

---

[72] posset] potuit D

[73] Theiner, VMS I 63 No. 15 ' . . . propter heresim'; Guillaume le Breton, *Gesta Phil. Aug.* c. 216: 'comitem . . . et eius filium damnatos de heresi . . . ' (cf. at n. 50, above); *Chronicon S. Martini Turonensis* (c. 1225): ' . . . Raimundus quoque comes Tolosanus et filius suus Raimundus tanquam heretici condempnantur' (ed. O. Holder-Egger, MGH SS 26 [1882] 466.26-7). Some recent writers, who otherwise give very fine interpretations of the case against Raymond, still describe the sentence as establishing *inter al.* his 'guilt' as a heretic: so Tillmann, *op. cit.* (n. 51) 198; Hageneder, 'Studien . . . ' (*cit.* n. 51) 160 (but more cautiously *ibid.* n. 75: 'als hereticus und ruptarius oder deren Förderer'); id., 'Das päpstliche Recht . . . ' 69 n. 52. Correctly Evans, *op. cit.* 307: 'guilty of harboring heretics and *routiers*'; see also Belperron, *op. cit.* (n. 48) 307, 309 ('jugement de Salomon'). — For the relations between the disposal of Raymond's case and the general legislation of the council (const. 3) on the forfeiture of rulers' rights by negligence in uprooting heresy see Hageneder, 'Studien . . . ' 162ff.

[74] de peccatis] deportatus D (!)

[75] uel—competentem *om.* D (not noted in Friedberg's *app. crit.*)

[76] Cf. his letter in Innocent's *Reg.* 12.109 (PL 216.142A-B), the letter of the papal leg-

is to be given to him 'saluo per omnia catholicorum iure uirorum, mulierum et ecclesiarum . . . , ut eam teneat ab iis a quibus est de iure tenenda,'⁷⁷ that is, to be held as a fief from the king of France.⁷⁸ On the other hand, R 73.5-8 speaks only of a custody (' . . . ut terram . . . custodire idem comes usque ad mandatum suum deberet'), which is obviously a confusion with the next part of the *ordinatio* (see below) or with the custody that had been given to Montfort earlier in April (see above, at n. 52).

56-57 *Filius enim . . . expectans:* Unfortunately G is mutilated here by two omissions: the scribe left a blank after 'enim' and inadvertently dropped a line or more after 'expectans.' The *ordinatio* reads: 'residua terra que non fuit a crucesignatis obtenta custodiatur ad mandatum ecclesie per uiros idoneos . . . ut prouideri possit unico adolescenti filio prefati comitis Tolosani, si talem se studuerit exhibere quod . . .' etc;⁷⁹ but 'residua terra' is rather vague; Pierre des Vaux refers this to the count's possessions in the Provence.⁸⁰ The *Chanson* dwells at length in moving terms on Innocent's solicitude for the 'child' (vv. 3631-66).

57-59 *Multa talium . . . eundo:* In view of the colorful account of the *Chanson*, and of the chroniclers' hints at disagreement in the council (cf. at n. 67 above), one might have welcomed if G had reported some of these rampant rumors. For his classical quotations see the notes to the text.

6. The Dedication of the Church of S. Maria in Trastevere. Sunday, 15 November 1215

60 *Prima dominica post Martini:* This is 15 November 1215.

61-62 *Summus pontifex ad consecrandam ecclesiam b. Marie . . . conducitur:* The thirteenth-century part of the *Necrologium ecclesiae b. Mariae trans Tiberim*, first published in excerpt by H. Bresslau in 1885, and again in full by P. Egidi in 1908, has an entry under *xvii kal. dec.*: 'Eodem die dominus Innocentius papa III consecrauit eccl. s. Marie Transtiberim.'⁸¹ Roman topographers have therefore been aware that a consecration of the church took

---

ates, *Reg.* 12.108 (*ibid.* 140D), and the papal replies of 11-12 November 1209, *Reg.* 12.122, 123 (Potthast 3833-4; cf. Tillmann, *op. cit.* 190 and n. 19).

⁷⁷ uirorum] et *add.* D   ab iis *om.* D   de iure est *tr.* D

⁷⁸ Cf. Hageneder, 'Studien . . .' 160.

⁷⁹ comitis prefati *tr.* D

⁸⁰ *Hyst. Albig.* § 572 (c. 83).   Cf. Belperron, *op. cit.* 309; also Martin-Chabot's commentary, *Chanson* II 86 n. 2.

⁸¹ ed. H. Bresslau, in *Neues Archiv der Gesellsch.* etc. 11 (1885) 99-101, at p. 101; ed P. Egidi, *Necrologi e libri affini della provincia Romana* I (Fonti per la storia d'Italia; Rome 1908) 100-01. — Our thanks are due to Fr. Leonard Boyle, O. P. for having pointed out this text, together with other material on S. Maria in Trastevere.

place on some 15th of November in the pontificate of Innocent III,[82] but without paying any attention to the notice of the Fourth Lateran Council in one of the most widely read history books of the Middle Ages, the *Chronicon pontificum et imperatorum* of Martin of Troppau (Martinus Polonus, d. 1278): '... tempore huius concilii consecravit ecclesiam b. (*al.* sancte) Marie trans Tyberim.'[83] Martin is commonly belittled as uncritical by modern historians; for once, however, the eyewitness G proves him to be correctly informed.

61 *ad consecrandam ecclesiam:* S. Maria in Trastevere, the old *titulus Calixti* (*et Iulii*), was completely rebuilt by Innocent II, beginning in 1139.[84] When Innocent III proceeded now, over seventy years later, to a new consecration, he must have decided that canon law required this to be done. The common doctrine of canonists, as developped on the basis of Gratian's *Decretum*,[85] counted a rebuilding of the walls *a fundamentis* among the reasons that made an *iteratio consecrationis* necessary; also, in all cases where it was doubtful for lack of records whether a church had been consecrated before, a new consecration was in order. Of the reconstruction under Innocent II, Cardinal Boso says in his *Vita*, 'totam renovavit et construxit';[86] and 'novis muris funditus reconstruxit' is the expression used by the contemporary Benedict of St. Peter's (Benedictus canonicus) in his *Liber poli-*

---

[82] C. Cecchelli, *S. Maria in Trastevere* (Collezione Le Chiese di Roma; Rome s. a. [c. 1932]) 36; M. Armellini, *Le Chiese di Roma*, nuova ed. a cura di C. Cecchelli (Rome 1942) II 786; and cf. the standard guide books.

[83] ed. H. Weiland, MGH SS 22 (1872) 438.13; incorporated in the 15th-century continuation of the *Liber Pontificalis*, ed. L. Duchesne II (Paris 1892; reprinted 1955) 452, *Vita* of Innocent III.

[84] Cf. Armellini-Cecchelli II 785. The date of completion (Innocent II died in 1143) is uncertain. N. Maurice-Denis and R. Boulet, *Romée ou le pélerin moderne à Rome* (3rd ed. Paris 1950) 657 give the years 1140-48, basing themselves probably on the last lines of the inscription of the pope's tombstone in S. Maria in Trastevere; ... QVI· PRESEn/TEM· ECCLesiAM· AD· HO/NOREm· DEI· GENETRICIS:/MARIE·SICVT·ESt·A·FVn/DAMEnTis·SVmpTibus· propriis·RE/NOVAVIT: sub·Anno·Domini·M°·C°:XL:7C·A D:M:CXL/VIII: (ed. Duchesne, *Lib. pont.* II 385 n.2; Armellini-Cecchelli 788 [I have expanded the abbreviations, except for the uncertain A D: which appears as AD in Duchesne]). But this inscription dates from the 14th century when the remains of Innocent II were transferred to the church from the Lateran basilica, and the meaning of 'etc. ad (A.D.?) m.cxlviii' remains obscure.

[85] *De cons.* D. 1 cc. 16, 18, 19, 24; cf. Rufinus, *Summa decretorum, de cons.* D.1 c.18 (ed. H. Singer, Paderborn 1902, p. 543) and—to cite only some of Innocent's contemporaries—Johannes Teutonicus, *Glossa ordinaria, de cons.* D.1 c.18 v. *altaria*, c.24 v. *innovata*; id. *Apparatus Comp. III, de dedic. eccl.* 3.31.3 (= X 3.40.4) v. *reconciliari* (Munich MS lat. 3879, fol. 232va); Tancred, *Gl. ord. Comp. III, ad loc.* (MS Vat. lat. 1377 p. 195^b); later, Bernard of Parma, *Gl. ord.* X 3.40.4 v. *reconciliari*, and (incorporating Tancred's gloss) Hostiensis, *Summa*, tit. *de consecr. eccl.* § *Et an sit iteranda* (ed. Venice 1570, fol. 306va no. 5.)

[86] *Lib. pont.* II 384.

THE FOURTH LATERAN COUNCIL 145

ticus.⁸⁷ But the tradition of rededication is confused. We can eliminate what G. Vasi, the teacher of Piranesi, wrote in the eighteenth century of S. Maria in Trastevere, in the text which accompanies his engravings of the *Magnificenze di Roma*: ' ... Innocenzo II. nato in questo Rione, nell'anno 1139. rinnovò la Chiesa tutta, ... e consacrolla con l'intervento di tuti li Padri del Concilio III. [*sic*] Lateranense generale';⁸⁸ obviously he applied to Innocent II the information from Martinus Polonus on Innocent III, and thereby managed to confuse two popes and three councils. However, the *Necrologium* of our church has two entries which must be taken into consideration:

> 9 Jan. (v. id. Ian.); Consecratio eccle. s. Marie   (13th cent.: erased)⁸⁹
> 22 May (xi. kal. Iun.); Dedicatio basilice s. Marie trans Tyberim per manum Alexander pontificis et cum episcopi .iiii. cardinalis .ii. scole Lateranensis omnibus   (12th cent.)⁹⁰

The meaning of the erased thirteenth-century notice is obscure, most probably it was a mere error; but the other entry, in the twelfth-century stratum, could reasonably be referred only to Alexander III.⁹¹ Scanning that pope's itinerary, we would then have to choose between the years 1161, 1166, 1167, 1178, 1179. Still, the record must somehow have been suspected in Innocent III's day. If this piece of mangled Latin was all the information available, it was certainly 'nec certa scriptura nec testis ... e quibus consecratio sciatur' as canon law required it.⁹² (In 1295 another jurist-pope, Boniface VIII, was to proceed similarly in reconsecrating S. Clemente, where the new structure had been completed and in use by 1125.⁹³)

61-62 *que ad Oleum fundentem nuncupata est:* The story of the *fons olei* which according to Dio Cassius 48.43 gushed forth at the military hospice (*taberna meritoria*) on or near this site in the year 753 A.U.C. was interpreted by Eusebius as a symbol of the graces that flowed to the nations from the coming of Christ;⁹⁴ it is mentioned in connection with S. Maria in Trastevere

---

⁸⁷ Cited *ibid.* n.1 and, in the full context, by C. Vogel, *Lib. pont.* III (1957) 138 from the edition of Duchesne-Fabre, *Le Liber Censuum de l'église Romaine* II (Paris 1910) 141ff. (at p. 169). On Benedict's *Liber politicus* (= *polyptychus*), its MSS, and the use made of it in the *Liber censuum*, cf. Duchesne, *Lib. cens.* I (1905) 3-4. The work was dedicated to Innocent II; Mabillon published part of it (not including the passage here quoted) as *Ordo* XI = PL 78.1026ff.

⁸⁸ *Delle Magnificenze di Roma antica e moderna Libro terzo, che contiene le Basiliche e Chiese antiche di Roma* (Rome 1753) p. xlviii.

⁸⁹ Bresslau, *art. cit.* 100; Egidi, *op. cit.* 88-9.

⁹⁰ Egidi 94 (without notes on the Latin of the entry); not in Bresslau's excerpts.

⁹¹ So cited in Armellini-Cecchelli II 786 n.2.   ⁹² *De cons.* D.1 c.16.

⁹³ Cf. L. Boyle, 'The Date of the Consecration of the Basilica of San Clemente,' *Archivum Fratrum Praedicatorum* 30 (1960) 417-27.

⁹⁴ *Chronicon*, PG 19.521 = PL 27.542.

IX

in the *Mirabilia* literature of the earlier Middle Ages, in the *Liber pontificalis* ('s. M. in Transtiberim ubi oleum fluxit'), and the *Liber censuum* ('ubi terra manavit oleum').[95] Pietro Cavallini placed the *taberna meritoria* and the oil well in his mosaic of the Nativity (1291) in the apse.[96] But G is the only source to indicate that the church was actually called by this title, 'Our Lady of the flowing oil.'

62-78 *honorificentissime conducitur . . . ad palatium reducitur:* The writer shows himself here at his literary best, in the way he describes the papal procession (62-6), the enthusiasm of the people (66-8), and the festive decoration of Trastevere (68-73). He decides to be brief about the consecration itself, which lasted almost all day (73-6), and the return of the procession in the evening (76-8).

62-66 *Romanorum nobilissimi . . . precedebant:* In the procession the heads of the Roman nobility precede clergy and people; the festive attire and music are described in biblical terms,[97] but the rare word *barrire* 'to roar like an elephant' (65) is unusual in such a context.

66-68 *Pueri . . . indesinenter:* In order to describe the quasi-liturgical participation of the people meeting the procession, G borrows effectively from the first antiphon for the distribution of the palms on Palm Sunday: 'Pueri Hebraeorum portantes ramos olivarum obviaverunt Domino clamantes et dicentes, Hosanna in excelsis.' The chant, of course, differs here; and the term 'pueri,' dictated by the model, need not be taken literally.

68 *ex altera parte pontis:* Trastevere.

69-73 *lampades . . . numerus:* The Italian style of street decoration and illumination on church festivals is still much the same today.

7. The Feast of the Dedication of Sts. Peter and Paul.
18 November 1215

80 *ad ecclesiam b. Petri et Pauli:* This refers, somewhat incorrectly, to St. Peter's basilica (cf. line 83); the title of the feast day, 'in dedicatione ba-

---

[95] *Mirabilia urbis Romae* cc. 8, 31; *Graphia aurea urbis* c.39: ed. R. Valentini and G. Zuchetti, *Codice topografico della città di Roma* III (Fonti per la storia d'Italia; Rome 1946) pp. 26, 64, 94; and in derivative texts, *ibid.* 125, 189. By mistake, the editors also cite (*ibid.* 26) the *Passio s. Calixti,* AS Oct. VI 439-40: this is a confusion with the Bollandists' introduction, AS *cit.* 422E. — *Lib. pont.* II 323 = III 168 (*Vita* of Calixtus II); *Lib. censuum* I 272. — Cf. C. Cecchelli, 'Fons olei,' *Capitolium* 1 (1925) 535-9 (not seen; reference kindly supplied by Dr. Peter Herde); Cecchelli, *S. Maria in Trastevere* 8-9; F. Castagnoli, C. Cecchelli *et al., Topografia e urbanistica di Roma* (Rome 1958) 244-5.

[96] Cf. Armellini-Cecchelli 790; Maurice-Denis and Boulet, *Romée* 661; Cecchelli *locc. citt.* (preceding note). Reproduction, e. g. in *Enciclopedia Italiana* 9 (1931) pl. CLXX (opposite P. Toesca's article, p. 547).

[97] Cf. notes 11-13 to the text (above, III).

THE FOURTH LATERAN COUNCIL 147

silicarum SS. Petri et Pauli' (cf. the Roman calendar for 18 November) explains the careless contraction in G.

8-10. *Second Session: The Question of the Empire; Proceedings on Otto's IV's Request for Absolution. 20 November 1215*

For this session, Richard of San Germano (R 71.5-72.43) has been thus far the only source of substantial value.[98] This is now supplemented by G, and it is only natural that the Sicilian and the German eyewitness should report in detail on the dramatic proceedings of this day: actually they both dwell at greater length on this than on any other session.[99] There exist strong parallels between the two accounts, but also significant disagreements, especially as regards the sequence of events in the agitated session and its conclusion.

8. *The Motions Introduced; First Clashes; Speech of the Marquess of Montferrat*

84 *vi. feria post octauam Martini:* Friday, 20 November; so also R 71.5-6, who calls this, however, 'ten days' after St. Martin's (cf. above, to line 14).

84-85 *iterum sollempnizatum est concilium*: More in R 71.7-12: the pope ascends the throne; silence is ordered, trumpets are sounded; short allocution of the pope.

85-86 *primum episcopus Palermitanus . . . fecit:* R 71.12 gives the initial of his name, B(erardus), but does not mention the reading of Frederick's letter. The object of the letter and the archbishop's speech are left quite undetermined in G, while R has 'super facto domini regis F. in Romanum imperatorem electi . . . est locutus' (71.14-6). From this, and from the final pronouncement of Innocent in the third session (G 181-3, R 73.12-15), it becomes apparent that Berard of Palermo was instructed to petition the pope in council for approbation of Frederick's imperial election by the German princes (Frankfurt, 5 December 1212; royal coronation by Archbishop Siegfried of Mainz, 25 July 1215).

---

[98] There exists a late, and substantially correct, summary in Jean Le Long's Chronicle of St. Bertin's, Ypres (14th cent.): ' . . . In hoc consilio lecte fuerunt epistole Othonis imperatoris quarti, sed excommunicati, ad s. concilium destinate quibus humiliter petebat absolvi. Sed multis ibidem racionibus ostensum est tam a domino papa quam a marchione Montisferrati quod absolvi non deberet' (ed. Holder-Egger, MGH SS 25.831, with note 13 pointing to the parallel in R). The direct source of the monk of Ypres cannot be determined.

[99] In the columns of Garufi's edition, R gives 74 lines to sess. II, as against 21 for sess. I (not counting the verbatim insertion of the opening sermon) and 22 for sess. III. In G the proportions are: 65 lines (of our edition) for sess. II, 24 for sess. I, and 46 for sess. III (not counting 46 lines for the events between sessions and 9 for those after the council).

86-88 *Postmodum quidam Mediolanenses . . . admitterentur:* Cf. R 71.18-21: 'Mediolanenses quidam . . . impetrata licentia uerbum uolebant facere pro Ottone.' The Milanese ambassadors, as G and R will presently tell us, were to plead for the absolution of the ex-Emperor ('quondam imperatoris' G 87) Otto IV from the several-years-old sentence of excommunication.[100] The aim of the Guelf diplomatic move was transparent—and it will be seen that Frederick's ambassadors came prepared to counter it—: if Otto were absolved by the pope in a formal session of the council, his repudiation and deposition by the German princes (Nuremberg, September 1211) and Frederick's subsequent election could be challenged; the question of the imperial succession would thus be kept in abeyance. The matter, then, was not as harmless as it would appear from the *Annales Placentini Guelfi,* according to which the ambassadors of the cities of Milan, Piacenza, Cremona, and Pavia came to the council, 'sperantes et credentes discordiam que est inter dominum Ottonem imperatorem et Fredericum Sicilie regem accordari debere pariter et pacisci'[101] — as though after all that had happened, after the battle of Bouvines and Frederick's coronation as *rex Romanorum*, one could still speak of a mere *discordia* to be settled by reconciliation between 'the Emperor Otto' and the 'King of Sicily.'

89-90 *multi archiepiscopi . . . reclamabant:* On the storm that broke loose at this point cf. also R. 71.21-22: 'quorum principium uerbi tumultus (tumultum *ed.*) contra clamantium impediuit.'

90 *et precipue marchio de Munferrato*: From here on the two accounts differ. According to R 71.22-36, the pope restores quiet ('ad maioris tamen imperium est sedatus' 22-3) and the Milanese ambassadors obtain permission to speak; they produce and read Otto's letter, to which then the Marquess of Montferrat replies (R 72.1ff). G, on the contrary, has the Marquess rise immediately after the shouting to make his formal and evidently prepared speech, in which he raises two sets of *exceptiones* (the technical term is used later on, in G 111): three procedural points to bar the admission of the Milanese as Otto's *legati* (G 91-5), and seven substantive arguments against Otto's absolution (95-105). Pope Innocent, after overruling the procedural *exceptiones*, comments on the substantive ones (106-111), and only then is Otto's letter read (111-119).

---

[100] According to the recent investigation by A. Haidacher, 'Über den Zeitpunkt der Exkommunikation Ottos IV. durch Papst Innozenz III.,' *Römische historische Mitteilungen* 3 (1960) 132-85, the complex chronological problem is to be answered thus: conditional *excommunicatio latae sententiae*, 18 January 1210 (Potthast 3880, with correction, II p. 2052); solemn declaratory sentence, 18 November 1210 (Potthast 4213, with wrong date; cf. Böhmer-Ficker-Winkelmann, *Regesten des deutschen Kaiserreichs* 5 iii [=BFW; Innsbruck 1892] No. 6099); repeated on Holy Thursday 1211 (Potthast *ante* 4213; BFW 6101b).

[101] ed. G. H. Pertz, MGH SS 18 (1863) 431.25-8.

THE FOURTH LATERAN COUNCIL 149

It is difficult to decide here which witness reports the proper sequence of events: either of them could have been mistaken in writing down afterwards what he remembered of the tumultuous day. But if we consider the quasi-judicial nature of the session, G is more convincing. Montferrat's challenge of the ambassadors' right to appear for the ex-emperor would in a formal trial have to be pleaded by way of *exceptiones dilatoriae*, and such were to be pleaded *in initio litis*,[102] i.e. before the adversaries could present their case; while in R 72.31-3 this challenge comes up only towards the end of the session: 'marchio ... ordine turbato responsi [i. e. when it was out of turn for him to speak] adiecit quod ipsi Mediolanenses uerbum facere pro Oddone non poterant' (did he raise the point here a second time?). As for Montferrat's denial of Otto's right to be absolved—technically a set of *exceptiones peremptoriae*—its proper moment would have been less rigidly fixed even in a formal trial;[103] but considering that G has more precise and complete information than R on the substance of these *exceptiones*, on the pope's intervention, and on the Milanese rejoinder (see below), we are probably entitled to accept his whole account of the order of procedural moves as more correct.

91-95 *Prima ... secunda ... tercia ... diuerteret:* Only one of these three reasons—abetting of heretics—has a parallel in R's report on the *ordine turbato* reply (see above) of the Marquess to the Milanese rejoinder later on in the session:' ... et ex eo maxime quod eorum ciuitas Patarenos foueret in fidei christiane contemptum' (R. 72.35-7). Of the other two, the charge of perjury remains unspecified in G; the third indicates that the Guelf cities attempted to make Frederick's conciliar delegate change sides, i. e. to commit technical prevarication.

95-96 *vii. de causis:* R has only six arguments given by Montferrat against an absolution of Otto (72.4-23); they are furthermore presented in a partly different sequence = G Nos. 1, 2, 7, 4, 6, 5, (No. 3 missing).

96-97 *Prima ... absolutionem:* R No.1 (72.6-8) mentions only the fact that Otto had not kept his previous oath[104] to the Roman Church; according to G, Montferrat said more pointedly that for this reason a new security by oath (*cautio iuratoria*) would be insufficient.

---

[102] Cf. Gratian, C.3 q.6 p.c.2, and the *Ordines iudiciarii* in general, e.g. Ricardus Anglicus c.38 (ed. L. Wahrmund, *Quellen zur Geschichte des römisch-kanonischen Processes im Mittelalter* 2.3 [Innsbruck 1915] p. 89); Tancred 2.5.1 (ed. F. Bergmann, *Pillii, Tancredi, Gratiae Libri de iudiciorum ordine* [Göttingen 1842] p. 140).

[103] According to Gratian *loc. cit.* also 'in initio litis'; but cf. the modifications and qualifications in the *Ordines*, e.g. Ricardus Anglicus *loc. cit.*, Tancred 2.5.3 (p. 143).

[104] The oath is in the *Regestum de negotio imperii*, ed. F. Kempf (Miscell. hist. pont. 12.21; Rome 1947) No. 192, p. 405.

97-98 *Secunda . . . satisfacere:* In R No. 2 (72.9-11) the nature of the *damna Romanae ecclesiae illata* is spelt out more clearly: 'quia propter que anathematis est uinculo innodatus[105] adhuc detinet nec reddidit ut iurauit'; i. e. the non-restitution of territories held by Otto in central Italy (the vexed question of the so-called *recuperationes*).

98-100 *Tercia . . . detineat occupata:* No parallel in R; the invasion of Frederick's Sicilian lands is meant.

100-101 *Quarta . . . captiuauerit:* R No. 4 (72.15-17) does not identify the bishop ('legatum alium episcopum') whom Otto had seized and put in chains. The capture of Bishop Otto of Münster and his captivity are told by several chroniclers;[106] thus, emendation of the scribal blunder 'Manifestime episcopum' in G (see *app. ad lin.* 100) was indicated.

101-102 *Quinta . . . fecerit:* Again, R No. 6 (72.21-3) gives no name ('quia quoddam monialium monasterium . . . destruxerit . . . '); for Quedlinburg (G 101) cf. the *Annales Marbacenses* s.a. 1213[107] and Otto's testament of 1218 (see below, to lines 142-5).

102-104 *Sexta . . . dixerit:* Cf. R No.5 (72.18-20); the Guelfs' use of the derisive term 'Pfaffenkönig' for young Frederick is well known.

104-105 *Septima . . . porrexerit:* Winkelmann[108] thus was correct in assuming that the less explicit passage in R No. 3 (72.12-14 'episcopum quemdam . . . nisus est fouere') must be referred to Bishop Waldemar of Schleswig, whose postulation to the metropolitan see of Bremen Innocent had rejected in 1208, excommunicating him at the same time. By 4 November 1208 Waldemar was deposed from his original see, and in July 1209 the pope had asked Otto IV, then emperor-elect, to expel the intruder. But the next year, when Innocent confirmed the postulation of Bishop Gerard of Osnabrück—the brother of Otto of Münster—to the see of Bremen, 'dux Bernardus (as we read in the *Annales Stadenses*) Woldemarum quasi ex voluntate imperatoris Bremam reduxit.'[109] More specifically we learn from G that the ex-emperor had invested the intruder with the *regalia* of the archbishopric—a charge of Montferrat's which Otto's spokesmen did not deny (see G 145-6).

---

[105] que *om. Garufi*   innodato *Garufi*.
[106] *Chron. regia Coloniensis*, ed. Waitz, MGH SS *in usum schol.* (1880) 291, 293; cf. 235, 236; *Annales Stadenses*, ed. I.M. Lappenberg, MGH SS 16 (1859) 356.
[107] ed. Pertz, MGH SS 17 (1861) 173.
[108] *Op. cit.* (above, I n. 16) II 423.
[109] Potthast 3299, 3300 (postulation quashed, excomm.; cf. also 3256, 3354); 3530 (deposition); 3760-1 (mandate to Otto); 4116-18 (confirm. of Gerard, 30 October 1210); *Annales Stadenses*, MGH SS 16.355. Cf. Eubel, *Hierarch. cath.* I 145, 455; also H. Krabbo,' Die deutschen Bischöfe auf dem vierten Laterankonzil,' *Quellen und Forsch. aus ital. Arch. und Bibl.* 10 (1907) 292-3: Gerard was unable to attend the council.

9. Intervention of the Pope; Otto IV's Letter

106-107 *Tandem . . . compescuit:* This intervention of Innocent III is very different in tone from what we read in R 72.24-5 after Montferrat's speech, 'Que omnia summus pontifex auscultans aura benigna et approbans . . . ': in G, the pope at this point restrains ('compescuit') the Marquess 'et alios contra dominum Ottonem clamantes'—the last clause may refer back to the clamor by 'innumerable prelates' before Montferrat's speech (G 89-90) or else may indicate more shouting after he ended.

107-109 *dicens quod . . . audiantur:* The pope goes on to say that the guilty as well as the innocent must be heard by the council. This 'culpabilis et inculpabilis' we have to understand in the light of canonical procedure: regardless of the merits of Otto's case, he is entitled—through his proctors—to a hearing. In other words, the pope here overrules by a *sententia interlocutoria* the procedural objections (*exceptiones dilatoriae*) raised against the Milanese spokesmen.

109-110 *adhiciens etiam . . . recipiendus esset:* This conclusion of the procedural ruling is a remarkable instance of Innocent's highly personal and unceremonious manner of speech, here capping a biblical allusion (Ps. 48. 3) with a joke on the Devil's repentance—breaking perhaps into *volgare*,[110] as could be inferred from the continuation 'et in latino sermone . . . '(110). — If all this is missing in R, we have to remember that Richard of San Germano records only the second part of Montferrat's speech, not his preliminary exceptions of which the pope disposes here, and that according to R the Milanese had already introduced Otto's letter before that speech (cf. above, to line 90).

110-111 *Et in latino . . . interpretari cepit:* The pope's judicial summing-up of Montferrat's arguments against the ex-emperor's case (technically, his *exemptiones peremptoriae*) is also reported in R 72.25-6: ' . . . ea per ordinem ipsis Mediolanensibus de uerbo explicauit (replicauit *ed.*) ad uerbum'; but it is there differently colored by the preceding 'auscultans aura benigna et approbans.' Innocent's great ability to sum up facts and arguments in judicial hearings was often admired by his contemporaries.[111]

111-113 *Quibus expletis . . . imperatoris:* For the different order of proceeding reported by R see above, to line 90.

113-116 *premissa salutatione . . . exhibitionem:* The full initial greeting here recorded confirms the list of addressees given in R 71.26-9. But whether Otto's letter was indeed directed, as R 71.29-31 has it, to the cardinals etc. 'ac toti sacri concilio ad sui excusationem in modum querele contra dominum

---

[110] There are instances of his having done so on other occasions, cf. Tillmann, *op. cit.* (n. 51) 50 n. 64, 154 n. 11.

[111] Testimonies in Tillmann 49f.

papam,' i.e. whether Otto really tried to appeal from pope to council, is very doubtful: what follows has rather the ring of a humble petition ('supplicando deuote' G 116-7; 'ut ... supplicare deberent' R 71.35). Even though it is true that Otto had friends in the cardinals' college,[112] he can not have been under the illusion that the council might entertain a *querela contra papam*.

116-119 *In sequentibus ... spoponderint:* R 71.31-6 likewise specifies four points in Otto's letter: (1) petition to intercede for his absolution, (2) protestation of repentance, (3) promise to abide by whatever the pope will order him to do ('stare mandatis' G 118; 'ad mandatum ipsius cum iuramento seruandum' R 71.32-3); and (4) the offer of an oath to be taken by his ambassadors as sureties ('quod ... pro ipso spoponderint' G 118-9; 'adiecta insuper quam placeret ei [*sc.* papae] fideiussoria cautione' R 71.34-5). Both *spondere* and *cautio fideiussoria* are technical terms for suretyship, in contrast to the *cautio iuratoria* by Otto himself of which Montferrat had spoken (G 96).[113]

10. *Defense of Otto; End of the Session*

120-147 *Perlectis litteris ... postulauit:* The speech in defense of Otto is not given in R, where we read (always keeping in mind that R reports a different sequence of events) that after the pope's summing-up of Montferrat's arguments the Milanese want to reply (72.28-30); but the Marquess 'eorum principio obstitit' and speaks again, 'ordine turbato responsi' (71.30-31). According to G, however, the spokesman of the Milanese *nuntii* presents a point-by-point rebuttal, first of the three objections raised against their own qualification (G 121-30), then of the objectons against Otto's request for absolution (131-47).

121-30 *Contra primum ... debita:* Only the second of Montferrat's three preliminary points, the alleged abetting of heretics (G 92), is countered in this rebuttal by something more substantial that a mere denial of facts: the speaker describes the measures taken in Milan against heretics and those who harbor them ('quoniam ubicumque ... dare oporteret' 124-8). On the first point, the alleged perjury of the *nuntii*, proof to the contrary is offered (122-3) but never forthcoming.

131-45 *Contra articulos ... perceperint:* The speaker attempts a specific defense of Otto against Montferrat's seven *articuli* only on the first, second, and fifth count (lines 96, 97, 101 above); on two of these the pope pronounces immediately: (1) That Otto broke his sworn promises is a fact which admits

---

[112] Cf. Winkelmann, *Philipp von Schw. und Otto* II 421 with n. 6; more material in Tillmann 149.

[113] Cf. *Dig.* 2.2.3.3; 17.1.6, 46 etc.(*spondere*); *Dig.* 18.1.72 pr.; 35.3.3.1 (*cautio fideiussoria*); Cod. 1.49.1.1; 12.21.8.1 (*cautio iuratoria*).

THE FOURTH LATERAN COUNCIL 153

of no debate ('respondit papa quod ei constaret' 133), consequently the spokesman has to change his plea to a petition for forgiveness and an offer of amends ('Penitet igitur . . . , querit ueniam et offert satisfactionem' 134-5). (2) Concerning the satisfaction for the *damna ecclesiae Romanae illata*, Innocent rejects the offer of the Guelf cities ('quod Mediolanenses, Placentini et alie ciuitates . . . parate sint . . . satisfacere' 136-9) to guarantee Otto's obligation by oath and hostages: all their riches, the pope decides, would never suffice for reparation (139-41).

142-145 *respondit quod claustrum non destruxerit . . . inde perceperint:* The defense on the fifth count corresponds to the restitution Otto was to order later in his testament, 18 May 1218, c.4: 'Castrum in Quidelinburch destrui volumus antequam abbatissae reddatur; destructa vero munitione locus cum ecclesia restituatur abbatissae . . . '[114]

145-147 *Super aliis . . . postulauit:* This general plea for forgiveness and absolution includes an admission of the facts ('licet ipsum Ottonem penitus excusare nequiuerit') charged in the remaining four *articuli* (Montferrat's Nos. 3, 4, 6, 7).

147-148 *Et hec . . . hoc modo:* If it is difficult to understand how R could have missed, or why he should have suppressed, the whole Milanese speech with Innocent's two interventions, it is equally difficult to explain why G concludes with a mere 'et hec . . . gesta sunt hoc modo' and passed over the wild scene described by R 72.28-43 at the end of the session: Montferrat cuts off the Milanese—purportedly even before they can make their plea— and speaks again, out of turn;[115] the Milanese shout back and call him a liar (72.39-40); and while both parties hurl insults at each other (41), the pope raises his hand, 'et egredientibus ceteris ipse ecclesiam est egressus' (42-3). Did our German leave the session before it got out of control? Nothing but speculation is possible on these contradictions between the two reports; but R and G are in agreement on one point: the second session closed without a final decision on the issues so dramatically presented. This decision was to be announced only in the third session, ten days later.

11-13. Third Session. 30 November 1215
11. The Dogmatic Decrees

149 *in die beati Andree:* Monday, 30 November; cf. R 72.43-5 'die uero lune ultimo mensis Nouembris, in festo scil. b. Andree.'

150-151 *summo mane missa celebrata . . . dispositis:* Cf. the description of sess. I, lines 16-19 above.

---

[114] ed. L. Weiland, MGH *Const.* 2 (1896) 52.
[115] Only at this point has R him introduce an objection against their right to appear for Otto, see above, to line 90.

154

151-152 *in eminentiorem . . . ascendens:* Cf. *ibid.* lines 24-5. More solemnly R 72.46-73.2: 'tertio se manifestauit dominus papa egrediens tamquam sponsus de thalamo suo (cf. Ps. 18.5), et ascendens sedit pro tribunali, cui centuriones suberant et tribuni' (cf. Exod. 18.21, 25; Num. 31.14, 48, 52 and concordances).

152-158 *sancte Trinitatis fidem . . . clamando 'Reprobamus':* In these lines G reports an elsewhere unrecorded detail of the conciliar procedure used for promulgating the two dogmatic constitutions, c.1 (*Firmiter*) on the Creed and c.2 (*Damnamus*) on the teachings of Joachim of Fiore and Amaury de Bène. In both instances the pope had the text read out ('recitari fecit' 153, 'quibus recitatis' 153, 156); then the formal question was put to the assembly ('Creditis hec per omnia?' 153-4, 'An reprobatis . . . ?' 157) and the decrees were adopted by acclamation ('Credimus' 154, 'Reprobamus' 158). All this is differently presented by R, according to whose account (73.2-12) the session began with a sermon of Innocent III, 'Ipso prius loquente prout spiritus dabat eloqui illi' (73.2-3; cf. Act. 2.4), in which the pope first spoke of the case of Raymond of Toulouse, pronounced the sentence concerning the latter's lands, (72.3-8)[116] and then condemned the book of Joachim of Fiore, 'sicut in primo [*sic*] constitutionum capitulo continetur' (8-12).

That Innocent preached a sermon in the third session is certain. It was of course not the spurious 'Sermo II in concilio generali Lateranensi habitus' which is printed in the great conciliar collections, from the Roman edition to Mansi,[117] but—as Luchaire was first to observe[118]—a sermon once extant in the lost Register of Innocent's eighteenth year, summarized in the *rubricella* of Reg. Vat. 8A:[119] 'Sermo de Trinitate in concilio, in quo sermone fuit reprobatus libellus sive tractatus Abbatis Joachim contra Magistrum P. Lumbardum': a sermon that dealt with the Trinitarian creed and the censure of the abbot's book, obviously in preparation of the two dogmatic constitutions. Since the report of R misses out on the principal subject of Innocent's sermon—he mentions the Trinity only later on, in his summary of the condemnation of Joachim's books[120]—and calls the second constitution the first, there is good reason to suspect that he has contracted several events of the session into one. We should certainly follow R, as an eyewitnesss when he assigns the sentence in the case of Raymond to the third session:

---

[116] Cf. § 5 above; esp. to lines 50-52, 54-5.

[117] *Ed. Rom.* (intercalated pages, cf. n. 15 above); Mansi 22.973ff.

[118] A. Luchaire, 'Un document retrouvé' *ap.* Hefele-Leclercq 5 ii.1723; cf. also M. Maccarrone, 'Il IV Concilio Lateranense,' *Divinitas* 5 (1961) 270-98, at 288 n.25.

[119] Theiner, VMS I 63 No. 14.

[120] R 73.8-11 'librum Ioachim seu tractatum dampnauit quem contra magistrum Petrum Lombardum ediderat de unitate seu essentia Trinitatis'; this is almost verbatim from the opening words of the constitution (cf. COD 207.7-9).

in this he finds at least indirect support by the Chronicler of St. Martin's of Tours (c. 1225), who, without specifying any sessions, speaks of this sentence in a context which suggests the third.[121] But the adjudication of the Albigensian lands was a practical and disciplinary *ordinatio*, and it is hard to believe that such a sentence should have formed part of a papal sermon designed to introduce the council's dogmatic decrees. The early chronicler of Reinhardsbrunn (*Historiae*, 1209-15) was evidently more correctly informed when he wrote that the pope 'in sermone lepido de fide, de spe, de caritate et de omnibus fidei articulis tam multa disseruit.'[122]

152 *sancte Trinitatis fidem et singulos fidei articulos:* This encompasses the contents of const. 1: Trinity, Creation and fall, Incarnation, Passion and Resurrection, Last Judgment, Church, Eucharist, Baptism, and Penance.[123]

154-156 *Postmodum dampnati ... et reprobate ... Parisiensis:* The *reprobatio* of the (lost) treatise of Joachim on the Trinity and of the teachings of Amaury de Bène is enacted in const. 2;[124] but what is meant by the words, 'postmodum dampnati sunt omnes heretici' which precede this in G? If it is not only a literary phrase, i.e., if there was actually any reading of a general condemnation of 'all heretics'—as also the chronicler of St. Martin's of Tours indicates at this point[125]—it certainly did not become part of the censure of Joachim and Amaury as promulgated (c.2); and according to G himself the question put to the council was merely, 'An reprobatis sententias Ioachim et Emelrici?' A general condemnation is found, however, at the beginning of the third constitution of the council, which legislated far-reaching canonical measures against heretics and their abettors:[126]

Excommunicamus igitur[127] et anathematizamus omnem heresim extollentem se aduersus hanc sanctam orthodoxam catholicam fidem quam

---

[121] *Chron. S. Mart.* reports on the council in this sequence: constitutions (below, G 184), crusading statute (G 159-60), 'condemnation' of Raymond and his son, excommunication of other heretics (G 154-5), reprobation of Joachim's book and the teaching of Amaury (G 155-6): ed. O. Holder-Egger, MGH SS 26 (1882) 466-7. Cf. n. 125.

[122] ed. Holder-Egger, *Cronicon Reinhardsbr.* MGH SS 30.588.28-9; *Chronica s. Petri Erford.* SS 30.384. On the *Historiae* as source, cf. at n.3 above.

[123] Mansi 22.981-2; COD 206-7; X 1.1.1. For bibliography, see COD 207 n. 1.

[124] Mansi 22.981-6; COD 207-9; X 1.1.2. For bibliography, see COD 207 n.2, 209 nn. 1-3; Maccarrone, *art. cit.* 286-8; also M. Bloomfield, 'Joachim of Flora,' *Traditio* 13 (1957) 249-309, at 254-6.

[125] Raimundus quoque ... condempnantur (see above, n. 73), multique alii heretici < et ? > fautores eorum gladio anathematis feriuntur. Libellus enim (*al.* etiam) vel tractatus de Trinitate quem abbas Joachim ... edidit reprobatur et perversissimum dogma magistri Amorici ... condempnatur' (MGH SS 26.467.26-31).

[126] Mansi 22.986E; COD 209.10-14. For historical analysis of c.3 cf. Hageneder, 'Studien ... ' (n. 51 above) 163-7.

[127] igitur *om. edd.* (supplied here from A. García's forthcoming new edition).

superius exposuimus, condempnantes uniuersos hereticos quibuscumque rationibus censeantur, facies quidem habentes diuersas, sed caudas ad inuicem colligatas, quia de uanitate conueniunt in idipsum . . .

It is not impossible that this preamble was originally read at the point indicated by G and by St. Martin's chronicler (such a preamble would indeed fit smoothly between the end of the Creed in c.1 and the opening words, 'Dampnamus *ergo* et reprobamus libellum . . . ' of c.2) and that it was subsequently shifted to c.3 only in the written publication of the constitutions. But the few words in G and the French chronicle are perhaps too narrow a basis for this conjecture.

12. *The Crusade; Excommunication of the English Barons; A German Manoeuver; Confirmation of Frederick II*

159-160 *Postea . . . inducta:* The 'negocium s. Crucis' was then taken up for discussion ('tractatum est'), that is, continued from session I (lines 33-6 above); not mentioned for session III in R, but without a specific day by some other chroniclers.[128] The *firmissima pax* which was decreed on 30 November according to G corresponds to the sections prohibiting tournaments for three years (§ *Licet autem*) and enjoining general peace and truce for four years (§ *Quia vero ad hoc negotium*) in the constitution *Ad liberandam*;[129] these sections are not found in the draft transcribed by Roger of Wendover.[130] We may assume that also other sections of the *expeditio* which had not already been enacted in the first session—presumably all those which are not in Wendover's text[131]—belong to the last day of the council and are implied in the phrase 'de negocio s. Crucis et expedicione signatorum,' although one cannot be certain that every part of the official text published after the council was actually read in the sessions.

160-168 *Qua occasione . . . contulerit:* The sentence of excommunication pronounced against the rebel barons 'nuper in concilio generali' was dispatched on 16 December 1215 in a papal mandate to three English prelates who were to publish and execute it (Potthast 5013);[132] it was also announced on 30 January 1216 to the archbishop of Bourges and his suffragans with the man-

---

[128] Reinerius Leod. *Ann.* ed. Pertz, MGH SS 16.674.49-54 (cf. n. 28 above); *Chron. s. Martini Turon.* ed. Holder-Egger. MGH SS 26.467.4-26.

[129] Mansi 22.1066E-67B; COD 246.20-35; cf. also 243.35-8 (Mansi 1059E).

[130] See above, to lines 33-6 at n. 27.

[131] See tabulation in Appendix C: peace and truce; measures against aiding Corsairs and pirates; against trading with Saracens; ordinance on material and spiritual preparation; provision for revenue of clerics *in absentia*; enforcement of crusading vows.

[132] The best edition (with translation and notes) is in C. R. Cheney and W. H. Semple, *Selected Letters of Pope Innocent III concerning England (1198-1216)* (London-Edinburgh etc. 1953) No. 85, pp. 221-3.

THE FOURTH LATERAN COUNCIL 157

date to solicit help for King John (Potthast 5057), and probably sent to other ecclesiastical provinces in France as well.[133] The English conflict had come before the council because of the appeals against each other by King John and the barons: we have contemporary accounts of their moves before the council opened;[134] and there exists a number of Innocent III's pre-conciliar letters pertaining to the case between John and the barons, and between John and the bishops.[135]

From G we learn for the first time that the solemn conciliar excommunication took place in the third session; Innocent's letters sent after the council do not specify the day, nor do the chroniclers who otherwise supply significant detail: the so-called Walter of Coventry, who tells us that the barons' appeal was not heard in the council because they were excommunicates,[136] and Guillaume le Breton, who points out that opposition was voiced in the assembly: 'in eodem concilio excommunicavit idem papa multis contradicentibus barones Anglie et complices eorum.'[137] Richard of San Germano does not mention the excommunication of the English barons at all. It is odd that for him this important business should not have been worth recording.

160 *Qua occasione:* G expressly states that the sentence was pronounced in connection with the conciliar injunction of *firmissima pax* for the forthcoming Crusade. This timing reflects the mind of Innocent III as expressed in the sentence itself (see below), and repeatedly in earlier letters:[138] the barons' rebellion endangers the *negotium sanctae Crucis*.

161-163 *omnes barones . . . percelluntur:* Cf. the tenor of the sentence (Potthast 5013): ' . . . excommunicavimus et anathematizavimus . . . barones Anglie cum adiutoribus et fautoribus suis qui Iohannem illustrem regem Anglorum cruce signatum . . . persequuntur; . . . omnes qui ad occupandum vel invadendum regnum . . . operam vel opem impenderunt';[139] see also the

---

[133] *Sel. Letters* No. 87, pp. 226-7, cf. 226 n.1.

[134] See esp. Roger of Wendover, *Flores historiarum*, ed. Coxe III 323ff., 336ff.; ed. Hewlett II 138ff., 151ff.

[135] *Sel. Letters* Nos. 75 (19 March 1215; Potthast 4961), 79 (spring-summer 1215; pp. 205-6, not in Potthast), 80 (7 July 1215; Potthast 4992, misdated), 82 (24 August 1215; Potthast 4990), 83 (same day; Potthast 4991), 84 (4 November 1215; Potthast 5006, cf. 5005). For the last of these, confirming the suspension of Archbishop Stephen Langton, cf. M. Powicke and C. R. Cheney, *Councils and Synods with Other Documents Relating to the English Church* II (Oxford 1964) 47-9, with bibliography (page proofs kindly supplied before publication by Professor Cheney).

[136] *Memoriale* ed. W. Stubbs (Rolls Series; London 1872-3) II 228.

[137] *Gesta Phil Aug.* c. 216 ed. Delaborde (n. 50 above) I 306.

[138] Potthast 4992, 4990, 4991; see *Sel. Letters* 80, 82, 83 (at pp. 207-8; 212-3, 215; 217, 219).

[139] *Sel. Letters* No. 85, p. 221; cf. No. 87 (Potthast 5057) p. 227.

Annals of Rainier of Liège: ' . . . qui omnes barones Anglie et fautores eorum excommunicavit in generali consilio [sic], tunc quia idem rex signatus erat, tunc quia . . . ';[140] and Walter of Coventry: 'excommunicati . . . non solum ipsi [sc. proceres Angliae] sed omnes qui regem Angliae in hac parte infestabant cum adiutoribus et fautoribus eorum.'[141]

163-164 *Proposuitque . . . subsidium:* Apparently the pope made a speech ('proposuit') in announcing the excommunication. A similar remark is found in the letter to the archbishop of Bourges (Potthast 5057: ' . . . insurrexerunt in . . . regem viz. Anglie, qui crucis assumpto caractere tam magnifice et potenter ad terre sancte subsidium se parabat'),[142] but this was not part of the published sentence (Potthast 5013).

164-168 *et quod ipse . . . contulerit:* The sentence states this only briefly: ' . . . Iohannem . . . cruce signatum et vassallum Romane ecclesie' (Potthast 5013; cf. 5057 'ipsum regnum quod est sedis apostolice speciale').[143] In the conciliar speech as reported here by G, the reference to the terms of John's submission and to the kingdom as papal fief is more explicit; they are the terms of John's charter and oath incorporated in Innocent's great privilege of 21 April 1214,[144] which the pope had also called to memory in the encyclical of 24 August 1215, condemning *Magna carta*:[145] 'recipiens illud a nobis in feudum (= iure beneficiario, G 167) sub annuo censu mille marcarum.' Cf. also Rainier of Liège: 'tunc quia . . . signatus erat, tunc quia ipsum regnum ei resignauerat et ab ipso tributaliter acceperat.'[146]

168-178 *Quia uero . . . respondendo surrexerit:* In the episode of Archbishop Siegfried's intervention we have the most important piece of entirely new historical information afforded by G; it is remarkable not only because of the extraordinary German claims the narrator reveals, but also because of the way in which he describes with obvious delight the comical side of the incident, when the archbishop jumps up three times trying to make his point, in spite of the pope's telling him bluntly to be quiet.

Siegfried of Eppenstein had come to the metropolitan see of Mainz, and thus to the German arch-chancellorship, as a Guelf, being the candidate of Otto IV in the split election of 1200.[147] He was consecrated by the papal legate on 30 September 1201 and confirmed by Innocent III on 21 March

---

[140] MGH SS 16.674.39-41. [141] *Memoriale loc. cit.*
[142] *Sel. Letters* p. 226. [143] *Ibid.* pp. 221, 226.
[144] Potthast 4912; *Sel. Letters* No. 67, pp. 178ff.: promise of the feudal census, 'mille marchas sterlingorum' (180); 'concedentes in feudum' (papal charter, 181).
[145] Potthast 4990; *Sel. Letters* No. 82, p. 212.
[146] MGH *loc. cit.* (continued).
[147] For sources, see Will, *Regesten . . . der Mainzer Erzbischöfe* (above, I n.4) II (1886) 123 No. 1.

1202.[148] But by 1211 he emerged as one of the leaders of the princes' revolt which eventually led to Otto's deposition, and as papal legate in 1212 he published the excommunication of Otto and deposed Archbishop Dietrich of Cologne.[149] In December of that year he took part in the election of Frederick II and crowned him at Mainz; and it was he—with Cologne vacant— who performed the solemn coronation at Aachen on 25 July 1215.[150] Siegfried was familiar with the Curia from the years of his Roman exile, 1206-1208.[151] While it is known that he took part in the Lateran Council,[152] there has never been any indication thus far of a major role played by him, because it was the archbishop of Palermo and the Marquess of Montferrat who appeared as Frederick's ambassadors in the second session.

168-172 *ad imperatoriam . . . probare conabatur:* It is extremely interesting that a claim to imperial suzerainty over the *regnum Anglie* was raised at this point by the German arch-chancellor, for it shows that among the German magnates—whose rights Siegfried expressly stresses ('ne ius suum . . . principes imperii . . . amittant' G 169-70, 'quod . . . imperatori et principibus Alimanie de iure attineret' 171-2)—the twelfth-century Staufian ideology of world empire was still alive, and was taken seriously. After its early expression in the letter of Conrad III to Johannes Comnenus,[153] the imperial theory had come to speak in Barbarossa's day of the kings of Europe as *reguli* and *provinciales reges*;[154] and the designs of the Emperor Henry VI, toward the end of his life, were aimed at making the idea of world empire a

---

[148] *Ibid.* 126-7, Nos. 16, 21; Potthast 1643.

[149] Will, *Regesten* 149-50, Nos. 166-7, 170; p. 152 Nos. 178 (not in Potthast), 179, 183.

[150] *Ibid.* 154-5, Nos. 193-4; p. 161 No. 244.

[151] *Ibid.* 135-7, Nos. 75-89. A notice in the *Chronica regia Coloniensis* for 1208 makes him cardinal priest of S. Sabina, ' . . . Romam ad apostolicum se transtulit, ubi per biennium in ecclesia s. Sabine, ubi erat cardinalis, degens . . . ' (ed. Waitz, MGH *Script. in usum schol.* [1880] 226). This is accepted at face value by Will, *Regesten* No. 75, but cannot be confirmed by any other source: no papal document is subscribed by him during those years (cf. Potthast I p. 464 and Eubel I 46 for cardinals of S. Sabina under Innocent III). The title was apparently vacant between the death of Archbishop William of Reims (card. 1179-1202) and Archbishop Thomas of Naples (1216-43), and Siegfried is not addressed as cardinal in the papal letter, Potthast 3310 (Will p. 136 No. 83) nor in any later document.

[152] Will, *Regesten* 162-3, Nos. 257-8; cf. Krabbo, 'Die deutschen Bischöfe . . . ' (n. 109 above) 281-2; and the conciliar list of the Zurich MS cited II n. 30 above.

[153] Otto of Freising, in *Ottonis et Rahewini Gesta Friderici I imp.* 1.25, third ed. by G. Waitz and B. von Simson, MGH *Script. in usum schol.* (1912) 38.37-39.4: 'Ad haec Francia Hyspania Anglia Dania caeteraque regna imperio nostro adiacentia . . . nos frequentant, ad ea quae imperii nostri mandata sunt se prompta esse . . . affirmantes . . . '

[154] Rainald von Dassel, *ap.* Saxo Grammat. *an.* 1162, ed. G. Waitz, MGH SS 29 (1892) 114.19.

IX

160

reality.[155] All this has been often discussed, by the medieval canonists no less than by modern historians;[156] but Archbishop Siegfried's speech shows that this was not a mere question of academic debate and that the Staufian dreams had not died with Henry VI. One would like to know the proof he advanced ('probare conabatur' 172): it may have been the letter of King Henry II to Barbarossa which is quoted in Rahewin's part of the *Gesta Friderici I* (3.7: 'regnum nostrum . . . vobis exponimus, ut ad vestrum nutum omnia disponantur et in omnibus vestri fiat voluntas imperii . . . ');[157] it may have been the enfeoffment which the Emperor Henry VI had extorted from his royal prisoner, Richard I in 1193—if Roger of Hoveden's story of this and the subsequent release from the feudal oath is correct.[158]

In any event, Archbishop Siegfried's move was most inconsiderate, not to say stupid. One can only surmise that he made it without the knowledge of the young emperor-elect, whose cause the preposterous claim would have seriously damaged (cf. lines 178ff. below).[159] He certainly antagonized the pope, who had just finished praising King John for having taken his kingdom

---

[155] Cf. E. Kantorowicz, *Kaiser Friedrich der Zweite* (Berlin 1927) 12-15; B. Gebhard, *Handbuch der deutschen Geschichte* I (8th ed. by H. Grundmann, Stuttgart 1954) 332, 334 with bibliography.

[156] Cf. (to cite only a few modern interpretations) R. W. and A. J. Carlyle, *A History of Mediaeval Political Theory in the West* III (Edinburgh and London 1928) 173-6; R. Holtzmann, 'Der Weltherrschaftsgedanke des mittelalterlichen Kaisertums und die Souveränität der europäischen Staaten,' *Hist. Zeitschr.* 159 (1939) 251-64, esp. 255ff.; W. Holtzmann, *Das mittelalterliche Imperium und die werdenden Nationen* (Arbeitsgemeinschaft für Forschung des Landes Nordrhein-Westfalen 7; Köln-Opladen 1953), esp. 18-26; F. Kempf S. J., *Papsttum und Kaisertum bei Innocenz III.* (Miscell. historiae pontificiae 19; Rome 1954) passim (see Index s. vv. 'Kaisertum und Nationen'; 'Königserhebung durch Kaiser oder durch Papst'); F. Heer, *Die Tragödie des heiligen Reiches* (Stuttgart 1952) 240-45: 'Die staufischen reguli.' — For the canonists see W. Ullmann, 'The Development of the Medieval Idea of Sovereignty,' *English Historical Review* 64 (1949) 1-33; S. Mochi Onory, *Fonti canonistiche dell'idea moderna dello Stato* (Milan 1951); S. Kuttner, 'Papst Honorius III und das Studium des Zivilrechts,' *Festschrift für Martin Wolff* (Tübingen 1952) 79-101, at 95ff.; G. Post, 'Rex Imperator,' *Traditio* 9 (1953) 296-320; and 'Blessed Lady Spain,' *Speculum* 29 (1954) 198-209; both revised and enlarged in his *Studies in Medieval Legal Thought* (Princeton 1964) 453-93; B. Tierney, 'Some Recent Works on the Political Theories of the Medieval Canonists,' *Traditio* 10 (1954) 594-625, esp. 612-19: 'Regnum and Imperium'; Kempf, *op. cit.* 194-252.

[157] *Ed. cit.* (n. 153) 172.14-21.

[158] Roger of Hoveden, *Chronica* ed. W. Stubbs III (Rolls Series; London 1870) 202-3. Carlyle, *op. cit.* III 176 expressed doubts (confusion by Roger with a feudal oath for Richard's continental possessions?); but cf. R. L. Poole, *From Domesday Book to Magna Carta* (Oxford History of England 3; 1951) 336-7.

[159] Frederick II's own conception of the relation between the Empire and the *regna* was to develop in a very different direction, cf. Kantorowicz, *op. cit.* 515; W. Holtzmann, *op. cit.* 26.

in fief from the Roman Church (G 164-8); and the pope did not wait to show his annoyance (G 173-5). Already on an earlier occasion Siegfried of Mainz, when exercising his powers as a papal legate, had proved himself more zealous than prudent: 'Licet iniunctae tibi legationis ..., in quo etsi forte zelum habueris, non tamen secundum scientiam habuisti, cum ... processeris minus iuste,' Innocent had written him on 6 June 1213.[160]

170-171 *sancte Moguntine sedis archiepiscopus:* The solemn style, in comparison with the plain 'patriarcha Iherosolimitanus' (G 32), 'inter Compostellanum et Tolletanum episcopos' (41-2), 'episcopus Palermitanus' (85), may indicate some special reason the writer had for expressing his respect for the see of Mainz. If we consider that the Cistercian abbey at which his letter was copied was located in the archbishopric before and after its transfer from Aulesburg to Haina (1221)—Archbishop Siegfried himself dedicated the new church at Haina on 1 April 1224[161]—then it becomes very likely that our writer belonged, if not to the monastery itself, to the archdiocese of Mainz.

174-175 *Audias me modo, posthac audiam te:* Once more, we have here an example of Innocent's temperamental manner of speech (cf. lines 109-10). The colloquial *modo,* 'now,' points perhaps to an exclamation in *volgare.*

175-176 *tamquam promptus obediente filius:* Said with irony, in the light of the following, 'licet uero tribus uicibus ... surrexerit' (177-8).

178-180 *Verum quia ... credebatur:* The *commendatio et defensio regis Anglie* refers back to what Innocent III had said in announcing the sentence against the rebel barons ('Proposuitque ... contulerit,' 163-8), and it is interesting that this sentence should have caused speculation in the council hall on the outcome of the German question, still pending from the second session, in favor of Otto IV. Was it because Frederick II had come to the throne by a revolt of the German princes against Otto, and the Council fathers had the impression that the pope was now in a 'legitimistic' mood, even though he himself had fostered that revolt a few years earlier? Or was it because they knew, as we know it from a letter of King John's agent in Rome, Walter Mauclerc,[162] that the king had worked behind the scenes for his imperial nephew? But the *defensio regis Anglie* could also be understood as defense of John against the claims which the German arch-chancellor had brought forward, thereby unwittingly embarrassing his sovereign. What-

---

[160] PL 216.853A; Potthast 4746: Will, *Regesten* II 157 No. 211.
[161] Will 188, Nos. 469-70.
[162] Thos. Rymer, *Foedera* (ed. Record Commission; London 1816) I 120; cf. Winkelmann, *Philip von Schw. und Otto* II 421 and n.6 (correcting Rymer's date); Tillmann, *Papst Innoc.* 149 and n. 279; F. Kempf, 'Zu den Originalregistern Innocenz' III.' *Quellen und Forsch. aus ital. Arch.* 36 (1956) 127.

ever the speculations and rumors, this was the opportune moment for the pope to announce his decision in the question of the Empire.

181-183 *Nulli debet . . . uolumus et complebimus:* The tenor of the papal sentence is an approbation, or better ratification ('ratum habemus')[163] of 'what the princes of Germany and the Empire did concerning Frederick king of Sicily,' followed by the declaration that the pope intends to favor and further him in all things. The unnamed action ('quod . . . fecerunt') was of course the election and crowning of Frederick as *rex Romanorum*; from this point on, now ratified, the King of Sicily had become for Innocent the emperor-elect. Substantially the same is expressed by the other chroniclers: R 73.12-15 records for the third session, immediately after the dogmatic constitutions, that the pope 'predicti regis F. electionem per principes Alamannie factam legitime in imperatorem Romanum approbans confirmauit'; the Chronicle of Reinhardsbrunn has, at the same point of the proceedings, 'deinde Fredericum augustum futurum imperatorem publice declarauit.'[164]

Neither G nor R mention any decision on Otto IV's plea for absolution, over which the debates of session II had been broken off in an uproar. But if it is correct to assume that Otto's move was designed to reopen the question of legitimacy of Frederick's election (see above, to lines 86-8), the formal recognition of Frederick was all that was needed to deny the Guelf's petition; and if Otto should really have expected the council to overrule the papal excommunication (see above, to lines 113-6) and absolve him, silence was the most eloquent answer. There was no need nor room for renewing an excommunication that had been solemnly published years before. What Rainier of Liège writes in his Annals, 'Ottonem vero generali consilio [*sic*] excommunicatum et destitutum renuntiavit,'[165] has no foundation in the actual history of Otto's downfall; but Rainier's version was echoed in the fourteenth-century Annals of Jacques de Guise, who lets the emperor first be excommunicated at the council together with the English barons, and then deposed as rebel against the Roman Church.[166] Some modern writers still speak of a 'deposition' of Otto IV at the Lateran Council,[167] but this

---

[163] On 'approbation' in Innocent's political thought, as being not in the jurisdictional order of canonical *confirmatio* but based on a right to 'examine' the elect before imperial consecration, cf. Kempf, *Papsttum und Kaisertum* 105-34. The formula 'ratum habemus' is a new element in this complex set of concepts.

[164] MGH SS 30.588.29-30.   [165] MGH SS 16.674.45-6.

[166] 'Ibidem presidens barones Anglie . . . cum Othone qui fuerat imperator excommunicans, eundem Othonem depositum, quia ecclesie Romane rebellis extiterat, denunciavit . . . '; ed. E. Sackur, MGH SS 30.i (1896) 272.28-32.

[167] Winkelmann, *op. cit.* II 423-4; Hefele-Leclercq 5 ii.1319; Kantorowicz, *Kaiser Friedrich der Zweite* 68; F. Bock, 'Studien zu den Originalregistern Innocenz' III.,' *Archiva-*

THE FOURTH LATERAN COUNCIL 163

is a myth which reads history backwards from the deposition of Frederick II at Lyons in 1245.

13. *Conciliar Legislation; End of the Council*

184 *Deinde leguntur . . . pape:* The short sentence is all G has to say about the most important single body of disciplinary and reform legislation of the medieval Church; but probably our writer sent a set of the constitutions along with his letter.¹⁶⁸ R is equally short: 'Et sancta synodus lxx capitula promulgauit' (73.15-6). In fact, only a few medieval writers made an effort to summarize the Lateran legislation, or at least part of it: so the chronicler of St. Martin's of Tours (c. 1225), who briefly describes a selection of twenty-nine constitutions¹⁶⁹ and reveals some knowledge of canon law when he observes that much of this reconfirmed earlier *constituta*: 'multa constituit multaque constituta a retroactis temporibus confirmavit';¹⁷⁰ or Aubrey of Trois-Fontaines, who breaks off after enumerating cc.1-17: 'sequuntur et alia multa usque ad 70.'¹⁷¹ Others are satisfied with mentioning one or two of the conciliar measures,¹⁷² or with including some of them in a general account of Innocent as a legislator.¹⁷³ Roger of Wendover (who gives a wrong

---

lische Zeitschrift 50/51 (1955) 329-64 at 356ff. This whole construction has been refuted by H. Tillmann, 'Zur Frage des Verhältnisses von Kirche und Staat in Lehre und Praxis Innocenz' III.,' *Deutsches Archiv für die Erforschung des Mittelalters* 9 (1951-2) 140 and n. 17; Kempf, 'Zu den Originalregistern . . . ' 127; *Papsttum und Kaisertum* 271.

[168] Giessen MS fol. 47ʳ-58ᵛ; cf. pp. 117, 120, above.

[169] MGH SS 26.466-7; they are identified in the editor's notes: cc. 6, 11-13, 18, 20-25, 28, 29, 43-47, 50, 52, 59, 62-69. ' . . . hec et multa alia ibi instituta sunt que longum est enumerare' (467.3-4). Later on, the chronicler speaks also of the crusading statute, of the condemnation of heretics (c.3) and of Joachim's and Amaury's teachings (c.2). — Cf. also Luchaire, *Le Concile de Latran* (above, II n. 32) 62.

[170] MGH SS 26.466.14. It is not correct to say the chronicler of St. Martin's 'observed that the decrees lacked originality'—so M. Gibbs and J. Lang, *English Bishops and Reform* (Oxford 1934) 101, who evidently misunderstand Luchaire's remark (*loc. cit.*), ' . . . ne sont pas toutes originales'—nor to cite him as an example of the 'surprising ignorance' concerning the decrees among medieval chroniclers (*ibid.*).

[171] ed. P. Scheffer-Boichorst, MGH SS 23 (1874) 904.6-7.

[172] *Continuatio Annal. Rotomag.* (late 13th cent.), citing c.68 on the Jewish badge; *Annales Normannici* (same period): ' . . . multa utilia statuta sunt pertinentia ad statum universalis ecclesie,' mentions c.13 against foundation of new religious orders; the so-called Ménestrel de Reims (c. 1260) § 145: ' . . . mout de commandemenz qui estoient necessaire a seinte eglise,' cites a non-existing statute 'que une clochete seroit portee avec Corpus Domini' and c.16 on clerical dress (ed. Holder-Egger, MGH SS 26.502, 514, 530; cf. Luchaire, *op. cit.* 61-3). Also Salimbene, *Chronica* (c. 1282-88) says he read the pope's sermon *Desiderio desideravi* and 'omnia que ibi ordinata sunt' but singles out only c. 13; 'cetera que ibi ordinata fuerunt non scribo propter tedium et propter prolixitatem vitandam' (ed. Holder-Egger, MGH SS 32.i [1905] 22; cf. Gibbs and Lang *loc. cit.*).

[173] *Chronica minor auctore minorita Erphordiensi* (c. 1261) ed. Holder-Egger, MGH SS

IX

164

number for the constitutions) indicates that some of the prelates found the new legislation too burdensome: 'recitata sunt in pleno concilio capitula sexaginta (*al.* quadraginta) quae aliis placabilia videbantur, aliis onerosa.'[174] This may well have been the case; and medieval writers occasionally remark that the new constitutions were not always observed.[175]

We cannot enter here into the manuscript tradition of the Lateran corpus[176] nor into the history, still largely unexplored, of its genesis and composition. It is only a minor point that the traditional number of seventy constitutions seems at first sight to be contradicted by the *rubricella* for the entry in the lost part of Innocent's Register: 'Sequuntur multe ordinationes per diuersa capitula facte et ordinate in dicto concilio ... et sunt in summa lxviii capitula':[177] as G shows, the dogmatic decrees (cc. 1-2; G 152-8) were promulgated separately from the sixty-eight disciplinary constitutions (cc. 3-70). The drafting was done at the Curia, and G is quite correct in speaking of 'constitutiones domini pape': they were read and adopted, not debated in the council. This is reflected in the language of the constitutions ('sacra uniuersali synodo approbante ... ' c.5; 'sicut olim aperte distinximus et nunc sacri approbatione concilii confirmamus ... ' c.8; 'sacri approbatione concilii decernimus ... ' c.44; 'Sacro approbante concilio prohibemus ... ' c.47), as well as in the general rubrics of a number of manuscripts[178] and in the canonical collections (*Compilatio quarta* and Gregorian Decretals), where the individual pieces appear inscribed as 'Innocentius III in concilio generali.'

185-191 *cum iam ... terminauit:* The closing ceremonies are nowhere else recorded: exposition and adoration of the True Cross (185-7), *Te Deum* (187-8), collect (188-9), benediction (190-91).

---

24 (1879) 195. Luchaire, *op. cit.* 61, cites only a later derivative of this text, the *Flores temporum* of a Swabian Franciscan (*c.* 1292; SS 24.247-8). There some more statutes are inserted and the series is concluded by a purported constitution on the Octave of the Nativity B.M.V. Actually this belongs to Innocent IV and the First Council of Lyons (from *Chron. min. Erph.* p. 200, not recognized by the editor); cf. Potthast II 995 *post* num. 11731.

[174] ed. Coxe III 342; Hewlett II 156.

[175] Cf. Luchaire, *op. cit.* 63. — *Ann. Normann. loc. cit.* (on c. 13): 'quod paucis potuit temporibus observari'; Ménestrel de Reims *loc. cit.*:'et mout d'autre commandement qui ne sont mie bien tenu ni gardei'; Salimbene *loc. cit.* (on c.13): 'set ista constitutio propter prelatorum negligentiam servata non fuit ... '

[176] Cf. above, I n. 13.

[177] Theiner, VMS I 63 No. 14.

[178] Munich MS lat. 9596, p. 255: 'Incipit nouella Innocentii pape'; Prague Univ. XXIII. E. 59, fol. 1r: 'Hee sunt constitutiones edite a domino papa Innocentio iii. et confirmate in concilio generali'; Rouen MS 706, fol. 255r: 'Incipit noua constitutio domini Innocentii pape iii.'; Vatican MS Vat. lat. 3555, fol. 25v: 'Incipiunt constitutiones Innocentii pape'; Aix-en-Provence, Bibl. de Mèjanes MS 1683 (1548), fol. 3r: 'Institutiones domini Innocentii tercii'; etc. (From A. García's apparatus of the forthcoming edition.)

THE FOURTH LATERAN COUNCIL 165

185-186 *magnam partem de ligno ... allato:* Less than an hour earlier Innocent had enacted a conciliar constitution (c.62) against the trafficking in relics: as is well known, they flooded the West as a result of the Crusades, especially after the sack of Constantinople. It is therefore somewhat surprising that at this solemn moment he would expose for adoration (G 186-7), and give his final blessing (190) with, a relic of the True Cross that had been brought recently from the imperial city; for many may have asked themselves by what means it had been acquired. The pope could have chosen one of the older and more famous Roman relics: the particle for which Pope Hilary (461-68) had built the oratory of the Holy Cross at the Lateran;[179] or the particle kept at S. Croce in Gerusalemme which, according to a tradition at least as old as the first recension of the *Liber pontificalis* (and included in the office for the feast of the Finding of the Cross, 3 May), had been given by Constantine to the basilica in the Sessorian palace;[180] the particle in the reliquary at St. Peter's, sent by the Emperor Justin II (565-78) to Pope John III;[181] or the one deposited by Leo III or Paschal I in a coffer at the oratory of St. Lawrence (the *Sancta sanctorum*) and believed to be from the great relic in Jerusalem which the Emperor Heraclius had recovered in 628 in the Persian war.[182] But above all, this same coffer held a particle of the True Cross which was in use for the papal liturgy from the eighth to the fourteenth century, being carried in procession from the palace chapel to Santa Croce on Good Friday, and to the Lateran basilica on the feast of the Exaltation of the Cross (14 September); it is generally considered to be identical with the 'mirae magnitudinis et ineffabilis portio ligni dominicae crucis' which Pope Sergius (687-701) had found in St. Peter's.[183]

All these are mentioned in the *ordines* and the descriptions of the Lateran in the twelfth and thirteenth centuries, whereas the new relic from Constan-

---

[179] *Liber pontificalis* ed. Duchesne I (Paris 1886; repr. 1955) 242; Johannes Diaconus, *De ecclesia Lateranensi* c.10 (PL 194.1556) = c.13 ed. Valentini-Zuchetti, *Codice topografico* (n. 95 above) III 356. Cf. A. Frolow, *La relique de la Vraie Croix* (Paris 1961) Nos. 20, 357.

[180] *Lib. pont.* I 80, 179, 196 n.75; Frolow No. 27 (with recent bibliography, p. 177). Cf. *Breviarium Rom.* 3 May: Nocturn, *lectio* 6 (until the suppression of the feast in 1960).

[181] Frolow No. 34 (with bibliogr. pp. 180-1); cf. Duchesne, *Lib. pont.* I 378 n.28.

[182] Jo. Diaconus *loc. cit.*; cf. Frolow Nos. 78, 357.

[183] *Lib. pont.* I 374, with Duchesne's commentary 378 nn. 28-30 and C. Vogel's supplementary note III (1957) 97; Andrieu's *Ordo* XXIII (8th cent.): M. Andrieu, *Les Ordines Romani du haut moyen-âge* III (Spicilegium sacrum Lovaniense 24; Louvain 1951) 271; Benedict of St. Peter's, *Liber politicus* (before 1142; cf. n. 87 above) c. 74, ed. Duchesne-Fabre, *Liber censuum* II 159 (cf. p. 164 n.60) (= ed. Mabillon, PL 78.1053); Cencius, *Ordo* (13th cent.) § 28, ed. *Lib. cens.* I 296 (= Mab. *Ordo* XII, PL 78.1075). — Cf. Frolow Nos. 67, 79, 88 (with bibliography, pp. 215-6, on Paschal I's [817-24] now empty enameled reliquary in the Museo Sacro of the Vatican, but without mentioning the traditional identification with Pope Sergius' Cross), Nº. 357.

tinople seems to have been little noticed. Thus far it was attested only in 1311, in an inventory of the papal treasury drawn up under Clement V, where it is described as having the words 'Hic continetur lignum vivifice Crucis de Constantinopoli translatum ad Vrbem tempore Innocencii pp. tercii' engraved on the reliquary.[184] The testimony of G thus acquires a particular significance for the liturgical use of this relic soon after its arrival from Constantinople.

188-190 *hanc collectam . . . uoluntatem:* This prayer, found in the Roman Missal for the Sunday within the octave of the Ascension, does not appear in any of the known medieval conciliar *ordines*.[185]

192 *sollempniter tantum tribus diebus:* Cf. R 73.16-8: . . . propter causam Trinitatis summus pontifex s. synodum trina sexione compleuit.'

14. *The Weeks after the Council*

195-198 *Altera autem die . . . remanserunt:* In his *Historia minor*, Matthew Paris, writing in the mid-thirteenth century, maintains that Innocent III withheld the licence to depart until every prelate had paid him a subsidy; they all had to borrow the monies from the curial bankers on harsh terms before they could leave with the pope's blessing.[186] This story is in keeping with Matthew's anti-papal bias and the remarks he makes elsewhere on Innocent's 'insatiable greed.'[187] It is also typical of his method of historical invention,[188] being palpably made up from an incident which Matthew himself tells in the *Gesta abbatum s. Albani*. When Abbot William after the end of the council went to take leave from Innocent, the pope chided him for coming barehand-

---

[184] *Regestum Clementis papae V*, Benedictine ed. Appendix I (Rome 1892) p. 448; cf. Frolow Nos. 452, 682.

[185] Communication from Dr. Richard Kay, letter of 10 June 1963.

[186] *Hist. minor* ed. F. Madden II (Rolls Series; London 1866) 174; ed. Liebermann, MGH SS 28 (1888) 399.32-6; shorter in *Chron. majora* ed. H. R. Luard II (1874) 635. This was accepted at its face value by Winkelmann, *Philip von Schw. und Otto* II 424.

[187] *Chron. maj.* II 565.

[188] Without prejudice to his otherwise well-deserved reputation as a fine historian. On his works, their interrelation, chronology, use of source material, etc. see now R. Vaughan, *Matthew Paris* (Cambridge 1958). Of older studies, F. Liebermann's introduction to the selections edited by him for the MGH (SS 28.74-106) retains its great value. — Modern liturgical studies, for instance, should have taken notice of the information Matthew has to offer on discussions and decisions concerning the Mass at the IV Lateran Council: on the commemoration of local saints in the Canon ('in secreto missae') and the abolition of 'quaedam quae diu ante ea fuerant usitata,' *Gesta abbatum s. Albani* ed. H. T. Riley I (R.S. London 1867) 261-2; ed. Liebermann, MGH SS 28.438.26-39; this important passage is not mentioned in the pertinent sections of J. Jungmann, *Missarum sollemnia* (5th ed. Wien-Freiburg-Basel 1962) I 133, II 221-2, nor in S. J. P. Van Dijk and J. H. Walker, *The Origins of the Modern Roman Liturgy* (London-Westminster, Md. 1960) 95-112.

ed. The abbot offered fifty marks but was 'forced' to make it one hundred, which he had to borrow from the *usurarii curiae*—just as, he mused, the pope did to all prelates.[189] There is no reason to dispute Abbot William's nasty experience, but the incident probably belongs into another context[190] than that of papal scheming which Matthew first insinuates in the story of the *Gesta* ('levius tamen hoc tulit abbas et equanimius quia hoc idem fecit papa universis') and then goes on to state as a positive fact in the *Historia minor* ('papa vero prelatis petentibus licentiam repatriandi minime concessit, immo a singulis auxilium in pecunia postulavit ... '). The tale of payments extorted severally from the council fathers loses all semblance of probability when we read the factual report of G: a good many (*multi*) bishops and prelates departed on the first day (1 December) after the end of the council, a great number of them (*quamplures*) remained until Christmas, and some (*quidam*) until the beginning or the middle of Lent. These all stayed on 'pro specialibus negotiis in curia' — which is a plausible enough reason.

197 *et maxime de Alemannia:* So for instance Siegfried of Mainz, a charter of whom is dated from Rome, 18 December 1215.[191] Much of the German bishops' business in Rome was likely to be connected with practical matters that grew out of the recognition of Frederick II.

199 *usque ad mediam quadragesimam:* Mid-lent, Thursday of the third Lenten week, was 17 March 1216.

201-203 *Et testimonium ... eius:* To a medieval writer it did not appear to be in bad taste to confirm his own veracity with the words of St. John (19.35, 21.24); so did e.g. Willelmus Durantis, speaking of the preparation of the decrees in the Second Council of Lyons (1274).[192]

APPENDIX A

Two Unidentified 'Conciliar' Statutes

In the Giessen Codex the letter on the Lateran Council is followed by the traditional brief *Notitia* (fol. 60va) in another hand: and on fol. 60vb a third hand, not unlike a thirteenth-century chancery script, entered the following

---

[189] ed. Riley I 263-4; ed. Liebermann 438-9. The derivation of the generalized statement in the *Hist. min.* from the anecdote in the *Gesta* can be demonstrated almost word for word.

[190] Innocent greeted Abbot William with these words: 'Nonne es tu abbas s. Albani qui tot privilegiorum beneficia a nostra sede totiens obtinuisti?' (*Gesta* I 263); they suggest that a gift was expected of the abbot of St. Alban's, not in return for the licence to depart, but in connection with earlier favors granted to the abbey. — For a sober analysis of Innocent's attitude in matters of customary, expected, and requested gifts, see Tillmann, *Papst Innoc.* 39-44; on Matthew's allegations *ibid.* 294.

[191] Will, *Regesten* II 163 No. 258.

[192] Cf. Kuttner, 'Conciliar Law in the Making' (n. 24 above) 43.

IX

text (= Gs), which will be printed here side by side with sections of the *lex edictalis* promulgated by the Emperor Frederick II on 22 November 1220, during the rites of his coronation at St. Peter's (= F).[1]

Gs	F
(1) Quoniam ea que in meliuitano et kartaginensi concilio statuta sunt[2] in desuetudinem abierunt, statuit hoc sanctum concilium ut nullus omnino hominum clericum siue ecclesiasticam personam, cuiuscumque condicionis sit, in questione criminali uel ciuili ad iudicium seculare contra constitutiones inperiales et canonicas sanctiones trahere presumat. Quod si secus presumptum fuerit, actor consuetudinibus ciuitatum uel locorum non obstantibus a iure suo cadat, iudicatum non teneat et iudex ex tunc iudicii potestate nostra sit priuatus.[4]	4. Statuimus autem ut nullus ecclesiasticam personam in criminali questione uel ciuili trahere ad iudicium seculare presumat contra constitutiones imperiales et canonicas sanctiones. Quod si fecerit,[3] actor a iure suo cadat, iudicatum non teneat et iudex sit ex tunc iudicandi potestate priuatus.
(2) Item statuimus ut quecumque communitas uel persona, siue sit ecclesiastica siue secularis, temere per anni circulum iuris ordine obseruato in excommunicatione perstiterit, si clericus est omnibus beneficiis ecclesiasticis, siue habeant[5] curam animarum annexam siue non, ipso iure sit priuatus. Eodem modo laici, si per annum in excommunicatione perstiterint, feodis uel beneficiis que ab ecclesia tenent, siue sint temporalia siue perpetua, cum ipsorum fauctoribus, receptoribus adque defensoribus ipso iure sint priuati. Falsalli et ipsorum, si quos habeant, a fidelitate dominis suis prestita omnino sint absoluti. Nichilominus tamen banno imperiali ipsos subiacere decreuimus.	3. Item quecumque communitas uel persona per annum in excommunicatione propter libertatem ecclesie facta perstiterit, ipso iure imperiali banno subiaceat, a quo nullatenus extrahatur nisi prius ab ecclesia beneficio absolutionis obtenta.

---

[1] ed. L. Weiland, MGH *Const.* 2 (1896) 106-9, No. 85.
[2] Decr. Grat. C. 11 q.1 cc.42-43.
[3] *al.* factum fuerit
[4] An emendation is needed here: either 'iudicio ... sit priuatus' or, more probably, 'iudicii potestate auctoritate nostra sit priuatus' (homoiotel.).
[5] habeat Gs.

A connection between these two texts is suggested by the consideration that Gs, with the *bannus imperialis* at the end, would make no sense as a piece of canonical legislation.⁶ No matter how one might stretch the Innocentian doctrine of the pope's power in temporal matters 'certis causis inspectis' (*Per venerabilem*, Potthast 1794: X 4.17.13), no papal council and, *a fortiori*, no council of the German bishops—if one were to conjecture, for instance, that such an assembly was called after 1220 to 'canonize' and enlarge upon the provisions of Frederick's law—could have 'decreed' on its own authority to bring the ban of the Empire (*Reichsacht*) into operation for renitent excommunicates.⁷

The Giessen text would make sense, however, as a first draft of the *lex edictalis*. The emperor's law, as we know from a letter of Honorius III to Cardinal Nicholas of Tusculum, 10 November 1220, had been drafted for coronation day at the Roman Curia.⁸ On that day, the pope solemnly confirmed it, had it entered in the papal Register,⁹ and issued, still from St. Peter's as part of the ceremonies, a supplementary papal constitution.¹⁰ Shortly thereafter, Frederick ordered his law to be inserted in the Justinian Code,¹¹ and eventually Honorius III had both the imperial and the papal constitutions included in his official collection of decretals, the so-called *Compilatio quinta*, of 2 May 1226.¹²

In his penetrating study on the coronation laws of 1220, Professor De Vergottini has convincingly argued that Frederick promulgated the papal draft unchanged.¹³ But this does not exclude—in fact, the pope's letter to Cardinal Nicholas implies—that the curial text itself had gone through several stages before it was handed to the emperor-elect between 10 November and the cere-

---

⁶ A papal law could at the most request such a measure from the secular ruler; so Celestine III in his decretal *A nobis* with regard to the effects of degradation of clerics, JL 17639: '... per secularem comprimendus est potestatem ita quod ei deputetur exilium' (X 2.1.10; for the date, 15 April/25 Oct. 1191, see W. Holtzmann, 'La Collectio Seguntina,' *Revue d'histoire ecclésiastique* 50 [1955] 431, c.43).

⁷ Gs c.2 has a wider scope than c.7 of the *Privilegium in favorem principum ecclesiasticorum*, granted by Frederick II at Frankfurt, 26 April 1220, where the king (emperor-elect) pledges that *nostra proscriptio* will follow for every excommunicate whom, upon *denuntiatio* by the ecclesiastical judge, he finds to have persisted in the state of excommunication for six weeks (MGH Const. 2.90, No. 73 c.7). While the time span here is much shorter, the *Privilegium* requires in each case a royal sentence; in Gs (and in F c.3) the *bannus imperialis* follows automatically after a year, without a procedure of *denuntiatio*. For F c.3 see also below, n. 21.

⁸ Potthast 6395; Pressutti 2766; text in MGH *Const.* 2.104-5 No. 83.

⁹ *Reg. Hon.* 5.483; Potthast 6408; Pressutti 2786; the formula of confirmation is in MGH *Const.* 2.110 n.1.

¹⁰ Beg. 'Excommunicamus,' published in the letter *Noverit fraternitas tua*, 4 January 1221 (Potthast 6469; Pressutti 2945; text in X 5.39.49).

¹¹ MGH *Const.* 2.110 No. 86; for the distribution among the *authenticae* of *Cod. Just.* see the *editio stereotypa* of P. Krüger, 510ff.

¹² 5 *Comp.* 1.1.1. (Potth. 6469) and 2 (const. Freder. c.1); 1.3.4 (F c.8); 2.1.2 (c.5); 2.2.2 (c.4); 3.13.un. (c.9); 3.26.3 (c.2); 5.4.un. (cc.6-7); 5.12.4 (c.10); 5.18.3 (c.3).

¹³ G. De Vergottini, *Studi sulla legislazione imperiale di Federico II in Italia: Le leggi di 1220* (Milan 1952) 88-96.

mony at St. Peter's.[14] If we assume that Gs represents a portion of such an early draft, it would reveal an interesting development in Honorius' plans for the setting of the coronation; it would show that the pope originally planned everything to take place in a 'sanctum concilium' at which he and the emperor were to legislate in common for the good of Christendom, issuing joint decrees with ecclesiastical as well as secular sanctions.

In other words, Honorius III may have tried to imitate Lucius III's Council of Verona, which he would remember from the days when he was young Cencius, a canon of St. Mary's Major and in the service of Cardinal Hyacinth, the later Celestine III. At Verona in November 1184, Pope Lucius promulgated the sweeping constitution *Ad abolendam* against heretics 'de episcopali consilio et suggestione culminis imperialis ac principum eius,'[15] while Frederick Barbarossa in an imperial constitution, now lost,[16] proclaimed the enforcement of the papal measures by *proscriptio* — the ban of the Empire.

But if the conciliar setting at Verona was already an anachronism in its day,[17] a fusion of papal and imperial functions in one single conciliar enactment, such as suggested by the Giessen text, would have been even more out of step with the political realities of 1220. There was to be no 'sanctum concilium' at the coronation of Frederick II: separate constitutions were issued by the pope and the emperor, and the latter's *lex edictalis* consequently was stripped of the fastidious chancery language[18] as well as of the purely canonical elements[19] of the first draft—provided it is really a fragment of this draft that is preserved in Gs.

Moreover, if this interpretation of Gs is correct, the scope of the statute on the civil effects of excommunication became restricted in c.3 of the *lex edictalis:* not every excommunication will entail *ipso iure* the imperial ban after a year,[20] but only that which is pronounced for infringement of the liberties of

---

[14] Potthast 6395: ' ... studeatis ut capitularia que vobis mittimus presentibus interclusa, sub competentibus verbis, servata sententia, sub nomine regio in leges publicas redigantur nobisque mittantur ... in die coronationis sub imperiali nomine ... publicanda' (MGH *Const.* 2.104).

[15] JL 15109; X 5.7.9 (+ 3.38.23); cf. at n. 31 ed. Friedb.

[16] For testimonies cf. De Vergottini, *op. cit.* 42-3.

[17] Cf. *ibid.* 47ff.

[18] Gs c.1 lin. 4-5 nullus omnino hominum] nullus F   5 clericum siue *om.* F 6-7 cuiuscumque conditionis sit *om.* F   11 si secus presumptum fuerit] si fecerit (factum fuerit) F. — Gs c.2 lin. 2-4 siue sit ecclesiastica siue secularis temere per anni circulum] per annum F   19 ipsos subiacere decreuimus] subiaceat F

[19] Gs c.1 lin.1-4 Quoniam ea—concilium] Statuimus autem F Gs; c. 2 lin. 5-18 si clericus—sint absoluti *om.* F. — Also the clause 'iuris ordine observato' (Gs c.2.4) had no place in F c.3; it would have implied a right of the secular judge to reexamine the sentence.

[20] So Gs c.2; this does not go as far as the exaggerated promise made to Innocent III by Philip of Swabia in 1203: ' ... ut quicumque excommunicatus sit a domino apostolico, in banno statim sit imperiali' (MGH *Const.* 2.9 No. 8 c.9); but Innocent never pressed for this, cf. E. Eichmann, *Acht und Bann im Reichsrecht des Mittelalters* (Paderborn 1909) 120f. A common statute by Alexander III and Barbarossa in 1177 on *mutual* automatic operation of *excommunicatio* and *proscriptio* after a year is reported in the Chronicle of St. Michael's in Lüneburg (ed. Weiland, MGH SS 23.396) but deserves little credence; cf. Eichmann 31-2 (*contra*, De Vergottini, *op. cit.* 46ff., 105-6).

THE FOURTH LATERAN COUNCIL   171

the Church, i. e. pronounced for such legislative, judicial, and fiscal acts as
are forbidden in F c.1 and c.2.²¹ Neither did the papal counterpart to the imperial constitution resume the suppressed provisions of Gs. Honorius III's constitution of coronation day merely pronounced excommunication (1) of heretics and their abettors; (2) of all who observe, retain, apply, or enforce statutes or customs against ecclesiastical liberties. The pope thus supplemented cc. 6, 7, and 1 of the *lex edictalis*. There was no need for restating that vassals of a renitent excommunicate will be absolved from the obligations of their feudal oaths (Gs c.2 lines 15-18): this was settled canonical doctrine; Honorius himself had reaffirmed it a few years earlier in a ruling which was eventually incorporated into the Gregorian Decretals.²² And a general *ipso iure* forfeiture, after a year's lapse, of ecclesiastical benefices held by excommunicated clerics (Gs c.2 lines 5-9)—or of feudal benefices held from the Church by laymen (9-15)²³—did not become part of the common law of the Church.²⁴

The foregoing explanation of the Giessen text admittedly remains a hypothesis and does not solve all the problems. How, for instance, did a curial draft of the coronation laws—and only part of it—come to be copied in a book of the Cistercian abbey at Haina? The document might have been sent from Rome, perhaps by the same man who had written, four years earlier, the letter on the Lateran Council ... but here we enter the realm of pure speculation.

APPENDIX B

An Account Derived from Richard of San Germano
(cf. II n. 33 above)

MS Vat. lat. 3555 was first cited by J. Hardouin as one of the texts of the Lateran constitutions.²⁵ But he did not advert to the fact that this fourteenth-century codex includes also, after the conventional Notice of the council (fol. 61ᵛ) a somewhat longer account (fol. 62ʳ-63ʳ), which has thus far remained unpublished. It proves upon examination to be based on Richard of San Germano's long version (= R), but not entirely. Whoever compiled the text (= V) must have used the text of const. 2,²⁶ and at least one narrative source other than R

---

²¹ By the same token, the clause of G c.1 lin.11 13 'consuetudinibus non obstantibus' is lacking in F c.4: the *consuetudines* were already annulled in F c.1. (For Germany, F c.3 had the effect that the *Reichsacht* in cases of excommunication *propter libertatem ecclesiae facta* could now either follow after six weeks by denunciation procedure (n.7 above), or without this procedure after a year.)

²² C 15 q.6 cc.4-5, etc. — Honorius III, Potthast 7852=5462; Pressutti 351: 18 February 1217; 5 *Comp.* 5.16.2; X 5.37.13.

²³ For developments of forfeiture in the feudal law see Eichmann, *Acht und Bann* 85-6.

²⁴ Rather, a judicial sentence was needed in these cases; see the commentaries on X 1.14.8, e.g. Innocent IV, *Apparatus* nn. 1-2 *ad loc.* (ed. Venice 1570 p. 126); Johannes Andreae, *Novella* nn. 4, 12 *ad loc.* (ed. Venice 1581 [reprint Turin 1963] fol. 166ʳ); also Innocent III on fiefs, X 5.37.10.

²⁵ *Conciliorum collectio* ... 7 (Paris 1714) 15-16; cf. Mansi 22.979 n.1.

²⁶ See V 22-32.

which remains to be identified.[27] At one point this source bears a strong resemblance to the Giessen letter (G).[28]

Besides being a second-hand composition, V is a piece of poor workmanship, on two counts. It leaves off in the middle of session II, after recording the six charges which, according to R, the Marquess of Montferrat made against Otto IV. But what is more, V interpolates parts of the third session into the first[29] and gives this conflated 'first' session an abrupt ending which seems to be patterned after what R reports on the breaking-up of the second.[30] Thus we obtain a completely distorted view of the council; this is reflected in the table of contents of Vat. lat. 3555, fol. 67ᵛ; 'De duabus uniuersalibus eius [sc. concilii] sessionibus in ecclesia Lateranensi eodem [sc. Innocentio papa] presidente celebratis.'

In editing this curious text we have indicated the source material, line by line, in the apparatus.

In nomine Domini nostri Iesu Christi. Amen. Anno incarnationis ipsius mº.ccº.xvº. mense nouembri, decimo die intrante eodem mense, indictione iiij. in conspectu summi patris et secundi post Petrum apostolum principis, a solis ortu et occasu conuenientibus orbis prelatis in urbe de
5 mandato ipsius ad audiendam uocem sermonum eius, feria iiij. uenerabilis ille beati Martini dies festus occurrit, in quo patrum ipse pater ut placuit, ceu sedens doctorum in medio, primam fecit in Lateranensi ecclesia sessionem. In quem cum essent oculi eorum intendentes, postulantes de mensa propositionis illius pabulum sacietatis interne, ad eius
10 imperium hominum sedato tumultu, omnipotens sermo suus ad subditos de supernis sedibus uenit. Cuius initium tale fuit; 'Desiderio desideraui hoc pascha manducare uobiscum antequam moriar,' faciens nonnullos de pascha discursus, et presens illud pascha, quod in octauodecimo pontificatus sui tam gloriose tamque magnifice celebrauit, assimilans illi phase
15 quondam a rege Iosia in octauodecimo regni sui tempore celebrato.

---

[27] E. g. V 2-4 indictione — occasu; 5-7 feria iiij.—in medio; 16-21 Quem laudabiliter —subiturum (cf. n. 28), 29 Personam—illius.
[28] See V 19-21, apparatus.
[29] See the appar. to lines 16-18, 19-21, 22-32.
[30] Ibid. 32-34.

---

1 (fol. 62ʳ)   8 eorum] omnium R   8-9 prestolantes R

---

2 decimo die: ex R 62.12, cf. supra (IV) in comment. ad G 14. Sibimet ipsi contradicit V per vv. 'feria iiij.' (infra lin. 5) quae congruunt diei 11 nov. 1215   4 a solis ortu et occasu: cf. Ps. 112.3   4-5 conuenientibus—ipsius: cf. R 61.40-41 'conuocatis ad se ceteris orbis prelatis'   5 ad audiendam—eius: cf. Ps. 102.20   6 patrum ipse pater: ex R 62.23   7 sedens—in medio: cf. Luc. 2.46   7-8 primam—sessionem: cf. R 62.12 'in prima sexione quam fecit'   8-9 In quem—interne: ex R 62.24-7 9-10 ad eius—tumultu: cf. R 71.22-3 (sess. II)   10-11 omnipotens—uenit: ex R 62.28-9; cf. Sap. 18.15   11-12 Cuius initium—moriar: cf. R 62.29-33 'cuius tenor talis est: "Desiderio..." ' (Luc. 22.15) ... '; seqr. integer sermo (usque ad 70.36) 13-15 et presens—celebrato: cf. serm. Innoc. R 64.10-20 'Legitur enim ... ' (= Mansi 22.969C-D); 4 Reg. 23.23

IX

THE FOURTH LATERAN COUNCIL 173

Quem laudabiliter satis prosequens et laudabilius complens, nam spiritus erat qui loquebatur in eo, inter multa que contra hereticos de sancta Trinitate et catholica fide proposuit, fecit de succursu terre sancte principaliter mencionem, asserens se, ne quod aliis faciendum imponeret ipse
20 uitaret, preter grandes quas pro negocio ipso facere proponebat expensas, si de concilii foret consilio, laborem in propria persona subiturum.

Ioachim etiam Florensis abbatis librum seu | tractatum dampnauit quem contra magistrum Petrum Lombardum ediderat de Trinitate seu essencia Trinitatis, appellans ipsum hereticum et insanum, pro eo quod in suis
25 sentenciis dixerat quoniam quedam summa res est Pater et Filius et Spiritus Sanctus, et illa non est generans, neque genita, neque procedens. Unde dicebat illum non tam Trinitatem quam quaternitatem astruxisse in Deo, uidelicet illas tres personas et illam communem essenciam quasi quartam. Personam uero non condempnauit illius, pro eo quod omnia scripta sua
30 sibi transmisit suo uel approbanda iudicio uel corrigenda, dictans quandam epistolam, cui propria manu subscripsit, in qua fatebatur se illam fidem tenere quam Romana tenet ecclesia. Sic non est ipso die in concilio ultra processum, sed ad ipsius nutum, ceteri episcopi et prelati qui multitudine numerari non poterant, inclinato capite recesserunt.
35 Elapsis uero decem diebus, scilicet sexta feria prima post octauas beati Martini, iterum in preparato solio suo dominus papa conscendit prelatis presentibus uniuersis. Cumque de ipsius mandato esset silencium imperatum, hoc ipsum in tubis ductilibus tibicines acclamantes, Berardus Panormitanus archiepiscopus super facto domini regis Frederici in Ro
40 manum imperatorem electi impetrata licencia est locutus. Quod cum eleganter satis domino pape proponeret ab eius ore pendentibus uniuersis, Mediolanenses quidam, eo metam imponente sermoni, uerbum uolebant facere pro Oddone, quorum | principium tumultus contra clamancium impediuit. Ad maioris tamen imperium est sedatus. De cuius postea licencia

---

22 (fol. 62ᵛ)   38 Berī V   42 uolebat   43 (fol. 63ʳ)

16-17 *nam spiritus—in eo:* cf. Act. 6.10; R 73.2-3 (sess. III) 'prout spiritus dabat eloqui illi' (Act. 2.4)   17-18 *inter multa—proposuit:* cf. conc. Lat. c.1 (sess. III) cum rubr. X 1.1.1 'De summa Trinitate et fide catholica'   17 *contra hereticos:* vide supra in comment. ad G 154-6   18-19 *fecit—mentionem:* ex R 70. 38-40 (sess. I) ubi tamen agitur de sermone patriarchae Hierosolymitani   19-21 *asserens se—subiturum:* cf. G 33-6 (sess. I) 'Asseruit etiam—expendere'; vide supra in comment. ad loc.   19-20 *ne quod aliis—ipse uitaret:* cf. const. 'Ad liberandam' § 'Ne uero in humeros... nolimus' (Mansi 22.1062C; COD 244.30-31)   21 *si de concilii—subiturum:* cf. serm. Innoc. 'paratus iuxta consilium uestrum... laborem' (R 65.25-30; Mansi 970B-C)   22-24 *Ioachim—Trinitatis:* ex R 73.8-11 (sess. III); conc. Lat. c.2 (COD 207.7-9)   24-28 *ipsum hereticum—quartam:* ex conc. Lat. c.2 (COD 207.9-14)   29-32 *omnia scripta—ecclesia:* ibid. (209.1-4)   32-34 *Sic non—recesserunt:* cf. fin. sess. II R 72.41-3 'dominus papa manu innuit et egredientibus ceteris ipse ecclesiam est egressus' (vide supra in comment. ad G 147-8); fin. sess. I R 71.2-5 'sicque diei (dici *ed.*) illius sessio... est completa et prelati omnes ad maioris nutum (maiores nutu *ed.*) ecclesiam sunt egressi'   33-34 *qui—non poterant:* cf. supra in comment. ad G 19-22   35-63 *Elapsis uero—ex eodem:* fere verbotenus ex R 71.5 — 72.23

IX

174

   45 alter Mediolanensis est locutus ostendens in primis litteras quasdam et legens aureo ipsius Oddonis sigillo signatas, dominis cardinalibus et toti sacro concilio generaliter missas, in quibus nonnulla continebantur de sua excusacione, et quod redire libenter uolebat ad mandatum ecclesie, offerens ipsum cum iuramento seruare et insuper aliam dare summo pon-
   50 tifici qualem placeret libentissime caucionem. Vnde absolucionis gratiam ab eo postulabat. Quibus perlectis marchio Montis Ferrati cum licencia ex aduerso respondit Oddonem ab apostolica sede beneficium absolucionis impetrare non posse quod postulat, sex obiciens capitula contra ipsum. Primum uidelicet quod iuramentum apostolice sedi prestitum ut
   55 debuit non seruauit. Secundum, quia propter que anathematis est uinculo innodatus adhuc detinet nec reddidit ut iurauit. Tercium, quia episcopum quendam excommunicatum in maioris iniquitatis cumulum non est ueritus confouere. Quartum, quia quendam alium episcopum apostolice sedis legatum capere et uinculis mancipare presumpsit. Quintum, in con-
   60 temptum et ignominiam sancte Romane ecclesie regem uel imperatorem Fredericum regem appellauit presbiterorum. Sextum, quia monasterium quoddam monialium temere occupauit, et ipsis foris eiectis, municionem constituit ex eodem.

Appendix C

Roger of Wendover's Text of the *'Expeditio pro recuperanda terra sancta'*

(cf. IV above, at nn. 26-27)

    It has been argued above in the commentary on G 33-36 that the provisions of the const. 'Ad liberandam' as published after the council on 14 December 1215 (Potthast 5012) were originally read in part during the first, in part during the second session, and that Roger of Wendover's text [= W] represents a preliminary stage of the *Expeditio*, that is, the partial draft which was read in sess. I. A parallel printing of the two versions would be cumbersome and is not necessary to prove the point; instead, we present here a summary analysis of W (page references are to vol. III of Coxe's edition, with the page numbers of Hewlett's text [vol. II] in the Rolls Series added in parentheses) showing the additions, omissions, rephrasings, and changes of sequence in the official text (from Leonardi's edition in COD 243-47, cited by page and line). Purely verbal variants are not recorded, but for convenience the survey is divided into paragraphs, following the division in Mansi 22.1058E-67E [= M].

    The most telling symptons of a revision preceding the official publication will be found in the addition to several paragraphs of penal sanctions and other final clauses (§§ *Ad haec, Nos autem, Sane quia, Si qui vero*); the insertion of prefatory clauses (§§ *Ne vero, Sane quia*); the recasting of one section (§ *Iudaeos vero*), and the shifting of another to the beginning of the constitution, with a short general preamble added (§ *Ad liberandam*).

---

47 continebatur V

THE FOURTH LATERAN COUNCIL   175

§ *Ad haec* (M 1059E): prelates must preach the Crusade and urge princes, nobles, and communities, if they do not go in person, to send and finance troop contingents 'in remissionem peccatorum suorum' (indulgence).

W 342 (156-7) Ad haec sane nequid ... est expressum.

COD 244.9 sane *om.*
19-20 expressum] et ad maiorem cautelam etiam inferius exprimetur *add.*

§ *Huius remissionis* (M 1062B): indulgence for shipbuilders; admonition to *renuentes*.

W 342 (157) Sed etiam illos huius remissionis volumus esse participes qui propter ... fabricare.

COD 244.20 Sed—illos *om.*
20-21 participes qui] participes non solum eos qui naves proprias exhibent sed etiam illos qui

Renuentibus autem, et si qui ingrati fuerint ... redempti.

22-3 et si — fuerint] si qui forte tam ingrati fuerint domino Deo nostro

§ *Ne vero in humeros* (M 1062C): promise of papal assistance, naval and financial.

W 342-3 (157) Nos vero aliis exemplum praebere volentes triginta milia ... remanserunt.

COD 244.30-3 Nos — triginta] Ne vero in humeros hominum onera gravia et importabilia imponere videamur, quae digito nostro movere nolimus, similes illis qui dicunt utique sed non faciunt, ecce nos de his quae ultra necessaria et moderatas expensas potuimus reservare, triginta

§ *Cupientes autem* (M 1062E): crusading tax of one-twentieth on all clerical revenues for three years.

W 343 (157) Cupientes autem ... terrae sanctae,

COD 245.3-4 sanctae] per manus eorum qui ad hoc apostolica fuerint providentia ordinati *add.*

illis exceptis qui assumpto ... profecturi.

4-5 illis exceptis qui] quibusdam dumtaxat religiosis exceptis, ab hac praetaxatione merito eximendis, illis similiter qui

§ *Nos autem* (M 1063A): crusading tax of one-tenth on revenues of pope and cardinals: penal clause (not in W) for defrauding of tax.

W 343 (157) Nos autem ... persolvemus.

COD 245.8-10 persolvemus] sciantque se omnes ad hoc fideliter ... sententiam excommunicationis incurrant *add.*

§ *Sane quia iusto* (M 1063A): protection of crusaders' rights: no prefatory clause in W.

W 343 (157-8) Statuimus etiam ut omnes clerici sive laici post crucem assumptam

sub beati Petri ... maneant, necnon sub archiepiscoporum ... defensione et eorum bona omnia consistant,

ita ut donec ... quieta.

COD 245.10-14 statuimus — assumptam] Sane quia iusto iudicio coelestis imperatoris ... quorum personas et bona post crucem assumptam
15 maneant] suscipimus
necnon] statuentes ut
16 et—omnia *om.*
17 consistant] propriis nihilominus protectoribus ad hoc specialiter deputandis *add.*
19-20 quieta] et si quisquam contra praesumpserit, per censuram ecclesiasticam compescatur *add.*

§ *Si qui vero* (M 1063C): protection from usury.

W 343 (158) Si qui vero proficiscentium ... ecclesiastica districtione compellantur;

COD 245.23-5 eccl. — compellantur] eadem praecipimus districtione compelli. Quod si quisquam creditorum ... animadversione mandamus.

§ *Iudaeos vero* (M 1063D): protection from Jewish usury; special provisions (not in W) on amortization of principal, by Jews' income from the securities given.

W 343 (158) de Iudaeis hoc idem statuentes, per saecularem potestatem ut ad hoc faciendum inducantur.

COD 245.25-35 de Iudaeis — inducantur] Iudaeos vero ad remittendas usuras per saecularem compelli praecipimus potestatem, et donec illas remiserint, ab universis ... denegetur. His autem qui ..., compulsis Iudaeis proventus pignorum ... computare, cum huiusmodi ... non absorbet.

Porro ecclesiarum praelati qui ... cruce signatis et eorum procuratoribus aut familiis ... graviter puniendos.

36 procuratoribus aut *om.*

[§ *Caeterum quia cursarii* (M 1063E): measures against all who aid or who trade with Corsairs; § *Excommunicamus praeterea* (M 1066B): excommunication and other penalties against all who furnish arms, armaments, or ships to Saracens, who pilot their ships, etc.; § *Prohibemus insuper* (M 1066D): embargo on sailing to Saracen territories; § *Licet autem torneamenta* (M 1066E): prohibition of tournaments for three years; § *Quia vero ad hoc negotium* (M 1066E): injunction of general peace and truce for four years (see above, commentary on G 159-60). All this not in W.]

§ *Ad liberandam* (M 1058E): call for departure of the crusaders on 1 June 1216. Preamble not in W.

W 343-4 (158) Caeterum de virorum

COD 243.16-17 Caeterum] Ad liberandam terram sanctam de manibus impiorum ardenti desiderio aspirantes

THE FOURTH LATERAN COUNCIL

prudentium consilio	17-18 consilio] qui plene noverant circumstantias temporum et locorum *add*.
definimus ut ita ... conveniant in regnum Siciliae	18 definimus] sacro approbante concilio *praem*. (*om*. W *per homoiotel*.?)
alii apud Brundisium,	21 alii] sicut oportuerit et decuerit *add*.
alii apud Messanam, ubi et nos ... ... profecturus.	22 Messanam] et partes utrobique vicinas *add*.

[§ *Ad liberandam* continued (*Ad eundem quoque:* M 1059A): same term for those who go by land route; promise of sending a legate; admonition for spiritual preparedness; § *Ipsis autem clericis* (M 1059 C): provision of revenue for departing clerics; § *Ne igitur hoc sanctum* (M 1059C): all prelates are to enforce earlier and new crusading vows. All this not in W.]

§ *Nos igitur omnipotentis Dei* (M 1067B): Solemn announcement of crusading indulgence.

W 344 (158-9) Nos autem de omnipotentis Dei ... iuxta facultatem suam ...	COD 246.35 autem] igitur *de om*. 247.3 facultatem] et qualitatem *add*.
et qui in alienis expensis in propriis personis ... veniam peccatorum.	4 qui] illis similiter qui licet propriis] tamen *add*.
Huius quoque remissionis concedimus esse participes qui ad subventionem ... ministrabunt	5 concedimus] volumus et concedimus 7 participes] iuxta qualitatem subsidii et devotionis affectum omnes *add*.
aut circa praedicta consilium ... opportunum. Omnibus etiam proficiscentibus in hoc opere sancta et universalis synodus orationum et beneficiorum ... ad salutem. Amen.	8 circa praedicta *om*. 9 etiam] pie *add*. 10 opere] communi *add*. sancta et *om*. orationum et] omnium 12 Amen *om*.

Concordance I

W			COD
(1) 342-3	(156-8)	Ad haec sane—graviter puniendos	244.9-245.36
—	—	—	245.37-246.35
—	—	—	243.16-17
(2) 343-4	(158)	Caeterum de virorum—profecturus	243.17-25
—	—	—	243.25-244.9
(3) 344	(158-9)	Nos autem—salutem. Amen	246.35-247.12

Concordance II

COD	W	Paragraphs in M
243.16-17	-	Ad liberandam (preamble)
243.17-25	(2)	Ad liber. (continued)

243.25-244.9	-	Ad liber. (concluded), Ipsis autem, Ne igitur hoc sanctum
244.9-245.36	(1)	Ad haec ne quid, Huius remissionis, Ne vero in humeros, Cupientes, Nos autem, Sane quia iusto, Si quia vero, Iudaeos vero
245.37-246.35	-	Caeterum quia cursarii, Excommunicamus, Prohibemus, Licet autem, Quia vero
246.35-247.12	(3)	Nos igitur omnipotentis

*Universidad Pontificia de Salamanca
and Yale University*

Additional Note on d'Achéry's MS of the Albigensian Sentence (p. 140 above). — At a time when it was no longer possible to make substantial changes in the proofs of this article, reexamination of Paris MS lat. 12249 (on microfilm) by A. García, and new information kindly supplied on its provenance by Mme Jacqueline Rambaud-Buhot, Bibliothèque Nationale, have led us to conclude that the Paris MS is probably the codex from which d'Achéry took his text. The MS shows exactly the same peculiarities as the description and text he published: after a table of rubrics (fol. 107va-108rb) we find the brief Notice, with the same unusual ending 'In ea synodo — sequuntur' (108^v), followed by the Lateran constitutions (109^r-126^v) and the sermon 'Desiderio desideraui' (127^r-129^r, ends 'domino nostro Iesu Christo qui cum patre' [cf. R, p. 132 n. 15 above]; *oratio Innocentii papae* in d'A.); then the Albigensian sentence (129^{rv}) with the same title, the same poor reading 'Quantum ecclesia laborauit' (laborauerit *cett.*) and the same omission of two sentences after 'uidebitur expedire' (De negotio uero — dissoluatur *contin. cett.*) as in d'A. On fol. 129^v-130^r two additions follow (conc. Lat. c. 53 and 3 Comp. 3.27.2).

Par. lat. 12249 originally belonged to the Abbey of Préaux, diocese of Lisieux; see L. Delisle, *Le Cabinet des manuscrits* II (Paris 1874) 396; from there it went to St.-Maur-des-Fossés, where it was No. 29, and in 1716 it was acquired, with the other MSS of St.-Maur (cf. Delisle II 45, 74-8), by the Benedictines of St.-Germain-des-Prés. Mme Rambaud-Buhot, to whom we owe these indications, points out that on the other hand no MS containing acts of the IV Lateran Council is found in the old book lists for the Abbey of Lyre (Montfaucon, *Bibliotheca bibliothecarum* [Paris 1739] II 1256) and that d'Achéry could well have seen the MS from Préaux at St.-Maur-des-Fossés. If so, he would simply have been mistaken about the provenance of the book and we would be entitled to identify Par. lat. 12249 as his source.

X

JOHANNES TEUTONICUS, DAS VIERTE LATERANKONZIL UND DIE COMPILATIO QUARTA

I

Glossen des Johannes Teutonicus zu den Konstitutionen des vierten Laterankonzils (1215) sind bisher aus den Hss. Kassel, Landesbibliothek *Jur. 11 (unfoliiert; = K) und Florenz, Laurenziana *S. Croce IV sin. 2 (fol. 254-264ʳ; = L) bekanntgeworden;[1] ein weiteres Exemplar befindet sich in Graz, Universitätsbibl. *138 (fol. 233-246ʳ; = G).[2] Die entscheidende Frage, ob diese Glossen

---

[1] Vgl. KUTTNER, *Repertorium der Kanonistik* (Studi e Testi 71, Città del Vaticano 1937) 369 ff. — Die Florentiner Hs. (bisher nur aus Bandini bekannt und danach in *Repert.* 340, 352, 365, 369, 379 benutzt) enthält fol. 1-2 (in der alten Zählung unnumeriert): Fragment der *Comp. I* ohne Glossen, mit Florentiner Prozessnotizen fol. 1ᵛ am Rande. — fol. 3-78ᵛ (1-76 alter Zählung): *Comp. I*, bis fol. 47 (45) mit dem Apparat des Alanus (nicht rein; inc. ad *prooem.* v. *filii*: 'Arg. quod secundum conscientiam debemus iudicare...'; Zusätze von zweiter Hand aus Tancred; bricht im tit. *de iure patron.* c. *Querimonia* [3, 33, 11] ab); von fol. 47 ab mit Tancreds Apparat in zweiter Rezension, von anderer Hand. — fol. 79-129ᵛ (77-127 alter Zählung): *Comp. II* mit dem Apparat Tancreds in erster Rezension (vgl. KUTTNER, *Bernardus Compostellanus Antiquus*, in *Traditio* 1 [1943] 211 n. 15; unten IV n. 5) und erweiternden Zusätzen. — fol. 130-237ᵛ (128-235): *Comp. III*, unvollständig (bis 5, 15, un.), mit Tancreds Apparat. — fol. 238-252ᵛ (236-250): *Comp. IV*, unter Auslassung der Konzilsschlüsse (vgl. *Repert.* 379), mit dem Apparat des Johannes Teutonicus — fol. 254-264ᵛ (251-263): die *lateranischen Konstitutionen* mit dem Apparat des Johannes (davor fol. 253 ein halbes Blatt mit Rubrikenverzeichnis). — fol. 265 (262): *Arbor consanguinitatis* mit Glosse des Johannes Teutonicus, inc. 'Quod pictura arboris sit autentica probatur...' (über diesen Glossenapparat, der hier und in anderen Hss. rein, in manchen Hss. aber mit Damasusglossen kombiniert vorkommt [vgl. z. B. *Repert.* 378 zur Hs. Rouen *706], bleiben weitere Mitteilungen vorbehalten).

[2] G (ol. III. 138; 41/31) ist bisher nur aus FRIEDBERG, *Corp. iur. can.* II, xlvi (danach *Repert.* 341, 352, 366, 380) unzureichend bekannt; die Hs. enthält fol. 1-79ᵛ, 81-122ᵛ: *Compp I und II* mit Tancreds Apparaten in zweiter Rezension. — fol. 123-232ᵛ: *Comp. III* mit dem Apparat des Vincentius. — fol. 233-246ᵛ: *Conc. Lat.*

von Johannes als selbständiges Werk vor seinem Apparat zur Compilatio quarta (=Q) geschrieben wurden oder nur einen Auszug aus diesem Apparat darstellen, habe ich seinerzeit aufgrund von Selbstzeugnissen des Glossators (aber ohne Prüfung der Hss.) zugunsten der ersten Alternative beantwortet.³ Demgegenüber hat Gillmann nach eingehendem Studium der Hs. K (bei ihm als Ca bezeichnet) die entgegengesetzte Lösung vertreten.⁴

Nicht ohne Wehmut nehme ich heute eine Diskussion wieder auf, die, wäre es nach unser beider Wunsch gegangen, noch zu Lebzeiten des unvergesslichen Würzburger Meisters ihren Abschluss hätte finden sollen.⁵ Die erneute Untersuchung der strittigen Frage, durch die Ungunst der Zeiten um so viele Jahre verzögert, soll nicht polemischen Zwecken, sondern der Aufhellung eines grösseren Problemkreises dienen : nämlich dem Nachweis der hervorragenden Rolle, die Johannes Teutonicus bei der schulmässigen Rezeption und Bearbeitung der Gesetze aus den späteren Pontifikatsjahren Innozenz' III. gespielt hat.

Eine methodische und vergleichende Prüfung des Allegations-

IV mit dem Apparat des Joh. Teut. — fol. 246ᵛ-268ʳ: *Comp. IV* ohne die Konzilsschlüsse, unglossiert. — fol. 268ᵛ: Fragment einer *Quaestionensammlung,* inc. ' Quidam habuit causam aduersus alium super x. ....'; mit Allegationen aus Compp. I-III. Vielleicht *reportatio* aus der Schule des Laurentius (q. 2: '... Solutio. Laurentius dixit... '); einmal wird auch *R.* (Ricardus?) zitiert. — fol. 269-275ᵛ: *Casus* 'In prima parte istius (*al.* huius) capituli' zu Comp. III (vgl. *Repert.* 403), hier im Gegensatz zur meist anonymen Ueberlieferung im Explicit als 'casus nouissimarum secundum Vincentium' bezeichnet (die im *Repert.* 403 für Paris *3922 notierte Zuschreibung an Guido Brito beruht auf singulärer Kontamination der Casus 'In prima parte' mit dem fünften Buch der Casus 'Scribit dominus papa', für die Guidos Autorschaft auch anderwärts bezeugt ist: ibid. 404 f. Damit beheben sich die loc. cit. geäusserten Zweifel). — fol. 275ᵛ-281: *Casus* 'Cives Anconitani' zu Comp. II (vgl. *Repert.* 402). — fol. 281-288ᵛ: *Casus* ' Canones debent' zu Comp. I (ibid. 400). — fol. 289: *Arbor consang. et affin.* mit dem Johannes-Damasus-apparat (vgl. n. 1 oben), stark zerstört.

³ *Repert.* 370 f.; eine ähnliche Vermutung schon bei Schulte, *Geschichte der Quellen und Literatur* I, 256. — Ein weiteres Selbstzitat auch in gl. C. 2 q. 7 c. *Metropolitanum* (45): '... ut plene dixi in const. Ut debitus '.

⁴ *Hat Johannes Teutonikus zu den Konstitutionen des 4. Laterankonzils (1215) als solchen einen Apparat verfasst?* in *Archiv für kath. Kirchenr.* (AKKR) 117 (1937) 453-466.

⁵ Zur Korrespondenz hierüber vgl. Gillmanns Rezensionsabhandlung *Zur Inventarisierung der kanonistischen Handschriften aus der Zeit von Gratian bis Gregor IX.* (Mainz, 1938: Anhang [pp. 54-94] zum Sonderdruck von *Des Johannes Galensis Apparat zur Comp. III...* aus AKKR 118, 174-222) p. 91 f. Vgl. auch Kuttner, *La réserve papale du droit de canonisation,* in *Rev. hist. de droit français et étr.* 4ᵉ sér. 17 (1938) 209 n. 2.

stils der Glossen von K und Q führt Gillmann zu den folgenden Feststellungen: in einer Gruppe von Glossen beider Textzeugen verweisen die Allegationen unmittelbar auf die Konzilsschlüsse, ohne deren Einordnung in die Titel der Comp. IV zu berücksichtigen; insbesondere finden sich Fälle, in denen die Zitierweise mit *supra* und *infra* nur auf die Reihenfolge im Vulgattext passt, aber im Widerspruch zu der vielfach veränderten Reihenfolge in der Kompilation steht.[6] Andererseits ergibt eine zweite Gruppe von Glossen das umgekehrte Bild: sei es dass die Konstitutionen unter den entsprechenden Kompilationstiteln allegiert werden, sei es dass *supra* und *infra* nur der Kompilationsordnung, nicht der Vulgatordnung entsprechen, sei es endlich dass ausser den Konzilsschlüssen auch Dekretalen der Comp. IV angeführt werden.[7]

Das Glossenmaterial von K ist also in sich widerspruchsvoll, und seltsamerweise findet sich die selbe Inkonsequenz in den entsprechenden Glossen von Q. Daraus folgert Gillmann, dass es keinen ursprünglichen Apparat zu den Konzilsschlüssen als solchen gegeben hat: die Glossen der zweiten Gruppe könnten nur für Q geschrieben worden sein, und die Gegenargumente aus der ersten Gruppe seien mit der einfachen Erwägung zu beseitigen, dass Johannes bei Abfassung des Kompilationenapparates Q auch ein Exemplar der Konstitutionen (mit dem Apparat des Vincentius)[8] vor sich liegen hatte und gelegentlich zu Rate zog; dabei sei er dann gelegentlich von der Kompilationsordnung auf die Vulgatordnung seines Hilfstextes abgeirrt.[9] Mit anderen Worten, nach Gillmann ist der Allegationsstil der ersten Gruppe nur ein Resultat professoraler Zerstreutheit, und K nur ein nachträglicher Schreiberauszug aus Q.

Indessen hätte eine tiefergehende Textkritik—selbst wenn es ausser K keine Hs. der Konstitutionenglossen gäbe—von vornherein die Unhaltbarkeit dieser Lösung gezeigt. Bei aller unübertrefflichen Sorgfalt in der Aufdeckung und deskriptiven Analyse minutiöser Details, die Gillmann zeitlebens in seinen Handschriftenforschungen eigen war, lässt es sich nicht leugnen, dass eine gewisse Tendenz

---

[6] GILLMANN (*Hat Johannes...?*) 456-459.
[7] GILLMANN 459-465.
[8] Ueber den Konzilsapparat des Vincentius vgl. *Repert.* 369 f. Weitere Hss.: Admont, Benediktinerstift *22 (fol. 245-246; Fragment c. 69-Schluss); Rouen, Bibl. municipale *706 (E. 54; fol. 255-268ᵛ: vgl. KUTTNER, *Réserve papale* 209 n. 2, in Berichtigung von *Repert.* 374, 378).
[9] GILLMANN 465 f.

zur Vereinfachung komplexer Tatbestände ihn zuweilen die eigentlich textkritischen Probleme und Aufgaben nicht hat sehen lassen.[10] Der kontradiktorische Befund der Allegationen in KQ und das gelegentliche Schwanken der Hss. von Q sind zu verdächtig, als dass man mit einer harmonisierenden Theorie über die Schwierigkeiten hinweggleiten dürfte, ohne die Möglichkeit einer durch Kontamination verschiedener Rezensionen verderbten Ueberlieferung auch nur in Erwägung zu ziehen.

Im einzelnen ist zu bemerken: *a*) manche Allegationen aus Gillmanns zweiter Gruppe sind in Wahrheit in sich widerspruchsvoll oder doppeldeutig;[11] *b*) bei einigen Glossen stehen die entscheidenden, auf Dekretalen der Comp. IV verweisenden Stellen nur in Q, fehlen aber in K, ohne dass Gillmann diese auffallende, seiner Theorie widersprechende Differenz zu erklären versucht;[12] *c*) die Hss. von Q differieren zuweilen untereinander gerade an den kritischen Stellen oder weisen Spuren einer nicht auf Comp. IV passenden *lectio difficilior* auf:[13] so zitiert z. B. eine Hs. die Dekretale *Ad probandum* einmal aus der Sammlung des Alanus (1206) statt aus Comp. IV selbst; *d*) wenn Johannes in einem Fall mit den Worten 'ut dixi supra eodem' auf eine Glosse verweist, die in Q erst später ('unten') folgt, nach der Vulgatordnung des Konzils aber vorangehen müsste, so versagt die Abirrungshypothese: des Glossators Zerstreuung kann nicht so weit gegangen sein, dass er von einer eigenen, erst später zu schreibenden Anmerkung als *dixi supra* sprach;[14] *e*) in manchen Fällen endlich argumentiert Gillmann aus der Allegationsweise von Q-glossen, die in K gänzlich fehlen, mit denen sich also logischerweise überhaupt nichts beweisen lässt.[15]

---

[10] Vgl. G. Post, *The so-called Laurentius-Apparatus...*, in *The Jurist* 2 (Washington 1942) 5-31; Kuttner, *Bernardus Compostell.* (oben n. 1) 286 n. 35, 287 f. Die Beispiele sind vermehrbar.

[11] Widerspruchsvoll gl. Conc. c. 24 v. *collatione habita;* c. 34 c. *pauperibus;* c. 46 v. *nullo;* c. 56 v. *reprobamus.* Doppeldeutig gl. Conc. c. 24 v. *uiduatis;* c. 29 v. *de suis cogatur;* c. 58 v. *nec quicquam fraudis.* Vgl. (auch zu den folgenden Anmerkungen) die Analyse unten, II.

[12] Gl. Conc. c. 8 v. *excessus;* c. 35 v. *alioquin;* c. 53 v. *ex loci consuetudine.*

[13] Gl. Conc. c. 26 v. *ultra Italiam;* c. 46 v. *nullo;* c. 56 v. *reprobamus.*

[14] Gl. Conc. c. 38 v. *interlocutiones.* Ein ähnlicher Fall in gl. c. 56 cit. '... hoc dixi infra de decimis...', offensichtlich aus Konzilsordnung (*dixi supra*) und Kompilationsordnung (*dicam infra*) geflickt.

[15] Gl. Conc. c. 38 v. *presumatur;* c. 40 v. *super rebus;* c. 41 v. *bona fide;* c. 48 v. *defecerit.* Ganz fehl am Platze sind endlich die Dekretalenglossen Q 1, 3, 6 v. *per alios* und Q 2, 6, 1 v. *super hoc instrumento* (Gillmann 465), die ja notwendig erstmals zur Kompilation geschrieben sein müssen.

Eliminiert man alle textkritisch verdächtigen Stellen, so bleiben nur noch neun Glossen, die in KQ ohne Zweifel Gillmanns zweiter Gruppe beigezählt werden dürfen,[16] gegenüber dreissig teils zur ersten Gruppe gehörigen, teils zweifelhaften Fällen.[17] All das musste zu einer Vermutung für die Existenz zweier ursprünglich verschiedener Fassungen (Konzilsstil und Kompilationsstil) drängen, die in K und in Q auf verschiedene Weise miteinander vermischt zu sein scheinen (vgl. *b, c, e*). Bei den starken Indizien gegen die Reinheit von K bleibt es bedauerlich, dass Gillmann — dem ja einzelne Mängel der Hs. nicht entgangen waren — seine Ergebnisse nicht an der Florentiner Hs. (L) nachgeprüft hat. In der Tat wäre dann seine ganze Hypothese zusammengebrochen.

II

L enthält das Konzil mit johanneischen Glossen und Insertion (fol. 254, 257ᵛ-258ᵛ) einiger Vincentiusglossen.[1] Die Allegationen der Hauptschicht entbehren im Gegensatz zu KQ jeglichen Hinweises auf Comp. IV; doch hat eine jüngere Hand zuweilen solche Hinweise interpoliert. In der folgenden Analyse bedürfen Glossen, deren ausschliessliche Bezugnahme auf die Vulgatordnung der Konstitutionen statt auf Comp. IV bereits aus KQ feststeht (Gillmanns erste Gruppe),[2] keiner Beschreibung mehr.[3]

---

[16] Gl. Conc. c. 7 v. *excesserint;* v. *per capitulum;* c. 23 v. *de persona ydonea;* c. 24 v. *qui secreto;* v. *in loco;* c. 35 v. *si dicat;* c. 37 v. *ad remotos;* c. 52 v. *non utique uno;* v. *ad singulos gradus.*

[17] Vgl. oben n. 11-15; unten II n. 2.

[1] Zu c. 1 *Firmiter* finden sich z. B. die von Gillmann veröffentlichten Glossen des Vincentius ad vv. *credimus, sunt boni, compositus, uiam uite* (AKKR 109 [1929] 223-225).

[2] Gl. Conc. c. 6 v. *statuant;* c. 10 v. *subministrent;* c. 30 v. *correctionem;* v. *diligens inquisitio;* c. 33 v. *personaliter;* c. 35 v. *ex rationabili causa;* v. *in expensis;* c. 40 v. *continuatur;* c. 47 v. *possit probari;* v. *error sit;* v. *ualeat dubitari;* c. 53 v. *compellantur;* c. 69 v. *in usus pauperum*: vgl. Gillmann 456-459. Auch die an sich doppeldeutige Allegation in gl. c. 9 v. *prouideant* (Gillm. 456) bedarf keiner Bestätigung aus L.

[3] Für einzelne, von Gillmann oder mir benutzte Hss. von Q gelten die folgenden Siglen: Qa =Bamberg, Staatsbibl. *Can. 19 (P. II. 6); Qb =Vat. *Borgh. 264; Qi = Frankfurt, Stadtbibl. *28; für die Ausgabe des Ant. Augustinus steht die Sigle Qe. (Gillmann benutzt die Siglen *A, I, e* für Qa, Qi, Qe. Die weiteren von mir kollationierten vatikanischen Hss. — vgl. *Repert.* 381 — bieten keine bemerkenswerten Varianten).

c. 7 (*4Comp. de off. iud. ord.* 1, 13, 1) *Irrefragibili,* v. *excesserint*: ' Si forte fama ... ut j. e. (j. de accusat. *QK*) c. Qualiter. ' (L fol. 255rb; QK Gillm. 459). — L ' infra eodem ' verweist auf c. 8, das Titelzitat in QK auf *4Comp.* 5, 1, 4.

ibid. v. *per capitulum*: ' Nunquid in eo casu ... ex. iii. de elect. Cum in iure (*3Comp.* 1, 6, 18). [et est hoc expressum j. de concess. preb. non uac. Postulasti. *add. QK*] Nec obstat quod dicit lex ... ' (L eod.; QK Gillm. 461). — Der Zusatz der Rezension Q verweist auf die Dekretale *4Comp.* 3, 2, 2 (an. 1212; Potthast 4110) und ist in K übernommen, in L von der Zusatzhand unter der Glosse nachgetragen. — Varianten: infra] et *K;* Postulasti] Post translationem *Q*e.

c. 8 (*4Comp. de accus.* 5, 1, 4) *Qualiter,* v. *excessus*: ' Videamus ... ii. q. i. In primis (c. 7). [uel dic uerius ... ut s. e. Inquisitionis. *add. Q*] Si uero testes ... ' (L fol. 257^r; QK Gillm. 460 n. 5). — Zusatz in Q verweist auf *4Comp.* 5, 1, 2 (an. 1212; Po. 4628); fehlt in LK (von Gillmann für K ohne Erklärung notiert).

c. 23 (*4Comp. de elect.* 1, 3, 8) *Ne pro defectu,* v. *de persona ydonea ipsius*: ' Hic precepit ... ut probatur lxv. dist. Si forte (c. 9) [et s. e. Bone *add. QK*] et ff. de legatis ... ' (L fol. 258va; QK Gillm. 462). — Zusatz in Q verweist auf *4Comp.* 1, 3, 2 (an. 1215; Po. 4989); in K übernommen.

c. 24 (*4Comp. de elect.* 1, 3, 9) *Quia propter,* v. *uiduatis*: ' Per hoc patet quod loquitur ... canonicorum. [Set numquid ... ut s. e. Ne pro defectu. *add. QK*] Jo.' (L eod.; QK Gillm. 463). — Q fügt eine neue *quaestio* an und löst sie durch Allegation der const. *Ne pro defectu* = c. 23 = *4Comp.* 1, 3, 8 (von K übernommen). Doch bleibt die Allegation selbst für QK doppeldeutig, da sie gleichermassen auf die Konzils- wie auf die Kompilationsordnung passt.

ibid. v. *qui secreto*: [' Forte per iuramentum, ut s. e. (tit. *add. K*) Ad nostram.'] (QK Gillm. 463). — Zusatzglosse in Q (von K übernommen) mit Allegation von *4Comp.* 1, 3, 7 (an. 1205; Po. 2481); fehlt in L.

ibid. v. *collatione habita*: ' Ut uideatur ... numerus alium [ut dixi s. e. Bone. *add. QK*].' (L fol. 258va; QK Gillm. 465). — Der Zusatz in Q (von K übernommen) verweist auf eine eigne Glosse zu *4Comp.* 1, 3, 2. Den inneren Widerspruch, der dadurch entsteht, dass eine entsprechende Glosse garnicht existiert — gemeint ist vielmehr gl. c. *Scriptum est* (*4Comp.* 1, 3, 6: an. 1212: Po. 4577) — hält Gillmann 465 n. 1 für unerheblich.

ibid. v. *in loco*: ' Set quis est locus ... ut j. e. de rescr. (s. de rescr. *QK*) Nonnulli ... ut j. e. Nichil est ... et uarie locuntur iura de illa materia [prout notaui vii. q. i. Factus. Set hec questio soluitur s. e. c. i. *add. QK*]. Jo.' (L eod.; QK Gillm. 463). — L ' infra eodem de rescr. Nonnulli ' verweist auf c. 37 unter Beifügung der Kapitelsrubrik des

Vulgattextes (vgl. die Konzilienausgaben und die Rubrikenliste bei Potthast I, 437 f.), wie dies auch Vincentius in seinem Konstitutionenapparat gelegentlich zu tun pflegte (vgl. dazu Gillm. 460 n. 5); die zweite Allegation in L bezieht sich auf c. 26. Wegen der in Comp. IV veränderten Reihenfolge von cc. 24, 37 (*4Comp.* 1, 3, 9 und 1, 2, 5) hat Q die erste Allegation in 'supra de rescr.' geändert; die zweite dagegen (c. 26 = *4Comp.* 1, 3, 11) konnte unberührt bleiben. Der Zusatz in Q verweist auf c. *Coram* (1, 3, 1: Datum ungewiss; Po. 5027). K folgt Q, während sich in L ein Zusatz von zweiter Hand findet: 'set certum est quod extra prouinciam positi non uocantur, ut ex. iiii. Coram.'

c. 26 (*4Comp. de elect.* 1, 3, 11) *Nichil est*, v. *ultra Italiam*: 'Licet fines ... j. e. (s. de rescript. *QK*) Nonnulli.' (L fol. 259ra; QK Gillm. 460). — L verweist auf c. 37 ('infra'), Q auf *4Comp.* 1, 2, 5; übernommen in K. Spuren der L-rezension in Qab: 's. de rescr. j. e. Nonnulli' (vgl. Gillm. 460 n. 2).

c. 29 (*4Comp. de prebend.* 3, 2, 4) *De multa*, v. *de suis cogatur*: 'Si habet propria ... j. de sent. excomm. Sub interminatione.' (L eod.; QK eod.). — LK verweisen auf c. 49 unter der Rubrik (vor c. 47) des Vulgattextes (für dieselbe Zitierweise bei Vincentius vgl. Gillm. 460 n. 5). In Q konnte dies bei unverändertem Wortlaut für Hinweis auf *4Comp.* 5, 15, 6 benutzt werden.

c. 34 (*4Comp. de censib.* 3, 18, 4) *Quia plerique*, v. *pauperibus*: 's. cap. prox. contra et j. de sent. exc. Sub interminatione.' (L fol. 259vb; Q Gillm. 466 n. 1; fehlt in K). — L 'supra cap. prox.' bezieht sich auf c. 33 *Procurationes* (= *4Comp.* 3, 18, 2); d. h. Johannes kontrastiert c. 34 '... tantundem cogatur pauperibus elargiri' mit c. 33 '... et ecclesiae quam taliter aggrauauit tantundem impendet'. Die in Q unveränderte Allegation ist sinnlos, da dort 'cap. prox.' auf *4Comp.* 3, 18, 3 (Conc. c. 46 *Aduersus*) bezogen werden muss. Für die Allegation von c. *Sub interminatione* vgl. oben zu c. 29.

c. 35 (*4Comp. de appell.* 2, 12, 3) *Ut debitus*, v. *si dicat*: 'Id est si alleget ... ut ex. i. de rescr. Si autem (*1Comp.* 1, 2, 7). [Et hoc intelligo ... ut xvi. q. iii. Placuit (c. 8) et s. e. Oblate ... constat. *add. QK*] Et intellige quando secundus ...' (L eod.; QK Gillm. 462). — Zusatz in Q (übernommen von K) verweist auf *4Comp.* 2, 12, 1 (an. 1209, Po. 3775); in L von jüngerer Hand mit der gebotenen Aenderung '... et ex. iiii. de app. Oblate' nachgetragen.

ibid. v. *alioquin*: 'Hic manifeste uidetur ... possit uti, [ut s. de fide instr. Cum Johannes *add.* Q] C. de app. Eos (7, 62, 6).' (L eod.; QK Gillm. 460 n. 5). — Zusatz in Q verweist auf *4Comp.* 2, 8, un. (bei Po. 3872 auf c. 1206-1209 datiert: vgl. aber unten III n. 15); fehlt in LK (von Gillmann für K ohne Erklärung notiert). Kontamination in Qa: '... ut C. de fide instr. ...'

c. 37 (*4Comp. de rescr.* 1, 2, 5) *Nonnulli*, v. *ad remotos*: ' Nota quod remotus ... ex. iii. de elect. Cum inter (*3Comp.* 1, 6, 3). [j. de elect. Nichil est. *add. QK*] Sunt autem duo ... ' (L fol. 260ra; QK Gillm. 460). — Zusatz in Q verweist auf c. 26 in der Kompilationsordnung, *4Comp.* 1, 3, 11; in K übernommen.

c. 38 (*4Comp. de probat.* 2, 6, 3) *Quoniam contra*, v. *interlocutiones*: ' Licet scribi ... an interlocutiones transeant in rem iudicatam dixi s. e. Cum cessante. Jo.' (L fol. 260rb; Q Gillm. 465 n. 5; fehlt in K). — LQ ' dixi supra eodem ' verweist auf c. 36; im Kompilationsstil müsste es ' dicam infra de appell. Cum cessante ' (*4Comp.* 2, 12, 4) heissen, und in der Tat machen die Hss. Qai ' Emendations '-versuche in dieser Richtung (so auch Vat. *Ottob. 1099, Vat. *lat. 1377 und *2509). Dass Gillmanns Abirrungshypothese hier für die konzilsmässige Zitierweise versagt, ist oben (I, Text zu Anm. 14) erörtert worden.

ibid. vv. *dilationes, negligentiam, presumatur* wird dreimal 'j. e. Sacro' allegiert (L eod.; Q Gillm. 466 n. 1; fehlt in K). — LQ ' infra eodem ' verweist auf c. 47; im Kompilationsstil müsste es ' j. de sent. exc. Sacro' (*4Comp.* 5, 15, 5) heissen. Von Gillmann wegen des Ausfalls der Glossen in K ohne Würdigung notiert; so auch das folgende Beispiel.

ibid. v. *presumatur*: ' Numquid ergo ... admittuntur testes, C. de probat. Cum precibus (4, 19, 8). [j. de fide instr. Cum Johannes. *add. Qie*] Nam et partes ... ' (L eod.; Q Gillm. eod.; fehlt in K). — Zusatz in Qie wie zu c. 35 v. *alioquin* oben.

c. 40 (*4Comp. de arbit.* 1, 18, 1) *Contingit*, v. *super rebus*: ' Per hoc non determinatur ... ex. i. de cons. et aff. Ex litteris, in fine (*1Comp.* 4, 14, 2). [Tamen ... in spiritualibus, ut j. c. prox. *add.* Q] Jo.' (L fol. 260ra; Q Gillm. 466 n. 1; fehlt in K). — Zusatz in Q verweist auf die Dekretale *Per tuas* (*4Comp.* 1, 18, 2: an. 1214-15; Po. 4957); ein entsprechender Zusatz ' Tamen ... ut ex. iiii. de arbitris. Per tuas, in fine ' ist in L von jüngerer Hand nachgetragen.

c. 41 (*4Comp. de prescript.* 2, 10, 3) *Quoniam omne*, v. *bona fide*: ' Arg. contra ... ut presumatur titulus. [Set contra j. de decim. Dudum. *add.* Q].' (L fol. 260rb; Q Gillm. 466 n. 1; fehlt in K). — Zusatz in Q verweist auf *4Comp.* 3, 9, 3 (an. 1215; Po. 5298).

c. 46 (*4Comp. de censib.* 3, 18, 3) *Aduersus consules*, v. *nullo*: ' Sic ergo non ualet ... ut s. e. (j. de heret. QK) Excommunicamus ... ut ex. al. de sent. et de iud. (s. de sent. et re iud. QK) Ad probandum ... ' (L fol. 261ra; QK Gillm. 460 n. 5). — L ' supra eodem ' verweist auf c. 3, QK ' infra de hereticis ' auf *4Comp.* 5, 5, 2. Die zweite Allegation (Po. 5023) ist in L der Sammlung des Alanus (c. 1206) entnommen: Alan. 2, 17, 8 (erste Redaktion 2, 15, 8 — über die beiden Fassungen der Sammlung siehe unten III); in QK auf *4Comp.* 2, 11, 2 geändert. Doch behält

Qe die *lectio difficilior* ' ut ex. Al. ... ' bei, was Gillmann verzeichnet, ohne Verdacht gegen die Ursprünglichkeit von KQai zu schöpfen, und ohne dem inneren Widerspruch in Qe (zwei verschiedene Allegationsweisen in einer Glosse!) Beachtung zu schenken.

c. 48 (*4Comp. de appell.* 2, 15, 5) *Cum speciali*, v. *defecerit*: [' Videtur ergo quod appellans ... ut s. de probat. Quoniam... '] (Q Gillm. 460 n. 5). — Zusatzglosse mit Allegation von *4Comp.* 2, 6, 3 (= c. 38); fehlt nicht nur in LK, sondern auch in Qi.

c. 52 (*4Comp. de testib.* 2, 7, 6) *Licet ex quadam*, v. *non utique uno*: ' Quia si mille ... duobus. [arg. contra ista j. qui matrim. accus. poss. Cum in tua. add. *QK*] Jo. ' (L fol. 262rb; QK Gillm. 461). — Zusatz in Q (übernommen in K) verweist auf *4Comp.* 4, 4, un. (an. 1212; Po. 4614). Die Hs. Qi bricht nach ' ... contra ista ' ab (Gillm. 462 n. 1).

ibid. v. *ad singulos gradus*: ' Numquid ergo tenetur ... a fratribus [ut j. de cons. et aff. Tua *add. QK*]. Set quid si testes ... ' (L fol. 262va; QK Gillm. 462). — Zusatz in Q (übernommen in K) verweist auf *4Comp.* 4, 3, 2 (an. 1212; Po. 4379).

c. 53 (*4Comp. de decim.* 3, 9, 5) *In aliquibus*, v. *ex loci consuetudine*: ' Sic ergo consuetudo ... ut xi. di. In his rebus (c. 7). [Et istud intelligo ... ut s. de prescript. Quoniam. Jo. *add. Q*]. ' (L eod.; QK Gillm. 460 n. 5). — Zusatz in Q verweist auf *4Comp.* 2, 10, 3 (= c. 41); fehlt in LK (von Gillmann für K ohne Erklärung notiert).

c. 56 (*4Comp. de pact.* 1, 15, un.) *Plerique*, v. *reprobamus*: ' Hoc dixi s. e. (dixi j. de decimis *Q*) In aliquibus ... ' (L fol. 262vb; Q Gillm. 466 n. 1; fehlt in K). — L ' supra eodem ' verweist auf c. 53, das Titelzitat in Q auf *4Comp.* 3, 9, 5. Doch verrät das in sich widerspruchsvolle ' dixi infra ' die Herkunft der Q-glosse aus einer nur oberflächlich geänderten Konzilsfassung; vgl. oben I, n. 14.

c. 58 (*4Comp. de priuil.* 5, 12, 8) *Quod nonnullis*, v. *nec quicquam fraudis*: ' Per hoc uidetur ... ut s. c. prox. ' (L fol. 263rb; QK Gillm. 464). — LKQ ' supra c. proximum ' verweist auf const. *Ut priuilegia* = c. 57 = *4Comp.* 5, 12, 7: die Allegation in der Konzilsordnung konnte unverändert für die Kompilationsordnung stehen bleiben, ist also doppeldeutig. Zwar hat der Schreiber der Konstitutionen in K die Vulgatordnung eigenmächtig geändert, indem er c. 57 und c. 56 vertauschte (57. 56. 58), sodass also das Zitat für K — und nur für K — nicht passt. Seltsamerweise hat Gillmann daraus gefolgert, dass die Glosse sich nur auf die Kompilationsordnung bezieht. Die Kongruenz mit der echten Konzilsordnung wird bei ihm nicht erwähnt.

Mit der vorstehenden Analyse ist der Beweis erbracht, dass Johannes Teutonicus die lateranischen Konstitutionen ursprünglich als solche glossiert hat. Bezugnahmen auf Comp. IV sind diesen

Glossen fremd: sie finden sich nur in Zusätzen oder Aenderungen, die mit der Einarbeitung der Konzilsglossen in den Kompilationenapparat Q zusammenhängen. Gillmanns scheinbare Gegenargumente erklären sich durch die Tatsache, dass die Konzilshs. K nicht wie L den reinen Konstitutionenapparat, sondern eine *recensio mixta* aus diesem und aus Q aufweist. Die Grazer Konsilshs. (G) habe ich einstweilen nicht kollationieren können; eine gewisse Vermutung spricht aber dafür, dass sie die konzilsmässige Rezension der Glossen enthält. Denn die in Comp. IV nicht rezipierte Kreuzfahrerkonstitution *Ad liberandam* (nach c. 70) ist hier gleichfalls mit johanneischen Glossen versehen.[4]

Für das Vorhandensein zahlreicher Allegationen aus dem Vulgattext des Konzils in Q bedarf es hiernach nicht mehr der gekünstelten Abirrungs- und Zerstreuungshypothese. Vielmehr ergibt sich, dass Johannes, als er die Comp. IV glossierte und dabei seine eigenen Konzilsglossen dem neuen Apparat einverleibte, in manchen Fällen die notwendigen Aenderungen des Allegationsstils vorzunehmen vergass. Solche Nähte und Unebenheiten lassen auf eine gewisse Hast schliessen, die bei der Umredigierung obgewaltet haben muss: eine Erscheinung, die mit der nun zu erläuternden Entstehungsgeschichte der Comp. IV zusammenhängt.

III

Die Compilatio quarta[1] entsprang dem Bedürfnis der Schule, drei Gruppen von innozentianischen Texten zusammengefasst in das den Dekretalisten geläufige Buch- und Titelschema zu bringen: erstens die lateranischen Konstitutionen, zweitens eine Reihe von älteren Dekretalen, die in der offiziellen Comp. III übergangen waren, endlich die seit dieser Sammlung erlassenen Dekretalen der späteren Pontifikatsjahre. Zwar war schon gelegentlich der Versuch gemacht worden, die Konzilsschlüsse allein, ohne Abweichen von der ursprünglichen Ordnung, in fünf *partes* zu zerlegen, jeden Teil

---

[4] Inc. v. *impiorum*: 'Siue saracenorum siue paganorum...'; expl. v. *contriti*: 'Quia non penitenti non dimittitur peccatum, xxiiii. q. i. Legatur (q. 2 c. 2). Jo.'
— Gillmann 465 n. 4 hatte das Fehlen von Glossen zur const. *Ad liberandam* in K als Indiz gegen einen originalen Konzilsapparat betrachtet.

[1] Ergänzungen und Berichtigungen zur Handschriftenliste (*Repert.* 375-381) können im gegenwärtigen Zusammenhang unterbleiben.

wiederum durch Auswahl einiger Rubriken des Vulgattextes in Titel zu zergliedern, und das Ganze im justinianischen Geschmack als ' Novellen' zu präsentieren : so in der Hs. *S. Croce III sin. 6 (fol. 97-107ᵛ) ² der Laurenziana (deren aus Vincentius-, Damasus- und unsignierten Glossen zusammengestellter Apparat³ noch näherer Untersuchung bedarf);⁴ so auch ein anonymes Proömium ' Questionum articuli' zu den Konzilsschlüssen, das in der Hs. Lissabon, Bibl. Nacional *Alcob. 381 (fol. 225)⁵ irrtümlich der Comp. IV vorangeschickt wird.⁶ Aber auf die Dauer war doch

---

² Die bisher nur unvollkommen aus Bandini bekannte Hs. (danach *Repert.* 340, 369, 378) enthält fol. 1-2ᵛ : Fragment einer *Dekretalensammlung* saec. XII aus der Familie der Bambergensis (vgl. KUTTNER, *Traditio* 1, 285 n. 30); die Blätter sind vertauscht, fol. 1ʳ durch Rasur unkenntlich; Ordnung und Titelrubriken stehen der *Coll. Lipsiensis* am nächsten (fol. 2ʳ⁻ᵛ=*Lips.* 52, 15-30; 53, un.; 55, 1-7. fol. 1ᵛ = *Lips.* 59, 5-6, 16-23). — fol. 3-96ᵛ: *Comp.* I mit Tancreds Apparat erster Rezension (vgl. *Trad.* 1, 311 n. 15). — fol. 97-107ᵛ : *Conc. Lat. IV* mit Mischapparat. — fol. 108-Schluss: *Comp. IV* mit Glosse des Joh. Teutonicus.

³ In Ergänzung früherer Angaben (*Repert.* 369; *Réserve papale* [oben I n. 5] 209 n. 2) hier nur soviel, dass die Vincentiusglossen zahlreich und zum Teil kritisch verarbeitet, die Damasusglossen weniger zahlreich sind. Die Hauptmasse der Glossen gehört dem Redaktor des Apparates, der sich mit den Bologneser Disputationsübungen (*quaestiones dominicales*, in gl. c. 11 v. *pauperes*, v. *unius prebende*) und der Kurialpraxis (gl. c. 35 v. *exposita*: '... contra probat cotidiana consuetudo curie') wohl vertraut zeigt und sogar Äusserungen des Papstes aus dem Konsistorium zu berichten weiss (gl. c. 23 v. *alterius*: '... set papa innocentius ita interpretatus est illa iura in quadam disputatione'). Mit Hilfe seiner zahlreichen Selbstzitate (*de hoc dixi, notaui* etc.) aus Glossen zu Compp. I-III liesse er sich wohl leicht identifizieren; doch ist mir zur Zeit ausreichendes Vergleichsmaterial unzugänglich.

⁴ Rubr. *Prima pars nouellarum. de fide catholica et summa trin.* (c. 1); *de hereticis* (c. 3) usw. Pars II: cc. 5-22 in 6 Titeln; III: cc. 23-34 in 4 Titeln; IV: cc. 35-49 in 7 Titeln; V: cc. 50-*Ad liberandam* in 9 Titeln.

⁵ Die bisher nur ungenau bekannte Hs (vgl. *Repert.* 342, 353, 367, 380, 385) enthält fol. 1-76ʳ, 76ᵛ-116ᵛ, 117ʳ-224ʳᵃ: *Compp. I-III* mit Tancreds Apparaten, und zwar zu Comp. II in erster Rezension (vgl. *Trad.* 1, 311 n. 15); Zusatzschichten zu Compp. I und II. — fol. 224ʳᵇ-224ᵛ: fünf *Dekretalen Honorius' III;* Nr. 1-3 sind Trennstücke von *Super speculam* (Pressuti 2267) mit einem Glossenapparat 'Nota in causis ecclesiasticis' von Joh. Teutonicus und Willielmus Vasco (vgl. *Trad.* 1, 337 n. 43). — fol. 225-256ᵛ: *Comp. IV* mit dem Apparat des Joh. Teutonicus, darin ad c. 1 *Firmiter*, v. *qui omnes* unser Proömium. — DENIFLES Angabe (*Die Universitäten des Mittelalters* I, 108 n. 226; vgl. *Repert.* 385), die Hs. enthielte auch Comp. V, muss auf einem Irrtum beruhen.

⁶ ' Questionum articuli non poterant legibus comprehendi... Ideo presentes constitutiones, quas nouellas appellamus, sunt promulgate a sancta synodo [in] uniuersali sub domino Innoc. iij. patre perspicacissimi ingenii et summe intelligentie, cui a longissimis temporibus non fuit inuentus similis in cathedra piscatoris, qui ecclesiam exaltaret et obseruaret legem excelsi. Diuiduntur autem nouelle iste in .v. partes. In prima parte tractat de fide catholica (c. 1) et reprobatione

eine weniger oberflächliche Systematisierung und eine Kombination der konziliaren mit der bisher nicht genügend erfassten Dekretalengesetzgebung des Papstes erwünscht.

Das auf die Zeit vor Comp. III zurückgehende Material (44 Dekretalen) ist fast ausschliesslich unter Benutzung dreier älterer Sammlungen zusammengestellt.[7] Dreissig dieser Dekretalen lassen sich in der Sammlung des Alanus von 1206 nachweisen;[8] nur in geringerem Maasse wurden die Sammlungen Gilberts (1202-3; fünf Stücke) und Bernhards von Compostella (1208; vier Stücke) herangezogen.[9] Für Alanus hielt sich die Comp. IV nicht an den ersten Entwurf, wie er in der Fuldaer Hs. *D. 14 (=W) vorliegt,[10] sondern an die besser geordnete zweite Rezension (A=Vercelli, Kapitelsbibliothek *LXXXIX, fol. 51-136; Salzburg, St. Peter *a.

---

hereticorum (cc. 2-3) et quorumdam rituum grecorum (c. 4). In secunda...' usw. Die fünf Teile stimmen mit denen der Florentiner Hs. überein, die Titeleinteilung ist aber etwas verschieden (pars II: 5 Titel; III: 4 Titel; IV: 5 Titel; V: 5 Titel).

[7] Eingehende Forschungen zu den Quellen der Comp. IV fehlen; für die im Text folgenden Beobachtungen sind die Angaben von R. VON HECKEL, *Die Dekretalensammlungen des Gilbertus und Alanus...*, in *Zeitschr. der Savigny-Stift. Kan. Abt.* 29 (1940), 116-357, und H. SINGER, *Die Dekretalensammlung des Bernardus Compostellanus antiquus*, in *Wiener SB*, 171 (1914), Nr. 2, vielfach von grossem Nutzen gewesen.

[8] Aus Heckels Analyse ergeben sich 31 (vgl. p. 174); die Differenz beruht auf dem sogleich zu erörternden Unterschied zwischen den zwei Alanusrezensionen: denn *4Comp.* 3, 7, un. kommt zwar in der vorläufigen Fuldaer Fassung (app. 102), aber nicht in der endgültigen Alanussammlung vor und dürfte am ehesten mit *Bern. Compost.* 2, 14, 1 verwandt sein, vgl. Singer, op. cit. 25 n. 73; Heckel, op. cit. 333.

[9] *Gilb.* 1, 3, 6; 9, 5; 18, 4; 2, 8, 2; app. 6 (*4Comp.* 1, 3, 3; 5, 6, 1; 1, 16, 1; 2, 4, 1; 3, 1). *Bern.* 1, 8, 13; 17; 21, 6; 2, 14, 1 (*4Comp.* 1, 3, 5; 7; 12, 4; 3, 7, un.). Comp. IV hat zwar mit Gilbert 3 weitere (vgl. HECKEL 174) und mit Bernhard 13 weitere Stücke (vgl. SINGER *loc. cit.*; KUTTNER, *Trad.* 1, 330) gemeinsam. Doch liegen in all diesen Fällen — vielleicht mit Ausnahme von *Gilb.* app. 13, das sekundär zur Ergänzung von *Al.* 2, 18 (16) 4 für *4Comp.* 3, 13, 2 benutzt sein mag — keine direkten Quellenbeziehungen vor, wie sich teils aus Textvergleich, teils aus der Erwägung ergibt, dass überall wo Alanus bereits als primäre Quelle gegeben war, dem parallelen Vorkommen in anderen Sammlungen keine Bedeutung zukommt. Aus derselben Erwägung scheidet die ältere Sammlung Rainers von Pomposa (vgl. *Repert.* 310; eine weitere Hs. in Paris *lat. 3922A, fol. 235-242: *Trad.* 1, 328 n. 6) trotz acht gemeinsamer Stücke als Quelle für Comp. IV aus.

[10] W ist jetzt ausführlich von Heckel beschrieben; bereits im *Hist. Jahrb. der Görresges.* 57 (1937) 86 n. 3, 259, hat Heckel die bis dahin herrschende Ansicht Schultes (Fuld. *D. 14 sei eine ' vermehrte ' Sammlung, der in Fuld. *D 5 enthaltene Auszug sei die Originalfassung) widerlegt. Vgl. auch *Réserve papale* (oben I n. 5) 198 n. 5. Zur Konzeptnatur von W vgl. HECKEL, *Die Dekretalensammlungen* ... 138.

IX. 18, fol. 169-243),[11] die auch sonst in Bologna benutzt zu werden pflegte.[12]

Immerhin dürfte der Redaktor die genannten Vorlagen gelegentlich an anderen, sekundären Quellen kontrolliert haben;[13] aber nur fünf Dekretalen der Comp. IV, die mit Sicherheit aus den Jahren vor Comp. III stammen,[14] sind nicht in Gilbert, Alanus,

---

[11] Vgl. zu A einstweilen *Trad.* 1, 289 n. 52; 313 n. 26; 318 f.; 327 n. 5. Für seine Analyse von W hat Heckel von meinen Mitteilungen über A mehrfach Gebrauch machen können, vgl. HECKEL, *op. cit.* 118 n. 2; 149; 162 n. 1; 177. Die Benutzung von A durch Comp. IV ergibt sich aus dem Parallelismus z. B. der folgenden Kapitel:

4Comp	A	W app.
1, 3, 4	1, 6, 14	15
4, un.	7, un.	61
6, 1	9, 3	55
2	4	1, 7, 3

[12] Der Beweis dafür kann hier nur angedeutet werden. (*a*) Für Bernhard von Compostella vgl. *Trad.* 1, 327 n. 5. — (*b*) Comp. II hat von ihren 12 bei W und Gilb. nicht nachweisbaren Stücken (vgl. HECKEL 173 n. 1) 6 aus A: *2Comp.* 2, 1, 2 (A 2, 1, 2); 3, 18, 1 (3, 16, 6); 3, 22, 4-5 (3, 19, 3-4: beachte den Parallelismus); 5, 20, un. (6, 3, 1); 5, 22, 1 (6, 7, un.), während von den 11 vorinnozentianischen Stücken des Anhangs von W, die in Comp. II nicht wiederkehren (vgl. HECKEL *loc. cit.*), 10 auch in A fehlen (nur W app. 76 = A 2, 5, 4); ferner verrät Comp. II sich durch die Doublette *Cura* (*Quia*) *suscepti* JL 17626: *2Comp.* 5, 8, 2 *de cler. pugn. in duello* (= *Gilb.* 5, 6, 2 h. t.) = *2Comp.* 5, 16, un. *de purg. vulg.* (= A 5, 19, 1 h. t.). — (*c*) Die *Coll. Estensis*, ein Konkurrenzunternehmen zur Comp. II (vgl. *Trad.* 1, 310 f.) enthält 5 Stücke, die nur aus A, nicht aus W stammen können. — (*d*) Die Allegationen Tancreds aus Alanus (die ich noch in *Repert.* 457 ff. aus Schultes mangelhafter Beschreibung der Fuldaer Hss. zu identifizieren unternahm) passen durchweg besser auf A als auf W, nämlich: 'in alano ex. de suppl. negl. prel. Licet dilecti': A 1, 9, 3 (W app. 55); 'ex. alani de suppl. negl. Litteras': A 1, 9, 4 (W 1, 7, 3); 'ex. tit. alani de elect. Offitii tui': A 1, 6, 14 (W app. 15); 'ex. alani eod. tit. (de sent. exc.) Quante presumptionis': A 5, 23, 1 (W app. 96); 'infra de sent. et re iud. alani Ad probandum': A 2, 17, 8 (W 2, 15, 8). Das gleiche gilt für Alanuszitate überhaupt bei den Glossatoren; nur an einer Stelle in Tancreds *Ordo iudic.* (ed. Bergmann 152 lin. 2-3) wird mit 'ut ex. Alan. de consang. c. Quod uero' auf die in A fehlende, zweifelhafte Dekretale W 4, 11, 3 = app. 108 (Alex. III? Inn. III?) hingewiesen. — (*e*) Alanus selbst hat die Sammlung in der Rezension A mit einem Glossenapparat versehen (Cod. Vercell.), den er und andere Glossatoren (Albertus, Joh. Galensis) später zur Kommentierung von Compp. II und III ausgebeutet haben.

[13] Die dadurch zuweilen entstehenden Textdifferenzen gegenüber W und Gilb. haben Heckel (p. 175) zu einer äusserst konservativen Beurteilung des Quellenverhältnisses veranlasst: nur ein Teil (24) der gemeinsamen Dekretalen (36) stamme 'sicher' oder 'vielleicht' aus Gilb. und W. Aber Heckels eigene Analyse der restlichen Stücke rechtfertigt solche Uebervorsicht nicht; auch ergibt sich aus A oft stärkere Uebereinstimmung mit Alanus als aus W zu vermuten war.

[14] *4Comp.* 2, 1, 1 (an. 1206-7: Po. 3018); 3, 3, 1 (an. 1204: Po. 2360); 4, 3, 1 (1209 iun. 26: Po. 3753); 5, 11, un. (an. XII? XI? Po. 3663); 5, 16, 2 (1209 febr. 16: Po. 3656). Friedberg hatte zwar *4Comp.* 5, 11 un. irrig als Trennstück von Po. 1806

X

621

oder Bernhard nachweisbar.[15] In diesem Zusammenhang ist zu betonen, dass der übliche Zeitansatz für Comp. III auf das Jahr 1210 ungenau ist. Die offizielle Sammlung enthält nämlich aus dem zwölften Registerjahr (1209 febr. 22 — 1210 febr. 21) nur sechs oder sieben[16] Stücke, alle aus dem ersten Drittel dieses Jahres (die jüngsten vom 30. April und vom 29. Juni : Po. 3718, 3756).[17] Wann die fertige Sammlung mit der Bulle *Devotioni vestrae* nach Bologna gesandt wurde, lässt sich nicht sagen;[18] aber angesichts der Tatsache, dass Peter von Benevent die Arbeit bereits im Sommer 1209 abgeschlossen haben muss,[19] wird man für das Publikationsdatum kaum über den Herbst dieses Jahres, keinesfalls über das Ende des zwölften Regierungsjahres hinabgehen dürfen. Die in Comp. IV enthaltenen sechs Dekretalen aus dem zwölften Registerband (vom 26. Juni 1209 ab)[20] gehören also, mit Ausnahme der ersten, bereits

---

(an. 1203) angesehen, doch ergibt sich die Zugehörigkeit zu Po. 3663 aus dem Register (XI, 265: vgl. PL 215, 1580C). Der Zeitansatz der Dekretale (ein anderes Trennstück in *3Comp*. 1, 18, 11) bleibt ungewiss: sie befindet sich unter den 16 Briefen Po. 3660-75, die ohne Rücksicht auf ihre Chronologie am Ende des XI. Registerbandes eingetragen sind, ist aber dort ausdrücklich 'anno XII' datiert (vgl. HECKEL, op. cit. 160).

[15] Zwei weitere Dekretalen gehören nur scheinbar in diesen Zusammenhang: *4Comp*. 1, 16, 2 (an. 1203 laut Po. 2075) ist in Wahrheit den Jahren 1210-11 zuzuweisen (vgl. DENIFLE, *Universitäten des MA*. 86 n. 153); und bei *4Comp*. 2, 8, un. hat sich Po. 3872 zu seinem Zeitansatz (1206-9) nur durch die Tatsache verleiten lassen, dass in dieser Dekretale eine Urkunde inseriert ist, deren Datum in den Hss. zwischen 1206 und 1208 nov. 4 schwankt. Danach hätte 1206(-9) lediglich als terminus a quo angegeben werden dürfen; den term. ad quem liefert die erste Rezension von Tancreds Apparaten zu Compp. I und II (1210-15), in denen Po. 3872 ad *1Comp*. 2, 3, 17 v. *dumtaxat*; *2Comp*. 2, 10, 3 v. *assertionem testium* als 'extra titulos' oder 'extra innoc.' allegiert wird.

[16] Wenn nämlich Po. 3663 (*3Comp*. 1, 18, 11) wirklich ins zwölfte Jahr gehört; vgl. oben n. 14.

[17] Po. 3684 (*3Comp*. 3, 33, 7); 3692 (1, 7, 3); 3698 (3, 25, 3); 3704 (2, 12, 14); 3718 (5, 23, 10); 3756 (3, 19, 3: von Baluze und Friedberg irrig als Trennstück von Po. 3660 behandelt, vgl. Heckel 160; 312) — und vielleicht Po. 3663. Dagegen sind die in Friedbergs Liste (*Compp. ant.* p. xxvi) folgenden höheren Potthastnummern 3865-71 alle zeitlich ungewiss; und Po. 3880 (bei *3Comp*. 4, 8, 1) ist ein Druckfehler für Po. 388.

[18] Das öfters angegebene Datum '28. Dez. 1210' beruht auf Verlesung, vgl. *Repert*. 355 n. 2.

[19] Man beachte, dass den 6 (7) Dekretalen des 12. Jahres 21 (in 23 Kapitel verteilte) Dekretalen des 11. Jahres gegenüberstehen, nämlich die bei Friedberg p. xxvi verzeichneten Nrn. zwischen Po. 3305 und 3655 (*Reg.* XI, 3-255). Die ungewissen Nrn. 3660 ff. (vgl. oben n. 14) bleiben dabei ausser Ansatz.

[20] Po. 3753 (*4Comp*. 4, 3, 1: 1209 iun. 26); 3757 (5, 6, 2: iul. 1); 3775 (2, 12, 1); 3791 (2, 5, un.); 3792 (3, 13, 1); 3886 (2, 2, 2; 3, 18, 1; 5, 16, 1: 1210 ian. 23).

zu dem nach Redaktionsschluss der Comp. III entstandenen Material.

Für die nach Comp. III erlassenen Dekretalen Innozenz' III. wurden in der Schule mehrfach private, unsystematische Sammlungen in ungefähr chonologischer Ordnung angelegt: so die kleine Sammlung der Hs. Vat. *Pal. 658 (15 Nummern)[21] und eine bisher unbekannte von mindestens 35 Nummern in Prag, Universitätsbibl. *Lobkowitz 439.[22] Aus derartigen Zwischenkompilationen, und nicht aus dem Register,[23] dürfte der Verfasser der Comp. IV sein Material der Jahre 1209/10-1215 (43 Dekretalen in 57 Kapiteln,[24] dazu 17 einstweilen undatierbare:[25] insgesamt 74 Stücke) zumeist geschöpft haben. Aus der Zeit nach dem Konzil ist nur eine Dekretale nachweisbar.[26] Was endlich die Konzilsschlüsse selbst angeht, so bringt er 69 von den 70 Konstitutionen, in 71 Kapitel verteilt.[27]

---

[21] Vgl. *Repert.* 308; in c. 1 ist dort Po. 3663 statt Po. 1806 zu lesen (vgl. oben n. 14).

[22] Die Prager Hs. ist bei P. LEHMANN, *Mitteilungen aus Handschriften* III, in *Münchener SB* 1931-32 Heft 6, p. 21 f. kurz beschrieben, ihr kanonistischer Inhalt aber dort ungenau bestimmt. fol. 1-23ᵛ: *Conc. Lat. IV*, unglossiert; fol. 24-45: die *Coll. Pragensis* mit 35 Kapitelsinitialen; doch sind mehrere Stücke willkürlich kontaminiert (z. B. fol. 41: Po. 3656 und 5031). Beginnt c. 1: Po. 3663 (*4Comp.* 5, 11, un.); c. 2: Po. 3775 (2, 12, 1); c. 3: Po. 3753 (4, 3, 1); c. 4: Po. 3757 (5, 6, 2); c. 5: Po. 5029 (2, 7, 1); c. 6: Po. 3872 (2, 8, un.)... c. ult. (35?): Po. 4844 (2, 7, 4: 1213 nov. 6). Beachte die Parallelen *Prag.* 1, 2, 4, 6: *Pal.* 1-4. — Vom übrigen Inhalt der Hs. (LEHMANN, *loc. cit.*) ist das zeitgenössische Federporträt Innozenz' III. bemerkenswert.

[23] Registerbenutzung vermuten ohne Grund G. POST, *Parisian Masters as a Corporation*, in *Speculum*, 9 (1934), 434 n. 3; HECKEL, *Histor. Jahrb.* 55 (1935), 289 n. 35.

[24] Hierbei sind die in *Coll. Prag.* und *Pal.* vertretenen, aber vor Comp. III liegenden Potthastnummern (3663, 3753 usw.) nicht mitgezählt, wohl aber Po. 2075 und 3872 (oben n. 15). Das übrige ergibt sich aus Friedbergs Liste, wo freilich die in den gegenwärtigen Zusammenhang gehörenden Dekretalen *4Comp.* 1, 2, 4 (Po. 4873); 1, 3, 6 (4577); 2, 5, un. (3791); 2, 11, 3 (4195); 4, 3, 2 (4379); 5, 14, 1 (4143); 5, 15, 1 (4826) nicht — oder nicht richtig — bestimmt sind. Geteilt werden Po. 4614 (viermal); 3886, 4006, 4072, 4379, 4820 (je dreimal); 4722 (zweimal).

[25] Nach Abzug der bei Potthast oder Friedberg undatierten, aber aus Alanus oder sonst (vgl. n. 24; für *4Comp.* 3, 3, 1: Po. 2360) bestimmbaren Stücke verbleiben Po. 5021-22, 5024-29, 5031-32, 5037-41 und *4Comp.* 2, 1, 2; 2, 7, 2. Für manche von diesen lässt sich die ungefähre chronologische Einordnung aus *Coll. Prag.* ahnen.

[26] *4Comp.* 5, 5, 1 (1215 dec. 14: Po. 5009), in *Repert.* 372 übersehen. Dagegen bleibt die scheinbar jüngere Dekretale 3, 9, 3 (an. XVIII? XIX? Po. 5298) unbestimmt.

[27] Ausser der unnumerierten Kreuzfahrerkonstitution ist c. 42 ausgelassen; geteilt sind c. 40 (*4Comp.* 1, 18, 1; 2, 4, 2) und c. 62 (3, 17, 2; 5, 14, 5). Friedbergs abweichende Angaben sind falsch.

IV

Von allen bisher aufgestellten Vermutungen über die Person des Verfassers der Comp. IV ist die von Maassen und Kantorowicz vorgeschlagene Zuweisung an Johannes Teutonicus[1] die einzige, für die sich erhebliche Gründe, und gegen die sich keine erheblichen Gegengründe vorbringen lassen. Hinfällig ist dagegen die gelegentlich vertretene These, Comp. IV sei eine offizielle kuriale Sammlung — denn das Fehlen einer Promulgationsbulle, die nur zögernde Anerkennung durch die Bologneser Schule (worüber näheres unten), und vor allem das Schweigen über Comp. IV in Tancreds klassischem Abriss der Geschichte der Dekretalensammlungen bis zum Tode Innozenz' III. entziehen solch willkürlicher Annahme jeglichen Boden.[2] Hinfällig ist auch Gillmanns Theorie von einer Urheberschaft des Alanus,[3] die (wie anderwärts nachgewiesen) auf Missdeutung gewisser bei Tancred vorkommender 'extra Alani'-zitate beruht[4] und übrigens schon daran scheitert, dass die Hinweise auf Alanus sich bereits in der ersten, vorlateranischen Rezension von Tancreds Apparaten zu Compp. I und II finden,[5] also mit Comp. IV nichts zu tun haben können.

Für Johannes Teutonicus waren bisher zwei Zeugnisse bekannt: der Bericht des Johannes de Deo in seinem *Principium decretalium* (nach 1245), an der entscheidenden Stelle allerdings in der einzigen Hs. (Par. lat. 4489) verstümmelt, jedoch von Kantorowicz sinngemäss ergänzt;[6] und die Rubrik der Hs. Admont *22 (fol. 246ᵛ):

---

[1] Vgl. R. VON SCHERER, *Handbuch des Kirchenrechts*, I (Graz, 1886) 289 n. 43; H. KANTOROWICZ, *Das Principium decretalium des Johannes de Deo*, in *Zeitschr. der Savigny-Stift. Kan. Abt.* 12 (1922), 431 f.; dazu zögernd *Repert.* 372.

[2] Vgl. *Repert.* 373, 358.

[3] *Wer ist der Verfasser der Compilatio IV?* in AKKR 116 (1936) 127-157.

[4] *Repert.* 372 n. 2; 457-462. Zustimmend HECKEL, op. cit. 175. Zum Nachweis der Alanuszitate in A vgl. oben III n. 12 d.

[5] Von der ersten Rezension der beiden Apparate (*Repert.* 328, 346) sind bisher insgesamt 16 Hss. (7 für Compp. I-II, 6 für Comp. I, 3 für Comp. II) nachgewiesen worden: GILLMANN, *Zur Inventaris.* (oben I, n. 5). 82-85; KUTTNER, *Réserve papale*, 203 n. 3; 222; *Trad.* 1, 311 n. 15; vgl. oben I n. 1; III nn. 2, 5, 15. Zur zweiten Rezension gehören z. B. alle bei GILLMANN, AKKR 105 (1925) 493 f. und AKKR 116, 146 ff. mitgeteilten Allegationen der lateranischen Schlüsse; das Vorkommen der Alanuszitate in der ersten Rezension ergibt sich aus den von mir geprüften Hss., z. B. Vat. *lat. 2509, *Urb. 178, *Borgh. 264 (kollationiert *Repert.* 457 ff.).

[6] KANTOROWICZ, *loc. cit.* Zur Lesung des Kontextes vgl. aber unten n. 16.

'Incipit compilacio magistri Johannis theotonici'.⁷ Inzwischen konnte ich mich durch Autopsie von dem unanfechtbar zeitgenössischen Charakter der Admonter Rubrik überzeugen,⁸ und die anfänglichen Zweifel an der Zuverlässigkeit des Johannes de Deo lassen sich nicht mehr aufrecht erhalten. Vielmehr entstammt der Bericht des Portugiesen offenbar einer Bologneser Schultradition, für die nunmehr ein weiteres, wohl um einige Jahre älteres Zeugnis ans Licht gekommen ist. Die Hs. Vat. *Borgh. 45 (fol. 23ʳ⁻ᵛ) ⁹ enthält nämlich ein anonymes Dekretalenprincipium, inc. 'Ceterum quia unius cuiusque', das aus der Zeit zwischen der Erhebung des Magister Zoën auf den bischöflichen Stuhl von Avignon (1243) ¹⁰

---

⁷ *Repert.* 372, nach P. BUBERL, *Die illuminierten Hss. in Steiermark*, I (Beschreibendes Verzeichnis der illum. Hss. in Oesterreich, IV, Leipzig, 1911), p. 94.
⁸ Die Admonter Hs. (in *Repert.* 341, 352, 366, 379, 384 aus Buberls Katalog herangezogen) enthält fol. 1-85ᵛ: *Comp. I* mit Tancreds Apparat in erster Rezension (vgl. *Réserve papale*, 203 n. 3) und postlateranischen Zusätzen von Tancred (Rez. II); *f., fi., phi.* (wohl Philipp von Aquileja: vgl. *Trad.* 1, 281 n. 16, ii); *W.* (Willielmus Vasco: *ibid.* 337 n. 42); *Ja.* (Jacobus von Albenga: *ibid.* 335 n. 20); *R.* (Rodulphus Anglicus? Robertus de Anglia? vgl. *ibid.* 326 n. 32; Raymund von Peñafort?); *G.* (Guido Brito? Gilbert?). Einmal werden auch Damasus und Ambrosius zitiert, fol. 21ᵛ: 'Mag. da. et amb. et fi. intelligunt'. — fol. 86-128ᵛ: *Comp. II* mit Tancreds Apparat in erster Rezension; Zusätze wie zuvor (Siglen *t., f., W.*); ferner sind die Notabilien des Paulus Ungarus (*Repert.* 411) und die Casus 'Quesiuit anchonitanus' (*Repert.* 402) begonnen, aber nicht fortgeführt. — fol. 129-244ᵛ: *Comp. III* mit dem Apparat des Joh. Teutonicus und gelegentlichen Zusätzen aus Tancred. — fol. 245-246ʳ: Fragment der *lateranischen Konstitutionen* (c. 69 bis Schluss) mit Vincentius' Apparat (vgl. oben I n. 8). — fol. 246ᵛ-270: *Comp. IV* mit Joh. Teutonicus' Apparat und Zusatzglossen (gelegentlich *f., W.* wie oben; meist aber unsigniert). — fol. 271-311: *Comp. V* mit einem Fragment (bis fol. 297ᵛ) des Apparats des Jacobus von Albenga. Als Anhang die Dekretale *Exhibita nobis Nicolai* Honorius' III. (vgl. *Repert.* 303; ed. *Bibl. Casin.* IV, 70) mit dem bisher nicht überlieferten Datum 'apud urbem ueterem v. idem (!) septembr. pont. nostri anno quinto' (Orvieto, 1220 sept. 9). Es wäre zu prüfen, ob sie mit dem in nachgregorianischen Extravagantensammlungen unter dem Namen Alexanders IV. überlieferten Stück gleichen Anfangs (vgl. PHILLIPS, *Kirchenrecht*, IV, 347 n. 5; SCHULTE, *Wiener SB*, 55, 734; FRIEDBERG, *Corp. iur. can.* II, col. liii nr. 15, col. lv nr. 39) identisch ist.
⁹ Auf den sonstigen Inhalt der Miscellanhandschrift kann hier nicht eingegangen werden.
¹⁰ *Princ. Borgh.* § 14: '...magister zen tunc canonicus bononiensis et demum episcopus auignionensis'. Zur Biographie Zoëns vgl. HAURÉAU, in *Notices et extraits*, 24, II (1876) 158 ff.; L.-H. LABAUDE, *Avignon au XIIIᵉ siècle: l'évêque Zoen Tencarari et les Avignonais*, Paris, 1908; *Gallia christiana noviss.* VII (1920), 167-211. Als Elekt begegnet der Magister erstmals 1241 mart. 27 (Labaude 83 f.; *Gall. chr. noviss.* nr. 488); die Konsekration fand 1243 zwischen sept. 7 und 21 statt (*Gall. chr. noviss* nr. 511, 512; sept. 7-oct. 13 bei Labaude 85 n. 1, wo sonstige chronologische Schwierigkeiten erörtert sind).

und der — im Gegensatz zu Johannes de Deo hier nicht erwähnten — Novellensammlung Innozenz' IV. von 1245 [11] stammt. Der einstweilen nicht zu ermittelnde Autor [12] hat seine historischen Notizen vielfach aus denselben Quellen wie nach ihm Johannes de Deo geschöpft: [13] so z. B. den Bericht über Tancred als Redaktor und Zoën als Glossator der Comp. V; [14] so die Anekdote über den Zornausbruch Gregors IX. im Konsistorium, der den Anlass zur Inangriffnahme der amtlichen grossen Dekretalenkompilation gegeben haben soll; [15] so vor allem die Notiz über Comp. IV:

Princ. Borgh.	*Joh. de Deo* [16]
(§ 12) ... et uocatus fuit tertius liber.	... et uocatur liber innocencij ⟨siue liber tertius decretalium.
(§ 13) Post illam uero magister Joan. theothonicus accepit constitutiones concilii inocentii	Processu temporis Johannes Teutonicus accepit constitutiones concilij innocencij⟩

---

[11] Für Joh. de Deo vgl. KANTOROWICZ, op. cit. 423, 441, 443 f.

[12] Zu keinem Ergebnis führt ein Vergleich mit den Angaben des Johannes Andreae (*Novella*, ad v. *Gregorius*: vgl. den Abdruck bei Schulte, *Gesch. der Quellen und Lit.* II, 550 ff.) über die Proömia acht wichtiger Gregorianenkommentare. Danach sollen Philippus und Goffredus, ähnlich wie Vincentius, ohne ihren Namen zu nennen, mit der Herleitung des Naturrechts aus der Schöpfung begonnen haben. Das möchte auf unser *Princ. Borgh.* zutreffen (s. den Text im Anhang). Mit Goffredus de Tranos Anfangsglosse 'Gregorius nonus uolens' ist es aber jedenfalls nicht identisch, und von Philippus weiss Joh. Andreae weiter zu berichten, dass er Gregor IX. mit den Worten 'quod non sedit excellentioris ingenii vel eminentioris scientie in cathedra piscatoris' gepriesen habe. *Princ. Borgh.* dagegen hat 'pater eminentissime scientie et perspicentissimi ingenii' (§ 16), was aus Vincentius' Epithet für Innozenz III. (vgl. LASPEYRES, *Bernardi Papiensis... Summa*, Ratisb., 1860, p. 356) stammt.

[13] Nicht immer: über Differenzen vgl. die Noten zum Abdruck im Anhang.

[14] *Princ. Borgh.* § 14; Joh. de Deo ed. KANTOROWICZ 434 ff.; 443 (mit teilweise verfehlter Emendation: vgl. n. 16 unten).

[15] *Princ. Borgh.* § 15; Joh. de Deo, ibid. 436 ff.; 443. Vgl. die Noten zum Abdruck im Anhang.

[16] Ergänzungen von mir. Der 'unerhört schlechte Text' (Kantorowicz, 420) der Pariser Hs. hat offensichtlich drei Lücken. Die zweite ergänzt K. richtig 'fecerat' (pp. 430, 443 o); bei der ersten vermutet er mit Recht ein Homöoteleuton, aber seine Restitution ('...liber innocencij et ⟨postea uocatus fuit liber tertius decretalium. Processu temporis Ioh. Teutonicus composuit alium librum innocencij et⟩ quasdam decretales...': pp. 431, 443l-l) ist sprachlich nicht glücklich und übergeht die wichtigen lateranischen Schlüsse. Bei der dritten Lücke endlich musste selbst ein Meister der Emendationskunst an dem völlig verderbten Satzfragment 'Sed quia' rell. scheitern: K. schlägt es zum folgenden und konjiziert: 'Sed quia Honorius papa uoluit retractare uiam predecessorum, progressu temporis

et quasdam decretales quas idem inocentius fecerat in sex annis sui regiminis usque ad concilium, et conpillauit eas et glosauit: et uocatus fuit quartus liber decretalium.	et quasdam decretales quas inocencius ⟨fecerat⟩ in .vj. anno (!) sui regiminis usque ad concilium, et glosauit et compilauit et uocatus est liber quartus decretalium.
Set quia dominus papa illam conpillationem noluit approbare, ira sucensus recessit de curia.	Sed quia papa uoluit (?) . stractare (?) uiam successam (?) recessu (?) ⟨de curia.
(§ 14) Postmodum magister tangredus, tunc canonicus bononie et demum arcidiaconus ...	Processu⟩ temporis transigus (!) de bononia archidiaconus ...

Weitere quellenmässige Bestätigung für diese Nachricht darf aus anderen, bisher nicht untersuchten Texten erwartet werden;[17] hier interessiert uns vor allem die starke innere Glaubwürdigkeit der knappen Erzählung von dem Misserfolg des Kompilators an der Kurie, die mit einem Schlage eine Reihe bisher nicht recht verständlicher literargeschichtlicher Phänomene aufs beste erklärt:

1. Johannes Teutonicus muss mit grosser Eile gearbeitet haben, um Kompilation und Apparat in der kurzen Zeitspanne zwischen dem Konzil (November 1215) und dem Tod des Papstes (16. Juli 1216) herzustellen und in Rom zur Approbation vorzulegen; insbesondere wenn man bedenkt, dass er zunächst die Konzilsschlüsse in der Vulgatordnung glossierte und gleichzeitig an der Fertigstellung seines Dekretapparates arbeitete.[18] Damit erklären sich

---

Tancredus...' (pp. 434 f., 443*p-t*). In Wahrheit liegt auch hier Homöoteleuton vor: 'recessu (*scr.* recessit)... processu', und von den vorangehenden, teilweise schwer lesbaren (K. 436, 443*q-r*) Worten darf man 'noluit' (statt 'uoluit') und 'ira succensus' (statt 'uiam successam') sicher vermuten; bei 'stractare' ist wenigstens ein Buchstabe erloschen: 'approbare' bleibt möglich.

[17] Ein zweites Exemplar des *Princ. Borgh.* soll sich in einer Brüsseler Hs. befinden, wie mir Prof. J. Juncker kurz vor seinem Tode (Oktober 1938) mitteilte. Weiteren Aufschluss gibt vielleicht auch das noch nicht vollständig untersuchte, zu Lebzeiten Gregors IX. geschriebene Proömium 'Sicut omnium liberalium artium' der Hs. Bamberg Can. 64 (P. II, 18: vgl. einstweilen SCHULTE, *Wiener SB*, 68 [1871], 112 ff.; *Gesch. der Quellen und Lit.* II, 494; SECKEL, *Krit. Vierteljahrssch. für Gesetzgeb. und Rechtswiss.* 36 [N. F. 17, 1894], 370; GENZMER, *Zeitsch. der Sav.-Stift. Rom. Abt.* 55 [1935], 336 n. 1), das laut Schulte mit der Zurückführung des kanonischen (?) Rechts auf das Paradies beginnt, und die Geschichte der *Compilationes antiquae* gibt, 'jedoch etwas confus' (*Wiener SB* 68, 113).

[18] Zur Datierung des Dekretapparates vgl. *Repert.* 93 f. Spätere Niederschrift des Apparates zur Comp. IV (so *Repert.* 375) ist nach der Aussage des *Princ. Borgh.* nicht mehr haltbar.

die groben Flüchtigkeitsfehler, die den hastig aus dem Konstitutionenapparat übernommenen Glossen der Comp. IV anhaften.[19] Aus der grossen Eile begreift sich auch, dass das Material der neuen Sammlung nur in einem Stück über die Zeit des Konzils hinausreicht.[20]

2. Als terminus ad quem für die Redaktion der Comp. IV samt Apparat ergibt sich nunmehr der Frühsommer des Jahres 1216; doch wird Johannes mit der Veröffentlichung erst nach dem Tode Innozenz' III. hervorgetreten sein (Herbst 1216? 1217?),[21] um sich nicht weiteren Tadel aus Rom zuzuziehen. So wird es verständlich, dass er in den um diese Zeit bereits abgeschlossenen Apparat zum gratianischen Dekret nur wenige Hinweise auf Comp. IV nachträglich eingeflickt hat:[22] nach dem erlittenen Fehlschlag verspürte er begreiflicherweise keine Lust mehr, etwa die bereits niedergeschriebenen Allegationen von **Konzilsschlüssen**[23] auf die neue Sammlung umzuarbeiten. Erst in seinem etwas später beendeten Apparat zur Comp. III (c. 1217) hat Johannes die neue Sammlung mit grösserer Unbedenklichkeit nicht nur für Dekretalen-, sondern auch für Konzilshinweise benutzt.[24]

---

[19] Vgl. oben II, Analyse von gl. Conc. c. 24 v. *collatione habita*, cc. 26, 34, 38, 56; ferner alle Glossen in Gillmanns erster Gruppe (oben II n. 2).

[20] Vgl. oben III n. 26. Die Worte ' in sex annis sui regiminis usque ad concilium' (*Princ. Borgh.* und Joh. de Deo) sind also in dieser Hinsicht nicht ganz korrekt, während sie andererseits die Zeitspanne zwischen Comp. III und dem Konzil erstaunlich präzis bestimmen.

[21] In diesem Sinne sind die in *Repert.* 373 (Kompilation) und 375 (Apparat) vertretenen Datierungen zu modifizieren.

[22] Vgl. *Repert.* 94, mit Nachweisungen in nn. 1-2. Weiteres Material dieser Art ergibt sich aus GILLMANN, AKKR 116 (1936) 454 n. 2 Nr. 2. Von den dort mitgeteilten 8 Glossen der Trierer Hs. *906 waren die ersten 5 bereits aus anderen Hss. bekannt und erörtert (vgl. *Repert. loc. cit.* und p. 370); die 3 neuen — gll. C. 7 q. 1 c. 5 v. *que tunc;* 9 q. 2 pr. v. *Quod autem;* 11 q. 1 c. 18 v. *mox depositus* — bestätigen den bisherigen Befund: auch hier stehen die Allegationen aus Comp. IV als Selbstergänzungen am Ende der Glossen. Bei gl. C. 7 q. 1 c. 5 ist die Zusatznatur des Schlusspassus ' Extra prouinciam... ut ex. de elect. Coram lib. iiii. ' überdies handschriftlich gesichert: der Satz fehlt in Vat. *Pal. 625 und Vat. *lat. 1367 (hier vom Schreiber der Bartholomäusschicht nachgetragen).

[23] Ueber deren Entstehung durch Schreiber, die ' ex. in(nocentii) ' oft zu ' ex. iii. ' (oder ' ex. inn. ' zu ' ex. iiii. ') verlesen, sich aber dadurch verraten, dass die bei echten Kompilationenzitaten unerlässliche Titelangabe fehlt, vgl. *Repert.* 93 n. 3; 370 n. 6. Auch die von Gillmann mitgeteilte Lesart der Trierer Hs. zu gl. C. 2 q. 6 c. 6: '...ut ex. iiii. Ut debitus...' (AKKR 116, 454 n. 2 Nr. 2) gehört in diesen Zusammenhang.

[24] Für Allegationen von Dekretalen aus Comp. IV vgl. die Texte bei Gillmann, AKKR 116, 136-143; von Konzilsschlüssen als ' const. innoc. ' ibid. 131-136; aber

3. Warum der Papst dem neuen Dekretalenwerk die Approbation verweigerte, wissen wir nicht. Vielleicht wünschte er das lateranische Corpus als geschlossene Einheit zu erhalten; noch eher missbilligte er vielleicht die Aufnahme von Dekretalen der ersten zwölf Registerbände aus Privatsammlungen, da die Rezeption solcher Stücke einer Kritik an der offiziell in Comp. III getroffenen Auswahl gleichkam. Wie dem auch sei, unser Text gibt den Schlüssel zu dem eigentümlichen, misstrauisch zögernden Verhalten der Bologneser Schule gegenüber der Comp. IV. Mit Ausnahme gelegentlicher Zusätze jüngerer magistri zum johanneischen Apparat [25] ist die Sammlung nämlich nicht weiter glossiert worden — die einzige unter den fünf Compilationes antiquae, die nur einen einzigen Apparat aufweist.[26] Die ' grossen ' Professoren (Tancred, Vincentius, Laurentius usw.) haben also über das Werk keine Vorlesungen gehalten. Nur die sekundäre Casus- und Notabilienliteratur [27] hat sich seiner angenommen; von grösseren Arbeiten sind die unvollendete Jugendschrift des Hl. Raymund (*Summa iuris,* c. 1218-1221) [28] und einige Quästionensammlungen der zwanziger Jahre [29] die ersten, in denen Comp. IV rückhaltlos zitiert wird.

Konzilsschlüsse werden aus Comp. IV alligiert in gll. *3Comp.* 3, 12, un. v. *respondere;* 3, 17, 2 v. *transierunt;* 3, 23, 1 vv. *exemptus, percipiunt* (vgl. ibid. 141 f.).

[25] Martinus von Zamora (Olmütz, Metropolitankapitel *589, dritte Schicht: inc. ' Nam dubius in fide hereticus est ', vgl. *Trad.* 1, 335 n. 24); Philippus von Aquileja und Willielmus Vasco (Admont *22: oben n. 8); anonyme Johannesschüler (Bamberg *Can. 19 [P. II. 6] und Frankfurt *28: vgl. Gillmann, AKKR 117, 453 n. 1). Anonyme Zusätze auch in Padua, Antoniana *II. 35.

[26] Die irrige Mitteilung (*Repert.* 374, 378) über einen Apparat des Vincentius in Rouen *706 (in Wahrheit Conc. Lat. mit seinem Apparat fol. 255-268^v; darauf Comp. IV mit dem johanneischen App. fol. 269-297) ist bereits in *Réserve papale,* 209 n. 2 korrigiert worden.

[27] Vgl. *Repert.* 406 f., 414 f. Eine weitere Hs. der Casus ' Primo dicitur ' in Klosterneuburg *1048 (fol. 117 ff.). Die Notabilien ' Nota arg. quod aliter ' (*Repert.* 414) stammen ausweislich der Hs. Olmütz *589 (dritte Schicht zu Comp. IV) von Martinus Zamorensis (vgl. *Trad.* 1, 335 n. 24); zur Biographie des Autors der Notabilien ' Nota iudicem ', Petrus Hispanus Portugalensis, vgl. jetzt *Trad.* 1, 317: er ist jedenfalls von dem älteren Petrus Hispanus verschieden und vielleicht mit Bischof Pedro Salvadores von Porto (1235-47) zu identifizieren.

[28] *Repert.* 438 ff.; ed. J. Rius Serra, Barcelona 1945 (mir nicht zugänglich).

[29] So vor allem die *Quaest. Borghesianae* (Vat. *Borgh. 261, fol. 103-110^v: *Repert.* 429 f.; zur Datierung ist nachzutragen, dass Honorius III, *Super speculam* in q. 22 zitiert wird) und die mit ihnen engverwandten *Quaest. Patavinae* (Padua, Antoniana *III. 68: vgl. *Trad.* 1, 321 n. 6 in Ergänzung zu *Repert.* 255) inc. ' In quadam prouincia laici percipiunt decimas '; ferner die Riesensammlung der Hs. Klosterneuburg *1048 (fol. 75-116^v) inc. ' Quidam cum infirmaretur uocauit ad se medicum ', in der sich unterer anderen auch von Tancred disputierte Quästionen finden (*Trad.* 1, 324 n. 22).

4. Die Geschichte von der Ablehnung der Sammlung in Rom muss demnach in Bologna bekannt gewesen sein. Tonangebend für das Verhalten der Universität war das 'Haupt' der Dekretalisten: Tancred. Nicht nur, dass er noch um 1220 im Prolog seines Apparates zur Comp. III lediglich von 'constitutiones concilii proxime celebrati et iura a domino Innocentio pp. iii. post xii. annum edita' spricht, die Comp. IV aber mit Schweigen übergeht;[30] sondern überdies hat er sich auch zu Allegationszwecken der Comp. IV in all seinen um diese Zeit veröffentlichten Apparaten[31] nur gelegentlich und ausnahmsweise bedient, indem er die Konzilsschlüsse stets als solche, die älteren Dekretalen stets aus Alanus, und die neueren meist als 'extra titulos' oder 'extra in(noc.)' anführt.[32] Alle Erklärungsversuche chronologischer Natur — etwa dass Tancred die Arbeit an diesen Apparaten zu einer Zeit begonnen habe, als die Comp. IV noch nicht vorlag, und nach deren Erscheinen die bereits geschriebenen Partien eben nicht mehr umgearbeitet habe[33] — vermögen hier nicht zu befriedigen: sollte der Magister noch im Jahre 1220, mindestens drei Jahre nach Erscheinen der Kompilation, wirklich aus blosser Bequemlichkeit die inkonsequente Vielfalt des Zitierstils nicht beseitigt und die Geschichte der Dekretalensammlungen im Prolog nicht vervollständigt haben? Das ist besonders unwahrscheinlich, wenn man bedenkt, dass es sich bei seinen Apparaten zu Compp. I und II damals bereits um zweite, revidierte Auflagen handelte.

Das Principium des Cod. Borgh. schafft hier erwünschte Klarheit. Wegen ihrer Ablehnung durch Innozenz III. wurde eben die

---

[30] *Repert.* 358.

[31] Für 1220 als terminus a quo auch der Apparate zu Compp. I und II (zweite Redaktion) vgl. GILLMANN, *Zur Inventaris.* (oben I n. 5) 85; auch schon G. POST, in *Anniversary Essays in Mediaeval History by Students of Chas. H. Haskins* (Boston-New York, 1929) 263 n. 30.

[32] Eine erneute Nachprüfung der von GILLMANN, AKKR 110, 131 ff. ohne kritische Unterscheidung gesammelten Allegationsformen ergibt übrigens, dass in den Apparaten zu Compp. I und II die Comp. IV überhaupt nicht benutzt ist (Gillmanns Beispiele AKKR 109. 638 n. 2; 116, 146 n. 3; 147 n. 1; 148 n. 7 sind alle kritisch verdächtig und haben in den vatikanischen Hss. keine Titelallegationen), im App. Comp. III aber nur dort, wo es sich um Glossen handelt, die Tancred aus Joh. Teutonicus übernimmt (vgl. die Beispiele AKKR 116, 131 n. 5, 134 n. 3 usw. bis 142 nn. 4, 6; 145 n. 2; *Zur Inventaris.* 91 n. 2). Eine weniger zurückhaltende Stellungnahme scheint nur in den *Quaest. Claustroneob.* (oben n. 29) vorzuliegen, wobei aber zu bedenken ist, dass es sich nicht um von Tancred selbst redigierte, sondern um reportierte Disputationen handelt.

[33] So *Repert.* 328 n. 3, 358, 373, 462.

neue Sammlung des Johannes Teutonicus in Bologna zunächst nicht als vollwertige Ergänzung zu den drei rezipierten Kompilationen angesehen — ein Parallelfall zu dem Missgeschick, das dem Spanier Bernhard im Jahre 1208 mit seiner Compilatio Romana widerfahren war [34] — und daher von Tancred, soweit möglich, bewusst ignoriert. Erst in den zwanziger Jahren dürfte sich ihre Anerkennung als *liber quartus* oder *compilatio quarta* durchgesetzt haben. Das grosse Ansehen ihres Redaktors und Glossators, dem die Schule ja immerhin die Glossa ordinaria zum gratianischen Dekret verdankte, trug schliesslich den Sieg über die etwas peinliche Entstehungsgeschichte davon.

Anhang: [1] *Cod. Vat. Borgh. 45, fol. 23ʳ ᵛ*

Hec dicuntur in principio decretalium. ꝛ.

(1) § Ceterum quia unius cuiusque rei potissima pars est principium, ut ff. de orig. iuris l. i. (*Dig.* 1, 2, 1), ideo de principio huius libri et origine iuris primum est uidendum. ad cuius euidentiam est sciendum quod in principio mundi creauit deus celum et terram. ultima die sui operis creauit hominem ad ymaginem et similitudinem suam, ut xxxiij. q. v. Hec ymago (c. 13), et creauit ipsum in perfecta, idest uirili etate, sc. xxx. annorum, ut de pen. di. ii. § Adam [2] (p. c. 30). et cum eo creauit ius naturale, ut dicitur in principio (D. 1 pr.), quo iure regebantur homines ante legem mosaycam, quod hiis consimilibus ys(idorus) ferebat:

    quod tibi uis fieri mihi fac, quod non tibi, noli.
    sic potes in terris uiuere iure poli. [3]

---

[34] Ein seltsamer Zufall will es, dass eine bisher unbekannte Hs. von St. Florian (*XI. 346, fol. 131-154) beide Sammlungen kombiniert, indem sie eine gekürzte Comp. IV mit einem Anhang aus Bernhards Comp. Rom. versieht (nachzutragen zur Benutzungsgeschichte der Comp. Rom. in *Trad.* 1, 331 ff.).

[1] Textabdruck nach meiner Abschrift aus dem Jahre 1939; nochmalige Nachprüfung am Original war mir nicht möglich. Die Schrift des Cod. Borgh. ist zum grossen Teil fast erloschen und nur unter der Quarzlampe zu entziffern. Paragraphenzählung von mir; in der Hs. beginnen neue Absätze bei §§ 8, 9, 10, 11, 12, 13, 14. Die mannigfachen literargeschichtlichen Zusammenhänge des *Princ. Borgh.* mit anderen zeitgenössischen Proömien können hier nicht erörtert werden; gelegentliche Hinweise auf die nächstverwandte Schrift, das *Principium* des Johannes de Deo, geschehen unter Angabe der Seitenzahlen bei Kantorowicz (oben IV n. 1).

[2] Adam] Romanos *Ms.* (verweist auf dict a. c. 30, sachlich unzutreffend).

[3] Das Distichon ist Gemeingut der Dekretalisten des 13. Jhdts., vgl. z. B. Hostiensis, *Summa* (prol. n. 6). Die Zuweisung an 'Ysidorus' erklärt sich aus der Tatsache, dass Grat. D. 1 ff. (über Naturrecht, Gewohnheit, positives Recht usw.) durchweg aus Isid. *Etym.* stammt.

de quo iure legitur in principio decretorum: ' humanum genus duobus regitur, naturali uidelicet ' etc.

(2) Verum quia homo per peccatum percussus in naturalibus amittens gratiam eiectus est de paradiso, ut de pen. di. ii. [4] Adam (p. c. 30), et quia peccata hominum et malitie superexcicuerant et multiplicate erant, necessarium fuit ut conderentur iura, ut eorum metu humana coherceretur audacia: ideo facte sunt leges, ut iiii.di. Facte sunt (c. 1), et sic post legem naturalem scriptam in corde hominis subsecuta fuit lex mosayca. de qua lege habes vii.di. Moyses (c. 1) et c. sequenti, et xxxij. q.ii. [5] Moyses (c. 9). ex qua lege secute fuerunt ecclesiastice constitutiones et humane rationabiliter promulgate, et ceperunt constitutiones iste a iustificationibus quas dominus tradidit moysi dicens: ' si emeris seruum ebreum ' vii.di. § i. (pr.)

(3) Post quam legem secuta fuit lex prophetica, de qua lege ⟨legitur⟩ de cons. di.ij. Reuera (c. 69) et di.iiij. Queris (c. 129), et in principio decretorum, Humanum genus, in fine. et tunc contingeba⟨n⟩t omnia in figura que postmodum completa fuerunt tempore gratie, sc. quando dei filius nos docuit precepta euangelica. et ex his duabus legibus constat uetus testamentum.

(4) Demum nato dei filio secuta est lex euangelica, idest precepta iiiij. euangeliorum. de qua lege legitur ij. q.i. Si peccauerit (c. 19).

(5) Post legem euangelicam secuta est lex apostolica, ut sunt epistole Pauli, canones apostolorum, de quibus legitur xv. et xvj.di. per totum. et ex hiis duabus legibus constat nouum testamentum, in quo ueritas manifestata est, ut infra de cellebr. miss. Cum marthe, § Ceterum (X. 3, 41, 6).

(6) Demum, ut gloria, decus et honor romane ecclesie plenius prefulgeret, secuta est lex canonica, in qua continentur opuscula sanctorum patrum, decreta et decretales: que dicuntur filie sue, sc. [6] decretorum, ex eo quod a decretis ortum et originem habuerunt. dicuntur tamen proprie decretales que fiunt ⟨per papam⟩ [7] ad consultationem subditorum: xviiij.di. c.i. et xv.di. Sacrosancta (c. 3 § 16).

(7) Set quia summorum pontificum omnia gesta in uno corpore non poterant conpaginari, xviiij.di. Si romanorum (c. 1), ideo diuersi pontifices diuersas conpillationes fecerunt in quibus decretales suas epistolas conpaggarunt. de quibus conpillationibus sic teneatis:

(8) Post conpillationem decretorum factam a magistro Gratiano tam

---

[4] de pen. di.ii.Adam] *corr. in marg. ex* l.di. infra e. adam *Ms.*
[5] q.ii] et q̄m̄ *Ms.*
[6] sc.] sorores *Ms.* — Vgl. Joh. de Deo 425 (442).
[7] *add. marg.* — Vgl. Joh. de Deo 426 (442) (auch dort wird im folgenden D. 15 c. 3 *Sancta* als *Sacrosancta* zitiert: 442 *g*).

ex dictis sanctorum patrum quam ex legibus inperatorum, multe constitutiones et decretales epistole a diuersis pontificibus manauerunt, quedamque capitula et leges remanserunt de corpore canonum, legum et diuinarum scripturarum, de quibus Nicholaus fecit mentionem xix.di. Si romanorum (c. 1). [8] Quas magister Bernardus, tunc prepositus et demum episcopus papiensis, recollegit et additis decretalibus allexandri ipsas ad communem utillitatem, et maxime studentium, sub certis titulis collocauit: et ista fuit prima conpillatio et uocabatur primus liber. [9]

(9) Post illam conpillationem quedam alie decretales a diuersis pontificibus emanarunt, sc. a domino cellestino, lucio et urbano, quas magister Gislibertus ad instar prime conpillationis sub certis titulis collocauit. [10]

(10) Post illam uero magister Allanus anglicus de dictis decretalibus et de quibusdam Jnno. iij. fecit quamdam aliam conpillationem. [11]

(11) Postmodum magister [alanus] Bernardus Conpostellanus de predictis decretalibus et de quibusdam aliis quas sumpsit de registro domini Jnoc. iij. fecit quamdam aliam conpillationem: et dicebatur secundus liber decretalium. [12]

(12) Verum quia magister obmiserat quasdam constitutiones et decretales, idem Jnnocentius per magistrum P. beneuentanum notarium

---

[8] Vgl. Joh. de Deo 426 (443).

[9] Auch Joh. de Deo 427 erwähnt nur Alexander III. unter den in Comp. I vertretenen Päpsten und übergeht den Originaltitel 'Breviarium extravagantium'. Kantorowicz's gegenteilige Konjektur (443c) ist hinfällig.

[10] Statt der Erwähnung der Päpste Coelestin III., Lucius III., Urban III. (unvollständig!) hat Joh. de Deo 428 (443) hier 'fecit aliam compilationem de dictis decretalibus et de quibusdam innocencii' — also ähnlich wie *Princ. Borgh.* § 10 für Alanus.

[11] Die Notiz über Alanus (an der 'de dictis decretalibus' als unzutreffend zu beanstanden ist; denn Gilbert und Alanus ergänzen einander) fehlt bei Joh. de Deo, der (429, 443) stattdessen von einer Sammlung spricht, in der 'quidam doctor, nomen eius nescimus' nebst 'predictas decretales' solche von Alexander, Urban III., Gregor VIII., Lucius, Coelestin und Innozenz zusammengestellt habe, 'et uocatur liber secundus decretalium'. Die Deutung auf Comp.II (Joh. Galensis; so Kantorowicz) ist naheliegend und wohl richtig. Immerhin bleibt die Möglichkeit, dass Alanus gemeint war und dass nach 'predictas decretales et alias... et innocencij compilauit' durch Homöoteleuton eine Notiz über Bernhard von Compostella in der Pariser Hs. ausgefallen ist: denn in *Princ. Borgh.* §11 wird, wenn auch unrichtig, das Prädikat 'secundus liber decretalium' dieser Sammlung gegeben.

[12] Die falsche Bezeichnung der *Comp. Romana* als Comp.II ist merkwürdig; man wäre geneigt, nach 'aliam conpillationem' Abirrung auf den Schluss eines verlorenen Satzes über die wirkliche Comp.II zu vermuten. Allein die zweimalige Beteuerung, vor Gregor IX. habe es sieben Dekretalensammlungen gegeben (§§14, 17), spricht gegen eine solche Konjektur.

suum iussit fieri quamdam aliam conpillationem: et uocatus fuit tertius liber.[13]

(13) Post illam uero magister Joan. theothonicus accepit constitutiones concilii inocentii et quasdam decretales quas idem inocentius fecerat in sex annis sui regiminis usque ad concilium, et conpillauit eas et glosauit: et uocatus fuit quartus liber decretalium. Set quia dominus papa illam conpillationem noluit approbare, ira sucensus recessit de curia.[14]

(14) Postmodum magister tangredus, tunc canonicus bononie et demum arcidiaconus, ad instantiam honorii pape conpillauit alium [15] librum: et uocatus fuit quintus liber. quem magister zen, tunc canonicus bononiensis et demum episcopus auignionensis glosauit.[16] et sic, si bene attendas, vij. fuerunt conpillationes, et quelibet illarum habebat quinque libros sub se.[17]

(15) Tempore procedente, cum allegaretur quadam die illa decretalis 'Coram' de elect. (X. 1, 6, 35) coram domino Gregorio viiij.[18] que uagabatur extra conpillationes predictas, idem dominus G. ira commotus dixit quia destruerent librum decretalium, et ex tunc mandauerunt domini chardinales nepotibus et amicis eorum bononie, ut non deberent studere in decretalibus, set tantum in legibus uel decretis quousque ipse idem dominus greg. disponeret de conpillatione ipsius libri.[19]

(16) Et sic processu temporis idem dominus G., pater eminentis-

---

[13] Besser als Joh. de Deo 429 (443). Anlass der offiziellen Sammlung war freilich nicht die Auslassung von Dekretalen, sondern die Aufnahme gewisser Stücke 'quas Romana curia refutabat' durch Bernhard (vgl. Tancred; SINGER, *Wiener SB*, 171, II, 29 ff.).

[14] Vgl. oben IV.

[15] alium] quintum *Ms*.

[16] Vgl. Joh. de Deo 434 (443); oben IV n. 10 (zur Datierung des *Princ. Borgh.*) und n. 16 (zu Kantorowicz's verfehlter Emendation 'Sed quia Honorius papa uoluit retractare...').

[17] Ungenau: Alanus hat sechs Bücher.

[18] Die Hs. liest 'illa decretalis coram de elect. dominus Gregorius viiij.' rell. Sinn und Syntax verlangen eine Emendation: die Textverderbnis ist wohl haplographisch zu erklären.

[19] Vgl. Joh. de Deo 436, 439 (443); Kantorowicz's Emendationen sind freilich vielfach irrig (bes. 443 *w, x, y, z, a*). — Bekanntlich verwirft Johannes Andreae die ganze Anekdote, weil die Dekretale *Coram* ja deutlich in *4Comp.* 1, 3, 1 gestanden habe (*Novella*, prooem. v. *compilationes*). Aber das Wesentliche und Glaubhafte der Geschichte liegt — wie schon Kantorowicz p. 437 richtig hervorhebt — darin, dass die Dekretale im Konsistorium zunächst vergeblich in der unübersichtlichen Masse der fünf Kompilationen gesucht wurde: eine Pointe, die freilich der Autor. des *Princ. Borgh.* (wie auch der Gewährsmann des Joh. Andreae) durch den pedantischen Erklärungsversuch 'que uagabatur extra conpillationes predictas' verdorben hat.

sime scientie et perspicentissimi ingenii, [20] attendens quod in predictis conpillationibus siue libris decretalium multe erant decretales epistole quarum alique propter nimiam similitudinem, alique uero propter sui prolixitatem confusionem studentibus generabant, alique uero uagabantur extra conpillationes seu libros predictos tamquam incerte: ad communem utillitatem, presertim studentium, per fratrem raymundum penitentiarium et capellanum suum iussit presentem conpillationem fieri, superfluis et contra⟨r⟩iis resecatis, a⟨d⟩ditis quibusdam suis decretis et constitutionibus, per quas nonnulla que in prioribus erant dubia declarantur. [21]

(17) Et hec fuit causa et origo presentis conpillationis. et si bene aduertas, vij. fuerunt conpillationes predicte absque conpillatione[m] decretorum. et per ea que dicta sunt distinguntur tria tempora: sc. tempus ante legem, et tempus sub lege, et tempus gratie. de quibus legitur infra titulo proximo, Firmiter credimus, § Hec sancta trinitas (X. 1, 1, 1 § 1). Hiis igitur prelibatis nunc ad litteram accedamus.

---

[20] Vgl. zu diesem Epithet oben IV n. 12; III n. 6.

[21] Von '... multe erant decretales epistolae' an eine Paraphrase aus der Bulle *Rex pacificus*.

XI

Die Konstitutionen des ersten allgemeinen Konzils von Lyon

SUMMARIUM. — I. De Innocentii IV collectione authentica (25. aug. 1245) constitutionum in Concilio Lugdunensi promulgatarum et de eiusdem pontificis ulteriore legislatione. — II. De reliquis constitutionum testimoniis, nempe de Chronicis Matthaei Parisiensis et de Registro Vaticano. — III. Recensentur varia conamina quae adhuc constitutionibus Conc. Lugd. restituendis adhibita fuerunt. — IV. An et quale momentum historicum Registro et Matthaeo attribuendum sit, et quidnam de constitutionum confectione aut conici aut e fontibus desumi queat. — V. De relationibus inter Collectionem authenticam, Registrum et Matthaeum tabulae statuuntur comparativae. Ex triplici traditione duodecim constitutionum, ex duplici traditione decem aliarum et ex simplici reliquarum duarum constitutionum traditione explicatur publicationis authenticae origo. — VI. Proponitur conclusio.

Quatuor digressiones. — I. De Innocentii IV apparatu super Collectione prima et secunda novellarum suarum. — II. De chronologia quarumdam novellarum tertiae Collectionis. — III. De galero rubro Cardinalium. ╱ - IV. An Goffredus de Trano canonista fuerit Cardinalis.

Es ist eine merkwürdige, aber wenig beachtete Tatsache, dass über die Konstitutionen, die Innozenz IV. auf dem ersten Konzil von Lyon 1245 erliess, allenthalben in Geschichtsdarstellungen und Quellensammlungen grosse Unklarheit und Verwirrung herrscht. Ueber dem vorwiegenden Interesse an dem historischen Hauptereignis der Synode, der Absetzung Kaiser Friedrichs II., ist ihre gesetzgeberische Arbeit von der Forschung durchaus vernachlässigt worden, und so machen wahllose Aneinanderreihung wirklicher und falscher Kanones auf der einen, völlige Ignorierung der Kanones auf der anderen Seite das Bild des Standes unserer Kenntnisse aus ([1]), ein Bild, dem nur wenige und kaum beachtete Ansätze zu

---

([1]) Für ersteres vgl. die Zusammenstellung unten p. 81 ss.; letzteres z.B. bei ODORICUS RAYNALDUS, *Annales Ecclesiastici ab anno MCXCVIII...*, Romae 1646 XIII p. 596-602 (an. 1245 nn. 24-57), bei E. KANTOROWICZ, *Kaiser Friedrich der*

kritischer Auslese der echten Konzilsschlüsse gegenüberstehen. Neuere Erkenntnisse auf dem Gebiet der Dekretalengeschichte des 13. Jahrhunderts liefern uns indessen einen Anhalt, die *question fort embrouillée* (²) einer genaueren Untersuchung zu unterziehen.

I.

Wir wissen nämlich nunmehr seit den Forschungen von Édouard Fournier (³), dass Innozenz IV. am 25. August 1245, wenige Wochen nach der Schlussitzung (17. Juli) des Konzils, eine amtliche Sammlung erliess, die er mit der Bulle

> *Cum nuper in concilio Lugdunensi quasdam constitutiones super certis articulis duxerimus promulgandas...*

an die Universitäten zum Gebrauch *tam in iudiciis quam in scholis* übersandte (⁴). Die neuen Konstitutionen, 22 an der Zahl, waren mit Titelrubriken versehen, nach deren Massgabe sie unter die entsprechenden Titel der gregorianischen Dekretalensammlung eingereiht werden sollten.

Diese *Collectio I* enthält folgende Stücke:

De rescriptis
1. *Cum in multis*
2. *Presenti*
3. *Dispendia*

De electione
4. *Statuimus ut si quis*
5. *In electionibus*

Zweite, Berlin 1927 p. 546-549 und Ergänzungsband p. 227, bei AG. THEINER, *I due concilii generali di Lione del 1245 e di Costanza del 1414...*, Roma 1861. A. FOLZ, *Kaiser Friedrich II. und Papst Innozenz IV., Ihr Kampf in den Jahren 1244 und 1245*, Strassburg 1905, sonst die eingehendste Untersuchung über das Konzil, tut die Konstitutionen p. 99 mit einem Satze ab.

(²) So bezeichnet sie mit Recht F. VERNET, Art. *Lyon* im *Dictionnaire de Théologie catholique* IX 1926 col. 1365.

(³) FOURNIER, *L'accueil fait par la France du XIIIe siècle aux Décrétales Pontificales*, in *Acta Congressus Iuridici Internationalis... Romae 12-17 novembris 1934* III, Romae 1936 p. 247-267 (auch als Sonderdruck Lille 1935); ders., *Questions d'Histoire du Droit canonique*, Paris 1936. Vgl. auch ST. KUTTNER, *Decretalistica*, in *Zeitschrift der Savigny-Stiftung für Rechtsgeschichte, Kanonistische Abteilung* 26 (1937) p. 436-470.

(⁴) FOURNIER, *L'accueil* p. 258-260. KUTTNER, *Decretalistica* p. 441.

De officio et potestate iudicis delegati
6. *Statuimus ut conservatores*

De officio legati
7. *Officii*

De iudiciis
8. *Iuris*

De litis contestatione
9. *Exceptionis*

De restitutione spoliatorum
10. *Frequens*

De dolo et contumacia
11. *Actor*

De eo qui mittitur in possessionem...
12. *Eum qui*

De confessis
13. *Statuimus ut positiones*

De exceptionibus
14. *Pia consideratione*

De sententia et re iudicata
15. *Cum eterni*

De appellationibus
16. *Cordi nobis*
17. *Legitima*

De homicidio
18. *Pro humani*

De sententia excommunicationis
19. *Cum medicinalis*
20. *Solet a nonnullis*
21. *Statuimus ut nullus*
22. *Quia periculosum.*

Hätte nun nicht der weitere Gang der Gesetzgebung Innozenz' IV. diese Sammlung als solche rasch in Vergessenheit geraten lassen, so wäre die Reihe der Kanones von Lyon niemals zweifelhaft geworden. Allein bereits am 21. April 1246 folgte die amtliche *Collectio II,* bestehend aus 10 eigenartig zurechtgeschnittenen Trennstücken der am 17. März ergangenen Dekretale *Romana ecclesia* und aus einer von Innozenz erneuerten Dekretale Gregors IX., insgesamt 11 Nummern ([5]). Die beiden Sammlungen wurden alsbald in der Schule meist nicht getrennt gehalten, sondern durch Ineinandergliederung ihrer Titelrubriken nach der Ordnung des Liber Extra zu einer neuen Sammlung von 33 Nummern verschränkt (*Coll. I+II*), wie es den Anforderungen von Praxis, Unterricht und literarischer Bearbeitung entsprach ([6]). Innozenz IV. hat diese Umbildung seiner beiden Sammlungen gutgeheissen, wenn nicht gar selbst angeregt, indem er — was bisher nicht bekannt ist — die 33 Stücke in dieser neuen Form glossierte ([7]).

Die Sammlung von 33 Nummern bildete in den Jahren nach 1246 den Ausgangspunkt verschiedener privater Erweiterungen durch Anhänge und Einschübe echter, aber nicht authentisch zum Schul- und Gerichtsgebrauch publizierter Dekretalen; und die Unsicherheit, die durch das Kursieren zahlreicher derart interpolierter Exemplare entstand, veranlasste dann den Papst zur amtlichen Feststellung von nunmehr 41 definitiven Novellen (Konstitutionen und Dekretalen) in der Bulle *Ad explicandos* vom 9. September 1253 (*Collectio III*) ([8]). Dieser rasche Entwicklungsgang macht es

([5]) *Decretalistica* p. 439 mit Literaturangaben. Näheres über diese Sammlung und über *Romana ecclesia* wird demnächst eine Dissertation von P. J. KESSLER bringen.

([6]) *Decretalistica* p. 444 s.

([7]) Vgl. dazu *Exkurs I,* unten p. 110 ss. — Auch der Apparat des BERNHARD VON COMPOSTELLA dürfte ursprünglich nur zu Coll. I + II geschrieben sein, *Decretalistica* p. 456. Die endgültige Redaktion zur Coll. III veranstaltete Bernhard erst nach dem Tode Innozenz' IV.; denn in der Gl. zu c. *Quia cunctis* (Coll. III 28) ad v. *non possit* schreibt er: *Quia per talem indulgentiam multum impediebatur iurisdictio..., dominus alex. indulgentiam huiusmodi omnino revocavit... in decre. Ad futuram memoriam* (Cod. Vatic. * Pal. lat. 629 fol. 269vn). Gemeint ist die Dekretale *Quia pro qualitate* Alexanders IV. vom 18. August 1255, bei A. POTTHAST, *Regesta Pontificum Romanorum...,* Berolini 1874-75 (abgekürzt Po.) n. 15989, die später von Clemens IV. in milderer Form erneuert wurde. Vgl. JOH. ANDREAE, gl. ad c. *Ne aliqui* (Sext. V, 7, 5).

([8]) FOURNIER, *L'accueil* p. 262, *Questions* p. 33 s.; KUTTNER, *Decretalistica* p. 437 s.; Po. 15129, E. BERGER, *Les Registres d'Innocent IV,* Paris 1884 ss. n. 7756.

erklärlich, dass die authentische Coll. I, die Sammlung der *nuper in concilio Lugdunensi* verkündeten Konstitutionen, nur so selten in Handschriften begegnet: bisher sind nur Arras, Stadtbibl. 541 und (vermutungsweise) Pressburg, Domkapitel 13 (Jur. 210) bekannt geworden ([9]). Nach eigner Kenntnis kann ich jetzt noch Innsbruck, Universitätsbibl. *70 (fol. 335^v-338^r) und Wien, Nationalbibl. *2073 (fol. 238^v-242^v) hinzufügen ([10]).

Nun hätte an sich, trotz des raschen Aufgesogenwerdens der Coll. I, die Reihe der Lyoner Konstitutionen aus der endgültigen Coll. III ablesbar bleiben können, wenn diese Sammlung durch authentische Inskriptionen die Herkunft der einzelnen Stücke angezeigt hätte. Unglücklicherweise legte aber Innozenz IV. in der Bulle *Ad explicandos* nur Zahl, Reihenfolge und Titelrubriken der 41 Kapitel amtlich fest, während er im übrigen von der bewährten Publikationsweise seiner Vorgänger (Innozenz III., Honorius III., Gregor IX.) abwich und statt des vollen Textes der Sammlung nur die Initien der Kapitel, ohne Text und ohne Inskriptionen mitteilte ([11]). So enstand in den Handschriften bald Verwirrung durch falsche Inskriptionen, die den Weg zur Erkenntnis der Kanones von Lyon versperren mussten.

([9]) Vgl. *Decretalistica* p. 443 s.

([10]) Autopsie einer Hs. ist stets durch ein * vor der Signatur gekenzeichnet. — In der Innsbrucker Hs. fehlt ein Blatt zwischen fol. 335 und 336, sodass der Text in Coll. I c. 4 abbricht und erst in c. 10 wieder einsetzt. fol. 336^r-337^r sind mit Glossen aus dem Apparat Innozenz' IV. versehen. Nach dem letzten Kapitel (*Quia periculosum*) hat eine fremde Hand einen Anhang mit einem Trennstück von *Romana ecclesia* (= Coll. III 39) begonnen. — Die Wiener Hs. geht fol. 241^v ohne Unterbrechung in einen Anhang über, der die Dekretale Gregors IX. *Non solum* (Po. 10202, 10204; vgl. dazu *Decretalistica* p. 438^7 a.E.) und 5 Trennstücke von *Romana ecclesia* (= Coll. III 19. 8. 6. 11. 13) umfasst; fol. 242^v hat eine spätere Hand noch ein weiteres Trennstück (= Coll. III 30) und Glossen hinzugefügt. Ueber Besonderheiten der Coll. I in der Wiener Hs. s. unten pp. 104, 109. — Teile der Coll. I inseriert auch die stark lückenhafte Hs. der Gregorianen in St. Florian XI. 598 unter die entsprechenden Titel. Weitere Hss. entdeckte P. J. Kessler, der über seine Funde zur Traditionsgeschichte der Novellen im Rahmen der oben erwähnten Diss. berichten wird. — Die Angabe der *Tabulae Codicum mss... in Bibl. Palat. Vindob. asservatorum* I, 1864 p. 97 für die Hs. Wien 566, fol. 41^r-63^r: *Decisiones Concilii Lugdunensis, tempore Innocentii IV habiti* ist irrig; es handelt sich dort um Conc. Lugd. II 1274 (Mitteilung von Herrn Prof. Köstler).

([11]) Vgl. die Abdrucke der Bulle aus dem Register (zitiert *Decretalistica* p. 437^3), etwa den letzten von G. Battelli, *Acta Congr. Iurid. Internat.* III p. 473-475, der übrigens auch noch nicht ganz fehlerfrei ist.

XI

Erst durch die kürzliche Auffindung der Coll. I sind wir also wieder in der Lage, die 41 Stücke der Coll. III, die fast alle von Bonifaz VIII. in den Liber Sextus (1298) rezipiert worden sind, mit Sicherheit nach ihrer Herkunft zu gruppieren.

Coll. III	Liber Sextus	Coll. I
1. *Cum in multis*	I, 3, 2	1
2. *Presenti*	—	2
3. *Dispendia*	I, 3, 3	3
4. *Statuimus ut si quis*	I, 6, 1	4
5. *In electionibus*	I, 6, 2	5
6. *Romana ecclesia.. Edictum*	I, 8, 1	—
7. *Grandi*	I, 8, 2	—
8. *Romana ecclesia.. Cum Remensis*	I, 13, 1	—
9. *Statuimus ut conservatores*	I, 14, 1	6
10. *Officii*	I, 15, 1	7
11. *Romana ecclesia.. Prohibemus*	I, 16, 1	—
12. *Iuris*	II, 1, 1	8
13. *Romana ecclesia.. Nec appellationis*	II, 2, 1	—
14. *Exceptionis*	II, 3, 1	9
15. *Frequens*	II, 5, 1	10
16. *Actor*	II, 6, 1	11
17. *Eum qui*	II, 7, 1	12
18. *Statuimus ut positiones*	II, 9, 1	13
19. *Romana ecclesia.. In appellationis*	II, 10, 3	—
20. *Ad hec quia.. Presentium*	II, 10, 2	—
21. *Pia consideratione*	II, 12, 1	14
22. *Cum eterni*	II, 14, 1	15
23. *Ad apostolice*	II, 14, 2	—
24. *Abbate sane*	II, 14, 3	—
25. *Cordi nobis*	II, 15, 1	16
26. *Legitima*	II, 15, 2	17
27. *Romana eccl... Cum suffraganeorum*	II, 15, 3	—
28. *Quia cunctis*	III, 7, 1	—
29. *Dudum*	III, 9, 1	—
30. *Romana ecclesia.. Statuimus*	III, 20, 1	—
31. *Pro humani*	V, 4, 1	18
32. *Volentes*	V, 7, 1	—
33. *Romana ecclesia.. Licet autem*	V, 9, 1	—

XI

Die Konstitutionen des ersten allgemeinen Konzils von Lyon

Coll. III	Liber Sextus	Coll. I
34. *Romana ecclesia.. Questoribus*	V, 10, 1	—
35. *Cum medicinalis*	V, 11, 1	19
36. *Solet a nonnullis*	V, 11, 2	20
37. *Statuimus ut nullus*	V, 11, 3	21
38. *Quia periculosum*	V, 11, 4	22
39. *Romana ecclesia.. Ceterum*	V, 11, 5	—
40. *Dilecto*	V, 11, 6	—
41. *Veniens*	V, 12, 1	—

Die Konstitutionen der Coll. I werden aus der vorstehenden Tabelle ersichtlich; der Coll. II entstammen die Trennstücke der Dekretale *Romana ecclesia* und die Dekretale *Ad hec*, also die Nummern 6. 8. 11. 13. 19. 20. 27. 30. 33. 34. 39. Die restlichen acht Stücke stehen ausserhalb der beiden älteren Sammlungen; ihre Daten lassen sich nur zum Teil ermitteln ([12]):

7. *Grandi*: 1245 iul. 24 (Berger, Registres d'Innocent IV n. 1389)
23. *Ad apostolice*: 1245 iul. 17 (Berger n. 1367)
24. *Abbate sane*: 1252 ian. 18 - iun. 18
28. *Quia cunctis*: 1246 dec. 18 - 1250
29. *Dudum*: ?
32. *Volentes*: 1250 ian. 28 - 1251 mart. 4
40. *Dilecto*: 1247 iul. 8 - 1253 sept. 9
41. *Veniens*: ?

Sechs von ihnen (7. 24. 28. 29. 40. 41) sind Dekretalen, Entscheidungen von Einzelfällen, denen erst die Publikation in der amtlichen Sammlung von 1253 allgemeine Geltung verschaffte; während c. 32 *Volentes* eine allgemeine Konstitution über die Grenzen der Exemtionsprivilegien darstellt und c. 23 *Ad Apostolice*, mit der Inskription *Innocentius IV sacro presente concilio ad rei memoriam sempiternam*, in gekürzter Fassung die Absetzungssentenz gegen Friedrich II. enthält, das berühmteste und politisch wichtigste Aktenstück des Konzils von Lyon, das aber als Urteilsspruch in das nur allgemeine Kirchengesetze enthaltende Konstitutionenwerk der Coll. I nicht aufgenommen worden war.

([12]) Vgl. des näheren *Exkurs II*, unten p. 116.

II.

Vermöge der Coll. I sind wir also im Stande, die Nummern 1-5. 9. 10. 12. 14-18. 21. 22. 25. 26. 31. 35-38 der definitiven Novellensammlung Innozenz' IV. als die authentischen Konstitutionen von Lyon anzugeben. Aber während dies Erkenntnismittel erst in den letzten Jahren wieder entdeckt worden ist, stehen zwei andere Quellen der Forschung seit Jahrhunderten zur Verfügung. Beide sind freilich in sich unvollkommen und ergänzen auch einander nicht zur vollen Reihe der 22 Konzilsschlüsse; beide geben ausserdem ihre Kanoneslisten in Verbindung mit anderen Akten des Konzils von Lyon. Diese beiden Quellen sind der zeitgenössische, berühmte Konzilsbericht des englischen Chronisten Matthäus Paris († 1259), und die 17 *Institutiones factae in concilio generali apud Lugdunum* aus dem vatikanischen Register Innozenz' IV.

1. Der Bericht der *Chronica maiora* des Matthäus Paris war das erste Quellenstück über das Konzil von Lyon 1245, das überhaupt in einer Konziliensammlung erschien: nämlich 1606 in der Sammlung des Severin Binius, der dies wertvolle Zeugnis aus der 1571 durch Erzbischof Parker veranstalteten Erstausgabe des Matthäus abdruckte ([13]). Aus Binius ging dies Stück in die späteren Konziliensammlungen, bis herab zu Mansi, über ([14]).

Matthäus fügt in seinen dramatischen Bericht eine Reihe von

([13]) SEV. BINIUS, *Concilia generalia et provincialia quotquot reperiri potuerunt...*, Coloniae Agrippinae 1606 III 2 p. 1482-1489. — *Matthaei Paris Monachi Albanensis Angli Historia Maior...*, Londini 1571. Ueber die mehr als anfechtbare Qualität des von Parker hergestellten Textes vgl. im allgemeinen die Ausgabe von H. R. LUARD, *Matthaei Parisiensis... Chronica maiora* (= Rerum Britann. medii aevi Script. 57) II, London 1874 p. xxii ss., und für die Partien über das Konzil: IV (1877) p. xvii.

([14]) BINIUS, ed. 2 Colon. 1618 III 2 p. 727-732; *Conciliorum omnium generalium et provincialium Collectio Regia*, Parisiis 1644 XXVIII p. 453-472; PH. LABBE und Gabr. COSSART, *Sacrosancta Concilia ad Regiam editionem exacta...*, Paris 1671 XI 1 col. 658-671; J. HARDOUIN, *Acta Conciliorum* VII, Parisiis 1714 col. 395-406; NIC. COLETI, *Sacrosancta Concilia...* XIV, Venetiis 1731 col. 65-78; J. D. MANSI, *Sacrorum Conciliorum nova et amplissima Collectio* XXIII, Venetiis 1779 col. 633-647.

Dokumenten des Konzils ein: das Urteil gegen Friedrich II. ([15]), sodann einen langen Erlass *Afflicti corde* in Sachen des heiligen Landes und der Kreuzfahrer ([16]). Auf diese beiden, politisch-kirchliche Zeitfragen betreffenden Aktenstücke folgen unter der Rubrik *Constitutiones* 19 Kanones, die den grössten Teil der authentischen Konstitutionen, aber in anderer Ordnung, und zum Teil mit erheblichen Textabweichungen enthalten ([17]):

M 1. *Ecclesiastica censura* = Coll. I 21 (III 37). Die in der authentischen Fassung mit den Worten *Statuimus ut nullus* beginnende Konstitution ist bei M durch eine Arenga *Ecclesiastica censura iudices dampnabiliter abutuntur...* (*sancimus ut iudicum nullus*) eingeleitet.

M 2. *Eum qui* = Coll. I 12 (III 17).

M 3. *Exceptionis* = Coll. I 9 (III 14).

M 4. *Expediendis* = Coll. I 2 (III 2). Die in der authentischen Fassung mit dem Wort *Presenti* beginnende Konstitution ist bei M ebenfalls durch eine Arenga eingeleitet: *Expediendis causarum negotiis obscuritas est invisa...*, die auch in privaten Erweiterungen der innozentianischen Sammlung gelegentlich begegnet ([18]).

M 5. *Actor* = Coll. I 11 (III 16).

M 6. *Dispendia* = Coll. I 3 (III 3)

M 7. *Iuris* = Coll. I 8 (III 12).

M 8. *Statuimus ut positiones* = Coll. I 13 (III 18).

M 9. *Cum actus legitimi* = Coll. I 5 (III 5) ([19]). Auch diese Konstitution beginnt bei M mit einer Arenga, die in der authentischen Fassung *In electionibus* fehlt: *Cum actus legitimi dies et conditiones abhorreant sanctione legali...*

M 10. *In multis* = Coll. I 1 + 6 (III 1 + 9). M hat die beiden authentischen Konstitutionen *Cum in multis* und *Statuimus ut conservatores* verständnislos kontaminiert und den Text verstümmelt: er beginnt *In* (statt *Cum in*) und lässt den ganzen wichtigen Schlusssatz *quo-*

---

[15] ed. LUARD IV p. 445-455.
[16] *ibid.* p. 456-462.
[17] *ibid.* p. 462-472.
[18] Vgl. z.B. *Decretalistica* p. 451 num. 2, Anm. p. 452.
[19] Eine in Parkers Ausgabe am Schluss dieses Kapitels in den Text geratene Randglosse über das Kurfürstenkolleg (*Magnates Alemanniae, non tamen electores...*, vgl. ed. LUARD IV p. 455) druckte BINIUS$_1$ p. 1488 noch mit ab; in der zweiten Ausgabe p. 730 liess er sie richtig fort .

rum nomina — *variari* der ersten Konstitution ([20]) fort; von den sonstigen Varianten ist *ultra tres vel quatuor dietas* (!) *in iudicio* (!) *non trahantur* sinnlos; offenbar stellt das eingefügte *dietas* eine Abirrung auf Conc. Later. IV c. 37 dar (X 1, 3, 28: ... *ne quis ultra duas dietas extra suam diocesim... ad iudicium trahi possit;* in Briefen Innozenz' IV unzähligemale allegiert [21]) — in der Konstitution von Lyon handelt es sich aber nicht um Tagereisen, sondern um Personen! — Der Anfang der zweiten Konstitution ist bei der Verschmelzung zu *Statuentes ut si conservatores* entstellt.

M 11. *Statuimus ut si aliquis* = Coll. I 4 (III 4) pr. und § 1.

M 12. *Adicimus* = Coll. I 4 (III 4) § 2 — fin. Die Teilung der Konstitution *Statuimus* durch M, der vor § *Adicimus* eine neue Rubrik setzt, ist sinnlos, denn das zweite Stück kann ohne Beziehung auf das vorangehende garnicht verstanden werden. Selbst wenn man den störenden Fehler *in forma proponit* bei M 12 korrigiert und dann die Bestimmung über den liest, der *non plene probaverit quod in formam opponit* und *quod in personam obicit,* erkennt man doch noch nicht, dass es sich keineswegs um allgemeine prozessuale Einreden, sondern um Anfechtung von Wahlen, Postulationen und Provisionen handelt; es sei denn, man weiss, dass eben M 12 in Wahrheit ein Teil von M 11 ist.

M 13. *Officii* = Coll. I 7 (III 10).

M 14. *Frequens* = Coll. I 10 (III 15).

M 15. *Pia consideratione* = Coll. I 14 (III 21).

M 16. *Cum eterni* = Coll. I 15 (III 22).

M 17. *Cordi nobis* = Coll. I 16 (III 25).

M 18. *Cum excommunicatio sit medicinalis* = Coll. I 19 (III 35) *Cum medicinalis*.

M 19. *Solet autem a nonnullis* = Coll. I 20 (III 36) *Solet a nonnullis*.

Von den 22 Konstitutionen der Coll. I fehlen also bei Matthäus drei Nummern (17. 18. 22 = Coll. III 26. 31. 38); in der Teilung der Kapitel weicht M durch eine Kontamination (M 10) und eine Zerreissung (M 11. 12) von der amtlichen Sammlung ab, und drei Nummern (M 1. 4. 9) zeichnen sich durch Präambeln aus, die in der amtlichen Fassung fehlen.

[20] Vgl. den Text bei AEM. FRIEDBERG, *Corpus Iuris Canonici* II, Lipsiae 1881 col. 938.

[21] Vgl. BERGER, *Registres* IV (Indices) p. 127 col. 3 s. v. Dieta.

2. Die 17 *Institutiones* aus dem vatikanischen Register wurden wenige Jahre nach Binius, 1612 im vierten Bande der römischen Konzilienausgabe Pauls V. zum ersten Male veröffentlicht ([22]) und gingen seither gleichfalls in alle Konziliensammlungen über ([23]). Sie enthalten nur einen geringeren Teil der authentischen Konstitutionenreihe als Matthäus, aber darüber hinausgehend eine Anzahl von Beschlüssen, die in der amtlichen Sammlung nicht publiziert worden waren:

R 1. *Cum in multis* = Coll. I 1 (III 1).
R 2. *Presenti* = Coll. I 2 (III 2).
R 3. *In electionibus* = Coll. I 5 (III 5).
R 4. *Statuimus ut conservatores* = Coll. I 6 (III 9).
R 5. *Iuris* = Coll. I 8 (III 12).
R 6. *Exceptionis* = Coll. I 9 (III 14).
R 7. *Actor* = Coll. I 11 (III 16).
R 8. *Dispendia* = Coll. I 3 (III 3).
R 9. *Eum qui* = Coll. I 12 (III 17).
R 10. *Statuimus ut positiones* = Coll. I 13 (III 18).
R 11. *Legitima* = Coll. I 17 (III 26).
R 12. *Statuimus ut nullus* = Coll. I 21 (III 37).
R 13. *Cura nos*: eine allgemeine Verordnung über Vermögensverwaltung der Kirchen, im einzelnen: Richtlinien für Inventaraufnahme, Schuldentilgung, Darlehensnahme, Rechnungslegung.
R 14. *Arduis mens*: eine Ausschreibung von Sonderabgaben zur Unterstützung des lateinischen Kaisertums in Konstantinopel.
R 15. *Perennis*: eine Bitte an alle Geistlichen, testamentarische Verfügungen zugunsten des heiligen Landes bei Beicht- und Pfarrkindern zu erwirken.
R 16. *Christianae*: Vorkehrungen gegen den Tartareneinfall.
R 17. *Afflicti*: der auch bei Matthäus (vor den Konstitutionen) überlieferte Erlass zur Regelung der Verhältnisse der Kreuzfahrer.

Von den 22 authentischen Konstitutionen fehlen im Register also zehn (Coll. I 4. 7. 10. 14. 15. 16. 18. 19. 20. 22 = Coll. III 4. 10. 15.

([22]) Τῶν ἁγίων οἰκουμενικῶν Συνόδων τῆς Καθολικῆς Ἐκκλησίας τόμος τέταρτος. *Conciliorum generalium Ecclesiae Catholicae Tomus Quartus, Pauli V. Pont. Max. auctoritate editus*, Romae 1612 p. 73-78.

([23]) BINIUS₂ III 2 p. 723-726, *Ed. Regia* XXVIII p. 432-452, LABBE XI 1 col. 645-658, HARDOUIN VII col. 386-395, COLETI XIV col. 52-64, MANSI XXIII col. 619-632.

21. 22. 25. 31. 35. 36. 38). Dass andererseits R 13-17 in der amtlichen Sammlung nicht auftauchen — einzelne von ihnen begegnen indessen zuweilen in privaten interpolierten Sammlungen ([24]) —, erklärt sich daraus, dass es sich in diesen fünf Stücken um Beschlüsse über praktische Zeitfragen, um administrative und politische Erlasse, nicht um Setzung von allgemeinen Rechtsnormen handelt. Die nicht-juristische Natur dieser Konzilsdekrete schloss sie ebenso von der Aufnahme in das amtliche « Gesetzbuch » aus, wie dies seinerzeit beim letzten Kanon der Lateransynode von 1215 der Fall gewesen war ([25]), oder wie zunächst auch das Urteil gegen Friedrich II. nicht in die amtliche Sammlung kam.

3. Mit den 22 Konstitutionen, dem Urteil gegen den Kaiser und den fünf Erlassen R 13-17 liegt fast das ganze Werk des Konzils von Lyon vor uns. Hinzu kommt nur noch eine liturgische Anordnung über die Oktav des Festes von Mariä Geburt, von der wir durch zeitgenössische Zeugnisse und Berichte wissen ([26]). Dagegen kann die allgemeine verbreitete Ansicht, auf das Konzil von Lyon gehe auch der rote Hut der Kardinäle zurück, nicht als gesicherte historische Tatsache gelten ([27]).

III.

Nachdem die Liste der 22 Konstitutionen von Lyon nunmehr endgültig feststeht, müssen wir, ehe wir die sich aufdrängende Frage nach dem Verhältnis der drei voneinander abweichenden Quellen (Coll. I, M und R) prüfen können, einen Ueberblick über die bisherigen Rekonstruktionsversuche geben, die vor der Wieder-

---

([24]) Vgl. z.B. für *Arduis* und *Cura*: *Decretalistica* p. 452.
([25]) *Expeditio pro recuperanda terra sancta*, bei MANSI XXII col. 1058-1067.
([26]) Vgl. ausser den bei POTTHAST II p. 995 nach n. 11731 zitierten Quellen etwa noch *Monumenta Erphesfurtensia, Cronica minor*, ed. Holder-Egger (*Script. Rer. Germ.*), Hannoverae 1899 p. 659.
([27]) Vgl. dazu *Exkurs III*, unten p. 120. — Nach ONOFRIO PANVINIO, *De varia R. Pontificis creatione* (1553-1562; München, Staatsbibl. lat. 149, fol. 47; Vatic. lat. 6107 II, fol. 297) soll auch das « Papstwahldekret » *Quia frequenter* auf dem Konzil von Lyon erlassen worden sein. Vgl. die Widerlegung von H. SINGER, *Zeitschr. der Savigny-Stiftung, Kan. Abt.* 6 (1916) p. 29 ss., der nachweist, dass die Konstitution *Quia frequenter* niemals promulgiert worden ist.

auffindung der Coll. I von Historikern, Kanonisten und Konziliographen angestellt worden sind und vermöge deren das Bild des Gesetzgebungswerkes von Lyon bisher so vielfach geschwankt hat ([28]). Da nahezu alle Novellen Innozenz' IV. in derartige Rekonstruktionsversuche hineingezogen worden sind, bringen wir im folgenden die verschiedenen Listen zur besseren Uebersicht stets in der Numerierung der Coll. III, auch wo die betreffenden Konziliographen aus dem Liber Sextus schöpften, und heben die Fehlzuschreibungen stets durch Kursivdruck der Nummern hervor.

1. Wir haben schon (p. 74) angedeutet, dass die Verwirrung der Inskriptionen bereits in den Hss. der Coll. III beginnt, hervorgerufen durch die Publikationsweise Innozenz' IV., der in der Bulle *Ad explicandos* nur Titelrubriken und Initien, aber nicht die Inskriptionen und den Text der Novellen festlegte. Falsche Inskriptionen mussten sich in die Hss. umsomehr einschleichen, als die meisten von ihnen am Kopf der Sammlung die Bulle *Cum nuper in concilio Lugdunensi* beibehielten ([29]), die in Wahrheit nur zur Coll. I gehört hatte, an der Spitze der Coll. III aber den Anschein erwecken konnte, als gehörten alle 41 Novellen dem Konzil an. Für die infolgedessen auftretenden Schwankungen genügt es, die von einander unabhängigen Editionen Boehmers (1747) aus der Hs. Berlin, Staatsbibl. lat. fol. 7, und Mansis (1748 und 1779) aus den Hss. Lucca, Domkapitel *138 und *139, sowie eine weitere beliebige Hs., etwa Vatic. *Pal. lat. 629 miteinander zu vergleichen ([30]). Dass alle drei Texte die Coll. III nicht in reiner Form, sondern um eine in vielen Hss.

([28]) Einen derartigen Ueberblick gibt bereits VERNET, *Dict. théol. cath.* IX col. 1366 s., aber nicht vollständig und nicht immer genau.

([29]) *Decretalistica* p. 450. — Aus diesem Tatbestand sind viele falsche Folgerungen gezogen worden, so etwa von J. FR. VON SCHULTE, *Geschichte der Quellen und Literatur des Canonischen Rechts* II, Stuttgart 1877 p. 30; H. DENIFLE, *Chartularium Universitatis Parisiensis* I, Parisiis 1889 p. 189; G. BATTELLI (oben n. 11) p. 472; VERNET col. 1368.

([30]) J. H. BOEHMER, *Corpus Iur. Can.*, Halae Magdeb. 1747 II, *Appendix* col. 351-368; J. D. MANSI, *Sanctorum Conciliorum... Collectio nova, seu Collectionis Conciliorum... Supplementum* (Schmutztitel: *Ad Concilia Veneto-Labbeana Supplementum*) II, Lucae 1748 col. 1073-1098 = MANSI, *Coll. Amplissima* XXIII col. 651-674. — Zu Boehmers Hs. B e r l i n lat. fol. 7 (BOEHMER II p. xxx, xxxiii) vgl. VAL. ROSE, *Verzeichnis der lateinischen Hss. der Königl. Bibliothek zu Berlin* II 2, Berlin 1903 p. 568 s. num. 625. Von Mansis Hss. wusste man bisher nur, dass es sich um zwei Codices des Domkapitels zu L u c c a handelt (Mansi, *Suppl.* II col. 1071-1072, *Ampliss.* XXIII col. 649-650). Wie ich jetzt feststellen

frühzeitig auftauchende Interpolation *Non solum* vermehrt, enthalten (³¹), ist für unsere Frage unerheblich.

Folgende Kapitel (³²) der Coll. III weisen in den drei Textzeugen die Konzilsinskription auf:

Boehmer: 1-3. *Cum inter* (6). 9. *11.* 12.*13.* 14-18. *19. 20.* 22. 23. 25. 26. *27-30.* 31. *32-34.* 35. 38. *39. 41.*
Mansi: 2. 3. 5. 9. 12. 16. 23.
Pal.: 2. 3. 5. 9. 12. *13.* 16-18. 22. 23. 25. 26. *29.* 37.

Das Absetzungsurteil (23) ist also überall als Konzilswerk erkennbar; von den 22 Konstitutionen stehen aber bei Mansi nur 6, in Pal. 12, bei Boehmer 16. Dagegen hat Boehmer die Einführungsbulle der Coll. II (*Cum inter*) und 13 Stücke falsch inskribiert, sodass im ganzen 17 richtige 14 falschen Zuschreibungen gegenüberstehen. Auch Pal. hat 2 falsche Inskriptionen.

2. Bei diesem Sachverhalt ist es nicht verwunderlich, dass auch im Liber Sextus Fehler und Schwankungen in den Inkriptionen begegnen. Von den 41 Nummern der Coll. III hatte Bonifaz VIII. 40 rezipiert; es fehlte lediglich c. 2 *Presenti* und damit eine Lyoner Konstitution. Von den restlichen 40 Nummern werden in den Hss., die der Edition Friedbergs zugrundeliegen (³³), und in der Editio

---

kann, hat Mansi die um *Non solum* erweiterte Coll. III aus Cod. Luc. * 138, fol. 284 ss. entnommen und mit Cod. Luc. * 139, fol. 229 ss. verglichen, welcher die sog. Sammlung von 37 Nummern (vgl. *Decretalistica* p. 446 s.) enthält: es fehlen in ihm nämlich nicht nur, wie Mansi am Rande vermerkt (*Suppl.* II col. 1075, 1090, 1097; *Ampliss.* XXIII col. 652, 667, 673) die cc. *Grandi, Non solum, Dilecto*, sondern auch cc. *Ad Apostolice* und *Abbate*. Die Aenderungen, die Mansi am Text von Luc. 138 aufgrund von Luc. 139 vornahm, betreffen vor allem die Stellung einiger Kapitel. — Im handschriftlichen Inventar des Kapitelsarchivs von Lucca (und danach bei FR. BLUME, *Bibliotheca librorum manuscriptorum italica*, Gottingae 1834 p. 69) war Cod. 138 irrtümlich unter Nr. 137 und Cod. 137 (Dekretalen Gregors IX.) unter Nr. 138 verzeichnet; das Inventar ist jetzt berichtigt. Die in meinem *Repertorium der Kanonistik*, Città del Vaticano 1937 pp. 110, 320, 365, 379 aufgrund von Blumes Liste gemachten Angaben werde ich bei anderer Gelegenheit berichtigen. — Zu Cod. Vat. * Pal. 629 vgl. *Decretalistica* p. 450¹.

(³¹) Vgl. *Decretalistica* p. 438.
(³²) In der Zählung der Tabelle oben p. 75, nicht in der bei Boehmer und Mansi durch die Interpolation *Non solum* verschobenen Zählung.
(³³) *Corp. Iur. Can.* II, *Prolegomena* col. lii, Codd. A-G.

Romana alles in allem als Konzilsstücke bezeichnet (die mit * verse=
henen nur in Friedbergs Hss., nicht in ed. Rom.):

1. 3. 4. 9*. *11.* 12. 14. 15. 16*. 17*. 18. *19.* 21-23. 25. 26*. *27*.* 31. *32.* *34.* 35-38. *39*.*40.

Die irrigen und die in ed. Rom. fehlenden richtigen Herkunfts=
bezeichnungen sind in Friedbergs Hss. vertreten, wie folgt ([34]):

11 : AG	9* : ABC
19 : —	16* : CEFG
27* : G	17* : A - G
32 : G	26* : A - F
34 : G	(36 : steht ed. Rom., fehlt C)
39* : ACF	
40 : ABCDE	

Von den 21 rezipierten Konstitutionen tragen mithin die richtige
Inskription bloss 15 in ed. Rom.; 17 in D, G; 18 in AB, EF, C;
überall ausserdem die Nov. 23. Dem stehen an falschen Inskriptio=
nen gegenüber: 1 in BDE, F; 2 in C; 3 in A; 4 in G; 5 in ed. Rom.

3. Johannes Andreae unternahm um 1346 in seinen *Additiones
in Speculum Guil. Durantis* den ersten Versuch, aus dem Sextus
die Lyoner Kapitel abzulesen ([35]); seine Liste umfasst folgende 16
Novellen:

1. 4. 12. 15-17. 21-23. 25. 26. 31. 35-38,

das heisst 15 Konstitutionen und das Absetzungsurteil Nov. 23,
wenigstens aber keine Fehlzuschreibungen.

4. Binius brachte in der ersten Ausgabe seiner Konziliensamm=
lung (1606) ausser dem Abdruck aus der Chronik des Matthäus Pa=
ris (M) noch eine Initienliste von 19 Kapiteln des Sextus, die dem

---

([34]) Vgl. die Noten zu den Inskriptionen der betreffenden Kapitel: FRIED-
BERG II col. 978, 985, 1000, 1003, 1015, 1093, 1094, 1095.

([35]) Zu *Speculum* IV part. I, rubr. *de summa trin. et fide cath.* (ed. Lugduni
1547 III fol. 29ra): ... *Inno. iiij. omisit* (hanc rubricam) *in suo concilio lugdu=
nensi, ubi multas constitutiones valde necessarias edidit, ut in vj. patet...*

Konzil entnommen seien (³⁶). In der zweiten Ausgabe (1618) übernahm er die gesamten Texte aus dem vierten Bande (1612) der römischen Konzilienausgabe Pauls V. zum Conc. Lugd. (³⁷): die Einleitung der römischen Editoren, die Einberufungsschreiben Innozenz' IV., die sogenannte *Brevis nota eorum quae in primo concilio Lugdunensi generali acta sunt*, das Urteil gegen Friedrich II. und die 17 *Institutiones* (R). Hinter diesen Texten druckte Binius dann mit kleinen Umstellungen, Verbesserungen und Kürzungen (nämlich soweit die Texte bei M sich mit den Texten der römischen Ausgabe decken) das Material seiner ersten Ausgabe ab. Die Liste der 19 Initien aus dem Sextus erweiterte er auf folgende 25 Nummern (die mit * versehenen stehen erst in Binius₂ 1618):

1. 3. 4. 5*. 9*. *11*. 12. 14. 16*. 17*. 18. *19*. 21. 22. 25*. 26*. 31. *32*. *34*. 35-38. *39*. *40*,

sodass 19 richtigen von den im Sextus rezipierten 21 Konstitutionen (es fehlen Nov. 10. 15) 6 Fehlzuschreibungen gegenüberstehen (³⁸). — Den Schluss der Texte bei Binius machten einige Notae, die bereits in der ersten Ausgabe standen.

Die Kompilation von Binius₂ blieb massgebend für alle folgenden Konziliensammlungen; die verschwenderisch gedruckte Ed. Regia (Paris 1644) hielt sich Schrift für Schritt an Binius (³⁹), erlaubte sich nur zuweilen unbegründete «Verbesserungen» in den Lesarten.

5. Labbe und Cossart (1671) legten gleichfalls Binius zugrunde, nur dass sie anstatt seiner Liste von 25 Nummern des Sextus einen Text von 9 *Capitula Lugdunensis concilii a Binio non edita, collecta ex sexto decretalium* gaben (⁴⁰). Diese 9 Kapitel

11. *19*. 31. *32*. *34*. 37. 38. *39*. *40*

(³⁶) BINIUS₁ III 2 p. 1489 s.
(³⁷) BINIUS₂ III 2 p. 717-726 = *Ed. Rom.* IV p. 64-78. Ueber die Editionsgeschichte dieser Stücke werde ich ausführlicher in einer Untersuchung, *Die Akten des ersten allg. Konzils von Lyon und die römische Konzilienausgabe Pauls V.*, in *Miscellanea Historiae Pontificiae* (Univ. Gregoriana) vol. II 1939 berichten.
(³⁸) BINIUS₂ III 2 p. 732.
(³⁹) *Ed. Regia* XXVIII p. 413-474 = BINIUS₂ III 2 p. 717-732.
(⁴⁰) LABBE XI 1 col. 671-674.

mit frei erfundenen Rubriken sind das unglückliche Ergebnis des Versuchs, von den 25 Nummern bei Binius die im Abdruck von M und R edierten Stücke zu subtrahieren (⁴¹). Unglücklich: denn abgesehen davon, dass Labbe-Cossart die Identität von Nov. 37 mit R. 12 und M 1 übersahen, sind von den übrigen 8 Nummern nur 2 echte Konstitutionen, sechs dagegen Fehlzuschreibungen.

Hardouin strich in seiner Konzilienausgabe (1714) die Einleitung der römischen Editoren und Labbes 9 Kapitel ex Sexto, sowie die Noten des Binius (⁴²). Coleti (1731) stellte dagegen das ganze Bild wieder her, wie es bei Labbe-Cossart gewesen war (⁴³).

6. Auch ausserhalb des Kreises der Konziliensammlungen begegnen wir in dieser Zeit Versuchen zur Rekonstruktion der Kanones von Lyon. Joh. Cabassut schrieb in seiner *Notitia ecclesiastica historiarum conciliorum* (der 1680 erstmals erschienenen erweiterten Folioausgabe seines Bändchens *Notitia conciliorum sanctae ecclesiae* von 1668, das neben der grossen Ausgabe ständig weiter aufgelegt wurde) dem Konzil folgende Stücke zu (⁴⁴):

1. *Perpetuo*. 3-5. 9. 10. *11*. 12. 14. 16-18. *19*. 21. 15. 22. 23. 25. 26. 31. *32. Cum de diversis*. 34. 35-38. *39*. 40.

In der Absicht, zu ergänzen, *quae Binii... diligentiam effugerunt* (⁴⁵), behielt er dessen 25 Nummern mit allen Fehlern bei und fügte 5 Kapitel aus dem Sextus ein; drei richtige (10. 15. 23) und zwei falsche: die Konstitution *Perpetuo* Bonifaz' VIII. (! Sext. I, 5, 1) und die Stiftungsurkunde *Cum de diversis* Innozenz' IV. für das Generalstudium bei der Kurie (Sext. V, 7, 2; an. 1244-1245 [⁴⁶]). Im ganzen kommt Cabassut also auf 8 falsche und 22 richtige Nummern (21 Konstitutionen + Nov. 23), sodass dem Maximum an Fehlzuschrei-

(⁴¹) Von Binius' 25 Kapiteln sind Nov. 1. 3. 5. 9. 12. 14. 16-18. 26. 37 = R 1. 8. 3-7. 9-12, und Nov. 4. 21. 22. 25. 35. 36 = M 11 + 12. 15-19.

(⁴²) HARDOUIN VII col. 375-406.

(⁴³) COLETI XIV col. 39-84 = LABBE XI 1 col. 634-675.

(⁴⁴) Ich benutze JOH. CABASSUTIUS, *Notitia ecclesiastica historiarum conciliorum...*, ed. tertia Lugduni 1690 p. 466-473. — Die kleine *Notitia conciliorum s. ecclesiae* von 1668 und ihre Nachdrucke enthalten die Kanones nicht.

(⁴⁵) *Not. eccl.* p. 466 n. 8.

(⁴⁶) Zur Datierung vg. H. DENIFLE, *Die Universitäten des Mittelalters* I, Berlin 1885 p. 3¹¹, p. 302 s.

bungen immerhin auch die Zusammenstellung alles dessen, was an Lyoner Material im Sextus rezipiert war, gegenübertritt.

7. In einem nachgelassenen Werk Zeger Bernard Van Espens († 1728), dem *Commentarius in canones et decreta iuris veteris ac novi et in ius novissimum*, begegnen wir dem ersten Versuch, die Inskriptionen des Liber Sextus (nach der römischen Ausgabe), hauptsächlich durch Vergleich mit den Constitutiones bei Matthäus Paris, einer Kritik zu unterziehen ([47]). Nach Van Espens Ergebnissen sind wirklich lyonesisch die Novellen

1. 3-5. 9. 12. 14-18. 21-23. 25. 26. 31. 35-38,

was er in sechs Fällen lediglich den Inskriptionen entnimmt (1. 3. 4. 31. 37. 38; für Nov. 37 bestreitet er ausdrücklich, aber irrig das Vorkommen bei M [[48]]), in 12 Fällen dem Uebereinstimmen von Inskriptionen und M (12. 14-18. 21-23. 25. 35. 36); in zwei Fällen (5. 9) argumentiert er gegen die fehlenden Inskriptionen aus M; ein Kapitel endlich (26) stützt er auf die Autorität des Binius ([49]): hier hätte aber, wie überhaupt, die Liste des Registers herangezogen werden müssen. — Andererseits verwirft Van Espen als nicht-konziliar die Novellen

10. 11. 19. 32. 34. 39. 40,

davon Nov. 10 zu Unrecht. Er beruft sich gegen M auf die Unmöglichkeit der Wendung: *nisi hoc alicui specialiter duxerimus indulgendum* für ein konziliares Dekret, da so nur der Papst sprechen könne ([50]). Aber die Voraussetzung zugegeben, so ist doch der Schluss nicht zwingend. Mit derselben Begründung hätte Van Espen die Nov. 1 *Cum in multis* als Konzilsstück verwerfen müssen, da diese Konstitution die Auslegung einer Klausel, *que frequenter in litteris nostris inseritur*, betrifft: auch hier kann, rein sprachlich genommen, nur der Papst redendes Subjekt sein. Aber nichts steht dem entgegen, derartige Konstitutionen auf Konzilien zu verkünden.

([47]) VAN ESPEN, *op. cit.*, Lovanii 1759 pp. 505, 506-514.
([48]) *ibid.* p. 513.
([49]) *ibid.* p. 511.
([50]) *ibid.* p. 507.

Mit den übrigen Zurückweisungen ist Van Espen im Recht: 11. 19. 34. 39. 40 werden als Dekretalen erkannt, für c. 32 kann er sich auf das — an sich nicht schlüssige — Schweigen bei M berufen, trifft aber im Ergebnis das richtige.

Alles in allem hätte Van Espens kritischer Versuch mehr Beachtung verdient, als er gefunden hat. Seine Liste ist die erste seit Johannes Andreae, die gänzlich frei von Fehlzuschreibungen ist; und richtig weist er dem Konzil immerhin 20 Konstitutionen und Nov. 23 zu, sodass von dem im Sextus rezipierten Material nur Nov. 10 fehlt.

8. Die Wiederauffindung der Coll. III der Novellen Innozenz' IV. durch Boehmer (*Corpus iuris canonici* II, 1747) und Mansi (Supplementum zu Coleti, 1748) brachte keine Klärung in die Frage nach den Lyoner Schlüssen, sondern verwirrte eher den Tatbestand noch mehr. Infolge der irreführenden Rubriken — *Incipiunt decretales domini Innocentii pape quarti edite in concilio lugdunensi* (Berlin lat. fol. 7); *Incipiunt decretales novissime compilate per dominum Innocentium iiii. in concilio lugdunensi* (Lucca 138) — und der Präambel *Cum nuper,* die sie in ihren Hss. vorfanden ([51]), hielten beide Herausgeber die Sammlung im Ganzen für auf dem Konzil veröffentlicht ([52]). Boehmer nimmt nur c. 7 *Grandi* aus ([53]); Mansi, der wohl sah, dass eine grosse Anzahl der Novellen ihrer Natur nach nicht gut Konzilskanones sein könnten, aber an der Gesamtpromulgation auf dem Konzil festhielt, half sich durch die Unterscheidung von *canones quos tunc primo Innocentius condidit* — das seien die in der Sammlung ausdrücklich als Konzilskanones inskribierten — und solchen, *quos antea a se promulgatos in eamdem constitutionum suarum complexionem revocavit* ([54]). Als er dann

---

([51]) Zur Berliner Rubrik vgl. ROSE, *Verzeichnis der lat. Hss.* II 2 p. 569; BOEHMER hat zu *Lugdunensi* noch *I* gesetzt. — MANSIS andere Hs. (Lucca 139) ist *Incipiunt nove constitutiones jño. iiij.* rubriziert.

([52]) BOEHMER II p. xxx, MANSI, *Suppl.* II col. 1071-1072. Ungenau das Referat bei VERNET col. 1366 s.

([53]) BOEHMER II p. xxxi n. 103. Die Anmerkung ist sprachlich recht ungeschickt formuliert, und man könnte den Eindruck gewinnen, als wolle Boehmer auch die Nov. 8. 13. 19. 23. 24. 28. 29. 41 ausnehmen. Aber die Worte *Idem dicendum de...* beziehen sich nicht auf die über c. *Grandi* gemachte Bemerkung: *quod tamen ex concilio Lugdunensi haud desumptum,* sondern auf die Beobachtung über die Verstümmelung dieser Dekretale in Coll. III und Sextus.

([54]) MANSI, *Suppl.* loc. cit.

1779 im XXIII. Bande seiner Konziliensammlung sein Supplementum von 1748 (nämlich die Coll. III, eine *Adnotatio* zu den Annalen des Raynaldus und zwei Briefe von kaiserlicher Seite) hinter Coletis Texten wiederabdruckte (⁵⁵), strich er dafür Labbes neun *capitula a Binio non edita*. Seine Auffassung über die konziliare Veröffentlichung der Novellensammlung hielt er fest (⁵⁶).

9. Hefele machte dagegen 1863 in seiner Konziliengeschichte den Versuch, zu einer Aussonderung der Konzilsstücke aus der Sammlung Innozenz' IV. zu gelangen, indes mit weniger Geschick als seinerzeit Van Espen. Er gibt zunächst die 17 *Institutiones* des Registers (die er irrig für einen Teil der *Brevis nota* hält) (⁵⁷), und sodann folgende Novellen (⁵⁸):

4. 11. 15. *19.* 21-23. 25. 31. *32. 34.* 35. 36 38. *39. 40. Venerabilibus*,

also sieben falsche Nummern, darunter die in den Novellen garnicht enthaltene Dekretale *Venerabilibus* (Po. 15454; Sext. V, 11, 7) vom 11. Juli 1254. Leclerq hat in der französischen Ausgabe der Konziliengeschichte dies Kapitel durch die ebenfalls nicht zum Konzil gehörende Nov. 41 ersetzt (⁵⁹). — Die restlichen 10 richtigen Stücke ergeben, zusammen mit R 1-12 der *Institutiones*, 21 Konstitutionen + Nov. 23; es fehlt Nov. 10 *Officii*.

10. Potthast beginnt seine Konzilsregesten (⁶⁰) gleichfalls mit R 1-17 (ohne die Herkunft aus dem Register zu erwähnen) und lässt X *aliae constitutiones* folgen:

4. 15. 21. 22. 25. 31. *32.* 35. 36. 38,

sodass nur ein falsches Kapitel blieb. Nov. 23 steht richtig unter besonderer Nummer (Po. 11733) ausserhalb der Serie der Konsti-

---

(⁵⁵) MANSI, *Ampliss.* XXIII col. 649-682 = *Suppl.* II col. 1071-1108. Die Anmerkung stammt aus der von Mansi besorgten Ed. Lucensis der *Annales Ecclesiastici* (vgl. oben p. 70 n. 1) des RAYNALDUS, Lucae 1747 II p. 324 s.
(⁵⁶) *Ampliss.* XXIII col. 647, 649-650.
(⁵⁷) CARL JOSEPH VON HEFELE, *Conciliengeschichte* V, ₁Freiburg 1863. Ich benutze die zweite, von A. KNÖPFLER besorgte Auflage, Freiburg 1886 p. 1114-1120.
(⁵⁸) *ibid.* p. 1121-1123.
(⁵⁹) HEFELE-LECLERQ, *Histoire des Conciles* V 2, Paris 1913 p. 1675.
(⁶⁰) POTTHAST, *Regesta* II, Berol. 1875 p. 996.

tutionen. Dagegen ist Po. 11732 *Cum actus legitimi* (M 9) als Doublette von R 3 (Nov. 5) zu streichen; die Identität ist Potthast ebenso entgangen wie schon Binius und fast allen anderen Konziliensammlungen ([61]). Nov. 10 fehlt und ist zu Unrecht als zeitlich unbestimmbares Stück in Po. 15121 (1243-53) registriert.

11. Gegenüber Potthast hat J.-B. Martin, *Conciles et Bullaire du diocèse de Lyon* (Lyon 1905) n. 1079 den Tatbestand noch einmal sehr verwirrt. Seine Liste von 39 (nicht 38, wie er behauptet) Nummern:

Nov. 1. 2. 5. 9. 12. 14. 16. 3. 17. 18. 26. 37. Cura. Arduis. Perennis. Christianae. Afflicti. *11. 19. 31. 32. 34.* 38. 39. 40. *6-8. 13. 20. 24.* 26. *27-29.* Non solum. *30. 33. 41.*

verrät ihre kompilatorische Natur: Der erste Abschnitt (bis *Afflicti*) stellt R 1-17 dar; die folgenden acht (11 .... 40) sind Labbes *capitula a Binio non edita*, nur ohne das bereits in R vorhandene c. 37; sogar Labbes selbsterfundene Rubriken kehren bei Martin wieder. Der Rest (6 ... 41) erweckt den Eindruck, als sei geradezu der Versuch gemacht worden, die nicht zu Conc. Lugd. gehörigen Stücke aus den Novellen zusammenzutragen: nur Eine richtige Zuschreibung steht 13 falschen gegenüber, und die richtige ist eine Doublette! Dafür fehlen acht echte Konstitutionen (4. 10. 15. 21. 22. 25. 35. 36), die Martin bei M 11-19 hätte bezeugt finden können. Nov. 23 steht dagegen, wie bei Potthast, unter besonderem Regest (n. 1089). Insgesamt bietet also Martin n. 1079: 19 falsche Zuschreibungen, eine Doublette, 19 richtige Zuschreibungen, worunter aber nur 14 von den 22 *Constitutiones* ([62]).

12. In den entgegengesetzten Fehler war Friedberg, *Corpus iuris canonici* II (1881), *Prolegomena* col. L verfallen: übervorsichtig wagt er im Quellenverzeichnis zum Liber Sextus nur die durch R 1. 3. 5-12 bezeugten Kapitel (= Nov. 1. 5. 12. 14. 16. 3. 17. 18.

([61]) BINIUS III 2 ₁p. 1488, ₂p. 730, *Ed. Regia* XXVIII p. 464, LABBE XI 1 col. 666, COLETI XIV col. 73, MANSI XXIII col. 642. Nur HARDOUIN VII col. 402 und VAN ESPEN p. 507 haben die Identität erkannt.

([62]) MARTIN n. 1080-1082 wiederholt überflüssigerweise R. 14. 16. 17; n. 1084 = Po. 11732 ist zu streichen; n. 1069 scheint die Dekretale *Grandi* (Coll. III 7) vom 24. Juli 1245 als Konzilswerk bezeichnen zu wollen.

26. 37) dem Konzil zuzuweisen, sodass nicht nur das im Sextus nicht rezipierte R 2 (Nov. 2), sondern aus unerfindlichem Grund auch R 4 (Nov. 9) fehlt. — Aehnlich übervorsichtig ist F. Vernet im *Dictionnaire de théologie catholique* IX (1926) col. 1367 s. Indem auch er allen Zeugnissen ausser dem Register misstraut, will er zu R 1-17 nur noch die Absetzungssentenz Nov. 23, ferner Nov. 31 *Pro humani* (die im Text als einzige unter den Konstitutionen die Formel *sacro approbante concilio* enthält) und Po. 11732 *Cum actus legitimi*, das er nicht als Doublette von R 3 erkennt ([63]), hinzufügen.

IV.

Allen diesen schwankenden Versuchen gegenüber sind wir nun durch die Coll. I in der Lage, die Liste von 22 Konstitutionen als die einzig authentische Reihe der Kanones von Lyon darzutun. Aber mit dieser grundlegenden Feststellung sind die traditionsgeschichtlichen Probleme doch noch nicht erschöpft. Es bleibt die Frage nach dem historischen Verhältnis der Coll. I zu den Ueberlieferungen des Registers und der Chronik des Matthäus zu erörtern. Denn obwohl diese beiden Ueberlieferungen nicht vollständig sind — R enthält nur 12, M nur 19 unserer Konstitutionen — und obwohl M sogar erhebliche Abweichungen in der Redaktion der einzelnen Kanones aufweist, wären doch R und M durch die Wiederauffindung der Coll. I nur dann als historische Quellen wertlos geworden, wenn ohne Zweifel feststünde, dass beides irgendwelche Auszüge aus der amtlichen Sammlung wären.

Allein eine solche bequeme Annahme hält nicht stand. Was R anlangt, so wäre es kaum begreiflich, wie die päpstliche Kanzlei dazu käme, aus einer amtlich publizierten Sammlung nur einen willkürlichen Auszug zu registrieren, das Versendungsschreiben zu unterdrücken und fünf nicht mitpublizierte Konzilsstücke (R 13-17) mitaufzunehmen. Und ebenso unbegreifflich wäre es, wenn M die amtliche Sammlung gekannt, sich aber trotzdem die Mühe gemacht hätte, in einem «Auszug» ihre Ordnung künstlich zu verwirren und zu einigen Texten Präambeln hinzuzudichten.

([63]) V̲ERNET col. 1369, wo auch die Oktav von Mariae Geburt und die Verleihung des roten Hutes erwähnt werden.

Lässt man aber die Exzerpthypothese fallen, so müssen R und M anderweitige Quellenbedeutung haben. Dem Kanzleistück R ist ein hoher Quellenwert auch immer zuerkannt worden; dagegen gilt es, sich vor dem oft begangenen Fehler der Geringschätzung von M zu hüten (wohin er führt, lehrt das Beispiel Friedbergs und Vernets): so wie der Konzilsbericht des Matthäus für die Kenntnis der bewegten Verhandlungen trotz mancher Ungenauigkeiten dem Kirchen- und dem Profanhistoriker unentbehrlich bleibt, so sollte auch der Kanonist an der Serie der *Constitutiones* bei M unbeschadet ihrer Mängel nicht vorbeigehen. Dass der lebhafte, wenn auch nicht immer zuverlässige Chronist über die Vorgänge zu Lyon sehr eingehende Informationen von englischen Konzilsteilnehmern besass, dürfte ausser Zweifel stehen ([64]).

Irgendwelchen quellenmässigen Wert können aber R und M nur dann besitzen, wenn man von der Beobachtung ausgeht, dass Coll. I erst mehrere Wochen nach der letzten Sitzung (17. Juli) am 25. August 1245 publiziert wurde, und dass mithin chronologisch Raum für die Hypothese besteht, die amtliche Publikation durch die Bulle an die Universitäten gebe die Konstitutionen überarbeitet, in einer endgültigen Redaktion wieder, nicht aber in der Form, in der sie auf dem Konzil durch Verlesung promulgiert worden waren.

Ein solcher Unterschied zwischen « Promulgation » durch Verkündung an die Konzilsväter, und « Publikation » durch Versendung an die Universitäten — wobei erst durch die Publikation mit dem Rezeptionsbefehl die Konstitutionen rechtlich in Kraft treten und bis dahin redaktionelle Aenderungen möglich bleiben — stände, wenn wir ihn in Lyon vermuten dürfen, in der mittelalterlichen Konziliengeschichte nicht vereinzelt. Er ist uns nämlich bekannt aus der Geschichte des allgemeinen Konzils von Vienne 1311-1312, mit dessen Konstitutionen es sich noch ungleich komplizierter verhält als mit denen von Lyon 1245. Die Publikationsgeschichte der Vienner Konstitutionen, und damit der Clementinen, können wir jetzt durch die hervorragenden Forschungen von Ewald Müller als geklärt betrachten, soweit Klärung überhaupt möglich ist ([65]):

([64]) Vgl. zur Bewertung des Konzilsberichts bei Matthäus zusammenfassend W. E. LUNT, *The Sources for the first Council of Lyons, 1245* in *English Historical Review* 33 (1918 p. 72-78) p. 76.

([65]) Zum folgenden vgl. EWALD MÜLLER O. F. M., *Das Konzil von Vienne 1311-1312*, Münster 1934 (*Vorreformationsgeschichtliche Forschungen*, hrsg. von Hch. Finke, XII) p. 396-408, besonders p. 404 ss.

In der dritten Sitzung des Konzils (6. Mai 1312) liess Clemens V. eine Reihe von Konstitutionen verlesen und erklärte eine weitere Reihe von Dekreten, die noch nicht endgültig formuliert und daher nicht verlesen wurden, für so gut wie verlesen, *pro lectis, ordinatis et constitutis* ([66]). Alle Konstitutionen jedoch sollten erst mit der Versendung der endgültigen Fassung an die Universitäten Gesetzeskraft erlangen. Die Promulgation auf dem Konzil diente also nur dem Zweck, den konziliaren Charakter der Konstitutionen in einer vorläufigen Fassung zu sichern; sie sollten inhaltlich und formell noch von einer Kommission durchgearbeitet und mit anderen, ausserkonziliaren Erlassen des Papstes vereint als *Liber Septimus* publiziert werden.

Zu dieser endgültigen Publikation ist Clemens V. bekanntlich nicht mehr gekommen. Als die Umarbeitung und Einordnung der Schlüsse von Vienne in das Dekretalenschema beendet war, liess Clemens die verbesserte und vermehrte Sammlung am 21. März 1314 im Konsistorium zu Monteux bei Carpentras abermals verlesen, schob aber ihre Inkraftsetzung (mit geringen Ausnahmen [[67]]) wiederum bis zur Versendung an die Hochschulen heraus: diese allein sollte also erst den Akt der authentischen Publikation des Gesetzestextes darstellen. Aber ehe sie erfolgte, starb Clemens V. am 20. April 1314. Die wenigen Hss. der Clementinen, die — nach uns bekanntem, aber wegen des erweiterten Umfangs abgewandeltem Muster — mit der Publikationsbulle

> *Cum nuper in generali concilio Viennensi et ante et post quasdam constitutiones super certis articulis duximus promulgandas...*

beginnen ([68]), stellen die Textstufe von Monteux (nach Umarbeitung und zweiter Verlesung, aber vor der amtlichen Publikation) dar, die keine Gesetzeskraft erlangte. Wie bekannt, hat dann erst Jo-

---

([66]) MÜLLER p. 390, p. 687 n. 25 (aus der Hs. München lat. 2699).

([67]) MÜLLER p. 403.

([68]) Text in DENIFLE, *Chartul. Univ. Parisien.* II 1, Paris 1891 p. 169. MÜLLER p. 396^{39}. — Das Lyoner Muster Innozenz' IV. und seine erste Wiederholung durch Gregor X. (in der Versendungsbulle *Cum nuper* vom 1. November 1274 für die Konstitutionen des II. Konzils von Lyon, Po. 20951) sind MÜLLER p. 398 entgangen. — Zur Erweiterung *Cum nuper... et ante et post...* finden sich übrigens schon Analogien in interpolierten, durch Extravaganten vermehrten Hss. der Novellen Innozenz' IV; ein Beispiel bei E. FOURNIER, *Questions d'hist. du droit can.* p. 39.

hann XXII., nach nochmaliger Revision, die Aussendung der Clementinen an die Universitäten am 25. Oktober 1317 mit der Bulle *Quoniam nulla* vollzogen und damit die Konstitutionen des Vienner Konzils in Kraft gesetzt.

Wir haben diese Vorgeschichte der Clementinen hier in Erinnerung gebracht, um die Möglichkeiten einer stufenweisen Entstehung amtlicher Konzilsakten aufzuzeigen. In der Tat gelangen wir nur dann zu einer befriedigenden Erklärung für R und M, wenn wir zugeben, dass es schon in Lyon ähnlich gegangen sein kann wie 67 Jahre später in Vienne: dasss nämlich auf dem Konzil die Kanones in noch nicht endgültiger Formulierung und Ordnung verkündet wurden. Für eine solche Sachlage spricht ausser dem zeitlichen Abstand der Publikation von der Schlussitzung auch der Befund der erhaltenen Berichte über das Konzil von Lyon.

Die Mehrzahl der zeitgenössischen Chroniken und Annalen erwähnt überhaupt nichts vom Erlass der Konstitutionen, geschweige denn von Verhandlungen über sie. Einzig der Continuator V der *Chronica Regia Coloniensis* vermerkt zum Jahre 1245 ([69]):

... *in eodem concilio statuit domnus papa quasdam institutiones, que sub titulis competentibus referuntur postmodum inserte nove decretalium compilationi,*

und noch knapper der Continuator I von Gilberts *Chronicon pontificum et imperatorum* ([70]):

... *ubi deposuit Fridericum imperatorem et conposuit multas constituciones.*

Aber auch die ausführlicheren Berichte, die uns über die Konzilssitzungen überliefert sind, erweisen sich für die Frage der Konstitutionen als merkwürdig dürftig. Dass die politisch-satirische Allegorie vom Pfau (Pavo) ([71]) in der Schilderung des Konzils die kanonistische Tätigkeit übergeht, nimmt nicht Wunder, wohl aber, dass auch aus der sonst so sorgfältigen, in den Kreisen der päpstlichen Kanzlei entstandenen sog. *Brevis nota* ([72]) **nichts über Bera-**

([69]) Ed. WAITZ in *Script. Rer. Germ.*, Hannoverae 1880 p. 287.

([70]) Ed. HOLDER-EGGER in *Mon. Germ. Script.* XXIV, 1879 p. 136.

([71]) Ed. Th. G. VON KARAJAN, in *Denkschriften der Kaiserl. Akademie der Wissenschaften* II 1, Wien 1851 p. 111-117. F. W. E. ROTH in *Romanische Forschungen* 6 (1891) p. 46-54.

([72]) Erstmals in der römischen Konzilienausgabe erschienen, *Concil. gener.*

tung und Verkündung der Konstitutionen hervorgeht. Einzig Matthäus Paris ist etwas ergiebiger.

Zunächst erwartet man eine Ankündigung der gesetzgeberischen Arbeit in der Rede zu finden, die der Papst am 28. Juni in der Eröffnungssitzung über das Konzilsprogramm hielt. Aber während Br(evis nota), M(atthäus) und ein dritter Bericht (in den von H. Cole herausgegebenen *Articuli et Petitiones Praelatorum Angliae* [73]) über die vier politisch-kirchlichen Themata, die Innozenz ankündigte, zusammenstimmen — Bedrängung Konstantinopels durch die schismatischen Griechen, des hl. Landes durch die Sarazenen, Ungarns durch die Tartaren, und die Verfolgung der Kirche durch Kaiser Friedrich —, gehen sie über den fünften Punkt, die innerkirchlichen Fragen, auseinander (74). Nach M hätte der Papst die Bekämpfung einiger neuer Häresien ins Programm gestellt, nach Br die *difformitas praelatorum et subditorum* (also allgemeine Kirchenreform), nach dem englischen Dokument endlich *de ordinacionibus et constitucionibus totius generalis ecclesie* gesprochen. Da zu Lyon weder Reformdekrete, noch Ketzerdekrete beschlossen wurden, dürfte die letzte Version des Programms die einzig richtige sein; aber wie geringen Raum müssen die *ordinaciones* und *constituciones* nachher in den Verhandlungen eingenommen haben, wenn M und Br sie in der Programmrede so falsch darstellen!

Ob überhaupt Verhandlungen über die Konstitutionen stattfanden, können wir nach den vorliegenden Quellen nicht einmal mit Bestimmtheit sagen (75). Das englische Dokument schweigt gänzlich, aus Br dagegen erfahren wir, dass am 17. Juli, zu Beginn der dritten (letzten) Session, die mit der feierlichen Absetzung des

---

IV, 1612 p. 68-69; zuletzt in *Mon. Germ. Const.* II, 1896 p. 513-516 (ed. L. WEILAND). Zur Text- und Editionsgeschichte dieses Berichtes vgl. ausführlich meine oben n. 37 angekündigte Untersuchung.

(73) Sir HENRY COLE, *Documents illustrative of English History in the Thirteenth and Fourteenth Centuries...*, London 1844 p. 351 ss.; für die Geschichte des Konzils erstmals verwertet von W. E. LUNT (oben n. 64) p. 73 ss.

(74) *Brevis Nota*, in *Concil. general. ed. Rom.* IV p. 68, MANSI XXIII col. 610 s., *Mon. Germ. Const.* II p. 514. — MATTH. PARIS, ed. LUARD IV p. 434 s. — *Articuli et Petitiones*, COLE p. 351. — Vgl. LUNT p. 77.

(75) Zweifelnd schon VAN ESPEN (oben p. 87) p. 505.

Kaisers schloss, der Papst ein liturgisches Dekret über die Oktav von Mariae Geburt erliess und sodann

> *quasdam constitutiones quae pro recuperatione terrae sanctae, ac alias quae pro subsidio Romani Imperii, et etiam alias quae contra Tartaros factae fuerant, fecit legi* ([76]).

Dies ist der einzige Punkt, an dem Br überhaupt irgendetwas von Konstitutionen erwähnt, aber die Stelle bezieht sich, so wie sie dasteht, nur auf die Erlasse R 14-17 (*Arduis, Perennis, Christianae* und *Afflicti*), nicht auf die eigentlichen, juristischen Konstitutionen. Vermutlich sind indessen auch sie zu diesem Zeitpunkt des Konzils verlesen worden ([77]), und dann ist es charakteristisch, dass Br dies zu sagen vergisst: mehr als ein rasches formelles *fecit legi* kann hiernach kaum stattgefunden haben, Beratungen keinesfalls.

So bleibt die einzige Quelle, die über die Verkündung der Konstitutionen etwas mehr Aufschluss gibt, Matthäus Paris. Zwar nicht über den Zeitpunkt: M bringt die Erlasse *de negotio crucis* und die 19 *Constitutiones* wohl hinter seinem Bericht über die Verkündung des Absetzungsurteils ([78]), aber ohne dass es klar wird, ob er damit den chronologischen Verlauf der Schlussitzung wiedergeben will. Ist dies doch der Fall, so steht dem die deutliche Aussage der in äusseren Daten und Fakten stets zuverlässigeren *Brevis nota* gegenüber ([79]), dass nach der Verlesung des Urteils der Papst sich sogleich erhoben und ein Tedeum angestimmt habe, *quo hymno decantato per omnes fuit concilium dissolutum*.

Wichtig dagegen ist M nicht nur, weil hier der einzige Konzilsbericht vorliegt, der einen Text der erlassenen Konstitutionen mitteilt, sondern vor allem durch folgenden Schlussvermerk ([80]):

> *Cum autem haec statuta ad notitiam audientium pervenissent, in conspectu omnium sapientium placuerunt. Et in hoc tam*

---

[76] *Ed. Rom.* p. 69, MANSI col. 612, *Mon. Germ.* p. 516.

[77] So auch BERGER, *Registres* II, Paris 1887 p. xciv, wenigstens für die Reihe R 1-17.

[78] Ed. LUARD IV p. 456 ss.

[79] *Ed. Rom.* p. 69, *Mansi* col. 613, *Mon. Germ.* p. 516.

[80] Ed. LUARD IV p. 473. Schon VAN ESPEN p. 505 machte auf diesen Passus aufmerksam.

favorem quam gratiam dominus Papa promeruit universorum. Verumtamen quaedam eorum ante concilium, quaedam durante concilio, quaedam vero post concilium sunt statuta.

Ergab schon die Dürftigkeit des Berichtes in Br und das Schweigen in den anderen Quellen, dass die Verkündung auf dem Konzil keine grosse Rolle gespielt haben kann, so zeigen die Worte des Matthäus (denen irgend eine bestimmte Nachricht zugrundeliegen muss), dass die endgültige Redaktion der Kanones zur Zeit der Verlesung überhaupt noch nicht abgeschlossen war. Dass sie wirklich verlesen wurden, dürfen wir allerdings nach dem Wortlaut der Bulle vom 25. August, worin die Konstitutionen ausdrücklich als *nuper in concilio* promulgiert bezeichnet werden, wohl nicht bezweifeln, und auch M sagt ja mit Bezug auf die ganze Reihe, dass *haec statuta ad notitiam audientium pervenissent*. Aber diese Verlesung kann nur eine vorläufige Fassung und Ordnung der Beschlüsse zum Gegenstand gehabt haben, wenn M die einschränkende Bemerkung daran knüpft, dass ausser den schon *ante concilium* und den *durante concilio* verfassten Stücken einige aus der ganzen Reihe (*eorum*) erst *post concilium sunt statuta*. Will man nämlich den Widersinn vermeiden, der entstände, wenn noch nicht bestehende Konstitutionen den Hörern zur Kenntnis gekommen sein sollten, so kann das *quaedam (eorum) vero post concilium sunt statuta* hier nur heissen, dass die betreffenden Stücke erst nach dem Konzil ihre endgültige Fassung erhalten haben, auf dem Konzil aber in irgendeiner provisorischen Weise — sei es im Entwurf, sei es summarisch — mitgeteilt wurden. Dann konnten sie alle als Konzilsstücke gelten, ganz wie später zu Vienne die Stücke, die *pro lectis* erklärt wurden.

V.

Wenn tatsächlich in der Schlussitzung des Konzils nur eine solche provisorische Promulgation stattfand, so gewinnt die Existenz von Kanoneslisten, die von der amtlich promulgierten Coll. I abweichen und die als Exzerpte aus ihr nicht gut erklärbar sind, einen historischen Sinn. Wir kehren damit zur Untersuchung der

Institutiones in R und der *Constitutiones* in M zurück und legen folgende Tabellen zugrunde:

R	Coll. I	(Coll. III)	M		M	Coll. I	(Coll. III)	R
1	1	(1)	10*a		1*	21	(37)	12
2	2	(2)	4*		2	12	(17)	9
3	5	(5)	9*		3	9	(14)	6
4	6	(9)	10*b		4*	2	(2)	2
5	8	(12)	7		5	11	(16)	7
6	9	(14)	3		6	3	(3)	8
7	11	(16)	5		7	8	(12)	5
8	3	(3)	6		8	13	(18)	10
9	12	(17)	2		9*	5	(5)	3
10	13	(18)	8		10*	1+6	(1+9)	1+4
11	17	(26)	--		11	4a	(4a)	--
12	21	(37)	1*		12	4b	(4b)	--
13	—	—	--		13	7	(10)	--
14	—	—	--		14	10	(15)	--
15	—	—	--		15	14	(21)	--
16	—	—	--		16	15	(22)	--
17	—	—	(Luard p. 456)		17	16	(25)	--
					18	19	(35)	--
					19	20	(36)	--

Die erste Tabelle lehrt uns, dass R 1-12 (über die nicht-juristischen Stücke R 13-17 vgl. oben p. 81) auch in Coll. I (und III) eine Reihe bilden; eine unterbrochene Reihe nämlich, in der die Abfolge der Kanones von R zwar auseinandergezogen, aber mit Einer Ausnahme nicht verändert wird. Die Ausnahme betrifft Nov. 3, die in R nicht auf Nov. 2 = R 2, sondern auf Nov. Coll. I 11 (III 16) = R 7 folgt; eine Abweichung, die sich merkwürdigerweise in der sonst ganz anders geordneten Liste von M wiederholt: R 7. 8 = M 5. 6 = Coll. I 11. 3.

Aus der zweiten Tabelle erkennen wir, dass M im Verhältnis zur authentischen Sammlung und zu R in zwei Gruppen zerfällt: M 1-10 und M 11-19. Die erste Gruppe bringt 11 (in 10 zusammengefasste) Konstitutionen, die auch durch R vertreten sind, aber in einer völlig anderen Reihenfolge als R und Coll., und darüber hinaus mit vier erheblichen Rezensionsabweichungen, die wir hier durch * gekennzeichnet haben: die Präambeln in M 1. 4. 9, und die Kontamination zweier Stücke in M 10 (vgl. oben p. 78). Der Unterschied zu Coll. I ist hier also erheblich grösser als bei R, er erstreckt sich übrigens auch auf die Kapitelüberschriften, die hier, im Gegensatz zu R, von den Titelrubriken der Sammlung abweichen ([81]). Die zweite Gruppe dagegen, M 11-19, enthält ausschliesslich Konstitutionen, die in R fehlen, und diesmal in einer der Coll. I wesentlich näherstehenden Form: die 8 (in 9 zerlegten) Nummern bilden auch in Coll. I eine Reihe, und zwar so, dass (entsprechend wie für R 1-12) in Coll. die Abfolge der Kanones von M lediglich auseinandergezogen, aber nicht verändert wird.

Wir haben also

R 1 -12: intermittente Reihe in Coll.
R 13-17: fehlt in Coll.; Verordnungen nicht-juristischen Inhalts.
M 1 -10: keine Reihe in Coll., im Material durch R 1-10. 12 gedeckt, im Text wichtige Eigenheiten.
M 11-19: intermittente Reihe in Coll.

Wenn wir nun die beiden Reihen R 1-12 und M 11-19 sinngemäss ineinanderschieben, so ergibt sich mit

R = Coll. I 1. 2.   5. 6.   8. 9.   11. 3. 12 13.   17.   21
M =   4.   7.   10.   14. 15. 16.   19. 20.

ein der Coll. I sehr nahekommendes Bild, das nur in drei Punkten von der amtlichen Sammlung abweicht:

Coll. I 3   (III 3) steht hinter 11 (16).

([81]) M 1. *De sententia excommunicationis.* M 2. *De contumacia absentis punienda.* M 3. *Ut non impediatur litis contestatio per obiectum exceptionis peremptoriae, etc.* M 4. *Non committantur causae iudicibus delegatis, nisi in civitatibus vel locis famosis, ubi possit haberi peritorum copia.* M 5. *Actori qui contumax fuerit non dabitur citatio, nisi prius refundat et caveat defendendo literae.* M 6. *Ut propter plures et diversas personales actiones non trahatur quis ad diversos iudices.* M 7. *Ut non compellatur quis comparere in iudicio nisi in casibus in litera notatis.* M 8. *De positionibus negativis quae probari non possunt de officio iudicis delegati.* M 9. *Si eligat quis sub condicione vel alternatione vel incertis verbis, non valet.* M 10. *Ut per generalem clausulam, scil. ' quidam alii', non trahantur in iudicio ultra tres vel quatuor dietas.* — Nur die Rubrik von M 1 deckt sich mit dem Titel von Coll. I 19-22.

Coll. I 18 (III 31) fehlt.
Coll. I 22 (III 38) fehlt.

Aus diesem Tatbestand kann man meines Erachtens wichtige Schlussfolgerungen ziehen:

1. Für die Reihe R 1-12 können wir drei verschiedene Textordnungen feststellen, ausser R nämlich die auseinandergezogene Reihe in Coll. I und die gänzlich anders geordnete, aber immerhin geschlossene Gruppe M 1-10, in der nur eine Nummer (R 11) fehlt. Dann ergibt sich aber, bei Ablehnung der Exzerpthypothese, dass den drei Textordnungen auch drei verschiedene Redaktionsstufen entsprechen müssen, deren historische Folge sich aus folgenden Erwägungen ableiten lässt:

a) Coll. I enthält die definitive Ordnung.

b) R ist mit Coll. I verwandt durch Parallelität der Ordnung — mit einer Ausnahme, betreffend Nov. 3 — und Gleichheit der Textgestalt, bei quantitativem Zurückbleiben des Materials.

c) M 1-10 ist mit R verwandt durch Identität des Materials — mit einer Ausnahme, betreffend R 11 —, bei starker Differenzierung in Ordnung und Textgestalt.

d) M 1-10 weist keine direkte Aehnlichkeit mit Coll. I auf.

Mithin steht R in der Mitte zwischen M 1-10 und Coll. I. Dann wird M 1-10, als die der endgültigen fernststehende Form, auch notwendig zur ältesten; sie mag die Form und Ordnung darstellen, in der diese Kapitel auf dem Konzil verlesen wurden: noch ohne jede Rücksicht auf das Titelschema der Dekretalensammlungen, ungeordnet, ohne authentische Rubriken, und teilweise mit Präambeln versehen, die als rein rhetorisch bei der endgültigen Textfeststellung missfielen, während sie bei der Verlesung nicht unwirksam waren. Vorlage des Matthäus dürften dann für M 1-10 die Berichte von Konzilsteilnehmern gewesen sein, die umständlichen, summarienartigen Rubriken mögen Zutat des Chronisten sein. Das fehlende Stück R 11 dürfte sich bei der Konzilsverlesung noch in dieser Gruppe von Konstitutionen befunden haben; ob M seine Vorlage hier unvollständig wiedergegeben hat, oder ob die Vorlage bereits lückenhaft war, steht dahin.

R 1-12, als Mittelglied zwischen der konziliaren und der publizierten Redaktionsstufe, ist dann das Produkt einer ersten Umarbeitung dieser Kapitelgruppe, an der Kurie nach Konzilsschluss entstanden. Einige Präambeln wurden gestrichen (bei M 1. 4. 9), die Einzelstücke textlich gefeilt und nach dem Dekretalenschema angeordnet, wobei die Stücke die entsprechenden Titelrubriken (R 1. *De rescriptis*, R 2. *De eodem*, R 3. *De electione et electi potestate* usw.) erhielten. An einer wichtigen Stelle sieht man nun, dass diese redaktionelle Tätigkeit noch den Stempel einer unfertigen Vorstufe zur endgültigen Fassung trägt: das Kapitel *Dispendia* (Nov. 3) blieb, obgleich es bereits den Titel *De rescriptis* erhielt und also zu R 1. 2 gehört hätte, als R 8 hinter dem *De dolo et contumacia* rubrizierten R 7 *Actor* stehen. Damit weist R charakteristischerweise an der einzigen Stelle, an der es die Ordnung der Coll. I noch nicht erreicht, dieselbe Ordnung wie M (5. 6) auf; der beste Beweis für die Richtigkeit unserer Annahme, dass die M 1-10 zugrundeliegende Textstufe den Ausgangspunkt der redaktionellen Arbeit für R bildete.

Warum übrigens R hier mit der Einordnung zögerte, ergibt sich aus dem Inhalt des Kapitels: Bei mehreren Personalklagen gegen einen Beklagten soll der Kläger Justizbriefe nicht an verschiedene zu delegierende Richter beantragen; widrigenfalls werden die Briefe ungültig und der Kläger schuldet dem Beklagten Schadensersatz. Entsprechend sollen für eine Gegenklage Briefe nicht an andere als die bereits delegierten Richter erbeten werden ([82]). Es handelt sich also um ein Klägerdelikt, das in der Tat auch unter den Titel *De dolo* und hinter c. *Actor* (Klägerversäumnis) passen würde, da der Inhalt der Konstitution sogut das Prozessrecht wie das Recht der Reskripte betrifft. Dennoch trug die zweite Bedeutung schliesslich den Sieg davon, und der ursprüngliche, in R beibehaltene Zusammenhang von M 5. 6 wurde in der endgültigen Redaktion aufgegeben.

Was hier vor allem gezeigt werden sollte, ist der nur vermittelnde und vorbereitende Charakter, der der Redaktion R zukommt, und der so lange verkannt wurde, weil Textzeuge dieser Fassung

---

([82]) Sext. I, 3, 3.

eben das päpstliche Register ist (⁸³). Nach unserer Ueberzeugung ist aber R 1-12 nur aus Versehen ins Register geraten: es handelt sich um einen Entwurf der Redaktoren, die mit der Bearbeitung dieser Gruppe der Konzilsschlüsse (der Gruppe M 1-10) betraut waren, und nicht um ein aus der Kanzlei herausgegangenes Schreiben, das wirklich ins Register gehört hätte. Daher steht die ganze Serie auch so verdächtig, ohne Datum und mit der falschen Rubrik *Institutiones* (statt *Constitutiones*) *facte in concilio generali apud lugdunum*, am Schluss des Quaternio, der die *litterae curiales* des zweiten Jahres Innozenz' IV. enthält; und so lässt sich auch die Zusammenlegung mit den Konzilsstücken R 13-17 erklären, die man nirgendwo anders unterzubringen wusste, und von denen z.B. R 13 durch den wenig sachkundigen Registrator die garnicht passende Rubrik *De usuris* erhielt.

Dass eine solche, der authentischen Publikation nicht entsprechende Eintragung möglich war, ergibt sich aus der auch sonst für die Mitte des 13. Jahrhunderts nachweisbaren Gepflogenheit der Kanzlei, *litterae curiales* nicht nach dem Original, sondern nach Konzepten zu registrieren (⁸⁴).

2. Für die Gruppe M 11-19 konnten wir einen doppelten Unterschied zu M 1-10 feststellen: die bereits erreichte, als Reihe zu wertende Ordnungsparallelität zur Coll. I, und das Fehlen dieser Reihe in R. Damit ist aber zugleich gesagt, dass M 11-19 schon auf derselben redaktionellen Stufe wie R steht, und so erhebt sich die Frage, ob wir diese Reihe überhaupt noch als homogene Fortsetzung von M 1-10, d. h. als provisorische konziliare Fassung ansprechen dürfen. Denn M 11-19 weist alle Merkmale auf, die M 1-10 nicht, genauer noch nicht hat: die Ordnung nach dem Titelschema der Dekretalensammlungen, keine wesentlichen Textunterschiede zur amtlichen Sammlung, endlich auch anstelle der umständlichen Ka-

---

(⁸³) Nur MANSI, *Adnotatio* zu RAYNALDUS, *Annales Ecclesiastici*, ed. Lucensis 1747 II p. 324 = *Suppl.* II col. 1099 = *Ampliss.* XXIII col. 675 hält dafür, *acta illa Vaticana mutila esse*, aber mit falscher Begründung.

(⁸⁴) Vgl. HARRY BRESSLAU, *Handbuch der Urkundenlehre* I, ₂Leipzig 1912 p. 117. — Uebrigens ist R noch nach Erlass der Coll. I an der Kurie benutzt worden, nämlich zur Herstellung einer Kanzleiordnung (ed. M. TANGL, *Die päpstlichen Kanzleiordnungen von 1200-1500*, Innsbruck 1894 p. 55-59), die in c. 1 die Aussendungsbulle *Cum nuper*, in c. 2-9 acht Lyoner Konstitutionen und in c. 10-18 neun lediglich die Kanzlei betreffende Bestimmungen enthält (TANGL p. 56); c. 2-9 erweisen sich bei näherem Zusehen als identisch mit R 1-8.

pitelsummarien die authentischen Titelrubriken der Sammlung, wovon nur das erste, zerrissene Kapitel M 11 + 12 = Nov. 4 eine Ausnahme macht ([85]).

Will man trotz all dieser auffallenden Verschiedenheiten von M 1-10 und M 11-19 an der Homogeneität von M 1-19 festhalten, so kann man dafür nur Ein Argument geltend machen: den Ueberlieferungszusammenhang bei Matthäus Paris. Ein schwaches Argument; denn warum sollte der in Textverarbeitungen versierte Chronist nicht zwei verschiedene ihm vorliegende Quellenreihen zusammengefasst haben? Die festgestellten Unterschiede legen dies nahe, und sogar die eine Unstimmigkeit, die bezüglich der Titelrubriken in der Reihe M 11-19 geblieben war, passt vortrefflich zur Annahme kompilatorischer Arbeit: dass gerade M 11 + 12, also der Anfang der zweiten Quellenreihe, statt der erwarteten Titelrubrik *De electionibus* noch zwei Kapitelsummarien im Stile von M 1-10 aufweist, zeugt für die Absicht des Matthäus, die Ueberschriften zu vereinheitlichen. Aber die Absicht blieb unausgeführt, und damit die «Naht» sichtbar.

Die hiernach zu vermutende Ursprungsverschiedenheit von M 1-10 und M 11-19 lässt drei verschiedene historische Erklärungsmöglichkeiten zu: Entweder besass Matthäus unmittelbare Ueberlieferung nur für M 1-10 und wollte diese unvollständige Serie nachträglich aus der publizierten Coll. I ergänzen. Aber dann bliebe das Fehlen dreier Konstitutionen (Coll. I 17. 18. 22 = Coll. III 26. 31. 38) in der «Ergänzungsliste» unverständlich.

Oder M 11-19 stellt bereits ein Produkt nachkonziliarer Zwischenredaktion an der Kurie dar (analog der R-gruppe), welches Matthäus in seine Liste aufgenommen hat, weil die ursprüngliche, konziliare Form dieser Kapitel schon ihm nicht mehr erhalten war. Aber ein solcher Schluss von der Aehnlichkeit des redaktionellen Typus in M 11-19 und R 1-12 auf die Gleichartigkeit der Entstehung kann sich nur auf das Argument der Analogie, nicht auf irgendeinen Anhaltspunkt in den Quellen selbst stützen und ist daher historisch bedenklich.

([85]) M 11. *Ne aliquis impediat electiones vel postulationes.* M 12. *De poena deficientium in probatione.* M 13. *De officio legati.* M 14. *De restitutione spoliatorum.* M 15. *De accusationibus.* M 16. *De sententia et re iudicata.* M 17. *De appellationibus.* M 18. *De sententia excommunicationis.* M 19. *De eodem.* - Die Rubrik von M 15 beruht offenbar auf einem Versehen für *De exceptionibus.*

Als dritte Möglichkeit bleibt, dass die Gruppe M 11-19 bereits auf dem Konzil in dieser verhältnismässig fertigen Form verlesen wurde und es eine bloss provisorische konziliare Fassung (wie bei M 1-10) für sie niemals gegeben hat. Das würde heissen, dass diese Gruppe von der Kurie bereits fertig ausgearbeitet auf das Konzil mitgebracht wurde, also eine Zusammenstellung ursprünglich vorkonziliarer Konstitutionen ist. Für diese Hypothese sprechen mehrere gewichtige Gründe:

a) Für die Konstitutionen M 11-19 ist eine selbständige, gesonderte Ueberlieferung ausserhalb der Chronik des Matthäus, in Extravagantensammlungen nachweisbar. Zum Beispiel stehen in der Hs. Fulda, Landesbibliothek D. 10 (fol. 8^r-9^v), anschliessend an eine Abschrift der Sammlung von 33 Nummern mit dem Apparat des Papstes (Coll. I + II, oben p. 73), die Novellen 4. 10. 15. 21. 22. 25. 35. 36, scheinbar ein unmotivierter Auszug ([86]), in Wahrheit aber dieselbe Reihe wie M 11-19. Und die gleiche Zusammenstellung dieser acht Konstitutionen findet sich auch in anderen Dekretalenhss. ([87]), ist also keine bloss zufällige Einzelüberlieferung. Als ein späterer Auszug lässt sie sich, nach der amtlichen Veröffentlichung der Coll. I, nicht gut erklären, sehr wohl aber, wenn diese acht Konstitutionen bereits vor dem Konzil bekannt waren.

b) Die acht Konstitutionen sind aber in Cod. Fuld. ausserdem mit einem Glossenapparat des Gottfried von Trani (Sigle *G.*, *Go.*) versehen. Nun ist aber der bedeutende Kanonist höchstwahrscheinlich bereits Anfang April 1245, also vor dem Konzil, als Kardinaldiakon von S. Adriano verstorben ([88]). Doch selbst wenn er das Konzil überlebt hätte, bliebe es unbegreiflich, warum er statt der authentischen Sammlung die «Auswahl» von acht Konstitutionen glossiert haben sollte.

c) Ferner wird die Annahme eines vorkonziliaren Ursprungs der acht Stücke M 11-19 möglich durch die bereits (oben p. 97) zitierte Aeusserung des Matthäus selbst, der von den Konstitutionen mitteilt, dass *quaedam eorum ante concilium... sunt statuta*. Und damit deckt sich die Rubrik der Coll. I in der Hs. Wien *2073 (oben p. 74):

([86]) So habe ich noch *Decretalistica* p. 447 angenommen.

([87]) Nach freundlicher Mitteilung von Herrn Kessler, von dem genauere Angaben über eine Reihe bisher ungeprüfter Hss. der Innozentianen in der oben n. 5 angekündigten Dissertation zu erwarten sind.

([88]) Vgl. dazu *Exkurs IV*, unten p. 124.

Constitutiones domini pape innoc. iiii. in constitutione (!) *generali apud lugdunum promulgate, inter quas inseruntur quedam alie antea* (scr. aña) *conposite, prout exigit ordo rubricarum.*

d) Gewichtige Anhaltspunkte liefern uns ferner einige der in M 11-19 enthaltenen Konstitutionen selbst. Bezeugt ist die schon vorkonziliare Existenz zunächst für M 13 *Officii* = Coll. I 7 (III 10). Denn in einem Schreiben Innozenz' IV. vom 23. Februar 1244 an den Patriarchen von Jerusalem, apostolischen Legaten, steht: ... *non obstante constitutione a nobis edita, ut apostolice sedis legati, nisi cardinales existant, nullam potestatem habeant beneficia conferendi* ([89]). Ebendies macht aber den Inhalt der Konstitution *Officii* aus, die also damals schon als Einzelerlass bestanden haben muss. Damit finden auch die Beobachtungen Van Espens über die unkonzilsmässige Sprechweise des Kanons ([90]) ihre Erklärung. — Ueber die Konstitution M 15 *Pia* = Coll. I 14 (III 21) wissen wir aus dem *Ordo iudiciarius* (1263-66) des Aegidius de Fuscarariis, dass fr. Jacobus Buoncambio O. P., Vizekanzler der römischen Kirche vom 15. April 1239 bis zum 31. Mai 1244 (dem Tag seiner Ernennung zum Bischof von Bologna; 1244-1260), *interfuerat compilationi illius decretalis* (!) *Pia* ([91]). Mit *compilatio* muss hier die Redaktion des Stückes in der päpstlichen Kanzlei unter Mitwirkung des Vizekanzlers gemeint sein; denn die Mitwirkung des Bischofs von Bologna beim Konzil gerade für dieses eine Stück hervorzuheben, läge doch kein Anlass vor.

e) Ein letztes Argument können wir endlich aus der Coll. I entnehmen. Dem Schlusskapitel der authentischen Sammlung, Coll. I 22 *Quia periculosum* (III 38) ist nämlich ein Epilog angehängt, der mit den Worten

Huic etiam adicimus sanctioni, ut illud quod in constitutione ' Solet a nonnullis ' a nobis hactenus promulgata fuerat consti-

---

([89]) BERGER, Registres n. 476.
([90]) Vgl. oben p. 87.
([91]) AEGIDIUS DE FUSCARARIIS ed. L. WAHRMUND, *Quellen zur Geschichte des römisch-kanonischen Prozesses im Mittelalter* III 1, Innsbruck 1916 p. 65. Erster Hinweis bei PAUL M. BAUMGARTEN, *Von der apostolischen Kanzlei*, Köln 1908 p. 75 « nach gütiger Mitteilung des Herrn Dr. Göller ». Baumgarten, der auch die Daten der Vizekanzlerschaft des Jacobus bringt (BRESSLAU I₂ p. 251 will sie bis zum 2. Juni fortdauern lassen), geht übrigens zu weit, wenn er aus ihm ganz allgemein « einen der Kompilatoren der Dekrete Innozenz' IV. » macht.

> *tutum, ... ad episcoporum et archiepiscoporum sententias nullatenus extendatur...*

dem Kapitel M 19 *Solet* = Coll. I 20 (III 36) eine einschränkende interpretatio authentica gibt, und damit deutlich den Stempel eines nachträglichen amtlichen Zusatzes trägt. Dies eigenartige Verfahren (statt einer Umredigierung des Kapitels selbst) kann man doch wohl nur dadurch erklären, dass die Konstitution *Solet* einer Aenderung schon entzogen war, weil sie bereits für sich allein Rechtskraft besass; dann muss sie aber schon vor dem Konzil (*hactenus*) erlassen worden sein.

Lässt sich aber für drei Stücke der Reihe M 11-19 eine ursprünglich vorkonziliare Redaktion und Verbreitung annehmen (M 13. 15. 19), so wird damit unsere Hypothese vom vorkonziliaren Ursprung der ganzen Reihe — an deren Geschlossenheit bei der mannigfachen Sondertradition kein Zweifel besteht — im höchsten Grade wahrscheinlich, und M 11-19 ist als eine auf dem Konzil bloss erneuerte und in das Konstitutionenwerk einbezogene Gruppe älterer innozentianischer Konstitutionen anzusprechen.

3. Die beiden vorbereitenden Kapitelgruppen R 1-12 und M 11-19 umfassen beinahe, aber nicht ganz, den Bestand der in Coll. I publizierten Konzilskonstitutionen: es fehlen Coll. I 18 und 22 (III 31. 38). Nach dem Text der Publikationsbulle zur Coll. I hat die Möglichkeit auszuscheiden, dass diese beiden Stücke etwa garnicht dem Konzil angehörten; für die Konstitution I 18 *Pro humani* (III 31) schafft ausserdem die Formel *sacri approbatione concilii statuimus* im Text volle Gewissheit. Sind aber beides Konzilsstücke, so macht ihr Fehlen in R und M bei der von uns angenommenen mehrstufigen Entstehungsgeschichte der Coll. I keine Schwierigkeit: Das Fehlen besagt nichts weiter, als dass die endgültige Textredaktion dieser zwei Kapitel eben bei der Verlesung in der dritten Sitzung noch nicht feststand und dass bei der redaktionellen Vorbereitung der authentischen Sammlung die beiden Stücke aus irgendeinem Grunde eine Kapitelgruppe für sich bildeten ([92]).

([92]) Damit würde sich auch die Bemerkung des Matthäus Paris decken, dass von den Konstitutionen *quaedam vero post concilium sunt statuta* (oben p. 97), wenngleich grammatisch diese Aussage sich genau genommen nur auf *haec statuta, quaedam eorum*, d. h. auf Stücke aus der in M 1-19 wiedergegebenen Serie beziehen kann.

Nun wissen wir in der Tat aus der zwischen 1250 und 1253 geschriebenen Lectura des Hostiensis zu den Novellen, dass der Papst den ursprünglichen, also konziliaren, Text des c. *Quia periculosum* (I 22 = III 38) an einem wichtigen Punkte in der authentischen Fassung abgeändert hat, und können ferner nachweisen, dass Vornahme oder Nichtvornahme dieser Aenderung von Wichtigkeit für die Textgestaltung des c. *Pro humani* sein musste ([93]):

>Hostiensis ad c. Quia periculosum, v. interdicti vel suspensionis: *In textu fuit primo sic positum: ' excommunicationis et interdicti, vel suspensionis ', sed dominus noster illud verbum ' excommunicationis ' cancellavit; et cum quaereremus ab eo, quare hoc fecerat, respondit quod nimis favorabilis erat canon xvij. q. iiij. Si quis suadente. Attamen aliqui praesumpserant quod alius canon esset in causa, ille sc. quem habuistis supra de homic. extra. Pro humani, quia illo tempore occasione assissinorum timor et tremor venerat super multos, et ideo fuerat promulgatus, sicut fuit, et ibi de hoc cautum...*
>
>Ad c. Pro humani, v. praelatus: *Episcopus vel superior quicumque fuerit, excepto loquente, et hac de causa fuit decisum privilegium episcoporum quoad canones excommunicationum, ut notavi infra de sent. excom. Quia periculosum.*

Das Kapitel *Quia periculosum* dekretiert die generelle Exemtion der Bischöfe und höheren Prälaten von *ipso iure* eintretenden Zensuren, derart dass die *poena latae sententiae* sie nur noch dann treffen soll, wenn im betreffenden Strafgesetz die Bischöfe ausdrücklich eingeschlossen sind. Im usrprünglichen Text sollte sich nun nach dem Bericht des Hostiensis diese Sonderstellung auf Exkommunikation, Interdikt und Suspension erstrecken; in der authentischen Fassung strich Innozenz aber die Exkommunikation aus diesem Privileg; nach seiner privaten Aeusserung geschah diese sachliche — nicht bloss redaktionelle — Aenderung, weil sonst der für die Kirchenzucht grundlegend wichtige Kanon *Si quis suadente* (Exkommunikation *ipso facto* bei Gewalttaten gegen Kleriker) ni-

---

([93]) HOSTIENSIS, *Lectura*, ed. Venet. 1581 (*Henrici de Segusio Cardinalis Hostiensis... In Sextum Decretalium librum Commentaria*) fol. 35va und 28vb. — Vgl. über Ausgaben, Umfang und Entstehungszeit des Werkes: KUTTNER, *Decretalistica*, p. 460 s. Für den *terminus a quo* 1250 lässt sich noch ergänzend anführen, dass die *Lectura* sich auch auf die nicht vor diesem Jahre erlassene Nov. 32 *Volentes* (vgl. unten p. 118 s.) erstreckt.

mis favorabilis erat, d. h. mit dem blossen *Si quis* gewalttätige Prälaten nicht umfasst hätte und also zu «bequem» für sie gewesen wäre. In Kanonistenkreisen brachte man indessen die Textänderung auch mit der neuen Konzilskonstitution *Pro humani* über die Exkommunikation *ipso facto* beim Dingen von Assassinen in Zusammenhang, und nicht zu Unrecht; wenn das Assassinenunwesen auch nicht das Motiv der Textänderung in *Quia periculosum* für den Papst abgab, so bestand doch eine wichtige redaktionelle Beziehung zwischen den beiden Konstitutionen. Die Strafe in *Pro humani* sollte nämlich ausnahmslos für alle eintreten; wäre aber *Quia periculosum* unverändert geblieben, so hätte der Text von *Pro humani* an der Stelle ...*ut quicumque princeps, praelatus seu quaevis alia ecclesiastica saecularisve persona*... seinem Zweck nicht mehr genügt und in *ut quicumque princeps, episcopus, praelatus seu*... abgeändert werden müssen.

Diese komplexe Lage der beiden Kapitel macht es verständlich, warum sie beide in der Zwischenredaktion R 1-12 fehlen (in M 11-19 kann man sie ohnehin nicht vermissen, weil der Text von *Pro humani* einer Annahme vorkonziliaren Ursprungs widerspricht): Wegen eines grundsätzlich zu entscheidenden Problems hat Papst Innozenz das Kapitel *Quia periculosum* sich selbst zur endgültigen Inhalts- und Formgebung reserviert (*dominus noster illud verbum cancellavit!*), sodass es den Redaktoren, die mit der Bearbeitung jener Kapitelgruppe beauftragt waren, nicht anvertraut wurde. Das Kapitel *Pro humani* aber musste dann ebenfalls zurückgehalten werden, bis der Papst sich über den Wortlaut von *Quia periculosum* schlüssig geworden war.

VI.

Wie nach all diesen Vorbereitungen die endgültige Herstellung der amtlichen Coll. I vor sich ging, ist aus dem Vorangegangenen leicht abzulesen: Es lagen drei Kapitelgruppen vor: R 1-12; M 11-19; *Pro humani — Quia periculosum*. Die uns als solche überlieferten Gruppen R und M waren bereits nach dem Dekretalenschema der Titelrubriken in sich geordnet. In R war noch die Stellung von c. *Dispendia* zu korrigieren [94], dann konnten R und M nach Mass-

[94] Vgl. oben p. 101.

gabe ihrer Titelrubriken ineinandergeschoben, die zwei übrigen Konstitutionen ihrem Inhalt entsprechend eingefügt werden, und an den Schluss (Coll. I 22 *Quia periculosum*) wurde der Zusatz zum c. *Solet* aus der M-Gruppe (Coll. I 20) angehängt ([95]). Dies letztere blieb ohne Zweifel ein redaktioneller Schönheitsfehler, den später Bonifaz VIII. durch Streichung des Anhangs beseitigen zu müssen glaubte ([96]).

Eine Wiener Hs., Nationalbibl. *2189 (fol. 13ʳ-14ᵛ) gestattet uns übrigens, einen Blick in die Werkstatt der Redaktoren der Coll. I zu tun: Sie bringt unter der Rubrik *Constitutiones facte a dño. j. papa in concilio generali apud lugdunum* die folgenden 16 Nummern:

```
    Coll. III  1. 2. 3. 5. 9. 12. 14. 16. 17. 18. 26. 37. 38.    4 . 10. 15.
  = Coll. I    1. 2. 3. 5. 6.  8.  9. 11. 12. 13. 17. 21. 22.    4 .  7. 10.
  = R          1. 2. 8. 3. 4.  5.  6.  7.  9. 10. 11. 12. —       —   — —
  = M                                                           11+12. 13. 14.
```

Die Hs. gibt, unvollständig, den vorletzten Stand der Arbeiten, vor Ineinanderordnung des Materials wieder. R ist bereits durch die Umstellung von R 8 *Dispendia* korrigiert, das eine der beiden in RM fehlenden Kapitel angefügt; mitten in M bricht aber die Hs. ab.

Auch die oben pp. 74, 104 erwähnte Wiener Hs. der Coll. I, Nationalbibl. *2073 verdient in diesem Zusammenhang Beachtung, da sie die letzten Nummern der Coll. I, vor dem Anhang der Extravaganten, in folgender Umstellung bringt: 17. 19. 20. 21. 22. 18, also die beiden von Innozenz zur endgültigen Redaktion reservierten Konstitutionen 22 und 18 zusammen an den Schluss stellt.

Zusammenfassend können wir das Verhältnis von R, M und Coll. I wie folgt bestimmen.

a) Coll. I ist in vier Stufen entstanden:
Erlass einzelner Konstitutionen vor dem Konzil,
Verlesung in vorläufiger Form auf dem Konzil,
Vorbereitende Redaktion einzelner Kapitelgruppen,
Endgültige Redaktion durch Verflechtung der Gruppen und Vornahme letzter Korrekturen.

([95]) Vgl. oben p. 105.
([96]) Sext. V, 11, 4; vgl. FRIEDBERG, *Corp. iur. can.* II col. 1095.

b) Der Kapitelgruppen waren drei:
Erste Gruppe = Coll. I 1. 2. 3. 5. 6. 8. 9. 11. 12. 13. 17. 21,
Zweite Gruppe = Coll. I 4. 7. 10. 14. 15. 16. 19. 20,
Dritte Gruppe = Coll. I 18. 22.

c) Ausser der endgültigen Fassung sind erhalten:

für die erste Gruppe: die konziliare Verlesungsform in M 1-10 (eine Nummer der Gruppe fehlt); die vorbereitende Redaktion in R 1-12,

für die zweite Gruppe: die vorkonziliare Zusammenstellung in einigen Dekretalenhss., identisch mit der konziliaren Verlesungsform in M 11-19; keine weitere Zwischenredaktion,

für die dritte Gruppe: keine dieser Stufen, aber ein die Textgeschichte aufhellender Bericht bei Hostiensis.

EXKURS I (zu p. 73)

Der Glossenapparat Innozenz' IV. zu Coll. I + II seiner Novellen.

Schulte machte in seinen *Beiträgen zur Literatur über die Decretalen Gregors IX., Innozenz' IV., Gregors X.* ([1]) sieben Hss. namhaft, in denen er den Glossenapparat des Petrus de Sampson zu einer Reihe innozentianischer Novellen gefunden zu haben erklärte; eine achte, von ihm selbst an anderer Stelle genannte Hs. ([2]) hat er in dieser Liste vergessen. In meinem Aufsatz *Decretalistica* ([3]) habe ich mich auf Schultes Angaben verlassen und aus Katalogen zwei weitere Hss. hinzugefügt, gleichzeitig aber darauf hingewiesen, dass bezüglich der Initiums Unstimmigkeiten unter den Hss. bestehen, indem Schulte den Anfang zu c. *Cum in multis* nach einer ungenannten Hs. mit *Bene dicitur quia preter illos quatuor* angibt, während die Mehrzahl der Hss. mit *Nam omnes expressi in litteris convenientur preter illos quatuor* beginnt. Ueber den Umfang des Apparates liess sich aus Schultes Mitteilungen vermuten, dass er die aus Coll. I + II gemischte Sammlung von 33 Nummern umfasst.

([1]) *Sitzungsberichte der kais. Akademie der Wissenschaften in Wien, phil.-hist. Klasse* (= *Wiener SB*) 68 (1871 p. 55-127) p. 126.
([2]) *Wiener SB* 55 (1867) p. 770.
([3]) p. 456-457.

Nachdem ich inzwischen Gelegenheit hatte, einige Hss. durch Autopsie oder aufgrund mir zugänglicher Abschriftenproben nachzuprüfen, muss ich feststellen, dass Schulte eine grosse Verwirrung angerichtet und zwei ganz verschiedene Werke in eins zusammengeworfen hat.

I. Das Werk mit dem Anfang *Bene dixit* (nicht *dicitur*) *quia preter illos iiii. conveniri possunt omnes expressi* steht in folgenden Hss.:

> Firenze, Laurenziana *S. Croce V sin. 4 (fol. 80 ss.). (BANDINI, *Catal. Codicum latinorum Bibl. Mediceae-Laurentianae* IV, Florentiae 1777 col. 52, SCHULTE, *Wiener SB* 55 p. 770).
> Wien, Nationalbibl. *2083 (fol. 43ᵛ-45ʳ). (SCHULTE, *Wiener SB* 68 p. 126 s.).
> Wien, Nationalbibl. *2113 (fol. 74ᵛ-77ᵛ). Bisher unbekannt.

Es folgt in allen drei Fällen auf die Lectura des Petrus de Sampson zu den Gregorianen und ist in allen drei Fällen als sein Werk bezeugt. Cod. Laur. trägt die Rubrik *Incipit opus magistri p. sapsonis super novis decʳ.*, Wien 2113 weist oft die Sigle *p.* auf, Wien 2083 hat zwar weder Siglen noch Inskription, erscheint aber ohne Unterbrechung als Fortsetzung des Gregorianenkommentars, der hier (fol. 1) mit *Incipit summa magistri petri sāpsonis* rubriziert ist.

Es handelt sich nun bei dieser Schrift überhaupt nicht um einen Glossenapparat, wie man nach Schultes Angaben ([4]) annehmen muss, sondern um eine vom Dekretalentexte losgelöste, selbständig veröffentlichte (oder reportierte) Vorlesung, die oft nur in knapp gefassten Notizen ([5]), zuweilen in längeren Erörterungen besteht. Der Kommentar umfasst (auch hierüber sind Schultes Angaben, *Wiener SB* 68 p. 127 unzuverlässig) in Wien 2083: Nov. 1-6. 8-22. 25-39. 41, d. h. die sogenannte Collectio von 37 Nummern, die aus Coll. I, II und den Nummern 28. 29. 32. 41 besteht. Die Florentiner Hs. ist verstümmelt und bricht in Nov. 26 ab, in Wien 2113 fehlen die Nrn. 19. 31. Als *terminus a quo* ergibt sich 1250 (wegen c. 32 *Vo-*

([4]) Vgl. auch *Wiener SB* 68 p. 87 s.; *Geschichte der Quellen und Literatur des Canonischen Rechts* (= QL) II, Stuttgart 1877 p. 109.

([5]) Proben bei SCHULTE, *Wiener SB* 68 p. 88.

lentes [⁶]), als *terminus ad quem* wohl das Publikationsdatum der Coll. III: 9. September 1253.

II. Gänzlich verschieden von dieser Schrift ist der Apparat von Randglossen mit dem Anfang *Nam omnes expressi in litteris convenientur preter illos iiii.*, der sich in folgenden Hss. findet:

> Genf. Stadtbibl. 59. (SCHULTE, *Iter Gallicum*, in *Wiener SB* 59 [1868] p. 366; 68 p. 126).
> Angers, Stadtbibl. 377 (364. fol. 249 ss.). (SCHULTE, *Wiener SB* 59 p. 445; 68 p. 126).
> Fulda, Landesbibl. D. 10 (fol. 2-7^v). (SCHULTE, *Wiener SB* 68 p. 126).
> Wolfenbüttel, Landesbibl. Helmst. 437 (Kat. 472, fol. 32-37^v). (SCHULTE, loc. cit.).
> Leipzig, Universitätsbibl. 966 (fol. 255-260). (SCHULTE loc. cit.).
> Greifswald, Universitätsbibl. I. 4. (SCHULTE loc. cit.).
> London, British Museum Royal 11. B. V (fol. 14 ss.). (KUTTNER, *Decretalistica* p. 457).
> Cues, Hospital 232 (fol. 238-244^v). (*Decretalistica* p. 457).
> Wien, Nationalbibl. *2181 (fol. 62-69^v). Bisher unbekannt.

Ueberall ist, soweit ich feststellen kann, der Apparat zu der aus Coll. I + II gebildeten Sammlung von 33 Nummern gesetzt (⁷), wobei aber die Nrn. 10 und 31 (Coll. I 7. 18) unglossiert bleiben (⁸). Autor der Glossen, von denen keine sich mit den Erörterungen des Petrus deckt, ist Innozenz IV. selber; das lässt sich unschwer durch einen Vergleich mit den Druckausgaben des grossen Kommentars des Papstes zu den Gregorianen feststellen, in den ja Innozenz bekanntlich Erläuterungen zu seinen eigenen Novellen eingefügt hat (⁹). Ich gebe als Beispiel die Glossen zu den ersten beiden Kapiteln in Wien (und Fulda, soweit Seckels Notizen reichen):

(⁶) Vgl. dazu unten p. 118 s.

(⁷) Das ergibt sich aus SCHULTE, *Wiener SB* 68 p. 126 für die von ihm namhaft gemachten Hss., für Fulda aus den unveröffentlichten, mir zur Verfügung stehenden Notizen Emil Seckels, für Wien aus Autopsie. Für London gibt der Katalog von WARNER und GILSON, *Catalogue of Western Mss. in the old Royal and King's collections*, London 1921 I p. 346 nur 31 Nummern an. (?).

(⁸) So wenigstens Fulda und Wien. In Genf fehlt (nach SCHULTE, *Wiener SB* 59 p. 366) Nov. 15 statt Nov. 10. (?).

(⁹) Vgl. *Decretalistica* p. 462.

Cum in multis

v. generalem: *Nam omnes — illos iiii.* = ed. Venet. 1578 fol. 14 ᵇ
   ad h. c. gl. 2.
v. vel iiii: *Credimus tamen — ff. de liberali causa.* = ed. Venet. gl. 3.
v. citatorio: *Cuilibet illorum — illos iiii.* = ed. Venet. gl. 4.

Presenti

v. providendum: *Per hoc verbum — hac constitutione.* = ed. Venet.
   ad h. c. gl. 1.
v. dignitate: *De dignitate no. — de multa.* = ed. Venet. gl. 2 (fol. 14ᵛᵃ).
v. honorabilibus: *Sufficit quod — dominici* = ed. Venet. gl. 3.
v. civitatibus: *Sufficit enim — insignes.* = ed. Venet. gl. 4.
v. copia: *Tam pro advocatis — continuis.* = ed. Venet. gl. 5.
v. impune: *Et si contra talem — parcere.* = ed. Venet. gl. 8, erster Teil.

Im gedruckten Kommentar geht im c. *Cum in multis* eine Glosse *Idem videtur — inquirit* voran; im c. *Presenti* sind nach gl. 5 zwei kurze Worterklärungen eingeschoben und folgt in der letzten Glosse noch ein längeres Stück *Nobis videtur — copia peritorum*. Man sieht also, dass der gedruckte Kommentar reicher ist als der Apparat zu Coll. I + II, wie er ja auch eine grössere Anzahl von Novellen umfasst. Aber an der Identität des Autors ist kein Zweifel. Schulte kam überhaupt zu seiner irrigen Identifizierung mit Petrus de Sampson ([10]) lediglich durch die entfernte Aehnlichkeit des Initiums *Nam omnes expressi* mit dem Initium der Petrus-hss. (Inn.: *... omnes expressi... convenientur preter illos iiii.*; Petr.: *... preter illos iiii. conveniri possunt omnes expressi*), eine Aehnlichkeit, die indessen im Inhalt der kommentierten Konstitution liegt; und daraufhin erklärte er er die in Angers vorkommende Sigle *s.* als Abkürzung für Sampson ([11]). Aber wenn es sich hier überhaupt um eine Sigle handelt, kann sie nach Glossatorenbrauch nur einen Vornamen, und also Sinibaldus meinen.

Sollte es noch weiterer Bezeugungen für die Autorschaft Innozenz' IV. bedürfen, so kann man etwa auf Bernhard von Montmirat (Abbas Antiquus) verweisen, der in seiner Lectura zu den Novel-

---

([10]) *Wiener SB* 59 pp. 366, 445, anlässlich der Beschreibungen der Hss. Genf und Angers.
([11]) *loc cit.* p. 445.

len ([12]), in der er sonst nie seinen Lehrer Petrus de Sampson zu zitieren versäumt, zum c. *Cum in multis,* v. *generalem* ausdrücklich schreibt: *Nam omnes expressi in litteris convenientur preter eos iiij. inoc.* (Cod. Vatic. * lat. 2542, fol. 84ra). — Ein anderes Beispiel liefert die Lectura des Hostiensis ([13]) zum c. *Presenti,* v. *honorabilibus* (ed. Venet. 1581, fol. 3ra):

> *Hoc ideo dicit, quia non sufficit, quod sint collegiatae tenues, sicut sunt multae in Sicilia et Tuscia... Quid enim, si magni viri magnas causas agerent coram illitteratis clericis et pannosis? Vere risui parerent, secundum d(ominum) n(ostrum). ... r. sufficit quod sit cathedralis secundum d. n. ...*

womit fast wörtlich auf die Glosse *Sufficit quod ecclesie* zur selben Stelle in den Hss. Wien und Fulda Bezug genommen wird (= Innoc., ed. Venet. fol. 14va).

Für die Entstehungsgeschichte des grossen Kommentars des Papstes ist die Identifizierung seiner Glosse zu Coll. I + II von grosser Bedeutung. Wir wissen ja ohnedies, dass Innozenz IV. an seinem Gregorianenapparat viel herumredigiert und ihn auch nach der Herausgabe noch durch Zusätze erweitert hat, wie Diplovatatius im Vorwort zur Ed. Veneta (fol. † 2rb) schreibt:

> *Secundo adde, quod postea idem Innocentius ad dictum apparatum fecit additiones quas in libro hoc omnes appositas esse reperies...*

und wie sich auch aus Hss. ergibt ([14]). Der endgültige Abschluss kann übrigens (was ich, *Decretalistica* p. 463, übersehen habe) erst im letzten Lebensjahr erfolgt sein, da die Dekretale *Venerabilibus* (Sext. V, 11, 7; Po. 15454) vom 11. Juli 1254 kommentiert ist.

Nunmehr können wir aber mit Bestimmtheit sagen, dass die Novellenglossen ursprünglich nicht, wie in der endgültigen Fas-

---

([12]) Vgl. zu diesem Werke *Decretalistica* p. 461 s., zum Autor KUTTNER, *Wer war der Dekretalist Abbas antiquus?* in *Zschr. der Savigny-Stiftung, Kan. Abt.* 26 (1937) p. 471-489 und E. M. MEIJERS, *Responsa Doctorum Tholosanorum,* Haarlem 1938 p. VIII-IX.

([13]) Vgl. oben p. 107.

([14]) Vgl. etwa Vatic. *Urb. lat. 157, Rubrik: *In isto innocentio sunt posite et correcte a capite usque ad finem omnes additiones quas fecit innocentius post compilationem suam innocentii* (!), *et etiam sunt posite omnes additiones quas fecerunt super innoc. hos*(tiensis) *et g*(uido). Ungenau wiedergegeben bei C. STORNAJOLO, *Codices Urbinates latini* I, Romae 1902 p. 163. Die Zusätze sind in der Hs. am Rande stets durch *add. innocentii* gekennzeichnet.

sung, in den Gregorianenkommentar inseriert waren, sondern dass Innozenz zunächst einen Glossenapparat zu 31 Nummern der Coll. I + II veröffentlichte und erst später auch seine anderen Dekretalen und Konstitutionen glossierte, um schliesslich das Ganze in den grossen, vom Gesetzestext losgelöst heraussgegebenen *Apparatus in V libros Decretalium* einzufügen.

Die Erweiterung der ursprünglichen Novellenglosse ging wohl stufenweise vor sich; z.B. haben wir in Fulda D. 10, fol. 70-71^v (also getrennt von Coll. I + II, fol. 2-7^v) die vier Novellen 28. 29. 32. 41, d. h. die neuen Stücke der sonst vorkommenden Sammlung von 37 Nummern, mit einem Apparat von unsignierten Glossen, die nach Seckels Notizen mit *Iste prior erat exequtor alterius partis* beginnen und mit ... *debent integre soluere decimas. Repete que not. infra de v. s. Olim, tibi* schliessen. Mithin gehören sie (was mir, *Decretalistica* p. 458, entgangen war) Innozenz IV.: vgl. ed. Venet. fol. 155ra und fol. 236vb. — In Wien * 2075, fol. 79-93^v findet sich eine Form der Novellenglossen (ohne Dekretalentext), die dem Umfang der in den Gregorianenkommentar inserierten Stücke schon fast gleichkommt. — Die von Anfang an unterlassene Glossierung der Nov. 10 und 31 hat dagegen Innozenz nie nachgeholt; diese beiden Stücke fehlen auch im grossen Kommentar, während zwei Extravaganten (*Ut super appellatione* Sext. II, 15, 4 und *Venerabilibus* Sext. V, 11, 7) aufgenommen sind.

Man könnte versucht sein, diese überlieferungsgeschichtlich bezeugte Entwicklung mit einer Stelle bei Diplovatatius ([15]) in Zusammenhang zu bringen:

> *Et adde quod mens Innocentii fuit per dictum apparatum decretales glossis suis exornare. Sed praesentato apparatu per Bernardum Compostellanum suum capellanum, mutavit opinionem suam et voluit, quod glossae Bernardi insererentur in decretalibus, et de suo apparatu fecit volumen unum...*

und sie dahin zu interpretieren, dass Diplovatatius hier mit *decretales* die innozentianischen Novellen meine, deren Glossierung durch den Spanier Bernardus ([16]) den Papst von seinem ursprünglichen Plane abgebracht und zur Vereinigung seiner Novellenglossen mit dem Gregorianenapparat veranlasst habe. Allein da der Literar-

---

([15]) *Ed. Veneta*, fol. † 2vb.
([16]) Vgl. dazu *Decretalistica* p. 455 s. und oben p. 73 n. 7.

historiker von Pesaro notorisch auch sonst Bernhard von Compostella mit Bernhard von Parma, dem Glossator des Liber Extra durcheinandergebracht hat (¹⁷), darf man wohl überhaupt hinter seiner Mitteilung keine irgendwie glaubwürdige und historischer Auslegung zugängliche Nachricht vermuten (¹⁸).

EXKURS II (zu p. 76)

Zur Datierung einiger Novellen Innozenz' IV. in der Coll. III.

Die Daten von Nov. 7 und Nov. 23 lassen sich aus dem Register ablesen (1245 iul. 24 und iul. 17: BERGER, *Registres* n. 1389 und 1367). Es lassen sich ferner für die im Register fehlenden Stücke ermitteln:

24. *Abbate sane.* Die Dekretale ist *Preceptori hospitalis s. Joannis Hierosolymitani in Hispania et commendatori ac fratribus domus de Curvaria hospitalis eiusdem* adressiert und entscheidet einen Rechtsstreit zwischen den Johanniterrittern von Cervera und der Zisterzienserabtei Benifazá im Königreiche Aragon. Wir kennen nun aus diesem Prozess um die Ortschaft Rosel zwei Vorentscheidungen Innozenz' IV. vom 21. Mai 1250 und vom 18. Januar 1252, die J. DELAVILLE LE ROULX, *Cartulaire Général de l'Ordre des Hospitaliers de S. Jean de Jérusalem* II, Paris 1897, n. 2522 und n. 2583 mitteilt. In der zweiten dieser Zwischenentscheidungen werden die delegierten Richter angewiesen, die Parteien mit einer Frist von fünf Monaten zu zitieren, damit sie *per se vel per procuratores ydoneos conpereant coram vobis, facturi ac recepturi quod ordo dicta-*

(¹⁷) Vgl. den Abdruck der *Vita* des *Bernardus Compostellanus, patria Parmensis* (!) bei M. SARTI und M. FATTORINI, *De claris Archigymnasii Bononiensis professoribus* II, Bononiae 1772, Appendix p. 256 (In der 2. Ausgabe, Bononiae 1888/1896, sind die Viten aus Diplovatatius gestrichen).

(¹⁸) Ablehnend auch SCHULTE QL II p. 93, der übrigens zu Unrecht annimmt, die Mitteilung des Diplovatatius stamme aus Baldus. — Voreilige Folgerungen aus ihr ziehen L. WAHRMUND, *Archiv für katholisches Kirchenrecht* 79 (1899) p. 9¹⁴, H. KANTOROWICZ, *Archiv für Urkundenforschung* 13 (1933-35) p. 23 und G. BARRACLOUGH, *Dictionnaire de droit canonique* II (1937) col. 936 für die Datierung des Gregorianenapparates Bernhards von Parma.

verit rationis. So darf man vermuten, dass der Termin anberaumt wurde, um das inzwischen an der Kurie fertigzustellende Endurteil *Abbate sane* den Parteien am 18. Juni 1252 zu verkünden, und die Dekretale mithin auf 1252 ian. 18 - iun. 18 datieren. DELAVILLE LE ROULX n. 2610 nimmt allerdings den Termin vom 18. Juni 1252 und den 8. (!) September 1253, das Datum der Coll. III, als Grenzen an.

Zur Vorgeschichte des Prozesses sind zu vergleichen (freundlicher Hinweis von Herrn Prof. Vincke):

1157: Schenkung von Cervera an O. Hosp., falls das Gebiet den Mauren abgenommen werde, durch den Grafen von Barcelona (JOAQUÍM MIRET Y SANS, *Les Cases de Templers y Hospitalers en Catalunya*, Barcelona 1910 p. 93).

1171: Erneuerung der Schenkung durch König Alfons II von Aragon (*ibid.* p. 126).

1208: Schenkung des Gebiets von Benifazá mit Valumgraner, Fredes, Rosel *y otros adyacentes* an Don Guillermo de Cervera durch König Pedro II (J. L. VILLANUEVA, *Viage literario á las Iglesias de España*, IV, Madrid 1806 p. 153).

? Don Guillermo wird Mönch in Poblet und schenkt *à aquella casa estos mismos lugares* (*ibid*).

1229 iun. 14: König Jaime I bestätigt diese Schenkung (*ibid.*).

1233 aug. 13: Vertrag zwischen der Kirche von Tortosa und dem Kloster Poblet über den Bau eines Tochterklosters in Benifazá (*ibid.* p. 154).

1233 nov.: Bestätigung durch Jaime I und Anordnung des Klosterbaus (*ibid.*).

1246 oct. 14: König Jaime I schwört, zur Busse für die Misshandlung des Bischofs von Gerona die Kosten für Beendigung des Baus zu tragen (*ibid.* p. 159, Urkunde n. xxi p. 331; vgl. pp. 155 ss., 324 ss.).

28. *Quia cunctis*. Bernhard von Montmirat (Abbas Antiquus) gibt in seiner Lectura zu den Novellen den (in den Sammlungen beschnittenen) Tatbestand der Dekretale wieder, *sicut iacet in registro* ([1]). Mit eignen Worten berichtet ferner Hostiensis in seiner Lectura (ed. Venet. fol. 22vb) über den Streitfall. Der Prozess spielte

---

([1]) Codd. Vatic.* lat. 2542, fol. 86vb-87ra; *Borgh. 231, fol. 143^r. Vgl. *Decretalistica* p. 462.

zwischen einem gewissen Droco von Bourbon und dem Neffen des Papstes, Andreas; er ging um eine Pfründe in der Kirche von Chartres, die sogenannte *praepositura Normanniae*. Zugunsten des Droco lag ein Provisionsmandat vor, das während einer Sedisvakanz der Kirche von Chartres ausgeführt worden war; die weiteren Ereignisse spielten sich unter dem Pontifikat des neuen Bischofs ab, der zuvor Subdekan des Kapitels gewesen war. Daraus ergibt sich der *terminus a quo*: nach dem Tod Bischof Heinrichs von Chartres (1246 dec. 4: vgl. C. EUBEL, *Hierarchia catholica medii aevi* I ₂Monasterii 1913 p. 167); nach dem Provisionsmandat für Droco (1246 dec. 18: BERGER n. 2329-2330) und unter Bischof Matthäus de Champs (sed. 1247 apr.: EUBEL I p. 167). *Terminus ad quem* ist die erste Erwähnung des Nepoten Andreas als *praepositus Normanniae*, die man für das Jahr 1250 bei L. et R. MERLET, *Dignitaires de l'église Notre-Dame de Chartres*, Paris 1900 p. 250 findet. Innerhalb der Grenzen 1247-1250 spricht eine gewisse Wahrscheinlichkeit dafür, dass das Schreiben zu den verlorenen Stücken des sechsten oder in das gänzlich verlorene siebente Jahr der Registers (1248 iul.-sept.; 1249 iun. 28-1250 iun. 27 [²]) gehörte, da ja Bernhard von Montmirat einen Registertext kannte.

32. *Volentes*. Wir wissen aus der Lectura des Hostiensis (ed. Venet. fol. 30ra), dass die Abschnitte seiner Summa über Privilegien und Exemptionen bereits geschrieben waren, als die Konstitution *Volentes* erschien:

> ... *secundum hoc intellige quod notatur in summa eod. § fin. sub § 'Sed et dici potest'. Nec mireris de prolixitate posita ibi, quia totum illud notavimus antequam esset istud ius promulgatum, unde et in fine diximus: ' et comprobantur haec in authentica domini nostri extra eod. Volentes'. Et cum iura nova opiniones, quas sequimur, pro magna parte comprobent, et summa completa esset antequam iura nova venirent, in multis aliis locis summae idem poteris reperire.*

Die Summa ist in den Jahren 1250-1253 entstanden (³). Genauere Umgrenzung des Datums der Konstitution ermöglicht aber die Tat-

---

(²) Vgl. BERGER, *Registres* I p. viii s.
(³) *Decretalistica* p. 461¹.

sache, dass Innozenz IV. in einem Schreiben vom 4. März 1251, *Cum nuper duxerimus statuendum,* an das Generalkapitel von Citeaux (BERGER n. 5144) seine Konstitution über die Grenzen der Exemptionsprivilegien als *nuper* erlassen bezeichnet. Ein fast gleichlautendes Schreiben für die Johanniterritter erging am 18. März 1251 an den Kantor von Sens (DELAVILLE LE ROULX II n. 2556), sowie an den Grossmeister des Ordens (BERGER n. 5233). Der Brief an die Zisterzienser ist bei Po. 13967 irrig auf 1250 mai. 4 datiert (vgl. aber Po. 14222 a). — Da nun die genannten Schreiben auf besorgte Anfragen der Orden über die Tragweite der neuen Konstitution antworten, und da andererseits die Exemptionsprivilegien der Zisterzienser erst kürzlich, nämlich am 28. Januar 1250, durch eine Enzyklika (Po. 13912) uneingeschränkt in Erinnerung gebracht worden waren, darf man annehmen, dass die Anfrage von Citeaux nur durch ein nach dieser Enzyklika liegendes Ereignis veranlasst sein konnte; mithin ergibt sich für die Konstitution der Spielraum Ende Januar 1250 bis Februar 1251.

40. *Dilecto.* Die Dekretale ist bei Mansi (*Ampliss.* XXIII col. 673) *Innocentius IV fratri Johanni Lemovicensi* (scr. *Lemonic.*) *de ordine fratrum minorum, poenitentiario* (nostro) inskribiert. Der Tatbestand ist in den Sammlungen gänzlich fortgelassen, sodass zur Bestimmung des Datums ausser dem nichtssagenden Anfang *Dilecto filio decano Aurelianensi* (nicht etwa Adresse!) nur die selten überlieferte, aber auch in des Hostiensis Lectura (ed. Venet. fol. 36va) bezeugte Inskription an den Poenitentiar Johann von Limoges ([4]) in Betracht kommt. Wir wissen von diesem Franziskaner nur, dass er das Amt des Poenitentiars (wie es deren damals schon unter dem Kardinalpoenitentiar gab [5]) am 8. Juli 1247 noch nicht bekleidete (vgl. die Adresse von BERGER n. 3059), während er am 21. Januar 1251 mit dem Titel *poenitentiarius noster* angeredet wird (BERGER n. 4999). Die Dekretale kann, muss aber nicht in die Zwischenzeit fallen.

([4]) Nicht identisch mit *Jean de Limoges ou de Launha* in *Histoire Littéraire de la France* XVIII, Paris 1835 p. 393-395.
([5]) Vgl. E. GÖLLER, *Die päpstliche Pönitentiarie* I (*Bibl. des Kgl. Preussischen Historischen Instituts* III), Rom 1907 p. 129 ss.

XI

EXKURS III (zu p. 81)

Der rote Hut der Kardinäle.

Als Zeugnis für die allgemein angenommene Auffassung ([1]), Innozenz IV. habe den Kardinälen auf dem Konzil von Lyon den roten Hut zur Insignie bestimmt, kommt einzig Nicolaus de Carbio (Niccolò da Calvi), der Biograph des Papstes ([2]) in Betracht:

> ...Interim dictus pontifex, post concilium anno secundo, Cluniacum ivit cum rege Francie et ipsius fratribus locuturus; ubi domini cardinales primo capellos rubeos receperunt. In ipso concilio fuerat ordinatum ([3]).

Das als Bestätigung meist zitierte, um nahezu ein Jahrhundert jüngere Chronicon des venezianischen Dogen Andrea Dandolo (1343-1354):

> ...xvi. kalendas Augusti Federicum tamquam hostem ecclesiae damnat, ipsumque tam imperio quam Siciliae regno privat, et omnes vassallos eius absolvit a iuramento praestito, et constituit, ut cardinales, dum equitant, capellum rubeum portent, ut ab aliis discernantur, in signum quod prae ceteris, cum opor-

---

([1]) Vgl. von älteren: ALPHONSUS CIACONIUS (Alonso Chacon), *Vitae et Res gestae Summorum Pontificum et S. R. E. Cardinalium*, ed. 3, besorgt von AUG. OLDOINI, Romae 1677 II col. 101, dazu die ergänzende Note von VICTORELLI (dem Bearbeiter der zweiten Ausgabe von 1630) col. 105. — FRANC. PAGI, *Breviarium Historico-Chronologico-Criticum, illustriora Pontificum Romanorum gesta... complectens*, ₂Lucae 1729 II p. 176 s. — Von neueren: BERGER, *Registres* II p. cx⁴; J. B. SÄGMÜLLER, *Die Thätigkeit und Stellung der Cardinäle bis Papst Bonifaz VIII.*, Freiburg 1896 p. 164; J.-B. MARTIN, *Conciles et Bullaire... de Lyon*, 1905 n. 1068; H. GRAUERT, *Magister Heinrich der Poet...*, in *Abhandlungen der Bayrischen Akademie der Wissenschaften, phil.-hist. Kl.* 27 (1912) p. 107 s. und die üblichen Nachschlagewerke.

([2]) Vgl. über ihn F. PAGNOTTI, *Niccolò da Calvi e la sua Vita d'Innocenzo IV*, in *Archivio della R. Società Romana di Storia Patria* 21 (1898) p. 7-75; über seinen früher fälschlich mit *Nicolaus de Curbio* angegebenen Namen p. 34.

([3]) Ed. PAGNOTTI (*loc. cit.* p. 76-120) p. 97; die erste Ausgabe von E. BALUZE, *Miscellanea* VII, Parisiis 1715 p. 376 (wiederholt in *Baluzii Miscell.*, ed. MANSI, I, Lucae 1761 p. 200 und L. MURATORI, *Rer. Ital. Script.* III, Mediolani 1723 p. 592 η) hatte ein *sicut* vor *In ipso* eingeschoben.

> *tet, pro fide et ecclesia caput et vitam exponant; et octavam nativitatis...* (⁴)

kann als unmittelbares Zeugnis nicht gelten; und solange sich nicht eine ältere gleichartige Quellenaussage als wirkliche Vorlage für Dandolo nachweisen lässt, bleibt es wahrscheinlicher, dass er sich nur auf die Chronik des Guilelmus de Nangiaco (Guillaume de Nangis, † um 1300) stüzt (⁵):

> *Innocentius papa constituit, ut omnes cardinales Romane ecclesie portent in capite capellum rubeum, dum equitant, ut discernantur et cognoscantur ab aliis secum equitantibus, per hoc innuens, quod in persecucione fidei et iusticie Romana ecclesia, que caput est omnium aliarum, pre ceteris caput debet apponere, si necesse fuerit, cruentandum* (⁶).

Aber der französische Chronist bringt diese Notiz nicht zum Konzil, sondern zum Jahre 1252, wie auch der englische Dominikaner Nicolaus Trivet († 1328) erst für dieses Jahr eine Konstitution, *ut cardinales capellis rubeis uterentur,* notiert (⁷). — Ohne Zeitangabe findet sich eine derartige Anordnung Innozenz' IV. bei Jacobus de Voragine O. P. († 1298 als Erzbischof von Genua) im *Chronicon Januense* verzeichnet; er stellt sie zwischen zwei Ereignisse, deren erstes von allgemeiner, deren anderes aber von lokaler Bedeutung und mit besonderen persönlichen Erinnerungen des Chronisten verknüpft war; zwischen die Absetzung des Kaisers und den Aufenthalt des Papstes in Genua (Mai-Juni 1251) auf der Rückkehr nach Italien:

> *... qui postmodum Lugdunum per terram perrexit et ibi supradictum Federicum ab imperio deposuit. Iste Innocentius primus ordinavit, ut cardinales capellos rubros deferrent. Isto eodem anno, quo supradictus papa Innocentius Januam venit, inspirante gratia salvatoris ordinem praedicatorum intravimus, ubi nostra adolescentia...* (⁸).

Auf Jacobus de Voragine stützt sich zu Beginn des 14. Jahrhunderts der Bologneser Chronist Franciscus Pipinus:

(⁴) Ed. MURATORI, *Rer. Ital. Script.* XII, Mediolani 1728 col. 356.
(⁵) Vgl. BERGER, *Registres* II p. cx⁴, GRAUERT p. 108³.
(⁶) Ed. H. BROSIEN, *Mon. Germ. Script.* XXVI, Hannoverae 1882 p. 680.
(⁷) *Fr. Nicholai Triveti... Annales,* ed TH. HOG, Londini 1845 p. 241.
(⁸) Ed. L. MURATORI, *Rer. Ital. Script.* IX, Mediolani 1726 col. 48.

XI

Iste etiam Innocentius IV, ut scribit Jacobus de Varagine archiepiscopus Januensis (qui dicit se illo anno praedicatorum ordinem intrasse, quo idem Innocentius a Gallia Italiam repetens Januam venit) primus, ut cardinales pileos deferant ex rubro scarleto, instituit, hac de causa, ut recitari audivi a domino Petro de Columna cardinali... (⁹)

und knüpft nun daran eine Anekdote, als deren Gewährsmann er Kardinal Pietro Colonna, den bekannten unversöhnlichen Gegner Bonifaz' VIII. ([10]) nennt: Die Gräfin von Flandern habe anlässlich eines Besuches bei der Kurie (also wohl zu Lyon) einmal einen Abt für einen Kardinal, und am anderen Tage einen Kardinal für einen Abt gehalten und entsprechend begrüsst; *et papam adiens hanc specialem gratiam impetravit,* dass die Kardinäle künftig durch einen roten Hut ausgezeichnet sein sollten. Grossen Wert wird man dieser banalen Hofgeschichte nicht beimessen dürfen.

Keine chronologische Angabe bringt endlich die Prosainschrift auf dem Grabmal Innozenz' IV. im Dome zu Neapel: ... *quum purpureo primus pileo cardinales exornasset...* ([11]).

Nach alledem kann zwar kein Zweifel bestehen, dass der rote Hut den Kardinälen von Innozenz IV. zum Zeichen ihrer Würde gegeben wurde; aber diese Auszeichnung als einen Beschluss des Konzils von Lyon darzustellen, reicht das eine Zeugnis bei Nicolaus de Carbio nicht aus. Gegen ihn spricht vor allem das Schweigen der Konzilsberichte, und ganz besonders das Schweigen der sogenannten *Brevis nota* ([12]). Man hat schon öfters darauf hingewiesen, dass dieser kuriale Bericht mit besonderer Sorgfalt bei Fragen des Zeremoniells sich aufhält ([13]). So wäre es unbegreiflich, wenn der in den Kreisen der päpstlichen Kanzlei zu suchende Autor die Sitzordnung der Prälaten, unter Hervorhebung des Vorrangs der Kardinäle (auch der Kardinaldiakone) vor den Bischöfen, aufs genaueste

---

(⁹) Ed. MURATORI loc. cit. col. 666.

([10]) Kreiert 1288 durch Nikolaus IV., abgesetzt 1297 durch Bonifaz VIII., wiedereingesetzt 1306 durch Clemens V., gestorben 1326. Vgl. EUBEL, *Hierarchia cath. med. aevi* I p. 11.

([11]) Bei CIACONIUS-OLDOINUS II col. 104; die Inschrift ist restauriert durch Annibaldo da Capua, Erzbischof von Neapel 1578-1595.

([12]) Ueber sie oben p. 94 ss.

([13]) Vgl. Th. G. VON KARAJAN (oben p. 94[71]) p. 83, M. TANGL, in *Mittheilungen des Instituts für oesterreichische Geschichtsforschung* 12 (1891) p. 246 ss., W. E. LUNT (oben p. 92[64]) p. 75.

beschriebe (¹⁴), aber die Verleihung des roten Hutes überginge. Dies Schweigen muss man gegen Nicolaus de Carbio mit allem Nachdruck anführen.

Angesichts der Tatsache, dass andererseits der Biograph des Papstes auch einer seiner vertrautesten Familiaren war (¹⁵) und sich im allgemeinen als sorgfältig unterrichtet erweist, bin ich geneigt, die fragliche Stelle *In ipso concilio fuerat ordinatum* in der einzigen Pariser Hs. überhaupt für eine Interpolation zu halten. Schon sprachlich erscheint sie als merkwürdig abgehackter Nachtrag, wie wir aus der Ausgabe von Pagnotti jetzt sehen können, weswegen auch Baluze das Bedürfnis gefühlt hatte, sie durch *sicut* mit dem Vorangegangenen besser zu verknüpfen (¹⁶).

Aber was sagt denn Nicolaus eigentlich? Er setzt das Treffen zwischen Innozenz IV. und dem heiligen Ludwig zu Cluny im November 1245 irrig ins zweite statt ins erste Jahr nach dem Konzil (¹⁷), und teilt mit, dass bei dieser Gelegenheit die Kardinäle « zum ersten Male rote Hüte empfingen (*receperunt*). Auf dem Konzil war das angeordnet worden ». Dann hätte also Innozenz über ein Jahr (nach Nicolaus' Meinung!) gewartet, um diese Verfügung auszuführen? Und wenigstens erwartete man, dass die Kardinäle beim Treffen von Cluny den roten Hut zum erstenmale « trugen », nicht aber, dass er ihnen dort überhaupt erst « verliehen » wurde. Lässt man aber den sprachlich verdächtigen, historisch nicht gestützten Nachsatz fort, so gewinnt der Bericht des Biographen sofort an Glaubwürdigkeit (wobei nur der chronologische Irrtum bleibt).

Der rote Hut blieb längere Zeit, wohl noch das ganze 13. Jahrhundert über, das einzige Zeichen des Kardinalsranges; so sagt Magister Heinrich, der Verfasser des *Liber de statu Curiae Romanae* (1261-1264):

Vestibus incedunt communibus, attamen illud,
Quod caput insignit, ut rosa verna rubet (¹⁸);

(¹⁴) Vgl. *Concil. gener. ed. Rom.* IV p. 68, MANSI XXIII col. 610, *Mon. Germ. Const.* II p. 513.
(¹⁵) Vgl. PAGNOTTI, loc. cit. p. 36, und etwa die Urk. IV p. 54 vom. 22. Juni 1250, ...*ac per familiarem experientiam et familiaritatem expertam nobis carum admodum et acceptum...*
(¹⁶) S. oben n. 3.
(¹⁷) BERGER II p. CX⁴.
(¹⁸) Ed. GRAUERT p. 89, v. 617-618. Zur Abfassungszeit vgl. GRAUERT pp. 109 s., 146 ss., 508.

während die eigentlich rote Kleidung, ursprünglich Abzeichen der päpstliche Würde, noch den Legaten a latere vorbehalten war ([19]).

EXKURS IV (zu p. 104)

Der Kardinalat des Gottfried von Trani.

Drei Zeitgenossen des Kanonisten Gottfried von Trani bezeugen uns, er sei zu Ende seines Lebens Kardinal gewesen:

MATTHAEUS PARIS, zum Jahr 1245 ([1]):

Eodem quoque tempore obiit Galfridus de Trane cardinalis, quo non erat aliquis domino papae alius specialior vel utilior, vel scientia et moribus clarior.

BONAGUIDA ARETINUS, *De dispensationibus* ([2]):

... et in hac opinione est dñs. gof. quondam card., vir summe scientie et guill. et alii... (In den Druckausgaben lauten die entscheidenden Worte etwas anders: *... dominus Gof. vir summe scientie qui fuit cardinalis et alii plures...*).

NICOLAUS DE CARBIO, *Vita Innocentii IV,* c. 29 ([3]):

Sunt interim Lugduni mortui quinque venerabiles cardinales, utpote... dominus Goffredus de Trano (so die Hs., Pagnotti «verbessert» mit Baluze: *de Franco*) *Sancti Adriani diaconus cardinalis.*

Diese Stellen sind den Literarhistorikern des kanonischen Rechts seit langem bekannt; schon Diplovatatius wies auf die Aeus-

---

([19]) Vgl. SÄGMÜLLER p. 164 und ausser den dort zitierten Quellen etwa noch: HOSTIENSIS zu X: V, 33, 23 (*De privilegiis* c. *Antiqua*) ad v. *utens insigniis;* ed. Venet. 1581 fol. 87ra. INNOC. IV am 2. Dezember 1248 (BERGER n. 4225).

([1]) Ed LUARD IV p. 415.

([2]) Cod. Vatic.* lat. 2661, fol. 10va; Ausgaben: *Volumen XIIII Tractatuum ex variis Iuris Interpretibus collectorum,* Lugduni 1549 fol. 54va; *Tractatus illustrium... Iurisconsultorum XIIII,* Venetiis 1584 fol. 173v. Ueber den Autor vgl. jetzt G. BARRACLOUGH, *Dictionn. de droit can.* II col. 934-940, der die Schrift *De disp.* auf etwa 1250-55 datiert (col. 939).

([3]) Ed. PAGNOTTI p. 103, MURATORI III p. 592 s.

serung des Bonaguida hin (⁴), und so wird Gottfried allgemein als Kardinal bezeichnet (⁵).

Es gilt aber die Angaben der Lehrbücher noch zu präzisieren und gegen kritische Einwände zu sichern. Goffridus oder Goffredus, s. Adriani diaconus cardinalis, gehört zu den am 28. Mai 1244 promovierten Kardinälen (⁶); er wird bei Nicolaus de Carbio c. 13 unter denen erwähnt, die im Herbst 1244 zu Lande nach Susa (Segusia) reisten, um sich dort mit Innozenz IV. auf dem Wege nach Lyon zu treffen (⁷). In den Unterschriften der päpstlichen Urkunden begegnet er vom 23. Januar bis zum 21. März 1245 (⁸), dürfte also bald danach gestorben sein. Damit deckt sich die Angabe des Matthäus; denn *eodem quoque tempore* verweist auf die unmittelbar vorangehende Zeitangabe über den Tod eines englischen Barons, *septimana passionis Dominicae*. Der Passionssonntag des Jahres 1245 fiel auf den 2. April; danach läge das Todesdatum zwischen dem 3. und 8. April, also mehrere Monate vor der Eröffnung des Konzils (auf dem Sarti und Schulte die Erhebung des Kanonisten zum Kardinal überhaupt erst erfolgt sein lassen wollen).

Kardinal Gottfried wird als verstorben erwähnt in zwei päpstlichen Schreiben, die über die von ihm innegehabten Pfründen neue Verfügung treffen: BERGER n. 1309 (Po. 11686) vom 6. Juni, und BERGER n. 1460 vom 30. August 1245.

Die Identifizierung des Kanonisten, *quo non erat aliquis papae alius specialior vel utilior*, mit dem Kardinaldiakon ist hiernach wohlbegründet, und in diesem Zusammenhang verdient besonders der Brief des Papstes vom 6. Juni 1245 Beachtung, weil wir aus ihm erfahren, dass der Verstorbene zwei Kirchen in Trani zu Benefizium besass, die nunmehr seinem Neffen zugewandt werden sollen.

Nun erhebt sich aber andererseits das Bedenken, dass der Kar-

(⁴) Zitiert bei SARTI₂ (oben p. 116¹⁷) I p. 420³.
(⁵) SARTI₂ I p. 420; SCHULTE QL II p. 88; F. LAURIN, *Introductio in Corpus iuris canonici*, Friburgi 1889 p. 149; A. VAN HOVE, *Commentarium Lovaniense* I 1: *Prolegomena*, Mechliniae-Romae 1928 p. 247. Vgl. auch Jo. MAUBACH, *Die Kardinäle und ihre Politik in der Mitte des XIII. Jahrhunderts*, Bonn 1902 p. 20 s.
(⁶) Vgl. zu dieser Promotion NICOLAUS DE CARBIO c. 12, ed. PAGNOTTI p. 85, MURATORI III p. 592 γ. — MATTHAEUS PARIS ed. LUARD IV p. 354.
(⁷) Ed. PAGNOTTI p. 87, MURATORI III p. 592 γ.
(⁸) POTTHAST, *Regesta* II p. 1285 (mit der aus Nicolaus de Carbio, ed. Baluze-Muratori, entnommenen Benennung *de Franco*); BERGER n. 917, 979, 1004, 1105.

dinaldiakon von S. Adriano von manchen Schriftstellern als *Goffredus* (*Gotifredus*) *Castilionaeus* bezeichnet wird; zum erstenmale, soviel ich sehe, 1598 in der Biographie Innozenz' IV. von Paolo Pansa: *Goffredo Castiglione, nipote di Celestino...* (⁹), und mit eingehenderen Angaben von Alonso Chacon (Ciaconius) in seinen Papstviten, unter den Kardinälen Innozenz' IV (¹⁰):

> *Gotifredus Castilonaeus Mediolanensis diac. card. s. Adriani, ex subdiacono et capellano papae Honorii iij. A quo in Sardiniam legatus missus... Bullae Innocentii iv. Virziliacen. an. 1245* (¹¹). *Obiit paulo post creationem suam Lugduni, ibique sepultus. Hon. iij. an. 9* (¹²).

Der Kardinal von S. Adriano hätte demnach denselben Vor- und Zunamen gehabt wie Papst Coelestin IV. (1241 oct. 25 - nov. 10, zuvor Kardinal von S. Sabina), und so lässt Pansa ihn dessen Neffen, Chacon wenigstens seinen Landsmann sein. Aug. Oldoini machte dagegen in der von ihm veranstalteten 3. Ausgabe der Vitae des Ciaconius (1677) ohne ersichtlichen Grund aus dem Kardinal einen Verwandten des Stadtrömers Coelestin III. (Hyacinth Bobo-Orsini), liess ihn aber weiter aus Mailand oder Genua stammen (¹³). Als Mailänder erscheint Kardinal Goffredo Castiglione auch bei Phil. Argellati, *Bibliotheca Scriptorum Mediolanensium* (1745) I 2 col. 360 s.

Wie dem aber auch sei, man wird nicht einfach mit Eubel (¹⁴) Gottfried von Trani und Goffridus Castilionaeus für ein und dieselbe Person erklären können, sondern zunächst prüfen müssen, auf welcher quellenmässigen Bezeugung eigentlich die behauptete Existenz eines Kardinals Goffredo Castiglione beruht, und was sich etwa über seine Laufbahn und Person ermitteln lässt.

In den Urkunden Innozenz' IV. unterschreibt der Kardinal Gottfried stets nur *Ego Goffridus* (*Goffredus*) *s. Adriani diac. card.*, und auch der Papst selber nennt ihn nicht anders. Es gibt

---

(⁹) PAOLO PANSA, *Vita del gran Pontefice Innocenzo Quarto, ... da Tommaso Costo corretta...,* ₁Napoli 1598 (₂Napoli 1601) p. 97.

(¹⁰) ALPH. CIACONIUS, *Vitae et gesta Summorum Pontificum... necnon S. R. E. Cardinalium,* Romae 1601 p. 569; wiederholt in der zweiten, von VICTORELLI und UGHELLI besorgten Ausg., Romae 1630 col. 697.

(¹¹) BERGER n. 917.

(¹²) Vgl. zu *Hon. iij. an. 9* unten p. 128.

(¹³) CIACONIUS-OLDOINUS, *Vitae...* 1677 II col. 123.

(¹⁴) *Hierarchia* I p. 7; auch MAUBACH loc. cit.

nur ein einziges Dokument, welches seinen Namen mit Castiglione angibt, und auf dieses dürften alle von Pansa, Chacon usw. aufgestellten Behauptungen zurückgehen. Es handelt sich um eine Inschrift in S. Adriano, die, heute nicht mehr erhalten, im 17. Jahrhundert von Francesco Gualdi aufgezeichnet wurde, der sie *affissa al muro a piedi la chiesa mano dritta, con lettere fatte al l'antica e targa con capello cardinalizio, arme leone rampante coronato ondato che tiene un libro nelle branche* fand. Aus Gualdi ist sie publiziert bei Forcella ([15]):

> *Anno Jesu Christi nati millesimo ducentesimo quarto*
> *quadrageno tempore ss. patris Innocentii papae*
> *Quar. Dñus Gottifredus dictus Castilioneus spectabilis*
> *viri Joannis de Gottifredis ex dominis Frisinonis*
> *et Juliae Petri Leonis filius de regione Parionis*
> *Huius ecclesiae s.ti Adriani diaconus Cardinalis*
> *Honorii tertii olim in Sardineam Le-*
> *gatus. Ad honorem s. Agnetis suae do-*
> *mus advocate aram hanc marmore-*
> *am magnifice construi mandavit*
> *Rogate Deum pro eo*
> *Magister Iulianus refecit hoc opus.*

Die Echtheit dieser Inschrift ist schon von Oldoini, der sie (fehlerhaft) bereits in den Vitae abgedruckt hatte, bestritten worden, aber mit unzutreffenden Argumenten: der Stein sei 1204 datiert und hätte also den Pontifikat Innozenz' III., nicht Innozenz' IV. angeben müssen; ferner könne Goffredo Castiglione nicht Abkömmling der Herren von Frosinone sein und aus dem Stadtbezirk Parione (zwischen Via del Governo Vecchio und Via della Pace) stammen, da er Verwandter Coelestins III. (!) gewesen sei ([16]). — Der erste Einwand beruht auf der falschen Teilung *m. cc. quarto, quadrageno tempore* (= zur Fastenzeit), der zweite auf einer unbewiesenen Voraussetzung, die durch die Verwechslung von Coelestin IV. mit Coelestin III., der ja Stadtrömer war, noch verworrener wird. Oldoinis Kritik geht im *circulus vitiosus*; denn die Echtheit der Familienangaben auf der Inschrift bestreitet er aus Grün-

---

([15]) VINC. FORCELLA, *Iscrizioni delle chiese e d'altri edifici di Roma dal sec. XI fino ai giorni nostri* II, Roma 1873 p. 50 n. 140. — FRANC. GUALDI, in Cod. Vatic. lat. 8253 I, fol. 71.

([16]) CIACONIUS-OLDOINUS, loc. cit.

den, die nur im Namen Castiglione liegen, dieser aber ist in Wahrheit wiederum nur durch den Stein bezeugt.

Ist die Inschrift echt, so war der Kardinal von S. Adriano ein Römer aus dem Geschlecht der Gottifredi von Frosinone, Sohn des Johannes und der Julia Pierleoni; dann ist aber nicht nur jede Behauptung über seine Mailänder Herkunft und Verwandtschaft mit dem gleichnamigen Coelestin IV., sondern auch seine Identifizierung mit Gottfried von Trani hinfällig.

Allein die Inschrift erweist sich, wenn auch Oldoini mit seinen Argumenten Unrecht hatte, doch als unecht oder wenigstens verunechtet. Sie verrät sich nämlich durch die Identifizierung *Huius ecclesiae s. Adriani diaconus Cardinalis, Honorii tertii olim in Sardineam Legatus.* Ueber den Legaten Gottfried, den Honorius III. vormals nach Sardinien geschickt hatte, sind wir nämlich aus den päpstlichen Registern gut unterrichtet: er ist niemals Kardinal gewesen und war nicht Sohn des Johannes de Gottifredis von Frosinone.

> 1218 oct. 24 schreibt Honorius III. *Gottifredo clerico nato nobilis viri Theobaldi praefecti*, nimmt ihn unter seinen Schutz und bestätigt ihm ein Benefizium in Long-Kensington (*Longaichitoñ.*). P. PRESSUTTI *Regesta Honorii papae III*, Romae 1888-95, n. 1650.
>
> 1222 iun. 10 wird *G. capellanus Pontificis* in einem Schreiben des Papstes erwähnt. PRESSUTTI n. 4035.
>
> 1224 dec. 3 schwört Benedicta, Markgräfin von Massa etc. *domino Gottifredo prefecti urbis, domini pape subdiacono et capellano, totius Sardinie et Corsice legato* einen Treueid für die römische Kirche. *Mon. Germ. Ep. pont. s. XIII* (ed. RODENBERG) I, Berolini 1883 p. 187. (Auf dies in das Register Honorius' III. an. IX ep. 344 eingetragene Stück hatte sich schon Ciaconius bezogen, vgl. oben p. 126).
>
> 1225 iul. 11 entscheidet Honorius III. über eine *causa coram G. capellano Portificio agitata*. PRESSUTTI n. 5551.
>
> 1225 iul. 29: ebenso über eine Sache *coram G. capellano Pontificio qui auditor in hac causa deputatus fuit*. PRESSUTTI n. 5577.
>
> 1226 iun. 12 schreibt Honorius III. an Benedicta, darin wird *G. subdiaconus et capellanus Pontificius, Apostolice sedis legatus* genannt. PRESSUTTI n. 5992.

Gottfried, Sohn des Stadtpräfekten Theobald, wurde also 1218 vom Papst in seinen besonderen Schutz genommen und bald zu seinem Kaplan und Subdiakon gemacht; spätestens 1225 ist er *Auditor litterarum contradictarum*, nachdem er schon 1224 zum Legaten für Sardinien und Korsika ernannt worden war ([17]). Es ist nun interessant, dass in der feierlichen Urkunde der Markgräfin Benedicta das Amt seines Vaters wie ein Familienname, *Gottifredus Prefecti Urbis* gebraucht wird; und in der Tat ist in den Urkunden Gregors IX. diese Bezeichnung zum Namen *de Prefectis* oder *Prefecti* geworden ([18]):

> 1233 mai. 15: *Cum dilectus filius G. de Prefectis subdiaconus et capellanus noster...* L. AUVRAY, *Les Registres de Grégoire IX*, Paris 1890 ss., n. 1305.
>
> 1236 mai. 7 wird *G. de Prefectis subdiaconus et capellanus noster* erwähnt. AUVRAY n. 3153.
>
> 1236 iul. 21 teilt Gregor IX. dem Bischof und Kapitel von Tripolis mit, dass er *Gotifredo Prefecti subdiacono et capellano nostro* die Kantorei in der Kirche von Tripolis verliehen hat. AUVRAY n. 3270.
>
> 1238 apr. 1 schreibt Gregor IX. an den Rektor des Herzogtums Spoleto wegen Bestrafung der Bürger von Todi, die *dilectum filium G. de Prefectis subdiaconum et capellanum nostrum in castro Luniani* belagert hatten; ebenso an Gottfried selbst. AUVRAY n. 4224-26.

Steht hiernach bereits fest, dass der *Gottifredus dictus Castilioneus... viri Joannis... filius* in der Inschrift von S. Adriano zu Unrecht für den ehemaligen Legaten nach Sardinien ausgegeben wird, so kann man noch weitergehend feststellen, dass der ehemalige Legat, nämlich Gottifredus de Prefectis, Innozenz IV. auf seiner Flucht nach Lyon begleitete ([19]), im Jahre 1244 vom Kathedralkapitel von Bethlehem zum Bischof gewählt und am 24. Januar 1245 von Innozenz IV. bestätigt wurde ([20]). Die Konsekration des Elek-

---

([17]) Richtig FEL. CONTELORI, *De Praefecto Vrbis Liber*, Romae 1631 p. 82.

([18]) Die folgenden Daten ermittelte H. ZIMMERMANN, *Die päpstliche Legation in der ersten Hälfte des 13. Jahrhunderts* (Veröffentl. der Görres-Gesellschaft, Sektion f. Rechts- und Staatswiss. XVII), Paderborn 1913 p. 164^5, p. 308 num. 48.

([19]) NIC. DE CARBIO c. 13, ed. PAGNOTTI p. 87, MURATORI III p. 592 γ.

([20]) BERGER n. 956-958. Ueber Gottfried als Elekten vgl. *Gallia Christiana* XII, Parisiis 1770 col. 689; LOUIS CHEVALIER LAGENISSIÈRE, *Histoire de l'évêché de Bethléem*, Paris 1872 p. 78 ss.; Comte RIANT, *L'église de Bethléem et Varazze*

ten — der ja nur die Subdiakonatsweihe hatte — fand zu Lebzeiten Innozenz' IV. nicht mehr statt; in allen Schreiben des Papstes bis zum 27. Februar 1254 wird er als *Bethlemitanus electus* bezeichnet ([21]), und erst am 10. September 1255 schreibt Alexander IV. *G. Bethlemitano electo*, sich in den nächsten Quatembertagen zum Priester weihen zu lassen, und gestattet ihm *de gratia speciali*, den Empfang der Bischofsweihe bis zum Advent hinauszuschieben ([22]). Eine Legation des *Godefridus filius praefecti Romae, electus Beethlimitanus* nach Schottland erwähnt Matthäus Paris für das Jahr 1247 und knüpft daran eine beissende Bemerkung über die Geldgier der Kurialprälaten ([23]).

Die Unzuverlässigkeit der Inschrift von S. Adriano ist damit genugsam erwiesen; und es besteht kein Anlass, ihre Gleichsetzung von *Gottifredus dictus Castilioneus* mit dem Kardinaldiakon ernster zu nehmen als die mit dem Legaten Honorius' III, der niemals

---

en Ligurie, in *Atti della Società Ligure di Storia Patria* 17 (1885 p. 543-705) p. 573 ss.; R. RÖHRICHT, *Syria Sacra*, in *Zeitschrift des deutschen Palästina-Vereins* 10 (1887) p. 25.

([21]) Vgl. für *1245*: BERGER n. 837, 1066, 1079 (betreffend die zuvor innegehabte Pfründe in Tripolis; vgl. oben Gregor IX., AUVRAY n. 3270), 1531-1533, 1618. Für *1246*: BERGER n. 2025, 2039, 2052 (betreffend den Neffen Deodatus de Prefectis), 2057. Für *1248*: BERGER n. 3742 (betreffend Gottfrieds Pfründe in *Longkeincentonia*; vgl. oben Honorius III., PRESSUTI n. 1650), 3851, 4043. Für *1250*: Berger n. 5390. Für *1252*: Po. 14472. Für *1254*: BERGER n. 7344. — STREHLKE, *Tabulae ord. Theuton.*, Berolini 1869, worin sich p. 81, 82 noch zwei Bezeugungen für 1253 finden sollen (RIANT p. 576[1]), ist mir nicht erreichbar.

([22]) C. BOUREL DE LA RONCIÈRE, *Les Registres d'Alexandre IV*, Paris 1895 ss., n. 756. Von EUBEL I p. 135[6] (auch noch II p. xvi) unbegreiflicherweise als Schreiben an Gottfrieds Nachfolger Thomas ausgegeben. — RIANT p. 575[7] will bereits von etwa 1253 an einen anderen *G. electus* zwischen Gottfried und Thomas einschieben; denn der Elekt, der 1255 noch nicht die Priesterweihe hatte, könne unmöglich identisch mit Gottfried sein, welcher von Innozenz IV. und Nicolaus de Carbio als *capellanus et poenitentiarius papae* bezeichnet werde. Indessen ist dies nicht der Fall: Nicolaus nennt ihn lediglich Kaplan des Papstes (wozu er nicht Priester sein musste), und die von Riant für Innozenz IV. angeführten Zeugnisse, BERGER n. 1049 und Po. 13220 betreffen andere Personen: BERGER n. 1049 vom 11. Februar 1245 einen *capellanus G. de Romania*, den RIANT p. 575[1] mit Gottfried de Praefectis identifiziert hatte, obwohl dieser doch bereits am 24. Januar als Electus bestätigt war; Po. 13220 vom 17. Februar 1249 einen nach Polen entsandten *frater Goffredus poenitentiarius et capellanus apostolicus;* auch hier ist Riants Gleichsetzung (p. 573[5]) unmöglich, und jeder Grund für die Verdoppelung des *G. electus* entfällt.

([23]) Ed. LUARD IV p. 602.

Kardinal wurde. Wie der Stein zustande kam, ist heute, aus der Abschrift, schwer zu sagen; er dokumentierte wohl ursprünglich nur die Altarstiftung eines Privaten ([24]). Jedenfalls sollte der Name Goffredo Castiglione aus den Kardinalslisten für S. Adriano endgültig verschwinden und dem gutbezeugten Namen des Kanonisten aus Trani Platz machen.

([24]) Restauration des Steines im 15. Jahrhundert nimmt auch FORCFLLA II p. 50 aus epigraphischen Gründen an (vgl. vor allem die Schlusszeile: *...refecit*); vielleicht ist die Inschrift bei dieser Gelegenheit verunechtet worden.

XII

CONCILIAR LAW IN THE MAKING
The Lyonese Constitutions (1274) of Gregory X
in a Manuscript at Washington

I.

On the first of November 1274, Pope Gregory X published the legislation enacted in the II General Council of Lyons during the summer of the same year, by sending out the encyclical *Infrascriptas* addressed to all the faithful, and a special bull to the universities, *Cum nuper in concilio Lugdunensi* (1). The latter followed almost verbatim the wording used by Innocent IV in his bull *Cum nuper* (25 August 1245) on an analogous occasion after the close of the first Council of Lyons (2); and in view of the fact that publication by letter to the universities had been established, ever since the days of Innocent III (1209-10) (3) as the standard method of issuing a papal collection of law, the simultaneous dispatch in the form of an encyclical was, strictly speaking, unnecessary. In the canonical manuscripts of academic origin the *constitutiones novissimae*

---

(1) Potthast, *Regesta pontificum Romanorum* (Berlin 1874-5) nos. 20950-1; Denifle-Chatelain, *Chartularium universitatis Parisiensis* I (Paris 1889) 514 f. no. 449; J.-B. Martin, *Conciles et bullaire du diocèse de Lyon* (Lyon 1905) nos. 1900-1. Cf. É. Fournier, *L'accueil fait par la France du XIIIe siècle aux décrétales pontificales*, in *Acta Congressus iuridici internationalis... Romae 12-17 nov. 1934*, III (1936) 256; id., *Questions d'histoire du droit canonique* (Paris 1936) 7. Handbooks of the history of the sources of Canon law usually mention only *Cum nuper*: thus e. g. J. F. von Schulte, *Geschichte der Quellen und Literatur des Canonischen Rechts* (= Q L) II (Stuttgart 1877) 31; A. van Hove, *Prolegomena* (*Commentarium Lovaniense in Codicem iur. can.* I, 1; 2nd ed. Louvain 1945) 363.

(2) Cf. Fournier, *L'accueil* 258-60; Kuttner, *Decretalistica*, in *Zeitschrift der Savigny-Stiftung für Rechtsgeschichte* (= ZRG), *Kanon. Abt.* 26 (1937) 441; id., *Die Konstitutionen des ersten allgemeinen Konzils von Lyon*, in *Studia et documenta historiae et iuris* 6 (1940) 71-110; P. J. Kessler, *Untersuchungen über die Novellengesetzgebung Papst Innocenz' IV.* in *ZRG Kan. Abt.* 31 (1942) 145 f., 213 ff.; van Hove, *Proleg.* 362.

(3) For the date of the *Compilatio III* (probably in autumn, 1209) see Kuttner, in *Miscellanea Giovanni Mercati* 5 (*Studi e Testi* 125; Città del Vaticano 1946) 621.

of Gregory X are usually preceded by the introductory bull *Cum nuper*, with the address variously given as Bologna, Paris, Padua, as the case may be (4). Still, it is the letter *Infrascriptas* which alone we find prefixed to the official entry of the conciliar decrees in the papal register (5), and at least two canonists, Franciscus de Albano of Vercelli and Willielmus Durantis, chose this, and not *Cum nuper*, as the form on which to compose their commentaries (6).

Both official publications, identical but for the preamble, contain thirty-one statutes (*constitutiones*) arranged under fifteen rubrics which are taken from the traditional titles of the decretal law (7). The individual statutes are each inscribed as given by the pope in council (*Gregorius X in generali conc. Lugd.; Idem in eodem*), but both introductory bulls speak of statutes which the pope « has seen fit to promulgate recently in the General Council of Lyons and thereafter » (*nuper in*

---

(4) Cf. for Bologna I. H. Boehmer, *Corpus iuris canonici* (Halle 1747) II, p. (aa)ᵛ after col. 368; Schulte, *Die Dekretalen zwischen den "Decretales Gregorii IX" und "Liber Sextus Bonifacii VIII"*, in Sitzungsberichte der kais. Akademie der Wissenschaften, phil.-hist. Classe (= WSB) 55 (1867) 718 n. 47 and p. 776; QL II, 558 f. For Padua cf. Potthast 20951; Schulte, QL II, 161 n. 3 and p. 558; for Paris, Schulte, WSB 55, 718 n. 48; Denifle-Chatelain, *Chartul.* I no. 449 (with further material on the various forms of inscription).

(5) Potthast 20950; first printed in the Roman edition of the Ecumenical Councils, *Conciliorum generalium Ecclesiae catholicae Tomus Quartus* (Rome 1612) 95-104, and repeated in the great conciliar collections down to Mansi 24, 81-102; new edition in J. Guiraud, *Les registres de Grégoire X* (Paris 1892-1906) no. 576, pp. 241-50.

(6) For Franciscus de Albano see Fournier, *Questions* 14 and 19; as for Durantis, the first lemmata of his commentary are the words *Gregorius, servorum, universis* (ed. Simon Maiolus, *In sacrosanctum Lugdun. concilium sub Gregorio X Guilelmi Durantis... commentarius*, Fano 1569, fol. 1r-v); now, the word *universis* — on which Durantis observes: *nota quod papa se praemittit quando scribit universis* — occurs only in the address of *Infrascriptas*, which reads *Gregorius servus servorum dei universis Christi fidelibus...*, while *Cum nuper* is always addressed *...dilectis filiis universitati magistrorum et scholarium* etc.

(7) De summa trinitate et fide cath.: c. 1 *Fideli ac devota* (Liber Sextus 1.1.1); De elect.: cc. 2 *Ubi periculum*, 3 *Ut circa*, 4 *Avaritiae*, 5 *Quam sit ecclesiis*, 6 *Perpetuae*, 7 *Nulli licere*, 8 *Si quando*, 9 *Quamvis constitutio*, 10 *Si forte*, 11 *Sciant cuncti*, 12 *Generali constitutione*, 13 *Licet canon*, 14 *Nemo deinceps* (Sext. 1.6.3-15); De temporibus ordin.: 15 *Eos qui* (Sext. 1.9.2); De bigamis: 16 *Altercationis* (Sext. 1.12 un.); De officio iud. ord.: 17 *Si canonici*, 18 *Ordinarii locorum* (Sext. 1.16.2-3); De postulando: 19 *Properandum* (Sext. —); De iis quae vi met. ca. fiunt: 20 *Absolutionis* (Sext. 1.20 un.); De praebend. et dign.: 21 *Statutum felicis* (Sext. 3.4.3); De rebus eccl. non alien.: 22 *Hoc consultissimo* (Sext. 3.9.2); De relig. domibus: 23 *Religionum* (Sext. 3.17 un.); De censibus et procur.: 24 *Exigit perversorum* (Sext. 3.20.2); De immun. eccl.: 25 *Decet domum* (Sext. 3.23.2); De usuris: 26 *Usurarum voraginem*, 27 *Quamquam usurarii* (Sext. 5.5.1-2); De iniuriis: 28 *Etsi pignorationes* (Sext. 5.8 un.); De sent. excomm.: 29 *Constitutionem felicis*, 30 *Praesenti*, 31 *Quicumque* (Sext. 5.11.9-11).

generali concilio Lugdunensi et post duximus promulgandas), and already the contemporary canonists noted this apparent incongruity, observing that not all statutes as published had been promulgated in and by the council (8).

The words of the papal announcement, *in generali concilio... et post*, offer a valuable clue to the method employed by Gregory X: they indicate a process of law-making in which the « promulgation » in council represented only a preliminary stage, subject to alterations and enlargements before the final text of what the pope wished to be considered as the legislative work of the council was officially released in the form of a systematic collection. In choosing this method, Gregory followed the example set in 1245 by Innocent IV, and the same pattern was to be repeated at Vienne in 1311-12 by Clement V (9). But Innocent IV had allowed only six weeks to elapse between the last session of his council (17 July 1245) and the official publication (25 August); under Gregory X the intervening period was considerably lengthened (17 July 1274 to 1 November); and in the case of the Clementines the extreme slowness of the final redaction led to the unfortunate result that the publication took place only under the presiding pope's successor, John XXII, on 25 October 1317, over five years after the third session of Vienne (6 May 1312).

While for I Lyons and Vienne modern research has succeeded only with great difficulty in reconstructing the course of conciliar promulgation and later redaction, the story of the

---

(8) Durantis, ad v. *et post: hoc ideo dicit, nam quaedam ex eis fuerunt post celebratum concilium promulgatae...* (ed. Maiolus, fol. 1v). Boatinus of Mantua, ad v. Gregorius... *et post: videtur contrariari omnibus inscriptionibus que habent 'Gregorius X in concilio generali', 'idem in eodem' et sic de ceteris, nam inspectis inscriptionibus omnes decretales inducuntur facte in concilio lugdunensi, inspecta vero hac dictione 'post' videtur quod quedam facte fuerunt in concilio et quedam post...*: cf. Schulte, *Beiträge zur Literatur über die Decretalen Gregors IX.* etc., in WSB 68 (1871) 103. — Boatinus' commentary was not completed before 1277, since Cardinal Simon Paltinari, who died in this year (cf. Eubel, *Hierarchia cath. medii aevi* I [2nd ed. Münster 1913] 8), is mentioned as *dominus Symon bone memorie card. cum transiret Paduam...* (ad c. 15 *Eos qui*). Schulte, WSB 55, 779 and QL II, 160 n. 11 refers the passage to Simon de Brie and argues that it must have been written before 1281, when the latter became Pope Martin IV (d. 1285) and would no longer be styled as *cardinalis*. The reasoning is incomprehensible, since Boatinus speaks of a dead cardinal.

(9) On the preparatory stages of the legislation published after the close of I Lyons (1245) see Kuttner, *Die Konstitutionen* (n. 2 supra) esp. 91-110; for Vienne, see Ewald Müller, *Das Konzil von Vienne 1311-1312 (Vorreformationsgeschichtliche Forschungen*, ed. Finke, 12; Münster 1934) 396-408.

legislation of 1274 has been available in outline ever since a quasi-official, contemporary report on the council, the so-called *Brevis nota eorum quae in secundo concilio Lugdunensi generali gesta sunt*, became known by its inclusion in the Roman edition (1608-12) of the Ecumenical Councils. The text of this invaluable document, as printed by the *editores Romani* and reprinted with slight variations in the later collections, down to Mansi (10), is not based on the best of the extant MSS (11), but quite sufficient for our purpose (12). Originating as it does in the circles of the papal Chancery (13), the *Brevis nota* (BN) affords an authentic report of the conciliar proceedings. It tells how certain groups of decrees were read at the second, third, fifth, and sixth sessions — the fourth being entirely dedicated to the making of the union with the Greeks — and that at the end of the sixth session the pope promised further measures (*remedia opportuna*) on matters of reform, especially of parochial reform, which the pressure of other agenda had not allowed to be formulated *in ipso concilio*. The text accounts without difficulty for all but one of the thirty-one *constitutiones* published in November: cc. 2-12, 15-17, 19-31 were promulgated *in concilio* as follows (the order of BN is preserved):

sess. III (4 [7?] June) (14): cc. 3-9, 19, 15, 24, 29, 30;
sess. V (16 July): cc. 2, 10, 17, 20, 11, 28, 31, 12, 16, 25-27, 22, 21;
sess. VI (17 July): c. 23...

(10) *Ed. Rom.* (n. 5 *supra*) 4, 83-6; followed by Binius[2], the *ed. Regia*, Labbe, Hardouin, Coleti, and Mansi 24, 61-8. Cf. Martin, *Conc. et bull. de Lyon* (n. 1 *supra*) no. 1646, who overlooks however the *editio princeps*.

(11) It is a *recensio mixta* made from the same MSS and with the same methods as employed by the Roman editors for establishing the text of the corresponding *Brevis nota conc. Lugd. I* (for which see Kuttner, *L'édition romaine des conciles généraux et les actes du premier concile de Lyon* [*Miscell. hist. pontif.* III 5; Rome 1940] 21-33); i. e. they based themselves chiefly on the MS *Vat. lat.* 4734 (written c. 1370-78), fol. 81va-84vb, but introduced a number of readings from what I have called class B of the MSS (cf. *op. cit.* 25f.). The best and oldest MS, *Ottob. lat.* 2520, fol. 12-16 (cf. M. Tangl, in *Mittheilungen des Instituts für oesterreichische Geschichtsforschung* 12 [1891] 252f.) was unknown to the Roman editors (Kuttner, *op. cit.* 21f.).

(12) The edition of I. Carini, in *Spicilegio Vaticano I* (Rome 1890) 250-8, shows no improvement over the Roman text, since it only reproduces a late MS derived, by way of at least two intermediary copies, from *Vat. lat.* 4734; cf. *L'édition romaine* 34-8.

(13) Tangl, *op. cit.* 246 f. and 252 f.

(14) The commonly accepted date, 7 June, is that given by BN *ed. Rom.* 4, 84aD (Mansi 24, 64A) from *Vat. lat.* 4734 (= V) fol. 82v: *Eodem anno, mense vero Iunij, die eiusdem septima* (V: *vij°*), *in qua omnia facta sunt sicut in prima...*; the obviously defective sentence has never been challenged. The only sensible reading is found in *Ottob. lat.* 2520 (= O) fol. 13v; *Eodem anno... die eiusdem iiij*[o]

while cc. 13, 14, 18 are easily recognized as the decrees promised in the last session *super ordinatione ecclesiarum parochialium et super aliis* (15) ; they must consequently be the ones referred to as promulgated *post concilium* in the official documents of publication (16). They were expressly so designated by the glossator Willielmus Durantis, who, however, in the same context cited also c. 2 *Ubi periculum*, the famous statute on the conclave, as having been issued only after the close of the sessions (17). The renowned canonist was in a position to speak with authority, since he himself had taken an active share in the drafting of the Lyonese legislation (18): *...et qui vidit testimonium perhibet veritati* (Jo. 19.35), he quotes with questionable taste. It is therefore all the more surprising to find him at variance with the no less well informed BN, which not only positively assigned c. *Ubi periculum* to the fifth session but also went into unusual detail about the stormy antecedents of its promulgation (19). Whatever be the

facta est tercia sessio, in qua omnia rell.; it should therefore be followed also with regard to the date. As for the order of *constitutiones* presented by BN for *sess.* III (*...et postea lectae sunt constitutiones, scil. Vt circa electionem, Auaritiae caecitas rell.*), V and VI (*ed. Rom.* 86aD, 86bB; Mansi 67D, 68B; V fol. 84v; O fol. 15v-16r), there is complete agreement among O, V, and *ed. Rom.* — I owe the collations of the Vatican MSS to the kindness of Msgr. A. Pelzer.

(15) c. 13 *Licet canon* deals with the qualifications and residence required of parish rectors; c. 14 *Nemo deinceps*, with the conditions under which a vacant parish may be temporarily entrusted (*commendare*) to the care of a qualified person; c. 18 *Ordinarii*, with the plurality of benefices. Cf. BN *sess.* VI: *...alioquin dixit se dure acturum cum ipsis super reformatione morum. Super ordinatione uero ecclesiarum parrochialium* (transp. VRom), *ne fraudentur rectorum suorum presentia et quod* (om. VRom) *uiri idonei ponantur in eis, et super alijs dixit se cito, dante domino, apponere remedia opportuna: quod usque modo* (om. VRom) *in ipso concilio fieri non potuit...*

(16) This observation has been often repeated ever since Van Espen's *Commentarius in canones et decreta iuris veteris ac novi et in ius novissimum* (cf. *Opera*, ed. Louvain 1753; 4, 130-1, 137): the word (*et*) *post* is not, as Fournier, *L'accueil* (n. 1 *supra*) 256 f. believes, « un petit mot que personne n'a remarqué. »

(17) Durantis *loc. cit.* (n. 8 *supra*):... *post concilium promulgatae, viz. illa de elect. c. Ubi periculum et c. Licet canon et c. Nemo et illa de off. ord. c. Ordinarii, et qui vidit testimonium perhibet veritati.*

(18) Durantis ad *prooem.* v. *conc. Lugd.*: *in quo interfuimus et aliquas de infrascriptis edi procuravimus* (ed. Maiolus, fol. 1v, where the word *edi* is missing; cf. H. Singer, ZRG Kan. Abt 6 [1916] 22); and expressly for c. 9 *Quamvis*:... *hanc constitutionem promulgari in Lugd. conc. procuravi* (cf. also *Speculum iudiciale* ps. 1, *de legat.* § 4 n. 9) and c. 21 *Statutum*: *...ipse etiam hoc efficaciter procuravi.* Cf. E. Göller, *Zur Geschichte des zweiten Lyoner Konzils und des Liber Sextus*, in *Römische Quartalsschrift für christl. Altertumskunde und Kirchengesch.* 20, ii (1906) 82, 84, 87. An exaggerated account of Durantis' role in the council is given by Schulte, QL II, 145 f.

(19) *Ed. Rom.* 4, 85bD-86aA; Mansi 24, 66-7.

significance of Durantis' statement — and we shall have to return to this point later on (20) — there is no doubt that in some form the statute on the conclave was publicly read at the council.

While thus far the account given by BN tallies with the published *constitutiones*, historians have long since noted that there remain three puzzling discrepancies. No mention seems to be made in the former of the dogmatic canon *Fideli ac devota* (c. 1) on the procession of the Holy Ghost; on the other hand, BN lists two statutes which are not found in the official collection (21):

> *sess.* II (18 May): ...qua allocutione finita lecte a) sunt constituciones, scil. *Zelus fidei*, et licenciati sunt in ista sessione omnes b)...
>
> *sess.* VI (17 July): ...lecte sunt constituciones, scil. *Religionum diuersitas* c) et *Cum sacrosancta*, quibus lectis dominus papa alloquutus est concilium...

As to c. *Fideli*, a post-conciliar origin seems out of the question because of its context: the canon expressly reads, ...*nos...sacro approbante concilio dampnamus et reprobamus*. But a widespread opinion has identified this canon with the decree mentioned by BN for *sess.* II (22). This hypothesis is based on the conjectural reading *latae sunt constitutiones pro zelo fidei* which Bzovius, followed by Labbe and all later collections, substituted for the correct wording of the *editio Romana* (23). The « emendation » had obviously been prompted by the grammatical incongruity of the original, which speaks of *constituciones* in the plural but specifies only one initium, *Zelus fidei*. The substitution of a descriptive phrase, *pro zelo fidei*, certainly made smoother reading and could be understood as vaguely referring to a dogmatic canon.

(20) Cf. *infra* V, at n. 83, where also the various opinions of modern writers are discussed.

(21) *Ed. Rom.* 4, 84aA and 86bB (Mansi 24, 63C and 68B); V fol. 82r and 84v; O fol. 13r and 16r (MSS collated by Msgr. Pelzer) a) latae *VRom* b) omnes in ista sess. *VRom*   c) diversitatem *VRom*.

(22) Cf. e. g. Jos. Biner, *Apparatus eruditionis ad jurisprudentiam, praesertim ecclesiasticam* (Bologna 1754) 150a; Hefele-Knöpfler, *Conciliengeschichte* 6 (Freiburg 1890) 134; for repetition in more recent authors see nn. 27 ff. *infra*.

(23) Abr. Bzovius (Bzowski), *Annalium ecclesiasticorum... post Baronium...* tomus XIII (Cologne 1616) 719; Labbe-Cossart 11, 957A; Hardouin 7, 688C; Mansi 24, 63C. (Binius[2] 3, ii [1618] 740B retained the proper reading of the Roman edition).

Serious objections were, however, raised against this interpretation by Van Espen, who insisted that it would be strange if the council had pronounced a dogmatic definition of such crucial importance for the union with the Eastern Church without awaiting the arrival of the Greek spokesmen (24), i.e. before the fourth session (6 July), in which the latter solemnly recited the Emperor Michael's profession of faith and concluded the short-lived Union of Lyons. But the irrefutable argument of the Gallican scholar went unheeded for centuries. Two difficulties thus seemed to be disposed of with one stroke; as for the last remaining difficulty of BN, the statute *Cum sacrosancta*, scholars were satisfied with the assumption that it was lost (25).

The riddle of the missing texts was definitely solved over fifty years ago by Heinrich Finke in his suppletory and critical notes on the second edition of Hefele's *Conciliengeschichte*. Briefly, he was able to demonstrate that the initium *Cum sacrosancta* refers to the canon *Fideli* and that there exists a conciliar statute *Zelus fidei* of a quite different bearing (26). Unfortunately, Finke's slender volume did not find the wide attention it deserved: it remained unknown to the Abbé Martin, who in 1905 compiled his *Conciles et bullaire du diocèse de Lyon*, and even, more regrettably, to Dom Leclercq when he undertook the French editon of the respective volume of Hefele (1914); to F. Vernet, who in 1926 wrote the article on the Council of Lyons for the *Dictionnaire de théologie catholique*. All these standard reference works continued to repeat the old errors, describing c. *Cum sacrosancta* as being lost and the procession of the Holy Ghost as having been defined *pro zelo fidei* in *sess.* II (27); Vernet even went to some length to « prove »

---

(24) Van Espen, *op. cit.* (n. 16 supra) 116: ...*at eam editam fuisse ante adventum oratorum imperatoris Graecorum, qui demum post absolutam hanc* (i. e. the second) *sessionem advenerunt, non est verisimile*. A statement to the effect that c. *Fideli* was decreed by Greeks and Latins in common, is found — but without any reasons given — in Manuel Kalekas, *Adv. Graecos* (PG 152, 172) and in Bossuet's *Defensio declarationis cleri gallicani* 3.7.35 (*Opera* ed. Paris 1828; 42, 127).
(25) See e. g. Potthast ante n. 20863; Hefele-Knöpfler 6, 145.
(26) H. Finke, *Konzilienstudien zur Geschichte des 13. Jahrhunderts: Ergänzungen und Berichtigungen zu Hefele-Knöpfler « Conciliengeschichte » Band V und VI* (Münster 1891) 10-14. On the relation between BN and the printed statutes cf. *ibid*. 8 ff.; on an earlier, faulty attempt at reconstruction made by Kaltenbrunner, cf. *ibid*. 9 n. 1.
(27) Martin, *op. cit.*, nn. 1773, 1843; Hefele-Leclercq, *Histoire des conciles* 6, i (Paris 1914) 170, 181; F. Vernet, art. Lyon (*IIe concile oecouménique de*) in

that Van Espen's arguments to the contrary were invalid (28), and as late as 1941 M. Jugie asserted again in his *Schisme byzantin* that the Greeks were faced on their arrival with a dogmatic definition already pronounced (29). Some specialists, it is true, have put Finke's findings to profitable use (30), but among modern general works dealing *ex professo* with the canonical legislation of the Middle Ages, I find that only an American publication, H. J. Schroeder's *Disciplinary Decrees of the General Councils* (31), has conformed its report on the II Council of Lyons to the data which ought to have been common knowledge since 1891.

As to the details of the evidence: Finke found in a MS of Munich a summary of the Lyonese constitutions which epitomizes the first canon as follows: *Cum sacrosancta. Spiritus sanctus a patre et filio tamquam ex uno principio et una spiratione procedit* (32). The text of the canon, then, originally began with the words *Cum sacrosancta,* typical of a general arenga (33), and was thus read after the union, in the final

---

Dict. théol. cath. 9 (1926) 1379 ff. (although Finke's book is listed in the bibliography, col. 1391).

(28) *Op. cit.,* 1383 f.

(29) Jugie, *Le schisme byzantin* (Paris 1941) 260. More carefully G. Mercati, *Notizie di Procoro e Demetrio Cidone, Manuele Caleca e Teodoro Meliteniota...* (*Studi e Testi* 56; Città del Vaticano 1931) 140 n. 1: « ...precedette, come sembra, la venuta dei Greci ».

(30) e. g. Göller, *op. cit.* (n. 18 *supra*) 83; O. Holder-Egger in the notes of his edition of the Chronicle of St. Peter's at Erfurt (MGH, *Script. rer. germ.*, in-8⁰, Hannover-Leipzig 1899: cf. n. 124 *infra*); W. E. Lunt, *Papal Taxation in England...,* in *English Historical Review* 30 (1915) 401 f.; id. *Papal Revenues in the Middle Ages* (*Columbia Records of Civilization* 19; New York 1934) I, 40 etc. (see Index s. v. « Tenth »); *Financial Relations of the Papacy with England* (Cambridge, Mass. 1939) 312 ff.; see also C. Mirbt, art. *Gregor X.*, in *Realencyklopädie für prot. Theol. und Kirche* 7 (1899) 123, 125.

(31) (St. Louis-London 1937) 327-30. Unfortunately, Fournier (*L'accueil* 256 f. and *Questions d'hist.* [n. 1 *supra*] 7), is no exception to the rule.

(32) Munich MS *lat.* 213, fol. 128v; Finke, *op. cit.* 10. The text of this *Summula Monacensis* (better: *Notabilia*) had been published as early as 1867 by Schulte, WSB 55, 781, who gave the full rubric, *Constitutiones concilii generalis quod Gregorius papa X. Lugduni celebravit a. d. 1274, in quo Graeci ad unitatem* etc., copied the first few chapters, and noted that the work breaks off in c. 10; he did not recognize the critical value of the initium. Finke, on the other hand, was not aware of Schulte's earlier publication. For other material on the papal legislation of the 13th cent. in *Monac. lat.* 213 see Phillips, *Kirchenrecht* IV (1851) 520 ff.; Schulte *loc. cit.*; Kuttner, ZRG Kan. Abt. 26 (1937) 467; Kessler, *ibid.* 31 (1942) 284 n. 366; 33 (1944) 114-6; also (on the Provincial Council of Mayence 1233) Finke 30 n. 2 and pp. 32-5.

(33) Cf. the many listings of decretals beginning *Cum sacrosancta Romana ecclesia* in the Index of Jaffé's *Regesta*.

(sixth) session as indeed one would expect. In the officially published form, however, the canon immediately begins with the definition, *Fideli ac devota professione fatemur quod Spiritus Sanctus...*: the arenga had been cancelled in the course of final redaction, a procedure of which analogous instances are known from the First Council of Lyons (34).

Even more surprising was Finke's discovery, in a MS of Osnabrück, of a text of the statutes of 1274 opening with a lengthy decree, *Zelus fidei, fervor devotionis et compassionis pietas excitare debent corda fidelium*: the missing *constitutiones* of the second session (35). Also the incongruity of the plural form (*constitutiones*) was explained by the rediscovered text: *Zelus fidei* is actually a bundle of several statutes in one, including, after an exposition of the general purpose of the council, the following provisions (36):

1) the creation of various financial resources for the subsidy of the Holy Land, the foremost of which consists of the novel imposition, for six years, of a special tithe on all clerical incomes in Christendom. This famous crusading tenth, one of the most consequential innovations in the medieval system of papal finances (37), had been agreed upon by the prelates at the pope's bidding before the second session, as we are told by BN (38). Other provisions of the decree deal with the

---

(34) Cf. Kuttner, *Die Konstitutionen* (n. 2 *supra*) 78, 100 f.

(35) Osnabrück, Ratsgymnasium MS C. 1, fol. 124-126; cf. Finke, *op. cit.* 11-14. The contents of the miscellaneous codex are listed *ibid.* 1 n. 1; for its first item, the *Epitome Exactis regibus* (fol. 1-6), see also E. Seckel, *Beiträge zur Geschichte beider Rechte im Mittelalter* I (Tübingen 1898) 509. The fourth piece, *Super novellas domini Innocentii pp. IV* (fol. 67-69) has so far escaped the notice of all students (the present writer included) of the medieval literature on Innocent IV's legislation; neither has the collection of *extravagantes* (fol. 119-124: 38 decretals of Alexander IV, 3 of Urban IV, 6 of Clement IV, according to Finke *loc. cit.*) ever been analyzed.

(36) Edited by Finke, *op. cit.* 113-7; an English translation of sections 1 and 2 in Schroeder, *Disciplinary Decrees* 360-4. Since Finke used only Mansi's text of BN, he did not know that the original actually had cited the initium *Zelus fidei*: he therefore continued to speak of « die Constitutiones pro zelo fidei » (p. 113, also pp. 9 n. 1, 10), and Schroeder likewise considered *pro zelo fidei* as the « general title » of the statutes (p. 329).

(37) Cf. Lunt, as cited n. 30 *supra*. Finke's publication remained however unknown to A. Gottlob, *Die päpstlichen Kreuzzugssteuern des 13. Jahrhunderts* (Heiligenstadt 1892; cf. pp. 94 ff. on the Lyonese tenth) and *Kreuzablass und Almosenablass* (Kirchenrechtliche Abhandlungen 30-31; Stuttgart 1906).

(38) *Ed. Rom.* 4, 84aB (Mansi 24, 63D).

appropriation of certain ecclesiastical fines (39), with special offerings in churches, and with special taxes to be levied by the secular rulers;

2) repressive measures against the Corsairs and their abettors; against trading with the Saracens; proclamation of a six-years' truce; crusading indulgences, etc.; this entire section (beg. *Ceterum quia cursarii*) being a more or less literal re-enactment of Innocent III's c. *Ad liberandam* promulgated in the IV Lateran Council (c. 71) (40) and of Innocent IV's *Afflicti corde,* in the I Council of Lyons (c. 17 of the so-called *Institutiones*) (41);

3) beginning with a new arenga, *Non nobis,* an ordinance concerning the council itself: whereas the major prelates are enjoined not to depart without the pope's permission, the minor prelates who had not been personally and specially invited are given leave to withdraw; at the same time, however, they are to appoint a certain number of proctors, specified in a heretofore unusual manner by nations.

It is an astonishing fact that the text of c. *Zelus fidei* should have remained hidden for over six centuries, especially since the origin at the Council of Lyons of so far-reaching a measure as the crusading tenth was a matter of common knowledge, referred to as a conciliar resolution by contemporary chroniclers (42); by the *Brevis nota* — which in its report on the meeting that preceded the second session expressly adds the words, *sicut in constitutione habetur* (43); by Gregory X himself in his several letters appointing collectors or otherwise giving instructions for the execution of the decree (44); by local authorities, etc. One would expect, above all, that the pope had included the statute in his letters of publication on the first of November among the *constitutiones* (*quas*) *nuper in*

---

(39) i. e. those collected under the decretal X 5.26.2.
(40) Mansi 22, 1058 ff.; esp. 1063D-67.
(41) Berger, *Les registres d'Innocent IV* (Paris 1884-1919) n. 1368 c. 17; also Gregory IX, ep. *Rachel sum videns* (Mansi 23, 69). Cf. Finke, *op. cit.* 12 n. 1.
(42) Cf. e. g. those listed by Martin, *Conc. et bull. de Lyon* n. 1768.
(43) *loc. cit.* n. 38 *supra*.
(44) Cf. e. g. Guiraud, *Registres* nn. 494, 525, 541, 569-71, 578, 636, 652, 944, 966, 1041; for exemptions from the tenth, e. g. nn. 399, 409, 465, 552, 1042-3, 1056, 1059, 1069. Lunt, *Financial relations* 312 ff. discusses many of these letters; a translation of Guiraud n. 571 (with a comparative study of Boniface VIII's *Extrav. comm.* 3.7.un.) is given in Lunt, *Papal Revenues* II, 162-9.

generali concilio... duximus promulgandas. And yet, in deciding not to do so, Gregory X only followed the precedent established in 1245: when Innocent IV dispatched the twenty-two *constitutiones* of I Lyons which were to be universally used in schools and courts, he excluded from this series not only the sentence against Emperor Frederick II but also five pieces attested as conciliar decrees in the papal register (*Institutiones* cc. 13-17), for they represented only administrative and financial measures dictated by the practical and political needs of the times — of great actual importance, to be sure, but not in the nature of permanent laws for the Church universal (45). The same considerations evidently applied in 1274 to the c. *Zelus fidei*, which in many of its provisions resembles, and in one section even repeats, these particular *institutiones* of 1245 which had not become part of the general law.

BN accounts, then, for even more than the full number of the conciliar statutes published on 1 November 1274, in that it covers the thirty-one *constitutiones* and the cluster of ordinances promulgated in the second session but not included in the final redaction. From the characteristic differences between the report of BN and the official text we are entitled to conclude that BN was composed before 1 November: otherwise its author 1) would not have referred to *Zelus fidei* as one of the *constitutiones* in the same fashion as to the published ones, simply by its initium, i.e. he would not have assumed that to the future reader this text would be as generally accessible as any other of the statutes; 2) he would not have cited the canon on the procession of the Holy Ghost by an initium that is different from the one finally chosen; 3) he would probably have tried, in the reports on sessions III, V, VI, to cite the statutes of the respective sessions in the logical order which they finally received, rather than in the apparent disorder which his text presents; 4) he would have made some reference to the carrying out of the pope's plan for further reform decrees (cc. 13, 14, 18). In writing as he did, the author of BN must therefore have had the *constitutiones* before him in the Chancery in a preliminary, not in their final shape.

(45) Kuttner, *Die Konstitutionen* 81.

II.

From the *Lectura* of Franciscus de Albano we know some interesting details about the preparation of the conciliar statutes (46). Any of the prelates assembled at Lyons was entitled to hand in petitions (*capitula*) for remedial legislation on a specific subject in this form: *Supplicat talis prelatus quod super tali errore qui in sua provincia vel dyocesi servatur, provideatur*... These *capitula* were submitted for examination to the Chancery, the Apostolic Chamber, and the College of Advocates of the Curia; and after the proper choice among the opinions rendered by each of the three agencies (*Super tali facto consulit cancellaria quod ita provideatur...; Advocati vero ita consilium...; Camera autem sic consulit...*) the statute was formulated. A number of statutes seems to have been ready for promulgation by the end of May (47). We may further surmise that such general memoranda on reform as submitted by Humbert of Romans, Bishop Bruno of Olmütz, and others (48) underwent the same scrutiny as the *capitula*. Franciscus de Albano does not say to whom the actual drafting of the statutes fell, but we know that Willielmus Durantis, who at the time was one of the *auditores causarum s. palatii*, had a hand in at least some of them (49). Finally, as the analysis of BN shows, the legislation promulgated in the public sessions was subjected to further amendments before its official publication.

Additional evidence pointing to a preliminary stage of the conciliar texts was discovered by Canon É. Fournier, who

---

(46) Fournier, *Questions* (n. 1 *supra*) 21.

(47) Cf. the report of certain prelates who departed from the council about that time, as published from MS *Ottob. lat.* 2115 by O. Redlich, *Eine Wiener Briefsammlung zur Geschichte des deutschen Reiches* (*Mittheilungen aus dem Vaticanischen Archive* ed. Akademie der Wissenschaften, 2; Wien 1894) no. 23: *...ea que statuta sunt non sunt in tempore aliqua publicata, set eis qui remanserunt publicantur...*; this tallies with the report of BN which says that the statutes for *sess.* III (4 June) were read to the prelates sometime after *sess.* II (*ed. Rom.* 4, 84bA; Mansi 24, 64C). Note that the third session had been announced for 29 May but was prorogated (BN *ibid.* 4, 84aA,D; 24, 63B, 64A).

(48) Hefele-Leclercq 6, 164 ff.; J. Auer, *Studien zu den Reformschriften für das zweite Lyoner Konzil* (Freiburg 1910); K. Michel, *Das Opus tripartitum des Humbertus de Romanis* (2nd ed. Graz 1926); for the *Collectio de scandalis ecclesiae*, probably by Gilbert of Tournai, see A. Stroick, *Archivum francisc. histor.* 23 (1930) 3-31, 273-99, 433-66; ed. *ibid.* 24 (1931) 33-62. Cf. Schroeder, *Disciplinary Decrees* (n. 31 *supra*) 327.

(49) See n. 18 *supra*.

in 1934 gave a brief description of an old French translation of the Lyonese statutes found in MS franç. 491, fol. 295v-302, of the Bibliothèque nationale in Paris (50). The translation comprises twenty-six of the twenty-eight statutes actually promulgated in the sessions (c. 1 *Fideli* = *Cum sacrosancta* and c. 21 *Statutum* are missing) (51) but none of the three that were only announced (cc. 13, 14, 18); considerable differences from the published Latin text are mentioned by Fournier for c. 2 *Ubi periculum* and c. 22 *Hoc consultissimo* (52). There is no introductory bull and and no distribution by titles: one would like to know (53) whether the arrangement of the individual statutes corresponds to the order of BN.

More light can now be shed on the antecedents of the published text by a Latin MS fragment which the Library of the Catholic University of America purchased in 1947 from N.H. Christensen (Bloomfield, N.J.). The Washington MS (= W) consists of a single quire of nine vellum leaves, 22 × 16 cm (gathering: 0-9, 1-8, 2-7, 3-6, 4-5) without cover. It was formerly part of a collection of miscellaneous MSS, sewn into a medieval chained binding, which Mr. Christensen had obtained before the war in Zurich (54); the individual MSS once contained

(50) *L'accueil* (n. 1 *supra*) 256-8; on the MS see also p. 254.
(51) Fournier *loc. cit.* 257 speaks of 29 statutes and considers three as missing: since he failed to take cognizance of earlier researches (cf. nn. 16, 31 *supra*) he did not notice the identity of *Fideli* and *Cum sacrosancta*; nor did he recognize the fact that cc. 13, 14, 18 had been announced at the council and were not merely « d'autres décisions qu'il (le pape) ajoute à celles datant du concile ».
(52) See infra V, at nn. 80, 98.
(53) Photostats of the Paris MS could not be obtained in time before the completion of the present article. But see now Additional Note, p. 80 *infra*.
(54) The MSS are described as Nos. 2-7 in Mr. Christensen's Catalogue II, *The Library of a Scholar: Medieval & Renaissance Studies;* they will be numbered I-VI in this note (identifications supplied by the present writer are marked with an asterisk). — **I:** the original binding, containing 31 fols. (**1**) fol. 1-10v: *Helwicus Teutonicus (of Germar?) O. P., De dilectione dei et proximi, beg. Magister, quod est mandatum magnum in lege...*; ends *de novo infusos in prima consummata* (printed among the works of St. Thomas Aquinas; on the author see M. Grabmann, *Helwicus Theutonicus O. Pr. [Helwic von Germar?], der Verfasser der pseudothomistischen Schrift...,* in *Divus Thomas* 5 [Fribourg 1927] 401-10). (**2**) fol. 11-18v: anon. *De decem gradibus amoris*, beg. *Ut dicit Bernardus, magna res est amor, set sunt in eo gradus...*; ends *ubi in amore tuo eternaliter ardeam, qui vivis et regnas deus cum patre et sp. s. amen.* (**3**) fol. 19-28v: Innocent III, *De contemptu mundi.* (**4**) fol. 29-31v: Helwicus of Magdeburg O.F.M., *Decachordum*, beg. *Convertere animam meam in requiem tuam...*; ends incompl. in c. 10 *quod sub enigmate credidi, perfecte amabo, quod se...* (ed. F. Doelle, in *Beiträge zur Gesch. der sächsischen Franziskanerprovinz* 1 [1908] 68-80, 87-96). — **II:** 4 fols. containing **Honorius of Autun** (Ps. Augustinus), *De cognitione verae vitae*, beg. *Sapientia dei qui os muti...*;

in the volume are now unfortunately scattered among various owners (55). Some clues to the history of the miscellaneous codex are, however, provided by two sets of old entries on the inside of the chained cover, at present in the possession of Dr. L. Schopp in New York. There a fifteenth-century hand (A) has listed the original contents of the volume; the last entry reads: *Preces pro conuentu wiennensi*. In the eighteenth century another hand (B) noted that part of these contents were missing but that other items could be found instead in the book; among the latter, we read: *Gregorij PP. X. Decreta quaedam ex Conc. Lugd.* (56). The final entry of list A makes it possible to trace the provenance of the codex: it is mentioned indeed in an eighteenth-century catalogue of the Francis-

---

ends *sed spiritus sanctus corpus columbe condidit*. — **III:** 15 fols. containing an anonymous moral exposition of portions of Daniel, Kings, and Genesis, beg. *De penitentia. Daniellis iv. Ruit vox de celo* (Dan. 4.28)...; ends *dormivitque cum ea vi opprimens virginem* (Gen. 34.2). — **IV:** 71 fols. containing an anonymous treatise *de septem donis spiritus sancti* (incomplete; only pt. 1 *de dono timoris* and a portion of pt. 2 *de dono pietatis* are preserved) beg. *Quoniam multi subtiliter et utiliter elaboraverunt auctoritates diversas...*; ends *te moveat si recordatus fueris quia ille qui...*: this can be identified, from a reproduction of fol. 1r in the catalogue, as a *book of *exempla* abridged from Stephen de Bourbon's *Tractatus de diversis materiis praedicabilibus* (ed. A. Lecoy de la Marche, *Anecdotes historiques, légendes et apologues tirés du recueil inédit d'Étienne de Bourbon* [Paris 1877]; abbreviations of this work existed in great numbers in the 13th century, cf. J. Th. Welter, *L'exemplum dans la littérature religieuse et didactique du moyen âge* [Paris 1927] 221 n. 12). — **V:** the fragment of the Council of Lyons. — **VI:** 6 fols. containing a fragment of Ps. Dionysius Areopagita, *De caelesti hierarchia*, beg. *Calefacientes igitur nominantur et throni...*; ends *ut pulchrum et bonum amorem autem...*; with the commentary of Robert Grosseteste.

(55) MSS I and IV were sold to Dr. L. Schopp in New York; II and III, to the University of North Carolina, Chapel Hill, N. C.; V, to the Catholic University, Washington, D. C.; VI, to Professor S. H. Thomson of the University of Colorado, Boulder Colo. (Information kindly supplied by letter of Mr. Christensen).

(56) Lists A and B follow here, with the entries of hand B given in square brackets; numbers i-xiv supplied by the writer. — (i-ii) *Duo tractatus de amore* (= Ms I, 1-2). (iii) *Innocencius de miseria humane condicionis* (= MS I, 3). (iv) *Meditaciones helmerici ordinis fratrum Minorum* (= MS I, 4). [(v) *Liber Augustini de cognitione veri* (= MS II).] (vi) *De Penitencia* (= MS III). (vii) *Historia de Appollonio Tyro*. (viii) *Historia de Adriano imperatore*. (ix) *Historia de Secundo philosopho*. (x) *Hystoria de duobus pueris similibus, scil. Amico et Amelio*. (xi) *Tractatus de timore et caritate domini, quem dedit frater iacobus* (= MS IV). (xii) *Preces pro conuentu wiennensi*. [*NB. Multa hic notata non reperiuntur in hoc MS. Adest vero in eo* (xiii) *Tractatus de Septem Donis* (= xi = MS IV). (xiv) *Gregorij PP. X. Decreta quaedam ex Conc. Lugd.* (= MS V).] There can be but little doubt about the identity of Nos. xi and xiii; as to the lost Nos. vii-x, it is impossible to say which of the medieval versions they represented of the widely spread tales of Apollonius of Tyre, the Emperor Hadrian, Secundus the Philosopher, and Amis and Amile (for their occurrence in collections of *exempla* see Welter, *op. cit.* Index s. vv.).

can Convent (*Minoritenkloster*) of Vienna (57), where it was still seen in 1911 (58) and where its original nucleus (A) must have been as early as the fifteenth century. But at what time between the dates of lists A and B the additional quire containing the Washington fragment was sewn in (59), and whence it came, we are no longer able to say.

Written in a late thirteenth or early fourteenth-century French hand, in double columns of 34 lines each, W contains part of c. *Zelus fidei* and nineteen chapters, set off with red initials and severally inscribed, *Greg. x. ex concilio lugd.* The preserved text begins fol. 1v with the half-erased, faintly legible words: *terre predicte in subsidium sicut superius est ordinatum. § Ceterum quia cursarij...* (60), i.e. in the last sentence preceding the second section of *Zelus fidei*. The MS ends fol. 9vb in the midst of c. *Quamuis constitutio* (c. 9 of the official text) at the words, *liceat partibus ab huiusmodi ap // (pellationibus...)* (61). Fol. 1r has been completely rubbed off with such violence as to cause several holes, with partial loss of text also on the reverse. In the upper left corner of fol. 1r another hand has written in two lines the words, *Q(uonia)m d(ictu)m / est reg(e)nti* (? — possibly a guide for entering a text with this initium on the erased page).

By a comparison of the preserved portion of c. *Zelus fidei* with Finke's edition, the length of the missing first part can be computed at six columns, i.e. one folio (4 cols.) must have preceded fol. 1r (2 cols.). W may therefore have been a quintern, if the narrow strip of vellum which forms the counterpart of fol. 9 and is folded over fol. 1 can be considered the remnant of a page that has been cut off. But the text may as well have begun on the last folio of a preceding quire in the lost origi-

---

(57) Published by R. Wolkan, *Aus österreichischen Handschriftenkatalogen*, in *Zeitschrift des österr. Vereins für Bibliothekswesen* 15 (N.F. 2; 1911-12) 69-73; our MS appears as No. 19: *Tractatus de amore. Tractatus Innocentii de miseria hum. cond. Meditationes fratris Henrici. Liber Augustini de cognit. veri. Gregorii X. decreta de concilio Lugdun. Tractatus de 7 donis* (= MSS I. 1-4, II, V, IV).

(58) According to Wolkan (p. 69) the catalogue covers only 78 of the some hundred MSS actually found in 1911.

(59) The original nucleus itself was a result of accretions, as shown by the remark, *...quem dedit frater iacobus* in list A, No. xi. On the other hand, MS VI is mentioned neither in A nor in B: it seems to have been added after the 18th-century survey was made.

(60) Cf. ed. Finke 115 (middle).

(61) Guiraud, *Registres* p. 244b; ed. Rom. 4, 98aC; Mansi 24, 89B.

nal book; the council at any rate must have filled in this book more than one quire, since W ends in the midst of a sentence.

W presents the Lyonese constitutions arranged in three groups: fol. 1va-3ra: c. *Zelus fidei* (incomplete at the beginning), followed by two blank lines. — fol. 3ra-8ra: cc. 2, 10, 11, 17, 20, 31, 12, 16, 25, 22, 26 + 27 (in one), 23, followed by one and one-half blank columns. — fol. 8va-9vb: cc. 3, 4, 5, 6, 7, 8, 9... (breaks off incomplete). This order bears a striking resemblance to the account of BN:

W (i):	*Zelus fidei;*			
BN *sess*. II:	*Zelus fidei;*			
W (ii):	2, 10, 11, 17, 20,	31, 12, 16, 25,	22, 26+27,	23;
BN *sess*. V-VI: (V)	2, 10, 17, 20, 11, 28,	31, 12, 16, 25,	26, 27, 22, 21,	(VI) 23, 1;
W (iii):	3-9...			
BN *sess*. III:	3-9, 19, 15, 24, 29, 30.			

We have to recognize, then, W as related to the preliminary stage of redaction that underlies BN, i.e. as derived from an exemplar similar to the one used in the composition of BN at the Chancery. There is little doubt but that the lost final portion of W continued with cc. 19, 15, 24, 29, 30. The most obvious difference between the two texts lies in the fact that the statutes of session III come to stand in W behind those of sessions V-VI; one can only guess that the exemplar may have consisted of individual fascicles for the respective sessions and that the copyist of W confused their proper sequence. In session V, moreover, we notice transpositions in two places (17, 20, 11: 11, 17, 20; and 26, 27, 22: 22, 26 + 27); in each case the disturbance is enhanced by the fact that an omission (due to oversight?) follows the inversion. As for session VI, however, the ample space left after c. 23 suggests an intentional omission: it is remarkable that this should have happened precisely in the case of c. 1 *Fideli,* where a radical rewording had taken place during the interval between promulgation and publication. The general structure of W warrants the conclusion that we could have expected to read this canon here with its original, lost arenga, *Cum sacrosancta.* This assumption will be borne out by an analysis of the textual shape of the statutes preserved in W.

III.

A critical study of the individual texts in W will serve two distinct purposes. In the case of *Zelus fidei* it is a matter of determining the relative value of two MSS, W and Osnabrück C. 1 as edited by Finke (F), for the reconstruction of a decree which was never officially published (62). In the case of the statutes included in the official publication of 1 November 1274, there exists an authentic, definitive text (R) (63) and our task is rather to establish whether W, as a representative of the preliminary order observed in the conciliar promulgation, furnishes also evidence of a preliminary shape of the individual texts themselves; in other words, whether W presents readings which are to be considered, not merely variants of transmission, but testimony of another recension. If such a recension can be traced in W, it must needs be prior to R, by the same token by which the MS is « prior » in its external order.

This critical task is rendered difficult by the extremely poor quality of the copy. W teems with scribal errors and blunders, many of which show a complete disregard for elementary grammar and common sense. The frequency of such gross mistakes may be gleaned from the variants of the following statute, one of the shortest in the whole series:

R c. 8 (Rg 244b, Rr 98a-b, Rm 88); W fol. 9va

Si quando contigerit duabus electionibus celebratis *a)* partem alteram eligentium duplo maiorem numero inveniri, contra electores qui partem reliquam *b)* sic excedunt *c)*, ad extenuationem zeli, meriti vel auctoritatis ipsorum, reliquis vel electo ab eis aliquid opponendi *d)* omnem presenti decreto interdicimus facultatem. Si quid autem opponere voluerint quod votum illius cui opponitur nullum redderet ipso iure, id eis non intelligimus *e)* interdictum.

a) duarum electionum celebratio *W*   *b)* aliquam *W*   *c)* extendunt *W*
d) opponi *W*   *e)* idem eis intelligimus *W*.

---

(62) The copies mentioned by Lunt, *Financial relations* (n. 30 *supra*) 312 n. 1 as extant in three English cartularies have not been examined.
(63) In the following collations, the text of R is that of Guiraud's edition, *Registres* n. 576 (= Rg, cited by page and column); references to the *editio princeps* in ed. Rom. 4, 95 ff. (= Rr, cited by page, column, and marginal letter) and its most easily accessible reprint in Mansi 24, 81 ff. (= Rm, by column and marginal letter) have been added throughout.

The readings (a) and (d) are grammatically impossible; (b-c) *qui partem aliquam sic extendunt* is utter nonsense; (e) turns the meaning of the sentence into its contrary. (If one were to assume, for the sake of argument, that the legislator had originally planned to estop the minority even from charging an *ipso iure* nullity, he would have had to introduce this clause with an emphatic *Immo si quid...*, not with the adversative *Si quid autem...*).

A good many corruptions were obviously caused by the scribe's inability to decipher the exemplar; only some of the most glaring cases may be cited here:

R. c. 2: onusta] commixta *W* (the letter *o* is misread for an inverted *c*, which stands for *com-*; *nu* misread for *mi*)   commiserint] qui fuerit *W* (the abbreviation for *com* is misread for *q*, *mi* for *ui*, the long *s* for *f*, etc.)   c. 10: docuerit] detinet *W*   c. 17: inuenta] iniuria *W*   occasionem] ecclesie *W*   omne interesse] dicte terre interesse *W* (the abbreviation for *omne* is misread; the rest based on dittography)   c. 31: ad que committenda] absque committendo *W* c. 16: Altercationis] Lateranensis *W* (on erasure)   c. 25: conciones] contentiones *W*   canonis] curationis *W*   c. 22: sed constituendo] seu custodiendo *W*   restituendo] ostendendo *W*   c. 27: ydonee] donec *W*   c. 23: uerum etiam] metum autem *W*   c. 4: aliquorum] morum *W*   electi] clerici *W*   c. 5: magistra] magnarum *W*   licentiam] sententiam *W*   aliam] illam *W*   c. 6: motum] metum *W* c. 7 celata] collata *W*   pandatur] pendatur *W*

Omissions of words due to homoeographic slips are frequent, but sometimes we also find contractions of the text without rhyme or reason, e.g.:

R c. 2 (64)	W fol. 3ra
omnia que... a nostris sunt predecessoribus et precipue a felicis recordationis Alexandro papa tertio salubriter instituta...	ea que... a nostris predecessoribus a felicis recordationis Alexandro papa iiij. salubriter instituta... (65)

(64) Rg 241b; Rr 95bA; Rm 82A.
(65) Note that also some MSS of the collection *Cum nuper* give the name of the pope as Alexander IV, although Alexander III's decree *Licet de vitanda* (III Conc. Lat. c. 1; X 1.6.6) is clearly meant. On Schulte's erroneous assumption (WSB 55, 730) that Gregory X could have referred here to the much discussed c. *Quia frequenter* (which Schulte wrongly assigned to Alexander IV), see Friedberg, *Corpus iur. can.* II, 946 note c *ad loc.* (Sext. 1.6.3); Singer, *Das c. Quia frequenter, ein nie in Geltung gewesenes « Papstwahldekret » Innozenz IV.*, in ZRG Kan. Abt. 6 (1916) 5 ff. and 12 f.

R c. 22 (66)	W fol. 6va
Et nichilominus prelatos qui secus egerint ipso facto ab officio et administratione, clericos etiam qui scientes contra inhibitionem predictam aliquid esse presumptum, id superiori...	presumptim clericos uero dum id superiori...

R c. 3 (67)	W fol. 8vb
que appellantes, appellationis emisse tempore, verisimiliter ignorare potuerint et etiam ignorarint. Super huiusmodi autem ignorantia...	et uerisibile (sic) potuerint probare.Super huiusmodi autem ignorantia...

And yet, once the obvious scribal blunders are eliminated, it will be seen that W fulfills the expected critical purposes: the MS does add to our knowledge of *Zelus fidei* and provide us us with a clue to the « conciliar » text of the other statutes as distinct from their published form.

IV.

As stated above, the first section of *Zelus fidei*, with its important financial measures in aid of the Holy Land, is missing from W, save for a part of the last sentence. The second section, which repeats almost verbatim the provisions of Innocent IV's *Afflicti corde* and earlier identical decrees (68), offers in W only insignificant variants. In particular, W does not contain any more than F the usual clause enforcing the prohibition of tournaments which occurs in all the previous, corresponding enactments. Because Gregory X later mentioned this as part of his Lyonese decrees in a letter to King Rudolph, Finke suspected a lacuna in the Osnabrück MS (69). The agreement of W, however, raises the question whether one has not to assume a misquotation in Gregory's letter rather than a faulty archetype common to WF: for this latter explanation is barred by the differences between the two MSS in the third section of *Zelus fidei*, the decree *Non nobis*.

(66) Rg 247b; Rr 101bB; Rm 96A.
(67) Rg 243b; Rr 97bC; Rm 86D.
(68) Cf. note 41 *supra*.
(69) *Konzilienstudien* 14.

This ordinance ends in F with a list giving the numbers of proctors to be appointed for each nation by the minor prelates departing from the council. As W shows, Finke was correct in suspecting (70) the list in his MS to be incomplete. On the other hand, the list of W is defective also: only by combining the two texts can we obtain a fairly complete picture (see the edition below). Immediately after the list, W alone continues with a heretofore unknown provision outlawing immoderate subsidies and taxes imposed by the prelates on their subjects to cover their own expenses at the council.

The importance of *Non nobis* for the history of conciliar procedures, the additional matter in W, and the fact that Finke's publication is not easily accessible, warrant a new edition of the entire text (71).

Non nobis, sed domino damus gloriam *a)* et honorem (*cf. Ps. 113. 9*) et ipsi gratias reddamus *b)* quod ad tam sacrum concilium patriarcharum, primatum, *c)* archiepiscoporum, episcoporum, abbatum, priorum, prepositorum, decanorum, archydiachonorum et aliorum ecclesiarum prelatorum *d)* tam per se quam per procuratores ydoneos, necnon capitulorum, collegiorum et conuentuum procuratorum *e)* ad uocationem nostram *f)* copiosa multitudo conuenit. Sane licet pro felici prosecutione tanti negotij esset eorum consilium opportunum, et in ipsorum tanquam dilectorum filiorum presentia delectemur et quodammodo *g)* spirituali gaudio affluamus, contra nonnullos tamen eorum *h)* propter uaria incommoda que ipsorum copiositas *i)* ingerit, ne pre turba nimia se diutius comprimant et eorum absentia ipsis et ipsorum ecclesijs posset esse dampnosa, quadam prouida pietate commoti, de fratrum nostrorum consilio super hoc salubriter prouidere decreuimus, ut sic eorum *j)* grauaminibus occurratur, quod prosecutio huius negocij, quod feruenti spiritu et sollicitudine indefessa prosequimur, nullatenus derogetur. Omnes igitur patriarchas, primates, archiepiscopos, episcopos, *k)* abbates et *l)* priores per nos nominatim et specialiter euocatos sic remanere decreuimus, ut ante diffinitum concilium absque nostra speciali licentia non discedant. Ceteris uero abbatibus et prioribus non mitratis et aliis abbatibus et prioribus *m)* qui per nos non fuerunt *n)* nominatim *o)* et specialiter euocati, necnon prepositis, decanis, archydiaconis et alijs ecclesiarum *p)* prelatis ac quorumque *q)* prelatorum, capitulorum, collegiorum et conuentuum procuratoribus, recedendi ex dei et nostra benedictione *r)* clementer licentiam impertimur; mandantes ut

---

(70) *Ibid.* n. 1.

(71) W fol. 2rb-3ra; F pp. 116-7. In the MSS, no paragraph separates *Non nobis* from the preceding section; nor is the list of proctors set off, as has been done here for greater convenience. The spelling of W has been followed.

omnes taliter recedentes *s)* primitus, prout infra scribitur, procuratores sufficientes dimittant ad suscipienda nostra mandata et ea que in presenti nostro concilio *t)* ordinata sunt et in futurum auctore *u)* domino contigerit *v)* ordinari. Omnes, scilicet *w)*

>de regno Francie taliter recedentes quatuor,
>de regno Alamanie quatuor, *x)*
>de regnis Yspaniarum quatuor,
>de regno Anglie quatuor,
>de regno Scotie unum, *y)*
>de regno Sicilie duos,
>de Lambardia duos,
>de Tuscia unum,
>de terris ecclesie unum,
>de regno Norbeije unum
>de regno Sueuie unum,
>de regno Vngarie unum, *z)*
>de regno Dacie unum,
>de regno Boemie unum, *aa)*
>de ducatu Polonie unum,

procuratores sufficientes dimittant. *bb)* Ad hec ad nos ex quorundam relatione peruenit quod nonnulli archiepiscopi et episcopi alijque prelati, ea *cc)* occasione quod ipsos ad concilium mandauimus euocari, petentes a subditis immoderatum subsidium multa extorserunt ab eis, graues ipsis tallias inponentes; quorum aliqui, licet a subiectis multa exegerint, ad concilium non uenerunt. Verumtamen cum *dd)* nostre intentionis *ee)* non extiterit nec existat ut prelati ad concilium ueniendo sociarent obedire bonum cum grauamine subditorum, monemus prelatos omnes et singulos, eis firmiter innuentes, quatinus nullus eorum occasione premissa subditos suos tallijs uel *ff)* exactionibus grauare presumat. Si uero aliqui non uenerunt ad concilium et a subditis suis ea occasione aliquid exigerint, uolumus et precise mandamus quod ea occasione que receperunt ab eis restituant sine mora. Illi autem qui grauauerunt subditos ab eis subsidia immoderata petendo, eisdem satisfacere sine qualibet difficultate procurent, *gg)* mandatum nostrum taliter impleturi, quod non oporteat ut super hoc auctoritate nostra remedium apponatur.

a) set damus gl. dom. *F*   *b)* reddimus *F*   *c)* transp. post v. episcoporum *F*   *d)* prel. eccl. *W*   *e)* et proc. conu. *W*, conv. proc. *F*   *f)* advocatorum *(om. nostram) F*   *g)* quorundam *W*   *h)* contra — eorum] circa illos, tamen (tum *cod.*) *F*   *i)* multitudo et cop. *F*   *j)* om. *F*   *k)* om. *W*   *l)* om. *F*   *m)* non mitratis — prioribus *om. W propter homoeotel. (de re ipsa vide quae scripsit Brevis nota, ed. Rom. 84aA, Mansi 63C)*   *n)* fuerant *F*   *o)* nominati *FW*   *p)* eorum *W*   *q)* quorumlibet *F*   *r)* ex — bened.] dei gratia et bened. nostra *F*   *s)* qualiter *(corr.* equaliter) excedentes *W*   *t)* in presentia nostra concilio *F*   *u)* actore *F*   *v) FW,* contigerint *perperam Finke*   *w)* Mandamus scil. *F,* ut add. *Finke (qui integram sententiam alia manu adiectam esse monet p. 117 n. 3)*   *x)* om. *W,* iiii. *F*   *y)* de — unum *om. W*   *z)* de regno Sicilie — Vngarie unum *om. F*   *aa)* etc add. *F*   *bb) hic desinit F*   *cc)* ca *W*   *dd)* om. *W*   *ee) ex* interdictionis *corr. W*   *ff)* om. *W*   *gg)* procurrent *W*

V.

In the following collations of the statutes given in W after *Zelus fidei*, only those passages will be recorded which certainly or possibly are of critical value. Readings which, like the samples given above (III), are manifestly corrupt will be disregarded.

Ubi periculum (72)

R c. 2		W fol. 3ra-4va
presenti constitutione supplere sacro concilio approbante statuimus..	[1]	presenti constitutione supplere statuimus...
contenti singuli singulis tantummodo servientibus, clericis vel laicis...	[2]	uno tantummodo seruiente, clerico a) vel laico... a) clero W
nullo intermedio pariete seu alio velamine...	[3]	nullo intermedio pariete, cortina seu alio uelamine...
Nulli etiam fas sit ipsis cardinalibus vel eorum alicui nuntium mittere... (73)	[4]	Nulli sit etiam copia ipsis cardinalibus nuntium mittere...
Set si ad alios post sanitatem sibi redditam seu antea redire voluerit...	[5]	Set si ad alios sanitate sibi reddita redire uoluerit...
Porro si quando Romanum pontificem...	[6]	Ceterum si quando Romanum pontificem...
In hac etiam civitate, tam quoad expectationem absentium quam quoad habitationem communem, clausuram et cetera omnia, in domo episcopali vel alia qualibet eisdem cardinalibus deputanda, eadem observentur que...	[7]	In hac etiam ciuitate, in domo episcopali uel alia eisdem cardinalibus deputanda, omnia obseruentur que...

(72) Rg 241b-243b; [1] Rr 95bB, Rm 82B; [2] Rr 95bB-C, Rm 82 B-C; [3] Rr 95bC, Rm 82C; [4] Rr 96aA, Rm 82D; [5] Rr 96aE, Rm 83D; [6] Rr 96bA, Rm 83E; [7] Rr 96bB, Rm 84A; [8] Rr 96bB, Rm 84B; [9] *ibid.*; [10] Rr 96bC-D, Rm 84C-D; [11] Rr 96bD-97aE, Rm 84D-86A.

(73) The continuation in R (*vel scripturam. Qui vero contra fecerint, scripturam mittendo vel nuntium, aut cum aliquo...*) is marred by a homoeographic contamination in W (*uel scripturam, uel cum aliquo...*).

Preterea quia parum est iura condere...	[8]	Ad hec quia parum est iura *a)* condere... *a)* uota W
auctoritate nostra et eiusdem approbatione concilii...	[9]	auctoritate nostra et *a)* huius sacri concilij... *a)* uel W
Quod si forte in premissis vel circa ea fraudem commiserint aut ipsa diligenter non obseruaverint, cuiuscunque sint preeminentie, conditionis aut status, omni cessante privilegio eo ipso excommunicationis sint vinculo innodati...	[10]	Quod si premissa diligenter non obseruauerint aut fraudem in eis uel circa *a)* ea commiserint, *b)* cuiuscumque sint dignitatis, preeminentie, conditionis aut status, omni cessante priuilegio eo ipso sententiam excommunicationis incurrant... *a)* certa W *b)* qui fuerit W
Ceterum quia cum arbitrium *rell.* ieiuniorum indicant.	[11]	*deest*
deest	[12] [13]	In hijs autem omnibus et singulis nobis et nostris successoribus reseruamus plenam et liberam potestatem declarandi, addendi, detrahendi, prout communi utilitati *a)* uidebitur expedire. Nos itaque, attendentes sanctam et piam intentionem eiusdem summi pontificis, cum in predicta constitutione solum ad dei beneplacitum prosequendum et ad uniuersalis *b)* ecclesie prouisionem intendat nec in ea prosequatur aliquod suum interesse priuatum, presertim cum effectus *c)* constitutionis ipsius in id tempus excurrat quo *d)* ipse inter homines iam non erit; attendentes etiam quanta induxit pericula quasi recens et prolixa ecclesie Romane uaccatio, constitutionem eandem per quam periculis tantis occurritur *e)* acceptamus, aprobamus et eidem consentimus *f)* expresse. In cuius rei testimonium idem presens scriptum fecimus sigillo-

rum nostrorum munimine roborari. Datum Lugduni etc.

a) utilitate *W*   *b)* uniuersas *W*   *c)* affectus *W*   *d)* in — quo] tempus existimat quod *W*   *e)* occurratur *W*   *f)* idem censemus *W*

The final paragraph, *Nos itaque* [13] proves conclusively that W contains a conciliar text prior to R. We know from BN that Gregory X eventually defeated the strategy of the cardinals' opposition against the enactment of his law on the conclave, by causing the other prelates to put their seals to formal instruments of consent, made out separately by nations (*cedulae per regna et provincias*) before he proceeded to the promulgation of the statute on 16 July (*sess.* V) (74). The text of one of the *cedulae* was published by Kaltenbrunner in 1869 from an indirect copy of the original parchments which, eight in number, are today preserved in the Vatican Archives as part of the former Archives of the Castel S. Angelo (A.A arm. I. xviii, nos. 2187-2194; formerly arm. IX caps. VIII, nos. 1-8) (75). Identical, but for the names of the signatories, and dated, partly of 13 July, partly of 14 July (76), the documents are drawn up in the usual style of a *Vidimus* (77), with the full text of the papal statute inserted, and concluded by the bishops' declaration of approval, *Nos itaque rell.* — which we find reproduced, with some scribal mistakes, in W.

(74) BN *ed. Rom.* 85bD-86aA; Mansi 66-7. Cf. Finke, *Konzilienstudien* 3 f.; Martin, *Conc. et bull. de Lyon* n. 1809.

(75) F. Kaltenbrunner, *Actenstücke zur Geschichte des Deutschen Reiches...* (*Mittheilungen aus dem Vatic. Arch.* ed. Akad. der Wiss. 1; Wien 1869) no. 52, pp. 58-60, from « Collectio Platina Tom. I fol. 100, Cod. Vallicell. B 12, fol. 433a ». In a footnote (p. 58) Kaltenbrunner states that he has also seen, but not collated, the original documents. Their shelf-marks, as given above, I owe to the kindness of Msgr. Angelo Mercati, who moreover informs me (by letter of 31 December 1948) that Platina's collections, i. e. the apographs of papal documents made under his direction at the time of Sixtus IV (cf. also Raynaldi, *Annales eccles.* ad an. 1274 n. 27), are contained in three volumes of the Vatican Archives, now A. A arm. I. xviii nos. 1288-1290, but that Kaltenbrunner used instead Arm. XXXV t. 6-8 which, even as the *Vallicellianus*, contain only copies taken from Platina's apographs.

(76) The first date is that of the five documents signed by the bishops of Germany and Burgundy, the Provence, France, Spain, and the British Isles respectively; three were signed on 14 July by the Latin Patriarchs, the Italian bishops, and the Cistercian, Cluniac, and Premonstratensian abbots. Cf. Kaltenbrunner 59 f.

(77) *Universis presentes literas inspecturis... salutem in salutis auctore. Presente scripto fatemur nos vidisse ac diligenter inspexisse constitutionem domini nostri Gregorii divina providentia pape .x. subscripti tenoris...*.

If W, then, is to be considered a copy of the statute as signed by the prelates on 13 and 14 July, the readings of our MS acquire an unusual significance. In his edition of the German and Burgundian bishops' *cedula*, Kaltenbrunner had briefly passed over the inserted papal document, assuring the reader of its identity with the published text of *Ubi periculum* (78). W leads one to suspect that such is not the case: and indeed, as I am informed through the kindness of Msgr. Angelo Mercati, the eight originals in the Vatican Archives present the text of the statute which underlies W (of course, without the corruptions of the latter) (79), and not that of the register. We thus are in a position to confirm what É. Fournier had already inferred from the old French version (*Par. fr.* 491) of the Lyonese statutes (80): the historic law on the conclave, when first promulgated at the council — for no one will doubt that in the public session of July 16 it was read in that form to which the bishops had put their seals two (or three) days before — showed certain remarkable differences from the later, officially published text, which alone has come down in the collections. In some instances it is merely a matter of formal changes of wording (cfr. the variants numbered 2, 3, 4, 5, 6, 8, 10, above); but other points are worth the historian's attention:

a) In the original form, the basic provisions of *Ubi periculum* were introduced as a plain papal *constitutio,* without the clause, *sacro concilio approbante* (var. 1) but with the

---

(78) *Op. cit.* 59: « Es folgt die Constitution 'Ubi periculum' bei Mansi Conc. XXIV. 81-84 ».

(79) Apart from such mistakes in W as result from the notes to variants 2, 8, 9, 10 above, it is especially the final clause *Nos itaque* (var. 13) which has been corrected with the aid of Msgr. Mercati's collations. Here two more variants are found in Kaltenbrunner's edition (cf. also Finke, *op. cit.* 4 n. 3): *non solum* (instead of *solum*) *ad dei beneplacitum*; and *in eo* (instead of *in ea*) *prosequatur.* Only one Vatican document gives the absurd *non,* but no document has *in eo,* although some omit *in ea.* — In var. 3 above, the word *cortina* is found only in three of the original texts; in var. 4, the words *vel eorum alicui* (as in R) are present in all texts.

(80) *L'accueil* 257 (cf. *supra* at nn. 50-53). Fournier notes the absence of the last two paragraphs (our variant 11) and the presence of a different final clause (our var. 12; the French text lacks the bishops' declaration): *Mais en toutes ces coses u chascunes, à nous et à nos successeurs revvardons nos plaine et franke poesté de déclairier et de ajouster et de soustraire, ensi comme aucun porfit i sera vut à pourfiter.* He remains, however, unaware of the existence of the original documents.

bishops' declaration of approval at the end (var. 13). The council is mentioned only once in connection with a point of detail, dealing with the police power of the municipal government of the city where the conclave is to take place (var. 9): *auctoritate nostra et huius s. concilii;* since R gives the entire statute as approved in council, it has changed this into *a.n. et eiusdem approbatione conc.*

b) In the section which contemplates the eventuality of the pope's death *extra curiam*, it was deemed necessary in the official text (var. 7) to explain the original, brief *omnia observentur* in detail: *tam quoad expectationem rell.*

c) Two lengthy sections were added to the original statute after the promulgation in the official text (var. 11): the one (*Ceterum quia... observationes acceptas*) outlining the cardinals' grave obligation and declaring invalid all future pre-election promises, pacts, and oaths; the other (*Quia vero fidelibus... ieiuniorum indicant*) enjoining public prayers throughout the Church during the vacancy of the Holy See.

d) On the other hand, the original conclusion of the statute, which reserved to the pope and his successors the power of altering every and any provision of the new law by interpretation, addition, or repeal (var. 12), was struck out in the official redaction. This may, at first sight, seem astonishing in view of the fact that Gregory X himself, as we have just seen, made ample use of this power. The point is, however, that an express mention of the papal prerogative in this context might easily have lent an argument to the theorists of conciliar supremacy: could not such reservation be construed as implying that *per se* a law promulgated at a general council is beyond the reach of the pope, i.e. that a conciliar statute without this clause would be no longer subject to repeal or amendment by the pope alone? This possible interpretation in all likelihood prompted the redactors of R to cancel the sentence — although they could certainly not foresee that the problem would soon become one of practical importance in the very case of c. *Ubi periculum*: when in 1276 Hadrian V suspended, and his successor John XXI revoked the law of the conclave (81), the « conciliarist » objection was in-

---

(81) Potthast ante n. 21149; nn. 21151, 21162. Cf. Fournier, *Questions* 22 f.

deed put forward by some canonists but effectively refuted in Durantis' commentary by reference to papal supremacy (82). Recourse to a clause of reservation, had it still been in the text, might have been more convenient in the particular issue, but would have weakened the papal position on principle.

The rediscovery of the conciliar text of *Ubi periculum* solves also the riddle as to why Durantis, commenting on the words, *et post*, of the introductory bull of R, asserted the law of the conclave to be one of the Lyonese statutes which were issued only after the close of the council (83). As one of the pope's collaborators in the framing of the legislation, he must have had first-hand knowledge of the changes made in the conciliar text after the readings in the public sessions, and precisely in the case of *Ubi periculum* these changes amounted to more than a mere editorial recasting of words and phrases. Above all, the insertion in R of two lengthy and important paragraphs meant an enlargement of the original text by over one-third (84) and an addition of subject matter not contemplated in the first promulgation: to this extent, at least, the published version had actually become a post-conciliar enactment.

(82) Durantis ad c. *Ubi periculum*: ...*et praesens constitutio super hoc satis salubriter prouidebat, que cum tam solemni concilio approbante fuerat promulgata, mirum est quomodo absque universalis <vel> saltim particularis requisitione concilii fuerit reuocata...; frustra siquidem concilii approbatio et assensus requiritur, si sic sine concilio quod tam solemniter agitur reuocetur. Fieri* (the edition has *Sed;* corr. Singer, ZRG Kan. Abt. 6, 25 n. 2) *tamen potuit de plenitudine potestatis, secundum quam potest papa super omne concilium quicquid placet, ut supra eod. c. Significasti* (X 1.6.4). *Indulgeat ei deus qui causam prebuit reuocandi...* (ed. Maiolus fol. 6r). Cf. Joh. Andreae, *Glos. ord. ad Sext.* 1.6.3, v. *concilio*.

(83) Note 17 *supra*. The difficulty was rightly sensed by Göller, *Zur Geschichte* (n. 18 *supra*) 83, but he assumed (against BN) that *Ubi periculum* was not promulgated at all because of the resistance of the cardinals; thus also Schroeder, *Disciplinary Decrees* (n. 31 *supra*) 335. Vernet, *Dict. théol. cath.* 9, 1379 f. contrariwise rejects Durantis' statement as untrustworthy. Another explanation, which actually is none, was given by Singer, ZRG *Kan. Abt.* 6 (1916) 25 n. 2. He points to Durantis' words ad c. *Ubi periculum*, ...*que cum tam sollemni concilio approbante fuerat promulgata* (see n. 82) and argues that in the other passage, ad v. *et post*, the glossator did not want to say more than that the official publication took place after the council. This is besides the point because the same would apply to all 31 *constitutiones*, and Durantis names *Ubi periculum* expressly in conjunction with the three statutes which definitely were not read at the sessions. His words, *que cum tam rell.* repeat only what the official text says itself twice (see var. 1 and 9 *supra*): they do not contain an historical statement on the part of Durantis.

(84) Over one column in Guiraud's edition, as against three columns for the preceding matter.

Si forte (85)

R c. 10	W fol. 4va
subiciatur examini, cuius eventus examinandis aliis aut dabit initium aut negabit...	subiciatur examini, ex cuius apparebit euentu an *a)* sit ad discucienda cetera procedendum...

a) aut W

Sciant cuncti
(R c. 11, W fol. 4vb: no variants)

Si canonici (86)

R c. 17	W fol. 4vb-5ra
in instrumento publico vel patentibus litteris sigillorum suorum aut alterius autentici munimine roboratis...	in testimonio publico uel patentibus litteris sigillorum suorum munimine roboratis...

Canons who wish to declare a *cessatio a divinis* — the effect amounts to that of an interdict on their church (87) — have to state the legitimate cause in a public document; R adds to the original draft of c. 17 the alternative of having another authority's (instead of the capitular) seal affixed to the document. The variant *testimonio* is probably a misreading, easily explained on palaeographic grounds.

Absolutionis (88)

R c. 20	W fol. 5ra-b
excommunicationis sententie decernimus subiacere.	ipso facto excommunicationis sententie decreuimus subiacere.

Contrary to appearances, this is only a verbal change since R *subiacere* likewise indicates an *ipso facto* censure (89).

---

(85) Rg 244b; Rr 98bD; Rm 89D.
(86) Rg 245b; Rr 99bE; Rm 92A.
(87) Cf. Bernard of Parma, *Glos. ord.* ad X 1.31.13 v. *cessaverint*.
(88) Rg 247a; Rr 101aC; Rm 95B.
(89) Cf. Durantis ad v. *subiacere: est ergo canon late sententie, sed ante presentem constitutionem poterant excommunicari...*; Joh. Andreae, *Casus* ad h. c. (*Sext.* 1. 20 un.); gl. ad v. *excommunicationis*.

Quicumque (90)

R c. 31		W fol. 5rb-va
in excommunicationis sententiam incidant ipso facto.	[1]	eo ipso excommunicationis sententiam incurrant.
committere suo motu...	[2]	committere per se ipsos...

Generali (91)

R c. 12		W fol. 5 va-b
custodiam sive guardiam...	[1]	custodiam...
ministros in eis sollicite faciant abstinere quod...	[2]	ministros sic in eis sollicite faciant abstinere quod...

Altercationis
(R c. 16, W fol. 5vb: no variants)

Decet domum domini (92)

R c. 25		W fol. 5vb-6rb
flectant genua cordis sui, quod vel capitis inclinatione testentur.	[1]	flectant genua cordis sui; flectant et corporis, si patitur tunc facultas, uel capitis inclinatione testentur.
Attendantur in iocis ipsis intentis precordiis sacra solempnia...	[2]	Attendantur in eis intentis precordijs sacra missarum sollempnia...
Sint postremo... prorsus extranea...	[3]	Siue postremo... prorsus sint extranea...

The first variant of c. 25 offers a detail of liturgical interest: in the section on the reverence to be shown in church, especially during Mass, to the name of Jesus, the original text expressed the wish that the Apostle's word, *in nomine Jesu omne genu flectatur* (Phil. 2. 10), be devoutly complied with both spiritually and bodily, whenever possible, at every mention of the Holy Name.

(90) Rg 250a; Rr 104bB; Rm 102B-C. In R this canon, being the last of the series, ends with the date of publication. Note that variant 1 correponds to var. 10 in *Ubi periculum*.
(91) Rg. 245a; Rr 99aA, C; Rm 90A, C.
(92) Rg 248b; Rr 102bD, E; Rm 98E, 99A.

This intention was certainly in keeping with the well-attested personal piety of Gregory X (93), but the rubricists will have pointed out after the close of the sessions that to urge such actual genuflections would cause unending confusion in the liturgy of the Mass. (One will also remember that at the time kneeling was not even uniformly prescribed to honor the Real Presence (94)). The official text, which retained only the beautiful words, *flectant genua cordis sui*, taken from the apocryphal Prayer of Manasses (95), must have been formulated before 21 September 1274, because the statute is thus quoted in a papal letter of this date, addressed to the Dominican Order (96).

Hoc consultissimo (97)

R c. 22		W fol. 6rb-vb
triennio statuimus esse suspensos.	[1]	statuimus esse suspensos per triennium
cuiuscunque sint conditionis aut status...	[2]	cuiuscumque sint dignitatis aut status...

(93) Cf. the *Vita* in Muratori, *Rerum ital. script.* 3, 599-605; esp. Salimbene, *Chron.*: *...magnae religionis; ...circa divina fuit magnus zelator* (ed. Holder-Egger, MGH *Script.* 32, 488.37; 491.30). Less credence, however, is to be given the following statement of the *Estoire de Eracles Empereur* 34.26: *Cestui pape fist une antifone qui se commence 'Ave caro Christi cara', et commanda qu'on la cantast en toutes les yglises quant li prestres lieve li cors Notre Seignor, et dona .x. jors de pardon a tous ceaus qui la diroient ou auroient devotion* (ed. *Recueil des historiens des croisades, Occid.* 2, 473; cf. Martin, *Conc. et bull. de Lyon* n. 1824). The Eucharistic hymn *Ave caro Christi cara* (ed. F. J. Mone, *Lateinische Hymnen des Mittelalters* 1 [Freiburg 1853] n. 207; cf. A. Wilmart, *Auteurs spirituels et textes dévots du moyen âge latin* [Paris 1932] 366 n. 2) seems to have enjoyed considerable popularity: a shorter version is found, e. g., in *The Lay Folk's Mass Book* (ed. Simmons, *Early English Text Soc.* 1879) 288. It was nothing unusual during the Middle Ages to connect such devotional texts with the name of a pope: cf. Wilmart, *op. cit.* 367 n. 3 for the *Ave verum* (Mone n. 213; « Pope Leo ») and the *Ave sancta caro Christi* (Mone n. 220; « Pope Innocent »).

(94) Cf. E. Mangenot, art. *Élévation, in Dict. théol. cath.* 4, 2320-8 and the several pertinent studies of H. Thurston cited there.

(95) Cf. Durantis *ad loc.*: *haec verba sunt in libro Paralip. circa finem, ubi* (*ut* ed.) *dicitur, 'et nunc flecto genua cordis mei'* (ed. Maiolus fol. 86r); repeated by Guido de Baysio, *Comm. ad Sext.* 3.23.2, v. *cordis*. The more common reading of the Vulgate, *Or. Man.* 15, gives the singular, *genu*, as does the Greek text in *Constit. Apostolorum* 2.22.14: καὶ νῦν κλίνω γόνυ καρδίας μου, while the Latin *Didascalia* 2.22.14 has the plural, *genua* (ed. F. X. Funk, *Didascalia et Constitutiones Apostolorum*, Paderborn 1905; cf. *ibid.* p. 84 note, on the *Oratio Manassis*).

(96) Potthast n. 20926; cf. Ripoll, *Bullarium O. P.* 1 (Rome 1729) 524 no. 28.

(97) Rg 247a, b; Rr 101bB, C; Rm 96A, B. For a particularly bad corruption in the text of W for this statute, see *supra*, III at n. 66. With var. 2 here compare var. 10 of c. *Ubi periculum*.

While W does not offer any notable variants, we learn from the old French version discovered by Fournier that the text of c. 22 must originally have begun with an arenga *Testimonium Joseph* (98):

> Le tesmoignage de Joseph a l'estruisement des suivans li escriture vvarda, pour ce que des églises et des choses des églises le frankise li exemple de lui tiesmoignassent... Donques, de ciaus qui autrement faire, par damnable folie, s'enhardissent le hardiece renfernant par ce très conseilliet (= *Hoc consultissimo*) commandement...

The scriptural passage alluded to, Gen. 47. 20-26, is indeed a fitting introduction to a statute which bars the subjection of ecclesiastical immovables and rights to any form of lay overlordship, advowson, or patronage. But for reasons unknown, the opening sentences were cancelled in the post-conciliar redaction— and this even at an earlier date than the arenga *Cum sacrosancta* of the dogmatic canon *Fideli* (99): for the *Brevis-nota*, which cites the latter still with its original initium, refers to our statute by the first words of the official text, *Hoc consultissimo*, and W agrees with BN.

Usurarum voraginem - *Quamquam usurarii* (100)

R cc. 26-27	W fol. 6vb-7va
sancimus ut nec collegium, ... cuiuscunque sit... status, alienigenas et alios non oriundos de terris ipsorum publice pecuniam fenebrem exercentes... domos in terris suis... habitare permittat; set huiusmodi usurarios manifestos omnes infra tres menses de terris suis expellant, nunquam aliquos tales de cetero admissuri.	[1] sancimus *a)* ut nec collegium,... cuiuscumque sit... status, publice pecuniam fenebrem exercentes... domos in terris suis... habitare permittat *b)*; set infra tres menses ipsos usurarios manifestos de terris suis omnes expellant, ipsos uel alios ipso crimine similiter irretitos nunquam de cetero admissuri.

a) sanctimus *W*   *b)* permittant *W*

---

(98) Fournier, *L'accueil* 257 (Par. fr. 491).
(99) Cf. *supra*, at nn. 33-4.
(100) Rg 248b-249b; [1] Rr 103aC, Rm 99E; [2-5] Rr 103aD-E, Rm 99E-100B; [7] Rr 103aE, Rm 100B; [8-9] Rr 103bA, Rm 100C; [10-11] Rr 103bB-C, Rm 100D-E.

Nemo illis ad fenus exercendum domos locet vel sub alio titulo quocumque concedat.	[2]	*deest*
Qui vero contrarium fecerint, si persone fuerint ecclesiastice, patriarche, archiepiscopi, episcopi, suspensionis; minores vero persone singulares, excommunicationis; collegium autem seu alia universitas, interdicti sententiam ipso facto se noverint incursuros.	[3]	Qui uero contrarium fecerint archiepiscopi uel episcopi alijque maiores, suspensionis; minores uero, si singulares *a)* persone sint, excommunicationis; si autem alia uniuersitas, interdicti sententiam ipso facto se nouerint incursuros. *a)* regulares *W*
terre ipsorum, quandiu in eis iidem usurarii commorantur...	[4]	terre *a)* ipsorum in quibus jidem usurarij commorantur... *a)* tempore *W*
Ceterum si laici fuerint... compescantur.	[5]	Si uero laici fuerint... compescantur.
deest	[6]	Sententiam excommunicationis insuper incurrant omnes qui usurarijs manifestis ad fenus exercendum domos locarent uel sub quocumque alio titulo duxerint concedendas. Presenti quoque adicimus sanctioni ut quamquam *a)* usurarij manifesti de usuris quas *b)* receperint satisfacere... mandauerint... *a)* quicumque *W* *b)* om. *W*
(c. 27) Quamquam usurarii manifesti de usuris quas receperant satisfieri... mandaverint...	[7]	
si presto sint ipsi...	[8]	si presto fuerint *a)*... *a)* fuerit *W*
et rectori predicto modo cautionem huiusmodi..	[9]	et rectori caucionem huiusmodi...
alioquin aliam, recipientis cautionem huiusmodi arbitrio moderandam.	[10]	alioquin ex ipsius ordinarij arbitrio moderandam.
Omnes autem religiosos et alios qui manifestos usurarios contra presentis sancionis formam ad ecclesiasticam admittere ausi fuerint sepulturam, pene in Lateranensi concilio contra usurarios promulgate	[11]	Omnes autem religiosos et alios qui manifestos usurarios contra presentis constitutionis formam ad ecclesiasticam admittere ausi fuerint uel ad confessionem uel ad absolutionem uel ad communionem uel ad

statuimus subiacere. Nullus manifestorum usurariorum testamentis intersit aut eos ad confessionem admittat sive ipsos absolvat, nisi de usuris satisfecerint vel de satisfaciendo pro suarum viribus facultatum prestent, ut premittitur, ydoneam cautionem. Testamenta quoque manifestorum usurariorum aliter facta non valent, sed sint irrita ipso iure.

sepulturam, pene predicti concilij *a)* statuimus subiacere.

a) om. W

In view of the far-reaching importance of the Lyonese legislation on usury in the history of the later Middle Ages, it is of great interest to note the considerable changes which this particular text underwent during the months between its promulgation and publication. The testimony of W, though supported by little other evidence (101), is entirely credible.

a) As to form, the two statutes of R — one dealing with the residence of usurers (c. 26) and the other, with the modalities of testamentary restitution (c. 27) — prove to have been parts of one single text in the original promulgation (see var. 7). The division into two must have been decided before the time when the *Brevis nota* was composed in the Chancery, since *Usurarum* and *Quamquam* are separately listed in BN for the session of 16 July.

b) The original draft forbade the lease of dwellings to, and commanded the expulsion of, all usurers without distinction; the provisions of the official text contemplate only foreign and foreign-born usurers (var. 1: it seems to be out of the question that the words, *alienigenas—ipsorum* could be missing in W by scribal oversight only, since also in the following sentence W speaks of *ipsos usurarios, ipsos uel alios,* where R specifies *huiusmodi usurarios, aliquos tales*). There would have been little hope indeed of enforcing the more sweeping provision against native money-lenders also; besides, if we may

---

(101) Fournier, *L'accueil* 257 does not mention any peculiarities of the French version for cc. 26-27; a re-examination of the Paris MS would however be indicated.

trust the report of Franciscus de Albano (102), the council seems to have been asked specifically to curb the activities of the travelling merchants from Florence, Siena, Pistoja, Lucca, and Asti. At any rate, W tallies with the heretofore unexplained observation made by the Chronicler of Parma on a postconciliar change in the wording and scope of the statute: *et fuit ibi ordinatum quod nullus usurarius staret nisi in sua civitate, de quo concilium nichil scivit* (103).

c) In the conciliar text, excommunication was threatened indiscriminately to all (104) who rent or lease (105) houses to usurers (var. 6); in R, the corresponding prohibition (var. 2) does not contain a penal clause of its own, but is shifted before the general paragraph on censures and sanctions (var. 3-5); consequently it is covered by the same differentiation of censures which applies to other infringements of the statute: suspension for bishops etc., interdict for collegiate bodies, excommunication for individuals beneath episcopal rank.

d) In the section on testamentary restitution, the original draft gave to the Ordinary alone the power to establish the amount of the *cautio* (by surety, mortgage, etc. (106)) to be pledged in the case of indeterminate sums of usury (var. 10); R extends this power to all persons who are entitled to accept the pledge (*recipiens cautionem huiusmodi*), that is (107), the

---

(102) Quoted by Joh. Andreae ad h. c. (*Sext.* 5.5.1) pr.: *Dicit Franc. quod haec constitutio facta fuit propter Florentinos, Senenses rell.* The passage remains to be verified in the *Lectura* of Franciscus, MS St.-Omer 446, discovered by Fournier (*Questions d'hist.* 17 ff.).

(103) *Chronicon Parmense* ed. G. Bonazzi (*Rer. ital. script.*^{2} 9 ix; Città di Castello 1902) p. 30. In Muratori's edition (*Rer. it. script.* 9, 787) the crucial word *nisi* was omitted; the passage therefore remained incomprehensible to Finke, *Konzilienstudien* 10 n. 1.

(104) Including bishops, since Innocent IV's c. *Quia periculosum* (I *Conc. Lugd.* c. 22; *Sext.* 5. 11. 4) exempted them only from incurring general censures of interdict and suspension: to be included in a law threatening *ipso facto* excommunication, they need not be expressly named. (On the genesis of this canon see Kuttner, *Die Konstitutionen* [n. 2 *supra*] 107 f.).

(105) For the interpretation of *sub alio titulo concedat* see Joh. Andreae's gloss ad loc. (*Sext.* 5. 5. 1).

(106) Cf. Durantis ad c. *Quamquam* v. *idonee* (ed. Maiolus fol. 94v); Joh. Andreae *ad loc.* (*Sext.* 5. 5. 2.)

(107) The persons mentioned above are all named in the law; nevertheless Durantis ad v. *huius<modi>* writes: *scil. ordinarii qui est iudex in hoc casu* (ed. Maiolus *ibid.*). This interpretation is wrong.

bishop's vicar, the parish rector, or — with the Ordinary's mandate — the public notary (108).

e) The final provision of W against refractory religious and other ecclesiastics (var. 11) has been thoroughly reworded in the official text of c. 27. The verbal change from *pene predicti* <*concilii*> to *pene in Lateranensi concilio contra usurarios promulgate* became necessary once the original text of the statute was cut in two (in W, *predicti* refers back to the very beginning of c. *Usurarum* (109), which in R has become part of c. 26). Other changes, however, are of more substantial importance. In W, ecclesiastics are threatened with punishment, i. e. suspension (110), for admitting to the sacraments the usurer who has not made restitution or given the formal *cautio*, as well as for admitting his body to ecclesiastical burial; R restricts the censure (111) to the latter case while merely prohibiting, without a penal clause, the admittance of such a usurer to the sacrament of penance (communion is not mentioned, as self-evident). On the other hand, in the same sentence R not only forbids ecclesiastics to be present at the drawing of the usurer's will, but also adds a new clause invalidating the will itself if it should be made contrary to the provisions of the present statute. It is not without historical interest to note that this drastic measure, which was to give rise to much controversy — does the Church, outside the Papal States, have jurisdiction to declare testaments legally void (112)? — should have been absent from the conciliar text.

Religionum (113)

R c. 23	W fol. 7va-8ra
Sed quia non solum importuna petentium...	[1] Sed quia importuna petentium ...

(108) The statute uses the term *servus publicus*, on which see Durantis and Joh. Andreae *ad loc.*
(109) *Usurarum uoraginem... compescere cupientes constitutionem Lateranensis concilij contra usurarios editam... precipimus inuiolabiliter obseruari.* The reference is to c. *Quia in omnibus* (III Conc. Lat. c. 25; X 5. 19. 3).
(110) Cf. *Conc. Lat. cit.*
(111) Later increased to excommunication by Clement V: cf. *Clem.* 3. 7. 1.
(112) See the discussion in Durantis *ad loc.* (ed. Maiolus fol. 97v). For later, local re-enactments of the rule see T. McLaughlin. *The Teaching of the Canonists on Usury*, in Mediaeval Studies 2 (1940) 7 n. 74.
(113) Rg 247b-248a; [1] Rr 101bE, Rm 96D; [2] Rr 102aA, Rm 97A; [3] Rr 102aB, Rm 97B; [4-5] Rr 102aC, Rm 97C-D.

et quatenus processerant...	[2]	...et que processerant *a)*... *a)* precesserant W
nec de novo domum aut aliquem locum acquirant, nec domos seu loca que habent alienare valeant...	[3]	nec domos seu loca alia emant *a)* nec huiusmodi alienare ualeant... *a)* nec — emant *super ras.* W
Personis quoque ipsorum ordinum omnino interdicimus, quoad extraneos, predicationis et audiende confessionis officium aut etiam sepulturam.	[4]	Personis quoque *a)* ipsorum ordinum omnino predicationis *b)* et audiende confessionis officium nec non uel admittendi extraneos ad sepulturam aliquos interdicimus facultatem. *a)* Personas quorumcumque W *b)* predicantes W
Carmelitarum et Eremitarum s. Augustini ordines, quorum institutio dictum concilium generale precessit...	[5]	Carmelitarum et Heremitarum s. Augustini ordines, qui se asserunt ante dictum concilium institutos...

While the critical value of the first four variants is not above suspicion (114), var. 5 shows that at the time of the council (*sess.* VI) the pope's attitude towards the Carmelites and Austin Friars was much more reserved than when the final text was formulated: the origin of the two orders before the decisive date, the IV Lateran Council (1215), is presented as an allegation (*qui se asserunt*) in W, but as a fact in R. We know that Gregory X had sweeping plans of union with regard to religious and military orders in general (115); the reference to future plans was later eliminated from c. *Religionum* by Boniface VIII (*Sext.* 3. 17. 1), who also changed the provisional toleration of the Carmelites and Augustinians to definite approval (116).

(114) In var. 1, for instance, the omission of *non solum* may be a blunder, as is the distortion of the corresponding *uerum etiam* (which follows in the same sentence) into *metum autem*.

(115) See the several chronicles cited in Martin, *Conc. et bull. de Lyon* nn. 1818-9; also Joh. Andreae *ad loc.* (*Sext.* 3. 17. 1) v. *in solido*.

(116) RW: *Carmelitarum et Eremitarum... ordines... in suo statu manere concedimus, donec de ipsis fuerit aliter ordinatum. Intendimus siquidem tam de illis quam de reliquis... prouidere.* Bonif. VIII: *...in solido statu volumus permanere* (om. *donec — prouidere*). According to Friedberg's edition, *Corp. iur. can.* II, 1055 n. 7 ad loc., the oldest MS of the *Sextus* collated by him (A = Troyes 1716, ol. Clairvaux L. 22, dated 1301 A. D.; cf. *proleg.* col. lii) retains however the original text

Ut circa (117)

R c. 3

si quando aliqui electionibus, postulationibus vel provisionibus se opponunt, proponendo aliqua contra electionis, postulationis seu provisionis formam aut personas eligentium vel electi sive illius cui provisio erat facienda vel facta, et propter...

in huiusmodi litteris vel instrumentis...

potestatem sibi noverint interdictam...

super antiquis supervenerit probandi facultas aut aliqua antiqua in opponentium notitiam de novo pervenerint...

quod ad ea probanda se credunt sufficientes probationes habere. Illa sane que felicis recordationis Innocentius papa IIII contra non plene probantes ea que in formam vel personam obiecerant statuit, in suo volumus robore permanere.

W fol. 8va-b

[1] si quando aliqui electionibus, postulationibus uel prouisionibus huiusmodi se opponunt, proponendo *a)* uel opponendo aliqua contra electionis formam aut personas eligentium uel electi, et propter...

a) om. W

[2] in instrumentis et litteris supradictis...

[3] potestatem suam nouerint interdictam...

[4] super antiquis superuenerit probandi facultas aut eadem antiqua in opponentium noticiam de nouo peruenerint...

[5] quod ad ea probanda credunt se sufficientes. Hijs que *a)* per felicis recordationis Innocentium papam .iiij. contra non plene probantes ea que in formam uel personam obiecerunt statuta sunt, *b)* in suo robore duraturis *c)*.

a) queque *W* (quoque que *scr.?*)
b) stat. sunt *om. W*   *c)* duratur *W*

Avaritiae (118)

R c. 4

damnande ambitionis...

sub yconomatus vel procurationis nomine...

W fol. 8vb-9ra

[1] dampnose ambicionis...

[2] yconomatus uel procurationis nomine...

---

of R. This is all the more puzzling since the *Glossa ordinaria* of Joh. Andreae, completed probably in the same year 1301 (Gillmann, in *Archiv für kath. Kirchenrecht* 104 [1924] 55 n. 4), gives already a detailed account of the revision of the text (v. *in solido*).

(117) Rg 243b; [1] Rr 97bA, Rm 86B; [2-4] Rr 97bB, Rm 86C-D; [5] Rr 97C, Rm 86D-E. The reference in var. 5 is to I *Conc. Lugd. c. 4 Statuimus (Sext. 1. 6. 1).*
(118) Rg 243b-244a; [1] Rr 97bD, Rm 86E; [2] Rr 97bE, Rm 87B.

XII

Quam sit ecclesiis (119)

R c. 5		W fol. 9ra-b
electores... petere consensum ipsius, electus vero illum adhibere...	[1]	electores... petere consensum ipsius, electi consensum uero habere...
iure, si quod ei ex sua electione fuerat acquisitum...	[2]	interim *a)* si qua ex sua electione fuerint acquisita... *a)* intim W
nisi forsan ea sit electe persone conditio ut electioni de se celebrate absque superioris sui licentia, ex prohibitione seu quavis provisione sedis apostolice, consentire non possit.	[3]	nisi forsan talis sit electe persone conditio quod electioni *a)* de se celebrate absque superioris sui licentia consentire non possit. *a)* electionem W
infra huiusmodi trimestre tempus...	[4]	infra tale tempus...

Among the readings in W for cc. 3-5 some remain doubtful, and only in one case does the difference between the two texts amount to more than a revision of style; speaking of persons who need a permission to accept an election, the conciliar text of c. 5 (var. 3) contemplated only the *licentia superioris*, i. e. the case of religious or regulars, where the common law restricts the freedom of accepting any office (120); R adds the words, *ex prohibitione rell.* and thereby includes all cases where a permission is needed by a special provision of the Holy See.

The remaining statutes offer in W only corrupt readings, one of which may be cited here as an illustration of the many pitfalls in our MS:

Perpetuae (121)

R c. 6	W fol. 9rb-va
nisi adeo in eo perstiterint quod ex votis eorum comunis electio subsequatur, nequa-	nisi adeo in ea perstiterint quod ex uotis eorum communis electio subsequeretur *a)* ne-

---

(119) Rg 244a; [1] Rr 98aA, Rm 87C; [2-3] Rr 98aB, Rm 87D; [4] Rr 98aC, Rm 88A.
(120) Cf. Grat. D. 58; C. 16 q. 1 cc. 28, 33, 34.
(121) Rg 244a; Rr 98aD; Rm 88A-B.

quam eligendi potestate privantur, licet pro eo quod indignum nominando scienter contra conscientias suas agunt...	quaquam eligendi potestatem de cetero habeant pro eo quod indignum nominando scienter contra conscientias suas agunt...
	a) subsequaretur *W*

The possibility suggested at first sight by the reading of W — viz. that the council may have originally planned to deprive of their rights all electors who knowingly nominate an unworthy candidate — is ruled out by the *nisi*-clause, which in this case would mean that the electors retain their right precisely in the worst of contingencies, namely when through their insistence the unworthy candidate is actually elected. The reading, *nequaquam... potestatem de cetero habeant,* is therefore to be rejected.

Nulli licere
Si quando
Quamvis constitutio
(R cc. 7-9, W fol. 9va-b: no genuine variants) (122)

VI.

To sum up: notwithstanding its incompleteness and textual deficiencies, the Washington MS is a document of uncommon value. It affords an opportunity, rare in the history of medieval legislation, of catching a glimpse of conciliar law in the making. W shows that changes were made in the wording of many statutes during the months which elapsed between promulgation and publication, and in some instances these changes prove to be of no slight importance. This is particularly true of the great statute on the conclave and of that on usury; in the case of the former the divergencies between the published text and the conciliar original could have been known long ago, had the bishops' *cedulae* in the Vatican Archives ever been properly examined. Our MS is equally important for the reconstruction of the unpublished decree of

---

(122) What appears at first sight to be a variant in c. *Quamvis* (Rg 244b: *ceterum in premissis casibus...*; W fol. 9 vb: *ceterum in omnibus prem. cas.*) is actually a mistake in Guiraud's edition: the word *omnibus* does occur in R, though with a slight inversion (*...in prem. omn. cas.:* Rr 98bC, Rm 89B; *Sext.* I. 6. 10).

the second session, especially for restoring the list of nations to be represented at the council by proctors.

A critical edition of the Lyonese constitutions, reproducing both the conciliar and the official text, would be highly desirable. But before such an edition can be undertaken, a better copy, unmarred by the contaminations of W, would have to be found for the conciliar form. (In the case of *Ubi periculum*, of course, the Vatican originals will be decisive). A systematic search among the many MSS of the *constitutiones novissimae* of Gregory X may yield more than one copy which gives the statutes in the order of promulgation as reported by the *Brevis nota*: the MSS recorded in catalogues or otherwise have never been examined in this respect (123). Yet there can be little doubt that texts representing the order of BN were known in the Middle Ages: a faint echo of it can be found, e. g., in the Chronicle of St. Peter's of Erfurt (124). Any such copy would presumably present the readings which underlie W and, if it be complete, wold satisfy our curiosity as to some of the statutes that are omitted or lost in the latter: notably, the canon *Fideli* (*Cum sacrosancta*) on the procession of the Holy Ghost; or c. 19 *Properandum*, which, as we know from Durantis, aroused violent opposition among the advocates of the Curia (125) and was later omitted by Boniface VIII from the *Liber Sextus*; or c. 24 *Exigit perversorum*, of which we may now assume that the initium *Exigit multorum* given by BN is not merely a bad reading (126). Some MS may also yield the Latin text of the arenga *Testimonium Joseph* for c. 22 *Hoc consultissimo* and thus lead us to an even earlier stage of redaction than that of BN and the archetype of W.

A future editor would finally have to collate the text of

---

(123) One may assume that Finke would not have failed to notice any unusual order in the Osnabrück MS (nn. 35-6 *supra*).

(124) *Cronica S. Petri Erfordensis moderna*, ed. Holder-Egger (*Monumenta Erphesfurtensia saec. XII. XIII. XIV.* in MGH *Script. rer. germ.* in-8°, Hannover-Leipzig 1899) pp. 264 ff. The chronicler reports on the Lyonese legislation in the following order: *Zelus fidei* (sess. II; Holder-Egger 265 n. 1 observes that the chronicler may have known the text); cc. 23 (sess. VI), 15, 19, 24 (sess. III; cf. BN: 19, 15, 24) and 23 again; cc. 2, 17, 20 (sess. V; cf. BN: 2, 10, 17, 20) and 17 again; cc. 16, 26, 27, 22 (same session; cf. BN: 16, 25, 26, 27, 22).

(125) Cf. Durantis ad c. *Properandum*. v. *qui autem*: ...*ex quo uidimus aduocatos curiae in promulgatione huius constitutionis grauissime perturbari*... (ed. Maiolus fol 69r; cf. Maiolus' observations in his introduction, fol. **1v).

(126) *Ed. Rom.* 4, 84aE; Mansi 24, 64B; Mss V and O (n. 14 *supra*).

R (*Infrascriptas*) with the best among the numerous MSS of the collection sent to the universities (*Cum nuper*). Friedberg's critical apparatus to the pertinent chapters in the *Liber Sextus* includes readings of five arbitrarily selected copies of *Cum nuper* and is far from reliable. But even there, definite traces of the conciliar text as represented by W can be found; what is more, in some instances such readings appear in the *Liber Sextus* itself (127):

Ubi periculum
(R c. 2; *Sext.* 1. 6. 3)

[var. 5 *supra*] seu antea *Hbcd Sc cum R*, seu ante *S*, om. *He cum W* (cf. *Friedb. 947 n. 11 ad loc.*)

[10] Quod si forte in premissis *rell.* innodati *Hbcd cum R*, Quod si premissa *rell.* incurrant *Hae S cum W* (*om. v.* dignitatis, *quod tamen legitur in cod. Berol.*) (128) (cf. *Friedb. 948 nn. q, r ad loc.*)

Quicumque
(R c. 31; *Sext.* 5. 11. 11)

[1] in excommunicationis sententiam incidant (-unt *He*) ipso facto *Habde cum R*, eo ipso (ipso facto *Hc Sc*) sententiam excommunicationis incurrant *Hc S cum W* (cf. *Friedb. 1102 nn. 4, c ad loc.*) (129)

[2] suo motu *Hbc S cum R*, sua manu *Ha*, per se ipsos *Hd cum W*, om. *He* (cf. *Friedb. ibid. n. e*)

Decet domum
(R c. 25; *Sext.* 3. 23. 2)

[1] flectant genua *rell.* testentur *Habcd S cum R*, flectant corporis si id patiatur facultas *add. He Sa; cf.* W (cf. *Friedb. 1061 n. 5 ad loc.*)

(127) MSS used by Friedberg for Gregory X's collection: Munich *lat.* 14011 (= Ha), Breslau II. F. 30 (= Hb), Erlangen 464 (now MS 350; = Hc), Munich *lat.* 3202 (= Hd), Leipzig, Univ. 980 (= He). Cf. *Corpus iur. can.* II, *proleg.* coll. lv and lxxi-ii (at the latter place, Hd is erroneously given as *Monac. lat.* 539). Friedberg's references to Mansi (= Hf) are not pertinent for our purpose. As to his MSS of the *Sextus*, only Troyes 1716 (= A; cf. n. 116 *supra*) and Munich *lat.* 329 (= C) offer variants in the places discussed above. It should however be noted that Friedberg has made no complete collation of C, cf. *proleg.* col. lii. The reading of the *Sextus* and the two MSS will be given above with the sigla S, Sa, and Sc respectively.

(128) I. H. Boehmer, *loc. cit.* (n. 4 *supra*): variants from *Cod. Berol.* II (cf. his *proleg.* p. xxx), which today is MS Berlin *lat. fol.* 7.

(129) Friedberg's notation is not very clear, and demonstrably wrong as regards the word order: according to him, *Habde* and Mansi would read: *ipso facto in exc. sent. inc.* This is not true for Mansi (R), hence hardly true for *Habde*.

Ut circa
(R c. 3; *Sext.* 1. 6. 4)

[1] provisionibus *Hbcd S cum R*, huiusmodi add. *Hae cum W* (*cf. Friedb. 949 n. c ad loc.*)

Trifling as these data may seem, they suffice to demonstrate (see esp. *Ubi periculum* var. 10 and *Quicumque* var. 1) that the compilers of Boniface VIII's collection did not simply follow the papal register for the text of the Lyonese statutes. What sources they actually employed is a question of great interest, but it would be hazardous to attempt an answer on the narrow basis of MS evidence afforded in Friedberg's edition. And how, for instance, should one interpret the fact that precisely the oldest MS thus far examined of the *Liber Sextus* (130) repeats in c. *Decet domum* a clause which had been definitely discarded in R? Given the present state of our knowledge, one has to be satisfied with the observation that the genesis of the *Liber Sextus* remains largely unexplored. By investigating the transmission of the original, conciliar form of Pope Gregory X's Lyonese legislation, one may hope to solve at least some of the intricate problems in this promising field of research.

(130) Sa (= A). On its age and another obsolete reading it offers (in c. *Religionum*) see n. 116 *supra*.

Additional Note. After the present paper had been set up in print, the writer obtained from the Bibliothèque nationale photostats of the old French translation contained in Ms *Par. fr.* 491, fol. 295v-302v (cf. *supra* at nn. 50-53, 80, 98, 101). Its order of statutes is based on an interlacing juxtaposition of BN *sess.* V, III, and VI:

V: 2   10, 11   20, 17, 28, 31, 12, 16; 25-27; 22
III: 3-9   19, 15   24, 29, 30
VI: 23

The two missing canons (21 and 1) would have come to stand at the end, being the last ones of *sess.* V and VI respectively. Only the sequence of BN *sess.* V cc. 10, 17, 20, 11 (W: 10, 11, 17, 20) has been inverted. The French text of each statute is preceded by a Latin initium; note that the lemma for c. 24 is given as *Exigit multorum* (= BN), not *Exigit perversorum* (cf. n. 126 *supra*). On the otherwise lost arenga *Testimonium* for c. 22 see n. 98 *supra;* but cc. 26 *Usurarum* and 27 *Quamquam* are already separated.

The readings of W are represented in the translation of cc. 2 *Ubi periculum* (var. 3 has also the word *gourdine* = *cortina*, like W; var. 4 has the words *v a aucun diaus* = *vel eorum alicui*, like A: cf. n. 79 *supra*); 10 *Si forte;* 17 *Si canonici* (but our suspicion against the variant *testimonio* is confirmed by the French

CONCILIAR LAW IN THE MAKING 81

estrument); 31 *Quicumque* var. 2; 12 *Generali* var. 2; 25 *Decet domum* var. 1 *(flekissent... dou kief tesmoignent, flekissent encore dou cors se pooirs celi cose suefre:* position as in *He Sa,* see preceding page); 23 *Religionum* var. 4; 3 *Ut circa* var. 2, 4; 5 *Quam sit ecclesiis* var. 3.

In other cases, *cod. Par.* sides with R: cc. 20 *Absolutionis;* 31 var. 1; 12 var. 1; 25 var. 2-3; 26 and 27 (all except var. 9; *et gouuerneeur le caucion de tel manere,* as in W); 23 var. 1-2; 3 var. 1, 3, 5; 4 *Avaritiae;* 5 var. 1, 2, 4; 6 *Perpetuae.* Some cases remain uncertain: cc. 22 *Testimonium* = *Hoc consultissimo* (var. 1 *par .iij. ans Nos estaulisons estre souspendus* may be either W or R; the entire sentence in which var. 2 occurs is missing); 23 *Religionum* (var. 3: *ne de nouel maison v aucun liu naquierent ne maisons v lius* [= R] *de tell manjere* [= *huiusmodi* W] *estrangier puissent;* var. 5: the French equivalent of either relative clause [*quorum... precessit* R, *qui se... institutos* W] is missing, the entire context in *cod. Par.* being contaminated).

XIII

THE DATE OF THE CONSTITUTION « SAEPE », THE VATICAN MANUSCRIPTS AND THE ROMAN EDITION OF THE CLEMENTINES

The constitution *Saepe contingit* of Pope Clement V (1305-1314) is commonly recognized as the most important single piece of medieval legislation in the history of summary judicial procedure. A century and a half of complex developments — in papal responses, in statutory enactments, and in the often conflicting teachings of the glossators of both the civil and the canon law — had left a great number of ambiguities in the practical application of those procedures that were distinguished from the regular *ordo iudiciorum* as *de plano, summatim* or *simpliciter cognoscere, sine iudiciorum strepitu, sine forma iudicii,* or by similiar terms.[1] The constitution *Saepe* fixed once and for all the meaning of these clauses in a unified doctrine: henceforth the formalities that remained necessary and those that could be dispensed with in summary procedure were clearly defined for the theory and practice of both laws.

Given the historical importance of the constitution, it is all the more astonishing that by a quirk of textual transmission an erroneous notion on the time of its enactment should have prevailed among scholars for centuries. *Saepe contingit* forms the concluding chapter of the *Constitutiones Clementinae* (tit. *De verborum significatione,* 5. 11. 2); and in the official Roman edition of the *Corpus iuris canonici* (1582) it appears with the date appended, " Data Avinione xiij. Kalen. Decembris, Pontificatus nostri anno secundo ". Accordingly, students of the history of civil procedure by and large have placed the constitution in Pope Clement's second year, 19

---

[1] The stages of this development are discussed by CH. LEFEBVRE, *Les origines romaines de la procédure sommaire aux XII et XIII s.,* in *Ephemerides Iuris Canonici,* t. 12 (1956), pp. 149-197.

November 1306, without giving any thought to several obvious reasons why this cannot be true.² For one, the purported date is impossible in itself: Clement V did not take up residence at Avignon before 1309. The autumn of 1306 he spent mostly in Bordeaux and places close by; nearly all the letters of the second half of November that year were given from his native town of Villandraut.³ Furthermore, the constitution *Saepe* specifically refers back to an *alia constitutio nostra* concerning cases of summary procedure: this is the decree *Dispendiosam* which, as has always been known from the testimony of Johannes Andreae, was first promulgated at the Council of Vienne (1311-12).⁴ More precisely, the findings of Franz Ehrle and Ewald Müller have established that *Dispendiosam* belonged to a set of reform measures enacted in the third session of the Council on 6 May 1312.⁵

I.

With this day as *terminus a quo*, the problem of the date of *Saepe contingit* becomes part of the complicated post-conciliar history of the Clementine legislation. Between the close of the Council and the day when John XXII definitively published the *constitutiones plurimae* which his predecessor had issued " nedum in concilio Viennensi, quin etiam ante et post ipsum concilium ",⁶ a process of law-making repeated itself for which Innocent IV at the first, and Gregory X at the second Council of Lyons had set the pattern: the " promulgation " in council as a preliminary stage, subject to alterations and additions, until the final text of what the pope wishes to be regarded as legislative work of the council is released

---

² For a select list of manuals and treatises on canonical procedure giving the wrong date (if any), see LEFEBVRE, *op. cit.*, p. 149 n. 3, p. 151 n. 8. This includes even L. WAHRMUND'S editions of the treatises of Johannes Fasolus and Johannes de Lignano on summary procedure, in *Quellen zur Geschichte des römisch-kanonischen Prozesses im Mittelalter*, t. 4, Innsbruck 1925-1928, fasc. 5, p. xv; fasc. 6, pp. xii, xvii-xviii.

³ See the Benedictine edition of the *Regestum Clementis papae V*, Rome 1885-1892, Nos. 1517 ff. and the itinerary in R. FAWTIER and Y. LANHERS, *Tables des Registres de Clément V*, Paris 1948, p. 2.

⁴ JOH. ANDREAE, *Glossa ordinaria*, *Clem.* 5. 11. 2 v. *Saepe*. This was briefly pointed out by LEFEBVRE, *op. cit.* p. 149 n. 3.

⁵ Cf. F. EHRLE, *Ein Bruchstück der Acten des Concils von Vienne*, in *Archiv für Literatur- und Kirchengeschichte des Mittelalters*, t. 4 (1888), pp. 442, 462; E. MÜLLER, *Das Konzil von Vienne 1311-1312* (= Vorreformationsgeschichtliche Forschungen 12), Münster 1934, pp. 490, 626.

⁶ JOHN XXII, *Quoniam nulla*, 1 Nov. 1317 (*prooem. Clem.*).

The date of the constitution « Saepe »

in the form of a topical collection, by "publication" to the universities.[7] But what had taken only a few weeks in Lyons, 1245, and a few months in 1274, was to drag on for years after the Council of Vienne. While the post-conciliar commission charged with revising and completing the decrees [8] was engaged in its task, unauthorized versions had already been put in circulation; the finished product of the commission's labors was ready for publication by 21 March 1314, when Clement V had read it out at a public consistory in Monteux. But before the publication could be completed by distributing copies of the collected *Constitutiones* to the universities, the Pope died on 20 April. With grave doubts remaining, among canonists and at the curia, as to whether or not the collection had been published with legally binding force,[9] Pope John XXII

---

[7] Cf. S. KUTTNER, *Die Konstitutionen des ersten allgemeinen Konzils von Lyon*, in *Studia et Documenta historiae et iuris*, t. 6 (1940), pp. 70-131, esp. 91-110; *Conciliar Law in the Making*, in *Miscellanea Pio Paschini* (= Lateranum 15), Rome 1949, t. 2, pp. 39-81, esp. 41-54.

[8] P. VIOLLET, *Guillaume de Mandagout, Canoniste*, in *Histoire littéraire de la France*, t. 34 (1914), pp. 22, 60, accepts at its face value the assertion of the 17th-century writer MARCELIN FORNIER (*Histoire générale des Alpes Maritimes...*, ed. P. Guillaume, t. 2, Paris 1890, p. 111) that the revision of the decrees was entrusted to Guillaume de Mandagout. Viollet assumes that Fornier "très probablement" utilized a "témoignage contemporain de grande valeur, aujourd'hui perdu", the report of the redactor of the Cartulary of Embrun, and considers it intrinsically very convincing, since Guillaume had been one of the compilers of the *Liber Sextus*; admitting, however, that he might not have been the only one in charge of revising the decrees of Clement. The argument, based on the mere probability of Fornier's having used a 14th-century source of uncertain and unascertainable contents, is rather thin. Even if we assume that the redactor of the Embrun Cartulary said what he is supposed to have said, his information may have stemmed from the same error which we find in the title of the incunable GW 7091 (HR 5409, Rome 1478) of the Clementines (fol. 1v): "Compilatores huius libri fuerunt Guil'. Mandagoti episcopus Ebredunen̄. Et Berengarius episcopus Burdegalen̄. alias Biturien̄. postea Cardinalis, ut per Jo. an. in addi. specu. in quarta parte in ti. de electio". This title is based on a misconstruction of the passage where Johannes Andreae speaks of Guillaume de Mandagout's *Libellus de electionibus* and continues: "... quem libellum ... in quantum nova iura illum secuta, scil. Sexti, cuius praedicti ambo compilatores fuerunt, et Clementinarum, exigunt, brevissime reformavit (*leg.* reformavi?) ..." (*Additiones in Speculum* 4. 1 *de elect.*; ed. Venice 1577, t. 4, p. 83b. The emendation "reformavi" is Schulte's and has much to recommend it, cf. VIOLLET, *op. cit.* p. 53). One can see how an omission of the comma after "fuerunt" would cause the error of GW 7091. As for Pope Clement's commission, Joh. Andreae merely speaks of "per peritiores fecit illas recenseri" (*Glos. ord. Clem., prooem. v. de cetero*).

[9] *Glos. ord. loc. cit.*

more than three years later undertook the definitive publication in the usual form by sending it, after a few minor revisions,[10] to the universities on 1 November 1317 with his bull, *Quoniam nulla*.[11]

The question, then, is at which point in this long-drawn process the constitution *Saepe* was inserted in the Clementines for the purpose of determining by an authentic declaration the nature of the summary procedures that were envisaged in the constitution *Dispendiosam* as well as in other cases. It seems that the form in which *Dispendiosam* appears in *Clem.* 2. 1. 2 was already the result of post-conciliar revision of the original decree;[12] and *Saepe* must have been added at a late stage, as may be surmised from the fact that it was placed, not in the title *De iudiciis* behind the conciliar text which it interprets, but at the very end of the Clementines, under the catch-all title *De verborum significatione*. The most interesting piece of information on the genesis of *Saepe contingit*, however, comes from the pen of Johannes Andreae, who states in the *Glossa ordinaria* that it was he himself who had urged the enactment of such a *constitutio declaratoria* when the text of *Dispendiosam* became known:[13]

... hanc constitutionem verborum blanditiis non egentem glossandam aggredior: de cuius causa impulsiva pars fui. Ex quo enim scivi mandasse concilium Viennense, supra de iudiciis, Dispendiosam, existimans non tantum utile sed summe necessarium, verba de quibus hic loquimur declarari, dominos ac peritos curiae sollicitavi saepius pro constitutione declaratoria procuranda, quae desiderata se nunc exhibet.

---

[10] *Ibid.*: "... et aliquas correxit et mutavit". E. FRIEDBERG, *Prolegomena*, in *Corpus iuris canonici*, t. 2 (Leipzig 1881), col. lx-lxii, remains skeptical.

[11] On the date see *infra*, nn. 28-30. — The fullest study of the legislative history of the Clementines is that of MÜLLER, *Das Konzil von Vienne* (n. 5 *supra*), pp. 387-408, with bibliography. The *Dissertatiuncula de Concilio Viennensi* of PIETRO BALLERINI, in his *Vindiciae juris divini ac naturalis circa usuram, quae veluti liber septimus haberi possunt...* (= De jure divino et naturali circa usuram libri sex ... t. 2), Bologna 1747, pp. 66-77, is generally forgotten but still worth reading.

[12] JOH. ANDREAE, *Glos. ord.* is silent on this, but two independent sources — the account of Card. Jacobus Stefaneschi and the anonymous notes on Vienne of Munich MS lat. 2699 — mention a conciliar decree on summary procedure only for litigation concerning episcopal elections and benefices, whereas the text of *Clem.* 2. 1. 2 adds matrimonial cases and suits on tithes and usury. Cf. MÜLLER, *op. cit.* pp. 490 f., 626 f.

[13] *Glos. ord. Clem.* 5. 11. 2 v. *Saepe*.

He does not reveal the source of his knowledge of the earlier decree, but the expression " ex quo enim scivi mandasse concilium Viennense " points in all likelihood to his having seen one of the unauthorized copies of the decrees that were circulated, according to his own testimony, soon after the Council.[14]

In any event, his démarche must have been successful before Pope Clement's commission finished its work and before publication of the *Constitutiones* was initiated in the consistory of 21 March 1314. Or is it possible, as E. Müller has cautiously suggested,[15] that *Saepe* was a later addition and that it was not issued by Clement V at all? Certainly John XXII cannot have been its author: even if *Saepe* appears without inscription in some manuscripts,[16] none but Pope Clement was in a position to speak in it of *Dispendiosam* as " alia constitutio nostra "; also, the three known copies of the Clementines which remain as witnesses of the publication initiated at Monteux — that is, the three copies which begin with Clement's preamble *Cum nuper*[17] — all contain the constitution *Saepe*,[18] and this ought to rule out the remote possibility of the latter's having been drafted during the few weeks between the consistory and the Pope's death. Even if one were not satisfied with the evidence of these manuscripts — and it must be admitted that at least two, perhaps even all of them, show signs of contamination with the vulgate (Johannine) text[19] — the possibility of a post-consistorial addition could be argued only if there existed any hint of such a procedure in the general account which Johannes Andreae gives of the making of the Clementines, or in the passage where he speaks of the genesis of *Saepe contingit* in particular.[20]

Johannes Andreae knew of the " publication " of the collected

---

[14] *Ibid. prooem.* v. *de cetero*: "... tamen postea de facto fuerunt publicatae...".

[15] *Das Konzil von Vienne*, p. 627.

[16] Thus FRIEDBERG's MSS ADEG, cf. his note 1 *ad loc.*

[17] Marburg C. 3 (= Friedberg's B), Chartres 275 (ol. 318; =F), Kassel jur. 15 (=G); cf. FRIEDBERG, *Proleg.* col. lx, lxii; H. DENIFLE, *Chartularium Universitatis Parisiensis*, t. 2, Paris 1891, No. 708, p. 169. MS Chartres 275 has escaped complete destruction in World War II: according to the classification in *Manuscrits des bibliothèques sinistrées de 1940 à 1944* (= Catalogue général..., t. 53, Paris 1962), it belongs to the category of MSS " dont on a retrouvé des restes en très bon état ou en bon état, presque complet ". (Information kindly supplied by Mlle. Vielliard).

[18] This point has been made, although not in very clear terms, by LEFEBVRE, *Les origines romaines* (n. 1 *supra*), p. 149 n. 3.

[19] See Excursus A, *infra*.

[20] *Glos. ord. Clem., prooem.* v. *de cetero* and 5. 11. 2 v. *Saepe*.

constitutiones in the consistory;[21] he had seen a copy or copies of the text with the preamble *Cum nuper*;[22] and he was personally involved in the antecedents of the constitution *Saepe*. Evidently he took a special interest in this *constitutio declaratoria* of which he considered himself the intellectual father. In the *Glossa ordinaria* on the Clementines he introduces his comments on *Saepe* with a little preface of its own,[23] and this rather unusual form of presentation strongly suggests that he wrote and published these glosses separately, before completing and publishing in 1322 the *apparatus* on the whole body of the Clementine constitutions.[24] This is indeed asserted in the subscription of the Vatican MS Ross. lat. 591 (*Clementinae* with *glos. ord.*; saec. xiv), which must be based on some concrete historical information, even though the scribe puts down at the end a patently wrong figure for the year of completion:

Explicit apparatus domini Johannis Andree doctoris decretorum super clementinis. Et hanc glossam super ista decretali ' sepe ' publicauit in scolis publice legendo dictam decretalem. set istum apparatum sub anno (ānis MS?) domini M.CCC°XXIX. die prima mensis Martij. (fol. 67vb).

Given all these circumstances, we may safely use an *argumentum ex silentio* for corroborating the evidence of the three " Monteux " manuscripts: if *Saepe* had been of post-consistorial making, Johannes Andreae would not have failed to say so. The constitution must therefore be dated between 6 May 1312 and 21 March 1314, probably closer to the later date.

---

[21] *Gl.* v. *de cetero*.

[22] *Gl. prooem.* v. *Quoniam nulla*: " Est sciendum quod Clemens suo exordio ad instar Innocentii iiij. et Gregorii x. narrabat...".

[23] *Gl.* v. *Saepe*: " Quoniam secundum Quintilianum lib. 7 de oratoria institutione, 'optimarum rerum inventio, et si lenociniis verborum destituta sit, ipsa tamen sui natura satis ornatur' (*Inst. or.* 12. 1. 30), cui bene convenit ff. de in integ. restit. l. i. in princ. (*Dig.* 4. 1. 1), hanc constitutionem verborum blanditiis non egentem glossandam aggredior...".

[24] For the date see H. DENIFLE, *Die Entstehung der Universitäten des Mittelalters bis 1400*, Berlin 1885, p. 443 n. 915, correcting J. F. VON SCHULTE, *Die Geschichte der Quellen und Literatur des Canonischen Rechts*, t. 2, Stuttgart 1877, p. 217, where the year 1326 is given. Denifle's argument can still be strengthened by the observation that in the *Glos. ord.* Johannes Andreae makes no use of the *Apparatus* of Jesselin de Cassagnes, completed in 1323 (cf. note 47, *infra*).

II.

When Boniface VIII published the *Liber Sextus*, he had the date of promulgation, " Romae, apud sanctum Petrum, v. Nonas Martii, pontificatus nostri anno quarto ", placed at the very end of the book, after the last of the *Regulae iuris*, rather than affixed to the introductory bull *Sacrosanctae* itself.[25] There were precedents for such terminal dating ever since the days of Innocent IV.[26] With a complex piece of codification such as the Sext, this style served particularly well to bring home the point that the whole mass of statutes and decretals compiled in the book was formally to be considered a single enactment, embedded as it were in the text of the opening letter issued on that day, 3 March 1298.[27] Had John XXII followed the legislative example of Boniface VIII, we could expect to read a date of publication at the end of the Clementines, after the constitution *Saepe*. This time, however, the date was placed immediately after the introductory bull *Quoniam nulla*: " Data Avenione, kal. Novembris pontificatus nostri anno secundo " (1 November 1317).[28] In many manuscripts and in the printed editions this appears with the variant " viii. kal. Novembris " (25 Octo-

---

[25] The date after *De reg. iur.* is provided with ample glosses in JOH. ANDREAE'S *Ordinaria in Sextum*.

[26] For dates at the end of Innocent IV's three collections see P.-J. KESSLER, *Untersuchungen über die Novellen-Gesetzgebung Papst Innozenz' IV.* in *Zeitschrift der Savigny-Stiftung für Rechtsgeschichte*, Kan. Abt. t. 31 (1942), pp. 213 (Coll. I), 238 f. (Coll. II), 202 (Coll. III); for the collection of Gregory X see J. H. BOEHMER, *Corpus iuris canonici*, Halle 1747, t. 2, Appendix, fol. (aa)ᵛ after col. 368; DENIFLE, *Chartul. Univ. Par.* t. 1, Paris 1889, p. 515 n. 1 to No. 449; J. GUIRAUD, *Les registres de Grégoire X*, Paris 1892-1906, No. 576, p. 250. — By contrast, the date of Gregory IX's *Rex pacificus* is known only from the papal register (L. AUVRAY, *Les registres de Grégoire IX*, Paris 1896-1955, No. 2083; POTTHAST No. 9693); it does not appear in the MSS and editions of the Decretals (cf. FRIEDBERG, *Corp. iur. can.* t. 2, col. 1-4; DENIFLE, *Chartul. Univ. Par.* t. 1, p. 154, note to No. 104).

[27] It is commonly taught that the same doctrine underlies already the Decretals of Gregory IX, i. e. that every text in the compilation was to be construed as issued on the day of the bull *Rex pacificus*, 5 September 1234; but the 13th-century canonists did not think so, cf. S. KUTTNER, *Quelques observations sur l'autorité des collections canoniques dans le droit classique de l'Eglise*, in *Actes du Congrès de Droit canonique... Paris, 22-26 Avril 1947*, Paris 1950, p. 311-312.

[28] So Friedberg's codd. AEFH (col. 1131, n. 7 *ad loc.*) and the papal register, cf. A. COULON, *Jean XXII (1316-1334): Lettres secrètes et curiales relatives à la France*, Paris 1906, No. 433.

ber),[29] owing probably to an early error in the manuscript tradition: there is no reason to assume that the Clementines were published for different universities on two different days,[30] or that the official entry in the papal Register is wrong.

In any event, the line we find at the end of the Clementines in the Roman edition, " Data Avinione xiij. Kalen. Decembris, Pontificatus nostri anno secundo ", remains incongruous: as we saw, it cannot refer to *Saepe*, but neither can it be read as a publication date in the Bonifacian style, for the collection had definitely been sent out some weeks before 19 November 1317.

On that day, however, Pope John XXII issued the constitution *Execrabilis*.[31] One of the most important pieces of medieval legislation in the never-ending battle against the cumulation of benefices (and also a powerful instrument of papal reservations), it soon made its appearance among the *extravagantes* which copyists were in the habit of appending to the Clementine corpus. It was promptly taken up by the glossators: When Guillaume de Montlauzun wrote his *Apparatus super Clementinis* in 1319, he supplemented this commentary with an *apparatus* on three major constitutions concerning benefices, from the autumn of Pope John's second year: *Suscepti* (8 kal. Nov.), *Execrabilis* (13 kal. Dec.), *Sedes apostolica* (3 kal. Nov.).[32] A few years later, in 1325, Jesselin de Cassagnes included these three pieces in his collection, with apparatus of glosses, of

---

[29] So Friedberg's CDI, the Roman edition, and all modern manuals of the history of canon law.

[30] This was DENIFLE's assumption, *Chartul. Univ. Par.* t. 2, No. 754, p. 211. But the evidence of Friedberg's MSS suffices to refute it: A and C are addressed to Avignon, yet have different dates; D E H I are addressed to Bologna and likewise differ in their dating, *kal. nov.* or 8 *kal. nov.* — The case of *Quoniam nulla*, then, cannot be compared with the single known instance of double entry of a letter with two different dates in the register of John XXII: *Litteras vestras*, 7 *kal. dec. an.* 2 (COULON, *Lettres secrètes et curiales*, No. 450) and 7 *id. dec.* (No. 455, cf. Coulon's note, col. 367). The other instances Coulon cites, col. 208 and 629, are imaginary: *Salvator noster*, undated (No. 262; but Coulon supplies a false date, 7 *kal. iul. an.* 1, from the 16th-century printing in the *Extravagantes comm.* 3. 2. 5) = 5 *id. iul. an.* 1 (No. 306); *Execrabilis*, 13 *kal. dec. an.* 2 (entered only once in the register, MOLLAT, *Jean XXII (1316-1334)*: *Lettres communes*, Paris 1904-1947, t. 2, No. 8137), same date in *Extrav. Jo. XXII* 3. un. (except for one of Friedberg's MSS: 'iii. kal. dec.') and *Extrav. comm.* 3. 2. 4 (not 'kal. dec.' as Coulon wrongly claims, col. 629).

[31] MOLLAT, *Lettres communes*, No. 8137, see the preceding note.

[32] On the date, MSS, and editions, see P. FOURNIER, *Guillaume de Montlauzun, Canoniste*, in *Histoire littéraire de la France*, t. 35 (1921), pp. 477-479. The three constitutions are MOLLAT, Nos. 8131, 8137, 8132.

The date of the constitution « Saepe »

twenty *Constitutiones extravagantes domini Johannis xxii*.³³ But also thereafter, the three constitutions continued their separate existence, being copied time and again into manuscripts of the Clementines.³⁴ *Execrabilis* in particular is rarely absent from even the briefest appendices in these manuscripts.

An intrusion of the date line of *Execrabilis* into the textual transmission of the Clementines themselves could thus provide a plausible explanation for the false date attached to the constitution *Saepe* in the Roman edition. But if this is to be more than conjecture, we have to probe for evidence of such a contamination in the history of the Clementine text. The false date line, this much is certain, does not appear in any of Friedberg's nine manuscripts.³⁵ An inquiry into the Vatican manuscripts is therefore justified. To be sure, with its twenty-five codices of the Clementines in the various *fondi*,³⁶ the Vatican Library offers both more and less than what the Roman editors might have seen during the late 1570's in the libraries of the city.³⁷ Still, it seems reasonable enough to limit the search to the present-day Vatican collection: if these codices should not yield substantial clues to the wrong date in the Roman edition, it is extremely unlikely that this date would be based on manuscript evidence at all.

III.

In the survey that follows, the Vatican manuscripts will be arranged according to the variations they show at the end of the Clementines. Such variations are found with regard to the presence or absence of *extravagantes* — usually one or more of the three texts of John XXII mentioned above — but also exist as regards the conciliar decree *Exivi de paradiso*, on the interpretation of the Franciscan Rule. Published by Clement V at Vienne in the third

---

³³ Date, MSS, and editions: FOURNIER, *Jesselin de Cassagnes, Canoniste*, in *Hist. litt.* t. 35, pp. 354-355.

³⁴ Cf. SCHULTE, *Geschichte der Quellen* (n. 24 *supra*), t. 2, p. 52; Friedberg's MSS No. 4, 5, 6, 9, 10, 13, 14, 17 of the *Extravagantes* (*Corp. iur. can.* t. 2, col. lxvi-lxviii); for the Vatican MSS see below, III D, E.

³⁵ See *app. crit.* n. 9 *ad loc.* (col. 1200).

³⁶ I have based this survey on the indications in the handwritten *schedario* of the late lamented L. Guizard, without searching the old inventories for possible other copies.

³⁷ The edition was completed before 1 July 1580, the date of Gregory XIII's Breve *Cum pro munere*.

session, 6 May 1312,[38] it was placed in the collected constitutions directly before *Saepe*, as first chapter of the title *De verborum significatione*. It is known that *Exivi* settled nothing; the bitter conflict between Spirituals and Conventuals raged on throughout most of the pontificate of John XXII and eventually moved from the field of discipline into that of dogma.[39] In this explosive situation, and also because it would have been impossible to expound the text of the conciliar decision without discussing Nicholas III's earlier decree *Exiit qui seminat* (1279), on which all glosses were forbidden,[40] the glossators refrained from commenting on *Exivi*;[41] and copyists often omitted the constitution from its proper place in the Clementines.

Unless otherwise marked, the manuscripts here cited are fourteenth-century, standard university copies; inscriptions and subscriptions are only noted if they are of more than routine interest.

A. *Manuscripts preserving the vulgate order*: Exivi – Saepe; *no date, no extravagantes*.

VAT. LAT. 1401. *Clem(entinae)* with *Glos(sa) ord(inaria)* of Johannes Andreae and additional glosses, taken mostly from the *apparatus (lecturae)* of Jesselin de Cassagnes, Guillelmus de Monte Lauduno, Paulus de Liazariis.[42] Subscription, fol. 60rb: " finit texstus clementinarum scriptus et correctus per gofredum cum originali curie. Deo gratias ". Bolognese miniatures.

---

[38] *Regestum Clementis pp. V*, No. 8873.

[39] Cf. John XXII, *Cum inter nonnullos*, 12 November 1323 (MOLLAT, No. 20406; *Extrav. Jo. XXII* 14. 4).

[40] *Sext.* 5. 12. 3 § *Itaque sub poena*.

[41] This is Zabarella's explanation, *Lectura in Clem.* 5. 11. 1, v. *Exivi* (ed. Venice 1504, fol. 192rb), whose commentary was later used in the printed editions to fill the lacuna of the *Glos. ord.* for this chapter.

[42] The works of these three (for Jesselin see FOURNIER, *op. cit.* n. 33 *supra*, pp. 353-354; for Guillaume, id. *loc. cit.* n. 32 *supra*; for Paulus, SCHULTE, *Geschichte*, t. 2, p. 247) furnish the bulk of the material also in all other MSS described below as having sets of additional glosses (unless noted otherwise). The sigla *p.* or *pau.* and *g.* or *gui(l).* are easily recognized, but those for Jesselin appear in many different forms and spellings (cf. also SCHULTE, t. 2, p. 199; FOURNIER, *op. cit.* p. 348 n. 3); I have noted *Jecelinus, Jece., Je., Jesselinus, Gecellinus, Gescelinus, Genz., gen., Ge.* in the Vatican MSS. The form *Zenzelinus*, which has come into general use through the printed editions of the *Extravagantes Jo. XXII*, is by far the least well attested in the MS tradition.

Vat. lat. 2506. *Clem.* without glosses; running head: " L(iber) VII ".[43]
Vat. lat. 2507. *Clem.* with *Glos. ord.*
Vat. lat. 13267. *Clem.* with *Glos. ord.*
Pal. lat. 638. Quarto size. *Clem.* without glosses. Subscription: " Expliciunt constitutiones noue edite a domino Clemente papa quinto. Finis adest operis, intercedere posco laboris ".
Ross. lat. 590. *Clem.* with *Glos. ord.* Fol. 1 missing. Prehumanistic script saec. xv. Initials with gold leaf.
Ross. lat. 591. *Clem.* with *Glos. ord.* Late saec. xiv. For the subscription and its significance, see *supra*, p. 432.

B. *Manuscripts omitting* Exivi; *no extravagantes directly appended.*

Vat. lat. 1397. With French miniatures. – fol. 1-68 rb: *Clem.* with *Glos. ord.* and additional glosses.
— fol. 69 ra-122 vb: Guillaume de Montlauzun, *Apparatus* on *Clem.* (" Explicit apparatus vij. decr. clementis pape "); fol. 123 ra-130 rb: *Apparatus* on *Suscepti, Execrabilis, Sedes apostolica* (" Explicit apparatus extrauagantium domini Johannis pape xxij. amen "). Running head: " L' VII ".
— fol. 130 va-132 ra: (separately) Clement V, *Exivi*; John XXII, *Cum inter nonnullos*, on the poverty of Christ and the Apostles (Mollat, *Lettres communes*, No. 20406; in *Extrav. Jo. XXII* 14. 4 with the false year " anno vii."), here correctly dated " ij. ydus nouembris... anno octauo "; followed by a " Priuilegium Ludouici Regis " (ends fol. 132 rb).
— fol. 133 ra-171 rb: *Extravagantes Jo. XXII* with *Glos. ord.* of Jesselin de Cassagnes; 171 va-191 vb: more *extravv.* follow, partly with glosses.
Vat. lat. 1399. *Clem.* with *Glos. ord.* and copious additional glosses.
Vat. lat. 1403. *Clem.* with *Glos. ord.* Additional glosses mostly from Paulus de Liazariis.

---

[43] The designation of *Clem.* as *Liber VII* was neither official nor encouraged; cf. *Glos. ord. prooem.* v. *in unum volumen*: " non tamen sub nomine libri, unde male dicunt qui allegant septimum librum..."; it occurs nonetheless in the MS tradition, cf. G. Phillips, *Kirchenrecht*, t. 4, Regensburg 1851, p. 386f.; Schulte, *Geschichte*, t. 2, p. 48 n. 10. So also here and in other Vatican MSS: see Vat. lat. 1397, Barb. lat. 1494, Ross. lat. 565 (below, B); Vat. lat. 2505 (D), Borgh. 285 (E).

VAT. LAT. 2508. fols. 1-59 vellum, humanistic script *an*. 1469; preceded by 9 unnumbered paper folios, followed by a paper quire, fols. 60-68. – fol. 1-54^v (vel.) *Clem.* without glosses; only the inscription and the first three words of *Exivi* copied before " *De verborum significatione Rubrica.* Sepe contingit... " (52vb). Subscription: " Hee clementinę transcriptę fuerunt per me Johannem de Criuellis de Parma in anno 1469 studentem in Jure canonico Baptisterij parmensis Canonicum et Rm̃i domini legati bononiensis Cardinalis Reatini [44] Cappellanum et commensalem existentem ".

In the preceding paper quire, " Jo. de Criuell' de parma in omnibus Juuenis inter decretorum scolares licet minimus tamen indignus " entered two orations, naming in the first (fol. ⟨1⟩^{r}, beg. " Quia preposterius [*sic*] ordo prius humana subsidia petere...") his teachers, Andreas Siculus (Bologna), Stefanus Costa and Franciscus de Curte (Pavia); [45] the second oration (fol. ⟨1⟩$^{r\cdot v}$, beg. " Solent, Reuerende presul, Magnifice Commissarie...") was held on 15 October 1469 " in collegio omnium doctorum parmen. in ecclesia Maiori astante Rm̃o d. episcopo parmen. Commissario et alijs officialibus...", to introduce a *repetitio* on c. *Cum non ab homine, de Juditiis* (X 2. 1. 10); there follows (fol. ⟨2⟩^{r}) a list of what " Ordinarius uisitans debet interrogare..."; (fol. ⟨2⟩^{v}) a " Prologus fiendus per promouendum ad Jnsignia ante decimationem punctorum ", etc. — The material on fol. 60-68 includes a treatise *De balneis Porrete* (60^r-62^v); two *consilia* on election cases (63^r-65^v, 67$^{r\cdot v}$), the second signed " p̃nlipus de perusio ", probably Philippus de Franchis of Perugia; [46] and the constitution *Illius licet inmeriti* of Calixtus III, 21 August 1456 (12 kal. sept. an. 2).

VAT. LAT. 13266. *Clem.* with *Glos. ord.*; first folios missing (beg. *Clem.* 1. 6. 3).

BARB. LAT. 1494 (XXVI. 31). *Clem.* with *Glos. ord.* and additional glosses in several hands. Running head " L' VII ". Ends fol. 45ra (text), 45vb (gl.).

---

[44] Angelo Capranica, bishop of Rieti, cardinal priest of S. Croce (1460), bishop of Palestrina (1472), died 1478; see C. EUBEL, *Hierarchia catholica medii aevi*, t. 2, Münster 1914, p. 13. His legation to Bologna seems, however, to have ended in January 1468, according to EUBEL, p. 35 (App. I), No. 277.

[45] Cf. on these SCHULTE, *Geschichte*, t. 2, pp. 306, 405, 294 n. 1.

[46] Professor in Pavia (1461), Ferrara (1467), and again Pavia; died 1471 (SCHULTE, *op. cit.* p. 342).

The date of the constitution « Saepe » 439

Preceded by two unnumbered fly-leaves with various entries, among which copious notes (fol. ⟨i⟩ᵛ-⟨ii⟩ᵛ) taken from the " lectura super li. vj." of *Guill*(elmus de Montelauduno), by the same hand as one of the sets of additional glosses on *Clem.* – fol. 45ᵛᵃ-49ᵛ: numerous miscellaneous entries: forms for letters, petitions, precedents and problems for disputation (45ᵛᵃ " Quidam habens duas manus, unam aridam et aliam utilem, condempnatus fuit ad amissionem unius manus..."), etc. Many of the petitions are by " Sancius de Serrio (*al.* Sarrio) aprobatus in decretis ", addressed *inter al.* to Pope Urban (V) and Pope Benedict (XII); some are on behalf of this Sanchez by " Rector, doctores et uniuersi scolares (*al.* et uniuersitas) generalis studii Illerdensis " (46ʳ: petitions for license to remain *in studio*, licenses for benefices); a *littera testimonialis baccalaureatus* by " guillermus raymundi de monte catheno decanus ecclesie Illerd. et cancellarius generalis studii eiusdem..." attesting that " Johannes petri de serrjo ", bachelor of arts of the diocese of Zaragoza, was made bachelor of medicine " sub venerabili et discreto viro Petro Cabacol in artibus et medicina magistro ", dated Lérida, 3 June 1364; a petition in Catalan (47ʳ), " supplicaco al duch faedora: Molt alt senyor, ala v̄ra altea humilment..."; etc. Prayers, incantations for various illnesses, medical notes, (46ʳ) verses on flebotomy, verses in praise of cheese, etc. Further study of these leaves would be rewarding for the prosopography of the University of Lérida in the fourteenth century.

PAL. LAT. 643. *Clem.* with *Glos. ord.* First folio missing. At the end, after *Saepe* (fol. 79ʳᵃ), the scribe may have planned to continue: " Joh'es xxii. ad perpetuam rei memoriam. Explixit ". (*ibid.*) " Explicit apparatus domini Johannis Andree super constitutionibus Clementis quinti in concilio vien'. DEO GRACIAS ". Provenance: Bensheim.

fol. 79ᵛᵃ: incantation against eye diseases, partly in German: " ✠ In nomine patris etc. ✠ Adiuro te macula per deum altissimum per deum fortissimum ✠ per patrem ✠ et filium ✠ et spiritum sanctum viuum et verum... vt exeas et recedas et ad nichilum redeas ab oculis famuli dei N. Item te adiuro... et abii et laui et et [*sic*] vidi et credidi deo. Sancta Odilia do heilige Jungfrawe v̄n sencte Symeon dy geseyne dir deyn augen... ab isto periculo oculorum et ab omni periculo anime et corporis amen ".

PAL. LAT. 644. After a fragment from Justinian's Digest (fol. 1-2ᵛ), *Clem.* with *Glos. ord.* (3ʳ-83ʳᵇ) and additional glosses (only fol. 3-12).

ROSS. LAT. 565. Very elegantly written and decorated (French, saec. xiv).

— fol. 1-64ra: Guillaume de Montlauzun, *Apparatus* on *Clem.* and the three *extravagantes*. Subscription: " Explicit apparatus VII. Libri ", followed by verses.
— fol. 65^r-124vb: *Clem.* with *Glos. ord.* Running head " L' VII ".
— fol. 125ra-173rb: Jesselin de Cassagnes, *Apparatus* on *Clem.* The date, 7 September 1323,[47] here follows directly upon the end of the concluding *casus* of c. *Saepe,* before the subscription:

Casus. quale sit futurum officium iudicis habentis procedere de plano et simpliciter hic cauetur. Datum auinoñ. vij. idus Septembris. Anno a natiuitate dñi m⁰.ccc⁰.xxiij. Indictione xj. (*leg.* vj.) Pontificatus Sanctissimi patris domini Johannis diuina prouidentia pape xxij. anno viij.
Explicit apparatus domini Gescelini de Cassanhis iuris utriusque professoris domini pape capellani...

There follow some verses by another hand; fol. 173va, in a small cursive, the beginning of a " Constitutio benedicti pape facta anno domini m⁰ccc⁰xxx⁰ de professis canonicis uel monachis..."; fol. 174^v a late commentary fragment.

— fol. 175^r-177va (new quire): Clement V, *Exivi*, John XXII, *Suscepti*, *Execrabilis*, *Sedes* (all three dated), with the wrong subscription " Explicit Liber VII^{us} siue Constit'. Clem̃. a p̃p̃. Jo. edit'. ".
— fol. 178^r-230va: *Extravagantes Jo. XXII* with *Glos. ord.* of Jesselin de Cassagnes. The date, Avignon, 24 April 1325, here correctly forms the conclusion of the " Explicit apparatus magistri Jesselini de cassanis... ".
— fol. 230vb: " Hic incipit alia dec vtilis et bona. Ex debito... duxerimus disponendum. Explicit hic decr' bona et utilis ": the const. *Ex debito* of John XXII on the reservation of benefices, of uncertain date.[48]

---

[47] Cf. Fournier, *Hist. litt.* t. 35, p. 354 and n. 2.

[48] *Extrav. comm.* 1. 3. 4, not in the papal register. P. Hinschius, *Das Kirchenrecht der Katholiken und Protestanten in Deutschland,* t. 3, Berlin 1883, p. 130 n. 3, and G. Mollat, *La collation des bénéfices ecclésiastiques sous les papes d'Avignon,* Paris 1921, p. 28, assumed that this was the constitution for which John XXII gave oral instructions to the Vice-chancellor Gaucelme de Jean on 17 kal. Oct. an. 1 (15 Sept. 1316), as reported in Baluze's *Vitae Paparum Avenionensium,* Paris 1693, t. 1, p. 722 (citing MS Colbert 349 = Paris, B. N. lat. 3204) [= nouv. éd. par G. Mollat, Paris 1927, t. 2, p. 218] and by Dietrich von Nieheim (ed. Erler, *Liber cancelleriae vom Jahre 1380,* Leipzig 1888, p. 137). In later publications, Mollat cautiously refrained from assigning a date to *Ex debito*; see his article, *Réserve,* in *Dictionnaire de Droit cano-*

C. *Manuscripts which place* Exivi *at the end, outside the Clementine corpus.*

VAT. LAT. 1400. After a folio from the Digest: *Clem.* with *Glos. ord.* and additional glosses, ends fol. 60rb ("Expliciunt constitutiones clementis"); fol. 60va-62va: *Exivi de paradiso.*

VAT. LAT. 8121. Small octavo, containing *Liber Sextus* with *Glos. ord.* (fol. 2-239^v), *Clem.* with *Glos. ord.* (241-360^v; 356^v "Explicit textus Clementinarum"); *Exivi* (361-365^v). First folios of both *Sext.* and *Clem.* missing. The glosses in both collections are written, not in the margin, but as commentary after each chapter. — Written in Bourges, 1444, by Bruno Johannis of Deventer, diocese of Utrecht, province of Cologne, *decretorum doctor*, for his *Reverendissimus dominus*, Petrus de Monte, bishop of Brescia (1442-1457), legate *a latere* in France of Pope Eugene IV, in the fourteenth year of his pontificate; *Sext.* completed on 17 August, *Clem.* on the feast of the Conversion of St. Paul: thus the lengthy subscriptions (fol. 239^v and, with verbal variants, fol. 365^v). Owned later by Master Bernard of Perugia, O. P. (fol. 239^v, saec. xv), then by Master Leonard de Mansuetis, of the same Order and city (fol. 1^v, saec. xv).

PAL. LAT. 642. *Clem.* with *Glos. ord.* (fol. 1-52rb; gloss ends 52vb), followed by *Exivi* (ends 56vb). Completed in Pavia, 11 August 1460; humanistic-gothic script.

(For separate tradition of *Exivi*, joined with *extravagantes*, see also Vat. lat. 1397, Ross. lat. 565 [*supra*, B]; Vat. lat. 1398 [*infra*, E]).

D. *Manuscripts preserving the vulgate order,* Exivi – Saepe, *with the constitution* Execrabilis *appended and dated Avignon, 13 kal. dec. an. 2.*[49]

VAT. LAT. 1402. *Clem.* with *Glos. ord.* and additional glosses. Ends fol. 57rb: "... nec etiam irritandus. Idem [*sic*]"; "Explicit

---

nique, t. 7, fasc. 39 (1960), col. 636, also his *Un recueil d'extravagantes*, in *Revue de droit canonique*, t. 4 (1954), p. 248, where *Ex debito* appears as No. 38 of the collection of MS Vat. lat. 1171 (fol. 73-74: "Data Aven. etc."). — An early date, September 1316, seems out of the question: Guillaume de Montlauzun did not include *Ex debito* in his commentary (1319) on the *extravagantes* of 1317 on reservation of benefices, nor did Jesselin de Cassagnes incorporate it into his *Extrav. Jo. XXII* (1325); the constitution is not even discussed in the glosses of either of the two writers. This argues for a date *post* 1325.

[49] The scribe of Pal. lat. 643 (without *Exivi*, see above, B) may have contemplated this addition, too.

apparatus domini Johannis andree super Clementinis. Deo gratias "; fol. 57va-58vb: " Johannes episcopus seruus seruorum dei ad perpetuam rei memoriam. Execrabilis... Data auinioni xiij. kll'. decembris pont. nostri anno secundo etc̄. " (no gloss).

VAT. LAT. 2505. – Fly-leaf (fol. 1): " Diligenter Nota (*supra lin.*) substitutionum materiam secundum dy. Quod substitutionum sunt due species... dic quod non. D. Dy. Dy. ": the *summula* of Dinus de Mugello on testamentary substitution;[50] also some scattered entries. – fol. 1^v: moral and theological questions, " Primo queritur utrum a precepto soluendi (soluendo MS) decimas aliquis absoluatur per contrariam consuetudinem. Et uidetur quod sic... (ends:) et a precepto circumcixionis ". (No legal sources cited).

— fol. 2-64rb: *Clem.* with *Glos. ord.*; fol. 64va-66ra: *Execrabilis* with date, no gloss; subscribed " Explicit vij. liber Decretalium Domini Johannis pape xxij. " – that is, considered by the scribe as part of the Clementines.

ARCH. S. PETRI A. 38. This codex, interesting in many respects, came to St. Peter's from the library of Cardinal Giordano Orsini (d. 1438).[51]

— fol. 1-131vb: *Liber Sextus* with the *Glos. ord.* and very copious additions of Johannes Andreae; to a large extent, but not always, identical with the glosses of his *Novella in Sextum* and much richer than the *Additiones* in the printed editions of the *Glos. ord.*[52] Some of the glosses from the *Novella* are further expanded;[53] and some are preceded (especially in the title *de regulis iuris*,

---

[50] F. C. VON SAVIGNY, *Geschichte des römischen Rechts im Mittelalter*, t. 5, 2nd ed., Heidelberg 1850, p. 464.

[51] The Orsini coat of arms under a red hat is on fol. 1^r. In the inventory of the cardinal's books bequeathed to the Basilica, we find an entry, " Sextus et Clementine in eod. volumine et pulcri ": F. CANCELLIERI, *De secretariis veteris basilicae Vaticanae Liber I*, t. 2, Rome 1786, p. 908^b; this is our codex.

[52] The relation between the *Additiones* and the *Novella in Sextum* in the MS tradition has never been examined; the observations by SCHULTE, *Geschichte*, t. 2, pp. 218-219, are inadequate.

[53] Thus e. g. *Sext. De prebend. et dign.* c. *Cum in ecclesia* (3. 4. 25) v. *licet*: " Hic factum narrat – litteras. Jo. an. (=*Novella ad loc.*) Dictum arci(diaconi) placet Jo. kald. quod plene prosequitur de concess. preb. in iiij. obiectione " (fol. 75^v). No work of Johannes Calderini on the Sext is known; but among his many monographic treatises (cf. SCHULTE, *op. cit.* p. 250f.) there might have been one *De concessione prebende non vacantis*. His *repetitiones* on two decretals in that title (X 3. 8. 6 and 15) are printed in the *Repetitionum in Vniversas fere Iuris canonici partes... volumina sex*, Venice 1587, t. 4, fol. 240vb-246rb.

fol. 119ff.) by the words " Epy(logus) dicit ", " Epi. ponit ", introducing a short summation of a given gloss of the *Ordinaria*.[54] Still other additions, some of them citing the *Novella*, are signed *G*(uillelmus de Montelauduno), *Pau*(lus de Liazariis), *Lapus* (see also "... et de hiis uide hic latius in nouella ", unsigned, fol. 75vb).

— fol. 132$^{r\text{-}v}$: The forged *Professio fidei* of Boniface VIII, entered somewhat later (pre-humanistic gothic script, saec. xiv ex./xv in.) on the originally blank leaf, with the gloss " Quamuis hanc professionem legerem (legero MS)...". This hitherto unknown copy, which could well be older than any of those seen by modern scholars, gives a text with several scribal blunders, but nonetheless serves to correct in part Finke's edition of the gloss.[55]

---

[54] Cf. JOH. ANDREAE, *Novella in quinque decretalium libros*, prol. n. 9: " Venientes ad glossas invenient alia tria...: Primo scil. epilogum..., idest breviloquum modum summationis ipsarum. Secundo..." (ed. Venice 1581, t. 1, fol. 2vb); and cf. S. KUTTNER, Introduction to the reprint of the *Novella*, Turin 1963, t. 1, p. xii.

[55] On the so-called *Professio* of Boniface VIII (also on MSS, editions, and earlier bibliography) see M. SOUCHON, *Die Papstwahlen von Bonifaz VIII. bis Urban VI. und die Entstehung des Schismas von 1378*, Braunschweig 1888, pp. 193-205; G. BUSCHBELL, *Die Professiones fidei der Päpste*, in *Römische Quartalschrift für christliche Alterthumskunde und für Kirchengeschichte*, t. 10 (1896), at pp. 291-297, 421-438; idem, *Die römische Ueberlieferung der Professiones fidei der Päpste*, ibid. t. 14 (1900), pp. 131-136; H. FINKE, review of Souchon, in *Göttingische gelehrte Anzeigen*, 1890, pp. 960-968, at pp. 965ff.; idem, *Aus den Tagen Bonifaz VIII.* (= Vorreformationsgeschichtliche Forschungen 2), Münster 1902, pp. 54-65. The *Professio* was fabricated probably in the circle of Guillaume de Nogaret, c. 1310, but none of the MSS that have come to light antedate the reform councils of the early 15th century (FINKE, *Aus den Tagen*, p. 61f.). The copy in Arch. S. Petri A. 38 might be older but cannot be dated with certainty on palaeographic grounds; at any rate it represents a tradition which is independent from the context of conciliar controversy (Pisa and Constance) in which the *Professio* appears elsewhere. — The set of glosses in our MS is the same as that which FINKE edited in *Acta Concilii Constanciensis*, t. 2, Münster 1923, pp. 682-688, from several 15th-century MSS, with a shorter version from one MS printed in the opposite columns. The edition does not quite measure up to the usual excellence of Finke's work. At some points separate glosses and their lemmata are conflated into one continuous text (e. g. p. 685^b, *gl.* v. *Non deseram*: "... di. IIII 'cathecuminum' custodire et palam confiteri..." should be separated; *custodire* is a new lemma of the text; likewise in *gl.* v. *Conciliis*: "... in suis titulis pontificum, videlicet Leonis primi...", where *pontificum* is a new lemma). Several glosses are truncated by omission, usually but not always indicated by dots (...). The omitted passages are, however, often of particular interest for determining the glossator's sources. From St. Peter's MS, it can be established that the anonymous writer, in addition

— fol. 133ra-197rb: *Clem.* with *Glos. ord.* ("Finiunt constitutiones Clementis v."; "Explicit apparatus domini Johanis Andree super clementinis. Jo.") and a considerable stratum of additional glosses, beg. "Dic quod hic non est aliqua inculcatio..." (ad gl. *prooem.* v. *ethymologias*). They represent a forgotten work of Johannes Andreae himself: the *Additiones* or *Apostillae* to his *Glossa ordinaria* on the Clementines, a work of which Zabarella still knew ("post perfectum suum commentum... nonnullas apostillas adiecit super hoc toto volumine") but which has escaped all later writers. It is here enriched by some further additional gloss material.[56]

— fol. 197va-198rb: *Execrabilis*, with its date, no gloss.

E. *Manuscripts with two or three extravagantes appended.*

BORGH. 285. *Clem.* without glosses, inscribed "Incipit liber septimus decretalium". Ends in the vulgate order *Exivi-Saepe* (fol. 24rb "Explicit liber septimus decretalium"), followed by John XXII, *Sedes, Suscepti, Execrabilis*, each with its proper date, fol. 24rb-26ra.

VAT. LAT. 1398. — fol. 1-54vb: *Clem.* (omitting *Exivi*) with *Glos ord.* and additions by Baldus de Ubaldis (*bal., bald.*), a heretofore unknown product of his canonistic activities.[57]

— fol. 55ra-57vb (another hand): Clement V, *Exivi*, with rubric *De verb. sign.* and scattered glosses by Baldus (same hand as above); fol. 57vb-58vb: John XXII, *Suscepti, Execrabilis*, with their dates, no glosses.

— fol. 59ra-59rb (added leaf): "*Circa constitutionem predictam sc. Execrabilis Jnfrascripte dubietates et questiones emerserunt que fuerunt per conditorem earum interpretate et ad quamlibet*

---

to Gratian and the Decretals, used two books which were not normally in the hands of professional canonists of the later Middle Ages: the *Liber Pontificalis* and the *Pseudo-Isidorian Decretals* (the latter, from a MS of Hinschius's class C). To demonstrate this in detail would require a special study which must be left for another occasion.

[56] Joh. Andreae's *Apostillae in Clem.* and the further glosses of this MS will be discussed in an article to appear in the forthcoming volume of *Études* in honor of Gabriel Le Bras. — The quotation above is from Zabarella's prologue of his *Lectura in Clem.* (ed. Venice 1504, fol. 2rb; printed also in SCHULTE, *Geschichte*, t. 2, p. 553).

[57] On Baldus as a canonist, see SCHULTE, *Geschichte*, t. 2, p. 276; G. CHEVRIER, *Baldi de Ubaldi*, in *Dictionnaire de Droit canonique*, t. 2 (1937), col. 41.

The date of the constitution « Saepe »

earum responsum prout patet in fine uniuscuiusque. prima dubietas talis. In quibusdam ecclesis, puta auinioñ. leodixum et similibus... huius includantur ". These 18 *dubia* with official responses " per conditorem earum (*leg.* eius) " appear also, with a shorter rubric, in a collection of John XXII's *extravagantes*, in MS Vat. lat. 1171 (No. 48, fol. 84v-86v),[58] and also at the end of the *Apparatus* of Guillaume de Montlauzun on *Execrabilis* as printed in the *Extravagantes communes* 3. 2. 4.[59] – fol. 59rb-59va: Benedict XII, *Ceca cordis*, 18 December 1335.

(For separate tradition of the sequence *Exivi-Suscepti-Execrabilis-Sedes*, see also Ross. lat. 565 [*supra*, B]).

Of the manuscripts here reviewed,[60] 19 present the Clementines without *extravagantes* added (7 in the vulgate order, 9 without *Exivi*, 3 with *Exivi* displaced); 5 manuscripts add *extravagantes* (3 add *Execrabilis* alone, 1: *Sedes-Suscepti-Execrabilis*, 1: (*Exivi*)-*Suscepti-Execrabilis*), all five ending with *Execrabilis*,[61] and consequently with the date of the latter. But in none of the Vatican manuscripts can we trace a contamination of this date with the constitution *Saepe*. For a clue to the date line in the Roman edition we have to turn to the history of the incunabula.

IV.

The first printing of the Clementines, *Constitutiones Clementis pp. V vna cum apparatu dni. Jo. Andree*, appeared in Mainz, Johann Fust and Peter Schoeffer, 25 June 1460 (GW 7077 [HC 5410]). It placed *Exivi* (fol. 49r-50v) outside the Clementine corpus (colophon, fol. 18vb) — there was, as we have seen, good manuscript precedent for this — and added to this the constitution *Execrabilis* (fol. 51ra-va)

---

[58] MOLLAT, *Un recueil d'extravagantes* (note 48 *supra*), p. 248.

[59] I have not examined the MSS nor the editions (Hain 11595 [Rome 1475]; Paris 1517) of the *Apparatus* on the three constitutions from which the glosses of *Extrav. comm.* 1. 6 un., 3. 2. 4, 3. 3 un. are taken. The considerably shortened edition in the *Repetitionum in Vniversas fere Iuris Canonici partes... volumina sex*, Venice 1587, t. 6, pt. 2 (fol. 1-2vb, 23vb-26va), does not include the *dubia* and *responsiones*.

[60] Not including the incomplete MS, Vat. lat. 13264, which breaks off fol. 54v in *Clem.* 5. 9. 2.

[61] Unusual combinations are found for the separate tradition of *Exivi* among the " pure " MSS: *Exivi–Cum inter nonnullos* (Vat. lat. 1397), *Exivi–Suscepti–Execrabilis–Sedes* (Ross. lat. 565); cf. *supra*, B.

with its date, and Benedict XII, *Ad regimen* (= *Extrav. comm.* 3. 2. 13; fol. 51^{va-b}).[62]

Except for the Benedictine constitution, which was not resumed in later printings, GW 7077 set a pattern: the appendix consisting of *Exivi* and *Execrabilis*, with the date Avignon, 13 kal. dec. an. 2 at the end, was reprinted with the Clementines fifteen times between 1467 and 1483: GW 7078-7081, 7085-7094, 7096;[63] only five printings appeared that end with *Exivi* alone: GW 7082-7084, 7095, 7097.[64] Meanwhile, the thought of publishing the Clementines together with a larger number of *extravagantes* caught the fancy of printers: not so much in connection with Jesselin's glossed compilation of *Extravagantes Johannis XXII* — the *Gesamtkatalog der Wiegendrucke* cites only one example of this combination[65] — as with a selection of truly " extravagant " constitutions by various popes.

While printings of the classical model, *Clem.* with *Exivi* and *Execrabilis* appended, continued to appear — more precisely, in the same year 1476 which saw between 2 May and 10 September the four printings GW 7087-7090 — Nicholas Jenson published at Venice a new edition, prepared by Alexander Nevus (de Nevo), doctor of both laws and professor of *ius pontificium* in the University of Padua (GW 7098 [Hain 5417], *sine die*). Nevo returned *Exivi de paradiso* to its correct place in the Clementine corpus (fol. 2-70rb) and shifted *Execrabilis* to ninth place in a series of twenty divers *extravagantes* which begins with Boniface VIII, *Iniuncte nobis* (= *Extrav. comm.* 1. 3. 1) and ends with John XXII, *Sedes* (= *ibid.* 1. 6. 1) (fol. 70va-77rb).[66] But at the end of the Clementines, immediately after the last word of *Saepe contingit*, he left the terminal date stand which

---

[62] The Vatican Library copy, with numerous marginal notes saec. xvi, is kept among the MSS (Vat. lat. 2704); last folio missing.

[63] Four of these are in the Vatican Library: GW 7080 (HC 5412), Mainz 1471: Stamp. Ross. 296. — GW 7081 (HC 5413), Strasbourg 1471: Stamp. Ross. 934. — GW 7085 (Hain 5416), Rome 1473: Incun. S. 49. — GW 7091, vol. I (HR 5409), Rome, c. 1478: Incun. S. 155 (vol. II, *Extrav. Jo. XXII* with *Glos. ord.* [Hain 4556]: Incun. Prop. II. 231).

[64] One of these in the Vatican Library: GW 7082 (Hain 5414), Rome 1472: Incun. S. 8 and Stamp. Ross. 1835.

[65] GW 7091, see note 63 *supra*.

[66] Vatican Library copy: Stamp. Ross. 492 (fol. 1 missing). For identification of the *extravagantes* see the notice in GW, t. 6, col. 715. There are 10 of Boniface VIII, 3 of Benedict XI, 2 of Clement V, and 5 of John XXII, including *Suscepti, Execrabilis*, and *Sedes*. — For Alexander de Nevo see SCHULTE, *Geschichte*, t. 2, pp. 330-331, 304 n. 4.

The date of the constitution « Saepe »   447

until then had properly appeared on the last page of every earlier edition (and manuscript) that ended with *Execrabilis*: " Data auinione xiii. kal. decembris pont. nostri anno secundo " (fol. 70rb). Whether this was carelessness or — more probably — a humanist's conjectural " reconstruction " of a closing line to match the end of the *Liber Sextus* [67] we cannot tell any more; but after this it is rather amusing to read the claim to *exactissima diligentia* which follows then and there in the colophon.[68]

Nevo's text with its terminal date was faithfully copied in the editions to follow; not only in nine printings which adopted his arrangement of *extravagantes* (GW 7099-7107),[69] but also in the recension prepared three years later, with 29 *extravagantes* appended, by Petrus Albignanus Trecius J. U. D. of Padua (GW 7108): its text of the Clementines is a " seitengetreuer Nachdruck " of GW 7098.[70] Albignani's arrangement was reproduced as such eight times (GW 7109-7116), and nineteen times in editions which combine in two volumes Sext, Clementines, and the 29 *extravagantes* (GW 4864, 4886+7117, 4888-4903, 4905).[71] Finally, it was with Nevo's dating that the Clementines appeared as tome II in the three-volume edition of Jean Chappuis (Paris, Rembolt, 1500-1501: GW 4904 [HC 3627]), which fixed the definitive arrangement of the *Extravagantes Johannis XXII* and 74 *Extravagantes communes* (tome

---

[67] See *supra*, at n. 25.

[68] " Opus clementinarum ere atque industria Nicolai Jenson gallici Uenetijs impressum feliciter explicit: vna cum apparatu dñi Joannis Andree: per excellentissimum iuris utriusque doctorem dñm Alexandrum Neuum ius pontificium in patauino gymnasio ordinarie legentem exactissima diligentia emendatum. M.cccc.lxxvj ".

[69] Three exist in Vatican Library copies: GW 7101 (Hain 5428), Venice 1482: Incun. IV. 76 (2). — GW 7102 (Hain 5432), Venice 1484: Incun. IV. 7 (1). — GW 7103 (HC 5434), Venice 1485: Incun. IV. 244, IV. 258.

[70] So the notice in GW, t. 6, col. 722. The Vatican Library copy of GW 7108 (HC 5424), Venice 1479, is Stamp. Ross. 302.

[71] The Vatican Library has two of these: GW 4886+7117 (Hain 3616+ HR 5445), Venice 1490-1491: bound in one in Incun. S. 101. In this edition, instead of the usual distribution — vol. I, *Sextus*; vol. II, *Clem.* and *Extrav.* — the *Extravagantes* appear at the end of vol. I (GW 4886), and the Clementines alone form vol. II (GW 7117). — GW 4888 (H 5446, HC 3618), Venice 1491: Stamp. Ross. 2288, with some handwritten entries saec. xv in vol. II: fol. 52v-⟨53r⟩ (number misprinted: 47), a response by Franc. Gonzaga, Cardinalis Mantuanus, " Habita diligenti ", Rome, 27 March 1471, to the *jurisconsulti* of Mantua, on the const. *Ambitiosae* of Paul II (= *Extrav. comm.* 3. 4. un.); after fol. 57 (ult.) a note on papal dates, and Pius II, const. *Auctoritate apostolica*, 1461, 15 kal. dec. an. iv, forbidding ordinations without dimissorial letters, etc.

III) as it was repeated in other sixteenth-century printings, to be eventually adopted in the official Roman edition of 1582.

The *Correctores Romani* thus gave Nevo's mistake, which had been carried from one printing to another for a hundred years, the stamp of authenticity. We do not know who was in charge of the Clementines among the members of the Roman commission, since in contrast to the fair amount of information we possess on the materials used, the methods applied, and the persons engaged in the *emendatio* of Gratian's Decretum,[72] practically nothing is known of the work of the *Correctores* as regards the other parts of the *Corpus iuris canonici*. It is commonly said that the task of editing was in the hands of Francisco Peña (Pegna), Auditor of the Rota, and Sixtus Fabri O. P., Master of the Apostolic Palace, at least as far as the Decretals of Gregory IX are concerned. This is somewhat exaggerated in the case of Peña; for Fabri it is altogether wrong.[73] But whoever may have been responsible for the Clementines, we must conclude that he did his work from printed books, without bothering to collate the extant manuscripts.

EXCURSUS A

On the " Monteux " Text of the Clementines, with a Note on the Commentary of Pierre Bertrand

I. The observation that of the three manuscripts which begin with Pope Clement's preamble *Cum nuper* — Marburg C. 3, Chartres 275 (318), Kassel jur. 15 (= Friedberg's B, F, G) — at least two show signs of contamination with the vulgate text (cf. at note 19 *supra*; MÜLLER, *Das Konzil von Vienne*, p. 404) is not new but needs some further comment.

1) Cod. F presents both *Cum nuper* and John XXII's *Quoniam nulla* at the beginning (cf. FRIEDBERG, *Corp. iur. can.* t. 2, col. ⟨1129-30⟩ n. 1).

2) Cod. B omits in *Clem.* 1. 1. 1 (*De summa Trin. c. Fidei*) the sentence " textum vero b. Mathei—exponi " of the original version which John XXII, according to Johannes Andreae (*gl. Clem.* 1. 1. 1 v. *aperuit*), had canceled before the final publication of 1317. At this point, it is interesting to note that the original phrase is present, not only in the

---

[72] For bibliography, see A. VAN HOVE, *Prolegomena* (= Commentarium Lovaniense in Codicem iuris canonici I, 1), 2nd ed. Malines-Rome 1945, p. 347 n. 6.

[73] See Excursus B, *infra*.

The date of the constitution « Saepe »

two Monteux texts FG, but by an inverted contamination also in some MSS of the vulgate (ADE, cf. Friedberg's n. 9 *ad loc.*) Friedberg drew from this the conclusion that the glossator " contendit quidem nec tamen probavit " the change made by John XXII (*Prolegomena*, col. lxii; cf. MÜLLER, *op. cit.* p. 412); he does not consider the possibility of contamination of the MSS. It is certain that Johannes Andreae had seen copies of the Monteux text (cf. at note 22 *supra*).

With the scanty information we possess on the extent of John XXII's revisions, two other possible cases of contamination remain, however, doubtful:

3) In *Clem.* 1. 2. 1 (*De rescr.* c. *Abbates*) all three Monteux MSS contain, with the vulgate, the passage " nec occasione locorum—haberent ", provided we can rely on Friedberg's critical *apparatus* (but it should be remembered that of his nine MSS he collated CDEHI and FG only for passages in which he found variants in A or B; cf. *Proleg.* col. lxiv). Johannes Andreae and Jesselin de Cassagnes characterize this sentence as a post-conciliar addition; the latter is also quoted on this by Cardinal Pierre Bertrand (see below, II). But whereas Joh. Andreae's statement, " iste versus non fuit de prima compilatione concilii " (*gl.* 1. 2. 1 v. *nec occasione*), might well refer to the *compilatio* of Monteux, it could also refer to the original form of the conciliar decrees, and this seems to have been Jesselin's understanding, for he attributes the passage inserted " post concilium Viennense " to the men " quibus iste constitutiones in melius reformande commisse fuerunt ", that is, to Pope Clement's commission. The passage may therefore actually have been in the Monteux text.

4) In the original text of *Clem.* 3. 11. 2 § 1 (*De relig. domibus* c. *Quia contingit* § *Ut autem*) the prohibition of giving hospitals to secular clerics in benefice was followed by a further clause, according to Joh. Andreae: "... in prima tamen editione concilii hoc fuit prohibitum: 'nec laicis habentibus filios vel uxorem ex qua possent verisimiliter filios procreare talia loca conferentur', quod postea fuit sublatum " (*gl.* 3. 11. 2 v. *saccularibus*, fin.) — but here too, the words " in prima editione concilii " are ambiguous. None of the three Monteux texts — again, if we can trust Friedberg's selective *apparatus* — contains the canceled passage.

II. The remark of Cardinal Pierre Bertrand on a post-conciliar insertion in c. *Abbates* (*Clem.* 1. 2. 1) has long been known from its publication by BALUZE, *Vitae Paparum Avenionensium*, Paris 1693, t. 1, p. 683 (nouv. éd. par G. MOLLAT, Paris 1927, t. 2, p. 170). But Baluze's text, as taken from the cardinal's *Apparatus super Sextum et Clem.* in Paris MS lat. 4085 (cf. MOLLAT, t. 2, p. 285), that is, from the short version, is unsatisfactory: by omitting the final clause and the siglum of Jesselin de Cassagnes, it gives the wrong impression of being an original observation by Pierre Bertrand; by omitting a word in the first sentence, it arrives at an impossible grammatical construction; and by attaching the gloss to a wrong lemma, it leads to a false notion on the extent of the post-conciliar interpolation.

The text printed below is that of the hitherto unknown long version of Book I of the *Apparatus* in a codex which in 1557 belonged to Jacques Spifame, bishop of Nevers, and is now at Washington, Catholic University MS 195, acquired from H. P. Kraus, New York, in 1959. (On the *Apparatus*, its MSS and its two recensions see P. FOURNIER, *Le Cardinal Pierre Bertrand, Canoniste*, in *Histoire littéraire de la France*, t. 37 [1938], pp. 110-118; Fournier knew the long recension only for Books II and V, Paris MS lat. 4085A: at the time he wrote, the only trace left of Spifame's MS was in a bookdealer's sales catalogue [L. Gougy, c. 1920-22], and Fournier thought that it probably contained the short recension). A detailed study of the Washington MS must be left for another occasion.

(fol. 54va) *Nec uero*[a]: hic uersus[b] usque ad uerbum 'si quis' fuit post concilium Viennense additus per illos quibus iste constitutiones in melius reformande commisse fuerunt. Vnde per hoc dicas ipsas ligare a tempore missionis domini Iohannis pape, non a tempore prime publicationis, ut[c] plene dixi supra in prohemio. Geze.[d]

EXCURSUS B

Francisco Peña, Sixtus Fabri, and the Roman Edition of the Decretals

Manuals and other reference works of the history of canon law invariably tell us that among the *Correctores Romani* it was Peña and Fabri who were in charge of editing the Decretals, especially the Decretals of Gregory IX; cf. AE. L. RICHTER, *Lehrbuch des katholischen und evangelischen Kirchenrechts*, Leipzig 1842, § 79 n. 9 (= 8th ed. by R. DOVE and W. KAHL, Leipzig 1886, t. 1, p. 263); G. PHILLIPS, *Kirchenrecht*,

---

[a] Nec uero] Nec^v *W*(ashington), Nisi ubi *B*(aluze). — The reference is to the words "Nec (uero) occasione... haberent" (continues: "Si quis"), i. e. to the same passage as the gloss of Joh. Andreae *ad loc.* According to *B*, also the end of the preceding sentence, "nisi ubi et coram ... gubernatoribus hoc liceret" would be a post-conciliar insertion. But in *W* our gloss is preceded by two glosses on this very passage (v. *gubernatoribus*, v. *lice⟨re⟩t*); thus the lemma of *W* must be correct, even if the variant "Nec *uero* occasione" is not attested in Friedberg's *app. crit.* [b] uersus *om. B.* — Probably an oversight, since the masculine gender is retained in the predicate "fuit additus". [c] ut plene *et rell. om. B.* [d] Geze. (=Gezelinus) *in rubro W.* — The work of Pierre Bertrand is composed of ample quotations from other glossators, together with the author's own observations and comments, always with the respective names (in red, *W*) given at the end.

t. 4, Regensburg 1851, p. 344; Schulte, *Geschichte*, t. 2, p. 23; Friedberg, *Corp. iur. can.*, t. 2, col. xli; R. von Scherer, *Handbuch des Kirchenrechts*, t. 1, Graz 1886, p. 271 n. 19; F. Laurin, *Introductio in Corpus juris canonici*, Freiburg-Vienna 1889, p. 153f.; Van Hove, *Prolegomena* (note 72 *supra*), p. 361; A. M. Stickler, *Historia iuris canonici latini*, t. 1, Turin 1950, p. 250; P. Torquebiau, *Les Décrétales de Grégoire IX* (*Corpus iuris canonici*, II), in *Dictionn. de Droit can.* t. 4 (1949), col. 631.

The only information on the share of Francisco Peña (1540-1612), auditor of the Rota, comes from a note of Antonio Agustín, in his *Dialogi de emendatione Gratiani* 1. 20, where he places him at the end of the roster of *Correctores Romani*: " Franciscus Pegna Hispanus, cuius sunt additiones Decretalium sine nomine, quia templum Dianae incendisse visus est " (ed. Paris 1672, p. 238; ed. Duisburg 1677, p. 343). The sarcastic remark has often been criticized, so by Baluze in his note *ad loc.* (ed. Duisburg, p. 695f.); by F. Florent, *Praefatio de methodo et auctoritate collectionis Gratiani* (1641), in *Opera juridica*, Paris 1679, t. 1, p. 55; J. H. Boehmer, *Corpus iuris canonici*, Halle 1747, t. 2, p. xxviii n. 98 (p. xxix); C. S. Berardi, *Gratiani canones genuini ab apocryphis discreti*, Venice 1777, t. 1, p. xxxvii; see also H. Laemmer, *Melematum Romanorum Mantissa*, Regensburg 1875, p. 65 n. 1 (p. 66). But whether unjust or not, Agustín's remark attributes to Peña only the marginal notes in the Roman edition of the Decretals, not the recension of the text itself.

The name of Sixtus Fabri, O. P., Master of the Apostolic Palace from 1580 to 1583, General of the Order 1583-1589 (d. 1614), was first connected with the editing of the Decretals by Quétif and Echard, *Scriptores Ordinis Praedicatorum*, Paris 1719-1723, t. 2, col. 266[b]: " Jussu Gregorii XIII Decretales summorum Pontificum et Extravagantes ad codices MSS. recensuit, quae deinde correctiores prodierunt ". Ae. L. Richter, *De emendatoribus Gratiani*, Leipzig 1835, pp. 50-51, took it up from there, pointing to the mention made of Fabri in Gregory XIII's Breve *Cum pro munere pastorali* of 1 July 1580. From Richter's *Lehrbuch* of 1842 (see *supra*), where the source of attribution is no longer given, the statement about Fabri made its way into the modern standard works, being passed from one to another without citation of any evidence.

But Richter, as well as the learned Dominicans before him, had misunderstood the relevant passage in Gregory XIII's *Cum pro munere*:

> ... adhibitis nonnullis ex fratribus nostris sanctae Romanae Ecclesiae Cardinalibus, adiuncto etiam aliquorum doctrina et pietate insignium virorum studio, Decretum Gratiani nuncupatum absque glossis, necnon idem Gratiani Decretum cum Decretalibus Gregorii Papae Noni praedecessoris nostri, Sexto, Clementinis et Extrauagantibus... reuidendi, corrigendi et expurgandi curam demandauimus. Cum autem ipsum Decretum absque glossis a praefatis a nobis deputatis iam totum emendatum et correctum ac nonnullis annotationibus illustratum existat, ipsiusque maior pars a dilecto filio Paulo Con-

stabili, tunc sacri nostri Palatij Apostolici Magistro, una cum dictis Decretalibus felicis recordationis Gregorii Noni praedecessoris nostri iam impressis, recognita et approbata sit, reliquum vero eiusdem Decreti una cum annotationibus praedictis, tam absque glossis quam ipsum totum cum glossis, Sextumque et Clementinas simul et Extravagantes a dilecto filio Sixto Fabri, eiusdem Palatij nostri Apostolici Magistro, recognoscenda omnia et approbanda, in officina populi Romani... imprimi et impressa diuulgari iusserimus, ... (*Decretum Gratiani*, ed. Rom. fol. *a* 2; ed. Friedb. col. lxxix).

What the Pope has to say, then, is this: (1) All of the *Decretum* without glosses is now (1 July 1580) on hand as emended and annotated by the *correctores*; (2) the major part of this text has been examined and approved (*recognita et approbata*) by the former Master of the Palace (1573-1580), Paolo Constabili, together with the *Decretales Gregorii IX*, which are already printed; (3) orders have been given that the remainder of the *Decretum* without glosses, as emended and annotated, as well as the entire *Decretum* with its glosses, the *Sextus*, the *Clementinae*, and the *Extravagantes* be examined and approved by the present Master of the Palace, Sixtus Fabri, and then printed in the *Officina Populi Romani*.

(The whole *Corpus* with its glosses was published two years later, in 1582, and often reprinted; the text of the *Decretum* without glosses [= 1] appeared only in 1584, in a Roman and a Venetian printing: cf. A. ADVERSI, *Saggio di un Catalogo delle edizioni del " Decretum Gratiani" posteriori al secolo XV*, in *Studia Gratiana*, t. 6 [1959], Nos. 78 and 81, also p. 422. Quétif and Echard saw a copy of the Venice 1584 edition with the title, " Decretum Gratiani emendatum et notationibus illustratum. Major pars a F. Paulo Constabili Sacri Palatii apostolici magistro Gregorii XIII iussu editum " [*sic*]: *Scriptores O. P.* t. 2, col. 255[b]; not mentioned in ADVERSI, *loc. cit.*).

Sixtus Fabri thus never occupied himself with the edition of the Decretals of Gregory IX; in fact, they were already printed when he took office as Master of the Palace. It was his predecessor Constabili, Master of the Palace from 1573 to 1580, General of the Order from 1580 to his death in 1582 (QUÉTIF-ECHARD, col. 255[a]), who was connected with the Roman edition of the Decretals; Fabri was put in charge only where Constabili had left off: for the remainder of Gratian and for the post-Gregorian books. But what is more, neither of the two had anything to do with the recension of the text (" ad codices MSS. recensuit ", as QUÉTIF-ECHARD, t. 2, col. 266[b] would have it). Gregory XIII's Breve speaks of *recognoscere et approbare*, and from the context it is clear that the first of these terms is to be taken in its literal meaning, " to examine ", " to review ". As one would expect from the successive Masters of the Apostolic Palace, their function was that of pre-censorship: to examine, certify, and approve the finished text for printing and publication.

Washington, D. C.

RETRACTATIONES

I. Quelques observations sur l'autorité des collections canoniques

Since this paper was written in 1947, the meaning and functions of the official publication of collected decretals, from Innocent III to Boniface VIII, have often been discussed. See especially Sten Gagnér, *Studien zur Ideengeschichte der Gesetzgebung* (Studia iuridica Uppsalensia 1; Stockholm-Uppsala 1960) *passim*; S. Kuttner, 'Il Codice di diritto canonico nella storia', *Commemorazione del cinquantesimo della promulgazione del Codex iur. can. ... il 27 maggio 1967* (Roma s.d.) 17-39 (Engl. trans. in *The Jurist* 28 [1968] 239-54); G. Fransen, *Les décrétales et les collections de décrétales* (Typologie des sources du moyen âge occidental 2; Turnhout 1972); K.W. Nörr, 'Päpstliche Dekretalen und römisch-kanonischer Zivilprozess', *Studien zur europäischen Rechtsgeschichte*, ed. W. Wilhelm (Frankfurt 1972) 53-65; O. Hageneder, 'Papstregister und Dekretalenrecht', *Recht und Schrift im Mittelalter*, ed. P. Classen (Vorträge und Forschungen 23; Sigmaringen 1977) 319-47; and the challenging paper by K. Pennington, 'The Making of a Decretal Collection: The Genesis of Compilatio Tertia', *Proceedings of the Fifth International Congress of Medieval Canon Law, Salamanca 21-25 September 1976* (Mon. Iur. Can. ser. C vol. 6, Città del Vaticano 1980) 67-92.

p. 311 n.1: The expression 'trahi ad consequentiam' for an individual decision that will 'make general law' is based on Dig. 1.3.14 (=50.17.141) and Dig. 1.4.1.2.

p. 311 n.3: See also const. 'Tanta' §10 (=Cod. 1.17.2.10), for the intentions of Justinian as regards the Digest.

p. 312 n.1: The chronological argument was also used by Hostiensis, *Summa* 5.39 *de sent. excomm.* § Quis possit excommunicare, n.3 ad casum 14 (ed. Venice 1570 fol. 492va). But in a surprising anticipation of much later doctrines, Johannes Galensis observed in his gloss, written before 1215, on Innocent III's bull of promulgation for Comp. 3, that the argument 'hoc prius, illud posterius' could no longer be used since all the 'constitutiones' (note the Justinianic terminology) were here confirmed simultaneously: text in F. Gillmann, 'Johannes Galensis als Glossator . . .', *Archiv für kath. Kirchenr.* 105 (1925) 488ff. at 560 n.1.

II. Some Roman Manuscripts of Canonical Collections

p. 7 n.1: For part II of MS Vat. lat. 4977 see already F. Patetta, 'Contributi sulla storia del diritto romano nel medio evo', *Bullettino dell'Istituto di dir. rom.* 4 (1891/92) 285; repr. in *Studi sulle fonti giuridiche medievali*, ed. G. Astuti (Torino 1967) 157.

p. 7 n.3: The reference should be corrected to read *Diuersorum patrum sententie* . . . (Mon. Iur. Can. ser. B vol. 1; Città del Vaticano 1973) p. lxi.

p. 8 n.9: The fragment was mentioned in passing as an excerpt from Gratian by Patetta, 'Nota sopra alcuni Mss. delle Istituzioni di Giustiniano', *Bullettino* 4.44 = *Studi* 68 (cf. add. to p. 1 n.1 *supra*).

p. 9 and pp. 25-26: The *quaestio* 'Quidam uxorem duxit' is actually an abridged excerpt from Hugh of St. Victor's *De sacram.* 11.6 (PL 176.488-94), on which cf. G. Fransen, 'La formation du lien matrimonial au moyen âge', *Revue de dr. can.* 21 (1971) 106ff. at 115-17. See my note in *Bulletin of Med. Can. Law* N.S. 2 (1972) 5.

p. 11 n.19a: For the texts in Gratian C.19 q.3 and the canonists' comments, see now G. Melville, 'Zur Abgrenzung zwischen Vita canonica und Vita monastica . . .', *Secundum regulam vivere: Festschrift für P. Norbert Backmund* (Windberg 1978) 205-42.

p. 12 and pp. 26-28: Another copy of Pseudo-Jerome 'Inter alia' is found in San Daniele dei Friuli MS 203, fol. 158r-159r, see U.-R. Blumenthal, 'Codex Guarnerius 203', *Bulletin of Med. Can. Law* N.S. 5 (1975) 11ff. at 19.

p. 12 n.22: The end of Burchard's text in the MS from Monte Amiata is *Decr.* 19.48, as given here; H. Mordek's correction to 19.43 (in 'Nachrichten', *Quellen und Forsch. aus ital. Archiven* 53 [1973] 492) does not take into account that the last folios of the MS are misbound—i.e. that fol. 163-164 should precede fol. 162, which continues Burch. 19.43-48 etc.

p. 22f. (section iv)(1): My identification of Vat. lat. 6093 (saec. xii) with Antonio Agustín's *Liber B. Mariae Populeti* (No. 288 in the catalogue of his Latin MSS) is wrong. The whole paragraph needs rewriting, but this in turn requires a complete examination of the Tarragona MS 26. At present, only the following points are certain:

(1) As L. Gasparri has shown in 'Osservazioni sul codice Vallicelliano C.24', *Studi Gregoriani* 9 (1972) 469ff. at 508-9, the book Antonio Agustín called 'liber Gal.' in the autograph notes of this MS (on which cf. p. 18 *supra*) is today Vat. lat. 6093, the *Liber Tarraconensis* and once No. 287 of Agustín's *Bibliotheca latina* (In particular, where he cites by chapter *and* page, 'ex libro vet. Gal. V.c.53 p. 91', the citation fits no MS but Vat. lat. 6093).

(2) The name 'Liber (vetus) Gal.', which Mrs. Gasparri cannot explain, refers to Petrus Galesius (Pedro Galés), the interlocutor B. in the first book of Agustín's Dialogues (see *De emend. Grat.* 1.1 note 1 = ed. Baluze p. 1 marg. = *Opp.* 3.17 marg.), to whom this MS then belonged (*ibid.* 1.4: 'et tuus, B., Tarraconensis'; cf. 1.20, 'B. : . . et liber meus Tarraconensis', p. 201 = Baluze 228 = *Opp.* 3.102). Later Agustín acquired and annotated it with great care. Galesius died in prison at Zaragoza in 1595 before being sentenced by the Inquisition; see A. Morel Fatio, 'L'humaniste hétérodoxe catalan Pedro Galés', in his *Études sur l'Espagne* 4 (Paris 1925)

221-94 (first publ. 1902). This fact was still awkwardly glossed over by Mayáns in his biography of Agustín (see *Opp.* 2.lvi); and in the Yale copy of the Dialogues, the name of Galesius was everywhere erased by a former Spanish owner.

(3) The *Liber B. Mariae Populeti* (Poblet; No. 288 in the *Bibl. lat.*), from which Agustín had sent copies of individual texts to the *Correctores Romani* (see p. 23 *supra*) remains unidentified. Apparently, it is not the Tarragona MS 26, since the readings quoted by the *Correctores* from Agustín's copies of this *vetustus codex* do not correspond to those which I have collated (on microfilm) in the Tarragona MS. Besides, its provenance does not seem to be the monastery of Poblet, but that of Santas Creus, see P.F. Kehr, PU in Spanien 1.1 (Abh. Akad. Göttingen N.F. 18.2; Berlin 1926) 207-8.

p. 23 n.72: For correspondence of Agustín on the *Hispana*, see also *Opp.* 7.227-28 (to Pérez) and 216 (to Zuriga).

p. 24 n.73: On the Vallicelliana MS F.54, see also the papers by F. Patetta, 'Contributi sulla storia . . .' (cf. *supra*, addition to p. 1 n.2) 249-54; repr. in *Studi* 121-26; 'Nuove osservazioni sui manoscritti . . . del capitolare di Lamberto', *Riv. italiana per le scienze giur.* 11 (1891) 382-83; repr. in *Studi* 751-52; E.A. Lowe, 'A New List of Beneventan Manuscripts', *Collectanea in honorem A.M. Card. Albareda* II (Studi e Testi 220; Città del Vaticano 1962) 233; and Mordek, *loc. cit., supra* for p. 12 n.22.

pp. 25-28: See *supra*, additions to pp. 9, 12.

p. 29 app. font.: There is a third collection which begins the excerpt from Gregory with 'Volumus', the Collection of Jumièges (Rouen MS 704 fol. 150v), see P. Fournier in *Mélanges Fabre* (Paris 1902) 194n as cited by J.H. Erickson, 'The Collection in Three Books and Gratian's Decretum', *Bulletin of Med. Can. Law* N.S. 2 (1972) 71 n.23.

III. The So-called Canons of Nîmes (1096)

p. 177 n.14: Pisa 59 fol. 1-16 is a florilegium, described by G. Miccoli, 'Un florilegio sulla dignità e i diritti del monachesimo', *Bollettino stor. Pisano* 33-35 (1964-66) 117-29. The same collection is found in Florence, Laur. Conv. soppr. 91 (Badia Fior. 2685) pt. I (20ff.) saec. xii in.; it diverges from Pisa only after fol. 15v (Hieron.) of the latter. Thus, Florence 91 provides a *new* copy of St. Peter Damian's opusc. 28 . I owe this information to H. Mordek (letter of 15 June 1972).

p. 178 n.18: Vatican, Reg. lat. 982 is a composite MS of which fol. 35 is a single leaf (saec. xii). It is a fragment of a canonical or theological collection, which continues on the *recto*, 'Decretum urbani pape ex concilio nemaxensi' (=c.2 Nîmes), and on the *verso*, after other texts, 'Ex decretis Gregorii Pape': 'Oportet eos -- peccata soluere iuxta constitutum ccc. et xviii. patrum', which is identified by a marginal note in a seventeenth-century hand as 'Caput Concilij Nemausensis sub Vrbano' (i.e., c.3, but with the full ending as in the texts edited by Frank and by Constable (cited in note 3 *supra*).

p. 183: On the editions of the *De concordia* (1663, 1669, 1704, and Frankfurt 1708), see P. de Chiniac, in the new edition of Baluze's *Capitularia* (Paris 1780) col. 67a/b, with a biting judgment on de Marca.

On Gratian C.16 q.2 *Sane*: where Sirmond made the comment Baluze attributed to him has not been found.

p. 187: Paris, B.N. lat. 3860 is the 'quidam cod. s. Albini Andegavensis' from which Pierre de Marca edited the acts of Paschal II's Lateran Council of 1112. L. Weiland, MGH Const. 1.570 nos. 399-400 collated this edition as text no.4 (citing ed. Baluze 1663 II 357 of the *De concordia*); the readings he recorded can now be traced in the Paris MS (Letter from G. Fransen, October 1975).

p. 188: Arsenal MS 678 is probably of Umbro-Roman origin, according to H. Mordek, 'Bemerkungen zum mittelalterlichen Schatzverzeichnis von Porto/Rom', *Studia Grat.* 20 (1976) 231ff. at 239 n.30.

IV. Gerland of Besançon and the manuscripts of his 'Candela'

After this paper was published, during the summers of 1978 and 1979, Dr. U.-R. Blumenthal completed the difficult task of sorting out and cataloguing the papers and photostats of the late Friedrich Heyer (cf. p. 75 n.21 *supra*), now in Berkeley. This brought to light a bundle of notes on Gerlandus and photostats of selected pages from the Dijon MS (pp. 77, 81 *infra*) and also of Robert's article (p. 72), in addition to the copy of the unsigned letter from the *Mémoires de Trévoux* (p. 75 n.21) we had found earlier.

All these materials are a saddening testimony to Heyer's superb gift for research and his almost compulsive recoil from completing work for which he had meticulously assembled all that was needed. He traced nearly all the MSS discussed in this article and collected most of the existing bibliographical information. Substantial excerpts of texts from, and notes on authors quoted in the *Candela* show that Heyer at some time planned a major study.

p. 72: A considerable number of MSS of (the other) Gerland's *computus* is cited in Heyer's papers.

p. 74 n.17: On Hugo Metellus, *ep.* 33, see also F. Bliemetzrieder, 'L'oeuvre d'Anselme de Laon...' *Recherches de théol. anc. et médiév.* 7 (1935) 36 (Heyer).

p. 75: A further text to be studied in this context would be the *Magistri Gerlandi regulae super dialectica*, beg. 'Cum prolixitas et difficultas logice discipline', Orléans MS 260, mentioned in Heyer's notes from L. Delisle, 'Notice sur plusieurs manuscrits de la bibliothèque d'Orléans', *Notices et extraits* 31.1 (1884) 390.

p. 75 n.21: Before Kohler's catalogue notice for the Sainte-Geneviève MS, the *Lettre* of 1763 had already been cited and put to use by F.X. Laire, *Index librorum ab inventa typographia ad annum 1500* (Sens 1791) in his notes on Gerland, II 279-83. I owe this information and photocopies of the relevant pages to Professor Vernet of the École des Chartes (letter of 22 June 1977); see also pp. 77-78 *infra*. Heyer recorded Laire's book in his notes.

p. 76 n.22: Heyer also took notes from the Giessen MS 632 (saec. xviii) containing materials by H.C. Senckenberg.

p. 76 n.25: More material on the *Candela* printed in 1527, its author Peter Blommeveen of Leyden O. Carth., and its editor Johannes Gerecht of Landsberg (Joh. Justus Lansperger) O. Carth. was collected by Heyer.

pp. 77-78: The manuscript F.X. Laire had seen was that of the Dominicans of Troyes (now Paris, B.N. lat. 10623). The description he gave of it in the Besançon MS 1260 ('Pieces relatives à l'histoire de l'imprimerie'; see p. 77 n.28) is actually a draft in French for the printed notice in his *Index librorum* cited above, which is shorter. (I owe photostats of fols. 252r-255r of the Besançon MS to the kindness of Mlle. O. Paris, Conservateur des manuscrits.) Laire also was the first to quote Chifflet's information about an (unidentifiable) MS and to copy the document (cf. p. 78 n.35) at the end of the Dominicans' MS.

p. 79: MS Montpellier 403, which I inspected in 1976, contains only books I-VII.

V. The 'Extravagantes' of the Decretum in Biberach

p. 62: *Coll. Rotomagensis* is now called *Rotomagensis prima*.

p. 62f.: on JL 13162, see now M.G. Cheney, 'JL 13162 "Meminimus nos ex": One Letter or Two', BMCL 4 (1974) 66-70.

p. 66: The explicit of JL 9654 is 'finem imponat', not 'salutem' as printed.

p. 69: JL 11660 appears as an addition to C.16 q.1 c.45 in Paris, B.N. lat. 16899 ('Item Adrianus pp. Cantuar. aepo. Commisse'), and, marked *palea*, in Paris, B.N. lat. 3897, 15393, 16698, Mazar. 1290; Angers, Bibl. munic. 371. It is an addition to C.12 q.5 c.7 in Paris, B.N. lat. 3896. These occurences are noted from Mme. Rambaud's index to Decretum manuscripts. The majority of collections have the incipit 'Commisse', instead of 'Commissum'.

p. 71 (additional note): *Coll. 3 Dunelm.* is now called *1 Dun.*, and the reference here would be 1 Dun. 3.5-8 etc.; see C.R. Cheney and M.G. Cheney, *Studies in the collections of twelfth-century decretals*, from the papers of the late W. Holtzmann . . . (Mon. Iur. Can. ser. B vol. 3; Città del Vaticano 1979) 90, 78 n.8.

VI. The Decretal 'Presbiterum' (JL 13912) — A Letter of Leo IX

p. 133 n.4: See also the gloss in Cambridge, Gonville and Caius College 676 fol. 31r (bottom) on D.50, a great distinction on *crimen enorme* etc.: '... in heresi quandoque specialiter dispensatur ...; in homicidio: in extra (*blank space left*) hunc andream, que tamen non creditur decretalis. Presbiterum etiam istum ....'

p. 135: Another case in which *App.* attributes an earlier text wrongly to Alexander III addressing an English bishop is JL 14030, which certainly is conciliar and most likely belongs to 'Eugenius iii in concilio Remensi' (so *Tann.* 4.2.6, *Sang.* 3.5.2, *Erl.* 32.6, *Lips.* 32.8); cf. *canones Remenses* in *Sang.*; Singer, *Neue Beiträge über die Dekretalensammlungen* (SB Akad. Vienna 171.1 [1913]) 129 c.32.

VII. Collectio Francofortana

Three additional manuscripts of the Coll. Francofortana have since been found and are now listed in Cheney and Cheney, *Studies in the collections*... (cited *supra* in the addition to No. V p. 71) xxvii. A monograph on the collection is being prepared by Professor Peter Landau (Regensburg) from the papers of the late Walther Holtzmann.

p. 377 (JL [Ja.] 13937): For more recent studies on the career and work of Vacarius, see S. Kuttner and E. Rathbone, 'Anglo-Norman Canonists of the Twelfth Century', *Traditio* 7 (1949-51) 286-88; my paper of 1964, 'Dat Galienus opes et sanctio Justiniana', reprinted in Kuttner, *The History of Ideas and Doctrines of Canon Law in the Middle Ages* (London 1980) No. X at p. 241 and the articles of R.W. Southern and P. Stein cited in the 'Retractationes', *ibid.* p. 19 *ad loc.*

p. 393 ('Dilectus filius'): A definitive edition of this letter, based on better MSS, will soon appear: S. Chodorow and C. Duggan, *Decretales ineditae seculi XII* (Mon. Iur. Can. ser. B vol. 4; in press).

VIII. A Collection of Decretal Letters of Innocent III in Bamberg

p. 47: Addition to 'Notes on the Concordance' — *Bamb.* 12: text also in Paris, B.N. lat. 3922A, fol. 244rb (mutilated), Appendix to Rainier c.10, without inscription; not identified by S. Chodorow, 'An Appendix to Rainier of Pomposa's Collection', *Bulletin of Med. Can. Law* N.S. 3 (1973) 61.

p. 49 (Bamb. 17 section [5]): Other references to points that will be taken up 'in proximo generali concilio' occur in the pope's letters; see e.g., 'Sicut uolumus', No. 79 (Po. --) in C.R. Cheney and W. Semple, *Select Letters of Pope Innocent III concerning England (1198-1216)* (London-Edinburgh etc. 1953) p. 205.

p. 56 n.48: Add to the references M. Dykmans, *Les sermons de Jean XXII sur la vision béatifique* (Misc. Hist. Pont. 34; Rome 1973); A. Maier, 'Die Pariser Disputation des Geraldus Odonis über die Visio beatifica', *Arch. ital. per la storia della pietà* 4 (1965) 213-52.

IX. A New Eyewitness Account of the Fourth Lateran Council

pp. 118 n.18 and 122 n.31: The entry in Arch. Vat. Indice 254, fol. 13v for No. 162 of the lost Register of Innocent's 18th year contained indeed the notice of the Council 'Anno ab incarnatione uerbi . . .' as an official text. This results from a set of three excerpts from the Register made by the notary Paolo da Rieti in 1283 and certified with the seal of the *auditor causarum*. Professor C.R. Cheney kindly drew my attention to this document published by E. Martin-Chabot, 'Copies certifiées de bulles pontificales', *Mélanges d'arch. et d'hist. de l'École Fr. de Rome* 70 (1958) 433 (cf. p. 431). The second and third of these excerpts read:

> Item. Pateat omnibus evidenter quod in Regesto predicti domini Innocentii pape III. pont. ejus octavi decimi inter alia, hec specialiter continentur, viz. *Anno ab incarnatione Verbi . . . non fuit certus numerus comprehensus* et cetera.
>
> Item pateat omnibus evidenter quod in eodem Registro, ubi agitur de annotatione prelatorum qui interfuerunt concilio supradicto, inter alios hii taliter exprimuntur, videlicet *Innocentius Catholice Ecclesie episcopus, Gervasius Constantinopolitanus, Radolfus Jerosolimitanus patriarcha* et cetera.
>
> Ego Paulus de Raate (*leg.* Reate) . . .

This corresponds precisely to the consecutive entries for Nos. 162 and 234 of the Register in the *Indice*. Professor Cheney convincingly suggests that between the general notice and the list of signatories present, the seventy-one decrees themselves (cc.1-70 + 'Ad liberandam') were entered as Nos. 163-233 (letter of 4 September 1972).

p. 132: The source of all later editions of the pope's sermon 'Desiderio desideravi' was the edition of his *Opera* published in Cologne 1582, according to W. Imkamp, 'Sermo ultimus, quem fecit Dominus Innocentius papa tertius . . .', *Röm. Quartalsschr. für christl. Altertumskunde* 70 (1975) 149ff. at 150-52, where only four MSS (Vat. lat. 700, 10902, and two Subiaco MSS) are listed. Imkamp's publication is based (cf. p. 150 n.11) on an unpublished Lateran University thesis (1961) by G. Scuppa. The MS tradition must be much wider; in addition to the Giessen fragment and the Paris MS I have mentioned, there are at least, as A. García y García tells me, Cambridge, Pembroke 101, fol. 81vb-82vb; Lincoln 177, fol. 155ra-156rc; Paris lat. 1568, fol. 95vb-97vb, and probably many more. The fragment in Carpentras MS 31 (s.xiv), inscribed according to Imkamp 'In concilio pro successu terrae sanctae' (*sic*; *leg.* pro succursu t.s.) would rather seem to be the const. 'Ad liberandam'.

p. 136: Several illuminations in the Toledo codex *de primatu* etc. and the Latin text of the first page were published, with commentary, by R. Foreville, 'L'iconographie du XIIe concile oecuménique, Latran IV (1215)',

Mélanges offerts à René Crozet, ed. P. Gallais and Y.-J. Riou (Poitiers 1966) II 1121-30; however, the quality of both the plates and the transcription are inferior to F. Fita's publication, 'Santiago de Galicia . . .' of 1902, cited p. 136 n.38 *supra*. Copies of the 'Pars Concilij lateranij' from the Toledo codex are also in Madrid B.N. MS Dd. 47 (see P. Ewald, 'Reise nach Spanien . . .', *Neues Archiv* 6 [1880/81] 295ff.) and Rome, Vallicelliana C.23 fol. 71 (P.F. Kehr, 'PU in Rom: Die römischen Bibliotheken III', *Nachr. Göttingen* 1903 p. 126ff.), from Antonio Agustín's library.

p. 145: Benedict's *Liber politicus* was dedicated not to Innocent II but to Cardinal Guido of Castello, who was to be Innocent's successor in 1143 as Celestine II.

p. 146: The title 'S. Marie fundentis oleum' was actually used by the cardinal priest Baldwin, 1137-38 (see JL I p. 840) in subscribing Innocent II's letters JL 7836, 7887 (so also the forgery JL †7846), but his successor Gregory signed as 'presb. card. tit. S. Calixti', 1140-1154; in June 1153 once with the title 'S. Marie trans Tiberim', a designation that was to replace the Calixtus title only in the 1180's.

p. 151: Other instances of Innocent's quick-witted courtroom manner are given by C.R. Cheney, *Pope Innocent III and England* (Papsttum und Päpste 9; Stuttgart 1976) 6f. See also Pierre de Sampson, as quoted by Johannes Andreae, *Novella* X 3.32.7.

p. 160: The letter of King Henry II to Barbarossa quoted in Rahewin 3.7 has been given a different interpretation by H.E. Mayer, 'Staufische Weltherrschaft', *Festschrift Karl Pivec* (Innsbruck 1966) 267-78.

p. 167: An example for prelates staying in Rome after the Council 'pro specialibus negotiis' is found in Innocent's summons of the Austin canons (29 February 1216) to a General Chapter by letters entrusted to the abbot of S. Maria de Pratis (Leicester) 'qui propter hoc iuxta mandatum nostrum apud apostolicam sedem remansit' (Cheney and Cheney, *Letters of Pope Innocent III (1198-1216) concerning England and Wales* [Oxford 1967] no. 1056).

p. 167ff.: It is exaggerated to say of Frederick II's *lex edictalis* that some ('certaines') of the emperor's *Constitutiones* 'reprenaient mot à mot les statuts du IVe Concile du Latran' and that thus the conciliar statutes acquired as imperial *loi d'État* 'une universalité et une efficacité qu'ils n'avaient pas en fait comme disposition conciliaire': so R. Manselli, 'De la "persuasio" à la "coercitio",' *Le Credo, la morale et l'Inquisition* (Cahiers de Fanjaux 6; Toulouse 1971) 194. In fact, it is only one of the emperor's ten constitutions, c. 7 (Krüger 6-7), which repeats one of the conciliar constitutions (c.3), though shortened and rephrased. Even after its insertion among the *authenticae* of the Codex (post Cod. 1.4.19, 1.5.4) one could not call this text 'more universal' than that of the Council, considering the limited authority of the Empire and imperial law in Europe.

X. Johannes Teutonicus, das vierte Laterankonzil und die Compilatio quarta

p. 608 n.1: MS Florence Laur. S. Croce IV sin. 2, fol. 130r-237v, has Tancred's *Apparatus* to Comp. 3 only as far as 1.6.4, then Johannes Teutonicus.

pp. 608-17: The apparatus of glosses Johannes Teutonicus wrote on the conciliar constitutions has been repeatedly discussed and is now edited by A. García y García in the forthcoming *Constitutiones Concilii quarti Lateranensis una cum Commentariis glossatorum* (Mon. Ius. Can. ser. A vol. 2, Città del Vaticano 1980).

p. 618 (MS Florence, Laur. S. Croce III sin. 6): The authorship of Damasus for this apparatus of glosses has since been established by A. García y García in his article 'El Concilio IV de Latrán y sus comentarios', *Traditio* 14 (1958) 484ff. at 498-501 and in the Introduction of his forthcoming edition, *Constit. Concilii.*

p. 618: The Prologue 'Questionum articuli' in the Alcobaça MS should be emended to read 'Quoniam omnes questionum articuli' (the scribe mistook the first two words for a lemma from const. 1 *v.* 'Qui omnes', lin. 30 in Leonardi's edition, *Conc. Oecum. decreta,* Herder 1962; 3rd ed. 1973). It actually is the opening of the *Casus Parisienses* on the Council, cf. my notes in the Bulletin of the Institute, *Traditio* 13 (1957) 469 and 24 (1968) 491, on Theiner's garbled information (1836) and the rediscovery in MS Paris lat. 3931, fol. 86va-88va by Dr. Martin Bertram. The edition of the Prologue by I. da Rosa Pereira, 'Dois manuscritos alcobacenses da Primeira Compilação', *Lumen* 1962 (offprint pp. 11-12) is now superseded by García's forthcoming edition of the *Casus Parisienses* in *Constit. Concilii* (cited *supra*).

p. 618 n.6: Parallels to the words of praise for Innocent III in Vincentius and (for Gregory IX) Philippus are mentioned p. 625 n.12 *infra;* see also Vincentius's Apparatus on the *arbor consanguinitatis,* Worcester MS F. 122 fol. 1va/b '. . . quia non est inuentus similis illi qui legem conseruet . . .'

p. 619: For Alanus, see now S. Kuttner, 'The Collection of Alanus: A Concordance of its Two Recensions', *Rivista di Storia del dir. ital.* 26 (1953) 37-53.

p. 620 and n.14: The collections of Gilbert, Alanus, and Bernard of Compostella probably lack only three (not five) of the decretals in Comp. 4 that certainly antedate the official Comp. 3: see the observations of C.R. Cheney, 'Three Decretal Collections before Compilatio IV', *Traditio* 15 (1959) 477ff. on Coll. Pragensis cc.16 and 27, which suggest somewhat later dates for Po. 2360 and 3018.

p. 621 n.14 (end): The 16 letters entered arbitrarily at the end of the eleventh year in the Register (quire xiii) are Reg. xi.262-77 = Po. 3660-73, 3105, 3340. They were only enregistered there because of the ongoing work of drafting the official Comp. 3, which was to include nothing but decretals that could be found in the Register. Cf. F. Kempf, *Die Register Innocenz' III* (Miscell. hist. pontif. 9; Rome 1945) 95ff.

p. 621 n.17: Baluze's error on Po. 3765 (29 June 1210) as part of Po. 3660 is repeated by Kempf, *loc. cit.*

p. 622: In addition to the collections of Prague (new shelfmark: XXIII.E.59) and Vat. Pal. 658, C.R. Cheney, 'Three Decretal Collections' (cited *supra*), *Trad.* 15.464-83, analyzed *Abrincensis secunda* (Avranches MS 149, fol. 119r-126v); in 1972 I analyzed a fourth collection of this type, *Bambergensis secunda*, in a paper now reprinted in this volume, No. VIII. (The statistics given above, p. 622 n.25, of decretals in Comp.4 with/without ascertainable dates have to be slightly modified.)

p. 622 n.22: For the portrait of Innocent III see now G.B. Ladner, 'Eine Prager Bildniszeichnung Innocenz' III. und die Collectio Pragensis', *Studia Grat.* 11 (1967) 23-35; F. Kempf, 'Die Umschrift des Prages Miniaturbildnisses Innocenz' III.', *Storia et storiografia: Studi in onore di Eugenio Dupré Theseider* (Rome 1974) 661-67.

p. 622 n.23: The inscription 'Idem in registro C. tit. S. Laurentii presb. cardinali . . .' in 4 Comp. 1.3.4 does not indicate use of the Register; it comes from Alanus (rec. 2) 1.6.14, the compiler's source.

p. 622 n.27: Johannes Teutonicus omitted c.42 in Comp. 4 although he had glossed the constitution. As Professor Pennington kindly informs me, it is entered in Cordoba MS 10, fol. 282va as an addition (with Johannes's gloss) to 4 Comp. 2.2.4.

p. 623: On the *Principium* of Johannes de Deo see also A.D. de Sousa Costa, *Um mestre português em Bolonha no seculo XIII, João de Deus: Vida e obras* (Braga 1957) 137-42.

p. 624: Cordoba MS 10 fol. 274ra is likewise inscribed, 'Incipiunt quarte decretales a m'. jo. compilate' as Professor Pennington first noted. For a full description of the Cordoba MS see A. García y García, 'Canonistica Hispana (II)', *Traditio* 23 (1967) 507-11; A. García *et. al.*, *Catálogo de los manuscritos e incunables de la Catedral de Córdoba* (Salamanca 1976) 15-18. Pennington has also noted glosses signed by Philip of Aquileja and Marcoaldus (Marcoardus), two masters at Padua, among the additional layers of glosses on Comp. 4 in both the Admont and the Cordoba MSS. On Marcoaldus (Marquard von Ried) see now W. Stelzer, 'Österreichische Kanonisten des 13. Jahrhunderts', *Österr. Archiv für Kirchenr.* 30 (1979) 57ff. at 78-80; Pennington, 'The Making of a Decretal Collection' (cited p. 1 *supra*, 'Retractationes' No. I, 'Quelques observations . . .') 77 n.27.

p. 624 n.10: On Zoën see also P. Herde, 'Ein Pamphlet der päpstlichen Kurie gegen Kaiser Friedrich II. . . .', *Deutsches Archiv* 23 (1967) 468ff. at 477 n.122, 503 n.149, 506.

p. 626 n.17: The late Professor Juncker's communication in 1938 on a second copy of the *Principium Borgh.* in a Brussels MS was based on a slip of memory of what F. Heyer had mentioned to him. In 1960 the late

Professor Heyer (d. 1973) told me 'in strict confidence' that it was the now lost MS Breslau (Wroclaw) Univ. I. Q. 102, fol. 201rb-202ra, of which he owned a photostat, and that it was a very similar text, but not the same. The photos and notes from Heyer's estate are now in Berkeley (cf. *supra*, 'Retractationes' No. IV, 'Gerland of Besançon'); the *Principium* begins 'Quoniam tunc decens et amabile Deo principium comprobatur'. K. Pennington, 'The Making of a Decretal Collection', 72ff. discusses and prints some passages from it side by side with the parallels in *Borgh.* and Joh. de Deo.

The prologue 'Sicut omnium liberalium artium' in Bamb. can. 64 belongs to a work of *Casus et Notabilia decretalium*; a second copy exists in Paris, B.N. lat. 14470, fol. 41r-144r (from St. Victor). Schulte's judgment on the account the prologue gives ('etwas confus') is correct. The account reappears, with the same errors, in Vincent of Beauvais, *Speculum doctrinale* 7.49 (e.g. Paris, B.N. lat. 6428, fol. 158vb).

p. 628: A criticism of the official selection made in Comp. 3 could for instance be found in 4 Comp. 3.9.4 where Johannes placed a piece which had been omitted from the letter Po. 898 in 3 Comp. 3.23.2 and 2.1.1: he repeated part of 3 Comp. 2.1.1 and combined it with the 'new' piece.

p. 630-34 (text): A. Maier, *Codices Burghesiani Bibliothecae Vaticanae* (Studi e Testi 170; Città del Vaticano 1952) p. 55, gives the opening words as 'Sciendum quia . . .' and the end as 'nunc ad lecturam accedamus'. The first lines of our text are faded and the ink has partly flaked off, but under the ultraviolet lamp the first word is undoubtedly 'Ceterum'—the writer uses the rhetorical device of a low-key opening. In the last line, the correct reading is 'litteram' (spelled 'licteram').

XI. Die Konstitutionen des ersten allgemeinen Konzils von Lyon

These investigations on the genesis and publication of Innocent IV's first collection of *Novellae* were further developed by P.-J. Kessler, 'Untersuchungen über die Novellengesetzgebung Papst Innocenz IV. (I)', *Zeitschr. der Savigny-Stift. für Rechtsgesch. Kan. Abt.* 31 (1942) 142ff. at 213-33, discussing many additional MSS; id., 'Wiener Novellen: Supplementum novellisticum I', *Studia Grat.* 12 (1967) 91ff. at 93-95, 98-99; P. Gerbenzon, 'Description of a Manuscript at The Hague', *Traditio* 21 (1965) 513-15 (on MS s'Gravenhage, Koninkl. Bibl. 73.E.14); M. Bertram, 'Aus kanonistischen Handschriften der Periode 1234 bis 1298', *Proceedings of the Fourth International Congress of Med. Can. Law, Toronto . . . 1972* (Mon. Iur. Can. ser. C vol. 5; Città del Vaticano 1976) 24ff. at 35-36 (summary information on eleven further MSS for the pre-conciliar and conciliar material). One may further add: Angers 379, fol. 215va (an introductory gloss, 'Ad evidentiam dicendorum', on the history of Coll. I, kindly communicated by Professor Kessler, who plans to edit this text with a commentary; letter of 31 May 1978); Barcelona, Univ. MS 588, fol. 47ra-48vb (cf. F. Miquel Rosell, *Inventario general de manuscritos de la Bibl.*

Universitaria de B. [Madrid 1958]; to be examined); Nürnberg Stadtbibl. Cent. IV 99, prefixed to a MS of Liber Extra (communication from Professor Weigand, 27 March 1965); perhaps Uppsala C.570, fol. 84r-85v (cf. M. Andersson-Schmitt, *Manuscripta mediaevalia Upsaliensia* [Acta Bibl. R. Universitatis Upsal. 15; Uppsala 1970] No. 1559; to be examined).

p. 88 after section III 7 add.: Another, less satisfactory reconstruction is found in J. Biner, *Apparatus eruditionis ad Jurisprudentiam praesertim ecclesiasticam* . . . (3rd ed. Augsburg and Freiburg 1754) 185ff.

p. 91 After section III 12 add.: The most recent attempt at reconstruction before this article appeared was that by H.J. Schroeder, *Disciplinary decrees of the General Councils: Text, translation, and commentary* (St. Louis-London 1937) 301-23 (Engl.), 585-94 (Latin).

p. 94: On the correct date of publication of the Clementines, 1 November 1317, see the paper on const. 'Saepe', republished as No. XIII in this volume, pp. 433-34.

p. 100f.: The const. R 11 (Coll. I c.17 = III c.26) was already absent from Matthew's source, as shown by other traditions of M 1-10: thus in the *Casus* 'Si quis impugnans' (cf. Kessler, 'Untersuchungen . . . (I)' *Zeitschr.* . . . Kan. Abt. 32 [1943] 228-30; and '. . . (III)', *ibid.* 33.104-6); MSS Paris lat. 15400, St. Omer 459, and Vatican Arch. S. Pietro G. 18 of the *Novellae* (cf. Bertram, 'Aus kanonistischen Handschriften . . .' 35-36).

p. 105: A similar inscription, 'Constitutiones Innocentii pape .iiii. ante concilium lugdun. et in concilio cum glossa' in London, Lambeth Palace MS 103 fol. 289v; see M.R. James, *A descriptive Catalogue of the Manuscripts in the Library of Lambeth Palace* (Cambridge 1932) p. 171.

pp. 110-16: For Innocent IV's own glosses on his legislative work and for Petrus de Sampson as writer on the *Novellae* these pages are superseded by Kessler's 'Untersuchungen . . . (II)', *Zeitschr.* . . . Kan. Abt. 32 (1943) 354-76; see also O. Pontal, 'Quelques remarques sur l'oeuvre canonique de Pierre de Sampzon', *Annuarium hist. conciliorum* 8 (1976) 126-42, who proposes a revision of the list of his works and those of Bernard of Montmirat (pp. 133ff.; the evidence is unsatisfactory); and see Bertram, *op. cit.* 34.

Don Gonzalo García Gudal, dean of the chapter of Toledo, owned at the time of his election to the see of Cuenca (1273) an 'apparado de Inocencio sobre las decretales nuevas' and 'otro apparado de Inocencio sobre todas las decretales': M. Alonso Alonso, 'Bibliotecas medievales de los arzobispos de Toledo', *Razón y Fe* 123 (1941) 303.

p. 118: On the final section of const. 'Volentes', which also occurs as separate piece 'Sane quia de huiusmodi' among *extravagantes*, see Kessler, 'Untersuchungen . . . (II)', *Zeitschr.* . . . Kan. Abt. 32 (1943) 368f.; '. . . (III)', *ibid.* 34.67-69, 85; 'Wiener Novellen' 103 n.66, 109. For the antecedents of the decree *Volentes* see also Innocent IV 'In generali', 14 May 1245 (Po. 11633).

p. 129: Goffredus de Prefectis was *auditor* delegated for cases in 1225, not *auditor litterarum contradictarum*, see P. Herde, *Beiträge zum päpstlichen Kanzlei- und Urkundenwesen im 13. Jahrhundert* (Kallmünz 1961) 17 n.140; 2nd ed. (1967) 21 n.172; A. Paravicini Bagliani, *Cardinali di Curia e 'familiae' cardinalizie dal 1227 al 1254* (Padova 1972) I 276 n.1.

XII. Conciliar Law in the Making

In recent years more light has been thrown on the genesis of the Lyonese constitutions and related documents by the studies of Roberg, Franchi, Bertram, and Boyle, cited in the notes that follow below. It should, however, be stated from the outset that the original, conciliar shape of the *constitutiones* could have become known before I published this essay in 1949, had I paid greater attention ten years earlier to a letter by Rudolf Köstler written on 22 April 1939 in reply to a inquiry of mine about the First Council of Lyons, whose decisions—then the subject of my research—were contained in the Vienna MS 566 (from Salzburg), fol. 41r-63r, according to the printed catalogue. This entry was wrong, Köstler told me; the constitutions were those of Lyons II, in an unusual order, beginning with a letter 'Zelus fidei' of Gregory X, and followed by the provincial council of Salzburg (1274). At the time, I merely noted his correction (Lyons II, not I) in the article of 1940 here republished as No. XI, at p. 74 n.10; and I did not look at his letter again until it fell into my hands long after World War II, when I sorted out boxes of papers and notes that had been stored for me at the Vatican Library 'for the duration' after my somewhat hurried departure from Rome in the spring of 1940 when Italy entered the war.

It was not difficult, after rereading the forgotten part of Köstler's information, all these many years later, to conclude that the Vienna MS must contain, similarly to the Washington fragment, the Lyonese constitutions at their conciliar stage. Further correspondence with Professor Köstler before his death (11 February 1952), and collation of the photostats he obtained for me at the Nationalbibliothek, showed that the conciliar text is better preserved in the codex from Salzburg (=S) than in the Washington fragment. It will obviously be impossible here to supply in full the evidence from the collations I made in S; occasional references to its text must suffice.

One aspect of S, however, deserves particular attention: the provincial council of Salzburg, which follows immediately on fol. 63v sqq. (=Mansi 24.135-44) was held by Archbishop Friedrich and his suffragans specifically for spreading the knowledge of the 'statuta sacri generalis Concilii celebrati proxime in Lugduno' and urging their observance. The acts of Salzburg are elsewhere dated 31 October ('ii. kal. nouembris') 1274 (see Hartzheim's note reproduced in Mansi 24.135 n.1). This is the day preceding Gregory X's formal letters of publication—a fact historians do not seem to have noted. It means that the copy of the Lyonese statutes that served the bishops meeting in Salzburg must have been the one which Archbishop Friedrich had brought with him from Lyons, and thus a copy representing the earlier, conciliar redaction. It may well have been the source from which the scribe of S copied his text.

Let us finally note that a fifteenth-century canonist annotated S with references to the *Liber Sextus*, correctly identifying also those pieces that differ in their incipit or otherwise from the latter.

p. 40 n.4: The text in Boehmer's *Corpus* is found after col. 368 of the separately paginated appendix to vol. II (not after II 368).

p. 41 n.8: Vienna MS 2113, fol. 130vb offers a better reading for Schulte's quotation from Boatinus's *Lectura*: '. . . inspectis inscriptionibus omnes decretales uidentur (inducuntur *Sch.*) facte in concilio lugdunensi . . .'.

p. 42: The so-called *Brevis nota* has now been reedited from the best and oldest MS, Vat. Ottob. lat. 2250 (on which cf. p. 42 nn.11,14, and collations *passim*) under its original title *Ordinatio concilii . . .*, with critical apparatus, notes, and comments by A. Franchi O.F.M., *Il Concilio di Lione (1274) secondo la Ordinatio concilii generalis Lugdunensis* (Studi e testi francescani 33; Rome 1965). Franchi was not aware of the Harleian MS 3603 in the British Library, written in a curial hand (s.xiii ex./s.xiv in.), fol. 123v-125r: 'Incipit ordinacio concilii generalis facta Lugduni per dominum G. papam X^m.'; preceded on fol. 120r-123v by 'Casus spectantes ad penitentiarios domini pape', which lists their powers of absolving and dispensing as of 1290, 'in the third year of Nicholas IV'.

p. 42 n.11: MS Vat. lat. 4734 should not be considered the copy of the *Ordinatio* (BN) made for Gregory XI (1370-78), but a fifteenth-century copy made from that (lost) MS, according to M. Dykmans, review of Franchi, in *Gregorianum* 47 (1966) 639.

p. 42 n.14: Like the Ottobonianus, MS Harley 3603 gives the correct date, 4 June, for the third session. Further confirmation comes from a Vatican MS of the constitutions, Pal. lat. 832, fol. 36r-93v, discovered by Dr. M. Bertram; see his paper 'Aus kanonistischen Handschriften . . .', *Proceedings Toronto* (cited *supra*, 'Retractationes' No. XI) p. 37f. There we read after c.30 (sess. III): Datum Lugduni anno domini mcc.lxxiiii. tempore concilii generalis, scilicet in uigilia sancti Bonifacii martiris [=4 June]. Publicata sunt hec iii. non. [*leg.* ii. non.?] iunii.' As written, the date reckoned from the Nones would be self-contradictory (3 June).

p. 43: The duplication of the word *ecclesiarum* (lin. 3) is mistaken.

L. Boyle, 'The Date of the Commentary of William Duranti on the Constitutions of the Second Council of Lyons', *Bulletin of Med. Can. Law* N.S. 4 (1974) 39-47, interprets *procurauimus, procuraui* in Duranti's comments as 'lobbying for', rather than having a share in drafting some of the constitutions.

p. 46: The full text of *Cum sacrosancta* has now been published by B. Roberg from the *rotulus* at Durham, Dean and Chapter Muniments, Loc. I no. 60*, in his *Die Union zwischen der griechischen und der lateinischen Kirche auf dem II. Konzil von Lyon (1274)* (Bonner historische Forschungen 24; Bonn 1964) 247. I have collated the text with the Vienna MS (S) fol. 62v-63r (where already Köstler had noticed its presence). Three more MSS containing *Cum sacrosancta* are recorded by M. Bertram, 'Aus kanonistischen Handschriften . . .' p. 37.

p. 47f.: The Osnabrück MS is today at the Niedersächsisches Staatsarchiv, Depositum 58d. A full analysis in Roberg, *Die Union* 223ff., who edits from it seven documents of importance for the history of the union at 226-47, and points to another text of *Zelus fidei* in Oxford, Bodleian Library Auct. F.3.10, fol. 210r-211v (S.C. 2582, part E of a composite MS). I have collated S fol. 41r-45v; three further MSS in Bertram 37f. *Zelus fidei* is also recorded, without identification, as No. 1519 Uppsala, Univ. C.583, fol. 199v-202v, in the strangely organized catalogue by M. Andersson-Schmitt, *Manuscripta mediaevalia Upsaliensia* (Acta Bibl. R. Universitatis Upsal. 16; Uppsala 1970). Piecing together the contents of the MS from the shelfmark index (p. 151), one finds that the decree is followed by No. 1629 (=C.583, fol. 202v-216r), 'Fideli ac deuota. Gregorius qui in generali concilio lugdunensi . . .', apparently an unknown commentary on the constitutions. The other contents of the MS (cf. catal. Nos. 1574, 1577, 1580, 1689) point to Franciscan provenance, after 1281.

p. 48 n.44: For appointments and reports of *collectores* in Italy, see P. Guidi, *Rationes decimarum Italicae: Tuscia* I (Studi e Testi 53; Città del Vaticano 1932) preface.

p. 50 n.47: For the departure of many prelates see also Boatinus, *Lectura*, proem. v. *et post* (cf. p. 41 n.9 *supra*):

> . . . uel dic quod concilium Lugd. recepit quemdam tractum, quia cum omnes prelati uocati essent ad concilium et ibidem moram aliquam contraxissent expectantes Grecos qui citati nondum uenerant, quia hoc erat durum quod uniuersale concilium ibidem contraheret tantam moram, licentiati fuerunt multi prelati et quidam remanserunt ibidem ut Grecos uenientes ad concilium expectarent, et hoc est forte causa quare dicat 'in generali concilio et post' (Vienna MS 2113, fol. 130vb).

p. 51f. and nn.54,55: The Washington fragment at Catholic University has now the shelfmark MS 183. The two MSS at the University of North Carolina are not recorded in C.U. Faye and W.H. Bond, *Supplement to the Census of Medieval and Renaissance Manuscripts in the United States and Canada* (New York 1962). As to the other remnants of the codex from the *Minoritenkloster* in Vienna—i.e. those belonging in 1949 to Dr. L. Schopp (New York) and Prof. S.H. Thomson (Boulder, Colo.), both since deceased, nothing is known about their present location. This is particularly unfortunate in the case of the original binding (see p. 52), which was the only evidence for the make-up of the MS before it was dismembered.

p. 54: Going beyond the 'striking resemblance' of the order in W to the account of the *Ordinatio* (BN), S fully retains the order of the latter. The original sequence is less well represented in the Vatican MS Pal. lat. 832, fol. 86r-93v (on which see also the additional note to p.42 n.14 *supra*), as recorded by Bertram 37f., where more MSS are cited which show differences from the vulgate order. See also T. Schmid, 'Canon Law in Manuscripts from Medieval Sweden', *Traditio* 7 (1949/51) 444ff. at 448 for a fragment of this kind.

p. 57-59: For further MSS of *Zelus fidei* see the addition to p. 47f. *supra*. The whole cluster of decrees has been edited again by C. Leonardi, in *Conc. Oecum. decreta* (Herder 1962, 3rd ed. 1977), with the use of W as basic text for *Non nobis* (=1d). In S, fol. 41r-45v, the decree *Non nobis* is missing; according to Roberg, *Die Union* 223, it is shorter than W in the Bodleian MS Auct. F.3.10, fol. 210r-211v.

p. 60-65: The conciliar version, used also by Leonardi, *Conc. Oecum. decreta*, in the app. crit. of c.2 has now been fully edited by Roberg, 'Der konziliare Wortlaut des Konclave-Dekrets *Ubi periculum* von 1274', *Annuarium hist. concilior.* 2 (1970) 231ff. at 256-62, from the sealed originals in the Vatican Archives (cf. p. 62); variants of W, the Bodleian MS just cited (fol. 213r/v), and the Durham *rotulus* (cited in the addition to p. 46 *supra*) are given at 243-45. I have no significant variants to add from my collation of S, fol. 52r-54v.

p. 66 n.89: For Johannes Andreae, the reference should be given as gl. Sext. 1.20.un v. *Absolutionis beneficium*, and summary (or rubric) extracted from it in the editions.

p. 66 n.95: 'flectant genua cordis sui': Also the letter of St. Clement to the Corinthians c.57.1 gives the implicit quotation from *Oratio Manass.* in the plural, τὰ γόνατα . . .

p. 68f.: The const. *Hoc consultissimo* (c.22) has an arenga in S fol. 60r/v: 'Induxit olim necessitas . . . malitia excrescente conuersum, hoc consultissimo . . .', which differs from the arenga 'Testimonium in Joseph' quoted p. 69 from the old French translation, 'Le temoignage de Joseph'. We therefore have here two stages of revision before the final publication of the statutes. Both arengae were meanwhile found by M. Bertram in Paris MS lat. 14765, in the margins of c.22, one to the left, the other to the right; 'Induxit olim' also in MSS Rouen 717 and Vat. Pal. lat. 832: see Bertram 37f.

p. 72 n.102: The initial gloss by Joh. Andreae to Sext 5.5.1 as printed in the sixteenth-century edition is actually lifted from his *Novella, ad loc.* (ed. Venice 1581, fol. 144rb); see also his addition to gl. 'hoc ergo' (v. *alienigenas*) *ibid.* fol. 144vb.

p. 75: The reading 'queque' of W which I emended in item [5] is defensible when understood in the sense of 'whichever' (*quaequae*).

XIII. The Date of the Constitution "Saepe", the Vatican Manuscripts, and the Roman Edition of the Clementines

p. 429: A publication of the collection in the *audientia litterarum contradictarum* is reported by hearsay in Stephanus Hugoneti's *apparatus* on the Clementines, *proem.*: '. . . dicunt quod post premissa auditor contradictarum eas publicauit in audientia litterarum de mandato domini Clementis', Philadelphia, Univ. of Pennsylvania MS lat. 95, fol. 2va. This is probably a misunderstanding of what Johannes Andreae wrote in the *Glos. ord.* on John XXII's bull of promulgation, v. *de cetero*: '. . . et ut a domino Atrebatensi audiui, qui tunc contradictarum erat auditor, Clemens precepit eas in audientia publicari'. On the Philadelphia MS see N. Zacour, 'Stephanus Hugoneti and his Apparatus on the Clementines', *Traditio* 17 (1961) 527-30.

p. 432: The wrong date 1326 for Joh. Andreae's *Apparatus* is still given in the *New Catholic Encycl.* (1967) art. 'Clementines' 3.946, and in C. Mesini, 'Il "Liber secretus iuris pontificii" dello Studio di Bologna', *Apollinaris* 43 (1970) 373ff. at 401.

p. 433 n.23: Also several MSS for Oxford are correctly dated 1 November 1317, see L.E. Boyle, 'The Curriculum in the Faculty of Canon Law at Oxford . . .', *Oxford Studies presented to D.A. Callus* (Oxford 1964) 159 n.1.

p. 435: For Jesselin see now J. Tarrant, 'The Life and Works of Jesselin de Cassagnes', *Bulletin of Med. Can. Law* 9 (1979) 37-64.

p. 436 n.42: The three glossators and Johannes Andreae form also the basis of an apparatus compiled by Simon Vairet, see Schulte, *Geschichte* II 405; Fournier, 'Simon Vairet, canoniste', *Hist. litt. de la France* 35 (1921) 608, citing MSS and pointing in note 1 to another, anonymous compilation from Guillaume, Jesselin, and Paulus in Paris, Arsenal MS 697 (from St. Victor), fol. 150ff. (Dr. Jacqueline Tarrant drew my attention to these texts.)

p. 438: Johannes de Crivellis received his doctorate in canon law 24 September 1470, see C. Piana, *Ricerche su le Università di Bologna e di Parma* (Spicilegium Bonaventurianum) 423 No. 114; more on him pp. 427, 463 (Nos. 118, 168).

p. 439: The theme for disputation 'Quidam habens duas manus . . .' is taken from Bartholomaeus Brixiensis, *Quaest. dominicales* q.85.

p. 440: John XXII, const. 'Ex debito' is similarly labeled in the Berlin MS Hamilton 181 (after Clementines and *Extravagantes Jo. XXII*), fol. 111v: 'Explicit hec decretalis que est bona et utilis'.

On the forged *Professio fidei* of Boniface VIII see also F. Dvornik, *The Photian Schism* (Oxford 1948) 448-51. As for its date, I overlooked the convincing arguments for A.D. 1407 proposed by J. Lulvès, 'Die Entstehung der angeblichen Professio fidei Papst Bonifaz' VIII.', *Mitteil. des Instituts für österr. Geschichtsforsch.* 31 (1910) 375-91: the text was fabricated in order to influence Gregory XII.

p. 444f.: The *dubietates et questiones* on *Execrabilis* are also found, after four *extravagantes* of John XXII, in New York, Hispanic Society MS B 2565, fol. 90r-92v. They are not found in MSS Vat. lat. 1397 and Ross. lat. 565 of Guillaume's *Apparatus* on the three *extravagantes*, cited pp. 437, 440 *supra*.

p. 445: Dr. J. Tarrant kindly called my attention to two more Vatican MSS of the Clementines which I overlooked:

Vat. lat. 6055, part B of a composite MS, fol. 1r-78r: *Clem.* with *Glos. ord.*; *Exivi* placed at end, without gloss; fol. 78r-79v: John XXII, *Execrabilis.*

Chis. lat. E.VIII.242, fol. 1r-56v: *Clem.* with *Glos. ord.*, misbound and incomplete (fol. 21ra-38vb, 1ra-20vb: 1.5.un-3.13.3; 39ra-56va: 5.3.3-end); fol. 56va-58rb: John XXII, *Execrabilis.*

p. 446: GW 7091, *editio princeps* for the *Extravagantes Jo. XXII*, bears a striking similarity to MS Vat. lat. 6055 (see above, addition to p. 445) part C and was probably printed (Rome 1478) from a twin copy of this MS (communication of Dr. J. Tarrant).

p. 447: The first edition of Chappuis in vol. III of his *Corpus* (GW 4904) contained only 70 *Extravagantes communes*; he added the three *extrav.* of John XXII with William of Montlauzun's gloss and Benedict XII, *Vas electionis* with the gloss of Jo. Franciscus de Pavinis only in ed. 2 (Paris 1503). See Schulte, *Geschichte* II 63 n.9; A.M. Stickler, *Historia iuris canonici latini* I (Torino 1950) 270-71.

p. 451: For Antonio Agustín's remark about Peña in the *Dialogi*, add references to the original edition of Tarragona 1587 p. 214 and the original edition of Baluze's notes, Paris 1672 p. 434. Peña's marginal notes are not without critical interest, see e.g. his observation on *Glos. ord.* X 2.28.46 v. *explicare*: 'Haec glossula non habetur in vetustis codicibus, neque hoc fragmentum cuius meminit invenitur in veteri compilatione'.

ADDENDUM

This volume was ready for press when a major article by P. Johanek came to hand, 'Studien zur Überlieferung der Konstitutionen des II. Konzils von Lyon (1274)' in *Zeitschrift der Savigny-Stiftung für Rechtsgeschichte* 66 (1979) 149-216, too late to include in *Retractationes* XII the substantial amount of new manuscript evidence the author presents and discusses.

General Index

Three special indices follow below. Index 2: Councils and Synods, Index 3: Papal Letters, Index 4: Manuscripts. All items in the *Retractationes*, printed here after the last article, are indexed by the number of the article and the page(s) to which they refer, followed by the symbol R (thus II 7n R = article No. II, *retractatio* to p. 7 note).

Abailard (Abelard): IV 81
Abbas antiquus: see Bernard of Montmirat
Abbreviatio 'Quoniam egestas': V 67
Adrian IV, pope: VII 372-74
Aegidius de Fuscarariis: XI 105
Agustín, Antonio: II 7 *et passim*, 22f R; IX 136R; XIII 451
Alanus: VII 373n; X 608n
— (collection): I 311n; X 619R, 620n R, 623, 629f
Albero, archbishop of Trier: IV 74
Alexander II, pope: II 15n, 21f
Alexander III, pope: IX 145, 170n; VI 133-35; VII 372-78
Alexander IV, pope: X 624n; XI 130; XII 47n, 56n
Alexander Nevus (de Nevo): XIII 446-48
Amaury de Bène: IX 154f, 163n
Amis and Amile: XII 52n
Anders Sunesun, archbishop of Lund: VIII 50ff
Andrea Dandolo, doge: XI 120
Andrew, priest: VI 134f
Angelo Capranica, card.: XIII 438
Anselm of Havelberg: II 11n
Anselm of Lucca (collection): II 8 *et passim*
Apollonius of Tyre (story of): XII 52n
Arno of Reichersberg: II 11n
Augustinus (pseudo-): XII 51n

Baldricius: IV 74n
Baldus de Ubaldis: XIII 444
Baldwin, cardinal priest of S. Maria in Trastevere: IX 146R
Baluze, Étienne (Stephanus Baluzius): III 175 *et passim*; XIII 449, 451
Bartholomew, bishop of Exeter: VI 133-35
Benedict XII, pope: XIII 439, 445f
Benedict of St. Peter (Benedictus canonicus): IX 145R
Benedicta, Marchioness of Massa: XI 128f
Benifazá (Cist. abbey): XI 116f
Berardus, archbishop of Palermo: IX 120, 147, 159
Berengar, archbishop of Bordeaux: XIII 429n
Bernard of Compostella (antiquus): I 311n; X 619ff, 620n R, 630 et n 34
Bernard of Compostella (jr.): XI 73n
Bernard of Montmirat (Abbas antiquus): XI 110-16R, 113f, 117f
Bernard of Pavia (Papiensis): I 309; VII 372, 376; IX 116f
Biner, J.: XI 88R
Binius, Severinus: XI 84
Boatinus of Mantua: XII 41n, 41n R, 50n R
Boehmer, J.H.: XI 83, 88
Bonaguida of Arezzo: XI 124
Bouhier, Jean (library of): IV 79f

Boniface IV (pseudo-): II 10f; III 175
Boniface VIII, pope: XI 83; XIII 433, 443, 446; see also *Professio fidei*
Breviarium extravagantium: see *Compilatio prima*
Breviarium (13th c., anon.): VII 371n
Brevis nota (conc. I Lugd.): XI 84ff, 122
Brevis nota [BN] (= *Ordinatio concilii generalis*: II Lugd.): XII 42 *et passim*
Burchard of Worms: VII 372; VIII 41
Burdinus, Mauritius: IX 133n
Cabassut, J.: XI 86
Calixtus I (pseudo-): VI 134f
Calixtus II, pope: II 10, 16f, 20, 24
Calixtus III, pope: XIII 438
Carmelites: XII 74
Casamari, abbot: VIII 52
Casus Parisienses (to const. IV Lat.): X 618R
Casus Si quis impugnans: XI 100-101R
Celestine II, pope: IV 81
Celestine III, pope: V 70f; VII 376, XI 126ff
Cencius: IX 165n, 170
Cervera (priory of Hospitallers): XI 116f
Chacón, Pedro: II 9, 15, 17
Chanson de la croisade . . .: see Willielmus de Tudèle
Chappius, Jean: XIII 447
Chronica S. Petri Erfordensis: IX 130, 155n
Chronicon Parmense: XII 72
Clement III, pope: VII 372f, 378
Clement IV, pope: XII 47n
Clement V, pope: XI 93; XIII 427 *et passim*
Clementinae Constitutiones: XI 92ff, 94R; XII 41; XIII 427 *et passim*, 429R

Codex Justinianus: I 311n R; IX 167ff R
Collectiones canonum sive decretalium: see also Alanus, Anselm of Lucca, Clementinae, Deusdedit, Extravagantes, Gilbertus, Liber Sextus, Novellae, Novissimae constitutiones, Parisiense fragm.
Collectio LXXIV titulorum: II 7n R, 8
— *Abrincensis prima*: VI 134
— *Abrincensis secunda*: X 622R
— *Ambrosiana*: V 66, 68
— *Appendix Abbrev. 'Quoniam egestas'*: V 67, 71
— *Appendix concilii Lateranensis*: VI 133ff
— *Bambergensis secunda*: VIII 41; X 622R
— *Berolinensis prima*: V 66n
— *Caesaraugustana*: II 23
— *Cantabrigensis*: V 68; VI 133n
— *Cantuariensis prima*: V 63
— *Cheltenhamensis*: VI 133, 135
— *Cottoniana*: VI 134, 135
— *Cusana*: V 62ff, 71
— *Duacensis*: V 66n
— *Dunelmensis prima (=1, 2, 3 Dun.)*: V 71n, 71n R
— *Estensis*: X 620n
— *Florianensis*: V 68ff
— *Fontanensis*: V 64, 66
— *Francofortana*: V 62, 65, 68, 71; VI 133n, 134n; VII 371 *et passim*
— *Lipsiensis*: V 62, 65; VII 373
— *Lucensis*: V 68
— *Palatina*: X 622
— *Parisiensis secunda*: V 65f; VII 371, 374n
— *Petrihusensis*: VI 133-135
— *Polycarpus*: II 11f
— *Pragensis*: VIII 41f, 54n; X 620n R, 622

— *Roffensis*: V 63
— *Romana* (Bernard of Compostella): X 620n R
— *Rotomagensis prima*: V 62, 62R; VI 133n
— *S. Floriani*: X 630n
— *Tanneri*: I 134n
— *Wigorniensis*: VII 371n, 377
— *Wigorniensis altera*: V 64
Compilatio decretorum: see Laborans
Compilatio prima: I 311; IX 116f
Compilatio tertia: VIII 41; X 620n R, 621, 621n R
Compilatio quarta: VIII 42; IX 140, 164; X 608 *et passim*, 620n R, 622R, 622n R
Compilatio quinta: I 308; IX 165
Constabili, Paolo: XIII 452
Constitutiones conciliorum
  A sancto concilio decretum est (Mogunt. spur.): V 66
  Absolutionis (II Lugd. c.20): XII 66, 81n
  Ad apostolice (=Po. 11733= Berger 1367): XI 76, 89
  Ad liberandum (IV Lat. c.71): IX 118n R, 122n R, 133ff, 156, 174ff; X 617; XII 48
  Afflicti corde (I Lugd. c.17): XII 48, 57
  Altercationis (II Lugd. c.16): XII 67
  Auaritiae (II Lugd. c.4): XII 75, 81n
  Cum actus legitimi (I Lugd. c.5): XI 78
  Cum sacrosancta (II Lugd. c.1): XII 45ff, 46R, 54 (cf. Fideli ac deuota)
  Decet domum domini (II Lugd. c.25): XII 67, 79f, 81n
  Dispendiosam (Vienn. c.[6]): XIII 428, 430
  Ecclesiarum censura (cf. I Lugd. c.1): XI 78
  Exigit peruersorum (II Lugd. c.24): XII 78, 80n
  Exiui de paradiso (Vienn. c.penult.): XIII 435 *et passim*, 445R
  Expediendis (cf. I Lugd. c.2): XI 78
  Fideli ac deuota (II Lugd. c.1): XII 44ff, 51, 54, 69, 78
  Generali (II Lugd. c.12): XII 67, 81n
  Hoc consultissimo (II Lugd. c.22): XII 51, 68f, 68f R, 78, 81n
  In multis (I Lugd. c.9): XI 78f
  Induxit olim necessitas (II Lugd. c.22): XII 68f R
  Item statuimus ut quecumque communitas (unpubl. draft): IX 167 (ed. 168)
  Le temoignage de Joseph: see Testimonium in Joseph
  Licet canon (II Lugd. c.13): XII 43n
  Licet de uitanda (III Lat. c.1): XII 56n
  Nemo deinceps (II Lugd. c.14): XII 43n
  Non nobis (II Lugd. ante c.1): XII 48, 57 (ed. 58f), 57-59R
  Nulli licere (II Lugd. c.7): XII 77
  Oportet eos (Nîmes c.3): III 178n R
  Ordinarii (II Lugd. c.18): XII 43n
  Perpetuae (II Lugd. c.6): XII 76, 81n
  Placuit omnibus (Ps. Nicene): II 11
  Placuit omnibus residentibus (cap. spur.): II 11
  Placuit omnibus sanctis (cap. spur.): II 11
  Pro humani (I Lugd. c.18): XI 106ff
  Properandum (II Lugd. c.19): XII 78

Quam sit ecclesiis (II Lugd. c.5): 76, 81n
Quamquam usurarum (II Lugd. c.27): XII 69ff, 80n
Quamuis constitutio (II Lugd. c.9): XI 43n, 53, 77
Quia periculosum (I Lugd. c.22): XI 105ff
Quicumque (II Lugd. c.31): XII 67, 79, 81n
Quoniam ea que frequenter (unpubl. draft): IX 167 (ed. 168)
Religionum diuersitas (II Lugd. c. 23): XII 44, 73f, 81n
Saepe contingit(Vienn. c.ult.): XI 94R; XIII 427 *et passim*
Si canonici (II Lugd. c.17): XII 66, 81n
Si forte (II Lugd. c.10): XII 80n
Si quando (II Lugd. c.8): XII 55ff, 77
Statutum (II Lugd. c.21): XII 43n, 51
Sunt nonnulli (Nîmes c.2 spur.): III 175 *et passim*, 178n R
Testimonium (in) Joseph (II Lugd. c.22): XII 68f R, 69
Vbi periculum (II Lugd. c.2): XII 43, 51, 60, 63ff, 60-65R, 78f, 80n
Vsurarum uoraginem (II Lugd. c.26): XII 69-73, 80n
Vt circa (II Lugd. c.3): XII 75, 80, 81n
Zelus fidei (II Lugd. ante c.1): XII 44 *et passim*, 47f R, 57-59R
Corpus iuris canonici: I 308ff
Correctores Romani: II 22f R
Cossart, G.: XI 85
Cronicon of Reinhardsbrunn: IX 130, 132, 155n, 162
Damasus, glossator: X 608n, 618, 618R

Damasus, pope: II 11f, 26-28
Decretales, authority of: I 305ff; see also under Collectiones and under names of popes
de Marca, Pierre, archbishop of Paris: III 180, 182ff, 183R
De ordine legendi s. Scripturam: IV 81n
De privilegiis et primatu ecclesie Toletane: IX 136f
Deusdedit (collection): II 15n, 24f; V 65
Dietrich, archbishop of Cologne (Köln): IX 159
Digesta Justiniani: I 311, 311R, 311nn R
Dinus de Mugello: XIII 442
Dionysius Aereopagita (pseudo-): XII 52n
Diplovatatius, Thomas: XI 114ff, 124
Diuersorum patrum sententie: II 7n R, 8
Durantis: see Willielmus Durantis
Eadsige, archbishop of Canterbury: VI 135
Eleanor of Aragon/Toulouse: IX 139
Eric, king of Sweden: VIII 51
Eugenius II (pseudo-): II 11
Expeditio pro recuperanda terra sancta: IX 133f, 156, 174-178; see const. Ad liberandum
Extravagantes, unidentified collection: XII 47n
Extravagantes Biberach: V 61 *et passim*
Extravagantes communes: XIII 447, 447R
Extravagantes Jo. XXII: XIII 435 *et passim*
Fabri, Sixtus, O.P.: XIII 448, 450-52
Finke, Heinrich: XII 45-47
Fragmentum Parisiense (*primum* = Fragm. B): V 64, 67, 71

Franciscus Pipinus: XI 121
Fratres mendicantes, treatise on (anon. 15th c): VII 371n
Frederick II, emperor: IX 120 *et passim*, 167f R
Friedberg, E.: XI 90f
Friedrich, archbishop of Salzburg: XII R
Galesius, Petrus (Pedro Galés): II 22, 22f R
García Gudal, Gonzalo: see Gonzalo García Gudal
García de Loaysa: see Loaysa
Garlandus Bisuntinus: see Gerland of Besançon
Garlandus Chrysopolitanus: see Gerland of Besançon
Gaucelme de Jean: XIII 440n
General Councils, Roman edition of: XI 83f
Gerard, bishop of Osnabrück: IX 150
Gerland (author of *Computus*): IV 72f
Gerland of Besançon: IV 71 *et passim*
Gervase, archbishop of Heraclea: IX 135f
Gilbertus (collection): VII 373n; X 619f, 620n R
Glosses on Gratian: V 68f, 70f; VII 372n
Glossa Ordinaria (*Decretales Gregorii IX*): I 312n
Goffredo Castiglione: XI 125ff
Goffredus de Prefectis: XI 129R, 128ff
Goffredus de Trano: X 625n; XI 104, 124ff
Gomez, Luis: II 16, 18f
Gonzaga, Francesco: XIII 447n
Gonzalez Tellez, M.: I 306n
Gonzalo García Gudal, dean of Toledo, bishop of Cuenca: XI 110-16R

Gotifredus: see Goffredus
Gratian: II 8 *et passim*, 11n R; III 183R; V 61ff, 66, 69R; VI 134; VII 371, 372n, 373n, 375, 380; XIII 444n, 452
— Appendices: V 65, 68, 71
— *Decretum*, authority of: I 306ff
— *Paleae*: V 62 *et passim*
— and Roman law: V 64
Gregory I, pope (the Great): III 175; V 65, 68; IX 164, 171
Gregory I (pseudo-): II 11f
Gregory VII, pope: I 307n; II 7n; V 65, 68
Gregory IX, pope: I 308, 311ff; X 625n; XIII 433n, 448, 450, 452
Gregory X, pope: IX 133n; XII 39 *et passim*; XIII 428, 432n, 433n
Gregory XII, pope: XIII 433
Gregory XIII, pope: XIII 435n, 451f
Gregory, cardinal priest of S. Maria in Trastevere: IX 146R
Guido Brito: X 609n
Guido da Castello (Celestine II): IV 81; IX 145R
Hadrian (Adrian) IV, pope: VII 372-74
Hardouin, J.: XI 86
Haymo (Haimo) of Auxerre: V 65; IX 119
Haymo of Halberstadt (pseudo-): IX 119
Hefele, C.J. von: XI 89
Heinrich, magister (poet): XI 123
Helwicus of Magdeburg: XII 51n
Helwicus Teutonicus (? of Germar): XII 51n
Henry II, king of England: IX 160R
Henry VI, emperor: IX 159f
Henricus de Segusio (Hostiensis): XI 107, 114
Honorius III, pope: I 308; VIII 52; IX 135n, 169-71; XI 128
Honorius Augustodunensis (Ps.-Augustine): XII 51n, 51f R

Hostiensis (Henricus de Segusio): I 312n R; XI 107, 114
Hugo Metellus: IV 74f, 74n R
Hugh of St. Victor: II 9R, 25-26R
Incunabula
  GW 4886 (+7117): XIII 447
  GW 4888-4903: XIII 447
  GW 4904: XIII 447, 447R
  GW 4905: XIII 447
  GW 7077: XIII 445f
  GW 7078-7097: XIII 446
  GW 7091: XIII 446R
  GW 7098: XIII 446f
  GW 7099-7107: XIII 447
  GW 7108: XIII 447
  GW 7109-7116: XIII 447
  GW 7117 (+4886): XIII 447
  Hain 11595: XIII 445n
Initia operum
  Ad euidentiam dicendorum (Gloss on *Novellae Inn. IV*, anon.): XI R
  Antiquitate et tempore (*Summa Decreti*, anon.): IV 71, 81n
  Arg. quod secundum conscientiam debemus iudicare (Gloss on Comp. 1, Alanus?): X 608n
  Calefacientes igitur nominantur et throni (Ps.-Dionysius, *De caelesti hierarchia*): XII 52n
  Ceterum quia unius cuiusque (*Principium decretalium Borghesianum*): X 624, 630-34R
  Conuertere animam meam in requiem tuam (Helwicus of Magdeburg, *Decachordum*): XII 51n
  Cum prolixitas et difficultas logice discipline (Gerland, *Regulae super dialectica*): IV 75R
  Cunctis amantissimis (Petrus Damiani, opusc. 28): II 10f
  De penitentia: Daniellis iv. Ruit uox de celo (moral exposition, anon.): XII 51f R, 52n
  Desiderio desideraui (Innocent III, sermon): IX 132R
  Dic quod hic non est aliqua inculcatio (Joh. Andreae, *Apostillae*): XIII 444
  Gregorius nonus uolens (Goffredus de Trano, *Apparatus in Decretales Greg. IX*): X 625n
  Gregorius qui in generali concilio lugdunensi (Commentary on II Lugd., anon.): XII 47f R
  In prima parte istius (*al.* huius) capituli (*Casus Comp. III*, Vincentius?): X 609n
  In quadam prouincia laici percipiunt decimas (*Quaest. Patavinae*): X 628n
  Inter alia que scripsisti (Ps.-Jerome, Letter to Pope Damasus): II 11 (ed. 26ff)
  Isaias propheta nobili prosapia ortus (Haymo, *super Isaiam*): IX 119
  Magister Gratianus in hoc opere (*Summa Parisiensis*): IV 71, 81n
  Magister, quod est mandatum magnum in lege (Helwicus Teutonicus, *De dilect. Dei et proxime*): XII 51n
  Nam dubius in fide hereticus est (Martinus Zamorensis, Gloss on Comp. 4): X 628n
  Prima etas in exordio sui continet creationem mundi (*Chronicon mundi*, anon.): II 13
  Prima pars continet de Deo, de Trinitate et unitate (Gerland, *Candela*,tabula libri): IV 73
  Questionum articuli non poterant legibus comprehendi: see Quoniam omnes questionum articuli
  Quia preposterius [sic] ordo prius humana subsidia petere (Joh. de Criuellis, *oratio*): XIII 438

Quidam cum infirmaretur uocauit ad se medicum (*Quaest. Claustroneoburg.*): X 628n

Quidam habens duas manus (Barth. Brixiensis, *Quaest. dominicales*): XIII 439R

Quidam habuit causam aduersus alium super x. (*Quaest. Graecenses*): X 608n

Quidam uxorem duxit sine presentia testium (Quaest. *De his qui occulte nubunt* [from Hugh of St. Victor]): II 9 (ed. 25f), 9R

Quod pictura arboris sit autentica (Joh. Teutonicus, *Apparatus in Arborem consang.*): X 608n

Quoniam multi subtiliter et utiliter elaborauerunt auctoritates diuersas (*De septem donis spiritus sancti*, anon.): XII 52n

Quoniam omnes questionum articuli (*var.* Questionum articuli) non poterant legibus comprehendi (*Casus Parisienses Conc. IV Later.*): X 618, 618R

Quoniam tunc decens et amabile Deo principium comprobatur (*Principium decretalium*, anon.): X 626n R

Sapientia dei qui os muti (Honorius Augustodunensis [Ps.-Augustine], *De cognitione uerae uitae*): XII 51n

Sciendum quod diuiso populo (Haymo, *super Isaiam*): IX 119

Si quis impugnans (*Casus*): XI 100-101R

Sicut omnium liberalium artium (Prolog., *Casus et Notabilia decretalium*): X 626n R

Solent, Reuerende presul, Magnifice Commissarie (Joh. de Criuellis, *oratio*): XIII 438

Spiritus sanctus a patre et filio tamquam ex uno (*Notabilia Monacensia constit. Lugd. II* v. *Cum sacrosancta*): XII 46

Studiorum omnium theologia gubernatrix (Gerland, *Candela*, prolog.): IV 72

Tria consideranda sunt in electione (*Distinctiones*, anon.): VI 134n

Vt dicit Bernardus, magna res est amor, set sunt in eo gradus (*De decem gradibus amoris*, anon.): XII 51n

Videtur contrariari omnibus inscriptionibus (Boatinus, *Lectura constit. Greg. X* v. *et post*): XII 41n

Innocent II, pope: IV 73f; IX 144f, 145R

Innocent III, pope: I 308, 311ff; IX 115 *et passim*, 118n R, 122n R, 151R; X 608 *et passim*, 621n R, 622n R

Innocent IV, pope: XI 70 *et passim*, R, 110-16R; XII 39, 41, 47n, 48, 49, 57; XIII 428, 432n, 433

Ivo of Chartres: II 9f, 13, 15n, 24f; III 177; VII 372

Jacobus Buoncambio: XI 105

Jacobus de Albenga, glossator: X 624n

Jacobus Stefaneschi, card.: XIII 430n

Jacobus de Voragine: XI 121

Jenson, Nicholas (printer): XIII 446

Jerome (pseudo-): II 12, 26-28

Jesselin de Cassagnes: XIII 432n, 434, 435R, 436n, 441

Joachim of Fiore: IX 154f, 163n

John, king of England: IX 157f, 160f

John XXII, pope: XI 93f; XII 41; XIII 428 *et passim*

Johannes Andreae: I 309; XI 83; XII 66n R, 72n R; XIII 428 *et passim*, 429R, 432R

Johannes Calderini: XIII 442n
John Chrysostom: IV 83
Johannes de Criuellis de Parma: XIII 438, 438R
Johannes de Deo: X 623, 623R, 625f
Johannes Franciscus de Pavinis : XIII 447R
Johannes Galensis: I 312n R
Johannes Lemovicensis O.F.M.: XI 119
Johannes Teutonicus: I 311n; VIII 42ff; X 608ff *et passim*, 608-17R, 622n R
Justinian, Codex: I 311n R; IX 167ff R
— Digest: I 311, 311R, 311nn R
Labbe, Philippe: XI 85
Laborans, card.: I 307; VII 375n
Langton, Stephen: IX 123n, 157n
Leo I, pope: II 19
Leo III, pope: V 70
Leo IX, pope: V 70; VI 134n, 135; VII 376
Lex edictalis (Frederick II): IX 167ff, 167ff R
Liber Sextus: XII 78-81
Liber legis Scaniae: VIII 48
Litterae de iustitia: VII 375
Loaysa, García de: IX 136, 138
Lotharius, glossator, archbishop of Pisa: VIII 54n
Lucius III, pope: VII 372f; IX 170
Magna Carta: IX 158
Mansi, Giov. Dom.: XI 83, 88f
Manuel Kalekas: XII 45n
Marcellus II, pope: II 21n
Marcoaldus (Marquard von Ried): X 624R
Martin IV, pope: XII 41n
Martin, J.-B.: XI 90
Martinus Polonus (Martin of Troppau): IX 144f
Matthew, bishop of Amalfi: IX 130f

Matthew Paris: IX 134n, 166f; XI 77ff, 91ff, 124
Meaux Pontifical: IX 131
Michael, emperor: XII 45f
Michael Thomasius: see Thomasius, Michael
Montferrat , Marquess of : IX 147-53, 159, 172
Necrologium eccles. b. Mariae trans Tiberim: IX 143, 145
Nevus (de Nevo), Alexander: XIII 446-448
Nicholas III, pope: XIII 436
Nicolaus de Carbio (da Calvi): XI 120, 123f, 130n
Nicholas Jenson (printer): XIII 446
Nicolaus de Tudeschis (Panormitanus): I 308n
Notabilia Monacensia (conc. II Lugd.): XII 46
Novellae Innoc. IV, Coll. I: XI 71 *et passim*
Novellae Innoc. IV, Coll. II: XI 72
Novellae Innoc. IV, Coll. III: XI 72 *et passim*
Novissimae constitutiones Greg. X: XII 39 et passim
Oratio Manassis: XII 68n, 68n R
Ordinatio concilii generalis Lugdunensis II (=*Brevis nota*): XII 42 *et passim*, 42R, 54R
Ordo qualiter fit concilium apud Lemoviacam urbem: IX 131
Ormaneto, Niccolò, bishop of Padua: II 16, 18ff, 22
Otto, bishop of Münster: IX 150
Panormitanus (Nicolaus de Tudeschis): I 308n
Paolo da Rieti, notary: IX 118n R, 122n R
Parisetus (Parisetti), Hieronymus: II 13-15, 17
Parisiense fragmentum (*primum* = Fragm. B): V 64, 71

Paschal II, pope: II 12, 24; VIII 51
Paulus de Liazariis: XIII 436f, 443
Peña, Francisco: XIII 438, 450f, 451R
Petrus Albignanus Trecius: XIII 447
Peter of Benevento: X 621
Petrus Bertrandi (Pierre Bertrand): XIII 449
Petrus Cabacol, magister: XIII 439
Petrus Colonna, card.: XI 121
Petrus Damiani: II 10, III 177; III 177n R
Petrus Galesius (Pedro Galés): II 22, 22f R
Petrus de Monte, bishop of Brescia: XIII 441
Petrus de Sampson: XI 110ff, 110-16R
Philip II, king of Spain: II 17, 21n
Philip of Aquileja, glossator: X 618n R, 624n, 624R, 625n
Platina, Bartolomeo: XII 62n
Polycarpus: II 11f
Pontifical, Meaux: IX 131
— Roman: IX 131
Potthast, A.: XI 89
Préaux, abbey of (manuscripts): IX 178n
Preces pro conventu Wiennensi: XII 52
Principium decretalium Borghesianum: X 624ff (ed. 630-34), 626n R
Professio fidei of Boniface VIII: XIII 440R, 443n, 443n R
Pseudo-: see Augustinus (pseudo-), Jerome (pseudo-), etc.
Quaestiones Borghesianae: X 628n
Quaestiones Claustroneoburgenses: X 628n, 629n
Quaestiones Graecenses: X 608n
Quaestiones Patavinae: X 628n
'Quod latenter et per uim et illicite introductum est, nulla debet stabilitate subsistere' : V 65

Rainier of Liège: IX 134n, 139n, 158, 162
Rainier of Pomposa: X 619n
Raymond of Peñafort: VIII 42
Raymond VI of St.-Gilles, count of Toulouse: IX 138ff
Raymond VII of St.-Gilles, count of Toulouse: IX 139
Richard of S. Germano: IX 120 *et passim*
Robert of Flamborough: VIII 41
Robert Grosseteste: XII 52n
Rodrigo Jiménez, archbishop of Toledo: IX 136f
Roger of Hoveden: IX 160
Roger of Wendover: IX 133f, 156ff
Roman edition of General Councils: XI 83f
Roman Pontifical: IX 131
Rudolph, king of Germany: XII 57
Rufinus: V 70; VII 372n
S. Adriano, diaconal church: XI 126ff
S. Callisto (= S. Maria in Trastevere): IX 146R
S. Maria de Pratis (Leicester), abbot of: IX 167R
S. Maria in Trastevere: IX 143-46, 146R
'Sanctorum patrum' (cap. incert.): V 66
Sancius de Sarrio (Serrio): XIII 439
Schott, André, S.J.: II 9n
Secundus Philosophus (story of): XII 52n
Sega, Filippo: II 21
Senckenberg, H.C.: IV 76n R
Simon de Brie (Martin IV): XII 41n
Simon de Montfort: IX 139-43
Simon Paltinari, card.: XII 41n
Simon Vairet: XIII 436n R
Siricius, pope: II 12
Skånske Lov (Skånelag): VIII 48
St. Bénigne, abbey at Dijon (manuscripts): IV 77, 80

Stephen de Bourbon: XII 52n
Stephanus Hugoneti: XIII 429, 429R
Stephen Langton: IX 123n, 157n
Stephen of Tournai: V 62n; VII 373n
Summa Antiquitate et tempore: IV 71, 81n
Summa Inperatorie maiestati: VI 134n
Summa Magister Gratianus in hoc opere (=S. Parisiensis): IV 71n, 81n
Summula Monacensis: XII 46
Sylvester, pope (apoc. council): II 24
Tancred, glossator: X 608n, 608n R, 618, 623n, 625 *et passim*
Taxaquet: see Thomasius, Michael
Thierry of Chartres (Teodericus Carnotensis): IV 74
Thomas Aquinas (pseudo-): XII 51n
Thomasius, Michael: II 14, 17f, 20f
Urban II, pope: II 8 *et passim*; III 175 *et passim*
Urban IV, pope: XII 47n
Urban V, pope: XIII 439
Vacarius: VII 377, 377R
Van Espen, Zeger Bernhard: XI 87; XII 45
Vauluisant (Cist. abbey), manuscript (formerly H.13): IV 77, 80

Vernet, F.: XI 91
Vincent of Beauvais: X 626n R
Vincentius Hispanus, glossator: X 608n, 610, 614, 618n R, 624f, 628
Waldemar, bishop of Schleswig: IX 150
Willielmus Duranti(s): XII 40 *et passim*
Willielmus de Mandagout (de Mandagoto), bishop of Embrun: VII 371n; XIII 429n
Willielmus de Montlauzun (de Monte Lauduno), glossator: XIII 434 *et passim*, 447R
Willielmus de Nangis: XI 121
Willielmus de Nogaret: XIII 443n
Willielmus Raymundi de Monte Catheno: XIII 439
William of St. Alban's: IX 166f
Willielmus (Guilhem) de Tudèle: IX 132-39, 143
Willielmus Vasco: X 618n
Wulfstan, archbishop of Canterbury: VI 135
Zachary of Besançon (Chrysopolitanus): IV 73n
Zenzelinus: see Jesselin de Cassagnes
Zoën, magister, archbishop of Avignon: X 624f, 624n R

Index 2: Councils and Synods

Beauvais (1114): III 175
Bourges (1031): IX 131
Ephesus (431): II 8n
Lateran (1110): II 24
Lateran (1112): III 187R
Lateran, general, I (1123): II 10, 14n, 16f, 24
Lateran, general, III (1179): VII 372, 373n
Lateran, general, IV (1215): IX 115 *et passim*; X 608 *et passim*; XII 48, 74
Lyon, I (1245): IX 122, 133n, 134n, 163f; XI 70 *et passim*; XII 39, 41, 47f

Lyon, II (1274): IX 122, 133n, 167; XI 74n; XII 39 *et passim*; XIII 428f
Mayence (1233): XII 46n
Nîmes (1096): III 175 *et passim*
Reims (1148): V 70; VI 135R; VII 372
Salzburg (1274): XII R
Thionville (821): IV 76, 83
Tours (1163): V 67f, 71n; VII 373
Verona (1184): IX 170
Vienne (1311-12): XI 92f; XII 41; XIII 428 *et passim*
Westminster (1175): V 69

Index 3: Papal Letters

JK †131: V 66
JK †249: II 12n
JK †384: V 68
JK †869: V 65
JE 1259: V 65, 67f
JE †1366: II 12n
JE 1482: V 66
JE †1951: II 11; III 176, 187
JE †1996: II 10f, 23; III 176 *et passim*
JE 2306: II 12n
JE 2536: V 70
JL 3773: V 66
JL 4269: V 70
JL 4501: II 22

JL 4722: II 15n
JL 5153: V 65, 67f
JL 5154: V 65, 67f
JL 5740: II 25
JL 5741: II 25
JL 5742: II 25
JL 5760: II 12n
JL 5763: II 11n
JL 5778: II 11n
JL 5820: III 186
JL 6335: VIII 55n
JL 7532: IV 73f
JL 7836: IX 146R
JL †7846: IX 146R
JL 7887: IX 146R
JL 8289: V 66

JL 8959: V 65
JL 9654: V 66, 66R
JL 9655: V 69
JL 9667: V 68, 70
JL 10141: IX 137
JL 10444: V 66; VII 373n
JL 11660: V 69, 69R
JL 12668: VII 376f
JL 13162: V 62f R
JL 13798: VII 376f
JL 13804: V 68
JL 13843: VII 377
JL 13854: VII 377
JL 13878: VII 377
JL 13906: VI 133n
JL 13912: VI 133 *et passim*
JL 13917: VI 133n
JL 13937: VII 377, 377R
JL 13944: VII 376f
JL 13960: VII 378
JL 13994: V 69
JL †13999: V 69
JL 14030: VI 135R
JL 14061: V 71
JL 14072: V 62, 69
JL 14073: V 62, 69
JL 14074: V 62, 69
JL 14107: V 70
JL 14155: V 68
JL 14157: V 68
JL 14188: VII 278
JL 14312: V 64
JL 14346: VII 377
JL 15109: IX 170n
JL 16596: VII 373, 378
JL 16941: V 70R
JL 17626: X 620n
JL 17639: IX 169n; XIII 438

WH 382: V 66
WH 624a: II 12 (ed. 28f)
WH 691: V 68
WH 709: V 65
WH 1084: V 68

Po. 388: X 621n
Po. 898: X 628R
Po. 1643: IX 159n
Po. 1806: X 620n, 622n
Po. 2075: X 621n, 622n
Po. 2360: VIII 54n; X 620n, 620n R, 622n
Po. 2481: X 613
Po. 2508: IX 135n
Po. 3018: X 620n, 620n R
Po. 3105: X 621n R
Po. 3256: IX 150n
Po. 3299: IX 150n
Po. 3300: IX 150n
Po. 3305-3655: X 621n
Po. 3310: IX 159n
Po. 3340: X 621n R
Po. 3354: IX 150n
Po. 3360: X 622n R
Po. 3530: IX 150n
Po. 3655: X 621n
Po. 3656: X 620n, 622n
Po. 3660-3673: X 621n, 621n R
Po. 3660: X 621n R
Po. 3663: X 620n, 621n, 622n
Po. 3684: X 621n
Po. 3692: X 621n
Po. 3698: X 621n
Po. 3704: X 621n
Po. 3718: X 621n
Po. 3753: X 620n, 621n, 622n
Po. 3756: X 621n
Po. 3757: X 621n, 622n
Po. 3760: IX 150n
Po. 3761: IX 150n
Po. 3765: X 621n R
Po. 3775: X 614n, 621n, 622
Po. 3791: X 621n, 622n
Po. 3792: X 621n
Po. 3833: IX 142f
Po. 3834: IX 142f
Po. 3865-3871: X 621n
Po. 3872: X 614, 621n, 622n
Po. 3880: IX 148n; X 621n

Po. 3886: X 621n, 622n
Po. 4006: X 622n
Po. 4072: X 622n
Po. 4110: X 613
Po. 4116: IX 150n
Po. 4117: IX 150n
Po. 4118: IX 150n
Po. 4143: VIII 45, 53n; X 622n
Po. 4163: VIII 53n
Po. 4164: VIII 53n
Po. 4174: VIII 53n
Po. 4195: VIII 53n; X 622n
Po. 4213: IX 148n
Po. 4312: VIII 45, 53n
Po. 4337: VIII 54n
Po. 4360: VIII 45, 53n
Po. 4379: VIII 53n; X 616, 622n
Po. 4400: VIII 45, 53n, 54n
Po. 4401: VIII 53n
Po. 4517: IX 139n
Po. 4523: VIII 45, *47*, 53n
Po. 4577: VIII 53n; X 613, 622n
Po. 4587: VIII 54n
Po. 4598: VIII 45, 53n
Po. 4603: VIII 45, 53n
Po. 4614: VIII 53n; X 616, 622n
Po. 4628: VIII 46, 53n; X 613
Po. 4641: VIII 46
Po. 4678: VIII 44-47
Po. 4683: VIII 47
Po. 4722: VIII 43-46, 53n; X 622n
Po. 4746: IX 161n
Po. 4789: VIII 46
Po. 4820: VIII 46-49, 53n; X 622n
Po. 4844: VIII 54n; X 622n
Po. 4847: VIII 54n
Po. 4869: VIII 46
Po. 4873: VIII 46, 53n; X 622n
Po. 4874: VIII 53n
Po. 4900: VIII 52
Po. 4912: IX 158n
Po. 4956: VIII 54n
Po. 4957: VIII 54n; X 615
Po. 4961: IX 157n

Po. 4967: IX 139n
Po. 4968: IX 139n
Po. 4969: IX 139n
Po. 4974: VIII 47
Po. 4989: VIII 54n; X 613
Po. 4990: IX 157n, 158n
Po. 4991: IX 157n
Po. 4992: IX 157n
Po. 5005: IX 157n
Po. 5006: IX 157n
Po. 5009: VIII 54n; IX 139ff; X 622n
Po. 5010: IX 140n, 142
Po. 5011: IX 140n
Po. 5012: IX 133n, 174ff
Po. 5013: IX 156-58
Po. 5014: IX 140n
Po. 5015: IX 140n
Po. 5021: X 622n
Po. 5022: VIII 54n; X 622n
Po. 5023: X 615
Po. 5024: X 622n
Po. 5025: VIII 54n; X 622n
Po. 5026: X 622n
Po. 5027: X 614, 622n
Po. 5028: VIII 54n; X 622n
Po. 5029: X 622n
Po. 5031: X 622n
Po. 5032: X 622n
Po. 5037: X 622n
Po. 5038: VIII 47f, 51, 53n; X 622n
Po. 5039: X 622n
Po. 5040: X 622n
Po. 5041: X 622n
Po. 5057: IX 157f
Po. *5193-*5204: IX 135n
Po. 5289: VIII 52
Po. 5290: VIII 52
Po. 5291: VIII 51
Po. 5298: VIII 54n; X 615, 622n
Po. 5462: IX 171n
Po. 6395: IX 169n, 170n
Po. 6408: IX 169n
Po. 6469: IX 169n

Po. 7852: IX 171n
Po. 9693: XIII 433n
Po. 10202: XI 74n
Po. 10204: XI 74n
Po. 10561 (=Auvray 4224-26): XI 129
Po. 11633: XI 118R
Po. 11686 (=Berger 1309): XI 125
Po. 11732: XI 91
Po. 11733 (=Berger 1367): XI 76, 89
Po. 11751 (=Berger 1389): XI 76
Po. 13092 (=Berger 4225): XI 124n
Po. 13220 (=Berger 4371): XI 130n
Po. 14166 (=Berger 4999): XI 119
Po. 14472: XI 130n
Po. 15121: XI 90
Po. 15123 (=Abbati sane): XI 76, 116f
Po. 15129 (=Berger 7756=Ad explicandos): XI 73f
Po. 15454 (=Berger 7823): XI 89, 114
Po. 15989: XI 73n
Po. 20926: XII 68n
Po. 20950: XII 39-41, 79
Po. 20951: XI 93n; XII 39-41, 79
Po. 21151: XII 64n
Po. 21162: XII 64n

Pressutti 1650: XI 130n
Pressutti 2267: X 618n, 628n
Pressutti 4035: XI 128
Pressutti 5551: XI 128
Pressutti 5577: XI 128
Pressutti 5992: XI 128

Auvray 1305: XI 129
Auvray 3153: XI 129
Auvray 3270: XI 129f
Auvray 4224-26 (=Po. 10561): XI 129

Berger 476: XI 105
Berger 837: XI 130n
Berger 917: XI 125n
Berger 956-58: XI 129n
Berger 979: XI 125n
Berger 1004: XI 125n
Berger 1049: XI 130n
Berger 1066: XI 130n
Berger 1079: XI 130n
Berger 1105: XI 125n
Berger 1309 (=Po. 11686): XI 125
Berger 1367 (=Po. 11733): XI 76, 89
Berger 1368: XII 48n
Berger 1389 (=Po. 11751): XI 76
Berger 1460: XI 125
Berger 1531-33: XI 130n
Berger 1618: XI 130n
Berger 2025: XI 130n
Berger 2039: XI 130n
Berger 2052: XI 130n
Berger 2057: XI 130n
Berger 3059: XI 119
Berger 3742: XI 130n
Berger 3851: XI 130n
Berger 4043: XI 130n
Berger 4225 (=Po. 13092): XI 124n
Berger 4371 (=Po. 13220): XI 130n
Berger 4999 (=Po. 14166): XI 119
Berger 5390: XI 130n
Berger 7344: XI 130n
Berger 7756 (=Po. 15129=Ad explicandos): XI 73f
Berger 7823 (=Po. 15454): XI 89, 114

Guiraud 399: XII 48n
Guiraud 409: XII 48n
Guiraud 465: XII 48n
Guiraud 494: XII 48n
Guiraud 525: XII 48n
Guiraud 541: XII 48n
Guiraud 552: XII 48n
Guiraud 569-71: XII 48n

Guiraud 576 (=Po. 20950): XII 39-41, 79
Guiraud 578: XII 48n
Guiraud 636: XII 48n
Guiraud 652: XII 48n
Guiraud 944: XII 48n
Guiraud 966: XII 48n
Guiraud 1041: XII 48n
Guiraud 1042-43: XII 48n
Guiraud 1056: XII 48n
Guiraud 1059: XII 48n
Guiraud 1069: XII 48n

Abbati sane (=Po. 15123): XI 76, 116f
Ad explicandos (=Po. 15129= Berger 7756): XI 73f
Ad regimen (Benedict XII): XIII 446
Albericus miles (Innocent III): X 622n
Ambitiosae (Paul II): XIII 447n
Auctoritate apostolica (Pius II): XIII 447n
Auditis litteris (Innocent III): VIII 47, 50, 52ff
Cum inter dilectos (Innocent III): VIII 47f; X 622n
Cum inter nonnullos (John XXII): XIII 436n, 437
Cum nuper (Clement V): XI 93, 97; XIII 432, 448
Cum nuper (Gregory X): XI 93n; XII 39-41, 79
Cum nuper (Innocent IV): XI 71
De reformatione (Innoc. III [Cheney No. 1056]): IX 167R
Dilecto (Innocent IV): XI 76, 119
Dilectus filius (Adrian IV): VII 393R
Ex debito (John XXII): XIII 440f, 440R
Execrabilis (John XXII): XIII 434f, 437 *et passim*, 444f R
Exhibita nobis (Honorius III): X 624n
Exiit qui seminat (Nicholas III): XIII 436
Illius licet inmeriti (Calixtus III): XIII 438
Infrascriptas (Gregory X): XII 39-41, 79
Iniuncte nobis (Boniface VIII): XIII 446
Litteram uestrarum lectione (Paschal II): II 12 (ed. 28-29)
Litteris a tua fraternitate (Ps. Siricius): II 12
Placuit communi (Ps. Eugenius II): II 11
Quia cunctis (Innocent IV): XI 76, 117
Quia frequenter (Innocent IV): XI 81n; XII 56n
Quoniam nulla (John XXII): XIII 428n, 430, 433f, 448
Quoniam perniciosa (=JK †249)
Rachel sum uidens (Gregory IX): XII 48n
Sacrosanctae (Boniface VIII) XIII 433
Sane quia de huiusmodi: see Volentes
Saluator noster (John XXII): XIII 434n
Sedes apostolica (John XXII): XIII 434f, 437, 440, 444-47
Sicut uolumus (Innocent III): VIII 49R
Statuimus secundum priorem diffinitionem ut monasteria (Ps. Gregory): II 12
Suscepti (John XXII): XIII 434f, 437 *et passim*
Tua nos duxit (Innocent III): VIII 47, 49ff
Vas electionis (Benedict XII): XIII 447R
Volentes (Innocent IV): XI 76, 118f, 118R

Index 4: Manuscripts

Admont
Stiftsbibliothek
22: X 610n, 623f, 628n
90: IV 77, 81

Aix-en-Provence
Bibliothèque de Méjanes
1683 (1548): IX 164n

Angers
Bibliothèque Municipale
368: III 187f
371: V 69R
377 (364): XI 112
379: XI R

Arras
Bibliothèque Municipale
541: XI 74

Avranches
Bibliothèque Municipale
146: III 175
149: VI 137n; X 622R

Bamberg
Staatsbibliothek
Can. 19 (P.II.6): X 612ff, 628n
Can. 64 (P.II.18): X 626n, 626n R
Patr. 132 (Q.VI.42): VIII 41

Barcelona
Biblioteca Universitaria
588: XI R

Berlin
Deutsche Staatsbibliothek
Hamilton 181: XIII 440R
lat. fol. 7 (Rose 625): XI 82, 88; XII 79n

Bern
Stadtbibliothek
22: IX 118n

Besançon
Bibliothèque de la Ville
1260: IV 77n, 77-78R

Biberach an der Riss
Spitalarchiv
B 3515: V 61 *et passim*

Boulder, Colo.
Prof. S.H. Thomson (formerly):
XII 52n, 52n R

Bratislava (Pressburg, Pozsonyi)
Chapter Library (administered by the Central State Archive)
13 (Jur. 210): XI 74

Breslau: see Wroclaw

Bruxelles (Brussels)
Bibliothèque royale
1407: IX 117
1408: IX 117
1409: IX 117

Cambrai
Bibliothèque Municipale
556 (514): IX 118n

Cambridge
Corpus Christi College
450: IX 118n
Gonville and Caius College
676: VI 133n R
Pembroke College
101: IX 132R

Peterhouse
180: VI 133ff

Cambridge (Mass.)
Harvard Law Library
64: V 65

Carpentras
Bibliothèque Municipale
31: IX 132R

Chapel Hill
University of North Carolina
sine numero: XII 52n, 52n R

Chartres
Bibliothèque Municipale
275 (*ol.* 318): XIII 431n, 448

Città di Castello
Biblioteca Capitolare (formerly):
IV 77, 81

Córdoba
Biblioteca del Cabildo
10: X 622n R, 624R

Cues (Bernkastel)
Bibliothek des St. Nikolaus-
Hospital
229: VII 370n
232: XI 112

Darmstadt
Landesbibliothek
907: V 65

Dijon
Bibliothèque Municipale
195 (158): IV 77, 81

Durham
Cathedral Library
C. III. 1: V 71n; VI 135n
Dean and Chapter Muniments
Loc. I no. 60*: XII 46R, 60-65R

El Escorial
Biblioteca Real de San Lorenzo
a.II.12: IV 81n
ç.II.264: II 21n

Erlangen
Universitätsbibliothek
464 (now MS 350): XII 79n

Firenze (Florence)
Biblioteca Medicea Laurenziana
Conv. soppr. 91 (Badia Fior. 2685):
III 177n R
S. Croce III sin. 6: X 618, 618R
S. Croce IV sin. 2: X 608, 608n R,
612ff
S. Croce V sin. 4: XI 111
S. Marco 499: II 13

Frankfurt
Stadt- und Universitätsbibliothek
28: X 612ff, 628n
60 (*ol.* S. Bartholomäus): VII 370 *et
passim*

Fulda
Landesbibliothek
D.5: VII 373n; X 619n
D.10: XI 104, 112, 115
D.14: VII 373n; X 614

Genève (Genf)
Bibliothèque Municipale
59: XI 112

Giessen
Universitätsbibliothek
632: IV 76n R
1105: IX 115 *et passim*

Graz
Universitätsbibliothek
138 (III.38;41/31): X 608 et n.2, 617

Greifswald
Universitätsbibliothek
I.4: XI 112

Grenoble
Bibliothèque de la Ville
512: III 189n

Halle
Universitätsbibliothek
Ye.52: VII 372n

Huesca
Biblioteca Provincial
20: II 13

Innsbruck
Universitätsbibliothek
70: XI 74
90: V 65

Kassel
Landesbibliothek
Jur. 11: IX 18n, 140, 141n; X 608, 610ff
Jur. 15: XIII 431n, 448

Klosterneuburg
Chorherrstiftsbibliothek
1048: X 628n

Kues: see Cues

Leipzig
Universitätsbibliothek
966: XI 112
980: XII 79n
1242: VI 133n, 134n

Lincoln
Cathedral Chapter
177: IX 132R

Lisboa (Lisbon)
Arquivo Nacional da Torre do Tombo
Coll. Especial pte. II, caixa 43: IX 137
Biblioteca Nacional
Alcobaça 304 (173): IX 118n
Alcobaça 381: IX 131n; X 618 et n.5, 618R

London
British Library (formerly British Museum)
Cotton Vitellius E. xiii: VI 134n, 135
Egerton 2819 (*ol.* Phillips 11726): VI 134n
Egerton 2901: VI 133n
Harley 3603: XII 42R, 42n R
Royal 11.B.: XI 112
Lambeth Palace
103: XI 105R
210: IX 118n

Lucca
Biblioteca Capitolare Feliniana
138: XI 82, 83n, 88
139: XI 82, 83n, 88n

München (Munich)
Staatsbibliothek
lat. 213: XII 46
lat. 329: XII 79n
lat. 539: XII 79n
lat. 2699: XIII 430n
lat. 3202: XII 79n
lat. 3879: IX 144n
lat. 8596: IX 118n
lat. 9596: IX 164n
lat. 14011: XII 79n

Madrid
Biblioteca Nacional
Dd. 47: IX 136R
Vitr. 15 n.5 Hh.144: IX 136

Marburg
Universitätsbibliothek
C.3: XIII 431n, 448

Montpellier
Bibliothèque de la Faculté de Médicine
403 (Bouhier E.6): IV 73n, 77, 79n, 79R
H.19: IV 80n

Nürnberg
Stadtbibliothek
Cent. IV 99: XI R

Napoli (Naples)
Biblioteca Nazionale
XII.A.37-39: II 13; III 178n

New York
Hispanic Society
B 2565: XIII 444f R

Dr. L. Schopp (formerly): XII 52n, 52n R

Olomouc (Olmütz)
Metropolitan Chapter Library
589: X 628n

Orléans
Bibliothèque Municipale
260: IV 75R

Osnabrück
Niedersächsisches Staatsarchiv Depositum 58d (formerly Ratsgymnasium C.1): XII 47n, 47f R, 55-57, 78

Oxford
Bodleian Library
Auct. F.3.10 (S.C. 2582, part E): XII 47f R, 57-59R, 60-65R
Barlow 37 (Sum. cat. 6464): VI 134n, 135
e Mus. 82: IX 118n
Tanner 8: VI 134n

Merton College
B.I.7: IX 118n

Padova (Padua)
Biblioteca Antoniana
II.35: X 628n
II.68: X 628n

Paris
Bibliothèque Nationale
Baluze 7: III 180ff
franç. 491: XII 51, 69, 80n
lat. 1568: IX 132R
lat. 3204: XIII 440n
lat. 3860: III 186ff, 187R
lat. 3881: III 178
lat. 3896: V 69R
lat. 3897: V 69R
lat. 3922: X 608n
lat. 3922A: VI 133n, 134n; VIII 47R; X 619n
lat. 3931: X 618R

lat. 4085: XIII 449
lat. 4085A: XIII 450
lat. 4284: III 178n
lat. 4489: X 623, 625n
lat. 6428: X 626n R
lat. 10402: III 185n
lat. 10623: IV 77ff, 77-78R, 81
lat. 11579: II 12n
lat. 12249: IX 118n, 132, 140, 141n, 178n
lat. 13820: III 185n
lat. 14470: X 626n R
lat. 14618: IV 71, 77, 78n
lat. 14765: XII 68f R
lat. 15001: V 64, 67, 71
lat. 15393: V 69R
lat. 15400: XI 100-101R
lat. 16698: V 69R
lat. 16899: V 69R
lat. 18119: IV 77f

Bibliothèque de l'Arsenal
678: III 188, 188R
697: XIII 436n R

Bibliothèque Mazarine
1290: V 69R
4310 (711): III 178n, 186

Bibliothèque de Sainte-Geneviève
2768: IV 75n, 75n R, 77, 79

Philadelphia, Penn.
University of Pennsylvania
lat. 95: XIII 429R

Pisa
Seminario, Biblioteca Catariniana
59: II 10, III 177n, 177n R

Pistoia
Archivio Capitolare
135 (109): II 10

Pozsonyi: see Bratislava

Prague
University Library
XXIII.E.59 (*ol.* Lobkowitz 439): VIII 54n; IX 164n; X 622 et n.22, 622R

Pressburg: see Bratislava

Reims
Bibliothèque Municipale
692: VIII 53n, 54n

Rome
Biblioteca Casanatense
1910: IX 118n

Biblioteca Vallicelliana
C.18: II 23n
C.21: II 23n
C.23: IX 136R
C.24: II 8n, 14n, 18, 22f R
C.26: II 8n, 23n
F.54: II 23-25, 24n R

Rouen
Bibliothèque Municipale
704 (E. 49): III 178n
706: IX 118n, 140, 141n, 164n; X 608n, 610n, 628n
717: XII 68f R

S. Daniele del Friuli
Biblioteca Civica Guarneriana
203 (220): II 12n, 12R, 26-28R

Salamanca
Biblioteca Universitaria
2644: II 23

Salzburg
Stift St. Peter
a.IX.18: X 619f

St. Florian

Stiftsbibliothek
XI.346: X 630n
XI.598: XI 74n

St. Omer

Bibliothèque Municipale
459: XI 100-101R

Tarragona

Biblioteca Provincial
26: II 22, 22f R

Toledo

Biblioteca del Cabildo
15-21: IX 136, 138; see also Madrid, Biblioteca Nacional Vitr. 15 n.5 Hh.144
15-26: IX 118n
42-21: IX 137

Torino

Accademia delle Scienze
MM. V. 21: III 177

Biblioteca Nazionale
D.IV.33 (Pasini lat. 239): II 15n, III 179

Trier

Stadtbibliothek
906: X 627n

Troyes

Bibliothèque Municipale
668: IV 73, 77, 79f
1082: IV 77, 80f
1716: XII 79n

Uppsala

University Library
C.570: XI R
C.583: XII 47f R

Vaticano, Città del

Archivio segreto Vaticano
A.A. arm. I. xviii, nos. 1288-1290: XII 62n
A.A. arm. I. xviii, nos. 2187-2194 (*ol.* Arm. IX caps. viii, nos. 1-8): XII 62, 63
A.A. arm. XXXV + 6-8: XII 62n
Indice 254: VIII 42, 50; IX 118n, 118n R, 122, 122n R
Reg. Vat. 8: VIII 54n
Reg. Vat. 8A: VIII 52, 56n

Biblioteca Apostolica Vaticana
Vat. lat. 700: IX 132R
Vat. lat. 1171: XIII 441n, 445
Vat. lat. 1361: II 9-13, 25; III 178
Vat. lat. 1363: II 14, 15n
Vat. lat. 1364: II 10, 14f, 18
Vat. lat. 1367: X 627n
Vat. lat. 1377: IX 144n; X 615
Vat. lat. 1378: IX 131n
Vat. lat. 1397: XIII 437, 441, 444f R, 445n
Vat. lat. 1398: XIII 441, 444
Vat. lat. 1399: XIII 437
Vat. lat. 1400: XIII 441
Vat. lat. 1401: XIII 436
Vat. lat. 1402: XIII 441
Vat. lat. 1403: XIII 437
Vat. lat. 2505: XIII 437n, 442
Vat. lat. 2506: XIII 437
Vat. lat. 2507: XIII 437
Vat. lat. 2508: XIII 438
Vat. lat. 2509: X 615, 623n
Vat. lat. 2704: XIII 446n
Vat. lat. 3531: II 14f
Vat. lat. 3555: IX 118 *et passim*
Vat. lat. 3762: II 8n
Vat. lat. 3829: II 21
Vat. lat. 3831: II 10
Vat. lat. 3833: II 25
Vat. lat. 3958: II 22n
Vat. lat. 3968: II 15n
Vat. lat. 4734: XII 42n, 42n R
Vat. lat. 4886: II 7n, 21f

Vat. lat. 4887: II 23n
Vat. lat. 4889: II 13n, 14, 21n
Vat. lat. 4890: II 13n, 14, 21n
Vat. lat. 4891: II 13n, 14
Vat. lat. 4892: II 13n, 14
Vat. lat. 4893: II 13n
Vat. lat. 4894: II 13n
Vat. lat. 4895: II 8
Vat. lat. 4897: II 8n
Vat. lat. 4913: II 17n
Vat. lat. 4961: II 21n
Vat. lat. 4977: II 7-9, 7n R
Vat. lat. 4979: II 7n, 22
Vat. lat. 4983: II 7, 14-19
Vat. lat. 4985: II 8n
Vat. lat. 4988: II 8n
Vat. lat. 5003: II 8n, 21
Vat. lat. 5890: II 14n
Vat. lat. 6055: XIII 445R, 446R
Vat. lat. 6093: II 8n, 22, 22f R
Vat. lat. 6252: II 16
Vat. lat. 6381: II 8n, 14-20
Vat. lat. 8121: XIII 441
Vat. lat. 8922: II 9n
Vat. lat. 9867: III 186n, 187n
Vat. lat. 10902: IX 132R
Vat. lat. 13264: XIII 445n
Vat. lat. 13266: XIII 438
Vat. lat. 13267: XIII 437
Arch. S. Petri A.38: XIII 442, 443n
Arch. S. Petri C.110: VII 375n
Arch. S. Petri G.18: XI 100-101R
Barb. lat. 535: II 15
Barb. lat. 897: II 8n, 23
Barb. lat. 1450: II 12, 12R, 26-28R
Barb. lat. 1494: XIII 437n, 438
Borgh. 45: X 624ff
Borgh. 261: X 628n
Borgh. 264: X 612ff, 623n
Borgh. 285: XIII 437, 444
Chis. lat. E.VIII.242: XIII 445R
Ottob. lat. 224: II 16
Ottob. lat. 1099: X 615
Ottob. lat. 2115: XII 50n
Ottob. lat. 2250: XII 42R
Ottob. lat. 2461: II 8n

Ottob. lat. 2520: XII 42n
Pal. lat. 625: X 627n
Pal. lat. 628: X 622
Pal. lat. 629: XI 73n, 82ff
Pal. lat. 638: XIII 437
Pal. lat. 642: XIII 441
Pal. lat. 643: XIII 439, 441n
Pal. lat. 644: XIII 439
Pal. lat. 656: VII 380
Pal. lat. 658: X 622R
Pal. lat. 832: XII 42n R, 54R, 68f R
Reg. lat. 438: II 8n
Reg. lat. 448: IX 118n
Reg. lat. 972: III 178n
Reg. lat. 982: III 178n, 178n R
Reg. lat. 987: III 178f
Reg. lat. 1026: III 179
Ross. lat. 565: XIII 437n, 439, 441, 444f R, 445
Ross. lat. 590: XIII 437
Ross. lat. 591: XIII 432, 437
Urb. lat. 178: X 623n

Venice

Biblioteca Nazionale Marciana (S. Marco)
lat. IV.55: II 20

Vercelli

Biblioteca Capitolare
LXXXIX: X 619f

Vienna: see Wien

Washington, D.C.

Catholic University of America
183 (formerly s.n.): XII R, 51ff, 51f R
195: XIII 450

Wien (Vienna)

Minoritenkloster
19 (formerly): XII 52f

Nationalbibliothek
566: XI 74n; XII R
2073: XI 74, 104, 109
2083: XI 111
2113: XI 111; XII 41n R, 50n R
2181: XI 112
2189: XI 109

Wolfenbüttel

Landesbibliothek
Helmst. 437 (Kat. 2172): XI 112

Worcester

Cathedral Library
F. 122: X 618n R

Wroclaw (Breslau)

University Library
I.Q.102: X 626n R
II.F.30: XII 79n

Zürich

Zentralbibliothek
Car. C.148: VIII 56n; IX 118n, 122, 136f, 159n

This volume contains a total of 380 pages